The New York Times

ATLAS

OF THE WORLD

To John Marshall Colson
from
Grandpa Gub.
for your
geography lessons

PAPERBACK EDITION

TIMES BOOKS

RANDOM HOUSE

Maps and index prepared by
Bartholomew, Edinburgh

Design
Ivan Dodd

*The Publishers would like to extend
their grateful thanks to the following:*

Mrs. J. Candy, Geographical Research
    Associates, Maidenhead
Flag information provided and authenticated
    by the Flag Institute, Chester
Mr. P.J.M. Geelan, Place-name consultant
Mr. H.A.G. Lewis OBE, Geographical
    consultant to *The Times*

Manufactured in Italy
9 8 7 6 5 4 3

First U.S. Edition

This latest addition to *The New York Times Atlas of the World* range present
essential information about our much changed world in a handy format
Derived from the well-established and popular *New Family Edition* of *Th
New York Times Atlas of the World*, this *Paperback Edition* is designed t
allow rapid access to geographical information for use in the home, office
college and school.

The maps are clearly and logically presented with place-names given i
their anglicized (conventional) form where such a form is in current use. Th
index contains around 30,000 names which are keyed to the maps by a simpl
grid system.

Preceding the map section there is a guide to all the world's independen
countries (including those new states which have emerged in the early 1990's
and the major dependent territories. Every entry includes the national flag i
full colour, vital statistics such as capital city, area, population, currency an
religion. A concise commentary on the most important aspects of th
geography and economic life of the country accompanies the statistics.

An illustrated four-page feature covers geographical comparisons c
continents, oceans, lakes and islands. This is supplemented by a list of th
populations of the major metropolitan areas of the world, and of mountai
heights and river lengths.

In the names, in the portrayal of international boundaries and in the list c
states and territories, the aim has been to show the situation in the area at th
time of going to press. This must not be taken as endorsement by th
publishers of the status of the areas concerned. The aim throughout has bee
to show things as they are. In that way the *Paperback Edition* of *The Ne
York Times Atlas of the World*, will best serve the reader to whom, it is hope
it will be of interest and practical use.

Times Books 199

CONTENTS

INTRODUCTORY SECTION

States & Territories of the World *4–43*

Geographical Comparisons: *44–47*
Continents, metropolitan areas, mountain heights, islands, oceans, seas, rivers, drainage basins and lakes.

Abbreviations used on the maps *48*

THE MAPS

Key to Symbols on maps *1*
Nations of the World 1:70M *2,3*
Nations of Europe 1:15M *4,5*
England Wales 1:2M *6,7*
Scotland 1:2M *8*
Ireland 1:2M *9*
British Isles & the North Sea 1:5M *10,11*
Scandinavia & the Baltic 1:7.5M *12*
Netherlands Belgium 1:2.5M *13*
France 1:5M *14*
Spain Portugal 1:5M *15*
Italy & the Balkans 1:5M *16,17*
Germany & Central Europe 1:5M *18,19*
Eastern Europe 1:10M *20,21*
Nations of Asia & Australasia 1:40M *22,23*
Northern Asia 1:20M *24,25*
Eastern Asia 1:20M *26,27*
Japan Korea 1:5M *28,29*
South-East Asia, Mainland 1:10M *30*
Central China 1:10M *31*
Australia & South West Pacific 1:20M *32,33*
South-East Australia 1:7.5M *34*
New Zealand 1:5M *35*
Indian & Pacific Oceans 1:60M *36,37*
South Asia & Middle East 1:20M *38,39*
Turkey Syria Iraq Iran 1:7.5M *40,41*
Northern India 1:7.5M *42,43*
The Ganges Plain 1:4M *43*
Southern India 1:7.5M *44*
Israel Lebanon Cyprus 1:2.5M *45*
Nations of Africa 1:40M *46*
South Africa 1:7.5M *47*
Northern Africa 1:15M *48,49*
Central & Southern Africa 1:15M *50,51*
Atlantic Ocean 1:60M *52*
Nations of North America 1:35M *53*
Canada 1:15M *54,55*
United States of America 1:12.5M *56,57*
Western USA 1:5M *58,59*
North Central USA 1:5M *60,61*
South Central USA 1:5M *62,63*
USA & Canada: The Great Lakes 1:5M *64,65*
California & Hawaii 1:2.5M & 1:5M *66*
Florida & South East USA 1:5M *67*
USA: Atlantic Seaboard 1:2.5M *68*
Caribbean 1:10M *69*
Mexico & Central America 1:15M *70*
Nations of South America 1:35M *71*
Northern South America 1:15M *72,73*
Southern South America 1:15M *74*
South East Brazil 1:7.5M *75*
Polar Regions 1:40M *76*

INDEX

Abbreviations used in the Index *77*
Index to the maps *77–132*

AFGHANISTAN
STATUS: Islamic State
AREA: 652,225 sq km (251,773 sq miles)
POPULATION: 16,433,000
ANNUAL NATURAL INCREASE: 2.5%
CAPITAL: Kabul
LANGUAGE: Pushtu, Dari
RELIGION: 90% Sunni, 9% Shi'a Muslim,
Hindu, Sikh and Jewish minorities
CURRENCY: Afghani (AFA)
ORGANIZATIONS: Col. Plan, UN

Afghanistan is a mountainous landlocked country in southwest Asia with a climate of extremes. In summer the lowland southwest reaches a temperature of over 40°C (104°F); in winter this may drop to -26°C (-15°F) in the northern mountains. The country is one of the poorest in the world with barely 10 per cent of the land suitable for agriculture. Main crops are wheat, fruit and vegetables. Sheep and goats are the main livestock. Mineral resources are rich but underdeveloped with natural gas, coal and iron ore deposits predominating. The main industrial area was centred on Kabul, but both Kabul and the rural areas have been devastated by civil war.

ÅLAND
STATUS: Self-governing Island Province of Finland
AREA: 1,505 sq km (581 sq miles)
POPULATION: 24,993
CAPITAL: Mariehamn

ALBANIA
STATUS: Republic
AREA: 28,750 sq km (11,100 sq miles)
POPULATION: 3,363,000
ANNUAL NATURAL INCREASE: 1.7%

CAPITAL: Tirana (Tiranë)
LANGUAGE: Albanian (Gheg, Tosk)
RELIGION: 70% Muslim, 20% Greek Orthodox,
10% Roman Catholic
CURRENCY: lek (ALL)
ORGANIZATIONS: UN

Albania is situated on the eastern seaboard of the Adriatic. With the exception of a coastal strip, most of the territory is mountainous and largely unfit for cultivation. The climate is Mediterranean along the coast, but cooler inland. Average temperatures in July reach 25°C (77°F) and there is 1,400 mm (55 inches) of rainfall annually. The country possesses mineral resources, notably chrome which is a major export, and deposits of coal, oil and natural gas. After decades of self-imposed political and economic isolation Albania shook off its own peculiar variant of communism in 1990. Administrative chaos and a massive fall in production ensued resulting in acute food shortages and widespread emigration. The country is one of the poorest in Europe with a backward rural economy and nearly half the labour force unemployed.

ALGERIA
STATUS: Republic
AREA: 2,381,745 sq km (919,355 sq miles)
POPULATION: 26,600,000
ANNUAL NATURAL INCREASE: 2.7%
CAPITAL: Algiers (Alger, El-Djezaïr)
LANGUAGE: 83% Arabic, French, Berber
RELIGION: Muslim
CURRENCY: Algerian dinar (DZD)
ORGANIZATIONS: Arab League, OAU, OPEC, UN

Physically the country is divided between the coastal Atlas mountain ranges of the north and the Sahara to the south. Algeria is mainly hot, with negligible rainfall, but along the Mediterranean coast temperatures are more moderate, with most rain falling during the mild winters. Arable land occupies small areas of the northern valleys and coastal strip, with wheat, barley and vines the leading crops. Sheep, goats and cattle are the most important livestock. Although oil from the southern deserts dominates the economy, it is now declining and natural gas output has increased dramatically. A virtual civil war has existed between the army and Islamic extremists which has caused the economy to deteriorate.

AMERICAN SAMOA
STATUS: Unincorporated Territory of USA
AREA: 197 sq km (76 sq miles)
POPULATION: 132,726
CAPITAL: Pago Pago

ANDORRA
STATUS: Principality
AREA: 465 sq km (180 sq miles)
POPULATION: 59,000
CAPITAL: Andorra la Vella
LANGUAGE: Catalan, Spanish, French
RELIGION: Roman Catholic majority
CURRENCY: French franc (FRF),
Andorran peseta (ADP)
ORGANIZATIONS: UN

Andorra, a tiny state in the Pyrenees between France and Spain, achieved fuller independence from these countries in 1993. The climate is alpine with a long winter, which lasts for six months, a mild spring and a warm summer. Tourism is the main occupation, with Andorra becoming an important skiing centre during the winter. Tobacco and potatoes are the principal crops, sheep and cattle the main livestock. Other important sources of revenue are the sale of hydro-electricity, stamps, duty-free goods and financial services.

ANGOLA
STATUS: Republic
AREA: 1,246,700 sq km (481,225 sq miles)
POPULATION: 10,770,000
ANNUAL NATURAL INCREASE: 2.9%
CAPITAL: Luanda
LANGUAGE: Portuguese, tribal dialects
RELIGION: mainly traditional beliefs,
Roman Catholic and Protestant minorities
CURRENCY: new kwanza (AOK)
ORGANIZATIONS: OAU, UN

Independent from the Portuguese since 1975, Angola is a large country south of the equator in southwest Africa. Much of the interior is savannah plateaux with average rainfall varying from 250 mm (10 inches) in the south to 1,270 mm (50 inches) in the north. Most of the population is engaged in agriculture producing cassava, maize and coffee. Most consumer products and textiles are imported. Angola possesses vast wealth in the form of diamonds, oil, iron ore, copper and other minerals. Apart from the production of oil, which is the biggest export, the economy has collapsed as a result of many years of civil war.

ABBREVIATIONS
The following abbreviations have been used. Codes given in brackets following the name of a currency are those issued by the International Standards Organization.

ANZUS	Australia, New Zealand, United States Security Treaty
ASEAN	Association of Southeast Asian Nations
Caricom	Caribbean Community and Common Market
CACM	Central American Common Market
CIS	Commonwealth of Independent States
Col. Plan	Colombo Plan
Comm.	Commonwealth
CSCE	Council for Security and Co-operation in Europe
ECOWAS	Economic Community of West African States
EEA	European Economic Area
EFTA	European Free Trade Association
EU	European Union
G7	Group of seven industrialized nations:– (Canada, France, Germany, Italy, Japan, UK, USA)
Mercosur	Common Market of the Southern Cone
NAFTA	North American Free Trade Agreement
NATO	North Atlantic Treaty Organization
OAS	Organization of American States
OAU	Organization of African Unity
OECD	Organization for Economic Co-operation and Development
OPEC	Organization of Petroleum Exporting Countries
UN	United Nations
WEU	Western European Union

ANGUILLA

STATUS: UK Dependent Territory
AREA: 115 sq km (60 sq miles)
POPULATION: 8,960
CAPITAL: The Valley

ANTIGUA AND BARBUDA

STATUS: Commonwealth State
AREA: 442 sq km (171 sq miles)
POPULATION: 65,962
ANNUAL NATURAL INCREASE: 1.0%
CAPITAL: St John's (on Antigua)
LANGUAGE: English
RELIGION: Anglican Christian majority
CURRENCY: E Caribbean dollar (XCD)
ORGANIZATIONS: Caricom, Comm., OAS, UN

The country consists of two main islands in the Leeward group in the West Indies. Tourism is the main activity. Local agriculture is being encouraged to reduce food imports and the growth of sea island cotton is making a comeback. The production of rum is the main manufacturing industry; there is also an oil refinery.

ARGENTINA

STATUS: Republic
AREA: 2,766,889 sq km
(1,068,302 sq miles)
POPULATION: 33,101,000
ANNUAL NATURAL INCREASE: 1.3%
CAPITAL: Buenos Aires
LANGUAGE: Spanish
RELIGION: 90% Roman Catholic,
2% Protestant, Jewish minority
CURRENCY: peso (ARP)
ORGANIZATIONS: Mercosur, OAS, UN

Relief is highest in the west in the Andes mountains, where altitudes exceed 6,000 m (19,500 ft). East of the Andes there are fertile plains known as the Pampas. In the northern scrub forests and grasslands of the Chaco hot tropical conditions exist. Central Argentina lies in temperate latitudes, but the southernmost regions are cold, wet and stormy. The economy of Argentina was long dominated by the produce of the rich soils of the Pampas, beef and grain. Agricultural products still account for some 40 per cent of export revenue, with grain crops predominating, despite a decline due to competition and falling world prices. Beef exports also decreased by over 50 per cent between 1970 and 1983, due to strong competition from western Europe. Industry is now the chief export earner. Industrial activity includes petrochemicals, steel, cars, and food and drink processing. There are oil and gas reserves and an abundant supply of hydroelectric power.

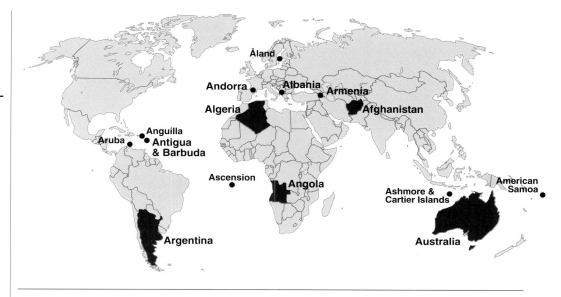

ARMENIA

STATUS: Republic
AREA: 30,000 sq km
(11,580 sq miles)
POPULATION: 3,686,000
ANNUAL NATURAL INCREASE: 1.2%
CAPITAL: Yerevan
LANGUAGE: Armenian, Russian
RELIGION: Russian Orthodox,
Armenian Catholic
CURRENCY: dram
ORGANIZATIONS: CIS, UN

Armenia is a country of rugged terrain, with most of the land above 1,000 m (3,300 feet). The climate, much influenced by altitude, has continental tendencies. Rainfall, although occurring throughout the year, is heaviest in summer. Agriculture is dependent upon irrigation and the main crops are vegetables, fruit and tobacco. Conflict over the disputed area of Nagornyy Karabakh, an enclave of Armenian Orthodox Christians within the territory of Azerbaijan, is casting a cloud over the immediate future of the country.

ARUBA

STATUS: Self-governing Island of
Netherlands Realm
AREA: 193 sq km (75 sq miles)
POPULATION: 68,897
CAPITAL: Oranjestad

ASCENSION

STATUS: Island Dependency of St Helena
AREA: 88 sq km (34 sq miles)
POPULATION: 1,117
CAPITAL: Georgetown

ASHMORE AND CARTIER ISLANDS

STATUS: External Territory of Australia
AREA: 3 sq km (1.2 sq miles)
POPULATION: no permanent population

AUSTRALIA

STATUS: Federal Nation
AREA: 7,682,300 sq km (2,965,370 sq miles)
POPULATION: 17,662,000
ANNUAL NATURAL INCREASE: 1.6%
CAPITAL: Canberra
LANGUAGE: English
RELIGION: 75% Christian,
Aboriginal beliefs, Jewish minority
CURRENCY: Australian dollar (AUD)
ORGANIZATIONS: ANZUS, Col. Plan,
Comm., OECD, UN

The Commonwealth of Australia was founded in 1901. The British Monarch, as head of state, is represented by a governor-general. It is the sixth largest country in the world in terms of area. The western half of the country is primarily arid plateaux, ridges and vast deserts. The central-eastern area comprises lowlands of river systems draining into Lake Eyre, while to the east is the Great Dividing Range. Climate varies from cool temperate to tropical monsoon. Rainfall is high only in the northeast, where it exceeds 1,000 mm (39 inches) annually, and decreases markedly from the coast to the interior which is hot and dry. Over 50 per cent of the land area comprises desert and scrub with less than 250 mm (10 inches) of rain a year. The majority of the population live in cities concentrated along the southeast coast. Australia is rich in both agricultural and natural resources. It is the world's leading producer of wool, which together with wheat, meat, sugar and dairy products accounts for over 40 per cent of export revenue. There are vast reserves of coal, oil, natural gas, nickel, iron ore, bauxite and uranium ores. Gold, silver, lead, zinc and copper ores are also exploited. Minerals now account for over 30 per cent of Australia's export revenue. New areas of commerce have been created in eastern Asia, particularly in Japan, to counteract the sharp decline of the traditional European markets. Tourism is becoming a large revenue earner and showed a 200 per cent growth between 1983 and 1988. This has slowed recently, although the Olympics Games, due to be held in Sydney in the year 2000, are expected to attract an additional 1.5 million overseas visitors.

STATES AND TERRITORIES

AUSTRALIAN CAPITAL TERRITORY
STATUS: Federal Territory
AREA: 2,432 sq km (939 sq miles)
POPULATION: 299,000
CAPITAL: Canberra

NEW SOUTH WALES
STATUS: State
AREA: 801,430 sq km (309,350 sq miles)
POPULATION: 6,009,000
CAPITAL: Sydney

NORTHERN TERRITORY
STATUS: Territory
AREA: 1,346,200 sq km (519,635 sq miles)
POPULATION: 168,000
CAPITAL: Darwin

QUEENSLAND
STATUS: State
AREA: 1,727,000 sq km (666,620 sq miles)
POPULATION: 3,113,000
CAPITAL: Brisbane

SOUTH AUSTRALIA
STATUS: State
AREA: 984,380 sq km (79,970 sq miles)
POPULATION: 1,462,000
CAPITAL: Adelaide

TASMANIA
STATUS: State
AREA: 68,330 sq km (26,375 sq miles)
POPULATION: 472,000
CAPITAL: Hobart

VICTORIA
STATUS: State
AREA: 227,600 sq km (87,855 sq miles)
POPULATION: 4,462,000
CAPITAL: Melbourne

WESTERN AUSTRALIA
STATUS: State
AREA: 2,525,500 sq km (974,845 sq miles)
POPULATION: 1,678,000
CAPITAL: Perth

AUSTRIA
STATUS: Federal Republic
AREA: 83,855 sq km (32,370 sq miles)
POPULATION: 7,910,000
ANNUAL NATURAL INCREASE: 0.6%
CAPITAL: Vienna (Wien)
LANGUAGE: German
RELIGION: 89% Roman Catholic, 6% Protestant
CURRENCY: schilling (ATS)
ORGANIZATIONS: Council of Europe, EEA, EFTA, OECD, UN

Austria is an alpine, landlocked country in central Europe. The mountainous Alps which cover 75 per cent of the land consist of a series of east-west ranges enclosing lowland basins. The climate is continental with temperatures and rainfall varying with altitude. About 25 per cent of the country, in the north and northeast, is lower foreland or flat land containing most of Austria's fertile farmland. Half is arable and the remainder is mainly for root or fodder crops. Manufacturing and heavy industry, however, account for the majority of export revenues, particularly pig-iron, steel, chemicals and vehicles. Over 70 per cent of the country's power is hydro-electric. Tourism and forestry are also important to the economy.

AZERBAIJAN
STATUS: Republic
AREA: 87,000 sq km (33,580 sq miles)
POPULATION: 7,398,000
ANNUAL NATURAL INCREASE: 1.0%
CAPITAL: Baku
LANGUAGE: 83% Azeri, 6% Armenian, 6% Russian
RELIGION: 83% Muslim, Armenian Apostolic, Orthodox
CURRENCY: manat
ORGANIZATIONS: CIS, UN

Azerbaijan gained independence on the break-up of the USSR in 1991. It is a mountainous country that has a continental climate, greatly influenced by altitude. Arable land accounts for less than 10 per cent of the total area, with raw cotton and tobacco the leading products. Major reserves of oil and gas exist beneath and around the Caspian Sea, which are as of yet fully undeveloped. The country includes two autonomous regions: Nakhichevan, which it is cut off by a strip of intervening Armenian territory and the enclave of Nagornyy Karabakh, over which long standing tensions escalated into conflict in 1992.

AZORES
STATUS: Self-governing Island Region of Portugal
AREA: 2,335 sq km (901 sq miles)
POPULATION: 237,100
CAPITAL: Ponta Delgada

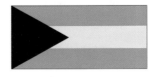

BAHAMAS
STATUS: Commonwealth Nation
AREA: 13,865 sq km (5,350 sq miles)
POPULATION: 262,000
ANNUAL NATURAL INCREASE: 1.9%
CAPITAL: Nassau
LANGUAGE: English
RELIGION: Anglican Christian majority, Baptist and Roman Catholic minorities
CURRENCY: Bahamian dollar (BSD)
ORGANIZATIONS: Caricom, Comm., OAS, UN

About 700 islands and over 2,000 coral sand cays (reefs) constitute the sub-tropical Commonwealth of the Bahamas. The island group extends from the coast of Florida to Cuba and Haiti in the south. Only 29 islands are inhabited. Most of the 1,000 mm (39 inches) of rainfall falls in the summer. The tourist industry is the main source of income and, although fluctuating through recession, still employs over 70 per cent of the working population. Recent economic plans have concentrated on reducing imports by developing fishing and domestic agriculture. Other important sources of income are ship registration (the world's fourth largest open-registry fleet), income generated by offshore finance and banking, and export of rum, salt and cement.

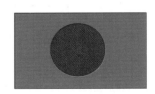

BAHRAIN
STATUS: State
AREA: 661 sq km (225 sq miles)
POPULATION: 539,000
ANNUAL NATURAL INCREASE: 3.2%
CAPITAL: Manama (Al Manāmah)
LANGUAGE: Arabic, English
RELIGION: 60% Shi'a and 40% Sunni Muslim, Christian minority
CURRENCY: Bahraini dinar (BHD)
ORGANIZATIONS: Arab League, UN

The sheikdom is a barren island in the Persian Gulf with less than 80 mm (3 inches) rainfall a year. Summer temperatures average 32°C (89°F). Bahrain was the first country in the Arabian peninsula to strike oil, in 1932. Oil still accounts for 60 per cent of revenue and gas is becoming increasingly important. Lower oil prices and decreased production is now causing the government to diversify the economy with expansion of light and heavy industry and chemical plants, and the subsequent encouragement of trade and foreign investment.

BANGLADESH
STATUS: Republic
AREA: 144,000 sq km (55,585 sq miles)
POPULATION: 118,700,000
ANNUAL NATURAL INCREASE: 2.2%
CAPITAL: Dhaka, (Dhākā, Dacca)
LANGUAGE: Bengali (Bangla), Bihari, Hindi, English
RELIGION: 85% Muslim, Hindu, Buddhist and Christian minorities
CURRENCY: taka (BDT)
ORGANIZATIONS: Col. Plan, Comm., UN

Bangladesh is one of the poorest and most densely populated countries of the world. Most of its territory, except for bamboo-forested hills in the southeast, comprises the vast river systems of the Ganges and Brahmaputra which drain from the Himalayan mountains into the Bay of Bengal, frequently changing course and flooding the flat delta plain. This land is, however, extremely fertile and attracts a high concentration of the population. The climate is tropical, and agriculture is dependent on monsoon rainfall. When the monsoon fails there is drought. Eighty-two per cent of the population are farmers, the

main crops being rice and jute. Bangladesh is the world's leading supplier of jute, which accounts for 25 per cent of the country's exports. The main industry and number one export is clothing . Natural gas reserves, under the Bay of Bengal, are beginning to be exploited.

BARBADOS

STATUS: Commonwealth State
AREA: 430 sq km (166 sq miles)
POPULATION: 259,000
ANNUAL NATURAL INCREASE: 0.3%
CAPITAL: Bridgetown
LANGUAGE: English
RELIGION: Anglican Christian majority,
Methodist and Roman Catholic minorities
CURRENCY: Barbados dollar (BBD)
ORGANIZATIONS: Caricom, Comm., OAS, UN

The former British colony of Barbados in the Caribbean is the most eastern island of the Antilles chain. The gently rolling landscape of the island is lush and fertile, the temperature ranging from 25–28°C (77–82°F) with 1270–1900 mm (50–75 inches) of rainfall per year. Sugar and its by-products, molasses and rum, are traditional cash crops. These are being overtaken in importance by tourism which provides an occupation for one-third of the population. This is a growth sector, although it has suffered recently from world recession. An oilfield supplies one-third of domestic oil requirements.

BELARUS

STATUS: Republic
AREA: 208,000 sq km (80,290 sq miles)
POPULATION: 10,280,000
ANNUAL NATURAL INCREASE: 0.5%
CAPITAL: Minsk
LANGUAGE: Belorussian, Russian
RELIGION: Roman Catholic, Uniate
CURRENCY: rouble
ORGANIZATIONS: CIS, UN

Belarus achieved independence in 1991. The country is mainly flat with forests covering more than one-third of the area. Swamps and marshlands cover large areas but, when drained, the soil is very fertile. The climate is continental with fairly cold winters (-7°C or 20°F). Grain, flax, potatoes and sugar beet are the main crops but livestock production accounts for more than half the value of agricultural output. Large areas of Belarus are thinly populated; most people live in the central area. The republic is comparatively poor in mineral resources and suffered terrible devastation during the Second World War. Post-war industrialization has been based on imported raw materials and semi-manufactured goods, concentrating on the production of trucks, tractors, agricultural machinery and other heavy engineering equipment. However, these industries are heavily reliant on imported Russian energy and output has declined since independence.

BELGIUM

STATUS: Kingdom
AREA: 30,520 sq km (11,780 sq miles)
POPULATION: 10,020,000
ANNUAL NATURAL INCREASE: 0.3%
CAPITAL: Brussels (Bruxelles/Brussel)
LANGUAGE: French, Dutch (Flemish), German
RELIGION: Roman Catholic majority, Protestant
and Jewish minorities
CURRENCY: Belgium franc (BEF)
ORGANIZATIONS: Council of Europe, EEA, EU,
NATO, OECD, UN, WEU

Over two-thirds of Belgium comprises the Flanders plain, a flat plateau covered by fertile wind-blown loess which extends from the North Sea coast down to the forested mountains of the Ardennes in the south. The climate is mild, maritime temperate with 720–1200 mm (28–47 inches) of rainfall a year. Over half the country is intensively farmed – cereals, root crops, vegetables and flax are the main crops and the country is nearly self-sufficient in meat and dairy products. Belgium's tradition as an industrialized nation dates back to the 19th century and Flanders has historically been famed for its textiles. The main industries now are metal-working (including motor vehicle assembly), chemicals, iron and steel, textiles, food and drink processing and diamonds. In recent years many companies have embarked on high-technology specialization including computer software, micro-electronics and telecommunications. Belgium is a trading nation, exporting more than half its national production. Most trade passes through the port of Antwerp, and an efficient communications network links it with the rest of Europe.

BELIZE

STATUS: Commonwealth Nation

AREA: 22,965 sq km (8,865 sq miles)
POPULATION: 230,000
ANNUAL NATURAL INCREASE: 2.6%
CAPITAL: Belmopan
LANGUAGE: English, Spanish, Maya
RELIGION: 60% Roman Catholic,
40% Protestant
CURRENCY: Belizean dollar (BZD)
ORGANIZATIONS: CARICOM, Comm.,
OAS, UN

Bordering the Caribbean Sea, in Central America, sub-tropical Belize is dominated by its dense forest cover. Principal exports are sugar cane, citrus concentrates and bananas. Since independence from Britain in 1973 the country has developed agriculture to lessen reliance on imported food products. Other commodities produced include tropical fruits, vegetables, fish and timber.

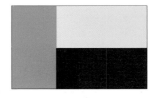

BENIN

STATUS: Republic
AREA: 112,620 sq km (43,470 sq miles)
POPULATION: 5,010,000
ANNUAL NATURAL INCREASE: 3.2%
CAPITAL: Porto Novo
LANGUAGE: French, Fon, Adja
RELIGION: majority traditional beliefs,
15% Roman Catholic, 13% Muslim
CURRENCY: CFA franc (W Africa) (XOF)
ORGANIZATIONS: ECOWAS, OAU, UN

Benin, formerly Dahomey, is a small strip of country descending from the wooded savannah hills of the north to the forested and cultivated lowlands fringing the Bight of Benin. The economy is agricultural, with palm oil, cotton, cocoa, coffee, groundnuts and copra as main exports. The developing offshore oil industry has proven reserves of over 20 million barrels.

BERMUDA

STATUS: Self-governing UK Crown Colony
AREA: 54 sq km (21 sq miles)
POPULATION: 74,837
CAPITAL: Hamilton

BHUTAN

STATUS: Kingdom
AREA: 46,620 sq km (17,995 sq miles)
POPULATION: 600,000
ANNUAL NATURAL INCREASE: 2.2%
CAPITAL: Thimphu
LANGUAGE: Dzongkha, Nepali, English
RELIGION: Mahayana Buddhist, 30% Hindu
CURRENCY: ngultrum (BTN), Indian rupee (INR)
ORGANIZATIONS: Col. Plan, UN

Bhutan is a small country in the Himalayan foothills between China and India, and to the east of Nepal. Rainfall is high at over 3000 mm (118 inches) a year but temperatures vary between the extreme cold of the northern ranges to a July average of 27°C (81°F) in the southern forests. Long isolated, the economy of Bhutan is dominated by agriculture and small local industries. All manufactured goods are imported.

BOLIVIA

STATUS: Republic
AREA: 1,098,575 sq km (424,050 sq miles)
POPULATION: 7,832,396
ANNUAL NATURAL INCREASE: 2.5%
CAPITAL: La Paz
LANGUAGE: Spanish, Quechua, Aymara
RELIGION: Roman Catholic majority
CURRENCY: Boliviano (BOB)
ORGANIZATIONS: OAS, UN

Bolivia, where the average life expectancy is 51 years, is one of the world's poorest nations. Landlocked and isolated, the country stretches from the eastern Andes across high cool plateaux before dropping to the dense forest of the Amazon basin and the grasslands of the southeast. Bolivia was once rich, its wealth based on minerals (in recent decades tin) but in 1985 world tin prices dropped and the industry collapsed. Oil and gas and agriculture now dominate the economy. Crops include soya, cotton, coca (cocaine shrub), sugar and coffee. Mining is still important, with the emphasis on zinc.

BOSNIA-HERZEGOVINA

STATUS: Republic
AREA: 51,130 sq km (19,736 sq miles)
POPULATION: 2,900,000
ANNUAL NATURAL INCREASE: 0.2%
CAPITAL: Sarajevo
LANGUAGE: Serbo-Croat
RELIGION: Muslim, Christian

CURRENCY: dinar
ORGANIZATIONS: UN

Bosnia-Herzegovina achieved independence in April 1992, but international recognition did not spare the Republic from savage ethnic warfare between Muslims, Serbs and Croats. Partitioning of the country into a new federation acceptable to all warring parties appears to be a necessity for peace. Before the war Bosnia's economy was based predominantly on agriculture – sheep rearing and the cultivation of vines, olives and citrus fruits. The country is mainly mountainous with the Sava valley in the north being the only lowland of consequence. The climate is Mediterranean towards the Adriatic, but continental and cooler inland.

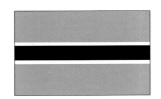

BOTSWANA

STATUS: Republic
AREA: 582,000 sq km (224,652 sq miles)
POPULATION: 1,291,000
ANNUAL NATURAL INCREASE: 3.4%
CAPITAL: Gaborone
LANGUAGE: Setswana, English
RELIGION: traditional beliefs majority,
Christian minority
CURRENCY: pula (BWP)
ORGANIZATIONS: Comm., OAU, UN

The arid high plateau of Botswana, with its poor soils and low rainfall, supports little arable agriculture, but over 2.3 million cattle graze the dry grasslands. Diamonds are the chief export, providing 80 per cent of export earnings. Copper, nickel, potash, soda ash, salt and coal are also important. The growth of light industries around the capital has stimulated trade with neighbouring countries.

BRAZIL

STATUS: Federal Republic
AREA: 8,511,965 sq km (3,285,620 sq miles)
POPULATION: 156,275,000
ANNUAL NATURAL INCREASE: 2.2%
CAPITAL: Brasília
LANGUAGE: Portuguese
RELIGION: 90% Roman Catholic,
Protestant minority
CURRENCY: cruzeiro real (BRC),URV
ORGANIZATIONS: Mercosur, OAS, UN

Brazil is the largest country in South America with the Amazon basin tropical rain forest covers roughly a third of the country. It is one of the world's leading agricultural exporters, with coffee, soya beans, sugar, bananas, cocoa, tobacco, rice and cattle major commodities. Brazil is an industrial power but with development limited to the heavily populated urban areas of the eastern coastal lowlands. Mineral resources, except for iron ore, do not play a significant role in the

economy at present, but recent economic policies have concentrated on developing the industrial base – road and rail communications, light and heavy industry and expansion of energy resources, particularly hydro-electric power harnessed from the three great river systems. Unlike other South American countries Brazil still has a serious inflation rate, introducing the 'real', on 1 July 1994 (the fifth new currency in a decade), in an attempt to slow the rate down.

BRITISH ANTARCTIC TERRITORY

STATUS: UK Dependent Territory
AREA: 1,544,000 sq km (599,845 sq miles)
POPULATION: no permanent population

BRITISH INDIAN OCEAN TERRITORY

STATUS: UK Dependency comprising the
Chagos Archipelago
AREA: 5,765 sq km (2,225 sq miles)
POPULATION: 266,000

BRUNEI

STATUS: Sultanate
AREA: 5,765 sq km (2,225 sq miles)
POPULATION: 270,000
ANNUAL NATURAL INCREASE: 3.2%
CAPITAL: Bandar Seri Begawan
LANGUAGE: Malay, English, Chinese
RELIGION: 65% Sunni Muslim, Buddhist and
Christian minorities
CURRENCY: Brunei dollar (BND)
ORGANIZATIONS: ASEAN, Comm, UN

The Sultanate of Brunei is situated on the northwest coast of Borneo. Its tropical climate is hot and humid with annual rainfall ranging from 2500 mm (98 inches) on the narrow coastal strip to 5000 mm (197 inches) in the mountainous interior. Oil and gas reserves, mostly offshore, are the basis of the Brunei economy. Half the oil and nearly all the natural gas (in liquefied form) are exported to Japan.

BULGARIA

STATUS: Republic
AREA: 110,910 sq km (42,810 sq miles)
POPULATION: 8,467,000
ANNUAL NATURAL INCREASE: 0.0%
CAPITAL: Sofia (Sofiya)
LANGUAGE: Bulgarian, Turkish
RELIGION: Eastern Orthodox majority,
Muslim minority
CURRENCY: lev (BGL)
ORGANIZATIONS: Council of Europe, EFTA,
OIEC, UN

Bulgaria exhibits great variety in its landscape. In the north, the land from the plains of the Danube slope upwards into the Balkan mountains (Stara Planina), which run east-west through central Bulgaria. The Rhodope mountains dominate the west, with the lowlands of Thrace and the Maritsa valley in the south. Climate is continental with temperatures ranging from -5°C (23°F) in winter to 28°C (82°F) in summer. The economy is based on agricultural products, with cereals, tobacco, cotton, fruits and vines dominating. Wine is a particularly successful export. Nuclear power is the main domestic power source, however the reactors are becoming elderly and other sources of energy are being sought, in particular oil and gas in the Black Sea. The heavy industry sector, which thrived in close association with the former USSR, is declining.

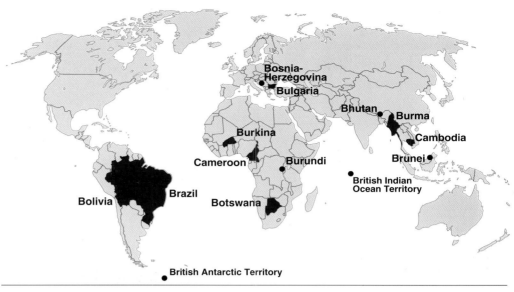

BURKINA

STATUS: Republic
AREA: 274,122 sq km (105,811 sq miles)
POPULATION: 9,490,000
ANNUAL NATURAL INCREASE: 2.8%
CAPITAL: Ouagadougou
LANGUAGE: French, Moré (Mossi), Dyula
RELIGION: 60% animist, 30% Muslim, 10% Roman Catholic
CURRENCY: CFA franc (W Africa) (OXF)
ORGANIZATIONS: ECOWAS, OAU, UN

Situated on the southern edge of the Sahara, Burkina, previously known as Upper Volta, is a poor, landlocked country with thin soils supporting savannah grasslands. Frequent droughts, particularly in the north, seriously affect the economy, which is mainly subsistence agriculture with livestock herding, and the export of groundnuts and cotton. There is virtually no industry. Some minerals are exported and manganese exports began in 1993.

BURMA (MYANMAR)

STATUS: Union of states and divisions
AREA: 678,030 sq km (261,720 sq miles)
POPULATION: 42,330,000
ANNUAL NATURAL INCREASE: 2.2%
CAPITAL: Rangoon (Yangon)
LANGUAGE: Burmese
RELIGION: 85% Buddhist. Animist, Muslim, Hindu and Christian minorities
CURRENCY: kyat (BUK)
ORGANIZATIONS: Col. Plan, UN

Much of Burma (renamed Myanmar by its military leaders in 1989) is covered by tropical rainforest divided by the central valley of the Irrawaddy, the Sittang and the Salween rivers. The western highlands are an extension of the Himalaya mountains; hills to the east and south are a continuation of the Yunnan plateau of China. The economy is based on the export of rice and forestry products. The irrigated central basin and the coastal region to the east of the Irrawaddy delta are the main rice-growing areas. Hardwoods, particularly teak, cover the highlands. There is potential for greater exploitation of tin, copper, gold, oil and natural gas deposits.

BURUNDI

STATUS: Republic
AREA: 27,835 sq km (10,745 sq miles)
POPULATION: 5,786,000
ANNUAL NATURAL INCREASE: 2.9%
CAPITAL: Bujumbura
LANGUAGE: French, Kirundi, Swahili
RELIGION: 60% Roman Catholic, animist minority
CURRENCY: Burundi franc (BIF)
ORGANIZATIONS: OAU, UN

This small central African republic is densely populated and one of the world's poorest nations. Although close to the equator, temperatures are modified because of altitude. Coffee is the main export, followed by tea, cotton and manufactured goods. The country has a history of ethnic fighting between the Hutu farming people, who make up 85 per cent of the population, and the Tutsi, originally pastoralists, who have dominated the army and the running of the country. Massacres of thousands of people in 1993-4 resulted from ethnic war, ignited by a Hutu election victory marking an end to 31 years of Tutsi domination.

CAMBODIA

STATUS: Kingdom
AREA: 181,000 sq km (69,865 sq miles)
POPULATION: 12,000,000
ANNUAL NATURAL INCREASE: 2.7%
CAPITAL: Phnom Penh
LANGUAGE: Khmer
RELIGION: Buddhist majority, Roman Catholic and Muslim minorities
CURRENCY: reil (KHR)
ORGANIZATIONS: Col. Plan, UN

Cambodia, in southeast Asia, is mostly a lowland basin. Over 70 per cent of the country is covered by the central plain of the Mekong river. The climate is tropical, with average annual temperatures exceeding 25°C (77°F). Monsoon rainfall occurs from May to October. These provide ideal conditions for the country's rice production and fish harvesting. The economy has been damaged since the 1970s by almost constant civil war. Power shortages hamper industrial development, the roads are badly damaged and land mines buried in the countryside make farming hazardous.

CAMEROON

STATUS: Republic
AREA: 475,500 sq km(183,545 sq miles)
POPULATION: 12,198,000
ANNUAL NATURAL INCREASE: 3.0%
CAPITAL: Yaoundé
LANGUAGE: English, French
RELIGION: 40% Christian, 39% traditional beliefs, 21% Muslim
CURRENCY: CRA franc (C Africa) (XAF)
ORGANIZATIONS: OAU, UN

Cameroon, in west Africa, is situated between the Gulf of Guinea in the south and the shores of Lake Chad in the north. In the south, coastal lowlands rise to densely forested plateaux, whereas further northwards savannah takes over, and aridity increases towards the Sahara. Oil products, once the main export, have declined in importance and now agricultural products account for most export revenue. Coffee, cocoa, bananas and avocados are the main cash crops. Mineral resources are underdeveloped but Cameroon is one of Africa's main producers of bauxite (aluminium ore) and aluminium is smelted at Edea.

CANADA

STATUS: Commonwealth Nation
AREA: 9,922,385 sq km (3,830,840 sq miles)
POPULATION: 28,866,000
ANNUAL NATURAL INCREASE: 1.4%
CAPITAL: Ottawa
LANGUAGE: English, French
RELIGION: 46% Roman Catholic,
Protestant and Jewish minorities
CURRENCY: Canadian dollar (CAD)
ORGANIZATIONS: Col. Plan, Comm., G7, OAS,
OECD, NATO, NAFTA, UN

Canada is the world's second largest country stretching from the great barren islands of the Arctic north to the vast grasslands of the central south, and from the Rocky Mountains in the west to the farmlands of the Great Lakes in the east. This huge area experiences great climatic differences but basically a continental climate prevails with extremes of heat and cold particularly in the central plains. The Arctic tundra of the far north provides summer grazing for caribou. Further south coniferous forests grow on the thin soils of the ancient shield landscape and on the extensive foothills of the Rocky Mountains. In contrast, the rich soils of the central prairies support grasslands and grain crops. The Great Lakes area provides fish, fruit, maize, root crops and dairy products; the prairies produce over 20 per cent of the worlds wheat; and the grasslands of Alberta support a thriving beef industry. Most minerals are mined and exploited in Canada with oil and natural gas, iron ore, bauxite, nickel, zinc, copper, gold and silver the major exports. Recently, diamonds have been discovered in the Northwest Territories. The country's vast rivers provide huge amounts of hydro-electric power but most industry is confined to the Great Lakes and St Lawrence margins. The principal manufactured goods for export are steel products, motor vehicles and paper for newsprint. The USA is Canada's main trading partner, taking 80 per cent of exports. Following a free trade agreement (NAFTA) in 1993 between the USA, Canada and Mexico, even closer economic ties will be made with the USA.

ALBERTA
STATUS: Province
AREA: 661,190 sq km (255,220 sq miles)
POPULATION: 2,672,000
CAPITAL: Edmonton

BRITISH COLUMBIA
STATUS: Province
AREA: 948,565 sq km (366,160 sq miles)
POPULATION: 3,570,000
CAPITAL: Victoria

MANITOBA
STATUS: Province
AREA: 650,090 sq km (250,935 sq miles)
POPULATION: 1,117,000
CAPITAL: Winnipeg

NEW BRUNSWICK
STATUS: Province
AREA: 73,435 sq km (28,345 sq miles)
POPULATION: 751,000
CAPITAL: Fredericton

NEWFOUNDLAND AND LABRADOR
STATUS: Province
AREA: 404,520 sq km (156,145 sq miles)
POPULATION: 581,000
CAPITAL: St John's

NORTHWEST TERRITORIES
STATUS: Territory
AREA: 3,379,685 sq km (1,304,560 sq miles)
POPULATION: 63,000
CAPITAL: Yellowknife

NOVA SCOTIA
STATUS: Province
AREA: 55,490 sq km (21,420 sq miles)
POPULATION: 925,000
CAPITAL: Halifax

ONTARIO
STATUS: Province
AREA: 1,068,630 sq km (412,490 sq miles)
POPULATION: 10,795,000
CAPITAL: Toronto

PRINCE EDWARD ISLAND
STATUS: Province
AREA: 5,655 sq km (2,185 sq miles)
POPULATION: 132,000
CAPITAL: Charlottetown

QUEBEC
STATUS: Province
AREA: 1,540,680 sq km (594,705 sq miles)
POPULATION: 7,226,000
CAPITAL: Quebec

SASKATCHEWAN
STATUS: Province
AREA: 651,900 sq km (251,635 sq miles)
POPULATION: 1,002,000
CAPITAL: Regina

YUKON TERRITORY
STATUS: Province
AREA: 482,515 sq km (186,250 sq miles)
POPULATION: 33,000
CAPITAL: Whitehorse

CANARY ISLANDS
STATUS: Island Provinces of Spain
AREA: 7,275 sq km (2,810 sq miles)
POPULATION: 1,493,784
CAPITAL: Las Palmas (Gran Canaria) and
Santa Cruz (Tenerife)

CAPE VERDE
STATUS: Republic
AREA: 4,035 sq km (1,560 sq miles)
POPULATION: 350,000
ANNUAL NATURAL INCREASE: 2.7%
CAPITAL: Praia
LANGUAGE: Portuguese, Creole
RELIGION: 98% Roman Catholic
CURRENCY: Cape Verde escudo (CVE)

ORGANIZATIONS: ECOWAS, OAU, UN
Independent since 1975, the ten inhabited volcanic islands of the republic are situated in the Atlantic 500 km (310 miles) west of Senegal. Rainfall is low but irrigation encourages growth of sugar cane, coffee, coconuts, fruit (mainly bananas) and maize. Fishing accounts for about 70 per cent of export revenue and all consumer goods are imported.

CAYMAN ISLANDS
STATUS: UK Dependent Territory
AREA: 259 sq km (100 sq miles)
POPULATION: 29,000
CAPITAL: George Town

CENTRAL AFRICAN REPUBLIC
STATUS: Republic
AREA: 624,975 sq km (241,240 sq miles)
POPULATION: 3,173,000
ANNUAL NATURAL INCREASE: 2.7%
CAPITAL: Bangui
LANGUAGE: French, Sango (national)
RELIGION: Animist majority, Christian minority
CURRENCY: CFA franc (C Africa) (XAF)
ORGANIZATIONS: OAU, UN

The republic is remote from both east and west Africa. It has a tropical climate with little variation in temperature. Savannah covers the rolling plateaux with rainforest in the southeast. To the north lies the Sahara Desert. Most farming is at subsistence level with a small amount of crops grown for export – cotton, coffee, groundnuts and tobacco. Hardwood forests in the southwest provide timber for export. Diamonds are the major export, accounting for over half of foreign earnings.

CHAD
STATUS: Republic
AREA: 1,284,000 sq km (495,625 sq miles)
POPULATION: 6,288,000
ANNUAL NATURAL INCREASE: 2.5%
CAPITAL: Ndjamena
LANGUAGE: French, Arabic, local languages
RELIGION: 50% Muslim, 45% animist
CURRENCY: CRA franc (C Africa) (XAF)
ORGANIZATIONS: OAU, UN

Chad is a vast state of central Africa stretching deep into the Sahara. The economy is based on agriculture but only the south, with 1,000 mm (39 in) of rainfall, can support crops for export – cotton, rice and groundnuts. Severe droughts, increasing desertification and border disputes have severely restricted development. Life expectancy at birth is still only 43 years. Salt is mined around Lake Chad where the majority of the population live.

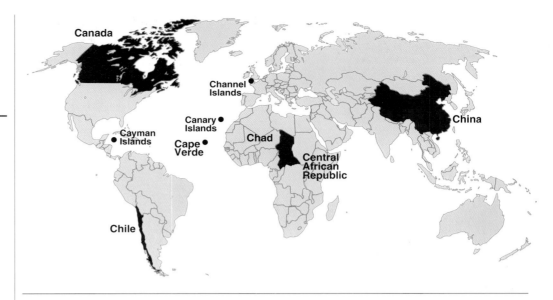

CHANNEL ISLANDS

STATUS: British Crown Dependency
AREA: 194 sq km (75 sq miles)
POPULATION: 145,796
CAPITAL: St Hélier (Jersey)
St Peter Port (Guernsey)

CHILE

STATUS: Republic
AREA: 751,625 sq km (290,125 sq miles)
POPULATION: 13,813,000
ANNUAL NATURAL INCREASE: 1.7%
CAPITAL: Santiago
LANGUAGE: Spanish
RELIGION: 85% Roman Catholic,
Protestant minority
CURRENCY: Chilean peso (CLP)
ORGANIZATIONS: OAS, UN

Chile is a long narrow country on the west coast of South America, stretching through 38° of latitude from the Atacama desert of the north to the sub-polar islands of Tierra del Fuego. Apart from a coastal strip of lowland, the country is dominated by the Andes mountains. Most energy is provided by hydro-electric power. The economy is based upon the abundance of natural resources with copper (the world's largest reserve), iron ore, nitrates, gold, timber, coal, oil and gas. Light and heavy industries are based around Concepción and Santiago. Traditional major exports are copper, fishmeal and cellulose. In the early 1990s farm production increased dramatically and food products now account for 29 per cent of export earnings.

CHINA

STATUS: People's Republic
AREA: 9,597,000 sq km (3,704,440 sq miles)
POPULATION: 1,154,887,381
ANNUAL NATURAL INCREASE: 1.3%
CAPITAL: Beijing (Peking)
LANGUAGE: Mandarin Chinese,
regional languages
RELIGION: Confucianist, Buddhist, Taoist,
Christian and Muslim minorities
CURRENCY: yuan (CNY)
ORGANIZATIONS: UN

The land of China is one of the most diverse on Earth and has vast mineral and agricultural resources. The majority of the people live in the east where the economy is dictated by the great drainage basins of the Yellow River (Huang He) and the Yangtze (Chang Jiang). Here, intensively irrigated agriculture produces one-third of the world's rice as well as wheat, maize, sugar, cotton, soya beans and oil seeds. Pigs are reared and fish caught throughout China. The country is basically self-sufficient in foodstuffs.

Western and northern China are much less densely populated as cultivation is restricted to oases and sheltered valleys. In the southwest, the Tibetan plateau averages 4,900 m (16,000 ft) and supports scattered sheep herding. To the north are Sinkiang and the desert basins of Tarim (Tarim Pendi) and Dzungaria, and bordering Mongolia the vast dry Gobi desert. In the far north only in Manchuria does a more temperate climate allow extensive arable cultivation, of mainly wheat, barley and maize.

The natural mineral resources of China are immense, varied and under-exploited. The Yunnan plateau of the southeast is rich in tin, copper, and zinc; Manchuria possesses coal and iron ore; and oil is extracted from beneath the Yellow Sea. The main industrial centres concentrate on the production of iron, steel, cement, light engineering and textile manufacturing.

With a population of over one billion, China has made tremendous efforts since the late 1970s to erase the negative economic effects of the collectivization policy implemented from 1955, and the cultural revolution of the late 1960s. In 1978 the Chinese leader, Deng Xiaoping, launched an economic revolution (creating special economic zones and encouraging foreign investment). The country is now experiencing phenomenal economic growth, a new consumer revolution and waves of entrepreneurial activities. A growing inequality in living standards between the rural provinces and the richer urban areas has led to a surge of migrants from the countryside to the cities.

ANHUI (ANHWEI)

STATUS: Province
AREA: 139,900 sq km (54,000 sq miles)
POPULATION: 57,600,000
CAPITAL: Hefei

BEIJING (PEKING)

STATUS: Municipality
AREA: 17,800 sq km (6,870 sq miles)
POPULATION: 10,900,000

FUJIAN (FUKIEN)

STATUS: Province
AREA: 123,000 sq km (47,515 sq miles)
POPULATION: 30,800,000
CAPITAL: Fuzhou

GANSU (KANSU)

STATUS: Province
AREA: 530,000 sq km (204,580 sq miles)
POPULATION: 22,900,000
CAPITAL: Lanzhou

GUANGDONG (KWANGTUNG)

STATUS: Province
AREA: 231,400 sq km (89,320 sq miles)
POPULATION: 64,400,000
CAPITAL: Guangzhou (Canton)

GUANGXI (KWANGSI-CHUANG)

STATUS: Autonomous Region
AREA: 220,400 sq km (85,075 sq miles)
POPULATION: 43,200,000
CAPITAL: Nanning

GUIZHOU (KWEICHOW)

STATUS: Province
AREA: 174,000 sq km (67,165 sq miles)
POPULATION: 33,200,000
CAPITAL: Guiyang

HAINAN

STATUS: Province
AREA: 34,965 sq km (13,500 sq miles)
POPULATION: 6,700,000
CAPITAL: Haikou

HEBEI (HOPEI)

STATUS: Province
AREA: 202,700 sq km (78,240 sq miles)
POPULATION: 62,200,000
CAPITAL: Schijiazhuang

HEILONGJIANG (HEILUNGKIANG)

STATUS: Province
AREA: 710,000 sq km (274,060 sq miles)
POPULATION: 35,800,000
CAPITAL: Harbin

HENAN (HONAN)

STATUS: Province
AREA: 167,000 sq km (64,460 sq miles)
POPULATION: 87,600,000
CAPITAL: Zhengzhou

HUBEI (HUPEH)

STATUS: Province
AREA: 187,500 sq km (72,375 sq miles)
POPULATION: 55,100,000
CAPITAL: Wuhan

HUNAN
STATUS: Province
AREA: 210,500 sq km (81,255 sq miles)
POPULATION: 62,100,000
CAPITAL: Changsha

JIANGSU (KIANGSU)
STATUS: Province
AREA: 102,200 sq km (39,450 miles)
POPULATION: 68,400,000
CAPITAL: Nanjing (Nanking)

JIANGXI (KIANGSI)
STATUS: Province
AREA: 164,800 sq km (63,615 sq miles)
POPULATION: 38,700,000
CAPITAL: Nanchang

JILIN (KIRIN)
STATUS: Province
AREA: 290,000 sq km (111,940 sq miles)
POPULATION: 25,100,000
CAPITAL: Changchun

LIAONING
STATUS: Province
AREA: 230,000 sq km (88,780 sq miles)
POPULATION: 39,900,000
CAPITAL: Shenyang

NEI MONGOL (INNER MONGOLIA)
STATUS: Autonomous Region
AREA: 450,000 sq km (173,700 sq miles)
POPULATION: 21,800,000
CAPITAL: Hohhot

NINGXIA HUI (NINGHSIA HUI)
STATUS: Autonomous Region
AREA: 170,000 sq km (65,620 sq miles)
POPULATION: 4,800,000
CAPITAL: Yinchuan

QINGHAI (CHINGHAI)
STATUS: Province
AREA: 721,000 sq km (278,305 sq miles)
POPULATION: 4,500,000
CAPITAL: Xining

SHAANXI (SHENSI)
STATUS: Province
AREA: 195,800 sq km (75,580 sq miles)
POPULATION: 33,600,000
CAPITAL: Xian (Xi'an)

SHANDONG (SHANTUNG)
STATUS: Province
AREA: 153,300 sq km (59,175 sq miles)
POPULATION: 83,430,000
CAPITAL: Jinan

SHANGHAI
STATUS: Municipality
AREA: 5,800 sq km (2,240 sq miles)
POPULATION: 13,400,000

SHANXI (SHANSI)
STATUS: Province
AREA: 157,100 sq km (60,640 sq miles)
POPULATION: 29,400,000
CAPITAL: Taiyuan

SICHUAN (SZECHWAN)
STATUS: Province
AREA: 569,000 sq km (219,635 sq miles)
POPULATION: 109,000,000
CAPITAL: Chengdu

TIANJIN (TIENTSIN)
STATUS: Municipality
AREA: 4,000 sq km (1,545 sq miles)
POPULATION: 9,100,402

XINJIANG UYGUR (SINKIANG-UIGHUR)
STATUS: Autonomous Region
AREA: 1,646,800 sq km (635,665 sq miles)
POPULATION: 15,600,000
CAPITAL: Urumchi (Ürümqi)

XIZANG (TIBET)
STATUS: Autonomous Region
AREA: 1,221,600 sq km (471,540 sq miles)
POPULATION: 2,300,000
CAPITAL: Lhasa

YUNNAN
STATUS: Province
AREA: 436,200 sq km (168,375 sq miles)
POPULATION: 37,800,000
CAPITAL: Kunming

ZHEJIANG (CHEKIANG)
STATUS: Province
AREA: 101,800 sq km (39,295 sq miles)
POPULATION: 42,000,000
CAPITAL: Hangzhou

CHRISTMAS ISLAND
STATUS: External Territory of Australia
AREA: 135 sq km (52 sq miles)
POPULATION: 1,275

COCOS (KEELING) ISLANDS
STATUS: External Territory of Australia
AREA: 14 sq km (5 sq miles)
POPULATION: 647

COLOMBIA
STATUS: Republic
AREA: 1,138,915 (439,620 sq miles)
POPULATION: 13,813,000
ANNUAL NATURAL INCREASE: 1.8%
CAPITAL: Bogotá
LANGUAGE: Spanish, Indian languages
RELIGION: 95% Roman Catholic,
Protestant and Jewish minorities
CURRENCY: Colombian peso (COP)
ORGANIZATIONS: OAS, UN

Colombia is bounded by both the Caribbean Sea and Pacific Ocean. The northernmost peaks of the Andes chain runs from north to south through its western half and the eastern plains, beyond the Andes, contain the headwaters of the Amazon and Orinoco rivers. Almost half of Colombia is covered by the Amazon jungle. Colombia has a tropical climate and temperatures that vary with climate. The fertile river valleys in the uplands produce most of the famous Colombian coffee. Bananas, tobacco, cotton, sugar and rice are grown at lower altitudes. Coffee has always been the major export crop, but manufacturing industry and oil, coal, gold and precious stones are becoming more dominant in the economy. An oil boom is predicted following the discovery of new oil fields at Cusiana and Cupiagua. Immense illegal quantities of cocaine are exported to the US and elsewhere.

COMOROS
STATUS: Federal Islamic Republic
AREA: 1,860 sq km (718 sq miles)
POPULATION: 585,000
ANNUAL NATURAL INCREASE: 3.7%
CAPITAL: Moroni
LANGUAGE: French, Arabic, Comoran
RELIGION: Muslim majority,
Christian minority
CURRENCY: Comoro franc (KMF)
ORGANIZATIONS: OAU, UN

The Comoro Islands, comprising Grand Comore, Anjouan, and Móheli, are situated between Madagascar and the east African coast. The climate is tropical and humid all year round, with a moderate average annual rainfall ranging from 1,000–1140 mm (40–45 inches). Less than half the land is cultivated and the country is dependent on imports for food supplies. The island's economy is based on the export of vanilla, copra, cloves and ylang-ylang essence (exported for the French perfume industry). Mangoes, coconuts and bananas are grown around the coastal lowlands. Timber and timber products are important to local development. There is no manufacturing of any importance.

CONGO
STATUS: Republic
AREA: 342,000 sq km (132,010 sq miles)
POPULATION: 2,690,000
ANNUAL NATURAL INCREASE: 3.3%
CAPITAL: Brazzaville
LANGUAGE: French, Kongo, Teke, Sanga
RELIGION: 50% traditional beliefs,
30% Roman Catholic, Protestant
and Muslim minorities
CURRENCY: CFA franc (C Africa) (XAF)
ORGANIZATIONS: OAU, UN

The Congo, Africa's first communist state still has strong economic ties with the west, especially France, its former colonial ruler. Situated on the coast of west Africa, it contains over

two-thirds swamp and forest, with wooded savannah on the highlands of the Bateké plateau near the Gabon border. Its climate is hot and humid with average rainfall of 1220–1280 mm (48–50 inches). Over 60 per cent of the population is employed in subsistence farming, while sugar, coffee, palm oil and cocoa are all exported. Timber and timber products are major exports but the main source of export revenue is oil from offshore oilfields. Mineral resources are considerable, including industrial diamonds, gold, lead and zinc. Manufacturing industry is concentrated in the major towns and is primarily food processing and textiles.

COOK ISLANDS
STATUS: Self-governing Territory Overseas in Free Association with New Zealand
AREA: 233 sq km (90 sq miles)
POPULATION: 18,617
CAPITAL: Avarua on Rarotonga

CORAL SEA ISLANDS
STATUS: External Territory of Australia
AREA: 22 sq km (8.5 sq miles)
POPULATION: no permanent population

COSTA RICA
STATUS: Republic
AREA: 50,900 sq km (19,650 sq miles)
POPULATION: 3,099,000
ANNUAL NATURAL INCREASE: 2.5%
CAPITAL: San José
LANGUAGE: Spanish
RELIGION: 95% Roman Catholic
CURRENCY: Costa Rican colón (CRC)
ORGANIZATIONS: CACM, OAS, UN

Costa Rica is a narrow country, situated between Nicaragua and Panama, with both a Pacific and a Caribbean coastline. Its coastal regions experience hot, humid, tropical conditions, but in upland areas its climate is more equable. The mountain chains that run the length of the country form the fertile uplands where coffee is grown and cattle are kept. Bananas, grown on the Pacific coast, and coffee are the major cash crops for export. Although gold, silver, iron ore and bauxite are mined, the principal industries are food processing and the manufacture of textiles and chemicals, fertilizers and furniture.

CROATIA
STATUS: Republic
AREA: 56,540 sq km (21,825 sq miles)
POPULATION: 4,764,000
ANNUAL NATURAL INCREASE: 0.4%

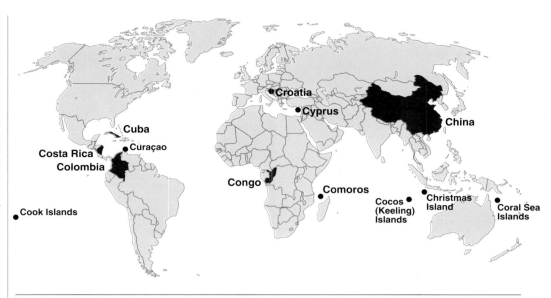

CAPITAL: Zagreb
LANGUAGE: Serbo-Croat
RELIGION: Roman Catholic majority
CURRENCY: kuna
ORGANIZATIONS: UN

Croatia is an oddly shaped country which runs in a narrow strip along the Adriatic coast and extends inland in a broad curve. Its climate varies from Mediterranean along the coast to continental further inland. Once part of the Yugoslavian Federation, Croatia achieved recognition as an independent nation in 1992 following the 1991 civil war between Serb and Croat factions. The conflict left the country with a damaged economy, disruption of trade, loss of tourist revenue and a huge reconstruction bill. Traditionally the fertile plains of central and eastern Croatia have been intensively farmed, producing surplus crops, meat and dairy products. The mountainous and barren littoral has been developed for tourism. Croatia used to be the most highly developed part of Yugoslavia, concentrating on electrical engineering, metal working, machine building, chemicals and rubber. Economic recovery is dependent upon political stability and an accommodation with the Serbs over the UN-supervised areas still under ethnic Serb control.

CUBA
STATUS: Republic
AREA: 114,525 sq km (44,205 sq miles)
POPULATION: 10,870,000
ANNUAL NATURAL INCREASE: 1.0%
CAPITAL: Havana (Habana)
LANGUAGE: Spanish
RELIGION: Roman Catholic majority
CURRENCY: Cuban peso (CUP)
ORGANIZATIONS: OIEC, UN

Cuba, the largest of the Greater Antilles islands, dominates the entrance to the Gulf of Mexico. It consists of one large and over 1,500 small islands, and is a mixture of fertile plains, mountain ranges and gentle countryside. Temperatures range from 22–28°C (72–82°F) and an there is an average annual rainfall of 1,200 mm (47 inches).

Sugar, tobacco and nickel are the main exports. Being a communist state, most of Cuba's trade has been with the former USSR and in the three years following the collapse of the Soviet Union the Cuban economy contracted by over 30 per cent (having lost its principal market for sugar, which it had bartered for oil, food and machinery). The economy was already suffering from US sanctions. Severe shortages of food, fuel and basic necessities were tolerated and in 1993 the government was forced to permit limited private enterprise and the use of American dollars.

CURAÇAO
STATUS: Self-governing Island of the Netherlands Antilles
AREA: 444 sq km (171 sq miles)
POPULATION: 707,000

CYPRUS
STATUS: Republic
(Turkish unilateral declaration of independence in northern area)
AREA: 9,250 sq km (3,570 sq miles)
POPULATION: 725,000
ANNUAL NATURAL INCREASE: 1.1%
CAPITAL: Nicosia
LANGUAGE: Greek, Turkish, English
RELIGION: Greek Orthodox majority, Muslim minority
CURRENCY: Cyprus pound (CYP), Turkish lira (TL)
ORGANIZATIONS: Comm., Council of Europe, UN

Cyprus is a prosperous Mediterranean island. The summers are very hot (38°C or 100°F) and dry, and the winters warm and wet. About two-thirds of the island is under cultivation and citrus fruit, potatoes, barley, wheat and olives are produced. Sheep, goats and pigs are the principal livestock. Copper is mined but the mining industry is declining. The main exports are manufactured goods, clothing and footwear, fruit, wine and vegetables. Tourism is an important source of foreign exchange.

CZECH REPUBLIC

STATUS: Federal Republic
AREA: 127,870 sq km (49,360 sq miles)
POPULATION: 10,330,000
ANNUAL NATURAL INCREASE: 0.3%
CAPITAL: Prague (Praha)
LANGUAGE: Czech
RELIGION: 40% Roman Catholic,
55% no stated religion
CURRENCY: Czech crown or koruna (CSK)
ORGANIZATIONS: Council of Europe,
OIEC, UN

Following the break up of Czechoslovakia, the Czech Republic came into being in January 1993. It is a country that lies at the heart of central Europe and has a diversity of landscapes. In Bohemia, to the west of the country, the upper Elbe drainage basin is surrounded by mountains. Moravia, separated from Bohemia by hills and mountains, is a lowland area centred on the town of Brno. The climate is temperate but with continental characteristics. Rain falls mainly in spring and autumn. This is historically one of the most highly industrialized regions of Europe, whose heavy industry once specialized in producing arms for the Soviet Union. Now the main products include cars, aircraft, tramways and locomotive diesel engines. There are raw materials (coal, minerals and timber) and a nuclear power station is being built to replace some polluting coal-fired stations.

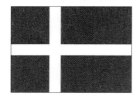

DENMARK

STATUS: Kingdom
AREA: 43,075 sq km (16,625 sq miles)
POPULATION: 5,181,000
ANNUAL NATURAL INCREASE: 0.1%
CAPITAL: Copenhagen (København)
LANGUAGE: Danish
RELIGION: 94% Lutheran, Roman Catholic minority
CURRENCY: Danish krone (DKK)
ORGANIZATIONS: Council of Europe, EU,
NATO, OECD, UN

Denmark is the smallest of the Scandinavian countries. It consists of the Jutland Peninsula and over 400 islands of which only one quarter are inhabited. The country is low-lying with a mixture of fertile and sandy soils, generally of glacial origin. Climate is temperate, with rainfall all the year round. Denmark's economy stems traditionally from agriculture and dairy products; bacon and sugar are still particularly important. An extensive fishing industry is centred on the shallow lagoons along the western coastline. Danish North Sea oil and gas provide self-sufficiency in energy and gas exports began in 1991. Food processing, beer, pharmaceuticals and specialist biotechnological equipment contribute to the industrial sector which provides 75 per cent of Danish exports.

DJIBOUTI

STATUS: Republic
AREA: 23,000 sq km (8,800 sq miles)
POPULATION: 467,000
ANNUAL NATURAL INCREASE: 2.9%
CAPITAL: Djibouti
LANGUAGE: French, Somali, Dankali, Arabic
RELIGION: Muslim majority,
Roman Catholic minority
CURRENCY: Djibouti franc (DJF)
ORGANIZATIONS: Arab League, OAU, UN

Situated at the mouth of the Red Sea, Djibouti consists almost entirely of low-lying desert. There are mountains in the north of which Musa Ālī Terara reaches 2,063 m (6,768 feet). Its climate is very hot all year with annual temperatures between 25–35°C (78–96°F). The annual rainfall is as low as 130 mm (5 inches). The land is barren so Djibouti's economy must rely on activities based on its deep natural port and position along a major shipping route. It therefore acts as a trade outlet for Ethiopia, as well as serving Red Sea shipping. Main exports are cattle and hides.

DOMINICA

STATUS: Commonwealth State
AREA: 751 sq km (290 sq miles)
POPULATION: 72,000
ANNUAL NATURAL INCREASE: -0.3%
CAPITAL: Roseau
LANGUAGE: English, French patois
RELIGION: 80% Roman Catholic
CURRENCY: East Caribbean dollar (XCD)
ORGANIZATIONS: Comm., OAS, UN

Dominica is located in the Windward Islands of the east Caribbean. It is mountainous and forested with a coastline of steep cliffs. Tropical rainforest covers nearly half of the island. The climate is tropical with average temperatures exceeding 25°C (77°F) and has abundant rainfall. Bananas are the major export, followed by citrus fruits, coconuts and timber. Coffee and cocoa production is developing. Tourism is the most rapidly expanding industry.

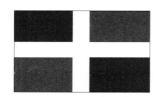

DOMINICAN REPUBLIC

STATUS: Republic
AREA: 48,440 sq km (18,700 sq miles)
POPULATION: 7,471,000
ANNUAL NATURAL INCREASE: 1.9%
CAPITAL: Santo Domingo
LANGUAGE: Spanish
RELIGION: 90% Roman Catholic,
Protestant and Jewish minorities
CURRENCY: Dominican peso (DOP)
ORGANIZATIONS: OAS, UN

The Dominican Republic is situated on the eastern half of the Caribbean island of Hispaniola. The landscape is dominated by a series of mountain ranges, thickly covered with rainforest, reaching up to 3,000 m (9,843 feet). To the south there is a coastal plain where the capital, Santo Domingo, lies. Minerals, in particular nickel, are important but agricultural products account for 70 per cent of export earnings. The traditional dependence on sugar has diminished, with coffee, tobacco and newer products including cocoa, fruit and vegetables gaining importance.

ECUADOR

STATUS: Republic
AREA: 461,475 sq km (178,130 sq miles)
POPULATION: 10,741,000
ANNUAL NATURAL INCREASE: 2.5%
CAPITAL: Quito
LANGUAGE: Spanish, Quechua,
other Indian languages
RELIGION: 90% Roman Catholic
CURRENCY: sucre (ECS)
ORGANIZATIONS: OAS, UN

Ecuador falls into two distinctive geographical zones, the coastal lowlands which border the Pacific Ocean and inland, the Andean highlands. The highlands stretch about 400 km (250 miles) north-south, and here limited quantities of maize, wheat and barley are cultivated. Ecuador's main agricultural export, bananas, coffee and cocoa, are all grown on the fertile coastal lowlands. The rapidly growing fishing industry, especially shrimps, is becoming more important. Large resources of crude oil have been found in the thickly-forested lowlands on the eastern border and Ecuador has now become South America's second largest oil producer after Venezuela. Mineral reserves include silver, gold, copper and zinc.

EGYPT

STATUS: Republic
AREA: 1,000,250 sq km
(386,095 sq miles)
POPULATION: 55,163,000
ANNUAL NATURAL INCREASE: 2.4%
CAPITAL: Cairo (El Qâhira)
LANGUAGE: Arabic, Berber, Nubian,
English, French
RELIGION: 80% Muslim (mainly Sunni),
Coptic Christian minority
CURRENCY: Egyptian pound (EGP)
ORGANIZATIONS: Arab league, OAU, UN

The focal point of Egypt, situated on the Mediterranean coast of northeast Africa, is the fertile, irrigated Nile river valley, sandwiched between two deserts. Egypt is virtually dependent on the Nile for water as average rainfall varies between only 200 mm (8 inches) in the north and zero in the deserts. Cotton and Egyptian clover are the two most important crops, with increasing cultivation of cereals, fruits, rice, sugar cane and vegetables. Agriculture is concentrated around the Nile flood plain and delta. In spite of this, however, Egypt has to import over half the food it needs. Buffalo, cattle, sheep, goats and camels are the principal livestock. Tourism is an important source of revenue together with the tolls from the Suez Canal. Major industries include the manufacture of cement, cotton goods, iron and steel, and processed foods. The main mineral deposits are phosphates, iron ore, salt, manganese and chromium. Egypt has sufficient oil and natural gas reserves for its own needs and exports crude oil. Gas is now replacing oil in Egyptian power stations in order to release more crude oil for export.

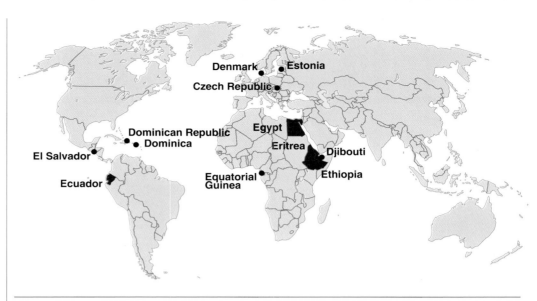

EL SALVADOR

STATUS: Republic
AREA: 21,395 sq km (8,260 sq miles)
POPULATION: 5,048,000
ANNUAL NATURAL INCREASE: 1.8%
CAPITAL: San Salvador
LANGUAGE: Spanish
RELIGION: 80% Roman Catholic
CURRENCY: El Salvador colón (SVC)
ORGANIZATIONS: CACM, OAS, UN

El Salvador is a small, densely populated country on the Pacific coast of Central America. Most of the population live around the lakes in the central plain. Temperatures range from 24–26°C (75–79°F) with an average annual rainfall of 1,780 mm (70 inches). Coffee provides about 50 per cent of export revenue. Other products include sugar, cotton, bananas and balsam. Industry has expanded considerably with the production of textiles, shoes, cosmetics, cement, processed foods, chemicals and furniture. Geothermal and hydro-electric resources are being developed and there are copper deposits as yet unexploited.

EQUATORIAL GUINEA

STATUS: Republic
AREA: 28,050 sq km (10,825 sq miles)
POPULATION: 369,000
ANNUAL NATURAL INCREASE: 2.3%
CAPITAL: Malabo
LANGUAGE: 85% Fang, Spanish, Bubi, other tribal languages

RELIGION: 96% Roman Catholic, 4% Animist
CURRENCY: CFA franc (C Africa) (XAF)
ORGANIZATIONS: OAU, UN

Independent from Spain since 1968, Equatorial Guinea consists of two separate regions – a mainland area with a tropical, humid climate and dense rainforest but little economic development, and the volcanic island of Bioko. Agriculture is the principal source of revenue. Cocoa and coffee from the island plantations are the main exports with wood products, fish and processed foods manufactured near the coast on the mainland.

ERITREA

STATUS: Republic
AREA: 91,600 sq km (35,370 sq miles)
POPULATION: 3,500,000
CAPITAL: Asmara (Āsmera)
LANGUAGE: Arabic, native languages, English
RELIGION: 50% Christian, 50% Muslim
CURRENCY: Ethiopian birr
ORGANIZATIONS: OAU, UN

Eritrea gained formal recognition of its independence from Ethiopia in 1993. The landscape consists of an arid coastal plain, which borders the Red Sea, and the highlands of the central area, which rise to over 2000 m (6,562 feet). There are few natural resources, with what industry there is being concentrated around Asmara. The consequences of continuing drought and the protracted civil war will affect the population and economy for some time to come.

ESTONIA

STATUS: Republic
AREA: 45,100 sq km (17,413 sq miles)
POPULATION: 1,516,000

ANNUAL NATURAL INCREASE: 0.2%
CAPITAL: Tallinn
LANGUAGE: Estonian, Russian
RELIGION: Lutheran, Roman Catholic
CURRENCY: kroon (EKR)
ORGANIZATIONS: Council of Europe, UN

With the mainland situated on the southern coast of the Gulf of Finland and encompassing a large number of islands, Estonia is the smallest and most northerly of the Baltic States. The generally flat and undulating landscape is characterised by extensive forests and many lakes. The climate is temperate. Agriculture, mainly livestock production, woodworking and textiles are also important. The economy is currently undergoing a transformation from central planning and state-ownership to a free market system based on private enterprise. Incorporated into the Soviet Union in 1940, Estonia regained its independence in 1991.

ETHIOPIA

STATUS: Republic
AREA: 1,023,050 sq km (394,895 sq miles)
POPULATION: 51,980,000
ANNUAL NATURAL INCREASE: 3.4%
CAPITAL: Addis Ababa (Ādīs Ābeba)
LANGUAGE: Amharic, English, Arabic
RELIGION: Ethiopian Orthodox, Muslim and animist
CURRENCY: birr (ETB)
ORGANIZATIONS: OAU, UN

Ethiopia's landscape consists of heavily dissected plateaux and plains of arid desert. Rainfall in these latter areas is minimal and unreliable, and drought and starvation are ever-present problems. Farming, in the high rural areas, accounts for 90 per cent of export revenue with coffee as the principal crop and main export together with fruit and vegetables, oil-seeds, hides and skins. Gold is mined on a small scale. The most important industries are cotton textiles, cement, canned foods, construction materials and leather goods. These are concentrated around the capital. In recent years the economy has been devastated by almost constant civil war.

FAEROES

STATUS: Self-governing Island Region
of Denmark
AREA: 1,399 sq km (540 sq miles)
POPULATION: 47,000
CAPITAL: Tórshavn

FALKLAND ISLANDS

STATUS: UK Crown Colony
AREA: 12,175 sq km (4,700 sq miles)
POPULATION: 2,121
CAPITAL: Stanley

FIJI

STATUS: Republic
AREA: 18,330 sq km (7,075 sq miles)
POPULATION: 758,275
ANNUAL NATURAL INCREASE: 1.8%
CAPITAL: Suva
LANGUAGE: Fijian, English, Hindi
RELIGION: 51% Methodist Christian,
40% Hindu, 8% Muslim
CURRENCY: Fiji dollar (FJD)
ORGANIZATIONS: Col. Plan, UN

A country of some 320 tropical islands, of which over 100 are inhabited, the Republic of Fiji is located in Melanesia, in the south-central Pacific Ocean. The islands range from tiny coral reefs and atolls to the two largest Vanua Levu and Viti Levu, which are mountainous and of volcanic origin. The climate is tropical with temperatures ranging from 16–33°C (60–90°F) and annual rainfall being 236 mm (60 inches). Fiji's economy is geared to production of sugar cane, which provides 45 per cent of export revenue. Coconuts, bananas and rice are grown and livestock raised. Main industries are sugar processing, gold-mining, copra processing and fish canning. Tourism is also an important revenue earner.

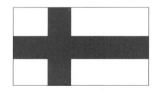

FINLAND

STATUS: Republic
AREA: 337,030 sq km
(130,095 sq miles)
POPULATION: 5,076,000
ANNUAL NATURAL INCREASE: 0.4%
CAPITAL: Helsinki
LANGUAGE: Finnish, Swedish
RELIGION: 87% Evangelical Lutheran,
Eastern Orthodox minority
CURRENCY: markka (Finnmark) (FIM)
ORGANIZATIONS: Council of Europe, EEA,
EFTA, OECD, UN

Finland is a flat land of lakes and forests. Over 70 per cent of the land supports coniferous woodland with a further 10 per cent being water. The Saimaa lake area is Europe's largest inland water system. Its soils are thin and poor on ice-scarred granite plateaux. Most of Finland's population live in towns in the far south because of the harsh northern climate. In the north temperatures can range from -30°C (-22°F) in the winter to 27°C (81°F) in summer. The Baltic Sea can freeze for several miles from the coast during winter months. There is 600 mm (24 inches) of rain per annum throughout the country. Forestry products (timber, pulp and paper) once dominated the economy (80 per cent in 1980) but now account for 40 per cent of the export total and engineering, in particular shipbuilding and forest machinery, is almost equal in importance. Finland is virtually self-sufficient in basic foodstuffs. The country depends heavily on imported energy, producing only 30 per cent of its total consumption (20 per cent by its four nuclear power stations).

FRANCE

STATUS: Republic
AREA: 543,965 sq km (209,970 sq miles)
POPULATION: 57,800,000
ANNUAL NATURAL INCREASE: 0.6%
CAPITAL: Paris
LANGUAGE: French
RELIGION: 90% Roman Catholic. Protestant,
Muslim, Jewish minorities
CURRENCY: French franc (FRF)
ORGANIZATIONS: Council of Europe, EEA, EU,
G7, NATO, OECD, UN, WEU

France encompasses a great variety of landscapes, ranging from mountain ranges, high plateaux to lowland plains and river basins. The Pyrenees, in the southwest, form the border with Spain and the Jura mountains, in the west, form a border with Switzerland. The highest mountain range is the Alps, south of the Jura. The Massif Central is the highest of the plateaux, which also include the Vosges bordering the plain of Alsace, and Armorica occupying the granite moors of the Brittany peninsula. The French climate is moderated by proximity to the Atlantic, and is generally mild. The south has a Mediterranean climate with hot dry summers, the rest of the country has rain all year round. (Paris has an average annual rainfall of 600 mm or 24 inches). Much of the French countryside is agricultural and it is estimated that one-third of the population derives an income from the land. France is self-sufficient in cereals, dairy products, meat, fruit and vegetables, and is a leading exporter of wheat, barley and sugar beet. Wine is also a major export. Over the past years there has been a steady drift of labour, mainly of younger people from the countryside to the industrialized areas. France is the fourth industrial power in the world after USA, Japan and Germany. It has reserves of coal, oil and natural gas, and is one of the world's leading producers of iron ore. It has large steel-making and chemical refining industries. Its vehicle, aeronautical and armaments industries are among the world's most important. Leading light industries are fashion, perfumes and luxury goods. Most of its heavy industry is concentrated in the major industrial zone of the northeast. In the past,

sources of energy have been provided from its reserves of fossil fuels, however in recent years other sources have increased in importance, such as nuclear power using uranium from French mines, tidal power, and hydro-electricity. Tourism is an important source of income, that will be further encouraged by the opening of the Channel Tunnel.

FRENCH GUIANA

STATUS: Overseas Department
of France
AREA: 91,000 sq km (35,125 sq miles)
POPULATION: 114,808
CAPITAL: Cayenne

FRENCH POLYNESIA

STATUS: Overseas Territory
of France
AREA: 3,940 sq km (1,520 sq miles)
POPULATION: 199,031
CAPITAL: Papeete

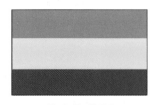

GABON

STATUS: Republic
AREA: 267,665 sq km (103,320 sq miles)
POPULATION: 1,012,000
ANNUAL NATURAL INCREASE: 2.7%
CAPITAL: Libreville
LANGUAGE: French, Bantu dialects, Fang
RELIGION: 60% Roman Catholic.
CURRENCY: CFA franc (C Africa) (XAF)
ORGANIZATIONS: OAU, OPEC, UN,

Gabon, which lies on the equator, consists of the Ogooué river basin covered with tropical rain forest. It is hot and wet all year with average annual temperatures of 25°C (77°F). It is one of the most prosperous states in Africa with valuable timber (mahogany, ebony and walnut) and mineral (manganese and uranium) resources. State-run plantations growing oil palms, bananas, sugar cane and rubber are also important. Gabon's economy, however, is heavily dependent on its oil industry. It is the third largest producer in sub-Saharan Africa after Nigeria and Angola. France supplies nearly half the country's imports and French influence is evident everywhere.

GAMBIA, THE

STATUS: Republic
AREA: 10,690 sq km (4,125 sq miles)
POPULATION: 1,026,000
ANNUAL NATURAL INCREASE: 3.2%
CAPITAL: Banjul
LANGUAGE: English, Madinka, Fula, Wolof

RELIGION: 90% Muslim,
Christian and animist minorities
CURRENCY: dalasi (GMD)
ORGANIZATIONS: Comm., ECOWAS, OAU, UN

The Gambia is the smallest country in Africa. An enclave within Senegal, it is 470 km (292 miles) long, averages 24 km (15 miles) wide and occupies land bordering the Gambia river. The climate has two distinctive seasons. November to May is dry but July to October sees monsoon rainfall of up to 1,300 mm (51 inches). The temperatures average about 23–27°C (73–81°F) throughout the year. Groundnuts and subsidiary products are the mainstay of the economy but tourism is developing rapidly. The production of cotton, livestock, fish and rice is increasing to change the present economic reliance on groundnuts.

GEORGIA

STATUS: Republic
AREA: 69,700 sq km (26,905 sq miles)
POPULATION: 5,471,000
ANNUAL NATURAL INCREASE: 0.5%
CAPITAL: Tbilisi
LANGUAGE: 70% Georgian, 8% Armenian,
6% Russian, 6% Azeri
RELIGION: Orthodox Christian
CURRENCY: coupon
ORGANIZATIONS: CIS

Georgia, covering part of the southern Caucasus, is a mountainous country with forests covering one-third of its area. The climate ranges from sub-tropical on the shores of the Black Sea, to perpetual ice and snow on the Caucasian crests. Rich deposits of coal are mainly unexploited. Cheap oil and gas imports, hydro-electric power and minerals, in particular rich manganese deposits, have led to industrialization successfully concentrated on metallurgy and machine-building. With the exception of the fertile plain to the east, agricultural land is in short supply and difficult to work. This is partly compensated by the cultivation of labour-intensive and profitable crops such as tea, grapes, tobacco and citrus fruit. The break-up of the Soviet Union brought independence for Georgia in 1991. The question of regional autonomy for the Abkhaz, Adzhar and South Ossetian minorities has repeatedly led to violent ethnic conflict in recent years, causing economic collapse.

GERMANY

STATUS: Federal Republic
AREA: 356,840 sq km (137,740 sq miles)
POPULATION: 81,051,000
ANNUAL NATURAL INCREASE: 0.6%
CAPITAL: Berlin
(seat of government Berlin/Bonn)
LANGUAGE: German

RELIGION: 45% Protestant
40% Roman Catholic
CURRENCY: Deutsch-mark (DM)
ORGANIZATIONS: Council of Europe, EEA, EU,
G7, NATO, OECD, UN, WEU

Germany has three main geographical regions: the Northern plain, stretching from the rivers Oder and Neisse in the east to the Dutch border; the central uplands with elevated plateaux intersected by river valleys and relieved by isolated mountains, gradually rising to peaks of up to nearly 1500 m (5000 feet) in the Black Forest: finally the Bavarian Alps stradling the Austrian border. With exception of the Danube, all German river systems run northwards into the North or the Baltic Seas. The climate is mainly continental with temperatures ranging from -3°–1°C (27–34°F) in January to 16°–19°C (61°–66°F) in July. Only in the north-western corner of the country does the climate become more oceanic in character. Germany on the whole has large stretches of very fertile farmland.

Politically, the division of Germany, a product of the post-1945 Cold War between the victorious Allies against Hitler, was rapidly overcome after the collapse of communism in Eastern Europe, and the unification of the two German states was effected in 1990. Economically, the legacy of 40 years of socialist rule in the East ensures that, in terms of both structure and performance, Germany will encompass two vastly different halves for a long time to come. Having lost its captive markets in what used to be the Soviet Bloc, the eastern economy then all but collapsed under the weight of superior western competition. The task of reconstruction is proving more difficult, more protracted and, most of all, more costly than expected. In the West, the Ruhr basin, historically the industrial heartland of Germany, with its emphasis on coal mining and iron and steel works, has long since been overtaken by more advanced industries elsewhere, notably in the Rhine-Main area and further south in the regions around Stuttgart and Munich. The rapidly expanding services sector apart, the German economy is now dominated by the chemical, pharmaceutical, mechanical engineering, motor and high-tech industries. To lessen the country's dependence on oil imports, an ambitious nuclear energy programme has been adopted. Although poor in minerals and other raw materials with the exception of lignite and potash, Germany has managed to become one of the world's leading manufacturers and exporters of vehicles,

machine tools, electrical and electronic products and of consumer goods of various description, in particular textiles. But the massive balance of trade surplus West Germany used to enjoy has now disappeared due to the sucking in of imports by, and the redistribution of output to, the newly acquired territories in the East.

GHANA

STATUS: Republic
AREA: 238,305 sq km (91,985 sq miles)
POPULATION: 15,959,000
ANNUAL NATURAL INCREASE: 3.3%
CAPITAL: Accra
LANGUAGE: English, tribal languages
RELIGION: 42% Christian
CURRENCY: cedi (GHC)
ORGANIZATIONS: Comm., ECOWAS, OAU, UN

Ghana, the west African state once known as the Gold Coast, gained independence from Britain in 1957. The landscape varies from tropical rainforest to dry scrubland, with the terrain becoming hillier to the north, culminating in a plateau averaging some 500 m (1,600 feet). The climate is tropical with the annual rainfall ranging from over 2,000 mm (79 inches) on the coast to less than 1,000 mm (40 inches) inland. The temperature averages 27°C (81°F) all year. Cocoa is the principal crop but although most Ghanaians farm, there is also a thriving industrial base around Tema, where local bauxite is smelted into aluminium. Tema has the largest artificial harbour in Africa. In recent years gold production has surged, Ghana having some of the world's richest gold deposits. Besides gold, Ghana's major exports are cocoa and timber. Principal imports are fuel, food and manufactured goods. Offshore oil has yet to be economically developed.

GIBRALTAR

STATUS: UK Crown Colony
AREA: 6.5 sq km (2.5 sq miles)
POPULATION: 31,000

GREECE

STATUS: Republic
AREA: 131,985 sq km (50,945 sq miles)
POPULATION: 10,269,074
ANNUAL NATURAL INCREASE: 0.4%
CAPITAL: Athens (Athínai)
LANGUAGE: Greek
RELIGION: 97% Greek Orthodox
CURRENCY: drachma (GRD)
ORGANIZATIONS: Council of Europe,
EC, NATO, OECD, UN

Greece is a mountainous country and over one-fifth of its area comprises numerous islands, 154 of which are inhabited. The climate is Mediterranean with temperatures averaging 28°C (82°F) in summer. The mountains experience some heavy snowfall during winter. Poor irrigation and drainage mean that much of the agriculture is localized. The main products of olives, fruit and vegetables, cotton, tobacco and wine are exported. The surrounding seas are important, providing two-thirds of Greece's fish requirements and supporting an active merchant fleet. Athens is the main manufacturing base and at least one quarter of the population lives there. Greece is a very popular tourist destination which helps the craft industries – tourism is a prime source of national income.

GREENLAND

STATUS: Self-governing Island Region
of Denmark
AREA: 2,175,600 sq km (836,780 sq miles)
POPULATION: 55,558
CAPITAL: Godthåb (Nuuk)

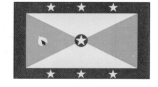

GRENADA

STATUS: Commonwealth State
AREA: 345 sq km (133 sq miles)
POPULATION: 95,343
ANNUAL NATURAL INCREASE: -0.2%
CAPITAL: St George's
LANGUAGE: English, French patois
RELIGION: Roman Catholic majority
CURRENCY: E Caribbean dollar (XCD)
ORGANIZATIONS: Caricom, Comm., OAS, UN

The Caribbean island of Grenada, whose territory includes the southern Grenadines, is the most southern of the Windward Islands. It is mountainous and thickly forested, with a settled warm climate and an average temperature of 27°C (81°F). Rainfall varies with altitude, ranging from 760 mm (30 inches) to 3,560 mm (140 inches) on the higher ground. The island is famous for its spices and nutmeg is the main export. Cocoa and bananas are also important, together with some citrus fruits and vegetables. Tourism is important and continues to expand.

GUADELOUPE

STATUS: Overseas Department
of France
AREA: 1,780 sq km (687 sq miles)
POPULATION: 406,000
CAPITAL: Basse-Terre

GUAM

STATUS: External Territory of USA
AREA: 450 sq km (174 sq miles)
POPULATION: 139,000
CAPITAL: Agaña

GUATEMALA

STATUS: Republic
AREA: 108,890 sq km (42,030 sq miles)
POPULATION: 9,745,000
ANNUAL NATURAL INCREASE: 2.9%
CAPITAL: Guatemala City (Guatemala)
LANGUAGE: Spanish, Indian languages
RELIGION: 75% Roman Catholic,
25% Protestant
CURRENCY: quetzal (GTQ)
ORGANIZATIONS: CACM, OAS, UN

The central American country of Guatemala has both a Pacific and a Caribbean coastline. The mountainous interior, with peaks reaching up to 4,000 m (13,120 feet), covers two-thirds of the country while to the north there is the thickly forested area known as the Petén. The northern lowland and the smaller coastal plains have a hot tropical climate, but the central highlands are more temperate. A rainy season lasts from May to October. Annual rainfall reaches up to 5,000 mm (200 inches) in some lowland areas but decreases to an average of 1,150 mm (45 inches) in the mountains. Agricultural products form the bulk of Guatemala's exports, notably coffee, sugar cane, cotton and bananas, but there is also a substantial industrial base. Manufacturing includes textiles, paper and pharmaceuticals. Mineral resources include nickel, antimony, lead, silver and in the north crude oil.

GUINEA

STATUS: Republic
AREA: 245,855 sq km
(94,900 sq miles)
POPULATION: 6,116,000
ANNUAL NATURAL INCREASE: 2.8%
CAPITAL: Conakry
LANGUAGE: French, Susu, Manika
RELIGION: 85% Muslim
10% animist, 5% Roman Catholic
CURRENCY: Guinea franc (GNF)
ORGANIZATIONS: ECOWAS, OAU, UN

Guinea, a former French colony, is situated on the west African coast. Its drowned coastline, lined with mangrove swamps, contrasts strongly with its interior highlands containing the headwaters of the Gambia, Niger and Senegal rivers. Agriculture occupies 80 per cent of the workforce, the main exports being coffee, bananas, pineapple and palm products. Guinea has some of the largest resources of bauxite (aluminium ore) in the world as well as gold and diamonds. Bauxite accounts for 80 per cent of export earnings.

GUINEA-BISSAU

STATUS: Republic
AREA: 36,125 sq km (13,945 sq miles)
POPULATION: 1,006,000
ANNUAL NATURAL INCREASE: 1.9%
CAPITAL: Bissau
LANGUAGE: Portuguese, Creole,
Guinean dialects
RELIGION: Animist and Muslim majority,
Roman Catholic minority
CURRENCY: Guinea-Bissau peso (GWP)
ORGANIZATIONS: ECOWS, OAU, UN

Guinea-Bissau, on the west African coast, was once a centre for the Portuguese slave trade. The coast is swampy and lined with mangroves, and the interior consists of a low-lying plain densely covered with rain forest. The coast is hot and humid with annual rainfall of 2,000–3,000 mm (79–118 inches) a year, although the interior is cooler and drier. Eighty per cent of the country's exports comprise groundnut oil, palm kernels and palm oil. Fish, fish products and coconuts also make an important contribution to trade.

GUYANA

STATUS: Co-operative Republic
AREA: 214,970 sq km (82,980 sq miles)
POPULATION: 808,000
ANNUAL NATURAL INCREASE: 0.3%
CAPITAL: Georgetown
LANGUAGE: English, Hindi, Urdu,
Amerindian dialects
RELIGION: Christian majority, Muslim
and Hindu minorities
CURRENCY: Guyana dollar (GYD)
ORGANIZATIONS: Caricom, Comm., UN

Guyana, formerly the British colony of British Guiana, borders both Venezuela and Brazil. Its Atlantic coast, the most densely-populated area, is flat and marshy, while towards the interior the landscape gradually rises to the Guiana Highlands – a region densely covered in rainforest. The climate is tropical, with hot, wet and humid conditions, which are modified along the coast by sea breezes. Agriculture, dominated by sugar and rice, is the basis of the economy. Bauxite deposits provide a valuable export and in the mid-1990s gold production increased.

HAITI

STATUS: Republic
AREA: 27,750 sq km (10,710 sq miles)
POPULATION: 6,764,000
ANNUAL NATURAL INCREASE: 2.0%
CAPITAL: Port-au-Prince
LANGUAGE: French, Creole
RELIGION: 80% Roman Catholic,
Voodoo folk religion minority
CURRENCY: gourde (HTG)
ORGANIZATIONS: OAS, UN

Haiti occupies the western part of the island of Hispaniola in the Caribbean. It is the poorest country in Central America. The country is mountainous with three main ranges, the highest reaching 2,680 m (8,793 feet). Agriculture is restricted to the plains which divide the ranges. The climate is tropical. Ninety per cent of the workforce are farmers and traditional exports have been coffee, sugar, cotton, and cocoa. In the early to mid-1990s national poverty worsened as a result of UN embargoes imposed against an illegal military regime. Thousands of Haitians fled the country. New sanctions in 1994 threatened to bring an end to all manufacturing and exporting activities.

HEARD AND McDONALD ISLANDS

STATUS: External Territory of Australia
AREA: 412 sq km (159 sq miles)
POPULATION: no permanent population
CAPITAL: Edmonton

HONDURAS

STATUS: Republic
AREA: 112,085 sq km (43,265 sq miles)
POPULATION: 5,462,000
ANNUAL NATURAL INCREASE 3.1%
CAPITAL: Tegucigalpa
LANGUAGE: Spanish, Indian dialects
RELIGION: Roman Catholic majority
CURRENCY: lempira (HNL) or peso
ORGANIZATIONS: CACM, OAS, UN

The central American republic of Honduras is a poor, sparsely populated country which consists substantially of rugged mountains and high plateaux with, on the Caribbean coast, an area of hot and humid plains, densely covered with tropical vegetation. These low-lying plains are subject to high annual rainfall, averaging 2,500 mm (98 inches), and it is in this region that bananas and coffee, accounting for over half the nation's exports, are grown. Other crops include sugar, rice, maize, beans and tobacco. There has been growth in new products such as shrimps, melons and tomatoes. Most industries are concerned with processing local products. Lead and zinc are exported.

HONG KONG

STATUS: UK Dependent Territory
AREA: 1,067 sq km (412 sq miles)
POPULATION: 5,920,000

HUNGARY

STATUS: Republic
AREA: 93,030 sq km (35,910 sq miles)
POPULATION: 10,289,000
ANNUAL NATURAL INCREASE: -0.6%
CAPITAL: Budapest
LANGUAGE: Hungarian (Magyar)
RELIGION: 60% Roman Catholic,
20% Hungarian Reformed Church, Lutheran
and Orthodox minorities
CURRENCY: forint (HUF)
ORGANIZATIONS: Council of Europe, OIEC, UN

Hungary is situated in the heartland of Europe. Its geomorphology consists mainly of undulating fertile plains with the highest terrain in the northeast of the country. The country is bisected north to south by the Danube. It has a humid continental climate, with warm summers that can become very hot on the plains, averaging 20°C (68°F), and cold winters, averaging 0°C (32°F). There is an annual rainfall of 500–750 mm (20–30 inches). Bauxite is Hungary's only substantial mineral resource, and less than 15 per cent of the gross national product is now derived from agriculture. The massive drive for industrialization has fundamentally transformed the structure of the economy since 1945. Both capital and consumer goods industries were developed, and during the 1980s engineering accounted for more than half the total industrial output. After a series of more or less unsuccessful attempts to introduce market elements into what essentially remained a centrally planned and largely state-owned economy, the communist regime finally gave up in 1989/90. However, their democratically elected successors have yet to prove that privatization and free competition will eventually bring general prosperity as well as political stability to what is now a profoundly troubled society.

ICELAND

STATUS: Republic
AREA: 102,820 sq km (39,690 sq miles)
POPULATION: 260,000
ANNUAL NATURAL INCREASE: 1.2%
CAPITAL: Reykjavík
LANGUAGE: Icelandic
RELIGION: 93% Evangelical Lutheran
CURRENCY: Icelandic krona (ISK)
ORGANIZATIONS: Council of Europe, EEA,
EFTA, NATO, OECD, UN

One of the most northern islands in Europe, Iceland is 798 km (530 miles) away from Scotland, its nearest neighbour. The landscape is entirely volcanic – compacted volcanic ash has been eroded by the wind and there are substantial ice sheets and lava fields as well as many still active volcanoes, geysers and hot springs. The climate is mild for its latitude, with average summer temperatures of 9–10°C (48–50°F), and vegetation is sparse. Fishing is the traditional mainstay of the economy. An average of some 1,540,000 tonnes of fish are landed each year and 80 per cent of Iceland's exports consist of fish and fish products. Tourism is becoming an increasing source of income.

INDIA

STATUS: Federal Republic
AREA: 3,166,830 sq km (1,222,395 sq miles)
POPULATION: 870,000,000
ANNUAL NATURAL INCREASE: 2.1%
CAPITAL: New Delhi
LANGUAGE: Hindi, English, regional languages
RELIGION: 83% Hindu, 11% Muslim
CURRENCY: Indian rupee (INR)
ORGANIZATIONS: Col. Plan, Comm., UN

Occupying most of the Indian subcontinent, India is second only to China in the size of its population. This vast country contains an extraordinary variety of landscapes, climates and resources. The Himalayas, in the north, are the world's highest mountain range with many peaks reaching over 6,000 km (19,685 feet). The Himalayan foothills, are covered with lush vegetation, water is in abundant supply (rainfall in Assam reaches 10,700 mm or 421 inches in a year) and the climate is hot, making this region a centre for tea cultivation. To the south lies the vast expanse of the Indo-Gangetic plain, 2,500 km (1,550 miles) east-west, divided by the Indus, Ganges and Brahmaputra rivers. This is one of the world's most fertile regions, although it is liable to flooding, and failure of monsoon rainfall (June to September) can result in severe drought. In the pre-monsoon season the heat becomes intense – average temperatures in New Delhi reach 38°C (110°F). Rice, wheat, cotton, jute, tobacco and sugar are the main crops. To the south lies the Deccan plateau, bordered on either side by the Eastern and Western Ghats, and in the northwest lies the barren Thar Desert. India's natural resources are immense – timber, coal, iron ore and nickel – and oil has been discovered in the Indian Ocean. There has been a rapid expansion of light industry, notably in the food processing sector, and the manufacturing of consumer goods. Nevertheless, 70 per cent of the population live by subsistence farming. Main exports by value are precious stones and jewelry, engineering goods, clothing, leather goods, chemicals and cotton. Tourism is a valuable source of revenue.

INDONESIA
STATUS: Republic
AREA: 1,919,445 sq km
(740,905 sq miles)
POPULATION: 187,870,000
ANNUAL NATURAL INCREASE: 1.8%
CAPITAL: Jakarta
LANGUAGE: Bahasa Indonesian, Dutch
RELIGION: 88% Muslim, 9% Christian,
Hindu and Buddhist minorities
CURRENCY: rupiah (IDR)
ORGANIZATIONS: ASEAN, Col. Plan,
OPEC, UN

Indonesia consists of thousands of islands in equatorial southeast Asia which include Kalimantan (the central and southern parts of Borneo), Sumatera, Irian Jaya (the western part of New Guinea), Sulawesi (Celebes) and Java. The climate is tropical: hot (temperatures averaging 24°C or 75°F per year), humid and subject to monsoons. Most of its people live along the coast and river valleys of Java, leaving parts of the other islands virtually uninhabited. It is a Muslim nation and has the fourth largest population in the world. Over three-quarters of the people farm and live in small villages. Oil and gas, manufactured goods and coal are the chief exports. Indonesia is also a leading supplier of forest products, palm oil, rubber, spices, tobacco, tea, coffee and tin. With the use of modern techniques, the country has achieved self-sufficiency in rice.

IRAN
STATUS: Republic
AREA: 1,648,000 sq km (636,130 sq miles)
POPULATION: 56,964,000
ANNUAL NATURAL INCREASE: 3.7%
CAPITAL: Tehran
LANGUAGE: Farsi, Kurdish, Arabic,
Baluchi, Turkic
RELIGION: Shi'a Muslim majority, Sunni Muslim
and Armenian Christian minorities
CURRENCY: Iranian rial (IRR)
ORGANIZATIONS: Col. Plan, OPEC, UN

Iran is a large mountainous country north of The Gulf. The climate is one of extremes with temperatures ranging from -20–55°C (-4–131°F) and rainfall varying from 2,000 mm (79 inches) to almost zero. Iran is rich in oil and gas and the revenues have been used to improve communications and social conditions generally. The war with Iraq between 1980 and 1988 seriously restricted economic growth and particularly affected the Iranian oil industry in The Gulf. Oil is the source of 85 per cent of Iran's revenue and thus when world oil prices fall, as in the early–mid 1990s, the economy suffers. Agricultural conditions are poor, except around the Caspian Sea, and wheat is the main crop though fruit (especially dates) and nuts are grown and exported. The main livestock is sheep and goats. Iran has substantial mineral deposits relatively underdeveloped

IRAQ
STATUS: Republic
AREA: 438,317 sq km (169,235 sq miles)
POPULATION: 19,410,000
ANNUAL NATURAL INCREASE: 3.3%
CAPITAL: Baghdad
LANGUAGE: Arabic, Kurdish, Turkoman
RELIGION: 50% Shi'a, 45% Sunni Muslim
CURRENCY: Iraqi dinar (IQD)
ORGANIZATIONS: Arab League, OPEC, UN

Iraq is mostly desert, marsh and mountain, but there are substantial areas of fertile land between the Tigris and the Euphrates. The two great rivers join and become the Shatt al-Arab which flows into The Gulf. The climate is arid with rainfall of less than 500 mm (20 inches) and summers are very hot (averaging 35° or 95°F). Iraq has a short coastline with Basra the only port. Light industry is situated around Baghdad, and there are major petro-chemical complexes around the Basra and Kirkuk oilfields. The war with Iran (1980–8) and the Gulf conflict (1991) wrecked the economy with exports of oil and natural gas, formerly accounting for 95 per cent of export earnings, severely restricted by sanctions. Meanwhile, Arabs living in the Tigris-Euphrates marsh regions are being deprived of their livelihood as the marshes are drained in government reclamation schemes.

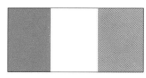

IRELAND
(EIRE)
STATUS: Republic
AREA: 68,895 sq km (26,595 sq miles)
POPULATION: 3,548,000
ANNUAL NATURAL INCREASE: -0.1%
CAPITAL: Dublin (Baile Átha Cliath)
LANGUAGE: Irish, English
RELIGION: 95% Roman Catholic, 5% Protestant
CURRENCY: punt or Irish pound (IEP)
ORGANIZATIONS: Council of Europe, EEA, EU,
OECD, UN

The Irish Republic, forming 80 per cent of the island of Ireland, is a lowland country of wide valleys, lakes and marshes, but with some hills of significance, such as the Wicklow Mountains, south of Dublin and Macgillicuddy's Reeks, in the southwest. The Irish climate is maritime and influenced by the Gulf Stream. Temperatures average 5°C (40°F) in winter to 16°C (60°F) in summer, with annual rainfall at about 1,400 mm (55 inches) in the west and half that in the east. There is much rich pastureland and livestock farming predominates. Meat and dairy produce is processed in the small market towns where there are also breweries and mills. Large-scale manufacturing, in which food processing, electronics and textiles have shown recent growth, is centred around Dublin, the capital and main port. The Irish Republic possesses reserves of oil and natural gas, peat and deposits of lead and zinc. A large zinc mine at Galmoy is expected to come into production in 1996.

ISRAEL
STATUS: State
AREA: 20,770 sq km (8,015 sq miles)
POPULATION: 5,287,000
ANNUAL NATURAL INCREASE: 2.7%
CAPITAL: Jerusalem
LANGUAGE: Hebrew, Arabic, Yiddish
RELIGION: 85% Jewish, 13% Muslim
CURRENCY: shekel (ILS)
ORGANIZATIONS: UN

Israel, in the eastern Mediterranean littoral, contains a varied landscape – a coastal plain, interior hills, a deep valley extending from the river Jordan to the Dead Sea, and the Negev semi-desert in the south. Efficient water management is crucial as two-thirds of rainfall, which falls mostly in the mild winters, is lost by evaporation. Fuel needs to be imported (mainly oil from Egypt). Economic development in Israel is the most advanced in the Middle East. Manufacturing, particularly diamond finishing, electronics and science based products are important, although Israel also has flourishing agriculture specializing in exporting fruit, flowers and vegetables to western Europe. The only viable mineral resources are phosphates in the Negev and potash from the Dead Sea.

ITALY

STATUS: Republic
AREA: 301,245 sq km (116,280 sq miles)
POPULATION: 56,767,000
ANNUAL NATURAL INCREASE: 0.2%
CAPITAL: Rome (Roma)
LANGUAGE: Italian, German, French
RELIGION: 90% Roman Catholic
CURRENCY: Italian lira (ITL)
ORGANIZATIONS: Council of Europe, EEA, EU,
G7, NATO, OECD, UN, WEU

Italy, separated from the rest of Europe by the great divide of the Alps, thrusts southeastwards into the Mediterranean Sea, in its famous boot-shaped peninsula. Including the large islands of Sicily and Sardinia, over 75 per cent of the landscape is either hill or mountain. The north is dominated by the plain of the river Po rising to the high Alps. Further along the peninsula the Apennine mountains run from north to south. Climate varies with altitude, but generally there is a Mediterranean regime in the south; in the north the climate becomes more temperate. Agriculture flourishes with cereals, vegetables, olives, and cheese the principal products and Italy is the world's largest wine producer. Tourism is a major source of revenue. In spite of the lack of mineral and power resources, Italy has become a trading nation with a sound industrial base. Manufacturing of textiles, cars, machine tools, textile machinery and engineering, mainly in the north, is expanding rapidly and accounts for nearly 50 per cent of the work force. This is increasing the imbalance between the north and south where the average income is far less per head, and where investment is lacking.

IVORY COAST (CÔTE D'IVOIRE)

STATUS: Republic
AREA: 322,465 sq km (124,470 sq miles)
POPULATION: 12,910,000
ANNUAL NATURAL INCREASE: 4.0%
CAPITAL: Yamoussoukro
LANGUAGE: French, tribal languages
RELIGION: 65% traditional beliefs,
23% Muslim, 12% Roman Catholic
CURRENCY: CFA franc (W Africa) (XOF)
ORGANIZATIONS: ECOWAS, OAU, UN,

Independent from the French since 1960, the Ivory Coast rises from low plains in the south to plateaux in the north. The climate is tropical with rainfall in two wet seasons in the south. Much of the population is engaged in subsistence agriculture. The two chief exports are cocoa and coffee. Other products include cotton, timber, fruit and tobacco. Gold mining began in 1990, diamonds are extracted and by 1995 the Ivory Coast is expected to become self-sufficient in oil and gas from the offshore fields.

JAMAICA

STATUS: Commonwealth State
AREA: 11,425 sq km (4,410 sq miles)
POPULATION: 2,469,000
ANNUAL NATURAL INCREASE: 0.8%
CAPITAL: Kingston
LANGUAGE: English, local patois
RELIGION: Anglican Christian majority.
Rastafarian minority
CURRENCY: Jamaican dollar (JMD)
ORGANIZATIONS: Caricom, Comm., OAS, UN

Jamaica, part of the Greater Antilles chain of islands in the Caribbean, is formed from the peaks of a submerged mountain range. The climate is tropical with an annual rainfall of over 5,000 mm (197 inches) on the high ground. There is a plentiful supply of tropical fruits such as melons, bananas and guavas. Principal crops include sugar cane, bananas, cocoa and coffee. Jamaica is rich in bauxite which, with the refined product alumina, is the main export. Major industries are food processing, textiles, cement and agricultural machinery. Since 1988 tourism has developed rapidly and is now the biggest single source of foreign earnings.

JAPAN

STATUS: Constitutional monarchy
AREA: 369,700 sq km (142,705 sq miles)
POPULATION: 123,653,000
ANNUAL NATURAL INCREASE: 0.4%
CAPITAL: Tokyo (Tōkyō)
LANGUAGE: Japanese
RELIGION: Shintoist, Buddhist,
Christian minority
CURRENCY: yen (JPY)
ORGANIZATIONS: Col. Plan, G7, OECD, UN

Japan consists of the main islands of Hokkaido, Honshu, Shikoku and Kyushu which stretch over 1,600 km (995 miles). The land is mountainous and heavily forested with small, fertile patches and a climate ranging from harsh to tropical. The highest mountain is Mt Fuji (Fuji-san) at 3,776 m (12,388 feet). The archipelago is also subject to monsoons, earthquakes, typhoons and tidal waves. Very little of the available land is cultivable. Most food has to be imported but the Japanese both catch and eat a lot of fish. The Japanese fishing fleet is the largest in the world. Japan is a leading economic power. Because of the importance of trade, industry has grown up around the major ports especially Yokohama, Osaka and Tokyo, the capital. The principal exports are motor vehicles, chemicals, iron and steel products and electronic, electric and optical equipment. Japan relies heavily on imported fuel and raw materials and is developing the country's nuclear power resources to reduce this dependence. Production of coal, oil and natural gas is also being increased. In the early–mid 1990s, after four decades of phenomenal growth, industrial output declined as Japan experienced its worst recession for half a century.

JORDAN

STATUS: Kingdom
AREA: 90,650 sq km (35,000 sq miles)
POPULATION: 4,291,000
ANNUAL NATURAL INCREASE: 5.8%
CAPITAL: Amman ('Ammān)
LANGUAGE: Arabic
RELIGION: 90% Sunni Muslim,
Christian and Shi'ite Muslim minorities
CURRENCY: Jordanian dinar (JOD)
ORGANIZATIONS: Arab League, UN

Jordan, one of the few kingdoms in the Middle East, is mostly desert, but has fertile pockets. The climate is predominantly arid. Temperatures rise to 49°C (120°F) in the eastern valleys but it is cooler and wetter in the west. Fruit and vegetables account for 20 per cent of Jordan's exports and phosphate, the most valuable mineral, accounts for over 40 per cent of export revenue. Amman is the manufacturing centre, processing bromide and potash from the Dead Sea. Other important industries are food processing and textiles.

KAZAKHSTAN
STATUS: Republic
AREA: 2,717,300 sq km (1,048,880 sq miles)
POPULATION: 17,035,000
ANNUAL NATURAL INCREASE: 1.0%
CAPITAL: Alma-Ata
LANGUAGE: Kazakh, Russian
RELIGION: Muslim majority, Orthodox minority
CURRENCY: tenge
ORGANIZATIONS: CIS, UN

Stretching across central Asia, Kazakhstan is Russia's southern neighbour. Consisting of lowlands, hilly plains and plateaux, with small mountainous areas, the country has a continental climate with hot summers (30°C or 86°F in July) alternating with equally extreme winters. Exceptionally rich in raw materials, extractive industries have played a major role in the country's economy. Vast oil and gas reserves near the Caspian Sea are now being exploited. Rapid industrialization in recent years has focused on iron and steel, cement, chemicals, fertilizers and consumer goods. Although three-quarters of all agricultural land is used for pasture, the nomadic ways of the Kazakh people have all but disappeared. Economic development during the Soviet period brought a massive influx of outside labour which swamped the indigenous population. The proportion of Kazakhs employed in the industrial sector has, until recently, been small, but with the move to towns and better training, the balance is starting to be redressed. Since Kazakhstan's independence in 1991, its economic prospects appear favourable; but the Soviet legacy includes many environmental problems, such as the ruthless exploitation of the Aral Sea for irrigation.

KENYA
STATUS: Republic
AREA: 582,645 sq km (224,900 sq miles)
POPULATION: 25,700,000
ANNUAL NATURAL INCREASE: 3.5%
CAPITAL: Nairobi
LANGUAGE: Kiswahili, English, Kikuyu, Luo
RELIGION: majority traditional beliefs,
25% Christian, 6% Muslim
CURRENCY: Kenya shilling (KES)
ORGANIZATIONS: Comm., OAU, UN

Kenya lies on the equator but as most of the country is on a high plateau the temperatures range from 10–27°C (50–81°F). Rainfall varies from 760–2,500 mm (30–98 inches) depending on altitude. Arable land is scarce but agriculture is the only source of livelihood for over three-quarters of the population. Tea, coffee, flowers and vegetables are the main products for export. Tea, however, has replaced coffee as the chief export and is second only to tourism as a source of foreign revenue. Manufacturing, centred at Nairobi and Mombasa, is dominated by food processing.

KIRGHIZIA (KYRGYZSTAN)
STATUS: Republic
AREA: 198,500 sq km (76,620 sq miles)
POPULATION: 4,502,000
ANNUAL NATURAL INCREASE: 1.7%
CAPITAL: Bishkek
LANGUAGE: Kirghizian, Russian
RELIGION: Muslim
CURRENCY: som
ORGANIZATIONS: CIS, UN

Located in the heart of Asia, to the south of Kazakhstan, Kirghizia is a mountainous country. Traditionally an agrarian-based economy with stock-raising prevalent, the country underwent rapid industrialization during the Soviet period becoming a major producer of machinery and, more recently, producing consumer goods. Valuable mineral deposits include gold, silver, antimony, mercury with the gold deposits believed to be among the world's largest. The cultivation of cotton, sugar beet, tobacco and opium poppies is expanding and provides the basis for a growing processing industry. Independence came unexpectedly in 1991, although Kirghizia had long wanted to control its own affairs.

KIRIBATI
STATUS: Republic
AREA: 717 sq km (277 sq miles)
POPULATION: 72,298
ANNUAL NATURAL INCREASE: 2.1%
CAPITAL: Bairiki (on Tarawa Atoll)
LANGUAGE: I-Kirbati, English
RELIGION: Christian majority
CURRENCY: Australian dollar (AUD)
ORGANIZATIONS: Comm., UN

Kiribati consists of 16 Gilbert Islands, eight Phoenix Islands, three Line Islands and Ocean Island. These four groups are spread over 5 million sq km (1,930,000 miles) in the central and west Pacific. The temperature is a constant 27°–32°C (80–90°F). The islanders grow coconut, breadfruit, bananas and babia (a coarse vegetable). Copra is a major export and fish, particularly tuna, accounts for one-third of total exports. Main imports are machinery and manufactured goods.

KOREA, NORTH
STATUS: Republic
AREA: 122,310 sq km (47,210 sq miles)
POPULATION: 22,618,000
ANNUAL NATURAL INCREASE: 1%
CAPITAL: P'yŏngyang
LANGUAGE: Korean
RELIGION: Chundo Kyo, Buddhism,
Confucianism, Daoism
CURRENCY: North Korean won (KPW)
ORGANIZATIONS: OIEC, UN

High, rugged mountains and deep valleys typify North Korea. Climate is extreme with severe winters and warm, sunny summers. Cultivation is limited to the river valley plains where rice, millet, maize and wheat are the principal crops. North Korea, rich in minerals including iron ore and copper, has developed a heavy industrial base. Industry has, however, since the early 1990s, been severely curtailed, firstly by the loss of Soviet aid following the break-up of the Soviet Union and then by losing imports through its isolationist policies and secretive nuclear industries. Its coal supplies, the main energy source for factories, are running out. Complete economic collapse is only salvaged by remittances from Koreans in Japan.

KOREA, SOUTH
STATUS: Republic
AREA: 98,445 sq km (38,000 sq miles)
POPULATION: 44,190,000
ANNUAL NATURAL INCREASE: 1.9%
CAPITAL: Seoul (Sŏul)
LANGUAGE: Korean
RELIGION: 26% Mahayana Buddhism,
22% Christian, Confucianism,
Daoism, Chundo Kyo
CURRENCY: won (KPW)
ORGANIZATIONS: Col. Plan, UN

The terrain of South Korea, although mountainous, is less rugged than that of North Korea. The flattest parts lie along the west coast and the extreme south of the peninsula. Its climate is continental temperature, with an average temperature range of -5°C (23°F) in winter to 27°C (81°F) in summer. The majority of the population live in the arable river valleys and along the coastal plain. Agriculture is very primitive, with rice the principal crop. Tungsten, coal and iron ore are the main mineral deposits. Despite having to import oil and industrial materials, the country is a major industrial nation producing iron and steel, textiles, aircraft, chemicals, machinery, vehicles and, in recent years, specializing in electronics and computers. South Korea, with Japan, leads the world in ship-building.

KUWAIT
STATUS: State
AREA: 24,280 sq km (9,370 sq miles)
POPULATION: 1,500,000
ANNUAL NATURAL INCREASE: -2.3%
CAPITAL: Kuwait (Al Kuwayt)
LANGUAGE: Arabic, English
RELIGION: 95% Muslim, 5% Christian and Hindu

CURRENCY: Kuwaiti dinar (KWD)
ORGANIZATIONS: Arab League, UN

Kuwait comprises low, undulating desert, with summer temperatures as high as 52°C (126°F). Since the discovery of oil, Kuwait has been transformed into one of the world's wealthiest nations, exporting oil to Japan, France, the Netherlands and the UK since 1946. The natural gas fields have also been developed. Other industries include fishing (particularly shrimp), food processing, chemicals and building materials. In agriculture, the aim is to produce half the requirements of domestic vegetable consumption by expanding the irrigated area. The invasion and attempted annexation of Kuwait by Iraq in 1990–1 had severe effects on the country's economy, but by 1994 the oil industry was restored to its pre-Gulf war efficiency.

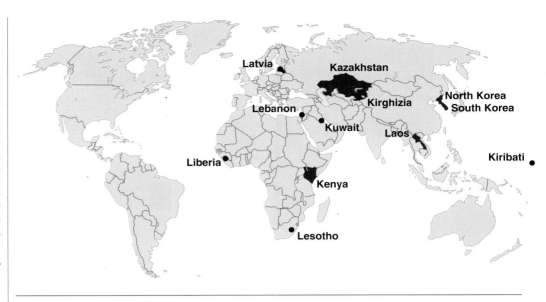

LAOS

STATUS: Republic
AREA: 236,725 sq km (91,375 sq miles)
POPULATION: 4,469,000
ANNUAL NATURAL INCREASE: 2.9%
CAPITAL: Vientiane (Viangchan)
LANGUAGE: Lao, French, tribal languages
RELIGION: Buddhist majority,
Christian and animist minorities
CURRENCY: kip (LAK)
ORGANIZATIONS: Col. Plan, UN

Laos is a landlocked, mostly mountainous and forested country in Indo-China. Temperatures range from 15°C (59°F) in winter, to 32°C (90°F) before the rains, and 26°C (79°F) during the rainy season from May to October. Most of the sparse population are subsistence farmers growing rice, maize, sweet potatoes and tobacco. Mineral resources include tin, iron ore, gold, bauxite and lignite. The major exports are coffee, tin and teak. Almost constant warfare since 1941 has hindered any possible industrial development, and Laos has become one of the world's poorest countries.

LATVIA

STATUS: Republic
AREA: 63,700 sq km (24,590 sq miles)
POPULATION: 2,577,000
ANNUAL NATURAL INCREASE: 0.0%
CAPITAL: Riga
LANGUAGE: Latvian, Lithuanian, Russian
RELIGION: Lutheran, Roman Catholic
and Orthodox minorities
CURRENCY: roublis (Latvian rouble), lats
ORGANIZATIONS: UN

Latvia is situated on the shores of the Baltic Sea and the Gulf of Riga. Forests cover more than a third of the total territory, a second third being made up of meadows and marsh, and there are some 4,000 lakes. Farmland supports dairy and meat production and grain crops. The country

possesses no mineral resources of any value. Industrial development has been sustained by a massive influx of Russian labour since Latvia's incorporation into the Soviet Union in 1940. Under the Soviets, Latvia was assigned the production of consumer durables such as refrigerators and motorcycles as well as ships, rolling stock and power generators. Latvia regained its independence in 1991. The main industries are now radio engineering, electronics, engineering, instruments and industrial robots.

LEBANON

STATUS: Republic
AREA: 10,400 sq km (4,015 sq miles)
POPULATION: 2,838,000
ANNUAL NATURAL INCREASE: 2.3%
CAPITAL: Beirut (Beyrouth)
LANGUAGE: Arabic, French, English
RELIGION: 62% Shi'a and Sunni Muslim,
38% Roman Catholic and Maronite Christian
CURRENCY: Lebanese pound (LBP)
ORGANIZATIONS: Arab League, UN

Physically, Lebanon can be divided into four main regions: a narrow coastal plain; a narrow, fertile interior plateau; the west Lebanon (Jebel Liban) and the Anti-Lebanon (Jebel esh Sharqi) mountains. It has a Mediterranean climate. Trade and tourism have been severely affected by civil war for 17 years from 1975. Agriculture accounts for nearly half of employment and cement, fertilisers, jewelry, sugar and tobacco products are all manufactured on a small scale.

LESOTHO

STATUS: Kingdom
AREA: 30,345 sq km (11,715 sq miles)

POPULATION: 1,836,000
ANNUAL NATURAL INCREASE: 2.7%
CAPITAL: Maseru
LANGUAGE: Sesotho, English
RELIGION: 80% Christian
CURRENCY: loti (LSL), S African rand (ZAR)
ORGANIZATIONS: Comm., OAU, UN

Lesotho, formerly Basutoland, is completely encircled by South Africa. This small country is rugged and mountainous, with southern Africa's highest mountain, Thabana Ntlenyana (3,482 m or 11,424 feet) to be found in the east of the Drakensberg. From these peaks the land slopes westwards in the form of dissected plateaux. The climate is generally sub-tropical although influenced by altitude; rainfall, sometimes variable, falls mainly in the summer months. Because of the terrain, agriculture is limited to the lowlands and foothills. Sorghum, wheat, barley, maize, oats and legumes are the main crops. Cattle, sheep and goats graze on the highlands.

LIBERIA

STATUS: Republic
AREA: 11,370 sq km (42,990 sq miles)
POPULATION: 2,580,000
ANNUAL NATURAL INCREASE: 3.1%
CAPITAL: Monrovia
LANGUAGE: English, tribal languages
RELIGION: traditional beliefs, Christian,
5% Muslim
CURRENCY: Liberian dollar (LRD)
ORGANIZATIONS: ECOWAS, OAU, UN

The west African republic of Liberia is the only nation in Africa never to have been ruled by a foreign power. The hot and humid coastal plain with its savannah vegetation and mangrove swamps rises gently towards the Guinea Highlands, and the interior is densely covered by tropical rainforest. Until the civil war, which ravaged the country, broke out in 1989 the country enjoyed some prosperity from its rubber plantations, rich iron ore deposits, diamonds and gold. Liberia has the world's largest merchant fleet due to its flag of convenience register and this is the only source of revenue relatively unscathed by the war.

LIBYA

STATUS: Republic
AREA: 1,759,540 sq km (679,180 sq miles)
POPULATION: 4,875,000
ANNUAL NATURAL INCREASE: 3.6%
CAPITAL: Tripoli (Ţarābulus)
LANGUAGE: Arabic, Italian, English
RELIGION: Sunni Muslim
CURRENCY: Libyan dinar (LYD)
ORGANIZATIONS: Arab League, OAU, OPEC, UN

Libya is situated on the lowlands of north Africa which rise southwards from the Mediterranean Sea. Ninety-five per cent of its territory is hot, dry desert or semi-desert with average rainfall of less then 130 mm (5 inches). The coastal plains, however, have a more moist Mediterranean climate with annual rainfall of around 200–610 mm (8–24 inches). In these areas, a wide range of crops are cultivated including grapes, groundnuts, oranges, wheat and barley. Only 30 years ago Libya was classed as one of the world's poorest nations but the exploitation of oil has transformed Libya's economy and now accounts for over 95 per cent of its exports.

LIECHTENSTEIN

STATUS: Principality
AREA: 160 sq km (62 sq miles)
POPULATION: 30,000
ANNUAL NATURAL INCREASE: 1.1%
CAPITAL: Vaduz
LANGUAGE: Alemannish, German
RELIGION: 87% Roman Catholic
CURRENCY: franken (Swiss franc)(CHF)
ORGANIZATIONS Council of Europe, EFTA, UN

Situated in the central Alps between Switzerland and Austria, Liechtenstein is one of the smallest states in Europe. Its territory is divided into two zones – the flood plains of the Rhine to the north and Alpine mountain ranges to the southeast, where cattle are reared. Liechtenstein's other main sources of revenue comprise light industry, chiefly the manufacture of precision instruments, and also textile production, food products, tourism, postage stamps and a fast-growing banking sector.

LITHUANIA

STATUS: Republic
AREA: 65,200 sq km (25,165 sq miles)
POPULATION: 3,742,000
ANNUAL NATURAL INCREASE: 0.7%
CAPITAL: Vilnius
LANGUAGE: Lithuanian, Russian, Polish
RELIGION: 80% Roman Catholic
CURRENCY: litas
ORGANIZATIONS: Council of Europe, UN

Lithuania is one of the three small ex-Soviet states lying on the shores of the Baltic Sea. The country consists of a low-lying plain with many lakes. Its climate is transitional, ranging between the oceanic type of western Europe and continental conditions. Temperatures range between -5--3°C (24–28°F) in winter to 17–18°C (62–66°F) in summer. There is on average 510 mm–610 mm (20–24 inches) of rainfall per year. Agriculture is dominated by beef and dairy produce; major crops are potatoes and flax. There is a large fishing industry. Industrial products include paper, chemicals, electronics and electrical goods. After almost 50 years' involuntary incorporation into the Soviet Union, Lithuania regained its independence in 1991. The economy is still linked to ex-Soviet countries and the change to a market economy is slow.

LUXEMBOURG

STATUS: Grand Duchy
AREA: 2,585 sq km (998 sq miles)
POPULATION: 395,200
ANNUAL NATURAL INCREASE: 0.8%
CAPITAL: Luxembourg
LANGUAGE: Letzeburgish, French, German
RELIGION: 95% Roman Catholic
CURRENCY: Luxembourg franc (LUF)
Belgian Franc (BEF)
ORGANIZATIONS: Council of Europe, EEA, EU, NATO, OECD, UN, WEU

The Grand Duchy of Luxembourg is situated between France, Belgium and Germany. The climate is mild and temperate with rainfall ranging from 700–1,000 mm (28–40 inches) a year. Just over half the land is arable, mainly cereals, dairy produce and potatoes. Wine is produced in the Moselle valley. Iron ore is found in the south and is the basis of the thriving steel industry. Other industries are textiles, chemicals and pharmaceutical products. Banking and financial services are growing sectors.

MACAU (MACAO)

STATUS: Chinese Territory under Portuguese Administration
AREA: 16 sq km (6 sq miles)
POPULATION: 374,000
CAPITAL: Macau

MACEDONIA
Former Yugoslav Republic of,

STATUS: Republic
AREA: 25,715 sq km (9,925 sq miles)
POPULATION: 2,066,000
ANNUAL NATURAL INCREASE: 1.1%
CAPITAL: Skopje
LANGUAGE: Macedonian, Albanian
RELIGION: Orthodox
CURRENCY: denar
ORGANIZATIONS: UN,
Council of Europe (non-voting member)

The landlocked Balkan state of the Former Yugoslav Republic of Macedonia is a rugged country crossed from north to south by the Vardar valley. The climate is continental with fine hot summers but bitterly cold winters. The economy is basically agricultural. Cereals, tobacco, fruit and vegetables are grown and livestock raised. Heavy industries include chemicals and textiles, which are the county's major employers. Following a Greek economic blockade in 1994, heavy industry – which had already declined through the loss of markets in other former Yugoslav republics – suffered further collapse.

MADAGASCAR

STATUS: Republic
AREA: 594,180 sq km (229,345 sq miles)
POPULATION: 12,827
ANNUAL NATURAL INCREASE: 3.1%
CAPITAL: Antananarivo
LANGUAGE: Malagasy, French, English
RELIGION: 47% animist, 48% Christian, 2% Muslim
CURRENCY: Malagasy franc (MGF)
ORGANIZATIONS: OAU, UN

Madagascar, the world's fourth largest island, is situated 400 km (250 miles) east of the Mozambique coast. The terrain consists largely of a high plateau with steppe and savannah vegetation and desert in the south. Much of the hot humid east coast is covered by tropical rainforest – here rainfall reaches 1,500–2,000 mm (59–79 inches) per annum. Although farming is the occupation of about 85 per cent of the population, only 3 per cent of the land is cultivated. Coffee and vanilla are the major exports, and the shellfish trade is growing rapidly. Much of Madagascar's unique plant and animal life are under increasing threat due to widespread deforestation, caused by the rapid development of forestry and soil erosion.

MADEIRA

STATUS: Self-governing Island Region of Portugal
AREA: 796 sq km (307 sq miles)
POPULATION: 253,400
CAPITAL: Funchal

MALAWI

STATUS: Republic
AREA: 94,080 sq km (35,315 sq miles)
POPULATION: 8,823,000
ANNUAL NATURAL INCREASE: 3.4%

CAPITAL: Lilongwe
LANGUAGE: Chichewa, English
RELIGION: traditional beliefs majority,
10% Roman Catholic, 10% Protestant
CURRENCY: kwacha (MWK)
ORGANIZATIONS: Comm., OAU, UN

Malawi is located at the southern end of the east African Rift Valley. The area around Lake Malawi is tropical and humid with swampy vegetation. In the highlands to the west and south-east conditions are cooler. Malawi has an intensely rural economy – 96 per cent of the population work on the land. Maize is the main subsistence crop, and tea, tobacco, sugar and groundnuts are the main exports. Malawi has deposits of both coal and bauxite, but they are under-exploited at present. Manufacturing industry concentrates on consumer goods and building and construction materials. All energy is produced by hydro-electric power.

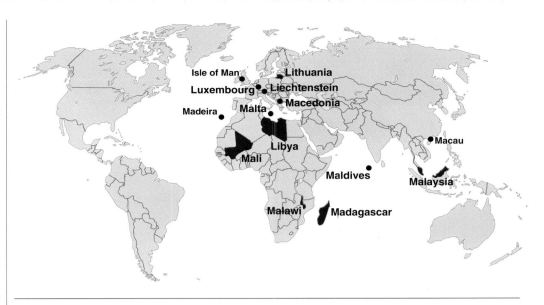

MALAYSIA
STATUS: Federation
AREA: 332,665 sq km
(128,405 sq miles)
POPULATION: 18,606,000
ANNUAL NATURAL INCREASE: 2.5%
CAPITAL: Kuala Lumpur
LANGUAGE: 58% Bahasa Malaysian,
English, Chinese
RELIGION: 53% Muslim, 25% Buddhist, Hindu,
Christian and animist minorities
CURRENCY: Malaysian dollar or ringgit (MYR)
ORGANIZATIONS: ASEAN, Col. Plan,
Comm., UN

The Federation of Malaysia consists of two separate parts; west Malaysia is located on the Malay Peninsula, while east Malaysia consists of Sabah and Sarawak on the island of Borneo 700 km (435 miles) across the South China Sea. Despite this distance, both areas share a similar landscape, which is mountainous and covered with lush tropical rainforest. The climate is tropical, hot and humid all the year round, with annual average rainfall of 2,500 mm (98 inches). At one time the economy was dominated by tin, rubber and timber. Now manufactured goods, in particular electronics, account for over two-thirds of the nation's exports in terms of value. Malaysia is rich in natural resources and other major exports include crude oil, timber, palm oil, pepper, rubber and tin. The fast-growing industrial sector demands increased power supplies which are being met by new power stations and hydro-electric power projects.

PENINSULAR
MALAYSIA
STATUS: State
AREA: 131,585 sq km (50,790 sq miles)
POPULATION: 15,286,098
CAPITAL: Kuala Lumpur

SABAH
STATUS: State
AREA: 76,115 sq km (29,380 sq miles)
POPULATION: 1,736,902
CAPITAL: Kota Kinabalu

SARAWAK
STATUS: State
AREA: 124,965 sq km (48,235 sq miles)
POPULATION: 1,583,000
CAPITAL: Kuching

MALDIVES
STATUS: Republic
AREA: 298 sq km (115 sq miles)
POPULATION: 238,363
ANNUAL NATURAL INCREASE: 3.3%
CAPITAL: Male
LANGUAGE: Dhivehi
RELIGION: Sunni Muslim majority
CURRENCY: rufiyaa (MVR)
ORGANIZATIONS: Col. Plan, Comm., UN

The Maldives are one of the world's poorest nations. They consist of a series of coral atolls stretching 885 km (550 miles) across the Indian Ocean. Although there are 2,000 islands, only about 215 are inhabited. The main island, Male, is only 1½ miles long. Fishing is the main activity and fish and coconut fibre are both exported. Most staple foods have to be imported but coconuts, millet, cassava, yams and fruit are grown locally. Tourism is developing and this is now the main source of revenue.

MALI
STATUS: Republic
AREA: 1,240,140 sq km (478,695 sq miles)
POPULATION: 9,818,000
ANNUAL NATURAL INCREASE: 2.8%
CAPITAL: Bamako
LANGUAGE: French, native languages
RELIGION: 65% Muslim,
30% traditional beliefs, 1% Christian
CURRENCY: CFA franc (W Africa) (XOF)
ORGANIZATIONS: ECOWAS, OAU, UN

Mali is one of the world's most underdeveloped countries. Over half the area is barren desert. South of Timbuktu (Tombouctou) the savannah-covered plains support a wide variety of wildlife. Most of the population live in the Niger valley and grow cotton, oil seeds and groundnuts. Fishing is important. Mali has few mineral resources, although a gold mine opened in 1994. Droughts have taken their toll of livestock and agriculture. Main exports are cotton, groundnuts and livestock.

MALTA
STATUS: Republic
AREA: 316 sq km (122 sq miles)
POPULATION: 364,593
ANNUAL NATURAL INCREASE: 0.7%
CAPITAL: Valletta
LANGUAGE: Maltese, English, Italian
RELIGION: Roman Catholic majority
CURRENCY: Maltese lira (MTL)
ORGANIZATIONS: Comm., Council of Europe, UN

Malta lies about 96 km (60 miles) south of Sicily, and consists of three islands; Malta, Gozo and Comino. It has a Mediterranean climate with summer temperatures averaging 25°C (77°F). About 40 per cent of the land is under cultivation with wheat, potatoes, tomatoes and vines the main crops. The large natural harbour at Valletta has made it a major transit port, and shipbuilding and repair are traditional industries. Principal exports are machinery, beverages, tobacco, flowers, wine, leather goods and potatoes. Tourism and light manufacturing are booming sectors of the economy.

MAN, ISLE OF
STATUS: British Crown Dependency
AREA: 588 sq km (227 sq miles)
POPULATION: 71,000
CAPITAL: Douglas

MARSHALL ISLANDS

STATUS: Self-governing state in Compact of Free Association with USA
AREA: 605 sq km (234 sq miles)
POPULATION: 48,000
CAPITAL: Majuro
LANGUAGE: English, local languages
RELIGION: Roman Catholic majority
CURRENCY: US dollar (USD)
ORGANIZATIONS: UN

The Marshall Islands, formerly UN Trust Territory under US administration, consist of over 1,000 atolls and islands which in total account for only 181 sq km (70 sq miles) but are spread over a wide area of the Pacific. The climate is hot all year round with a heavy rainfall averaging 4,050 mm (160 inches). Fishing, subsistence farming and tourism provide occupation for most. The economy is heavily dependent on grants from the USA for use of the islands as military bases.

MARTINIQUE

STATUS: Overseas Department of France
AREA: 1,079 sq km (417 sq miles)
POPULATION: 373,000
CAPITAL: Fort-de-France

MAURITANIA

STATUS: Islamic Republic
AREA: 1,030,700 sq km (397,850 sq miles)
POPULATION: 2,143,000
ANNUAL NATURAL INCREASE: 2.7%
CAPITAL: Nouakchott
LANGUAGE: Arabic, French
RELIGION: Muslim
CURRENCY: ouguiya (MRO)
ORGANIZATIONS: Arab League, ECOWAS, OAU, UN

Situated on the west coast of Africa, Mauritania consists of savannah, steppes and vast areas of the Sahara desert. It has high temperatures, low rainfall and frequent droughts. There is very little arable farming except in the Senegal river valley where millet and dates are grown. Most Mauritanians raise cattle, sheep, goats or camels. The country has only one railway which is used to transport the chief export, iron ore, from the mines to the coast at Nouadhibou. Mauritania has substantial copper reserves which are mined at Akjoujt. A severe drought during the last decade decimated the livestock population and forced many nomadic tribesmen into the towns. Coastal fishing contributes nearly 50 per cent of foreign earnings. Exports are almost exclusively confined to iron ore, copper and fish products.

MAURITIUS

STATUS: Republic
AREA: 1,865 sq km (720 sq miles)
POPULATION: 1,098,000
ANNUAL NATURAL INCREASE: 1.1%
CAPITAL: Port Louis
LANGUAGE: English, French Creole, Hindi, Bhojpuri
RELIGION: 51% Hindu, 31% Christian, 17% Muslim
CURRENCY: Mauritian rupee (MUR)
ORGANIZATIONS: Comm., OAU, UN

Mauritius is a mountainous island in the Indian Ocean. It has a varied climate with temperatures ranging from 7–36°C (45–97°F) and annual rainfall of between 1,530–5,080 mm (60–200 inches). The economy of Mauritius once depended wholly on sugar. Although this is still important, with tea as a second crop, earnings from the manufacturing of clothing now surpass those from sugar. Tourism and financial services are also expanding.

MAYOTTE

STATUS: 'Territorial collectivity' of France
AREA: 376 sq km (145 sq miles)
POPULATION: 85,000
CAPITAL: Dzaoudzi

MEXICO

STATUS: Federal Republic
AREA: 1,972,545 sq km (761,400 sq miles)
POPULATION: 89,538,000
ANNUAL NATURAL INCREASE: 1.8%
CAPITAL: Mexico City
LANGUAGE: Spanish
RELIGION: 96% Roman Catholic
CURRENCY: Mexican peso (MXP)
ORGANIZATIONS: NAFTA, OAS, OECD, UN

Mexico consists mainly of mountain ranges and dissected plateaux. The only extensive flat lands are in the Yucatan Peninsula. Temperature and rainfall are modified by altitude – the north is arid but the south is humid and tropical. Mexico has one of the world's fastest growing populations and, with extreme poverty in many rural areas, migration to the cities continues to be prevalent. One-third of the land is used for livestock ranching and only 20 per cent farmed. Communal farms were abolished in 1991 and peasants are encouraged, with private ownership, to vary crops from the traditional corn and beans. Mexico has great mineral wealth, e.g. silver, strontium and gold, but much is still unexploited. There are considerable reserves of oil, natural gas, coal and uranium. Ten years ago petroleum products accounted for 70 per cent of exports. Now oil accounts for 30 per cent and the major exports are manufactured goods from

an industrial base of vehicle production, steel, textiles, breweries and food processing. Other exports are coffee, fruit, vegetables and shrimps. Tourism brings in important foreign revenue. Trading should be enhanced by Mexico's decision to join the USA and Canada in the North American Free Trade Association (NAFTA).

MICRONESIA
Federated States of,

STATUS: Self-governing Federation of States in Compact of Free Association with USA
AREA: 702 sq km (271 sq miles)
POPULATION: 109,000
ANNUAL NATURAL INCOME: 2.4%
CAPITAL: Palikir
LANGUAGE: English, eight indigenous languages
RELIGION: Christian majority
CURRENCY: US dollar (USD)
ORGANIZATIONS: UN

Micronesia, a former UN Trust Territory administered by the USA, is a federation of 607 islands and atolls spread over some 3,200 km (2,000 miles) of the Pacific. Being near the equator, the climate is hot and humid all year round with a high annual rainfall of 9,300 mm (194 inches). Subsistence farming and fishing are the traditional occupations while income is derived from the export of phosphates and copper, a growing tourist industry and revenue from foreign fleets fishing within its territorial waters.

MOLDOVA

STATUS: Republic
AREA: 33,700 sq km (13,010 sq miles)
POPULATION: 4,356,000
ANNUAL NATURAL INCREASE: 0.6%
CAPITAL: Kishinev
LANGUAGE: Moldovan, Russian, Romanian
RELIGION: Orthodox
CURRENCY: rouble
ORGANIZATIONS: CIS, UN

A country of hilly plains, Moldova enjoys a warm and dry climate with relatively mild winters. Temperatures range from 5–7°C (23–26°F) during winter, to 20–23°C (68°–72°F) for summer and rainfall averages 305–457mm (12–18 inches) per year. It has very fertile soil, so arable farming dominates agricultural output with viticulture, fruit and vegetables especially important. Sunflower seeds are the main industrial crop; wheat and maize the chief grain crops. Traditionally, food processing has been the major industry but recently light machine building and metal working industries have been expanding. Moldova, part of the Soviet Union between 1939 and 1991, has close ethnic, linguistic and historical ties with neighbouring Romania. Any moves towards re-unification have been fiercely resisted by the Russian minority in the eastern region of Trans-Dniester.

MONACO

STATUS: Principality
AREA: 1.6 sq km (0.6 sq miles)
POPULATION: 28,000
ANNUAL NATURAL INCREASE: 1.4%
CAPITAL: Monaco-ville
LANGUAGE: French, Monegasque, Italian, English
RELIGION: 90% Roman Catholic
CURRENCY: French franc (FRF)
ORGANIZATIONS: UN

The tiny principality is the world's smallest independent state after the Vatican City. It occupies a rocky peninsula on the French Mediterranean coast near the Italian border and is backed by the Maritime Alps. The climate is Mediterranean. It comprises the towns of Monaco, la Condamine, Fontvieille and Monte Carlo. Most revenue comes from tourism, casinos, light industry and financial services. Land has been reclaimed from the sea to extend the area available for commercial development.

MONGOLIA

STATUS: People's Republic
AREA: 1,565,000 sq km (604,090 sq miles)
POPULATION: 2,310,000
ANNUAL NATURAL INCREASE: 2.8%
CAPITAL: Ulan Bator (Ulaanbaatar)
LANGUAGE: Khalkha Mongolian
RELIGION: some Buddhist Lamaism
CURRENCY: tugrik (MNT)
ORGANIZATIONS: OIEC, UN

Situated between China and the Russian Federation, Mongolia has one of the lowest population densities in the world. Much of the country consists of a high undulating plateau reaching 1,500 m (4,920 feet) covered with grassland. To the north, mountain ranges reaching 4,231 m (13,881 feet) bridge the border with the Russian Federation, and to the south is the vast Gobi desert. The climate is very extreme with January temperatures falling to -34°C (-29°F). Mongolia is predominantly a farming economy, based on rearing cattle and horses. Its natural resources include some oil, rich coal deposits, iron ore, gold , tin and copper. About half the country's exports originate from the Erdanet copper mine. The break-up of the Soviet Union in 1991 brought an end to a partnership whereby Mongolia supplied raw materials in exchange for aid. A year later communism was abandoned. The country is now forced to reform its economy, but is isolated and in need of investment.

MONTSERRAT

STATUS: UK Crown Colony
AREA: 106 sq km (41 sq miles)
POPULATION: 11,000
CAPITAL: Plymouth

MOROCCO

STATUS: Kingdom
AREA: 710,895 sq km
(274,414 sq miles)
POPULATION: 26,318,000
ANNUAL NATURAL INCREASE: 2.5%
CAPITAL: Rabat
LANGUAGE: Arabic, French, Spanish, Berber
RELIGION: Muslim majority, Christian
and Jewish minorities
CURRENCY: Moroccan dirham (MAD)
ORGANIZATIONS: Arab League, UN

One-third of Morocco consists of the Atlas Mountains, reaching 4,165 m (13,665 feet). Beyond the coastal plains and the mountains lies the Sahara. The north of the country has a Mediterranean climate with some winter rainfall, but elsewhere conditions are mostly desert like and arid. Agriculture has diversified in recent years and as well as tomatoes and citrus fruits exports now include a variety of fruit and vegetables. Morocco has considerable phosphate deposits, which in value account for a quarter of total exports. Manufacturing industries include textiles, leather, food processing and chemicals and a growing mechanical and electronic sector. Income from tourism and remittances from Moroccans abroad are the main sources of foreign revenue.

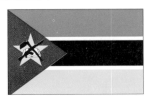

MOZAMBIQUE

STATUS: Republic
AREA: 784,755 sq km
(302,915 sq miles)
POPULATION: 14,872,000
ANNUAL NATURAL INCREASE: 2.7%
CAPITAL: Maputo
LANGUAGE: Portuguese, tribal languages

RELIGION: majority traditional beliefs,
15% Christian, 15% Muslim
CURRENCY: metical (MZM)
ORGANIZATIONS: OAU, UN

The ex-Portuguese colony of Mozambique consists of a large coastal plain, rising towards plateaux and mountain ranges which border Malawi, Zambia and Zimbabwe. The highlands in the north reach 2,436 m (7,992 feet). The climate is tropical on the coastal plain, although high altitudes make it cooler inland. Over 90 per cent of the population are subsistence farmers cultivating coconuts, cashews, cotton, maize and rice. Cashew nuts and shrimps are the main exports. Mozambique also acts as an entrepôt, handling exports from South Africa, and land-locked Zambia and Malawi. Natural resources include large reserves of coal, also iron ore, copper, bauxite, gold and offshore gas, but most are unexploited.

NAMIBIA

STATUS: Republic
AREA: 825,419 sq km
(318,614 sq miles)
POPULATION: 1,534,000
ANNUAL NATURAL INCREASE: 3.1%
CAPITAL: Windhoek
LANGUAGE: Afrikaans, German, English,
regional languages
RELIGION: 90% Christian
CURRENCY: Namibian dollar, SA rand
ORGANIZATIONS: Comm., OAU, UN

The southwest African country of Namibia is one of the driest in the world. The Namib desert, on the coast, has less than 50 mm (2 inches) average rainfall per year, the Kalahari, to the northeast, has 100–250 mm (4–10 inches). The vegetation is sparse. Maize and sorghum are grown in the northern highlands and sheep are reared in the south. Namibia, however, is rich in mineral resources, with large deposits of lead, tin and zinc, and the world's largest uranium mine. The rich coastal waters are the basis of a successful fishing industry.

NAURU
STATUS: Republic
AREA: 21.2 sq km (8 sq miles)
POPULATION: 9,919
ANNUAL NATURAL INCREASE: -0.3%
CAPITAL: Yaren
LANGUAGE: Nauruan, English
RELIGION: Nauruan Protestant majority
CURRENCY: Australian dollar (AUD)
ORGANIZATIONS: Comm. (special member)

Nauru, a small island only 19 km (12 miles) in circumference, is situated in the Pacific, 2,100 km (1,3000 miles) northeast of Australia. The flat coastal lowlands, encircled by coral reefs, rise gently to a central plateau. The country was once rich in phosphates which were exported to Australia and Japan. However these deposits will soon become exhausted.

NEPAL
STATUS: Kingdom
AREA: 141,415 sq km (54,585 sq miles)
POPULATION: 20,577,000
ANNUAL NATURAL INCREASE: 2.6%
CAPITAL: Katmandu (Kathmandu)
LANGUAGE: Nepali, Maithir, Bhojpuri
RELIGION: 90% Hindu, 5% Buddhist, 3% Muslim
CURRENCY: Nepalese rupee (NPR)
ORGANIZATIONS: Col. Plan, UN

Nepal is a Himalayan kingdom sandwiched between China and India. Some of the highest mountains in the world, including Everest, are to be found along its northern borders. The climate changes sharply with altitude from the mountain peaks southwards to the Tarai plain. Central Kathmandu varies between 2–30°C (35–86°F). Most rain falls between June and October and can reach 2,500 mm (100 inches). Agriculture concentrates on rice, maize, cattle, buffaloes, sheep and goats. The small amount of industry processes local products, with carpets and clothing showing particular economic growth.

NETHERLANDS
STATUS: Kingdom
AREA: 41,160 sq km (15,890 sq miles)
POPULATION: 15,269,000
ANNUAL NATURAL INCREASE: 0.7%
CAPITAL: Amsterdam
(seat of Government: The Hague)
LANGUAGE: Dutch
RELIGION: 40% Roman Catholic,

30% Protestant, Jewish minority
CURRENCY: gulden (guilder or florin) (NLG)
ORGANIZATIONS: Council of Europe, EEA, EU, NATO, OECD, UN, WEU

The Netherlands is exceptionally low-lying, with about 25 per cent of its territory being reclaimed from the sea. The wide coastal belt consists of flat marshland, mud-flats, sand-dunes and dykes. Further inland, the flat alluvial plain is drained by the Rhine, Maas and Ijssel. A complex network of dykes and canals prevents the area from flooding. To the south and east the land rises. Flat and exposed to strong winds, the Netherlands has a maritime climate with mild winters and cool summers. The Dutch are the leading world producers of dairy goods and also cultivate crops such as cereals, sugar beet and potatoes. Lacking mineral resources, much of the industry of the Netherlands is dependent on natural gas. Most manufacturing industry has developed around Rotterdam, where there are oil refineries, steel-works and chemical and food processing plants.

NETHERLANDS ANTILLES
STATUS: Self-governing Part of Netherlands Realm
AREA: 993 sq km (383 sq miles)
POPULATION: 191,311
CAPITAL: Willemstad

NEW CALEDONIA
STATUS: Overseas Territory of France
AREA: 19,105 sq km (7,375 sq miles)
POPULATION: 164,173
CAPITAL: Nouméa

NEW ZEALAND
STATUS: Commonwealth Nation
AREA: 265,150 sq km (102,350 sq miles)
POPULATION: 3,470,000
ANNUAL NATURAL INCREASE: 0.7%
CAPITAL: Wellington
LANGUAGE: English, Maori
RELIGION: 35% Anglican Christian,
22% Presbyterian, 16% Roman Catholic
CURRENCY: New Zealand dollar (NZD)
ORGANIZATIONS: ANZUS, Col. Plan,
Comm., OECD, UN

New Zealand consists of two main and several smaller islands, lying in the south Pacific Ocean. South Island is mountainous, with the Southern Alps running along its length. It has many glaciers and a coast line that is indented by numerous sounds and fjords. On the more heavily populated North Island, mountain ranges, broad fertile valleys and volcanic plateaus predominate. The overall climate is temperate, with an annual average temperature of 9°C (40°F) on South Island and 15°C (59°F) on the North Island. In terms of value the chief exports are meat, dairy produce and forestry products, followed by wood, fruit and vegetables. In the mineral sector there are deposits of coal, iron ore, oil and natural gas. Hydro-electric and geothermal power are well developed. Manufacturing industries are of increasing importance and in the early 1990s tourism expanded rapidly.

NICARAGUA
STATUS: Republic
AREA: 148,000 sq km (57,130 sq miles)
POPULATION: 4,130,000
ANNUAL NATURAL INCREASE: 2.8%
CAPITAL: Managua
LANGUAGE: Spanish
RELIGION: Roman Catholic
CURRENCY: cordoba (NIO)
ORGANIZATIONS: CACM, OAS, UN

Nicaragua, the largest of the Central American republics, is situated between the Caribbean and the Pacific. Active volcanic mountains run parallel with the western coast. The south is dominated by Lakes Managua and Nicaragua. Climate is tropical, with average daily temperatures in excess of 25°C (77°F) throughout the year. On the west coast wet summer months contrast with a dry period from December to April. Agriculture is the main occupation with cotton, coffee, sugar cane and fruit the main exports. Gold, silver and copper are mined.

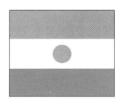

NIGER
STATUS: Republic
AREA: 1,186,410 sq km (457,955 sq miles)
POPULATION: 8,252,000
ANNUAL NATURAL INCREASE: 3.2%
CAPITAL: Niamey
LANGUAGE: French, Hausa and other
native languages
RELIGION: 85% Muslim, 15% traditional beliefs
CURRENCY: CFA franc (W Africa) (XOF)
ORGANIZATIONS: ECOWAS, OAU, UN

Niger is a vast landlocked southern republic. Apart from savannah in the south and in the Niger valley, most of the vast country lies within the Sahara desert. Rainfall is low, and decreases from 560 mm (22 inches) in the south to near zero in the north. Temperatures are above 35°C (95°F) for much of the year. Most of the population are farmers, particularly of cattle, sheep, and goats. Recent droughts have affected both cereals and livestock. The only significant export is uranium. and phosphates, coal, and tungsten are also mined. The economy depends largely on foreign aid.

NIGERIA
STATUS: Federal Republic
AREA: 923,850 sq km (356,605 sq miles)
POPULATION: 88,515,000
ANNUAL NATURAL INCREASE: 2.9%
CAPITAL: Abuja

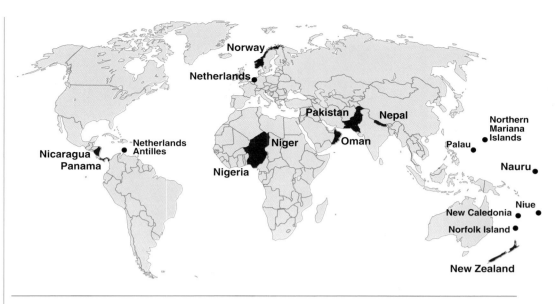

LANGUAGE: English, Hausa, Yoruba, Ibo
RELIGION: Muslim majority, 35% Christian, animist minority
CURRENCY: naira (NGN)
ORGANIZATIONS: Comm., ECOWAS, OAU, OPEC, UN

The most populous nation in Africa, Nigeria is bounded to the north by the Sahara and to the west, east and southeast by tropical rainforest. The southern half of the country is dominated by the Niger and its tributaries, the north by the interior plateaux. Temperatures average 32°C (90°F) with high humidity. From a basic agricultural economy, Nigeria is only slowly being transformed by the vast oil discoveries in the Niger delta and coastal regions, which account for 95 per cent of exports. Gas reserves are relatively underdeveloped.

NIUE

STATUS: Self-governing Territory Overseas in Free Association with New Zealand
AREA: 259 sq km (100 sq miles)
POPULATION: 2,267
CAPITAL: Aloli

NORFOLK ISLAND

STATUS: External Territory of Australia
AREA: 36 sq km (14 sq miles)
POPULATION: 1,977
CAPITAL: Kingston

NORTHERN MARIANA ISLANDS

STATUS: Self-governing Commonwealth of USA
AREA: 471 sq km (182 sq miles)
POPULATION: 45,200
CAPITAL: Saipan

NORWAY

STATUS: Kingdom
AREA: 323,895 sq km (125,025 sq miles)
POPULATION: 4,305,000
ANNUAL NATURAL INCREASE: 0.4%
CAPITAL: Oslo
LANGUAGE: Norwegian, Lappish
RELIGION: 92% Evangelical Lutheran Christian
CURRENCY: Norwegian krone (NOK)
ORGANIZATIONS: Council of Europe, EEA, EFTA, NATO, OECD, UN

Norway is a mountainous country stretching from 58° to 72°N. The climate along its indented western coast is modified by the Gulf Stream, with high rainfall and relatively mild winters. Temperatures average -3.9°C (25°F) in January and 17°C (63°F) in July. Rainfall may be as high as 1,960 mm (79 inches). Most settlements are scattered along the fjords, the coast and around Oslo in the south. Norway is rich in natural resources. Oil and natural gas predominate in exports, but are supplemented by metal products, timber, pulp and paper, fish and machinery. The advanced production of hydro-electric power has helped develop industry, particularly chemicals, metal products and paper.

OMAN

STATUS: Sultanate
AREA: 271,950 sq km (104,970 sq miles)
POPULATION: 1,637,000
ANNUAL NATURAL INCREASE: 3.8%
CAPITAL: Muscat (Masqaṭ)
LANGUAGE: Arabic, English
RELIGION: 75% Ibadi Muslim, 25% Sunni Muslim
CURRENCY: rial Omani (OMR)
ORGANIZATIONS: Arab League, UN

The Sultanate of Oman occupies the northeast coast of the Arabian peninsula, with an enclave overlooking the Strait of Hormuz. Its desert landscape consists of a coastal plain and low hills rising to plateau in the interior, and has two fertile areas; Batinah in the north and Dhofar in the south. Copper ores are being mined and exported and oil provides over 95 per cent of export revenue. New discoveries of gas suggest that this will eventually supplant oil in importance.

PAKISTAN

STATUS: Republic
AREA: 803,940 sq km (310,320 sq miles)
POPULATION: 119,107,000
ANNUAL NATURAL INCREASE: 3.1%
CAPITAL: Islamabad
LANGUAGE: Urdu, Punjabi, Sindhi, Pushtu, English
RELIGION: 90% Muslim
CURRENCY: Pakistan rupee (PKR)
ORGANIZATIONS Col. Plan, Comm., UN

The landscape of Pakistan is dominated by the river Indus which flows south through the country flanked by the plateau of Balochistan and the Sulaiman mountains to the west and the Thar desert to the east. The climate is arid with temperatures averaging 27°C (80°F). Rainfall can be

less than 127 mm (5 inches) in the southwest and only in the northern mountains does it reach appreciable amounts; 900 mm (36 inches). Over 50 per cent of the population are engaged in agriculture which is confined to the irrigated areas near rivers. Main crops are wheat, cotton, maize, rice and sugar cane. There are many types of low-grade mineral deposits, such as coal and copper, which are little developed. Main industries are textiles, food processing and oil refining but these only contribute about 20 per cent to the economy.

PALAU

STATUS: Self-governing state in Compact of Free Association with USA
AREA: 497 sq km (192 sq miles)
POPULATION: 15,450
CAPITAL: Babelthuap

PANAMA

STATUS: Republic
AREA: 78,515 sq km (30,305 sq miles)
POPULATION: 2,535,000
ANNUAL NATURAL INCREASE: 2.1%
CAPITAL: Panama City (Panamá)
LANGUAGE: Spanish, English
RELIGION: Roman Catholic majority
CURRENCY: balboa (PAB), US dollar (USD)
ORGANIZATIONS: OAS, UN

Panama is situated at the narrowest part of central American isthmus. Mountain ranges, reaching heights exceeding 3,000 m (9,800 feet), run the country's length. Much of its tropical forest has now been cleared, but some remains towards the border with Colombia. Its climate is tropical with little variation throughout the year. The average temperature is around 27°C (80°F). There is a rainy season from April to December. Most of its foreign income is earned from revenues derived from the Panama Canal and from a large merchant fleet that is registered in its name. Petroleum products, bananas and shrimps are the main exports.

PAPUA NEW GUINEA

STATUS: Commonwealth Nation
AREA: 462,840 sq km (178,655 sq miles)
POPULATION: 4,056,000
ANNUAL NATURAL INCREASE: 2.3%
CAPITAL: Port Moresby
LANGUAGE: English, Pidgin English,
RELIGION: Pantheist, Christian minority
CURRENCY: kina (PGK)
ORGANIZATIONS: Col. Plan, Comm., UN

Papua New Guinea (the eastern half of New Guinea and neighbouring islands) is a mountainous country. It has an equatorial climate with temperatures of 21–32°C (70–90°F) and annual rainfall of over 2,000 mm (79 inches). The country is rich in minerals, in particular copper, gold and silver, but development is restricted by rainforest and lack of roads. Exports include coconuts, cocoa, coffee, rubber, tea and sugar. Logging was once dominant but exports are now being reduced in order to preserve forest resources.

PARAGUAY

STATUS: Republic
AREA: 406,750 sq km (157,055 sq miles)
POPULATION: 4,500,000
ANNUAL NATURAL INCREASE: 2.9%
CAPITAL: Asunción
LANGUAGE: Spanish, Guarani
RELIGION: 90% Roman Catholic
CURRENCY: guarani (PYG)
ORGANIZATIONS: OAS, UN

Paraguay is a landlocked country in South America with hot rainy summers, when temperatures reach over 27°C (80°F), and mild winters with an average temperature of 18°C (64°F). Lush, fertile plains and heavily forested plateau east of the River Paraguay contrast with the scrubland of the Chaco to the west. Cassava, cotton, soya beans and maize are the main crops but the rearing of livestock – cattle, horses, pigs and sheep – and food processing, dominate the export trade. The largest hydro-electric power dam in the world is at Itaipú, constructed as a joint project with Brazil, and another massive hydro-electric development is being constructed at Yacyreta in conjunction with Argentina.

PERU

STATUS: Republic
AREA: 1,285,215 sq km (496,095 sq miles)
POPULATION: 22,454,000
ANNUAL NATURAL INCREASE: 2.1%

CAPITAL: Lima
LANGUAGE: Spanish, Quechua, Aymara
RELIGION: Roman Catholic majority
CURRENCY: new sol (PES)
ORGANIZATIONS: OAS, UN

Peru exhibits three geographical regions. The Pacific coastal region is very dry but with fertile oases producing cotton, sugar, fruit and fodder crops. This is the most prosperous and heavily populated area and includes the industrial centres around Lima. In the ranges and plateaux of the Andes and in the Amazon lowlands to the northeast, the soils are thin with the inhabitants depending on cultivation and grazing. Poor communications have hindered the development of Peru and there are great differences between the rich and poor. Peru has rich mineral deposits of copper, gold, lead, zinc and silver and there are oil and gas reserves in the interior.

PHILIPPINES

STATUS: Republic
AREA: 300,000 sq km (115,800 sq miles)
POPULATION: 65,650,000
ANNUAL NATURAL INCREASE: 2.3%
CAPITAL: Manila
LANGUAGE: Filipino (Tagalog), English,
Spanish, Cebuano
RELIGION: 90% Christian, 7% Muslim
CURRENCY: Philippine peso (PHP)
ORGANIZATIONS: ASEAN, Col. Plan, UN

The Philippine archipelago consists of some 7,000 islands and is subject to earthquakes and typhoons. It has a monsoonal climate, with up to 6,350 mm (250 inches) of rainfall per annum in some areas. This once supported tropical rain forest but, apart from Palawan island, this has now been destroyed. Fishing is important but small farms dominate the economy, producing rice and copra for domestic consumption and other coconut and sugar products for export. Main exports are textiles, fruit and electronic products. Remittances from Filipinos working overseas are important to the economy. There is high unemployment and the extent of poverty is widespread.

PITCAIRN ISLAND

STATUS: UK Dependent Territory
AREA: 45 sq km (17.25 sq miles)
POPULATION: 71
CAPITAL: Adamstown

POLAND

STATUS: Republic
AREA: 312,685 sq km (120,695 sq miles)
POPULATION: 38,310,000
ANNUAL NATURAL INCREASE: 0.4%
CAPITAL: Warsaw (Warszawa)

LANGUAGE: Polish
RELIGION: 90% Roman Catholic
CURRENCY: zloty (PLZ)
ORGANIZATIONS: Council of Europe,
OIEC, UN,

Much of Poland lies in the north European plain, south of the Baltic Sea. It is a land of woods and lakes, gently rising southwards from the coast towards the Tartry mountains in the south and Sudety mountains in Silesia. The climate is continental with short, warm summers and long severe winters, when average temperatures can drop below freezing point (32°F). Rainfall occurs mainly in the summer months and averages between 520 and 730 mm (21–29 inches). Both agriculture and natural resources play an important part in the economy and Poland is nearly self-sufficient in cereals, sugar beet and potatoes. There are large reserves of coal, copper, sulphur and natural gas. Its major industries are ship-building in the north and the production of machinery, transport equipment, metals and chemicals in the major mining centres of the south. Manufacturing industries in both the private and public sectors are expanding rapidly and the government is committed to a programme of economic reforms and privatization.

PORTUGAL

STATUS: Republic
AREA: 91,630 sq km (35,370 sq miles)
POPULATION: 9,846,000
ANNUAL NATURAL INCREASE: -0.7%
CAPITAL: Lisbon (Lisboa)
LANGUAGE: Portuguese
RELIGION: Roman Catholic majority
CURRENCY: escudo (PTE)
ORGANIZATIONS: Council of Europe, EEA, EU,
NATO, OECD, UN, WEU

Portugal occupies the western Atlantic coast of the Iberian Peninsula. The river Tagus, on whose estuary is Lisbon, divides the country physically. In the north the land lies mainly above 4,000 m (1,220 feet) with plateaux cut by westward flowing rivers. Here, the climate is modified by westerly winds and the Gulf Stream. This is reflected in the lush mixed deciduous/coniferous forests. Land to the south is generally less than 300 m (1,000 feet) and the climate becomes progressively more arid further south, with Mediterranean scrub predominating in the far south. A quarter of the population are farmers growing vines, olives, wheat and maize. Wines, cork and fruit are important exports. In industry the chief exports are textiles, clothing, footwear and wood products. Mineral deposits include coal, copper, kaolinite and uranium. Tourism is an important source of revenue, with many visitors coming to the Algarve region in the far south of the country.

PUERTO RICO

STATUS: Self-governing Commonwealth of USA
AREA: 8,960 sq km (3,460 sq miles)
POPULATION: 3,580,000
CAPITAL: San Juan

QATAR

STATUS: State
AREA: 11,435 sq km (4,415 sq miles)
POPULATION: 453,000
ANNUAL NATURAL INCREASE: 6%
CAPITAL: Doha (Ad Dawḥah)
LANGUAGE: Arabic, English
RELIGION: Muslim
CURRENCY: Qatari riyal (QAR)
ORGANIZATIONS: Arab League, OPEC, UN

The country occupies all of the Qatar peninsula in the Gulf and is a land of flat, arid desert. July temperatures average 37°C (98°F) and annual rainfall averages 62mm (2.5 inches). The main source of revenue is from the exploitation of oil and gas reserves. The North Field gas reserves are the world's largest single field and the development of these has a high priority.

RÉUNION

STATUS: Overseas Department of France
AREA: 2,510 sq km (969 sq miles)
POPULATION: 624,000
CAPITAL: Saint-Denis

ROMANIA

STATUS: Republic
AREA: 237,500 sq km (91,699 sq miles)
POPULATION: 22,767,000
ANNUAL NATURAL INCREASE: 0.1%
CAPITAL: Bucharest (Bucureşti)
LANGUAGE: Romanian, Magyar
RELIGION: 85% Romanian Orthodox,
CURRENCY: leu (ROL)
ORGANIZATIONS: Council of Europe, OIEC, UN

Romania is dominated by the great curve of the Carpathians, flanked by rich agricultural lowlands and has a continental climate. Forced industrialization has taken the economy from one based on agriculture to one dependent on heavy industry, notably chemicals, metal processing and machine-building. Since the fall of the communist dictatorship in 1989, most land has been privatized and there has been a re-emergence of Romania's traditional agriculture, with exports of cereals, fruit and wine. There are natural resources including oil, gas and minerals but industrial reform is slow and the economy is sluggish. Living standards are among the lowest in Europe.

RUSSIAN FEDERATION

STATUS: Federation
AREA: 17,078,005 sq km (6,592,110 sq miles)

POPULATION: 148,673,000
ANNUAL NATURAL INCREASE: 0.5%
CAPITAL: Moscow (Moskva)
LANGUAGE: Russian
RELIGION: Russian Orthodox,
Jewish and Muslim minorities
CURRENCY: rouble
ORGANIZATIONS: CIS, UN

Covering much of east and northeast Europe and all of north Asia, the Russian Federation (Russia) displays an enormous variety of landforms and climates. The Arctic deserts of the north give way to tundra wastes and taiga which cover two-thirds of the country. In the far south, beyond the steppes, some areas assume subtropical and semi-desert landscapes. The majority of the population live west of the north-south spine of the Urals but in recent decades there has been a substantial migration eastwards to the Siberian basin in order to exploit its vast natural resources. Massive oil fields off the east coast of Sakhalin north of Japan and also in the Russian Arctic (Timan Pechora basin) are now to be developed. Russia's extraordinary wealth of natural resources is a key factor in the country's speedy industrialization during the Soviet period. Heavy industry still plays a decisive role in the economy, while light and consumer industries have remained relatively under-developed. Agricultural land covers one-sixth of Russia's territory but there remains great potential for increase through drainage and clearance. By the mid-1980s the Soviet system was finally acknowledged to have reached an impasse, and the failure of the *perestroika* programme for reform precipitated the disintegration of the Soviet Union, which finally broke up in 1991. A transition from a state-run Communist economy to a market economy is taking place. Between 1992 and 1994 70 per cent of state-owned enterprises were privatized and farms are also starting to be re-organized.

RWANDA

STATUS: Republic
AREA: 26,330 sq km (10,165 sq miles)

POPULATION: 7,526,000
ANNUAL NATURAL INCREASE: 3%
CAPITAL: Kigali
LANGUAGE: French, Kinyarwanda (Bantu),
tribal languages
RELIGION: 50% animist, 50% Christian
(mostly Roman Catholic)
CURRENCY: Rwanda franc (RWF)
ORGANIZATIONS: OAU, UN

Small and isolated, Rwanda supports a high density of population on the mountains and plateaux east of the Rift Valley. It has a tropical climate with a dry season between June and August. Agriculture is basically subsistence with coffee the major export. Tin is mined and there are major natural gas reserves. Since 1990 a civil war has raged between the Tutsi and Hutu tribes, creating many thousands of casualties and well over one million refugees. The country has become reliant on foreign aid, and will require a massive international relief effort to avert disease and famine.

ST HELENA

STATUS: UK Dependent Territory
AREA: 122 sq km (47 sq miles)
POPULATION: 5,564
CAPITAL: Jamestown

ST KITTS-NEVIS

STATUS: Commonwealth State
AREA: 262 sq km (101 sq miles)
POPULATION: 40,618
ANNUAL NATURAL INCREASE: -0.4%
CAPITAL: Basseterre
LANGUAGE: English
RELIGION: Christian (mostly Protestant)
CURRENCY: E Caribbean dollar (XCD)
ORGANIZATIONS: CARICOM, Comm., OAS, UN

St Kitts-Nevis, in the Leeward Islands, comprises two volcanic islands: St Kitts and Nevis. The climate is tropical with temperatures of 16–33°C (61–91°F) and an average annual rainfall of 1,400 mm (55 inches). Main exports are sugar, molasses and cotton. Tourism is an important industry.

ST LUCIA

STATUS: Commonwealth State
AREA: 616 sq km (238 sq miles)
POPULATION: 136,000
ANNUAL NATURAL INCREASE: 1.9%
CAPITAL: Castries
LANGUAGE: English, French patois
RELIGION: 82% Roman Catholic
CURRENCY: E. Caribbean dollar (XCD)
ORGANIZATIONS: Caricom, Comm., OAS, UN

Independent since 1979 this small tropical Caribbean island in the Lesser Antilles grows coconuts, cocoa and fruit. Bananas account for over 40 per cent of export earnings. Main industries are food and drink processing and all consumer goods are imported. Tourism is a major growth sector.

ST PIERRE AND MIQUELON

STATUS: Territorial Collectivity of France
AREA: 241 sq km (93 sq miles)
POPULATION: 6,392
CAPITAL: St Pierre

ST VINCENT AND THE GRENADINES

STATUS: Commonwealth State
AREA: 389 sq km (150 sq miles)
POPULATION: 107,598
ANNUAL NATURAL INCREASE: 0.9%
CAPITAL: Kingstown
LANGUAGE: English
RELIGION: Christian
CURRENCY: E. Caribbean dollar (XCD)
ORGANIZATIONS: Caricom, Comm., OAS, UN

St Vincent in the Lesser Antilles comprises a forested main island and the northern part of the Grenadines. It has a tropical climate. Most exports are foodstuffs: arrowroot, sweet potatoes, coconut products and yams, but the principal crop is bananas. Some sugar cane is grown for the production of rum and other drinks. Tourism is well-established.

SAN MARINO

STATUS: Republic
AREA: 61 sq km (24 sq miles)
POPULATION: 24,003
ANNUAL NATURAL INCREASE: 1.2%
CAPITAL: San Marino
LANGUAGE: Italian

RELIGION: Roman Catholic
CURRENCY: Italian lira (ITL),
San Marino coinage
ORGANIZATIONS: Council of Europe, UN

An independent state within Italy, San Marino straddles a limestone peak in the Apennines south of Rimini. The economy is centred around tourism and the sale of postage stamps. Most of the population are farmers growing cereals, olives and vines and tending herds of sheep and goats.

SÃO TOMÉ AND PRÍNCIPE

STATUS: Republic
AREA: 964 sq km (372 sq miles)
POPULATION: 124,000
ANNUAL NATURAL INCREASE: 2.3%
CAPITAL: São Tomé
LANGUAGE: Portuguese, Fang
RELIGION: Roman Catholic majority
CURRENCY: dobra (STD)
ORGANIZATIONS: OAU, UN

This tiny state, independent from Portugal since 1975, comprises two large and several small islands near the equator, 200 km (125 miles) off west Africa. The climate is tropical with temperatures averaging 25°C (77°F) and rainfall of between 1,000–5,000 mm (40–197 inches). Cocoa (which provides 90 per cent of revenue), coconuts and palm oil are the main crops grown on the rich volcanic soil. Other foods and consumer goods are imported.

SAUDI ARABIA

STATUS: Kingdom
AREA: 2,400,900 sq km (926,745 sq miles)
POPULATION: 16,900,000
ANNUAL NATURAL INCREASE: 3.5%
CAPITAL: Riyadh (Ar Riyāḍ)
LANGUAGE: Arabic
RELIGION: 90% Sunni Muslim,
5% Roman Catholic
CURRENCY: Saudi riyal (SAR)
ORGANIZATIONS: Arab League, OPEC, UN

Saudi Arabia occupies the heart of the vast arid Arabian Peninsula. The country is mostly desert and there are no rivers which flow all year round. To the west, the Hejaz and Asir mountains fringe the Red Sea but even here rainfall rarely exceeds 380 mm (15 inches). Temperatures rise beyond 44°C (111°F) in the summer. The interior plateau slopes gently eastwards down to the Gulf and supports little vegetation. The southeast of the country is well named as the 'Empty Quarter'; it is almost devoid of population. Only in the coastal strips and oases are cereals and date palms grown. Oil is the most important resource – Saudi Arabia has a quarter of the world's known oil reserves – and export commodity and economic development is dependent on its revenue.

SENEGAL

STATUS: Republic
AREA: 196,720 sq km (75,935 sq miles)
POPULATION: 7,970,000
ANNUAL NATURAL INCREASE: 3.0%
CAPITAL: Dakar
LANGUAGE: French, native languages
RELIGION: 94% Sunni Muslim,
animist minority
CURRENCY: CFA franc (W Africa) (XOF)
ORGANIZATIONS: ECOWAS, OAU, UN

Senegal is a flat, dry country cut through by the Gambia, Casamance and Senegal rivers. Rainfall rarely exceeds 580 mm (23 inches) on the wetter coast. The interior savannah supports varied wildlife but little agriculture. Cultivation is mainly confined to the south where groundnuts account for nearly half of the agricultural output. Cotton and millet are also grown, but frequent droughts have reduced their value as cash crops. Phosphate mining, ship-repairing, textiles, petroleum products and food processing are the major industries. Both tourism and fishing are becoming increasingly important.

SEYCHELLES

STATUS: Republic
AREA: 404 sq km (156 sq miles)
POPULATION: 72,000
ANNUAL NATURAL INCREASE: 0.8%
CAPITAL: Victoria
LANGUAGE: English, French, Creole
RELIGION: 92% Roman Catholic
CURRENCY: Seychelles rupee (SCR)
ORGANIZATIONS: Comm., OAU, UN

This archipelago in the Indian Ocean comprises over 100 granite or coral islands. Main exports are copra, coconuts and cinnamon and in recent years tea and tuna. All domestic requirements, including most foodstuffs, have to be imported. Tourism has developed rapidly in the 1990s and is now the dominant sector in the economy.

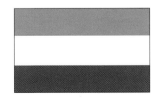

SIERRA LEONE

STATUS: Republic
AREA: 72,325 sq km
(27,920 sq miles)
POPULATION: 4,376,000
ANNUAL NATURAL INCREASE: 2.4%
CAPITAL: Freetown
LANGUAGE: English, Krio Temne, Mende
RELIGION: 52% animist, 39% Muslim and
8% Christian

CURRENCY: leone (SLL)
ORGANIZATIONS: Comm., ECOWAS, OAS, UN

Sierra Leone, a former British colony, has a coast dominated by swamps but is essentially a flat plain some 70 miles wide which extends to interior plateaux and mountains. Three-quarters of the population are employed in subsistence farming. Cash crops include cocoa and coffee but the main source of revenue is from minerals. Diamonds, gold, bauxite and iron ore are mined but the most important export is now rutile (titanium ore). Manufacturing in the form of processing local products has developed around Freetown.

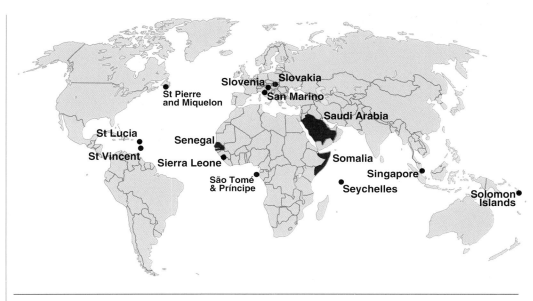

SINGAPORE

STATUS: Republic
AREA: 616 sq km (238 sq miles)
POPULATION: 2,874,000
ANNUAL NATURAL INCREASE: 1.2%
CAPITAL: Singapore
LANGUAGE: Malay, Chinese (Mandarin),
Tamil, English
RELIGION: Daoist, Buddist, Muslim, Christian
and Hindu
CURRENCY: Singapore dollar (SGD)
ORGANIZATIONS: ASEAN, Col. Plan,
Comm., UN

The republic of Singapore, independent from Britain since 1959, has been transformed from an island of mangrove swamps into one of the world's major entrepreneurial centres. The island, connected to Peninsular Malaysia by a man-made causeway, has a tropical, humid climate with 2,240 mm (96 inches) of rain per year. With few natural resources, Singapore depends on manufacturing precision goods, electronic products, financial services and activities associated with its port, which is one of the world's largest.

SLOVAKIA

STATUS: Republic
AREA: 49,035 sq km (18,932 sq miles)
POPULATION: 5,320,000
ANNUAL NATURAL INCREASE: 0.4%
CAPITAL: Bratislava
LANGUAGE: Slovak, Hungarian
RELIGION: Roman Catholic
CURRENCY: Slovak crown or koruna
ORGANIZATIONS: Council of Europe, UN

On 1 January 1993 Czechoslovakia ceased to exist and Slovakia and the Czech Republic came into being. Slovakia's geomorphology is dominated by the Tatry mountains in the north. Bratislava, the capital, lies in the extreme south-west, on the north bank of the Danube. Natural resources include iron ore, copper, antimony, mercury, magnesite and oil. Under Communism large manufacturing complexes developed,

many of which specialized in arms and tanks. The end of the Cold War in 1989 brought a collapse in demand for these products. This, and a decline in trade with the Czech Republic, has forced Slovakia to restructure existing industry and look to new developments such as aluminium smelting and car assembly.

SLOVENIA

STATUS: Republic
AREA: 20,250 sq km
(7,815 sq miles)
POPULATION: 1,990,000
ANNUAL NATURAL INCREASE: 0.7%
CAPITAL: Ljubljana
LANGUAGE: Slovene
RELIGION: Roman Catholic
CURRENCY: Slovenian tolar (SLT)
ORGANIZATIONS: Council of Europe, UN

The northernmost republic of the former Yugoslav federation, Slovenia, has always been one of the key gateways from the Balkans to central and western Europe. Much of the country is mountainous, its heartland and main centre of population being the Ljubljana basin. The climate generally shows continental tendencies, with warm summers and cold winters, when snow is plentiful on the ground. The small coastal region has a Mediterranean regime. Extensive mountain pastures provide profitable dairy-farming, but the amount of cultivable land is restricted. There are large mercury mines in the northwest and, in recent decades, this area has also developed a broad range of light industries. Combined with tourism, this has given the country a well-balanced economy. After a brief military conflict Slovenia won its independence in 1991.

SOLOMON ISLANDS

STATUS: Commonwealth Nation
AREA: 29,790 sq km (11,500 sq miles)

POPULATION: 349,500
ANNUAL NATURAL INCREASE: 2.9%
CAPITAL: Honiara
LANGUAGE: English, Pidgin English,
native languages
RELIGION: 95% Christian
CURRENCY: Solomon Islands dollar (SBD)
ORGANIZATIONS: Comm., UN

Situated in the South Pacific Ocean the Solomon Islands consist of a 1400 km (870 miles) archipelago of six main and many smaller islands. The mountainous large islands are covered by tropical rain forest reflecting the high temperatures, on average 22–34°C (72–95°F) and heavy rainfall, about 3,050 mm (120 inches). The main crops are coconuts, cocoa and rice, with copra, timber and palm oil being the main exports. Mineral deposits include reserves of bauxite, gold and phosphate, mined on the small island of Bellona south of Guadalcanal. Once a British protectorate, the Solomons became independent in 1978.

SOMALIA

STATUS: Republic
AREA: 6300,000sq km (243,180 sq miles)
POPULATION: 7,497,000
ANNUAL NATURAL INCREASE: 3.0%
CAPITAL: Mogadishu (Muqdisho)
LANGUAGE: Somali, Arabic, English, Italian
RELIGION: Muslim, Roman Catholic minority
CURRENCY: Somali shilling (SOS)
ORGANIZATIONS: UN, Arab League, OAU

Independent since 1960, Somalia is a hot and arid country in northeast Africa. The semi-desert of the northern mountains contrasts with the plains of the south where the bush country is particularly rich in wildlife. Most of the population are nomadic, following herds of camels, sheep, goats and cattle. Little land is cultivated but cotton, maize, millet and sugar cane are grown. Bananas are a major export. Iron ore, gypsum and uranium deposits are as yet unexploited. Five years of inter-clan warfare and a lack of coherent government have led to the collapse of the economy.

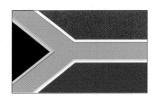

SOUTH AFRICA

STATUS: Republic
AREA: 1,220,845 sq km (471,369 sq miles)
POPULATION: 37,600,000
ANNUAL NATURAL INCREASE: 2.4%
CAPITAL: Pretoria (administrative)
Cape Town (legislative)
LANGUAGE: Afrikaans, English,
various African languages
RELIGION: mainly Christian, Hindu,
Jewish and Muslim minorities
CURRENCY: rand (ZAR)
ORGANIZATIONS: Comm., OAU, UN

The interior of South Africa consists of a plateau of over 900 m (2,955 feet) drained by the Orange and Limpopo rivers. Surrounding the plateau is a pronounced escarpment below which the land descends by steps to the sea. Rainfall in most areas is less than 500 mm (20 inches) and the land is increasingly drier towards the west. Agriculture is limited by poor soils but sheep and cattle are extensively grazed. Main crops are maize, wheat, sugar cane, vegetables, cotton and vines. Wine is an important export commodity. South Africa abounds in minerals. Diamonds, gold, platinum, silver, uranium, copper, manganese and asbestos are mined and nearly 80 per cent of the continent's coal reserves are in South Africa. Manufacturing and engineering is concentrated in the southern Transvaal area and around the ports. In 1994 the first ever multiracial elections were held resulting in Nelson Mandela coming to power. In a post-apartheid era, economic sanctions have been lifted, boosting exports, but the country faces adaptation, beginning with a rush of complicated land-ownership claims.

EASTERN CAPE

STATUS: Province
AREA: 174,405 sq km (67,338 sq miles)
POPULATION: 5,900,000
CAPITAL: East London

EASTERN TRANSVAAL

STATUS: Province
AREA: 73,377 sq km (28,311 sq miles)
POPULATION: 2,600,000
CAPITAL Nelspruit

KWAZULU-NATAL

STATUS: Province
AREA: 90,925 sq km (35,106 sq miles)
POPULATION: 8,000,000
CAPITAL: Durban

NORTHERN CAPE

STATUS: Province
AREA: 369,552 sq km (142,684 sq miles)
POPULATION: 700,000
CAPITAL: Kimberley

NORTHERN TRANSVAAL

STATUS: Province
AREA: 121,766 sq km (47,014 sq miles)
POPULATION: 4,700,000
CAPITAL: Pietersburg

NORTH WEST

STATUS: Province
AREA: 120,170 sq km (46,398 sq miles)
POPULATION: 3,300,000
CAPITAL: Klerksdorp

ORANGE FREE STATE

STATUS: Province
AREA: 123,893 sq km (47,835 sq miles)
POPULATION: 2,500,000
CAPITAL: Bloemfontein

PRETORIA-WITWATERSRAND-VEREENIGING (PWV)

STATUS: Province
AREA: 18,078 sq km (6,980 sq miles)
POPULATION: 6,500,000
CAPITAL: Johannesburg

WESTERN CAPE

STATUS: Province
AREA: 128,679 sq km
(49,683 sq miles)
POPULATION: 3,400,000
CAPITAL: Cape Town

SOUTHERN AND ANTARCTIC TERRITORIES

STATUS: Overseas Territory of France
AREA: 439,580 sq km (169,680 sq miles)
POPULATION: 180

SOUTH GEORGIA AND THE SOUTH SANDWICH ISLANDS

STATUS: UK Dependent Territory
AREA: 3,755 sq km (1,450 sq miles)
POPULATION: no permanent population

SPAIN

STATUS: Kingdom
AREA: 504,880 sq km (194,885 sq miles)
POPULATION: 39,166,000
ANNUAL NATURAL INCREASE: 0.5%
CAPITAL: Madrid
LANGUAGE: Spanish (Castilian), Catalan,
Basque, Galician
RELIGION: Roman Catholic
CURRENCY: Spanish peseta (ESP)
ORGANIZATIONS: Council of Europe, EEA, EU,
NATO, OECD, UN, WEU

Spain occupies most of the Iberian Peninsula, from the Bay of Biscay and the Pyrenees mountains in the north, to the Strait of Gibraltar in the south. It includes in its territory the Balearic Islands in the Mediterranean Sea, and the Canary Islands in the Atlantic. The mainland of Spain is mostly plateaus, often forested in the north, but becoming more arid and open further south. Climate is affected regionally by latitude and proximity to the Atlantic Ocean and Mediterranean Sea. Although the climate and terrain are not always favourable, agriculture is important to the Spanish economy. Wheat and other cereals such as maize, barley and rice are cultivated while grapes, citrus fruits and olives are important cash crops. Textile manufacturing in the northeast and steel, chemicals, consumer goods and vehicle manufacturing in the towns and cities have proved a magnet for great numbers of the rural population. The main minerals found are coal, iron ore, uranium and zinc. Tourism is of vital importance to the economy.

SRI LANKA

STATUS: Republic
AREA: 65,610 sq km (25,325 sq miles)
POPULATION: 17,405,000
ANNUAL NATURAL INCREASE: 1.5%
CAPITAL: Colombo
LANGUAGE: Sinhala, Tamil, English
RELIGION: 70% Buddhist, 15% Hindu, Roman
Catholic and Muslim minorities
CURRENCY: Sri Lanka rupee (LKR)
ORGANIZATIONS: Col. Plan, Comm., UN

The island of Sri Lanka is situated only 19 km (12 miles) from mainland India. The climate is tropical along the coastal plain and temperate in the central highlands. Annual rainfall averages only 1,000 mm (39 inches) in the north and east while the south and west receive over 2,000 mm (79 inches). The traditional economy of Sri Lanka is based on agriculture in which rubber, coffee, coconuts and particularly tea are dominant. The nation is also self-sufficient in rice. In recent years, however, manufacturing, especially of clothing and textiles, has become the main export earner. Gemstones and tourism are also important, but the tourist industry has suffered because of the activities of Tamil separatists.

SUDAN

STATUS: Republic
AREA: 2,505,815 sq km (967,245 sq miles)
POPULATION: 24,941,000
ANNUAL NATURAL INCREASE: 3.0%
CAPITAL: Khartoum
LANGUAGE: Arabic, tribal languages
RELIGION: 60% Sunni Muslim,
animist and Christian
CURRENCY: Sudanese pound (SDP)
ORGANIZATIONS: Arab League, OAU, UN

Sudan, in the upper Nile basin, is Africa's largest country. The land is mostly flat and infertile with a hot, arid climate. The White and Blue Niles are invaluable, serving not only to irrigate cultivated land but also as a potential source of hydro-electric power. Subsistence farming accounts for 80 per cent of Sudan's total production. Major exports include cotton, groundnuts, sugar cane and sesame seed. The principal activity is nomadic herding with over 40 million cattle and sheep and 14 million goats. However, economic activity has been damaged by the effects of drought and civil war.

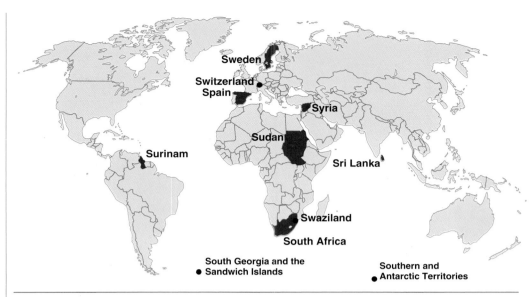

SURINAM

STATUS: Republic
AREA: 163,820 sq km (63,235 sq miles)
POPULATION: 438,000
ANNUAL NATURAL INCREASE: 2.5%
CAPITAL: Paramaribo
LANGUAGE: Dutch, English, Spanish,
Surinamese (Sranang Tongo), Hindi
RELIGION: 45% Christian, 28% Hindu,
20% Muslim
CURRENCY: Surinam guilder (SRG)
ORGANIZATIONS: OAS, UN

Independent from the Dutch since 1976, Surinam is a small state lying on the northeast coast in the tropics of South America. Physically, there are three main regions: a low-lying, marshy coastal strip; undulating savannah; densely forested highlands. Rice growing takes up 75 per cent of all cultivated land; sugar and pineapples are also grown, while cattle rearing for both meat and dairy products has been introduced. Bauxite accounts for 90 per cent of Surinam's foreign earnings. Timber resources offer great potential but as yet are largely untapped.

SWAZILAND

STATUS: Kingdom
AREA: 17,365 sq km (6,705 sq miles)
POPULATION: 823,000
ANNUAL NATURAL INCREASE: 3.4%
CAPITAL: Mbabane
LANGUAGE: English, Siswati
RELIGION: 60% Christian, 40% traditional beliefs
CURRENCY: lilangeni (SZL),
South African rand (ZAR)
ORGANIZATIONS: Comm., OAU, UN

Landlocked Swaziland in southern Africa, is a sub-tropical, savannah country. It is divided into four main regions: the High, Middle and Low Velds and the Lebombo Mountains. Rainfall is abundant, promoting good pastureland for the many cattle and sheep. Major exports include sugar, meat, citrus fruits, textiles, wood products and asbestos.

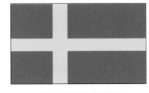

SWEDEN

STATUS: Kingdom
AREA: 449,790 sq km (173,620 sq miles)
POPULATION: 8,721,000
ANNUAL NATURAL INCREASE: 0.2%

CAPITAL: Stockholm
LANGUAGE: Swedish, Finnish, Lappish
RELIGION: 95% Evangelical Lutheran
CURRENCY: Swedish krona (SED)
ORGANIZATIONS: Council of Europe, EEA, EFTA,
OECD, UN

Glacial debris, glacier-eroded valleys and thick glacial clay are all dominant features of Sweden. Physically, Sweden comprises four main regions: Norrland, the northern forested mountains; the Lake District of the centre south; the southern uplands of Jönköping; the extremely fertile Scania plain of the far south. Summers are short and hot with long, cold winters. Temperatures vary with latitude; in the south from -3–18°C (27–64°F) and in the north from -14–14°C (7–57°F). Annual rainfall varies between 2,000 mm (79 inches) in the southwest, to 500 mm (20 inches) in the east. Over half the land area is forested resulting in a thriving timber industry, but manufacturing industry, particularly cars and trucks, metal products and machine tools, is well established. Mineral resources are also rich and plentiful – iron ore production alone exceeds 17 million tons a year. There are also deposits of copper, lead and zinc.

SWITZERLAND

STATUS: Federation
AREA: 41,285 sq km (15,935 sq miles)
POPULATION: 6,908,000
ANNUAL NATURAL INCREASE: 0.3%
CAPITAL: Bern (Berne)
LANGUAGE: German, French, Italian, Romansch
RELIGION: 48% Roman Catholic,
44% Protestant, Jewish minority
CURRENCY: Swiss franc (CHF)
ORGANIZATIONS: Council of Europe, EFTA,
OECD

Switzerland is a landlocked, mountainous country of great scenic beauty, situated in western Europe. The Alps traverse the southern half of the country, in which are to be found some of Europe's highest peaks. In the north the Jura mountains form a natural border with France.

Winters are cold with heavy snowfall in the highest regions. Summers are mild with an average July temperature of 18–19°C (64–66°F). Most rain falls in the summer months. Agriculture is based mainly on dairy farming. Major crops include hay, wheat, barley and potatoes. Industry plays a major role in Switzerland's economy, centred on metal engineering, watchmaking, food processing, textiles and chemicals. The high standard of living enjoyed by the Swiss owes much to the tourist industry. The financial services sector, especially banking, is also of great importance. Switzerland's history of neutrality has made it an attractive location for the headquarters of several international organizations.

SYRIA

STATUS: Republic
AREA: 185,680 sq km (71,675 sq miles)
POPULATION: 13,400,000
ANNUAL NATURAL INCREASE: 3.6%
CAPITAL: Damascus, (Dimashq, Esh Sham)
LANGUAGE: Arabic
RELIGION: 65% Sunni Muslim, Shi'a Muslim
and Christian minorities
CURRENCY: Syrian pound (SYP)
ORGANIZATIONS: Arab League, UN

Syria is situated in the heart of the Middle East. Its most fertile areas lie along the coastal strip on the Mediterranean Sea which supports the bulk of its population, and in the depressions and plateaux of the northeast which are cut through by the rivers Orontes and Euphrates. In the south the Anti-Lebanon mountains (Jebel esh Sharqi) is bordered to the east by the Syrian desert. While the coast has a Mediterranean climate with dry hot summers and mild winters, the interior becomes increasingly hot and arid – average summer temperatures in the desert reach 43°C (109°F). Rainfall varies between 220–400 mm (9–16 inches). Cotton is Syria's main export crop, and wheat and barley are also grown. Cattle, sheep and goats are the main livestock. Although traditionally an agriculturally-based economy, the country is rapidly becoming industrialized as oil, natural gas, salt, gypsum and phosphate are being exploited.

TAHITI

STATUS: Main Island of French Polynesia
AREA: 1,042 sq km (402 sq miles)
POPULATION: 199,031

TAIWAN

STATUS: Island 'Republic of China'
AREA: 35,990 sq km
(13,890 sq miles)
POPULATION: 20,600,000
ANNUAL NATURAL INCREASE: 1.5%
CAPITAL: Taipei (T'ai-pei)
LANGUAGE: Mandarin Chinese, Taiwanese
RELIGION: Buddhist majority, Muslim,
Daoist and Christian minorities
CURRENCY: New Taiwan dollar (TWD), yuan (CNY)
ORGANIZATIONS: none listed

Taiwan is separated from mainland China by the Taiwan Strait (the former Formosa Channel) in which lie the Pescadores. Two-thirds of Taiwan is mountainous, the highest point is 3,950 m (12,959 feet). The flat to rolling coastal plain in the western part of the island accommodates the bulk of the population and the national commerce, industry and agriculture. The climate is tropical marine, with persistent cloudy conditions. The monsoon rains fall in June to August, with an annual average of 2,600 mm (102 inches). Main crops are rice, tea, fruit, sugar cane and sweet potatoes. Industry has been founded on textiles but in recent years electronic products have gained in importance. The Taiwanese economy is inevitably influenced by its large neighbour and is likely to benefit from improving Chinese performance.

TAJIKISTAN

STATUS: Republic
AREA: 143,100 sq km (55,235 sq miles)
POPULATION: 5,465,000
ANNUAL NATURAL INCREASE: 3.0%
CAPITAL: Dushanbe
LANGUAGE: Tajik, Uzbek, Russian
RELIGION: Sunni Muslim
CURRENCY: Russian rouble
ORGANIZATIONS: CIS, UN

Situated in the mountainous heart of Asia, more than half the territory of Tajikistan lies above 3,000 m (10,000 feet). The major settlement areas lie within the Fergana valley in the west. The climate varies from continental to subtropical according to elevation and shelter. Extensive irrigation, without which agriculture would be severely limited, has made it possible for cotton growing to develop into the leading branch of agriculture, and on that basis textiles have become the largest industry in the country. Tajikistan is rich in mineral and fuel deposits, the exploitation of which became a feature of

economic development during the Soviet era. Preceding full independence in 1991 there was an upsurge of sometimes violent Tajik nationalism as a result of which many Russians and Uzbeks have left the country.

TANZANIA

STATUS: Republic
AREA: 939,760 sq km (362,750 sq miles)
POPULATION: 27,829,000
ANNUAL NATURAL INCREASE: 3.5%
CAPITAL: Dodoma
LANGUAGE: Swahili, English
RELIGION: 40% Christian, 35% Muslim
CURRENCY: Tanzanian shilling
ORGANIZATIONS: Comm., OAU, UN

Much of this east African country consists of high interior plateaux covered by scrub and grassland, bordered to the north by the volcanic Kilimanjaro region and Lake Victoria, to the west by Lake Tanganyika, by highlands to the south and by the Indian Ocean in the east. Despite its proximity to the equator, the altitude of much of Tanzania means that temperatures are reduced, and only on the narrow coastal plain is the climate truly tropical. Average temperatures vary between 19–28°C (67–82°F), and annual rainfall is around 570–1,060 mm (23–43 inches). The economy is heavily based on agriculture and subsistence farming is the main way of life for most of the population, although coffee, cotton, sisal, cashew nuts and tea are exported. Industry is limited, but gradually growing in importance, and involves textiles, food processing and tobacco. Tourism could be a future growth area.

THAILAND

STATUS: Kingdom
AREA: 514,000 sq km (198,405 sq miles)
POPULATION: 57,800,000
ANNUAL NATURAL INCREASE: 1.9%
CAPITAL: Bangkok (Krung Thep)
LANGUAGE: Thai
RELIGION: Buddhist, 4% Muslim
CURRENCY: baht (THB)
ORGANIZATIONS: ASEAN, Col. Plan, UN

Thailand is a land of flat undulating plains and mountains, consisting of the plains of the Chao Phraya and Mae Nam Mun river systems, fringed by mountains, a plateau in the northeast drained by the tributaries of the Mekong river, and the northern half of the Malay peninsula. From May to October, monsoon rains are heavy with an annual average rainfall of 1,500 mm (59 inches). The climate is tropical with temperatures reaching 36°C (97°F) and much of the country is forested. The central plain is well-served with irrigation canals which supply the paddy fields

for rice cultivation; Thailand is the world's leading exporter of this crop. Maize, cassava, sugar and rubber also contribute to the economy. Tin production has declined in importance in recent years and has, in part, been replaced by a small scale petro-chemical industry. Other industries of importance include textiles and clothing. Tourism, which grew at a record rate during the 1980s, has since levelled out after the military coup of 1991.

TOGO

STATUS: Kingdom
AREA: 699 sq km (270 sq miles)
POPULATION: 130,000
ANNUAL NATURAL INCREASE: 3.5%
CAPITAL: Lomé
LANGUAGE: French, Kabre, Ewe
RELIGION: Christian
CURRENCY: pa'anga (TOP)
ORGANIZATIONS: Comm.

Togo, formerly a German protectorate and French colony, is situated between Ghana and Benin in west Africa. A long narrow country, it has only 65 km (40 miles) of coast. The interior consists of mountains and high infertile tableland. The climate is tropical with an average temperature of 27°C (81°F). Most of Togo's farmers grow maize, cassava, yams, groundnuts and plantains, and the country is virtually self-sufficient in food stuffs. Phosphates account for half of export revenue. Cotton, cocoa and coffee are also exported.

TOKELAU ISLANDS

STATUS: Overseas Territory of New Zealand
AREA: 10 sq km (4 sq miles)
POPULATION: 1,577
CAPITAL: none, each island has its own administration centre

TONGA

STATUS: Kingdom
AREA: 699 sq km (270 sq miles)
POPULATION: 103,000
ANNUAL NATURAL INCREASE: 0.4%
CAPITAL: Nuku'alofa
LANGUAGE: Tongan, English
RELIGION: Christian
CURRENCY: pa'anga (TOP)
ORGANIZATIONS: Comm.

Tonga consists of an archipelago of 169 islands in the Pacific 180 km (112 miles) north of New Zealand. There are seven groups of islands, but the most important are Tongatapu, Ha'apai and Vava'u. All the islands are covered with dense tropical vegetation, and temperatures range from 11–29°C (52–84°F). Main exports are coconut products and bananas.

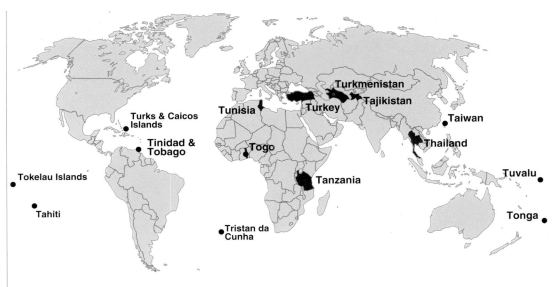

TRINIDAD & TOBAGO

STATUS: Republic
AREA: 5,130 sq km (1,980 sq miles)
POPULATION: 1,265,000
ANNUAL NATURAL INCREASE: 1.7%
CAPITAL: Port of Spain
LANGUAGE: English, Hindi, French, Spanish
RELIGION: 60% Christian, 25% Hindu,
6% Muslim
CURRENCY: Trinidad and Tobago dollar (TTD)
ORGANIZATIONS: Caricom, Comm., OAS, UN

Trinidad and Tobago, the southernmost Caribbean islands of the Lesser Antilles lie only 11 and 30 km (7 and 19 miles) respectively from the Venezuelan coast. Both islands are mountainous, the Northern Range of Trinidad reaching 940 m (3,084 feet) with its highest parts retaining tropical forest cover. The country has a humid, tropical climate with temperatures averaging 25°C (76°F) per annum. Rain falls mostly between June and December and varies between 1,300–3,000 mm (51–118 inches) annually. Sugar was once the mainstay of the economy but oil is now the leading source of revenue accounting for over 70 per cent of export revenue. There is also a petro-chemical industry based on significant gas reserves.

TRISTAN DA CUNHA

STATUS: Dependency of St Helena
AREA: 98 sq km (38 sq miles)
POPULATION: 295

TUNISIA

STATUS: Republic
AREA: 164,150 sq km (63,360 sq miles)
POPULATION: 8,401,000
ANNUAL NATURAL INCREASE: 2.0%
CAPITAL: Tunis
LANGUAGE: Arabic, French
RELIGION: Muslim
CURRENCY: Tunisian dinar (TND)
ORGANIZATIONS: Arab League, OAU, UN

Tunisia, on the southern shores of the Mediterranean is largely an arid, desert country of northern Africa. The eastern limits of the Atlas mountain range extend into northern parts of the country, which are separated from the Sahara desert to the south by a lowland belt of salt pans, called the Chott El Jerid. Average annual temperatures are in the range 10–27°C (50–81°F) and rainfall averages 380–500 mm (15–20 inches) in the north, but drops to virtually nothing in the south. The majority of the population live along the northeast coast. Wheat, barley, olives and citrus fruit are the main crops and oil, natural gas and sugar refining are the main industries. The tourist industry is expanding and is becoming increasingly important to the economy.

TURKEY

STATUS: Republic
AREA: 779,450 sq km (300,870 sq miles)
POPULATION: 59,869,000
ANNUAL NATURAL INCREASE: 2.2%
CAPITAL: Ankara
LANGUAGE: Turkish, Kurdish
RELIGION: 98% Sunni Muslim, Christian minority
CURRENCY: Turkish lira (TRL)
ORGANIZATIONS: Council of Europe, NATO,
OECD, UN

Turkey has always occupied a strategically important position linking Europe and Asia. It is a rugged, mountainous country particularly in the east. The central Anatolian plateau is bordered in the north by the Pontine mountains (Anadolu Dağlari) and in the south by the Taurus mountains (Toros Dağlari) which converge in the east, crowned by Mt Ararat (Büyük Ağri). Thrace, in European Turkey is flatter with rolling hills. Coastal regions exhibit Mediterranean conditions with short mild winters with some rainfall and long hot, dry summers. The interior is relatively arid with average rainfall in some places less than 250 mm (10 inches). The main crops are wheat and barley, but tobacco, olives, sugar beet, tea and fruit are also grown, and sheep, goats and cattle are raised. Turkey is becoming increasingly industrialized; textiles account for a third of exports and the car industry is developing. The nation now leads the Middle East in the production of iron, steel, chrome, coal and lignite. Tourism is a rapidly growing industry.

TURKMENISTAN

STATUS: Republic
AREA: 488,100 sq km (188,405 sq miles)
POPULATION: 3,714,000
ANNUAL NATURAL INCREASE: 2.5%

CAPITAL: Ashkhabad
LANGUAGE: Turkmen, Russian, Uzbek
RELIGION: Muslim
CURRENCY: manat
ORGANIZATIONS: CIS, UN

Situated in the far south of the former Soviet Union, Turkmenistan is a desert land except for the lowlands in the west along the Caspian shore, the mountains along its southern borders and the valley of Amudar'ya river in the north. The continental climate is responsible for great fluctuations in temperature, both during the day and throughout the year. Traditionally nomads, the Turkmen tribes under the Soviet regime, turned from pastoral farming to cotton-growing, made possible by extensive irrigation. Turkmenistan enjoys substantial natural resources, principally oil and gas but also potassium, sulphur and salt.

TURKS & CAICOS ISLANDS

STATUS: UK Dependent Territory
AREA: 430 sq km (166 sq miles)
POPULATION: 11,696
CAPITAL: Cockburn Town

TUVALU

STATUS: Special membership of the Commonwealth
AREA: 24.6 sq km (9.5 sq miles)
POPULATION: 10,090
ANNUAL NATURAL INCREASE: 1.5%
CAPITAL: Funafuti
LANGUAGE: Tuvaluan, English
RELIGION: 98% Protestant
CURRENCY: Australian dollar (AUD),
Tuvaluan coinage
ORGANIZATIONS: Comm., (special member)

Tuvalu consists of nine dispersed coral atolls, north of Fiji, in the Pacific Ocean. The climate is tropical; hot, with heavy annual rainfall exceeding 3,000 mm (118 inches). Fish is the staple food but coconuts and bread-fruit are cultivated. The sale of postage stamps abroad is, however, the largest source of revenue.

UGANDA

STATUS: Republic
AREA: 236,580 sq km
(91,320 sq miles)
POPULATION: 18,674,000
ANNUAL NATURAL INCREASE: 3.1%
CAPITAL: Kampala
LANGUAGE: English, tribal languages
RELIGION: 62% Christian, 6% Muslim
CURRENCY: Uganda shilling (UGS)
ORGANIZATIONS: Comm., OAU, UN

Uganda is bordered in the west by the great Rift Valley and the Ruwenzori mountain range which reaches 5,220 m (16,765 feet). In the east it is bordered by Kenya and Lake Victoria, from which the Nile flows northwards. Most of the country is high plateau with savannah vegetation although the lands around Lake Victoria have been cleared for cultivation and have become the most populated and developed areas. The climate is warm (21–24°C or 70–75°F), and rainfall ranges from 750–1,500 mm (30–59 inches) per annum. The Ugandan economy is firmly based on agriculture with a heavy dependence on coffee, the dominant export crop, and cotton. Fishing, from the waters of Lake Victoria is also important for local consumption.

UKRAINE

STATUS: Republic
AREA: 603,700 sq km (233,030 sq miles)
POPULATION: 52,194,000
ANNUAL NATURAL INCREASE: 0.3%
CAPITAL: Kiev (Kiyev)
LANGUAGE: Ukrainian, Russian
RELIGION: Russian Orthodox,
Roman Catholic (Uniate)
CURRENCY: karbovanets (coupon)
ORGANIZATIONS: CIS, UN

Ukraine consists mainly of level plains and mountainous border areas. The landscape is, however, diverse, with marshes, forests, wooded and treeless steppe. Deposits of 'black earth', among the most fertile soils, cover about 65 per cent of Ukraine. Grain, potatoes, vegetables and fruits, industrial crops (notably sugar beets and sunflower seeds) and fodder crops are grown. Food processing is important to the economy, and southern regions are renowned for wines. Ukraine is rich in mineral resources, such as iron ore, coal and lignite, and has large reserves of petroleum and gas. Extensive mining, metal production, machine-building, engineering and chemicals dominate Ukrainian industry, most of it located in the Donetsk basin and the Dnieper lowland. These two regions account for four-fifths of the urban population. Despite its natural wealth and industrial development, Ukraine has failed to respond to the economic needs of its independent status and has experienced sharp declines in agricultural and industrial output.

UNITED ARAB EMIRATES (UAE)

STATUS: Federation of seven Emirates
AREA: 75,150 sq km (29,010 sq miles)
POPULATION: 2,083,000
ANNUAL NATURAL INCREASE: 3.1%
CAPITAL: Abu Dhabi (Abū Ẓabī)
LANGUAGE: Arabic, English
RELIGION: Sunni Muslim
CURRENCY: UAE dirham (AED)
ORGANIZATIONS: Arab League, OPEC, UN

The United Arab Emirates (UAE), comprising seven separate emirates, are stretched along the southeastern coast of the Gulf. It is a country covered mostly by flat deserts with the highest land in the Hajar mountains of the Musandam Peninsula. Summer temperatures reach 40°C (104°F); meagre rains of 130 mm (5 inches) fall mainly in the winter. Only the desert oases are fertile, producing fruit and vegetables. The economic wealth of the UAE is founded on its huge reserves of hydrocarbons, mainly within the largest Emirate, Abu Dhabi, with smaller supplies in three others – Dubai, Sharjah and Ras al Khaimah. Natural gas and oil are the major exports for which Japan and the Far East are the major markets. Revenue gained from these has allowed the economy to grow rapidly, with there being huge investment in the service industries. It has a population that is overwhelmingly made up of foreign immigrants.

ABU DHABI

STATUS: Emirate
AREA: 64,750 sq km (24,995 sq miles)
POPULATION: 670,175

AJMAN

STATUS: Emirate
AREA: 260 sq km (100 sq miles)
POPULATION: 64,318

DUBAI

STATUS: Emirate
AREA: 3,900 sq km (1,505 sq miles)
POPULATION: 419,104

FUJAIRAH

STATUS: Emirate
AREA: 1,170 sq km (452 sq miles)
POPULATION: 54,425

RAS AL KHAIMAH

STATUS: Emirate
AREA: 1,690 sq km (625 sq miles)
POPULATION: 116,470

SHARJAH

STATUS: Emirate
AREA: 2,600 sq km (1,005 sq miles)
POPULATION: 268,722

UMM AL QAIWAIN

STATUS: Emirate
AREA: 780 sq km (300 sq miles)
POPULATION: 29,229

UNITED KINGDOM OF GREAT BRITAIN & NORTHERN IRELAND (UK)

STATUS: Kingdom
AREA: 244,755 sq km
(94,475 sq miles)
POPULATION: 57,998,400
ANNUAL NATURAL INCREASE: 0.3%
CAPITAL: London
LANGUAGE: English, Welsh, Gaelic
RELIGION: Protestant majority, Roman Catholic,
Jewish, Muslim, Hindu minorities
CURRENCY: pound sterling (GBP)
ORGANIZATIONS: Col. Plan, Comm.,
Council of Europe, EEA, EU, G7, NATO,
OECD, UN, WEU

The United Kingdom, part of the British Isles, is situated off the northwest European coast, separated from France by the English Channel. It includes the countries of England and Scotland, the principality of Wales, and the region of Northern Ireland in the north of the island of Ireland.

In broad terms Britain can be divided into the upland regions of Wales, Northern England and Scotland, characterized by ancient dissected and glaciated mountain regions, and the lowland areas of southern and eastern England where low ranges of chalk, limestone and sandstone hills are interspersed with wide clay vales. The highest point in the United Kingdom is Ben Nevis in the Grampians of Scotland at 1,344 m (4,409 feet).

The climate of the British Isles is mild, wet and variable. Summer temperatures average 13–17°C (55–63°F) and winter temperatures 5–7°C (41–45°F). Annual rainfall varies between 640–5,000 mm (26–200 inches) with the highest rainfall in the Lake District and the lowest in East Anglia.

Although only a tiny percentage of the nation's workforce is employed in agriculture, farm produce is important to both home and export markets. Seventy-six per cent of the total UK land area is farmland. The main cereal crops are wheat, barley and oats. Potatoes, sugar beet and green vegetable crops are widespread.

About 20 per cent of the land is permanent pasture for raising dairy and beef stock and 28 per cent, mainly hill and mountain areas, is used for rough grazing of sheep. The best fruit-growing areas are the southeast, especially Kent, East Anglia and the central Vale of Evesham. Fishing supplies two-thirds of the nation's requirements but overfishing and encroachment into territorial waters by other countries have created problems.

The major mineral resources of the UK are coal, oil and natural gas. Over two-thirds of deep-mined coal came from the Yorkshire and East Midlands fields and substantial reserves remain. However, the coal industry, which had already been in slow decline for some 30 years, collapsed rapidly in 1993–4 when many of the remaining pits were closed. The number of employees fell from 208,000 in 1983 to 18,000 in early 1994 and by mid-1994 only 16 deep coal mines remained in operation, compared with 50 pits two years earlier.

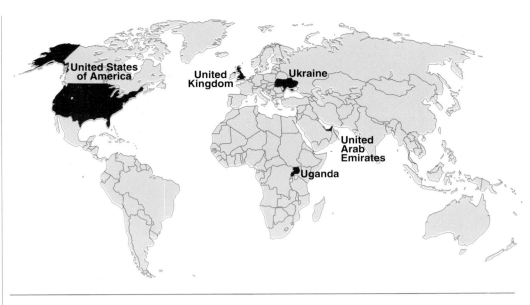

Before the 1970s Britain relied on imports from the Middle East for its oil supplies, but in 1975 supplies of oil and gas from the vast North Sea oil fields began to provide both self-sufficiency and enough to export. Some of the older fields are now nearly worked out and operating costs for these are rising. The major Scott Field came on-stream in 1993 and in 1994 approval was granted for the development of the Fife and Birch oil fields and the Armada gas fields.

Wind farms as a source of energy, often the subject of controversy with environmentalists, contribute less than 1 per cent of Britain's electricity.

Although the UK is an industrialized nation, the traditional mainstays of heavy industry such as coal, iron and steel and shipbuilding no longer figure prominently in the economy. Concurrent with the decline of heavy industry, there has been a substantial growth of light industries. High technology and electronic products predominate, as well as pharmaceuticals, motor parts and food processing. Tourism is an essential part of the economy, especially in London, and in five years up to 1993 the number of visitors to the UK rose by 22 per cent. Financial services is another expanding sector, the 'City' of London having the greatest concentration of banks in the world.

The UK is a trading nation. The balance of trade has changed during the last 30 years because of increasingly closer economic ties with Europe and the move towards a Single European Market. Consequently, trading with Commonwealth nations, particularly Australia, has assumed lower priority. In terms of value, the most important exports from the UK are machinery, chemicals and transport equipment, followed by food, beverages and tobacco, petroleum products, iron and steel.

The transport network in the UK is highly developed. Out of 362,357 km (225,164 miles) of public roads, 9 per cent are motorways and 13 per cent are other major roads. The railway network covers over 16,730 km (10,395 miles) and carries over 150 million tonnes of freight annually. The opening of the Channel Tunnel in 1994 has connected the motorway and rail networks of Britain with those of northern France and southern Belgium. The inland waterway system totals only 563 navigable kilometres (350 miles) but has potential to carry more than its present 4 million tonnes of goods annually.

ENGLAND
STATUS: Constituent Country
AREA: 130,360 sq km (50,320 sq miles)
POPULATION: 48,208,100
CAPITAL: London

NORTHERN IRELAND
STATUS: Constituent Region
AREA: 14,150 sq km (5,460 sq miles)
POPULATION: 1,573,282
CAPITAL: Belfast

SCOTLAND
STATUS: Constituent Country
AREA: 78,750 sq km (30,400 sq miles)
POPULATION: 4,998,567
CAPITAL: Edinburgh

WALES
STATUS: Principality
AREA: 20,760 sq km (8,015 sq miles)
POPULATION: 2,891,500
CAPITAL: Cardiff

UNITED STATES OF AMERICA (USA)
STATUS: Federal Republic
AREA: 9,363,130 sq km (3,614,170 sq miles)
POPULATION: 255,020,000
ANNUAL NATURAL INCREASE: 0.9%
CAPITAL: Washington D.C.
LANGUAGE: English, Spanish
RELIGION: Christian majority, Jewish minority
CURRENCY: US dollar (USD)
ORGANIZATIONS: ANZUS, Col. Plan, G7, NAFTA, NATO, OAS, OECD, UN

The United States of America is the world's fourth largest country after Canada, China and Russia with the world's fourth largest population. The 19th and 20th centuries have brought 42 million immigrants to its shores, and the population of the USA now has the highest living standard of any country in the world. The large land area covers a huge spectrum of different landscapes, environments and climates. The eastern coast of New England, where the European settlers first landed, is rocky, mountainous and richly wooded. South of New England is the Atlantic coastal plain, rising to the west towards the Appalachian mountain system. Beyond the Appalachians lie the central lowlands, a large undulating plain cut through by the Mississippi and Ohio rivers. Further west lie the Great Plains crossed by the Missouri, Red and Arkansas rivers and rising gently towards the mighty Rocky Mountains, a spine of mountains running south from Alaska. Beyond these lie the Great Valley of California, the coastal ranges and the Pacific coast.

Climatic variety within the United States is enormous, ranging from the Arctic conditions of Alaska to the desert of the southwest – winter temperatures in Alaska plummet to -28°C (-19°F); in Florida they maintain a steady 19°C (66°F). The centre of the continent is dry, but both the northwest Pacific and the New England Atlantic coast are humid with heavy rainfall. Many areas of the USA fall prey to exceptional, often disastrous, weather conditions: the northeastern seaboard is susceptible to heavy blizzards, the southern lowlands are vulnerable to spring thaw flooding and the Mississippi valley is prone to tornadoes.

The natural vegetation of the USA reflects its climatic diversity. The northwest coast is rich in coniferous forest, while the Appalachian mountain region is well endowed with hardwoods. In the arid southwest, vegetation is limited to desert scrub whereas the Gulf and South Atlantic coast are fringed with swampy wetlands. The central lowlands are endowed with rich black-earth soils (the agricultural heartland), gradually supplanted, towards the Rockies, by tall-grass prairie. The northeastern states of Illinois, Iowa, Indiana and Nebraska form the 'corn belt', which produces 45 per cent of the world's corn. Further west wheat supplements corn as the main crop. The northeastern states are predominantly dairy country, and the south is famous for cotton and tobacco. Rice is grown in Texas, California and Louisiana, and fruit and vegetables in Florida.

The USA consumes 25 per cent of all the world's energy resources but is well endowed with energy reserves. There are substantial coal resources, particularly in the Appalachians. The great rivers have been harnessed extensively for hydro-electric power. Oil and natural gas fields are found in Texas, Alaska, Louisiana and California and new deep-sea exploratory drilling is underway in the Gulf of Mexico. Oil production, however, has declined steadily since 1983.

The industrial base is diverse, the main industries being steel, motor vehicles, aerospace, chemicals, computers, electronics, telecommunications and consumer goods. The service industries (encompassing tourism and finance) are by far the biggest source of employment in the United States.

ALABAMA
STATUS: State
AREA: 131,485 sq km (50,755 sq miles)
POPULATION: 4,136,000
CAPITAL: Montgomery

ALASKA
STATUS: State
AREA: 1,478,450 sq km (570,680 sq miles)
POPULATION: 587,000
CAPITAL: Juneau

ARIZONA
STATUS: State
AREA: 293,985 sq km (113,480 sq miles)
POPULATION: 3,832,000
CAPITAL: Phoenix

ARKANSAS
STATUS: State
AREA: 134,880 sq km (52,065 sq miles)
POPULATION: 2,399,000
CAPITAL: Little Rock

CALIFORNIA
STATUS: State
AREA: 404,815 sq km (156,260 sq miles)
POPULATION: 30,867,000
CAPITAL: Sacramento

COLORADO
STATUS: State
AREA: 268,310 sq km (103,570 sq miles)
POPULATION: 3,470,000
CAPITAL: Denver

CONNECTICUT
STATUS: State
AREA: 12,620 sq km (4,870 sq miles)
POPULATION: 3,281,000
CAPITAL: Hartford

DELAWARE
STATUS: State
AREA: 5,005 sq km (1,930 sq miles)
POPULATION: 689,000
CAPITAL: Dover

DISTRICT OF COLUMBIA
STATUS: Federal District
AREA: 163 sq km (63 sq miles)
POPULATION: 589,000
CAPITAL: Washington D.C.

FLORIDA
STATUS: State
AREA: 140,255 sq km (54,1405 sq miles)
POPULATION: 13,488,000
CAPITAL: Tallahassee

GEORGIA
STATUS: State
AREA: 150,365 sq km (58,040 sq miles)
POPULATION: 6,751,000
CAPITAL: Atlanta

HAWAII
STATUS: State
AREA: 16,640 sq km (6,425 sq miles)
POPULATION: 1,160,000
CAPITAL: Honolulu

IDAHO
STATUS: State
AREA: 213,445 sq km (82,390 sq miles)
POPULATION: 1,067,000
CAPITAL: Boise

ILLINOIS
STATUS: State
AREA: 144,120 sq km (55,630 sq miles)
POPULATION: 11,631,000
CAPITAL: Springfield

INDIANA
STATUS: State
AREA: 93,065 sq km (35,925 sq miles)
POPULATION: 5,662,000
CAPITAL: Indianapolis

IOWA
STATUS: State
AREA: 144,950 sq km (55,950 sq miles)
POPULATION: 2,812,000
CAPITAL: Des Moines

KANSAS
STATUS: State
AREA: 211,805 sq km (81,755 sq miles)
POPULATION: 2,523,000
CAPITAL: Topeka

KENTUCKY
STATUS: State
AREA: 102,740 sq km (39,660 sq miles)
POPULATION: 3,755,000
CAPITAL: Frankfort

LOUISIANA
STATUS: State
AREA: 115,310 sq km (44,510 sq miles)
POPULATION: 4,287,000
CAPITAL: Baton Rouge

MAINE
STATUS: State
AREA: 80,275 sq km (30,985 sq miles)
POPULATION: 1,235,000
CAPITAL: Augusta

MARYLAND
STATUS: State
AREA: 25,480 sq km (9,835 sq miles)
POPULATION: 4,908,000
CAPITAL: Annapolis

MASSACHUSETTS
STATUS: State
AREA: 20,265 sq km (7,820 sq miles)
POPULATION: 5,998,000
CAPITAL: Boston

MICHIGAN
STATUS: State
AREA: 147,510 sq km (56,940 sq miles)
POPULATION: 9,437,000
CAPITAL: Lansing

MINNESOTA
STATUS: State
AREA: 206,030 sq km (79,530 sq miles)
POPULATION: 4,480,000
CAPITAL: St Paul

MISSISSIPPI
STATUS: State
AREA: 122,335 sq km (47,220 sq miles)
POPULATION: 2,614,000
CAPITAL: Jackson

MISSOURI
STATUS: State
AREA: 178,565 sq km (68,925 sq miles)
POPULATION: 5,193,000
CAPITAL: Jefferson City

MONTANA
STATUS: State
AREA: 376,555 sq km (145,350 sq miles)
POPULATION: 824,000
CAPITAL: Helena

NEBRASKA
STATUS: State
AREA: 198,505 sq km (76,625 sq miles)
POPULATION: 1,606,000
CAPITAL: Lincoln

NEVADA
STATUS: State
AREA: 284,625 sq km (109,865 sq miles)
POPULATION: 1,327,000
CAPITAL: Carson City

NEW HAMPSHIRE
STATUS: State
AREA: 23,290 sq km (8,990 sq miles)
POPULATION: 1,111,000
CAPITAL: Concord

NEW JERSEY
STATUS: State
AREA: 19,340 sq km (7,465 sq miles)
POPULATION: 7,789,000
CAPITAL: Trenton

NEW MEXICO
STATUS: State
AREA: 314,255 sq km (121,300 sq miles)
POPULATION: 1,581,000
CAPITAL: Sante Fe

NEW YORK
STATUS: State
AREA: 122,705 sq km (47,365 sq miles)
POPULATION: 18,119,000
CAPITAL: Albany

NORTH CAROLINA
STATUS: State
AREA: 126,505 sq km (48,830 sq miles)
POPULATION: 6,843,000
CAPITAL: Raleigh

NORTH DAKOTA
STATUS: State
AREA: 179,485 sq km (69,280 sq miles)
POPULATION: 636,000
CAPITAL: Bismarck

OHIO
STATUS: State
AREA: 106,200 sq km (40,995 sq miles)
POPULATION: 11,016,000
CAPITAL: Columbus

OKLAHOMA
STATUS: State
AREA: 177,815 sq km (68,635 sq miles)
POPULATION: 3,212,00
CAPITAL: Oklahoma City

OREGON
STATUS: State
AREA: 249,115 sq km (96,160 sq miles)
POPULATION: 2,977,000
CAPITAL: Salem

PENNSYLVANIA
STATUS: State
AREA: 116,260 sq km (44,875 sq miles)
POPULATION: 12,009,000
CAPITAL: Harrisburg

RHODE ISLAND
STATUS: State
AREA: 2,730 sq km (1,055 sq miles)
POPULATION: 1,005,000
CAPITAL: Providence

SOUTH CAROLINA
STATUS: State
AREA: 78,225 sq km (30,195 sq miles)
POPULATION: 3,603,000
CAPITAL: Columbia

SOUTH DAKOTA
STATUS: State
AREA: 196,715 sq km (75,930 sq miles)
POPULATION: 711,000
CAPITAL: Pierre

TENNESSEE
STATUS: State
AREA: 106,590 sq km (41,145 sq miles)
POPULATION: 5,024,000
CAPITAL: Nashville

TEXAS
STATUS: State
AREA: 678,620 sq km (261,950 sq miles)
POPULATION: 17,656,000
CAPITAL: Austin

UTAH
STATUS: State
AREA: 212,570 sq km (82,050 sq miles)
POPULATION: 1,813,000
CAPITAL: Salt Lake City

VERMONT
STATUS: State
AREA: 24,015 sq km (9,270 sq miles)
POPULATION: 570,000
CAPITAL: Montpelier

VIRGINIA
STATUS: State
AREA: 102,835 sq km (39,695 sq miles)
POPULATION: 6,377,000
CAPITAL: Richmond

WASHINGTON
STATUS: State
AREA: 172,265 sq km (66,495 sq miles)
POPULATION: 5,136,000
CAPITAL: Olympia

WEST VIRGINIA
STATUS: State
AREA: 62,470 sq km (24,115 sq miles)
POPULATION: 1,812,000
CAPITAL: Charleston

WISCONSIN
STATUS: State
AREA: 140,965 sq km (54,415 sq miles)
POPULATION: 5,007,000
CAPITAL: Madison

WYOMING
STATUS: State
AREA: 251,200 sq km (96,965 sq miles)
POPULATION: 466,000
CAPITAL: Cheyenne

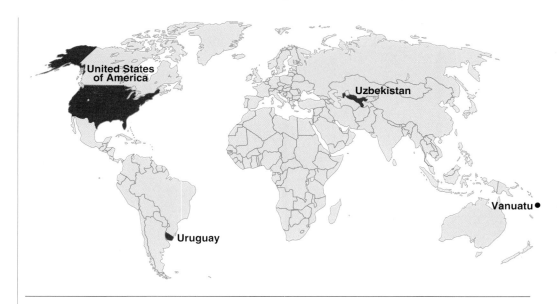

URUGUAY
STATUS: Republic
AREA: 186,925 sq km (72,155 sq miles)
POPULATION: 3,131,000
ANNUAL NATURAL INCREASE: 0.6%
CAPITAL: Montevideo
LANGUAGE: Spanish
RELIGION: Roman Catholic
CURRENCY: Uruguayan peso (UYP)
ORGANIZATIONS: Mercosur, OAS, UN

Uruguay is a small country on the southeast coast of south America. Geographically it consists firstly of a narrow plain, fringed with lagoons and dunes, skirting along the coast and the estuary of the river Plate. Further inland, rolling grassland hills are broken by minor ridges of the Brazilian highlands, which reach heights of no more than 500 m (1,600 feet). The climate is temperate and rainfall is spread evenly throughout the year at about 100 mm (4 inches) per month. Monthly temperatures average in the range of 10–22°C (50–72°F). The land has good agricultural potential, however most is given over to the grazing of sheep and cattle. The economy relies heavily on the production of meat and wool with 87 per cent of the area devoted to farming. Uruguay has no oil or gas reserves, and most of its energy requirements are obtained from hydro-electricity.

UZBEKISTAN
STATUS: Republic
AREA: 447,400 sq km (172,695 sq miles)
POPULATION: 20,708,000
ANNUAL NATURAL INCREASE: 2.4%
CAPITAL: Tashkent
LANGUAGE: Uzbek, Russian, Turkish
RELIGION: Muslim
CURRENCY: som
ORGANIZATIONS: CIS, UN

Established in 1924 as a constituent republic of the Soviet Union, Uzbekistan became an independent state in 1991. The majority of the country consists of flat, sun-baked lowlands with mountains in the south and east. The climate is markedly continental and very dry with an abundance of sunshine and mild, short winters. The southern mountains are of great economic importance, providing ample supplies of water for hydro-electric plants and irrigation schemes. The mountain regions also contain substantial reserves of natural gas, oil, coal, iron and other metals. With its fertile soils (when irrigated) and good pastures, Uzbekistan is well situated for cattle raising and the production of cotton. It is also the largest producer of machines and heavy equipment in central Asia, and has been specializing mainly in machinery for cotton cultivation and harvesting, for irrigation projects, for road-building and textile processing. During the Soviet period the urban employment market became increasingly dominated by Russians and other outsiders. The gradual emergence of better educated and better trained Uzbeks has generated fiercely nationalist sentiments.

VANUATU
STATUS: Republic
AREA: 14,765 sq km (5,700 sq miles)
POPULATION: 154,000
ANNUAL NATURAL INCREASE: 2.4%
CAPITAL: Port-Vila
LANGUAGE: Bislama (national), English, French, Melanesian languages
RELIGION: Christian
CURRENCY: vatu (VUV)
ORGANIZATIONS: Comm., UN

Vanuatu is a chain of some 80 densely forested, mountainous, volcanic islands, situated in the Melanesian south Pacific. Its climate is tropical, with a high rainfall and a continuous threat of cyclones. Copra, cocoa and coffee are grown mainly for export, with fish, pigs and sheep as well as yams, taro, manioc and bananas important only for home consumption. Manganese is the only mineral with deposits of economic value. Tourism is becoming important, particularly with Australian and Japanese visitors.

VATICAN CITY
STATUS: Ecclesiastical State
AREA: 0.44 sq km (0.17 sq miles)
POPULATION: 1,000
LANGUAGE: Italian, Latin
RELIGION: Roman Catholic
CURRENCY: Italian lira (ITL), Papal coinage
ORGANIZATIONS: none

The Vatican City, the headquarters of the Roman Catholic Church, is the world's smallest independent state. It is entirely surrounded by the city of Rome, occupying a hill to the west of the river Tiber. It has been the papal residence since the 5th century and a destination for pilgrims and tourists from all over the world. Most income is derived from voluntary contributions (Peter's Pence), tourism and interest on investments. The only industries are those connected with the Church.

VENEZUELA
STATUS: Republic
AREA: 912,045 sq km
(352,050 sq miles)
POPULATION: 20,410,000
ANNUAL NATURAL INCREASE: 2.5%
CAPITAL: Caracas
LANGUAGE: Spanish
RELIGION: Roman Catholic
CURRENCY: bolivar (VEB)
ORGANIZATIONS: OAS, OPEC, UN

Venezuela, one of the richest countries of Latin America, is divided into four topographical regions: the continuation of the Andes in the west; the humid lowlands around Lake Maracaibo in the north; the savannah-covered central plains (Llanos), and the extension of the Guiana Highlands covering almost half the country. The climate varies between tropical in the south to warm temperate along the northern coasts. The majority of the population live along the north coast. Venezuela's economy is built around oil production in the Maracaibo region; over three-quarters of export revenue comes from oil. Bauxite and iron ore are also important. The majority of employment is provided by industrial and manufacturing sectors of the economy.

VIETNAM
STATUS: Republic
AREA: 329,566 sq km (127,246 sq miles)
POPULATION: 69,306,000
ANNUAL NATURAL INCREASE: 2.3%
CAPITAL: Hanoi
LANGUAGE: Vietnamese, French, Chinese
RELIGION: Buddhist
CURRENCY: dong (VND)
ORGANIZATIONS: OIEC, UN

Situated on the eastern coast of the Indo-Chinese peninsula of southeastern Asia, Vietnam is predominantly a rugged, mountainous country. The north-south oriented mountainous spine separates two major river deltas: the Red River (Hong river) in the north and the Mekong in the south. Monsoons bring 1,500 mm (59 inches) of rain every year and temperatures average 15°C (59°F) annually. Rainforest still covers some of the central mountainous areas, but most has been cleared for agriculture and habitation. Rice is grown extensively throughout the north (Vietnam is the world's third largest exporter after the USA and Thailand) along with coffee and rubber in other parts of the country. Vietnam possesses a wide range of minerals including coal, lignite, anthracite, iron ore and tin. Industry is expanding rapidly, but decades of warfare and internal strife have impeded development. The US government has lifted its 20-year-old trade embargo, which will further help strengthen Vietnam's trade position.

VIRGIN ISLANDS (UK)
STATUS: UK Dependent Territory
AREA: 153 sq km (59 sq miles)
POPULATION: 16,749
CAPITAL: Road Town

VIRGIN ISLANDS (USA)
STATUS: External Territory of USA
AREA: 345 sq km (133 sq miles)
POPULATION: 101,809
CAPITAL: Charlotte Amalie

WALLIS & FUTUNA ISLANDS
STATUS: Self-governing Overseas Territory of France
AREA: 274 sq km (106 sq miles)
POPULATION: 14,100
CAPITAL: Mata-Uta

WESTERN SAHARA
STATUS: Territory in dispute, administered by Morocco
AREA: 266,000 sq km (102,675 sq miles)
POPULATION: 250,000
CAPITAL: Laayoune

WESTERN SAMOA
STATUS: Commonwealth State
AREA: 2,840 sq km (1,095 sq miles)
POPULATION: 170,000
ANNUAL NATURAL INCREASE: 0.5%
CAPITAL: Apia
LANGUAGE: English, Samoan
RELIGION: Christian
CURRENCY: tala (dollar) (WST)
ORGANIZATIONS: Comm., UN

Western Samoa constitutes a 160 km (100 mile) chain of nine south Pacific islands. The two largest islands, Savaii and Upolu, are mountainous and volcanic. Annual rainfall averages 2,500 mm (100 inches) per year and temperatures average 26°C (79°F) for most months. Only four of the islands are populated – Savaii, Upolu, Manono and Apolima. Main exports are copra, timber, coffee, cocoa and fruit. Western Samoa has some light industries, such as food processing, textiles and cigarette manufacture and a tourist trade is developing. Remittances from citizens abroad are, however, also very important to the economy.

YEMEN
STATUS: Republic
AREA: 527,970 sq km (328,065 sq miles)
POPULATION: 11,092,084
ANNUAL NATURAL INCREASE: 4.4%
CAPITAL: San'a (Şan'ā')
LANGUAGE: Arabic
RELIGION: Sunni and Shi'a Muslim
CURRENCY: Yemeni dinar and rial
ORGANIZATIONS: Arab League, UN

The Yemen Arab Republic and the People's Democratic Republic of Yemen were unified in 1990 to form a single state with its capital at San'a. Situated in the southern part of the Arabian Peninsula the country comprises several contrasting physical landscapes. The north is mainly mountainous and relatively wet with rainfall reaching 890 mm (35 inches) in inland areas which helps to irrigate the cereals, cotton, fruits and vegetables grown on the windward mountain sides and along the coast. The south coast stretches for 1,100 km (685 miles) from the mouth of the Red Sea to Oman. These southern regions are generally arid except along the coastal plain where irrigation schemes support some agriculture and away from the coast in the Hadhramaut valley where sufficient rainfall occurs for cereal cultivation. To the north of the Hadhramaut lies the uninhabited Arabian Desert. The population, most of whom are subsistence farmers or nomadic herders of sheep and goats, are concentrated in western regions. Until recently the only mineral exploited commercially was salt but since the discovery of oil in 1984 and 1991, that commodity is making an important contribution to the economy. Otherwise, industrial activity is limited to small scale manufacturing.

YUGOSLAVIA
Federal Republic of,
STATUS: Federation of former Yugoslav Republics of Serbia and Montenegro

AREA: 102,170 sq km (39,435 sq miles)
POPULATION: 10,479,000
ANNUAL NATURAL INCREASE: 0.8%
CAPITAL: Belgrade (Beograd)
LANGUAGE: Serbo-Croat, Albanian
and Hungarian
RELIGION: Orthodox Christian, 10% Muslim
CURRENCY: new Yugoslav dinar (YUD)
ORGANIZATIONS: UN (suspended)

Serbia and Montenegro are the last remaining elements of the Federal Republic of Yugoslavia. Until 1918, they were separate kingdoms. Union of the two, including Vojvodina, followed by unification with lands freed from the Turkish and Austro-Hungarian Empires, resulted in the creation of the Kingdom of Serbs, Croats and Slovenes, a name which was changed to the Kingdom of Yugoslavia in 1929. Yugoslavia became a Socialist Federal Republic in 1945. Economic difficulties from 1980 onwards, combined with regional and ethnic factors, culminated in the secession of Slovenia and Croatia in 1992. International recognition of their sovereignty did not deter Serbia, with the Serb-dominated army at its disposal, from armed incursion to secure areas inhabited by Serbians. Macedonia's claim for recognition was not so well received internationally because of Greek objection to the name Macedonia. Yet, it has ceased to be a part of Yugoslavia. No such impediment stood in the way of recognizing the independence of Bosnia-Herzegovina. Armed conflict intensified in this ethnically complex republic as rival factions fought to support their kinsfolk.

The climate is essentially continental with hot summers and cold winters. Agriculture, which is largely in private hands, features cotton and cereal cultivation on the fertile plains of Vojvodina in the north, livestock production in central Serbia and fruit and tobacco growing in Kosovo in the south. Industry, however, which had accounted for 80 per cent of economic wealth, has suffered severely from the effects of civil war and United Nations sanctions. Inflation is rife and only the black market flourishes.

MONTENEGRO
STATUS: Constituent Republic
AREA: 13,810 sq km (5,330 sq miles)
POPULATION: 664,000
CAPITAL: Podgorica

SERBIA
STATUS: Constituent Republic
AREA: 88,360 sq km (34,105 sq miles)
POPULATION: 9,815,000
CAPITAL: Belgrade (Beograd)

ZAIRE
STATUS: Republic
AREA: 2,345,410 sq km (905,330 sq miles)
POPULATION: 39,882,000
ANNUAL NATURAL INCREASE: 3.3%
CAPITAL: Kinshasa
LANGUAGE: French, Lingala, Kiswahili,
Tshiluba, Kikongo

RELIGION: 46% Roman Catholic,
28% Protestant, traditional beliefs
CURRENCY: zaire (ZRZ)
ORGANIZATIONS: OAU, UN

Zaire, formerly the Belgian Congo, lies astride the Equator and is Africa's third largest country after Sudan and Algeria. It is dominated by the drainage basin of the Zaire, Kasai, and Oubangui rivers, which join to flow into the Atlantic. The land gradually rises from these basins to the south and east, culminating in the Chaine des Mitumba or Mitumbar mountains. On its eastern border the great Rift Valley forms a natural boundary with Uganda and Tanzania. Tropical rainforest covers most of the basin. Zaire's climate is equatorial with both high temperatures, averaging 27°C (80°F) throughout the year, and high rainfall of about 1,500–2,000 (59–79 inches). The majority of the population is engaged in shifting agriculture. Cassava, cocoa, coffee, cotton, millet, rubber and sugar cane are grown. Although the nation possesses mineral wealth, particularly copper which alone has provided 40 per cent of foreign earnings, political turmoil has reduced the country to bankruptcy. The copper mines are closed and diamonds are the only source of income. Zaire faces expulsion from the IMF because of debt arrears.

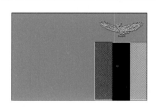

ZAMBIA
STATUS: Republic
AREA: 752,615 sq km (290,510 sq miles)
POPULATION: 8,638,000
ANNUAL NATURAL INCREASE: 3.5%
CAPITAL: Lusaka
LANGUAGE: English, African languages
RELIGION: 75% Christian, animist minority
CURRENCY: kwacha (ZMK)
ORGANIZATIONS: Comm., OAU, UN

Mineral-rich Zambia, is situated in the interior of southern central Africa. Its geography consists mainly of high rolling plateaus, with mountains to the north and northeast. In the south is the Zambezi river basin and the man-made reservoir of Lake Kariba, which forms Zambia's border with Zimbabwe. Altitude moderates the potentially tropical climate so that the summer temperature averages only 13–27°C (55–81°F). The north receives over 1,250 mm (49 inches) of rain per annum, the south less. Most of the country is grassland with some forest in the north. Farming is now mainly at subsistence level, as droughts have had an adverse effect on many crops, but some cattle rearing still takes on importance in the east. Copper remains the mainstay of the country's economy although reserves are fast running out. Lead, zinc, cobalt, cotton, groundnuts and tobacco are also exported. Wildlife is diverse and abundant and contributes to expanding tourism.

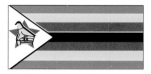

ZIMBABWE
STATUS: Republic
AREA: 390,310 sq km (150,660 sq miles)
POPULATION: 10,402,000
ANNUAL NATURAL INCREASE: 3.0%
CAPITAL: Harare
LANGUAGE: English, native languages
RELIGION: 58% Christian, traditional beliefs
CURRENCY: Zimbabwe dollar (ZWD)
ORGANIZATIONS: Comm., OAU, UN

Landlocked Zimbabwe (formerly southern Rhodesia) in south central Africa consists predominantly of rolling plateaux and valleys. A broad ridge of upland plateaux (the high veld) crosses east-west over the greater part of the country reaching heights of 1,200–1,500 m (3,940–4,920 feet). There are lowland areas (the low veld) formed by the valleys of the Zambezi and Limpopo rivers, in the north and south respectively. The climate varies with altitude and distance from the ocean. Rainfall across the country averages between 600-1,000 mm (24-39 inches). The exploitation of mineral deposits have traditionally supported the economy although recent years have seen a shift in the decline of chrome and coal and a rise in the importance of platinum, nickel and asbestos. Maize is the most important crop as it is the staple food of a large proportion of the population. Tobacco, tea, sugar cane and fruit are also grown. Manufacturing industry is slowly developing and now provides a wide range of consumer products.

North and Central America
25 349 000
9 785 000

CONTINENTS

land area 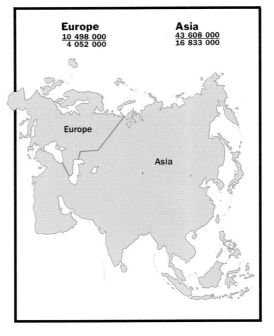 = 1 000 000 sq kms / 386 000 sq miles

Europe
10 498 000
4 052 000

Asia
43 608 000
16 833 000

Europe

Asia

Africa
30 335 000
11 709 000

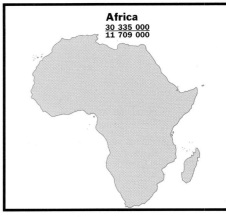

South America
17 611 000
6 798 000

Antarctica
13 340 000
5 149 240

Australasia
8 923 000
3 444 278

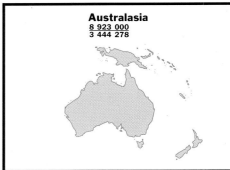

Population	City	Country
2,500,000	**Adibjan**	*Ivory Coast*
1,891,000	**Addis Ababa**	*Ethiopia*
3,297,655	**Ahmadabad**	*India*
3,380,000	**Alexandria**	*Egypt*
3,033,000	**Algiers**	*Algeria*
1,151,300	**Alma-Ata**	*Kazakhstan*
1,091,338	**Amsterdam**	*Netherlands*
3,022,236	**Ankara**	*Turkey*
1,390,000	**Anshan**	*China*
3,096,775	**Athens**	*Greece*
3,051,000	**Atlanta**	*USA*
896,700	**Auckland**	*New Zealand*
4,044,000	**Baghdad**	*Iraq*
1,779,500	**Baku**	*Azerbaijan*
2,414,000	**Baltimore**	*USA*
4,086,548	**Bangalore**	*India*
5,876,000	**Bangkok**	*Thailand*
1,625,542	**Barcelona**	*Spain*
10,900,000	**Beijing (Peking)**	*China*
1,500,000	**Beirut**	*Lebanon*
1,168,454	**Belgrade**	*Yugoslavia*
3,461,905	**Belo Horizonte**	*Brazil*
3,446,000	**Berlin**	*Germany*
2,310,900	**Birmingham**	*UK*
5,025,989	**Bogotá**	*Colombia*
12,571,720	**Bombay**	*India*
4,497,000	**Boston**	*USA*
1,803,478	**Brasília**	*Brazil*
950,339	**Brussels**	*Belgium*
2,350,984	**Bucharest**	*Romania*
2,992,000	**Budapest**	*Hungary*
12,200,000	**Buenos Aires**	*Argentina*
13,300,000	**Cairo**	*Egypt*
10,916,000	**Calcutta**	*India*
320,000	**Canberra**	*Australia*
2,350,157	**Cape Town**	*South Africa*
4,092,000	**Caracas**	*Venezuela*
3,210,000	**Casablanca**	*Morocco*
2,214,000	**Changchun**	*China*
1,362,000	**Changsha**	*China*
1,148,000	**Chelyabinsk**	*Russian Federation*
3,004,000	**Chengdu**	*China*
7,498,000	**Chicago**	*USA*
3,010,000	**Chongqing**	*China*
1,342,679	**Copenhagen**	*Denmark*
2,543,000	**Dalian**	*China*
4,135,000	**Dallas – Fort Worth**	*USA*
2,913,000	**Damascus**	*Syria*
1,657,000	**Dar-es-Salaam**	*Tanzania*
8,375,000	**Delhi**	*India*
4,285,000	**Detroit**	*USA*
6,105,160	**Dhaka**	*Bangladesh*
915,516	**Dublin**	*Republic of Ireland*
2,720,400	**Essen – Dortmund**	*Germany*
1,420,000	**Fushun**	*China*
383,900	**Geneva**	*Switzerland*
2,846,720	**Guadalajara**	*Mexico*
3,620,000	**Guangzhou (Canton)**	*China*
1,669,000	**Hamburg**	*Germany*

METROPOLITAN AREAS

Population	City	Country
1,412,000	**Hangzhou**	*China*
3,056,146	**Hanoi**	*Vietnam*
2,840,000	**Harbin**	*China*
2,099,000	**Havana**	*Cuba*
3,924,435	**Ho Chi Minh (Saigon)**	*Vietnam*
5,812,000	**Hong Kong**	*UK colony*
3,437,000	**Houston**	*USA*
4,280,000	**Hyderabad**	*India*
6,407,215	**Istanbul**	*Turkey*
9,000,000	**Jakarta**	*Indonesia*
608,000	**Jerusalem**	*Israel*
1,327,000	**Jilin**	*China*
2,415,000	**Jinan**	*China*
1,916,063	**Johannesburg**	*South Africa*
1,300,000	**Kābul**	*Afghanistan*
7,702,000	**Karachi**	*Pakistan*
1,947,000	**Khartoum**	*Sudan*
2,616,000	**Kiev**	*Ukraine*
3,505,000	**Kinshasa**	*Zaire*
1,711,000	**Kuala Lumpur**	*Malaysia*
5,689,000	**Lagos**	*Nigeria*
4,092,000	**Lahore**	*Pakistan*
1,566,000	**Lanzhou**	*China*
6,483,901	**Lima**	*Peru*
1,742,000	**Lisbon**	*Portugal*
9,277,687	**London**	*UK*
11,420,000	**Los Angeles**	*USA*
5,361,468	**Madras**	*India*
2,909,792	**Madrid**	*Spain*
2,578,900	**Manchester**	*UK*
8,475,000	**Manila – Quezon City**	*Philippines*
1,594,967	**Medellín**	*Colombia*
3,178,000	**Melbourne**	*Australia*
20,200,000	**Mexico City**	*Mexico*
1,814,000	**Miami**	*USA*
2,583,000	**Minneapolis – St Paul**	*USA*
1,633,000	**Minsk**	*Belarus*
2,521,697	**Monterrey**	*Mexico*
1,383,660	**Montevideo**	*Uruguay*
3,127,100	**Montréal**	*Canada*
8,957,000	**Moscow**	*Russian Federation*
1,236,000	**Munich**	*Germany*
2,095,000	**Nagoya**	*Japan*
1,503,000	**Nairobi**	*Kenya*
1,415,000	**Nanchang**	*China*
2,265,000	**Nanjing**	*China*
16,972,000	**New York**	*USA*
1,442,000	**Novosibirsk**	*Russian Federation*
1,106,000	**Odessa**	*Ukraine*
8,520,000	**Osaka-Kobe**	*Japan*
473,344	**Oslo**	*Norway*
921,000	**Ottawa**	*Canada*

Population	City	Country
9,318,000	**Paris**	*France*
4,941,000	**Philadelphia**	*USA*
2,287,000	**Phoenix**	*USA*
2,404,000	**Pittsburgh**	*USA*
3,015,960	**Pôrto Alegre**	*Brazil*
1,214,174	**Prague**	*Czech Republic*
3,797,566	**Pusan**	*South Korea*
2,230,000	**Pyôngyang**	*North Korea*
645,000	**Quebec**	*Canada*
2,060,000	**Qingdao**	*China*
1,281,849	**Quito**	*Ecuador*
3,295,000	**Rangoon**	*Burma*
2,859,469	**Recife**	*Brazil*
910,200	**Riga**	*Latvia*
9,871,165	**Rio de Janeiro**	*Brazil*
1,500,000	**Riyadh**	*Saudi Arabia*
2,723,327	**Rome**	*Italy*
1,388,000	**Sacramento**	*USA*
2,472,131	**Salvador**	*Brazil*
2,549,000	**San Deigo**	*USA*
5,240,000	**San Francisco**	*USA*
1,390,000	**San Juan**	*Puerto Rico*
4,628,000	**Santiago**	*Chile*
2,055,000	**Santo Domingo**	*Dominican Rept*
15,199,423	**São Paulo**	*Brazil*
10,627,000	**Seoul**	*South Korea*
13,341,896	**Shanghai**	*China*
4,763,000	**Shenyang**	*China*
2,874,000	**Singapore**	*Singapore*
1,221,000	**Sofia**	*Bulgaria*
2,507,000	**St Louis**	*USA*
5,004,000	**St Petersburg**	*Russian Federal*
1,669,840	**Stockholm**	*Sweden*
2,473,272	**Surabaya**	*Indonesia*
3,700,000	**Sydney**	*Australia*
2,228,000	**Taegu**	*South Korea*
2,720,000	**Taipei**	*Taiwan*
2,199,000	**Taiyuan**	*China*
452,000	**Tallinn**	*Estonia*
2,094,000	**Tashkent**	*Uzbekistan*
1,400,000	**Tbilisi**	*Georgia*
6,773,000	**Tehran**	*Iran*
1,135,800	**Tel Aviv**	*Israel*
9,100,000	**Tianjin**	*China*
11,609,735	**Tokyo**	*Japan*
3,893,400	**Toronto**	*Canada*
2,062,000	**Tripoli**	*Libya*
1,603,600	**Vancouver**	*Canada*
1,565,000	**Vienna**	*Austria*
593,000	**Vilnius**	*Lithuania*
1,655,700	**Warsaw**	*Poland*
4,293,000	**Washington DC**	*USA*
325,700	**Wellington**	*New Zealand*
652,000	**Winnipeg**	*Canada*
3,921,000	**Wuhan**	*China*
2,859,000	**Xian**	*China*
1,202,000	**Yerevan**	*Armenia*
726,770	**Zagreb**	*Croatia*
2,460,000	**Zibo**	*China*

MOUNTAIN HEIGHTS

metres	feet		
8,848	29,028	**Everest (Qomolangma Feng)**	
		China–Nepal	
8,611	28,250	**K2 (Qogir Feng) (Godwin Austen)**	
		India – China	
8,598	28,170	**Kangchenjunga** *India–Nepal*	
8,481	27,824	**Makalu** *China–Nepal*	
8,217	26,958	**Cho Oyu** *China–Nepal*	
8,167	26,795	**Dhaulagiri** *Nepal*	
8,156	26,758	**Manaslu** *Nepal*	
8,126	26,660	**Nanga Parbat** *India*	
8,078	26,502	**Annapurna** *Nepal*	
8,088	26,470	**Gasherbrum** *India–China*	
8,027	26,335	**Xixabangma Feng (Gosainthan)**	
		China	
7,885	25,869	**Distaghil Sar** *Kashmir, India*	
7,820	25,656	**Masherbrum** *India*	
7,817	25,646	**Nanda Devi** *India*	
7,788	25,550	**Rakaposhi** *India*	
7,756	25,446	**Kamet** *China–India*	
7,756	25,447	**Namjagbarwa Feng** *China*	
7,728	25,355	**Gurla Mandhata** *China*	
7,723	25,338	**Muztag** *China*	
7,719	25,325	**Kongur Shan (Kungur)** *China*	
7,690	25,230	**Tirich Mir** *Pakistan*	
7,556	24,790	**Gongga Shan** *China*	
7,546	24,757	**Muztagata** *China*	
7,495	24,590	**Pik Kommunizma** *Tajikistan*	
7,439	24,406	**Pik Pobedy (Tomur Feng)**	
		Kirghizia–China	
7,313	23,993	**Chomo Lhari** *Bhutan–Tibet*	
7,134	23,406	**Pik Lenina** *Kirghizia*	
6,960	22,834	**Aconcagua** *Argentina*	
6,908	22,664	**Ojos del Salado** *Argentina–Chile*	
6,872	22,546	**Bonete** *Argentina*	
6,800	22,310	**Tupungato** *Argentina–Chile*	
6,770	22,221	**Mercedario** *Argentina*	

metres	feet		
6,768	22,205	**Huascarán** *Peru*	
6,723	22,057	**Llullaillaco** *Argentina–Chile*	
6,714	22,027	**Kangrinboqê Feng (Kailas)**	
		Tibet, China	
6,634	21,765	**Yerupaja** *Peru*	
6,542	21,463	**Sajama** *Bolivia*	
6,485	21,276	**Illampu** *Bolivia*	
6,425	21,079	**Coropuna** *Peru*	
6,402	21,004	**Illimani** *Bolivia*	
6,310	20,702	**Chimborazo** *Ecuador*	
6,194	20,320	**McKinley** *USA*	
5,959	19,551	**Logan** *Canada*	
5,896	19,344	**Cotopaxi** *Ecuador*	
5,895	19,340	**Kilimanjaro** *Tanzania*	
5,800	19,023	**Sa. Nevada de Sta. Marta**	
		(Cristobal Colon) *Columbia*	
5,775	18,947	**Bolivar** *Venezuela*	
5,699	18,697	**Citlaltépetl (Orizaba)** *Mexico*	
5,642	18,510	**El'brus** *Russian Federation*	
5,601	18,376	**Damāvand** *Iran*	
5,489	18,008	**Mt St. Elias** *Canada*	
5,227	17,149	**Mt Lucania** *Canada*	
5,199	17,057	**Kenya (Kirinyaga)** *Kenya*	
5,165	16,945	**Ararat (Büyük Ağri Daği)** *Turkey*	
5,140	16,860	**Vinson Massif** *Antarctica*	
5,110	16,763	**Stanley (Margherita)** *Uganda–Zaire*	
5,029	16,499	**Jaya (Carstensz)** *Indonesia*	
5,005	16,421	**Mt Bona** *USA*	
4,949	16,237	**Sandford** *USA*	

metres	feet		
4,936	16,194	**Mt Blackburn** *Canada*	
4,808	15,774	**Mont Blanc** *France–Italy*	
4,750	15,584	**Klyuchevskaya Sopka**	
		Russian Federation	
4,634	15,203	**Monte Rosa (Dufour)**	
		Italy–Switzerland	
4,565	14,979	**Meru** *Tanzania*	
4,545	14,910	**Dom (Mischabel group)** *Switzerland*	
4,533	14,872	**Ras Dashen** *Ethiopia*	
4,528	14,855	**Kirkpatrick** *Antarctica*	
4,508	14,790	**Wilhelm** *Papua, New Guinea*	
4,507	14,786	**Karisimbi** *Rwanda–Zaire*	
4,477	14,688	**Matterhorn** *Italy–Switzerland*	
4,418	14,495	**Whitney** *USA*	
4,398	14,431	**Elbert** *USA*	
4,392	14,410	**Rainier** *USA*	
4,351	14,275	**Markham** *Antarctica*	
4,321	14,178	**Elgon** *Kenya–Uganda*	
4,307	14,131	**Batu** *Ethiopia*	
4,169	13,677	**Mauna Loa** *USA, Hawaii*	
4,165	13,644	**Toubkal** *Morocco*	
4,095	13,435	**Cameroon (Caméroun)** *Cameroon*	
4,094	13,431	**Kinabalu** *Malaysia*	
3,794	12,447	**Erebus** *Antarctica*	
3,776	12,388	**Fuji** *Japan*	
3,754	12,316	**Cook** *New Zealand*	
3,718	12,198	**Teide** *Canary Is*	
3,482	11,424	**Thabana Ntlenyana** *Lesotho*	
3,482	11,424	**Mulhacén** *Spain*	
3,415	11,204	**Emi Koussi** *Chad*	
3,323	10,902	**Etna** *Italy, Sicily*	
2,743	9,000	**Mt Balbi**	
		Bougainville, Papua New Guinea	
2,655	8,708	**Gerlachovsky stit (Tatra)**	
		Czech Republic	
2,230	7,316	**Kosciusko** *Australia*	

ISLANDS

land area ⬜ = 10 000 sq kms / 3 860 sq miles

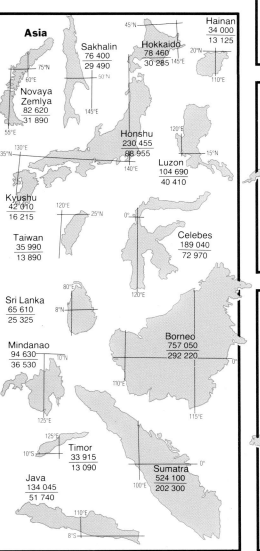

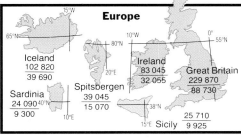

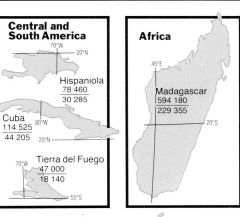

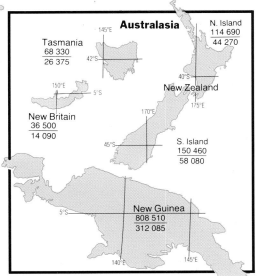

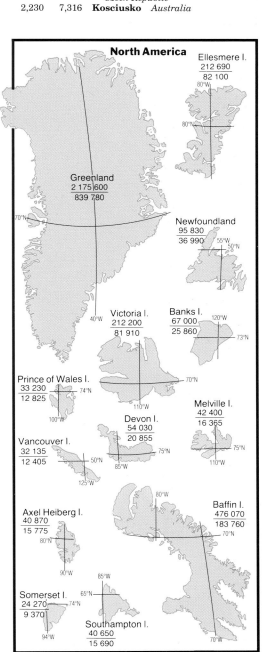

OCEANS AND SEAS

water area ☐ = $\dfrac{1\ 000\ 000\quad \text{sq km}}{386\ 000\quad \text{sq miles}}$

OCEAN FACTS AND FIGURES

The area of the Earth covered by sea is estimated to be 361,740,000 sq km (139,670,000 sq miles), or 70.92% of the total surface. The mean depth is estimated to be 3554 m (11,660 ft), and the volume of the oceans to be 1,285,600,000 cu. km (308,400,000 cu. miles).

INDIAN OCEAN

Mainly confined to the southern hemisphere, and at its greatest breadth (Tasmania to Cape Agulhas) 9600 km. Average depth is 4000 m; greatest depth is the Amirante Trench (9000 m).

ATLANTIC OCEAN

Commonly divided into North Atlantic (36,000,000 sq km) and South Atlantic (26,000,000 sq km). The greatest breadth in the North is 7200 km (Morocco to Florida) and in the South 9600 km (Guinea to Brazil). Average depth is 3600 m; the greatest depths are the Puerto Rico Trench 9220 m, S. Sandwich Trench 8264 m, and Romansh Trench 7728 m.

PACIFIC OCEAN

Covers nearly 40% of the world's total sea area, and is the largest of the oceans. The greatest breadth (E/W) is 16,000 km and the greatest length (N/S) 11,000 km. Average depth is 4200 m; also the deepest ocean. Generally the west is deeper than the east and the north deeper than the south. Greatest depths occur near island groups and include Mindanao Trench 11,524 m, Mariana Trench 11,022 m, Tonga Trench 10,882 m, Kuril-Kamchatka Trench 10,542 m, Philippine Trench 10,497 m, and Kermadec Trench 10,047 m.

Comparisons (where applicable)	greatest distance N/S (km)	greatest distance E/W (km)	maximum depth (m)
Indian Ocean	—	9600	9000
Atlantic Ocean	—	9600	9220
Pacific Ocean	11,000	16,000	11,524
Arctic Ocean	—	—	5450
Mediterranean Sea	960	3700	4846
S. China Sea	2100	1750	5514
Bering Sea	1800	2100	5121
Caribbean Sea	1600	2000	7100
Gulf of Mexico	1200	1700	4377
Sea of Okhotsk	2200	1400	3475
E. China Sea	1100	750	2999
Yellow Sea	800	1000	91
Hudson Bay	1250	1050	259
Sea of Japan	1500	1100	3743
North Sea	1200	550	661
Red Sea	1932	360	2246
Black Sea	600	1100	2245
Baltic Sea	1500	650	460

EARTH'S SURFACE WATERS

Total volume	c.1400 million cu. km
Oceans and seas	1370 million cu. km
Ice	24 million cu. km
Interstitial water (in rocks and sediments)	4 million cu. km
Lakes and rivers	230 thousand cu. km
Atmosphere (vapour)	c.140 thousand cu. km

to convert metric to imperial measurements:
1 m = 3.281 feet
1 km = 0.621 miles
1 sq km = 0.386 sq miles

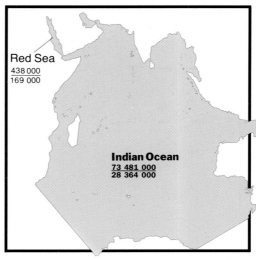

Red Sea
438 000
169 000

Indian Ocean
73 481 000
28 364 000

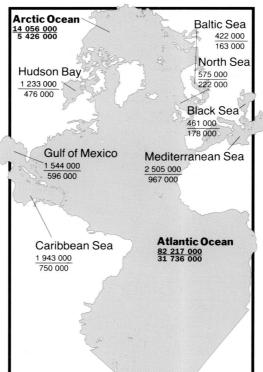

Arctic Ocean
14 056 000
5 426 000

Baltic Sea
422 000
163 000

Hudson Bay
1 233 000
476 000

North Sea
575 000
222 000

Black Sea
461 000
178 000

Gulf of Mexico
1 544 000
596 000

Mediterranean Sea
2 505 000
967 000

Caribbean Sea
1 943 000
750 000

Atlantic Ocean
82 217 000
31 736 000

FEATURES OF THE OCEAN BASIN

The majority of land drainage occurs in the Atlantic, yet this is the most saline ocean due to interchange of waters with its marginal seas. The continental margins (21% of ocean floors) are the most important economic areas.

	PACIFIC	ATLANTIC	INDIAN	WORLD
AVERAGE OCEAN DEPTH (metres) 3000 / 3500 / 4000				
OCEAN AREA (million sq km)	180	107	74	361
LAND AREA DRAINED (million sq km)	19	69	13	101
AREA AS PERCENTAGE OF TOTAL				
Continental margin	15.8	27.9	14.8	20.6
Ridges, rises and fracture zones	38.4	33.3	35.6	35.8
Deep ocean floor	42.9	38.1	49.3	41.9
Island arcs and trenches	2.9	0.7	0.3	1.7

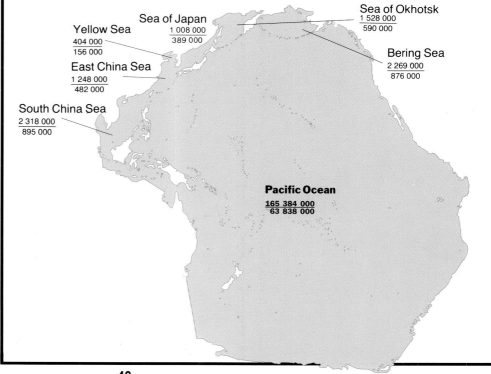

Sea of Japan
1 008 000
389 000

Sea of Okhotsk
1 528 000
590 000

Yellow Sea
404 000
156 000

Bering Sea
2 269 000
876 000

East China Sea
1 248 000
482 000

South China Sea
2 318 000
895 000

Pacific Ocean
165 384 000
63 838 000

RIVER LENGTHS

km	miles		
6,695	4,160	**Nile**	*Africa*
6,515	4,050	**Amazon**	*South America*
6,380	3,965	**Yangtze (Chang Jiang)**	*Asia*
6,019	3,740	**Mississippi-Missouri**	
		North America	
5,570	3,460	**Ob'-Irtysh**	*Asia*
5,550	3,450	**Yenisei-Angara**	*Asia*
5,464	3,395	**Yellow River (Huang He)**	
		Asia	
4,667	2,900	**Congo (Zaire)**	*Africa*
4,500	2,800	**Paraná**	*South America*
4,440	2,775	**Irtysh**	*Asia*
4,425	2,750	**Mekong**	*Asia*
4,416	2,744	**Amur**	*Asia*
4,400	2,730	**Lena**	*Asia*
4,250	2,640	**Mackenzie**	*North America*
4,090	2,556	**Yenisei**	*Asia*
4,030	2,505	**Niger**	*Africa*
3,969	2,466	**Missouri**	*North America*
3,779	2,348	**Mississippi**	*North America*
3,750	2,330	**Murray-Darling**	*Australasia*
3,688	2,290	**Volga**	*Europe*
3,218	2,011	**Purus**	*South America*
3,200	1,990	**Madeira**	*South America*
3,185	1,980	**Yukon**	*North America*
3,180	1,975	**Indus**	*Asia*
3,078	1,913	**Syrdar'ya**	*Asia*
3,060	1,901	**Salween**	*Asia*
3,058	1,900	**St Lawrence**	*North America*
2,900	1,800	**São Francisco**	
		South America	
2,870	1,785	**Rio Grande**	*North America*
2,850	1,770	**Danube**	*Europe*
2,840	1,765	**Brahmaputra**	*Asia*
2,815	1,750	**Euphrates**	*Asia*
2,750	1,710	**Pará-Tocantins**	
		South America	
2,750	1,718	**Tarim**	*Asia*
2,650	1,650	**Zambezi**	*Africa*
2,620	1,630	**Amudar'ya**	*Asia*
2,620	1,630	**Araguaia**	*South America*
2,600	1,615	**Paraguay**	*South America*
2,570	1,600	**Nelson-Saskatchewan**	
		North America	

RIVER LENGTHS & DRAINAGE BASINS

km	miles		
2,534	1,575	**Ural**	*Asia*
2,513	1,562	**Kolyma**	*Asia*
2,510	1,560	**Ganges (Ganga)**	*Asia*
2,500	1,555	**Orinoco**	*South America*
2,490	1,550	**Shabeelle**	*Africa*
2,490	1,550	**Pilcomayo**	*South America*
2,348	1,459	**Arkansas**	*North America*
2,333	1,450	**Colorado**	*North America*
2,285	1,420	**Dneper**	*Europe*
2,250	1,400	**Columbia**	*North America*
2,150	1,335	**Irrawaddy**	*Asia*
2,129	1,323	**Pearl River (Xi Jiang)**	*Asia*
2,032	1,270	**Kama**	*Europe*
2,000	1,240	**Negro**	*South America*
1,923	1,195	**Peace**	*North America*
1,899	1,186	**Tigris**	*Asia*
1,870	1,162	**Don**	*Europe*
1,860	1,155	**Orange**	*Africa*
1,809	1,124	**Pechora**	*Europe*
1,800	1,125	**Okavango**	*Africa*
1,609	1,000	**Marañón**	*South America*
1,609	1,095	**Uruguay**	*South America*
1,600	1,000	**Volta**	*Africa*
1,600	1,000	**Limpopo**	*Africa*
1,550	963	**Magdalena**	
		South America	
1,515	946	**Kura**	*Asia*
1,480	925	**Oka**	*Europe*
1,480	925	**Belaya**	*Europe*
1,445	903	**Godavari**	*Asia*
1,430	893	**Senegal**	*Africa*
1,410	876	**Dnester**	*Europe*
1,400	875	**Chari**	*Africa*
1,368	850	**Fraser**	*North America*
1,320	820	**Rhine**	*Europe*
1,314	821	**Vyatka**	*Europe*
1,183	735	**Donets**	*Europe*
1,159	720	**Elbe**	*Europe*
1,151	719	**Kizilirmak**	*Asia*

km	miles		
1,130	706	**Desna**	*Europe*
1,094	680	**Gambia**	*Africa*
1,080	675	**Yellowstone**	*North America*
1,049	652	**Tennessee**	*North America*
1,024	640	**Zelenga**	*Asia*
1,020	637	**Duena**	*Europe*
1,014	630	**Vistula (Wisla)**	*Europe*
1,012	629	**Loire**	*Europe*
1,006	625	**Tagus (Tejo)**	*Europe*
977	607	**Tisza**	*Europe*
925	575	**Meuse (Maas)**	*Europe*
909	565	**Oder**	*Europe*
761	473	**Seine**	*Europe*
354	220	**Severn**	*Europe*
346	215	**Thames**	*Europe*
300	186	**Trent**	*Europe*

DRAINAGE BASINS

sq km	sq miles		
7,050,000	2,721,000	**Amazon**	*South America*
3,700,000	1,428,000	**Congo**	*Africa*
3,250,000	1,255,000	**Mississippi-Missouri**	
		North America	
3,100,000	1,197,000	**Paraná**	*South America*
2,700,000	1,042,000	**Yenisei**	*Asia*
2,430,000	938,000	**Ob'**	*Asia*
2,420,000	934,000	**Lena**	*Asia*
1,900,000	733,400	**Nile**	*Africa*
1,840,000	710,000	**Amur**	*Asia*
1,765,000	681,000	**Mackenzie**	*North America*
1,730,000	668,000	**Ganges-Brahmaputra**	
		Asia	
1,380,000	533,000	**Volga**	*Europe*
1,330,000	513,000	**Zambezi**	*Africa*
1,200,000	463,000	**Niger**	*Africa*
1,175,000	454,000	**Yangtze**	*Asia*
1,020,000	394,000	**Orange**	*Africa*
980,000	378,000	**Yellow River**	*Asia*
960,000	371,000	**Indus**	*Asia*
945,000	365,000	**Orinoco**	*South America*
910,000	351,000	**Murray-Darling**	
		Australasia	
855,000	330,000	**Yukon**	*North America*
815,000	315,000	**Danube**	*Europe*
810,000	313,000	**Mekong**	*Asia*
225,000	86,900	**Rhine**	*Europe*

North and Central America

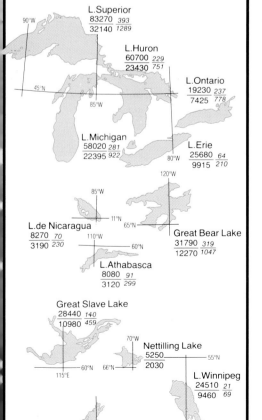

L.Superior 83270 *393* / 32140 *1289*
L.Huron 60700 *229* / 23430 *751*
L.Ontario 19230 *237* / 7425 *778*
L.Michigan 58020 *281* / 22395 *922*
L.Erie 25680 *64* / 9915 *210*
L.de Nicaragua 8270 *70* / 3190 *230*
Great Bear Lake 31790 *319* / 12270 *1047*
L.Athabasca 8080 *91* / 3120 *299*
Great Slave Lake 28440 *140* / 10980 *459*
Nettilling Lake 5250 / 2030
L.Winnipeg 24510 *21* / 9460 *69*
Reindeer Lake 6390 / 2470

INLAND WATERS

water surface area ☐ = 1 000 sq km / 386 sq miles

deepest point 229 metres / 751 feet

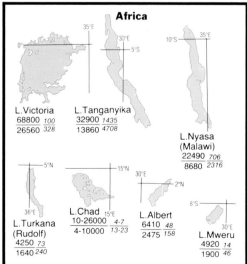

Africa

L.Victoria 68800 *100* / 26560 *328*
L.Tanganyika 32900 *1435* / 13860 *4708*
L.Nyasa (Malawi) 22490 *706* / 8680 *2316*
L.Turkana (Rudolf) 4250 *73* / 1640 *240*
L.Chad 10-26000 *4-7* / 4-10000 *13-23*
L.Albert 6410 *48* / 2475 *158*
L.Mweru 4920 *14* / 1900 *46*

South America

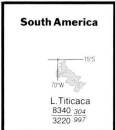

L.Titicaca 8340 *304* / 3220 *997*

Australasia

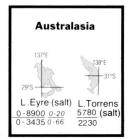

L.Eyre (salt) 0-8900 *0-20* / 0-3435 *0-66*
L.Torrens 5780 (salt) / 2230

Europe

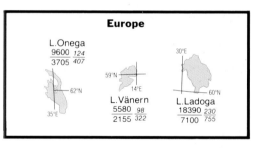

L.Onega 9600 *124* / 3705 *407*
L.Vänern 5580 *98* / 2155 *322*
L.Ladoga 18390 *230* / 7100 *755*

Asia

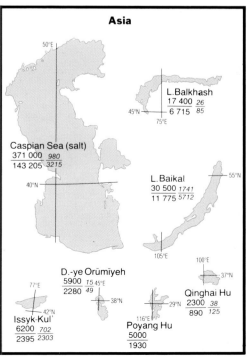

Caspian Sea (salt) 371 000 *980* / 143 205 *3215*
L.Balkhash 17 400 *26* / 6 715 *85*
L.Baikal 30 500 *1741* / 11 775 *5712*
D.-ye Orūmīyeh 5900 *15* / 2280 *49*
Issyk-Kul 6200 *702* / 2395 *2303*
Qinghai Hu 2300 *38* / 890 *125*
Poyang Hu 5000 / 1930

ABBREVIATIONS	FULL FORM	ENGLISH FORM
A		
a.d.	an der	on the
Akr.	Akra, Akrotírion	cape
Appno	Appennino	mountain range
Arch.	Archipelago	
	Archipiélago	archipelago
B		
B.	1. Bahía, Baía, Baie, Bay, Bucht, Bukhta, Bugt	bay
	2. Ban	village
	3. Barrage,	dam
	4. Bir, Bîr, Bi'r	well
Bol.	Bol'sh, -oy	big
Br.	1. Branch	branch
	2. Bridge, Brücke	bridge
	3. Burun	cape
Brj	Baraj, -i	dam
C		
C.	Cabo, Cap, Cape	cape
Can.	Canal	canal
Cd	Ciudad	town
Chan.	Channel	channel
Ck	Creek	creek
Co., Cord.	Cordillera	mountain chain
D		
D.	1. Dağ, Dagh, Dağı, Dağları	mountain, range
	2. Daryācheh	lake
Dj.	Djebel	mountain
Dr.	doctor	doctor
E		
E.	East	east
Emb.	Embalse	reservoir
Escarp.	Escarpment	escarpment
Estr.	Estrecho	strait
F		
F.	Firth	estuary
Fj.	Fjord, Fjörður	fjord
Ft	Fort	fort
G		
G.	1. Gebel	mountain
	2. Göl, Gölü	lake
	3. Golfe, Golfo, Gulf	Gulf
	4. Gora, -gory	mountain, range
	5. Gunung	mountain
Gd, Gde	Grand, Grande	grand
Geb.	Gebirge	mountain range
Gl.	Glacier	glacier
Grl	General	general
Gt, Gtr	Great, Groot, -e, Greater	greater
H		
Har.	Harbour, Harbor	harbour
Hd	Head	head
I		
I.	Ile, Ilha, Insel, Isla, Island, Isle Isola, Isole	island islands
In.	1. Inner	inner
	2. Inlet	inlet
Is	Iles, Ilhas, Islands, Isles, Islas	islands
Isth.	Isthmus	isthmus
J		
J.	Jabal, Jebel,	mountain
K		
K.	1. Kaap, Kap, Kapp	cape
	2. Kūh(hā)	mountain(s)
	3. Kólpos	gulf
Kep.	Kepulauan	islands
Khr.	Khrebet	mountain range
Kör.	Körfez, -i	gulf, bay
L		
L.	Lac, Lago, Lagoa, Lake, Liman, Limni, Loch, Lough	lake
Lag.	Lagoon, Laguna, Lagune, Lagoa	lagoon
Ld.	Land	land
Lit.	Little	little

ABBREVIATIONS	FULL FORM	ENGLISH FORM
M		
M.	1. Muang	town
	2. Mys	cape
m	metre, -s	metre(s)
Mal.	Malyy	small
Mf	Massif	mountain group
Mgne	Montagne(s)	mountain(s)
Mt	Mont, Mount	mountain
Mte	Monte	mountain
Mti	Monti	mountains, range
Mtn	Mountain	mountain
Mts	Monts, Mountains, Montañas, Montes	mountains
N		
N.	1. Neu-, Ny-	new
	2. Noord, Nord, Norte, North, Norra, Nørre	north
	3. Nos	cape
Nat.	National	national
Nat. Pk	National Park	national park
Ndr	Nieder	lower
N.E.	North East	north east
N.M.	National Monument	national monument
N.P.	National Park	national park
N.W.	North West	north west
O		
O.	1. Oost, Ost	east
	2. Ostrov	island
Ø	-øy	island
Oz.	Ozero, Ozera	lake(s)
P		
P.	1. Pass, Passo	pass
	2. Pic, Pico, Pizzo	peak
	3. Pulau	island
Pass.	Passage	passage
Peg.	Pegunungan	mountains
Pen.	Peninsula, Penisola	peninsula
Pk	1. Park	park
	2. Peak, Pik	peak
Plat.	Plateau, Planalto	plateau
Pov	Poluostrov	peninsula
Pr.	Prince	prince
P.P.	Pulau-pulau	islands
Pres.	Presidente	president
Promy	Promontory	promontory
Pt	Point	point
Pta	1. Ponta, Punta	point
	2. Puerta	pass
Pte	Pointe	point
Pto	Porto, Puerto	port
R		
R.	Rio, Río, River, Rivière	river
Ra.	Range	range
Rap.	Rapids	rapids
Res.	Reserve, Reservation	reserve, reservation
Resp.	Respublika	Republic
Resr	Reservoir	reservoir
S		
S.	1. Salar, Salina	salt marsh
	2. San, São	saint
	3. See	sea, lake
	4. South, Sud	south
s.	sur	on
Sa	Serra, Sierra	mountain range
Sd	Sound, Sund	sound
S.E.	South East	south east
Sev.	Severo-, Severnaya, -nyy	north peak
Sp.	Spitze	saint
St	Saint	saint
Sta	Santa	saint
Ste	Sainte	saint
Sto	Santo	strait
Str.	Strait	south west
S.W.	South West	
T		
T.	Tall, Tell	hill, mountain
Tg	Tanjung	cape
Tk	Teluk	bay
Tr.	Trench, Trough	trench, trough
U		
U.	Uad	wadi
Ug	Ujung	cape
Upr	Upper	upper

ABBREVIATIONS	FULL FORM	ENGLISH FORM
V		
V.	1. Val, Valle	valley
	2. Ville	town
Va	Villa	town
Vdkhr.	Vodokhranilishche	reservoir
Vol.	Volcán, Volcano, Vulkan	volcano
Vozv.	Vozvyshennost'	upland
W		
W.	1. Wadi	wadi
	2. Water	water
	3. Well	well
	4. West	west
Y		
Yuzh.	Yuzhno-, Yuzhnyy	south
Z		
Z	1. Zaliv	gulf, bay
	2. Zatoka	
Zap.	Zapad-naya, Zapadno-, Zapadnyy	western
Zem.	Zemlya	country, land

This page explains the main symbols, lettering style and height/depth colours used on the reference maps on pages 2 to 76. The scale of each map is indicated at the foot of each page. Abbreviations used on the maps appear at the beginning of the index.

BOUNDARIES

▬▬▬▬	International
▬ ▬ ▬ ▬	International under Dispute
▪ ▪ ▪ ▪ ▪ ▪	Cease Fire Line
─────	Autonomous or State
─────	Administrative
▬ ▬ ▬ ▬	Maritime (National)
─ ─ ─ ─	International Date Line

COMMUNICATIONS

▬▬▬▬	Motorway/Express Highway
▬▬▬▬	Under Construction
─────	Major Highway
─────	Other Roads
─ ─ ─ ─	Under Construction
─ ─ ─ ─	Track
→───←	Road Tunnel
→═══←	
─ ─ ─ ─	Car Ferry
─●─	Main Railway
─────	Other Railway
─ ─ ─ ─	Under Construction
→───←	Rail Tunnel
─ ─ ─ ─	Rail Ferry
─┼─┼─	Canal
⊕	International Airport
✈	Other Airport

LAKE FEATURES

	Freshwater
	Saltwater
	Seasonal
	Salt Pan

LANDSCAPE FEATURES

	Glacier, Ice Cap
	Marsh, Swamp
	Sand Desert, Dunes

OTHER FEATURES

	River
	Seasonal River
≍	Pass, Gorge
	Dam, Barrage
	Waterfall, Rapid
→───←	Aqueduct
	Reef
▲4231	Summit, Peak
.217	Spot Height, Depth
ᵕ	Well
△	Oil Field
▲	Gas Field
Gas / Oil	Oil/Natural Gas Pipeline
Gemsbok Nat. Pk	National Park
∴UR	Historic Site

LETTERING STYLES

CANADA	Independent Nation
FLORIDA	State, Province or Autonomous Region
Gibraltar (U.K.)	Sovereignty of Dependent Territory
Lothian	Administrative Area
LANGUEDOC	Historic Region
Loire **Vosges**	Physical Feature or Physical Region

TOWNS AND CITIES

Square symbols denote capital cities. Each settlement is given a symbol according to its relative importance, with type size to match.

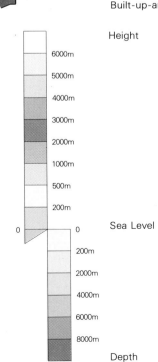

▣	⬤	**New York**	Major City
■	●	**Montréal**	City
▢	○	Ottawa	Small City
■	●	Québec	Large Town
▢	○	St John's	Town
▢	○	Yorkton	Small Town
▢	○	Jasper	Village
			Built-up-area

Height

6000m
5000m
4000m
3000m
2000m
1000m
500m
200m

0 — Sea Level — 0

200m
2000m
4000m
6000m
8000m

Depth

Population Key

Capitals | Cities & Towns
over 5 million
over 1 million
under 1 million

Colours used to denote countries
have no political significance

For more information about each country refer to the States and Territories section (page number in bold type). For large scale map refer to map section (page number in italic).

AFRICA
Algeria 4 *48*
Angola 4 *51*
Benin 7 *48*
Botswana 8 *51*
Burkina 9 *48*
Burundi 9 *50*
Cameroon 9 *48-49*
Cape Verde 10 *48*
Central African Republic 10 *50*
Chad 10 *49*
Comoros 12 *51*
Congo 12-13 *50*
Djibouti 14 *50*
Egypt 14-15 *49*

Equatorial Guinea 15 *48*
Eritrea 15 *50*
Ethiopia 15 *50*
Gabon 16 *50*
Gambia, The 16-17 *48*
Ghana 17 *48*
Guinea 18 *48*
Guinea-Bissau 18 *48*
Ivory Coast 21 *48*
Kenya 22 *50*
Lesotho 23 *51*
Liberia 23 *48*
Libya 24 *49*
Madagascar 24 *51*
Malawi 24-25 *51*
Mali 25 *48*
Mauritania 26 *48*
Mauritius 26 *51*
Morocco 27 *48*
Mozambique 27 *51*
Namibia 27 *51*

Niger 28 *48*
Nigeria 28-29 *48*
Rwanda 31 *50*
São Tomé & Príncipe 32 *48*
Senegal 32 *48*
Seychelles 32 *48*
Sierra Leone 32-33 *48*
Somalia 33 *50*
South Africa 34 *51*
Sudan 34 *49*
Swaziland 35 *51*
Tanzania 36 *50-51*
Togo 36 *48*
Tunisia 37 *48*
Uganda 38 *50*
Zaire 43 *50-51*
Zambia 43 *51*
Zimbabwe 43 *51*

AMERICA, North & Central
Antigua & Barbuda 5 *69*
Bahamas 6 *69*

Barbados 7 *69*
Belize 7 *70*
Canada 10 *54-55*
Costa Rica 13 *70*
Cuba 13 *69*
Dominica 14 *69*
Dominican Republic 14 *69*
El Salvador 15 *70*
Grenada 18 *69*
Guatemala 18 *70*
Haiti 19 *69*
Honduras 19 *70*
Jamaica 21 *69*
Mexico 26 *70*
Nicaragua 28 *70*
Panama 29 *70*
St Kitts-Nevis 31 *69*
St Lucia 32 *69*
St Vincent and the Grenadines 32 *69*
Trinidad & Tobago 37 *69*
United States of America 39-41 *56-57*

AMERICA, South
Argentina 5 *74*
Bolivia 8 *72-73*
Brazil 8 *72-73*
Chile 11 *74*
Colombia 12 *72*
Ecuador 14 *72*
Guyana 18 *73*
Paraguay 30 *74*
Peru 30 *72*
Surinam 35 *73*
Uruguay 41 *74*
Venezuela 42 *72*

ASIA
Afghanistan 4 *42*
Armenia 5 *41*
Azerbaijan 6 *41*
Bahrain 6 *41*
Bangladesh 6-7 *43*
Bhutan 8 *43*
Brunei 8 *27*

1:70 000 000
(45° N & S)

Burma **9** *30*	Nepal **28** *43*	Fiji **16** *33*	Croatia **13** *16*	Netherlands **28** *13*
Cambodia **9** *30*	Oman **29** *38*	Kiribati **22** *33*	Cyprus **13** *45*	Norway **29** *12*
China **11-12** *31*	Pakistan **29** *42*	Marshall Islands **26** *37*	Czech Republic **14** *18-19*	Poland **30** *18-19*
Georgia **17** *21*	Philippines **30** *27*	Micronesia,	Denmark **14** *11*	Portugal **30** *15*
India **19-20** *42-44*	Qatar **31** *41*	Federated States of **26** *36*	Estonia **15** *20*	Romania **31** *17*
Indonesia **20** *27*	Russian Federation **31** *24-25*	Nauru **28** *33*	Finland **16** *12*	Russian Federation **31** *20-21*
Iran **20** *41*	Saudi Arabia **32** *40-41*	New Zealand **28** *35*	France **16** *14*	San Marino **32** *16*
Iraq **20** *40-41*	Singapore **33** *30*	Papua New Guinea **30** *32*	Germany **17** *18*	Slovakia **33** *18-19*
Israel **20** *45*	Sri Lanka **34** *44*	Solomon Islands **33** *33*	Greece **18** *17*	Slovenia **33** *16*
Japan **21** *28-29*	Syria **35** *40*	Tonga **37** *33*	Hungary **19** *18-19*	Spain **34** *15*
Jordan **21** *40*	Taiwan **36** *31*	Tuvalu **37** *33*	Iceland **19** *12*	Sweden **35** *12*
Kazakhstan **22** *24*	Tajikistan **36** *39*	Vanuatu **41** *33*	Ireland **20** *9*	Switzerland **35** *16*
Kirghizia **22** *24*	Thailand **36** *30*	Western Samoa **42** *33*	Italy **21** *16*	Ukraine **38** *21*
Korea, North **22** *28*	Turkey **37** *40*	**EUROPE**	Latvia **23** *19*	United Kingdom **38-39** *6-9*
Korea, South **22** *28*	Turkmenistan **37** *38*	Albania **4** *17*	Liechtenstein **24** *16*	Vatican City **42**
Kuwait **22-23** *41*	United Arab Emirates **38** *41*	Andorra **4** *15*	Lithuania **24** *19*	Yugoslavia **42-43** *17*
Laos **23** *30*	Uzbekistan **41** *38*	Austria **6** *18*	Luxembourg **24** *13*	
Lebanon **23** *45*	Vietnam **42** *30*	Belarus **7** *19*	Macedonia **24** *17*	
Malaysia **25** *30*	Yemen **42** *38*	Belgium **7** *13*	Malta **25** *16*	
Maldives **25** *44*	**AUSTRALASIA**	Bosnia-Herzegovina **8** *16-17*	Moldova **26** *19*	
Mongolia **27** *26*	Australia **5-6** *32-34*	Bulgaria **8-9** *17*	Monaco **27** *14*	

A 40 B ② 30 C 20 70 D 10 E 0 F 10 G

Greenland (Den)
Cape Farewell

ICELAND
Reykjavík

Jan Mayen (Nor)

ARCTIC

Arctic Circle

NORWEGIAN SEA

Vesterålen
Lofoten
Narv

③

Trondheim

NORWAY

SWEDEN

Bergen

Uppsa
Oslo
Västerås

ATLANTIC

Faeroes

Rockall

Shetland

Orkney

Stavanger

Vänern Örebro Stockh
Borås Linköping Norrkö
Göteborg Jönköping

NORTH SEA

UNITED KINGDOM OF GREAT BRITAIN AND NORTHERN IRELAND
Dundee Aberdeen
Glasgow
Edinburgh
Belfast Newcastle
Middlesborough
IRELAND Blackpool Leeds Hull
Liverpool Manchester
Dublin Sheffield Derby
Cork Wolverhampton Nottingham
Birmingham Leicester Norwich
Northampton Oxford Reading Luton
Swansea Cardiff Bristol Ipswich
Plymouth Southampton London Brighton

Ålborg DENMARK
Århus Copenhagen Helsingborg
(København) Malmö
Odense Ölan
Bornholm
Kiel Rostock Schwerin
Lübeck
Bremerhaven Szczecin Gd
Wilhelmshaven Hamburg
Groningen Bremen GERMANY
Amsterdam Hannover Wolfsburg Berlin Gorzow Wlkp
's-Gravenhage Enschede Hildesheim Poznań
NETHERLANDS Paderborn Magdeburg Cottbus
Rotterdam Essen Dortmund Leipzig Dresden PO
Antwerp Düsseldorf Kassel Jena Zwickau Chemnitz Wrocław
BELGIUM Cologne (Köln) Erfurt
Brussels Bonn Frankfurt Plzen Prague CZECH REP
(Bruxelles) Koblenz Darmstadt Nürnberg (Praha) Brno

ATLANTIC OCEAN

④ 50

Isles of Scilly

English Channel
Channel Islands

Le Havre
Brest Caen Rouen Amiens Valenciennes
Lille Boulogne
Rennes Reims Luxembourg LUXEMBOURG
Lorient Le Mans Metz Mainz Heidelberg
St. Nazaire Orléans Nancy Strasbourg Stuttgart
Angers Troyes Heilbronn Augsburg
Nantes Tours FRANCE Dijon Freiburg Ulm Munich Vienna
Besançon Berne Mulhouse (München) (Wien)
Limoges Clermont- (Bern) Basle Salzburg
Bay of Ferrand Geneva Zurich AUSTRIA Bratisl
Biscay St-Étienne (Genève) SWITZERLAND Innsbruck G
Bordeaux Lyon Lausanne LIECHTENSTEIN
Valence Villeurbanne Bolzano Graz
La Coruña Gijón Oviedo Santander Baracaldo Toulouse Nîmes Novara Bergamo SLOVENIA HU
Vigo León Bilbao Vitoria Bayonne Pau Montpellier Rhône Turin Milan Brescia Udine Ljubljana
Logroño San Sebastián (Torino) (Milano) Verona Padova Trieste Zagreb
Oporto Burgos Zaragoza Marseilles Alessandria Piacenza Venice CROATIA
(Porto) PORTUGAL Valladolid (Marseille) Nice Genoa Parma Reggio (Venezia) BOSN
Salamanca ANDORRA Toulon (Genova) La Bologna Rimini HERZEGO
Sabadell Perpignan MONACO Spezia Florence San Marino
Lisbon Madrid Tarrasa Corsica (Firenze) Ancona Split
(Lisboa) SPAIN Alcalá de H. Zaragoza Tarragona (Corse) Bastia Livorno SAN MARINO
Badajoz Toledo Badalona ITALY Perugia
Barcelona Ajaccio Pisa Terni Pescara
Albacete Castellón de la P. Sassari Rome Bari
Córdoba Valencia Balearic Sardinia (Roma)
Faro Sevilla Granada Murcia Islands (Sardegna) Olbia Naples TYRRHENIAN
Huelva Elche Alicante Minorca (Napoli) Salerno SEA
Jerez de la F. Málaga Cartagena Ibiza (Menorca) Cosenza
Cádiz Almería Majorca Cagliari
Tangiers Ceuta (Sp.) Gibraltar (U.K.) (Mallorca) Palermo Messina
(Tanger) Tetouan Melilla (Sp.) MEDITERRANEAN Sicily Reggio di Calabria
Casablanca Rabat Oran Algiers (Sicilia)
(Alger) Syracuse

⑤

Madeira (Port.)

Canary Is.

MOROCCO

Marrakech

ALGERIA

TUNISIA

Tunis

MALTA

Baltic

ADRIATIC SEA

Saraj

Tarant

Bari

Foggia

D 10 E F 10 G

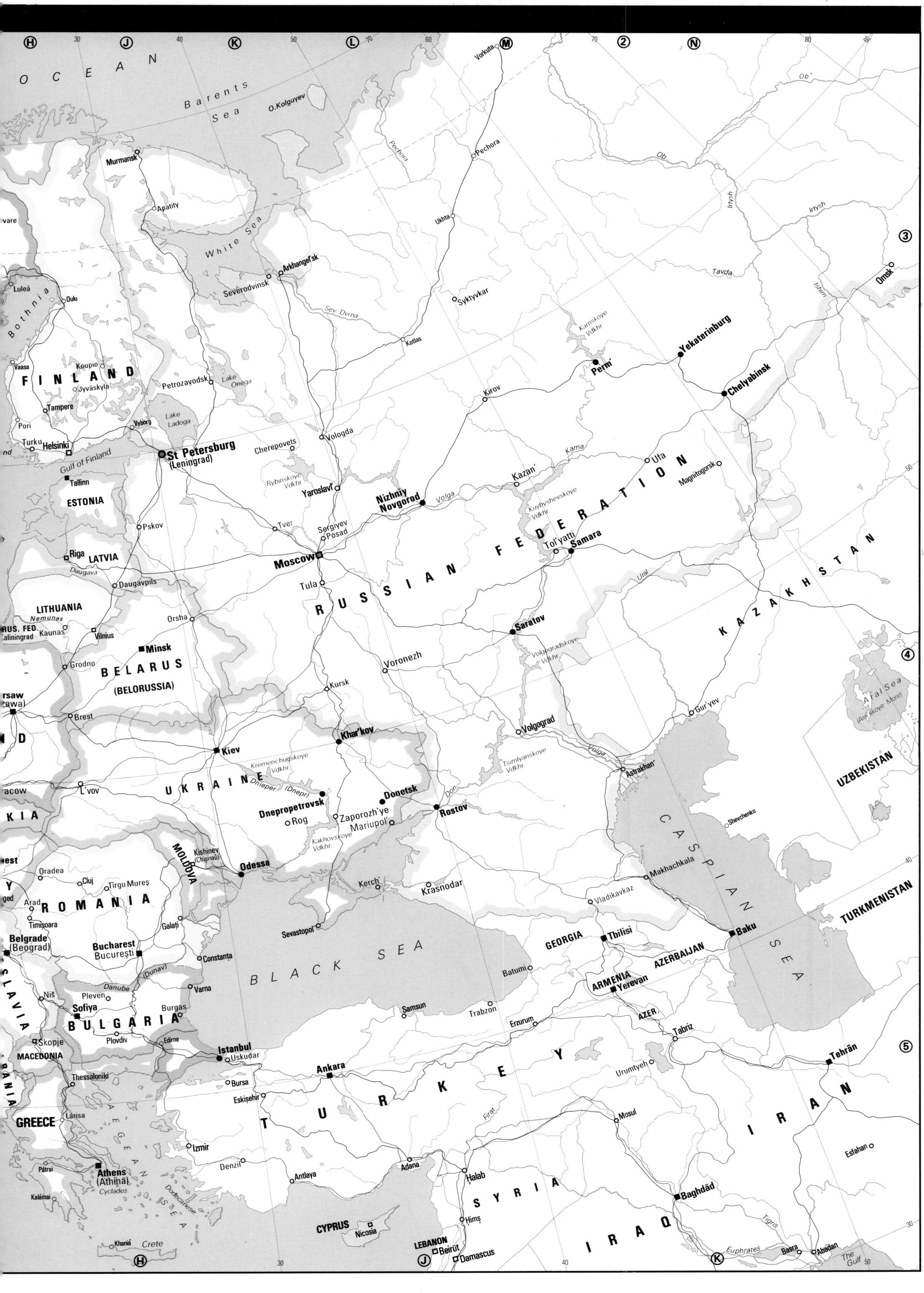

5

OCEAN

Barents Sea

O.Kolguyev

H 30 J 40 K 50 L 70 60 M 70 ② N 80 90

Murmansk

Pechora

Pechora

Vorkuta

Ob'

Irtysh

Irtysh

③

Apatity

White Sea

Severodvinsk

Arkhangel'sk

Ukhta

Tavda

Omsk

Sev. Dvina

Syktyvkar

Kotlas

Kamskoye Vdkhr.

Yekaterinburg

Luleå

Oulu

Kirov

Perm'

Vaasa

Koupio

Jyväskyla

Petrozavodsk

Lake Onega

Ufa

Chelyabinsk

FINLAND

Magnitogorsk

Tampere

Lake Ladoga

50

Pori

Vyborg

Cherepovets

Vologda

Kazan'

Kama

Turku

Helsinki

Gulf of Finland

St Petersburg (Leningrad)

Rybinskoye Vdkhr.

Kuybyshevskoye Vdkhr.

Tallinn

Yaroslavl'

Nizhniy Novgorod

Volga

Tol'yatti

Samara

ESTONIA

Pskov

Sergiyev Posad

Tver

RUSSIAN FEDERATION

KAZAKHSTAN

Riga

LATVIA

Moscow

Daugava

Tula

Ural

Daugavpils

④

LITHUANIA

Nemunas

Orsha

Saratov

Aral Sea

RUS. FED.

Kaunas

Kaliningrad

Vilnius

Voronezh

Volgogradskoye Vdkhr.

(Aral'skoye More)

Grodno

Minsk

Kursk

UZBEKISTAN

saw

awa

Brest

BELARUS

(BELORUSSIA)

Gur'yev

D

Warsaw

Kiev

Khar'kov

Volgograd

Volga

Kremenchugskoye Vdkhr.

cow

Cracow

L'vov

UKRAINE

Dnieper (Dnepr)

Donetsk

Don

Tsimlyanskoye Vdkhr.

Astrakhan'

Shevchenko

KIA

Dnepropetrovsk

Rog

Zaporozh'ye

Mariupol

Rostov

CASPIAN

TURKMENISTAN

Kakhovskoye Vdkhr.

Kishinev (Chisinău)

MOLDOVA

Odessa

Kerch'

Krasnodar

Makhachkala

SEA

est

Oradea

Cluj

Tirgu Mureş

Vladikavkaz

Baku

ged

Arad

Sevastopol'

ROMANIA

GEORGIA

Tbilisi

Timişoara

Galaţi

BLACK SEA

Batumi

ARMENIA

AZERBAIJAN

Belgrade (Beograd)

Bucharest

Bucureşti

Constanţa

Yerevan

AZER

Niš

Danube

(Dunav)

Varna

Samsun

Trabzon

Erzurum

Tabriz

Sofiya

Burgas

SLAVIA

Pleven

BULGARIA

⑤

Skopje

Plovdiv

Edirne

Istanbul

Urumiyeh

Tehrān

MACEDONIA

Thessaloniki

Uskudar

Ankara

IRAN

GREECE

Larisa

Bursa

TURKEY

Fırat

Mosul

Eskişehir

Izmir

Denzil

Adana

Halab

Esfahan

Athens (Athína)

Cyclades

Antalya

SYRIA

Baghdad

Kalámai

Khaniá

Crete

Dodecanese

CYPRUS

Nicosia

Hims

Tigris

AEGEAN SEA

H

30

J

LEBANON

Beirūt

Damascus

40

IRAQ

K

Euphrates

Basra

Abadan

The Gulf

50

30

40

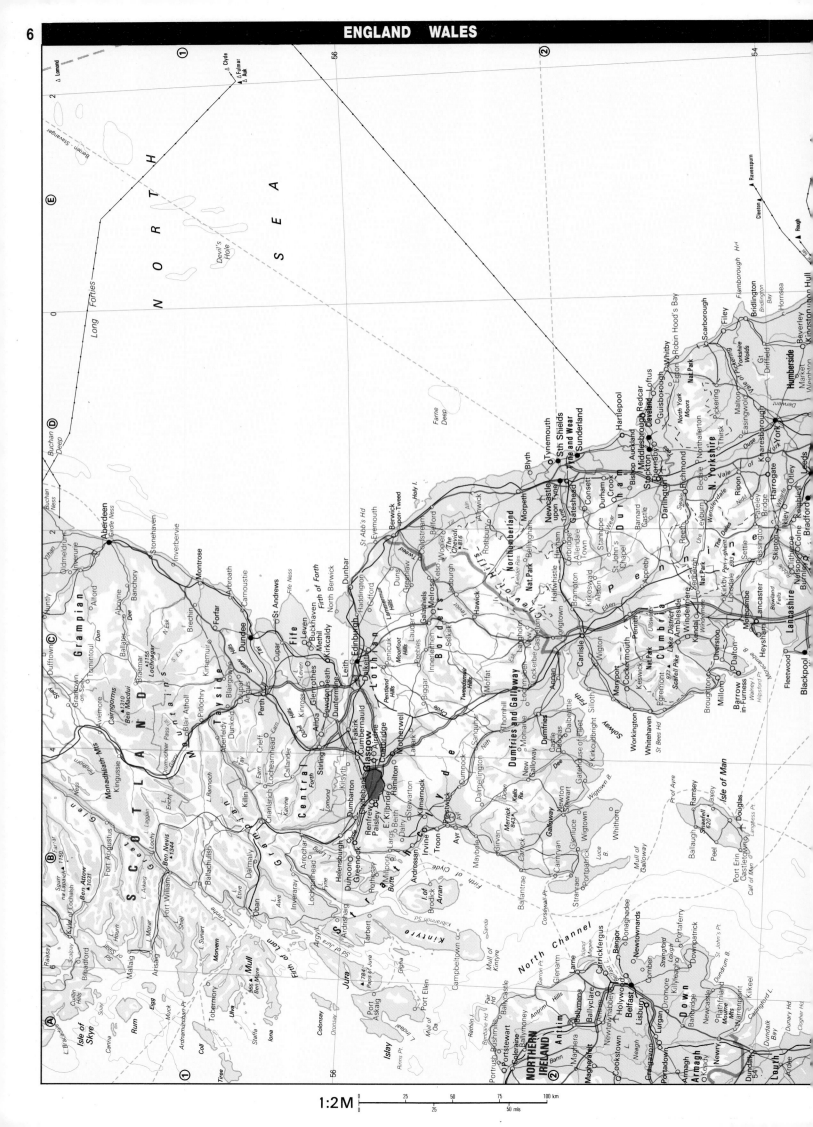

N O R T H   S E A

S C O T L A N D

NORTHERN IRELAND

1:2M

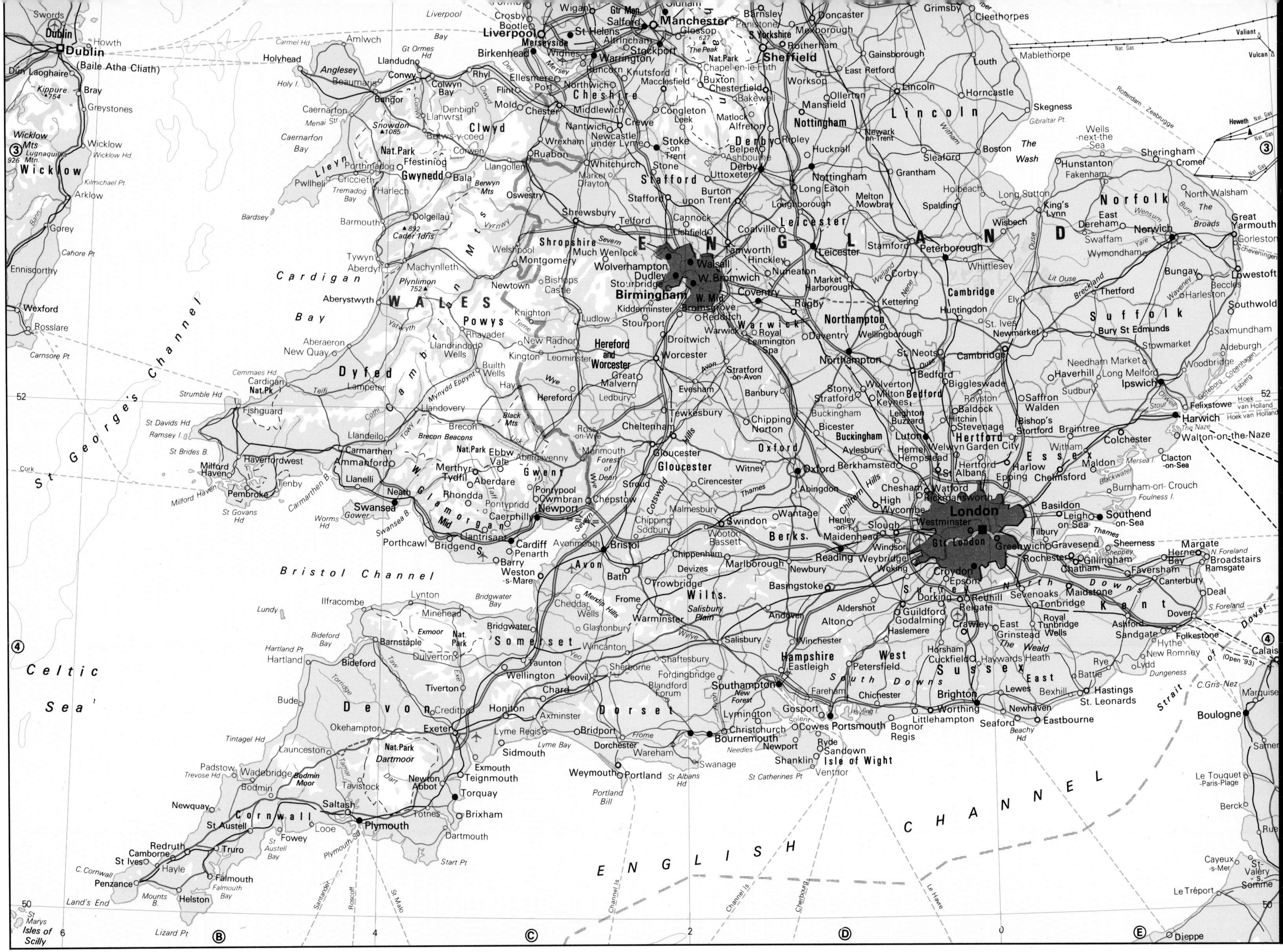
London
Birmingham
Manchester
Liverpool
Sheffield
Bristol
Cardiff
Swansea
Plymouth
Southampton
Portsmouth
Brighton
Dover
Norwich
Ipswich
Cambridge
Oxford
Reading
Leicester
Nottingham
Derby
Coventry
Northampton
Peterborough
Lincoln
Exeter
Dublin
(Baile Atha Cliath)
Wexford
Wicklow
E N G L A N D
W A L E S
Norfolk
Suffolk
Essex
Kent
East Sussex
West Sussex
Surrey
Hampshire
Dorset
Devon
Cornwall
Somerset
Wilts.
Berks.
Gloucester
Hereford and Worcester
Shropshire
Stafford
Cheshire
Warwick
Bedford
Hertford
Buckingham
Avon
Gwynedd
Clwyd
Powys
Dyfed
Gwent
Mid Glamorgan
W. Glamorgan
Isle of Wight
Isles of Scilly
ENGLISH CHANNEL
Bristol Channel
Cardigan Bay
St George's Channel
Celtic Sea
Strait of Dover
The Wash
Calais
Boulogne
Dieppe
Le Touquet -Paris-Plage
Cherbourg
Le Havre
St Malo
Roscoff
Channel Is
Land's End
Lizard Pt
B
C
D
E
3
4
50
52

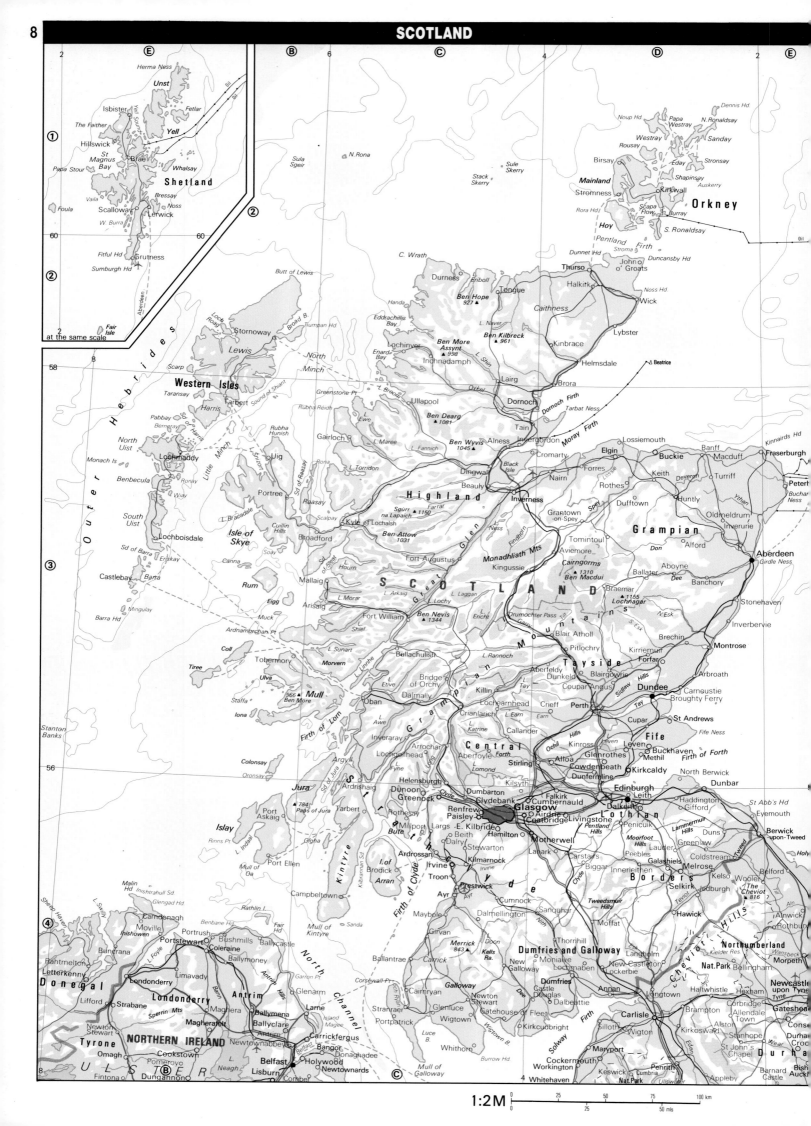

Shetland

Herma Ness
Unst
Isbister
The Faither
Fetlar
Yell
Hillswick
St Magnus Bay
Brae
Whalsay
Papa Stour
Bressay
Foula
Noss
Scalloway
Lerwick
Vaila
W. Burra
60
Fitful Hd
Fair Isle
Grutness
Sumburgh Hd
at the same scale

ORKNEY

Noup Hd
Papa Westray
N. Ronaldsay
Dennis Hd
Westray
Sanday
Rousay
Eday
Stronsay
Birsay
Shapinsay
Auskerry
Mainland
Kirkwall
Stromness
Scapa Flow
Burray
Hoy
S. Ronaldsay
Pentland Firth
Stroma
Dunnet Hd
John o' Groats
Duncansby Hd

C. Wrath
Durness
Eriboll
Tongue
Thurso
Halkirk
Ben Hope 927
Caithness
Noss Hd.
Wick
Handa
L. Naver
Eddrachillis Bay
Ben Kilbreck 961
Kinbrace
Lybster
Enard Bay
Ben More Assynt 998
Lochinver
Inchnadamph
L. Shin
Helmsdale
Lairg
Oykel
Brora
Beatrice
58
Butt of Lewis
Stornoway
Broad B.
Ullapool
Dornoch
Dornoch Firth
Tarbat Ness
Lewis
Greenstone Pt
Moray Firth
Western Isles
Rubha Réidh
L. Broom
Tain
Lossiemouth
Taransay
Harris
Sd of Harris
L. Maree
Ben Dearg 1081
Alness
Invergordon
Elgin
Banff
Macduff
Fraserburgh
Scarp
Ewe
Gairloch
Ben Wyvis 1045
Cromarty
Forres
Keith
Rothes
Turriff
Peter
Pabbay
Berneray
Rubha Hunish
L. Torridon
Dingwall
Black Isle
Nairn
Buchan Ness
North Uist
Uig
Rona
Beauly
Inverness
Dufftown
Huntly
Oldmeldrum
Inverurie
Monach Is
Lochmaddy
Portree
Sd of Raasay
Grampian
Benbecula
Wiay
Raasay
Scalpay
Sgurr na Lapaich 1150
Farrar
Grantown-on-Spey
Spey
Alford
Highland
South Uist
Isle of Skye
Broadford
Cuillin Hills
Ben Attow 1031
Kyle of Lochalsh
Fort Augustus
Monadhliath Mts
Aviemore
Tomintoul
Don
Aberdeen
Girdle Ness
Lochboisdale
Soay
Kingussie
Cairngorms
Ballater
Banchory
Sd of Barra
Eriskay
Canna
L. Hourn
Cairn
Ben Macdui 1310
Braemar
Dee
Barra
Rum
Mallaig
L. Morar
L. Arkaig
L. Lochy
L. Laggan
Lochnagar 1155
N. Esk
Stonehaven
Castlebay
Eigg
Arisaig
Ericht
Drumochter Pass
S. Esk
Inverbervie
Mingulay
Muck
Fort William
Ben Nevis 1344
Garry
Blair Atholl
Pitlochry
Brechin
Barra Hd
Ardnamurchan Pt
L. Shiel
Ballachulish
Tilt
Aberfeldy
Kirriemuir
Forfar
Montrose
Coll
Tobermory
Morvern
L. Etive
Bridge of Orchy
L. Rannoch
Dunkeld
Blairgowrie
Arbroath
Tiree
Ulva
966 Ben More Mull
Dalmally
Killin
L. Tay
Coupar Angus
Tayside
Carnoustie
Staffa
Iona
Oban
L. Awe
Lochearnhead
Crieff
Perth
Dundee
Broughty Ferry
Firth of Lorn
Crianlarich
L. Earn
Earn
Tay
Cupar
St Andrews
Stanton Banks
Colonsay
Oronsay
Inveraray
Arrochar
Callander
Central
Kinross
Leven
Fife
Fife Ness
56
Jura
784
Paps of Jura
Lochgoilhead
Aberfoyle
Forth
L. Katrine
Stirling
Oich
Alloa
Glenrothes
Buckhaven
Methil
Firth of Forth
Islay
Port Askaig
Sd of Jura
L. Lomond
Kilsyth
Cowdenbeath
Kirkcaldy
North Berwick
Rinns Pt.
Gigha
Helensburgh
Dumbarton
Falkirk
Cumbernauld
Dunfermline
Dunbar
Port Ellen
Kintyre
Dunoon
Greenock
Clydebank
Edinburgh
Leith
Haddington
St Abb's Hd
L. Indaal
Rothesay
Renfrew
Paisley
Glasgow
Airdrie
Coatbridge
Livingstone
Dalkeith
Lothian
Gifford
Eyemouth
Millport
Bute
Largs
E. Kilbride
Hamilton
Motherwell
Pentland Hills
Penicuik
Lammermuir Hills
Duns
Berwick-upon-Tweed
Ardrishaig
Tarbert
Ardrossan
I. of Arran
Brodick
Beith
Dalry
Stewarton
Lanark
Carstairs
Moorfoot Hills
Peebles
Lauder
Greenlaw
Coldstream
Kilbrannan Sd
Irvine
Kilmarnock
Irvine
Clyde
Biggar
Innerleithen
Galashiels
Borders
Kelso
Wooler
Troon
Prestwick
Ayr
Ayr
Cumnock
Tweedsmuir Hills
Melrose
Selkirk
Jedburgh
The Cheviot 816
Campbeltown
Sanda
Maybole
Dalmellington
Sanquhar
Moffat
Hawick
Teviot
Aln
Alnwick
Mull of Kintyre
Girvan
Doon
Merrick 843
Kells Ra.
Thornhill
Northumberland
Malin Hd
Inishtrahull Sd.
Fair Hd
Ballantrae
Carrick
New Galloway
Monaive
New Castleton
Lockerbie
Nat. Park
Bellingham
Morpeth
Sheep Haven
Rathlin I.
Portrush
Bushmills
Ballycastle
Dumfries and Galloway
Dumfries
Castle Douglas
Annan
Longtown
Hexham
Newcastle upon Tyne
Gateshead
L. Swilly
Carndonagh
Moville
Benbane Hd
Garron Pt
Stranraer
Corsewall Pt
Loch Ryan
Cairnryan
Newton Stewart
Glenluce
Gatehouse of Fleet
Dalbeattie
Kirkcudbright
Carlisle
Brampton
Alston
Corbridge
Allendale Town
Durham
Letterkenny
Londonderry
Limavady
Coleraine
Ballymoney
Antrim Hills
Glenarm
Larne
Wigtown
Wigtown B.
Maryport
Cockermouth
Workington
Keswick
Cumbria Nat. Park
Penrith
Ullswater
Stanhope
Bishop Auck
Lifford
Strabane
Sperrin Mts
Maghera
Magherafelt
Ballymena
Ballyclare
Island Magee
North Channel
Luce B.
Whithorn
Solway Firth
Burrow Hd
Silloth
Wigton
St John's Chapel
Wear
Donegal
Newton Stewart
Omagh
Cookstown
Pomeroyo
Antrim
Ballymena
Carrickfergus
Newtownabbey
Belfast
Bangor
Donaghadee
Newtownards
Holywood
Whitehaven
Keswick
Appleby
Barnard Castle
Tyrone
Northern Ireland
Fintona
Dungannon
Lisburn
Lisburn
Comber
Ulster
L. Neagh

1:2M

0 25 50 75 100 km
0 25 50 mls

1:2M

Herma Ness
Isbister *Unst*
St Magnus B.   *Fetlar*
Yell **Shetland**   Viking Bank
Whalsay
Lerwick
Foula   *Sumburgh Hd.*

Fair Isle

Westray   *Sanday*
N.Rona   *Sule Skerry*   *Rousay*   *Stronsay*
Sula Sgeir   *Stromness*   Kirkwall
Stack Skerry   **Orkney**
Hoy   *Scapa Flow*

Flannan Is   *Butt of Lewis*   C.Wrath
St Kilda   *Stornoway*   Thurso
Outer Hebrides   *Lewis*   ▲*Ben Hope 927*   *Duncansby Hd.*
Harris   Wick
N. Uist   Ullapool   ▲*Ben More Assynt 998*   Helmsdale

NORTH

SEA

The Minch

S.Uist   *Skye*   Dingwall   Dornoch   *Dornoch Firth*
Barra   *Kyle of Lochalsh*   L.Ness   Inverness   *Moray Firth*   Elgin   Banff   Fraserburgh
Mallaig   Fort Augustus   ▲*Ben Macdui 1309*   *Spey*   Peterhead
Rum   Fort William   ▲*Ben Nevis 1344*   **SCOTLAND**   *Don*   *Buchan Ness*
Coll   ▲*Ben Lawers 1214*   *Mts*   Braemar   *Dee*   Aberdeen
Tiree   *Ben*   Pitlochry   Stonehaven
Mull   Oban   *Grampian*   Perth   Dundee   Montrose
F.of Lorn   L.Awe   *Arbroath*   Long Forties
Colonsay   *Jura*   L.Lomond   Stirling   *F.of Tay*   St Andrews   Great Fisher Bank
Islay   Greenock   Kirkcaldy
Paisley   **Glasgow**   *F.of Forth*
Campbeltown   Irvine   Motherwell   Edinburgh   *St Abbs Hd.*
Malin Hd.   *Arran*   Kilmarnock   Galashiels   Berwick-upon-Tweed
Tory I.   *Rathlin I.*   Ayr   *White Coomb ▲822*   *Holy I.*
Aran I.   Coleraine   *F.of Clyde*   Girvan   Moffat   Hawick   Alnwick
▲*Errigal 752*   L.Foyle   *Merrick ▲843*   *Cheviots*   Morpeth
Londonderry   *N. IRELAND*   Dumfries   *Nith*   Blyth
Rossan Pt.   Ballymena   Stranraer   Newcastle upon Tyne
Donegal   L.Erne   Larne   Kirkcudbright   Carlisle   Gateshead   S. Shields
Erris Hd.   *Donegal B.*   Omagh   Belfast   *Solway Firth*   Penrith   Durham   Sunderland
Sligo B.   Enniskillen   Bangor   *Luce B.*   *Pennines*   Hartlepool
Achill I.   L.Conn   Sligo   Armagh   Portadown   ▲*Scafell Pike 977*   Darlington   Middlesbrough   Dogger Bank
Clew B.   Ballina   L.Neagh   Newry   *Isle of Man*   Kendal   *Yorkshire Moors*   Scarborough
Castlebar   L.Allen   Monaghan   Douglas   Barrow-in-Furness   *Ouse*   *Flamborough Hd.*
Slyne Hd.   L.Mask   Boyle   Cavan   Dundalk   Morecambe   Lancaster   Harrogate   York   Hull
L.Corrib   Roscommon   L.Ree   Longford   Drogheda   **IRISH SEA**   Blackpool   Bradford   Leeds   Spurn Hd.
Aran Is   Galway   Athlone   Mullingar   Preston   Huddersfield   Doncaster   Grimsby
Galway B.   *Shannon*   Monasterevin   **Dublin (Baile Átha Cliath)**   Bolton   **Manchester**   Humber
Ennis   L.Derg   Nenagh   Port Laoise   Dún Laoghaire   **Liverpool**   Birkenhead   Warrington   **Sheffield**   Lincoln
Mouth of the Shannon   **REP. OF IRELAND**   Bray   Holyhead   Chester   Crewe   Stoke-on-Trent   Nottingham
Kilrush   Carlow   *Wicklow Mts*   *Anglesey*   Shrewsbury   Derby
Dingle   Limerick   Tipperary   Kilkenny   Wicklow   Bangor   ▲*Snowdon 1085*   *Trent*   Leicester
Tralee   Clonmel   Arklow   Pwllheli   *Dee*   Wolverhampton   Coventry   Peterborough   Norwich   Great Yarmouth
Dingle B.   Killarney   *Blackwater*   *Barrow*   Waterford   Wexford   *Cardigan Bay*   Aberystwyth   **WALES**   **Birmingham**   Northampton   Bedford   Cambridge   King's Lynn   Lowestoft
▲*Carrauntoohill 1041*   Dungarvan   Rosslare   Worcester   **ENGLAND**   Ipswich   Felixstowe
Bantry B.   **Cork**   Youghal   *St George's Channel*   *St David's Hd.*   Fishguard   Builth Wells   *Wye*   Gloucester   Milton Keynes   Newmarket   Harwich   Colchester
Bantry   Pembroke   Carmarthen   Brecon   *Severn*   Oxford   Luton   Chelmsford
C.Clear   *Old Hd. of Kinsale*   Swansea   Newport   Swindon   Reading   **London**   Southend-on-Sea
Cardiff   **Bristol**   Bath   Windsor   *Thames*   Maidstone
Lundy I.   *Bristol Chan.*   Weston-super-Mare   Guildford   Canterbury   Dover
Barnstaple   Taunton   Salisbury   Winchester   Crawley   Folkestone   *Str. of Dover*
Bude   Exeter   Bournemouth   Southampton   Brighton   Hastings   Eastbourne
Newquay   *Dartmoor*   Weymouth   Portsmouth   *Isle of Wight*
Penzance   Truro   Plymouth   Torquay
Isles of Scilly   *Land's End*   Falmouth   *Prawle Pt.*
Lizard Pt.

ENGLISH CHANNEL

C. de la Hague
Alderney
Pte. de Barfleur
Guernsey   *Sark*   Cherbourg   Le Tréport   Dieppe   Amiens
Channel Is (To U.K.)   Valognes   St-Quentin
Jersey   St Helier   St-Lô   Bayeux   Le Havre   Fécamp   Rouen   Beauvais   Laon   Reims
Coutances   Caen   *Seine*   Bolbec   Compiègne   Charleville-Mézières
Granville   Deauville   Lisieux   Elbeuf   Louviers   Soissons   Fourmies
Golfe de St-Malo   **NORMANDY**   *Orne*   Evreux   Senlis   Château-Thierry   Épernay
Roscoff   St-Malo   *Mont St-Michel*   Argentan   Dreux   Mantes   Cergy-Pontoise   Meaux   Châlons-s.-M.
I.d'Ouessant   Morlaix   St-Brieuc   Dinan   Domfront   *Eure*   Versailles   **Paris**   Provins   Vitry-le-F.
Brest   **BRITTANY**   Châteaulin   Carhaix-Plouguer   Fougères   Mayenne   Chartres   Étampes   Melun   Romilly-s.-S.
Quimper   Loudéac   Pontivy   **MAINE**   Alençon   Rambouillet   Fontainebleau   Troyes   Sens
Quimperlé   Ploërmel   Vitré   Laval   Le Mans   Châteaudun   *Seine*   Chaumont
Concarneau   Rennes   *FRANCE*   *Bar-s.-A.*
Lorient   *Vilaine*

Calais   Dunkirk   Oostende   Bruges   Gent   **Antwerp (Antwerpen)**   Mechelen   Hasselt
Boulogne   St-Omer   Tourcoing   Roubaix   Kortrijk   Zeebrugge   **Brussels (Bruxelles)**   Leuven
Montreuil   Lille   Tournai   *Schelde*   Soignies   Namur   **BELGIUM**
Abbeville   Béthune   Lens   Douai   Valenciennes   Mons   Charleroi
Arras   Denain   Maubeuge   Vlissingen   's-Hertogenbosch   Breda   Tilburg   Eindhoven
Cambrai   Fourmies   *'s-Gravenhage*

Vlieland   *Terschelling*
Texel   Harlingen
Den Helder   Hoorn   Alkmaar   Zaandam   Haarlem   **Amsterdam**   Hilversum   Amersfoort
Leiden   Utrecht
The Hague ('s-Gravenhage)   **Rotterdam**   Dordrecht   *Lek*
Bergen   Sotra   Haugesund   Sunnhordland   Nordhordland

1:5M

0   50   100   150   200 km
0   50   100 mls

Iceland inset

25W   (A)   Arctic Circle   20   Grimsey   (B)   15   (C)

Bolungarvik   Drangajökull   Grimsey
Ísafjörður   Siglufjörður   Ólafsfjörður   Bakkaflói
Dalvík   Húsavík
*Gláma   Húnaflói   Saudárkrókur   Njarðvik
845   Blönduós   Akureyri
Biargtangar
Breiðafjörður   Akranes   Seyðisfjörður
Stykkishólmur   Langjökull   Hofs-   Neskaupstaður
jökull   Eskifjörður   65
I C E L A N D   Tungnafells-   Snæfell 1833
jökull   Óðáðahraun
Faxaflói   þjórsá   Vatnajökull
Reykjavik   Öræfajökull 2119
Kópavogur
Keflavik   Hafnarfjörður
Grindavik   Selfoss   Ingólfshöfði
Vestmannaeyjar   Mýrdalsjökull
Surtsey
at the same scale

Faeroes inset
(D) Faeroes (Faerøerne) (Den.)
Streymoy
Vágar   Tórshavn   62
Sandoy   (5)
Suduroy
at the same scale   7W   5

Main map labels

A R C T I C   O C E A N
B A R E N T S   S E A
N O R W E G I A N   S E A
Arctic Circle

Nordkapp   Honningsvåg   Vardø
Hammerfest   Vadsø
Søroya   Kirkenes
Tromsø   Alta   Nikel   Polyarnyy   Murmansk
Narvik   Kautokeino   Kola
Kebnekaise 2111   Monchegorsk   Apatity
Bodø   Kiruna   Kandalaksha
Fauske   Gällivare
Mo i Rana   Rovaniemi   Kemijärvi
Sandnessjøen   Kemi
Mosjøen   Boden   Oulu
Luleå
Brønnøysund   Piteå
Vilhelmina   Skellefteå   F I N L A N D
Rørvik   Umeå   Vaasa
Namsos   Kuopio
Steinkjer   Östersund   Örnsköldsvik   Jyväskylä
Kristiansund   Trondheim   Sundsvall   Tampere
Molde   Pori
Ålesund   Hudiksvall
Lillehammer   Gävle   Turku   Helsinki   St Petersburg (Leningrad)
Bergen   Hamar   Falun   Uppsala   Tallinn   Narva
Oslo   Västerås   Stockholm   E S T O N I A
Drammen   Örebro   Södertälje   Pärnu
Stavanger   Norrköping   Gulf of Riga   Pskov
Kristiansand   Linköping   Riga   L A T V I A
Göteborg   Jönköping   Gotland   Ventspils
Borås   Liepāja   Daugavpils
Ålborg   Kalmar   Šiauliai   Panevežys
Århus   Karlskrona   Klaipėda   L I T H U A N I A
D E N M A R K   Bornholm (Den.)   Kaliningrad   Kaunas   Vilnius
Copenhagen   Malmö   Gdynia   Minsk
North Sea   Odense   Gdańsk (Danzig)   B E L A R U S (BELORUSSIA)
Kiel   Rostock   Szczecin   P O L A N D
Hamburg   Lübeck   Poznań
Bremen   G E R M A N Y   Berlin   Warsaw

B A L T I C   S E A
Gulf of Bothnia
Gulf of Finland
Skagerrak
Kattegat

1:7.5M   0   100   200   300 km   50   100   150 mls

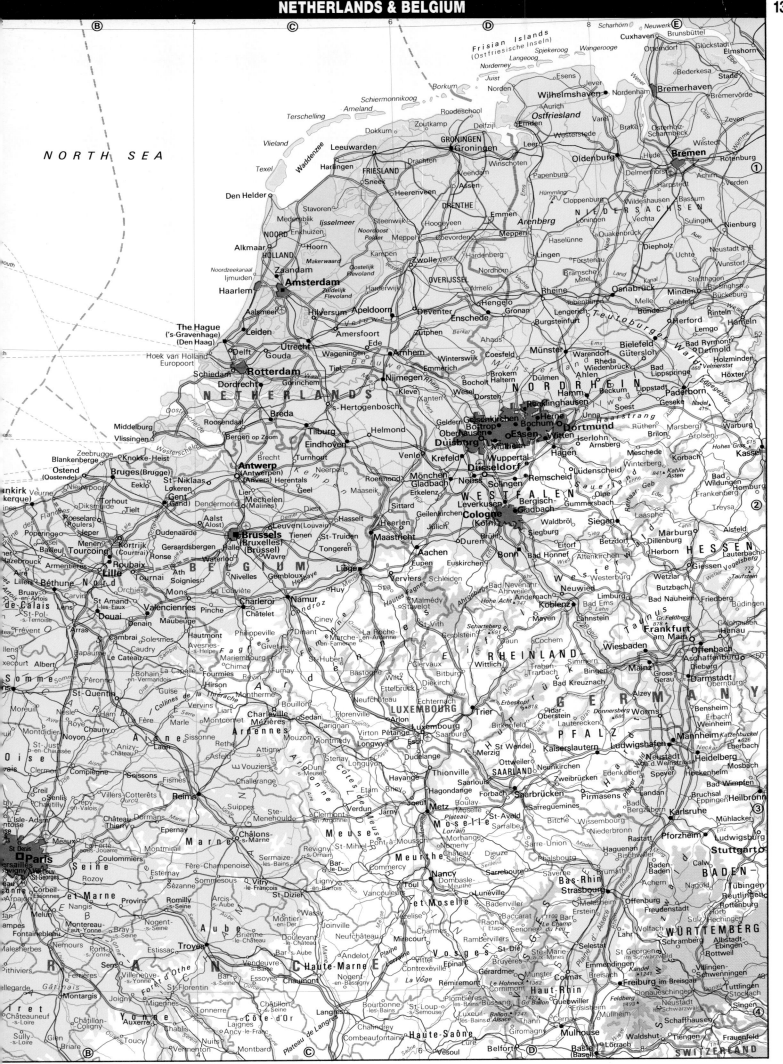

NORTH SEA

Frisian Islands
(Ostfriesische Inseln)

Scharhörn Neuwerk
Cuxhaven Brunsbüttel Elmshorn
Otterndorf Glückstadt
Borkum Wangerooge Bederkesa Stade
Spiekeroog Norderney Juist Langeoog Bremerhaven Bremervörde
Memmert Esens Wilhelmshaven Nordenham Osterholz- Zeven
Schiermonnikoog Jever Aurich Varel Braker Scharmbeck
Ameland Norden Emden Wilstedt
Terschelling Roodeschool Ostfriesland Westerstede Oldenburg Delmenhorst **Bremen**
Zoutkamp Delfzijl Leer Huder Rotenburg Achim Verden
Vlieland Dokkum GRONINGEN Papenburg Cloppenburg Wildeshausen Bassum
Waddenzee Leeuwarden Groningen Loningen Vechta Sulingen Nienburg
Den Helder Harlingen Drachten Keppeln Winschoten Lingen Quakenbrück Diepholz Uchte
Texel FRIESLAND Heerenveen Assen DRENTHE Meppen Haselünne NIEDERSACHSEN Neustadt a. R.
Medemblik Sneek Emmen Lingen Fürstenau Bramsche Stadthagen Wunstorf
Stavoren Hoogeveen Arenberg Nordhorn Ibbenbüren Melle Osnabrück Minden Bückeburg
Enkhuizen Steenwijk Meppel Coevorden Rheine Lengerich Bünde Herford
Ijsselmeer Noordoost Zwolle Hardenberg Burgsteinfurt Bielefeld Rinteln Hameln
Alkmaar Hoorn Polder Kampen Almelo Gronau Gütersloh Herford Lemgo
NOORD Makerwaard Oostelijk OVERIJSSEL Hengelo Münster Warendorf Ahlen Detmold Holzminden
Zaandam HOLLAND Flevoland Harderwijk Enschede Coesfeld Höxter
Haarlem **Amsterdam** Apeldoorn Deventer Winterswijk Ahaus Beckum Soest Paderborn
Zuidelijk Zutphen Berkel Dülmen Hamm Geseke Nadel
Aalsmeer Flevoland Veluwe Arnhem Emmerich Bocholt Haltern NORDRHEIN WESTFALEN
Leiden Amersfoort Wageningen Winterswijk Wesel Dorsten Recklinghausen Unna Ruthen Brilon Hohes Gras
The Hague Utrecht Ede Betuwe Xanten Gelsenkirchen Herne Dortmund Iserlohn Arnsberg Marsberg Warburg
(Den Haag) Gouda Tiel Waal Kleve Brokem Bottrop Bochum Witten Meschede Korbach Kassel
Delft Gorinchem Nijmegen Rhein Geldern Oberhausen Essen Hagen Winterberg
Schiedam Rotterdam Dordrecht s-Hertogenbosch Krefeld Duisburg Mülheim Lüdenscheid Sauerland Bad Wildungen
Hoek van Holland NETHERLANDS Wuppertal Solingen Remscheid Gummersbach Frankenberg Homburg
Europoort Breda Mönchen- Düsseldorf Bergisch- HESSEN
Middelburg Roosendaal Helmond Gladbach Neuss Gladbach Siegen Laasphe
Vlissingen Bergen op Zoom Tilburg Venlo Erkelenz Leverkusen Olpe Marburg Alsfeld
Zeebrugge Eindhoven Roermond Geilenkirchen Cologne Siegburg Dillenburg
Blankenberge Knokke-Heist Brecht Turnhout Maaseik Sittard Jülich (Köln) Eitorf Herborn Lauterbach
Ostend Bruges Antwerp Neerpelt Heerlen Düren Bonn Betzdorf Wetzlar Giessen Vogelsberg
(Oostende) (Brugge) (Antwerpen) Herentals Geel Maastricht Aachen Bad Honnef Altenkirchen Westerwald
Nieuwpoort Eeklo (Anvers) Lier Hasselt Eupen Euskirchen Neuwied Butzbach Frankfurt
Dunkirk Veurne St-Niklaas Mechelen Tongeren Verviers Schleiden Bad Neuenahr- Limburg Bad Nauheim Friedberg am Main
(Dunkerque) Diksmuide Lokeren (Malines) Leuven(Louvain) Liège Spa Ahrweiler Andernach Bad Nauheim Büdingen Offenbach
Roeselare Gent Aalst Tienen St-Truiden Hautes Fagnes Malmédy Hohe Acht Mayen Koblenz Bad Ems Aschaffenburg
Ieper (Roulers) (Gand) (Alost) Demer Huy Stavelot Scharteberg Cochem RHEINLAND- Lahnstein Wiesbaden GERMANY
Menen Kortrijk BELGIUM Brussels Namur Ciney St-Vith Daun Wittlich Traben- Simmern Mainz Hanau
Tourcoing (Courtrai) Ronse Geraardsbergen Brussels Condroz Marche- Gerolstein Trarbach Bingen Gross- Darmstadt
Lille Roubaix Oudenaarde Halle (Bruxelles) Gembloux La Roche- en-Famenne EIFEL Bitburg Diekirch Bad Kreuznach Gerau
Armentières Ath Waterloo Wavre (Brüssel) Charleroi Namur en-Ardenne Bastogne Clervaux Cochem Idar- Mosel Bensheim
Béthune Nord Tournai Nivelles Soignies St-Hubert Witz Bitburg LUXEMBOURG Oberstein Donnersberg Worms Erbach
Roeselare Mons Charleroi Philippeville Givet Dinant Marche Neufchâteau Ettelbruck Trier Kirn Alzey Weinheim
Béthune Valenciennes Pinche Châtelet Beaumont Couvin Rochefort Ardennes Bouillon Echternach Birkenfeld Bad Ems PFALZ Mannheim
St-Pol- Douai Denain Maubeuge Hautmont Chimay Fumay Revin Sedan Florenville Luxembourg St-Wendel Kaiserslautern Ludwigshafen
Arras Cambrai Solesmes Avesnes- Fourmies La Capelle Mézières Carignan Arlon Virton Pétange Merzig Zweibrücken Neustadt Heidelberg
Bapaume Le Cateau s-Helpe Hirson Montcornet Charleville- Mouzon Longuyon Esch Saarburg Homburg Speyer Mosbach
Albert Guise Liart Mézières Montmédy Longwy Dudelange Thionville Saarlouis Forbach Saarbrücken Pirmasens Landau Bruchsal Heilbronn
Somme Péronne Bohain- Vervins Rethel Stenay Esch Hayange Saarbrücken Sarreguemines Wörth Karlsruhe
St-Quentin en-Vermandois Thiérache Ardennes Neufchâteau Attigny Dun Metz St-Avold Bitche Mühlacker
Ham Sissonne Asfeld sur-Meuse Verdun Moselle Morhange Sarralbe Wissembourg Pforzheim
Chauny Laon Aisne Château- Clermont- Étain Bar-le-Duc Pont-à-Mousson Dieuze Sarre-Union Niederbronn Rastatt Ludwigsburg
Noyon Anizy-le-Château Thierry Suippes en-Argonne Jarny Nancy Château- Haguenau Stuttgart
Compiègne Soissons Fismes Ste- Clermont- St-Mihiel Meurthe Salins Seille Baden- BADEN-
Creil Senlis Villers Reims Menehould en-Argonne Commercy Toul Dombasle Sarrebourg Bas-Rhin Baden WÜRTTEMBERG
Cotterêts Ourcq Marne Revigny- Meuse Lunéville Saverne Achern
Crépy-en-Valois Château- Châlons-sur-Marne sur-Ornain Ligny- Strasbourg Offenburg Calw
Meaux Thierry Marne en-Barrois Vancouleurs Badonviller Brumath Nagold Tübingen
L'Isle-Adam Coulommiers La Ferté- Épernay Sermaize- Bar-le-Duc et-Moselle Badenviller Molsheim Lahr Freudenstadt Reutlingen
St-Denis sous-Jouarre les-Bains Meurthe Baccarat Sélestat Rottenburg
Paris Montmirail Vitry- Revigny Wassy Joinville Raon-l'Étape Le Champ Rottweil
Versailles Seine Provins le-François Bar-sur-Aube Neufchâteau Mirecourt Rambervillers du Feu St-Dié Ste-Marie- Obernai
Corbeil-Essonnes et-Marne Sézanne Fère-Champenoise Vitry Sommesous Andelot Épinal Vosges aux-Mines Emmendingen Villingen-
Melun Nangis Aube Brienne- Doulevant Neufchâteau Vittel Plaine Gérardmer Münster Colmar Breisach Schwenningen
Nogent- le-Château le-Château Chaumont La Vôge Remiremont Le Hohneck Haut-Rhin Freiburg im Tuttlingen
Fontainebleau Montereau- Bray- Essoyes Contrexéville Bruyères St-Dié Colmar Breisgau Donaueschingen Stockach
Faut-Yonne s-Seine Troyes Chaumont Luxeuil- Plombières- Bussang Guebwiller Feldberg Singen
Nemours Joigny Migennes Châtillon- les-Bains les-Bains Thann Neustadt Schaffhausen
Montargis Sens Haute-Marne Nogent- Haute-Saône Le Ballon Mülheim im Schwarzwald
Pont- en-Bassigny Langres d'Alsace Giromagny
sur-Yonne Chablis Côte-d'Or Haute-Saône Lure Cernay Waldshut Tiengen Frauenfeld
Gâtinais Auxerre Plateau de Langres Vesoul Mulhouse SWITZERLAND
Briare Toucy Vermenton Nuits Montbard Combeaufontaine Belfort Basel (Basle)

FRANCE

1:5M

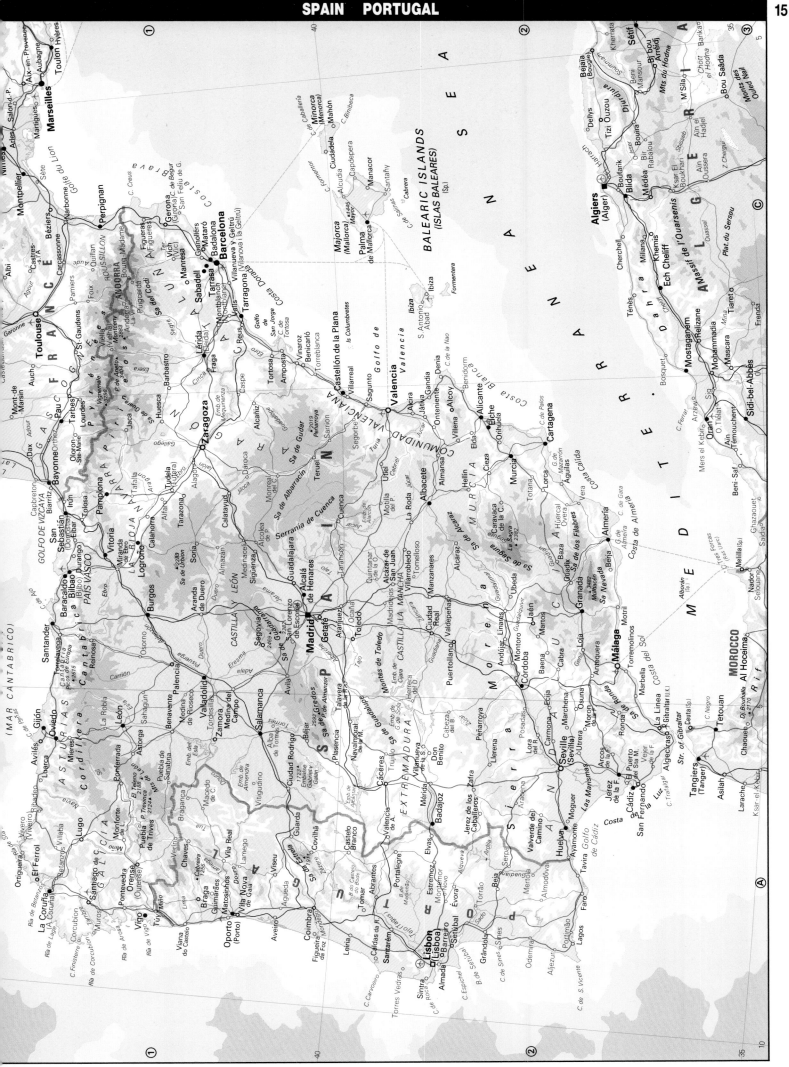

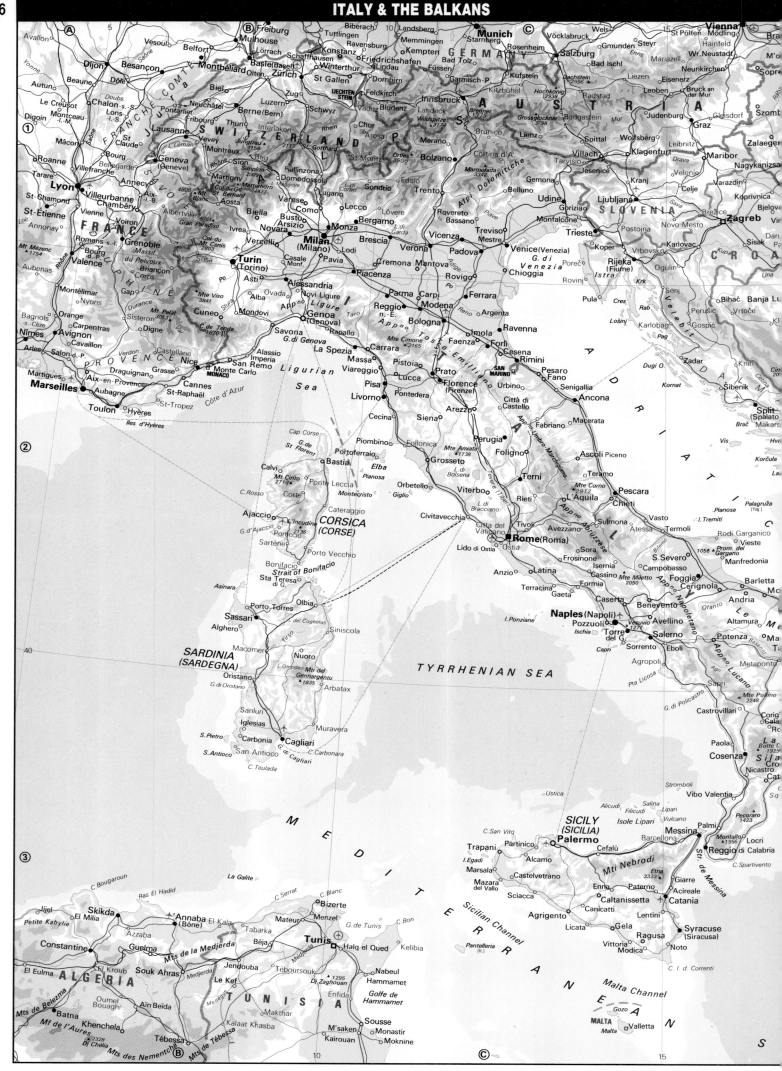

1:5M

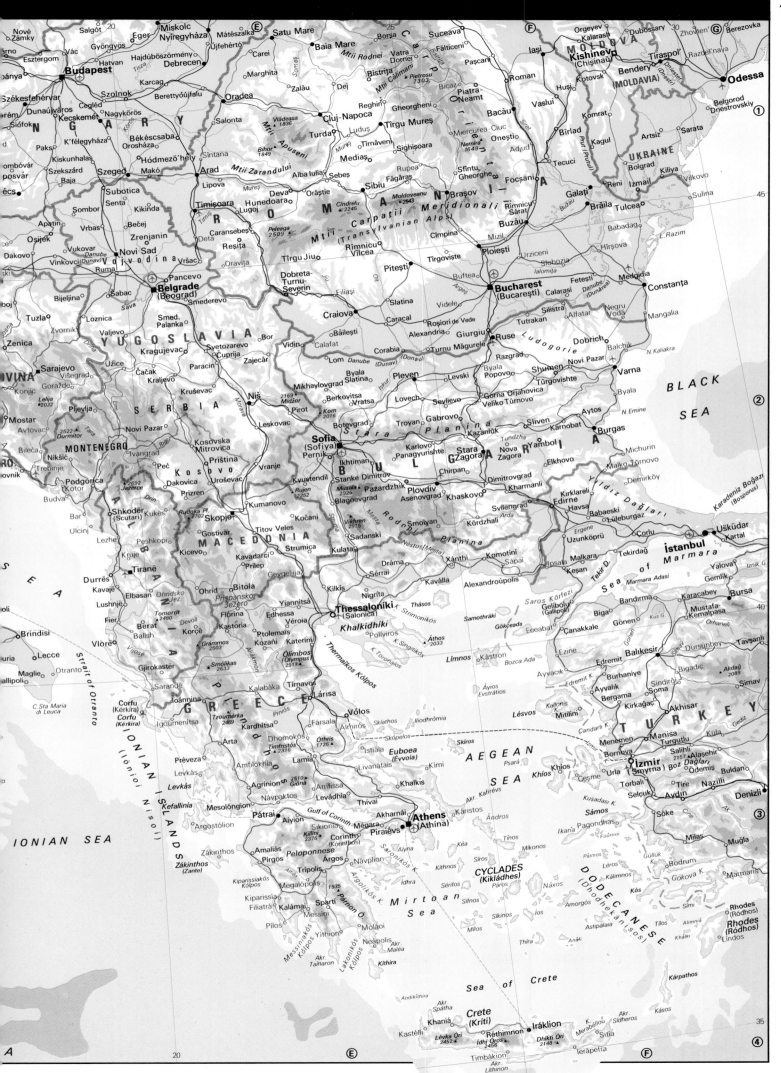

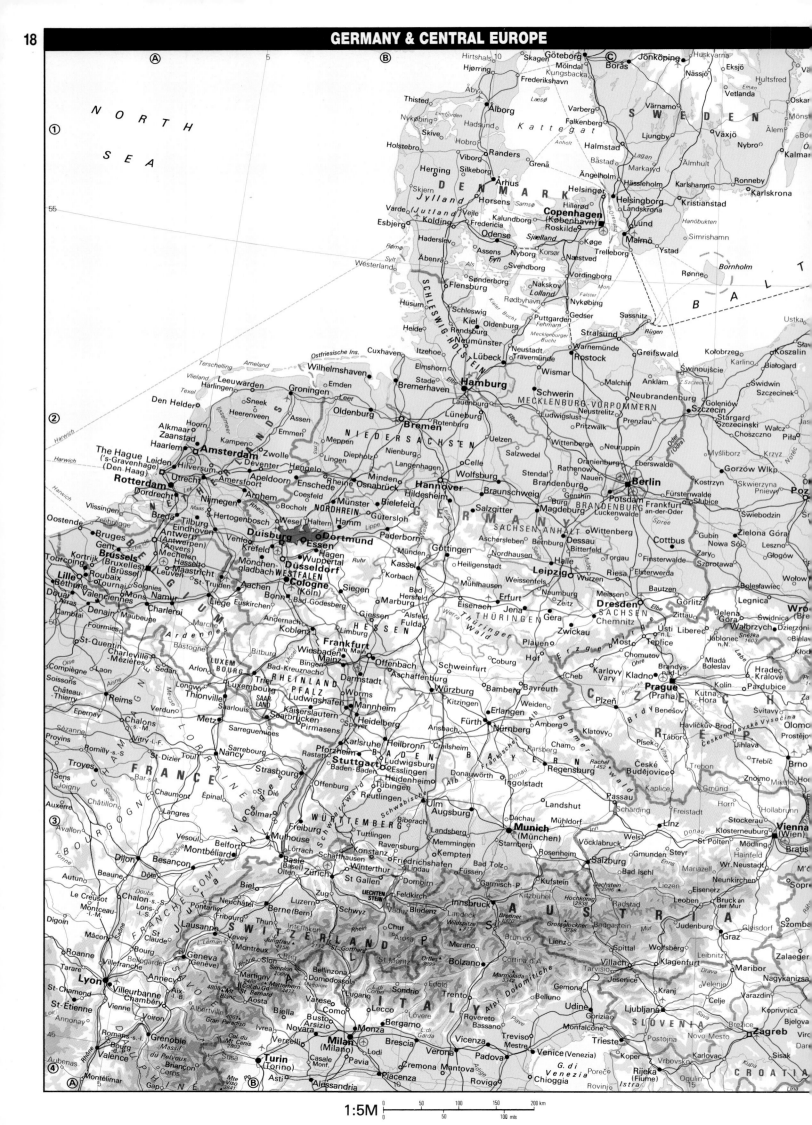

1:5M

0   50   100   150   200 km
0   50   100 mls

BARENTS SEA

(Barentsovo More)

Pechorskoye More

Ostrov Kolguyev

Novaya Zemlya

WHITE SEA (Beloye More)

NORWAY

Norwegian Sea

LAPLAND

FINLAND

Gulf of Bothnia

SWEDEN

Gulf of Finland

ESTONIA

LATVIA

LITHUANIA

BELORUSSIA (BELARUS)

RUSSIAN FEDERATION

Ural Mts

Zapadno Sibirskaya Nizmennost

Moscow (Moskva)

St Petersburg (Leningrad)

Stockholm

Helsinki

Minsk

Warsaw

Perm

Kazan

Izhevsk

Nizhniy Novgorod (Gorki)

Yekaterinburg

Chelyabinsk

Murmansk

Archangel

1:10M

0   100   200   300   400 km

0   100   200 mils

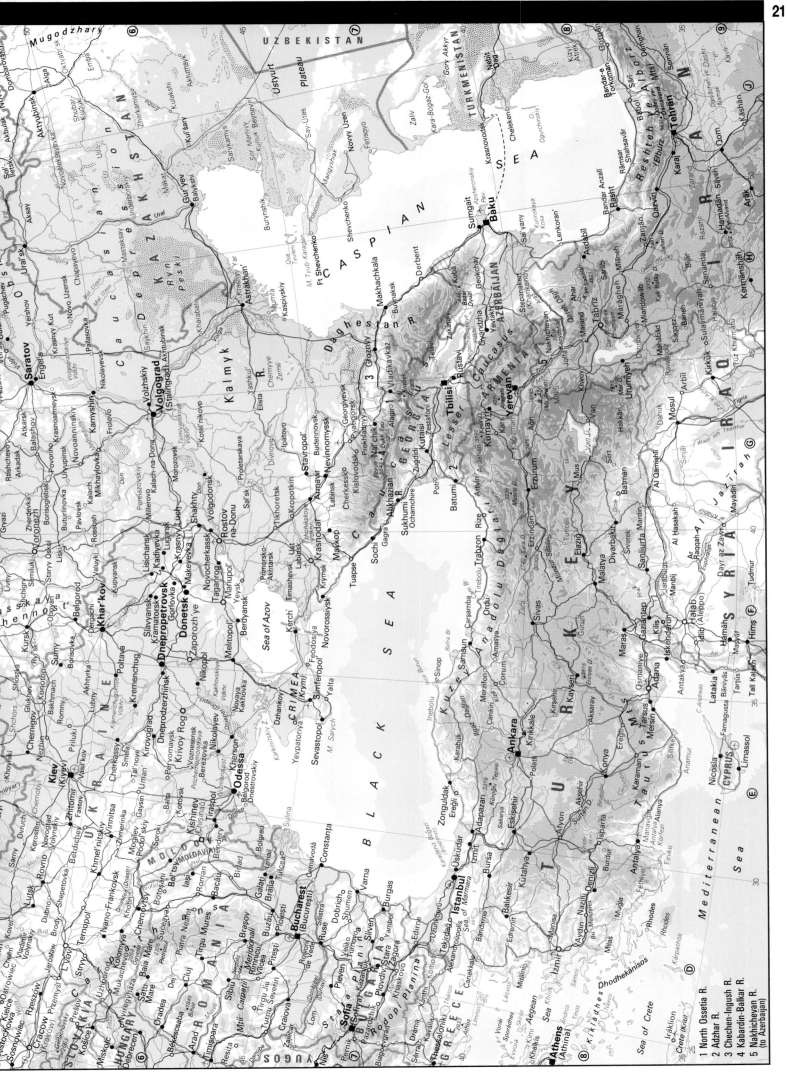

1 North Ossetia R.
2 Adzhar R.
3 Chechen-Ingush R.
4 Kabardin-Balkar R.
5 Nakhichevan R. (to Azerbaijan)

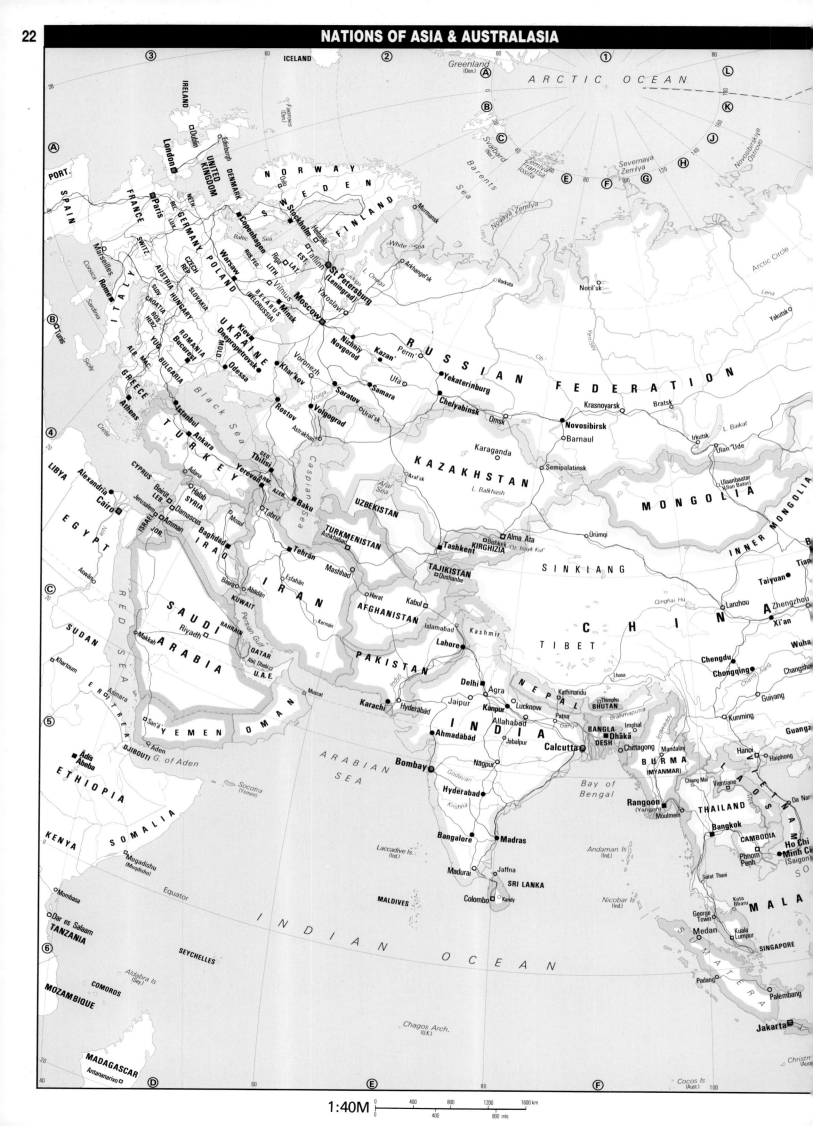

1:40M

U.S.A.
INTERNATIONAL DATELINE
Bering Sea
Magadan
Petropavlovsk Kamchatskiy
Sea of Okhotsk
Sakhalin
Kuril'skiye Ostrova
Khabarovsk
Hokkaidō
Sapporo
Harbin
Changchun
Vladivostok
JAPAN
Sea of Japan
Shenyang
Honshu
Tokyo
N.KOREA
Pyongyang
Nagoya
Ōsaka
Dalian
Seoul
S.KOREA
Pusan
Qingdao
Shikoku
Kita-Kyūshū
Kyūshū
Yellow Sea
Nanjing
Shanghai
Tropic of Cancer
Taipei
TAIWAN
PACIFIC OCEAN
Luzon
PHILIPPINES
Manila
Mindanao
Palawan
Davao
Sandakan
Sabah
Bandar Seri Begawan
Manado
Halmahera
Irian Jaya
Seram
Balikpapan
Sulawesi
INDONESIA
Ujung Pandang
Surabaya
Bali
Flores
Timor
Kupang
Darwin
Sumba
AUSTRALIA

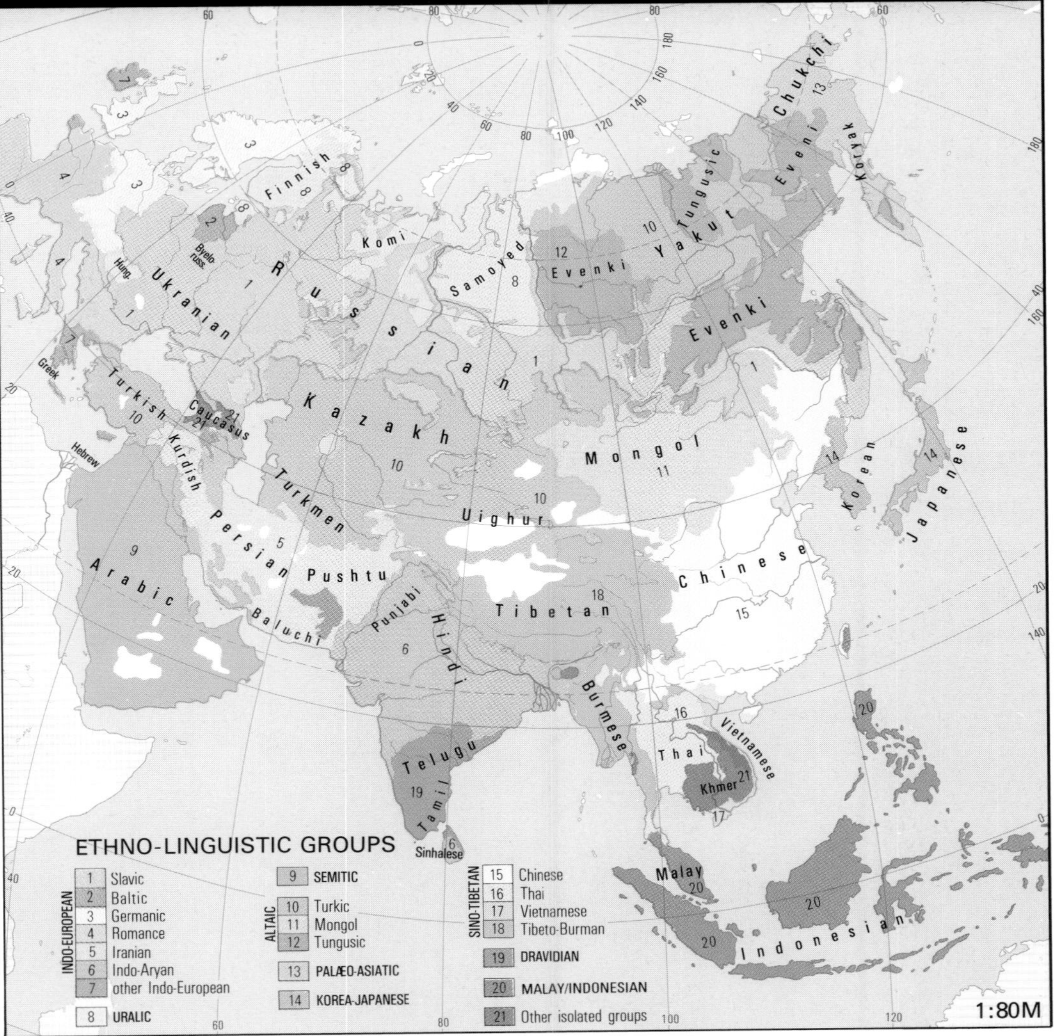

ETHNO-LINGUISTIC GROUPS
INDO-EUROPEAN
1 Slavic
2 Baltic
3 Germanic
4 Romance
5 Iranian
6 Indo-Aryan
7 other Indo-European
8 URALIC
9 SEMITIC
ALTAIC
10 Turkic
11 Mongol
12 Tungusic
13 PALÆO-ASIATIC
14 KOREA-JAPANESE
SINO-TIBETAN
15 Chinese
16 Thai
17 Vietnamese
18 Tibeto-Burman
19 DRAVIDIAN
20 MALAY/INDONESIAN
21 Other isolated groups
Finnish
Komi
Byelo russ
Hung
Ukranian
Russian
Samoyed
Evenki
Yakut
Tungusic
Eveni
Chukchi
Koryak
Greek
Turkish
Caucasus
Kurdish
Kazakh
Hebrew
Turkmen
Uighur
Mongol
Korean
Japanese
Persian
Pushtu
Arabic
Baluchi
Punjabi
Hindi
Tibetan
Chinese
Burmese
Thai
Vietnamese
Khmer
Telugu
Tamil
Sinhalese
Malay
Indonesian
1:80M

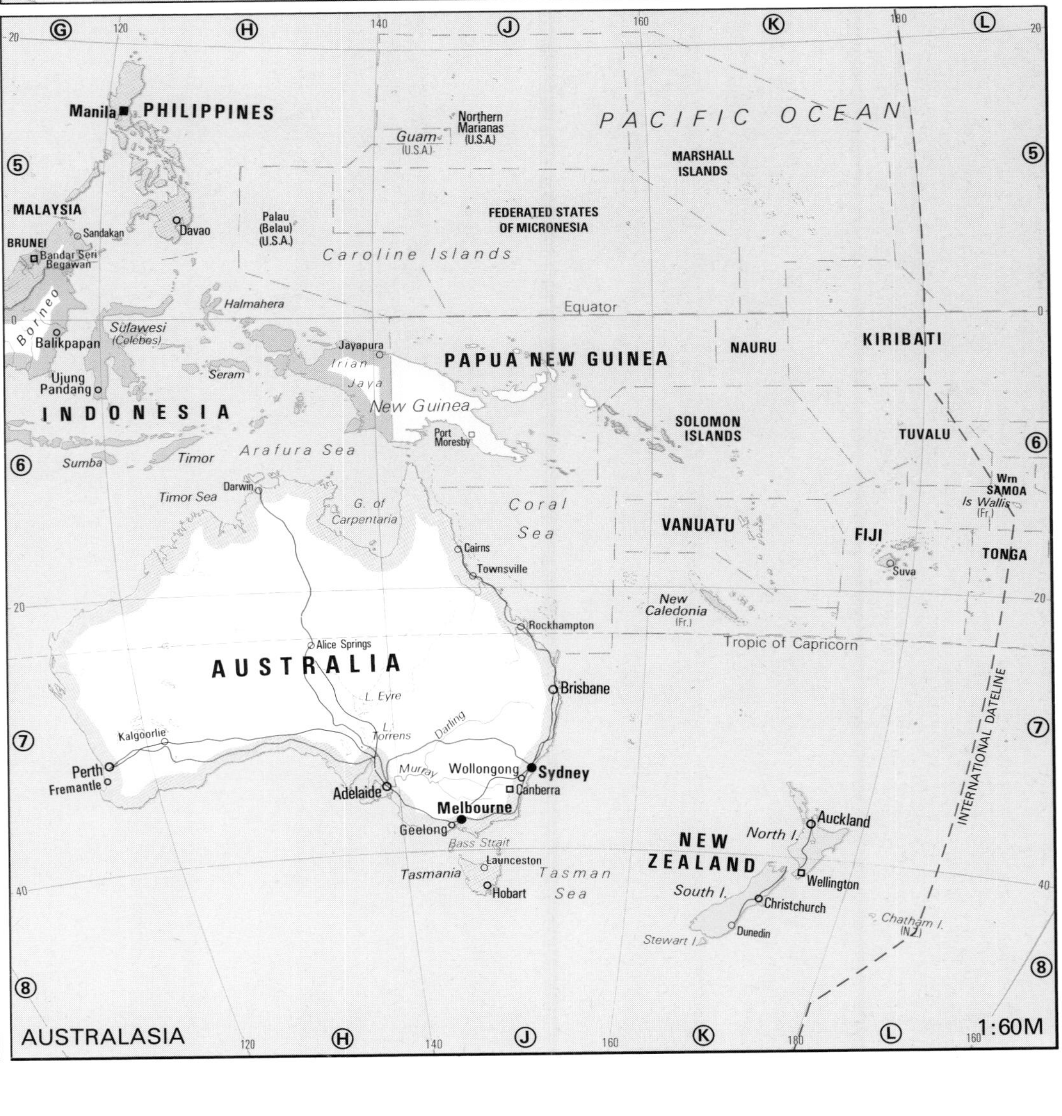

Manila
PHILIPPINES
PACIFIC OCEAN
Guam (U.S.A.)
Northern Marianas (U.S.A.)
MARSHALL ISLANDS
MALAYSIA
BRUNEI
Bandar Seri Begawan
Sandakan
Davao
Palau (Belau) (U.S.A.)
FEDERATED STATES OF MICRONESIA
Caroline Islands
Halmahera
Borneo
Equator
Balikpapan
Sulawesi (Celebes)
Jayapura
Irian Jaya
PAPUA NEW GUINEA
NAURU
KIRIBATI
Seram
Ujung Pandang
INDONESIA
New Guinea
Port Moresby
SOLOMON ISLANDS
TUVALU
Sumba
Timor
Arafura Sea
Darwin
Timor Sea
G. of Carpentaria
Coral Sea
VANUATU
FIJI
Wrn SAMOA
Is Wallis (Fr.)
TONGA
Cairns
Townsville
Suva
New Caledonia (Fr.)
Rockhampton
Alice Springs
Tropic of Capricorn
AUSTRALIA
L. Eyre
Brisbane
L. Torrens
Darling
Kalgoorlie
Perth
Fremantle
Murray
Wollongong
Sydney
Adelaide
Canberra
Melbourne
Geelong
Bass Strait
Launceston
Tasmania
Hobart
Tasman Sea
NEW ZEALAND
North I.
Auckland
Wellington
South I.
Christchurch
Dunedin
Stewart I.
Chatham I. (NZ)
INTERNATIONAL DATELINE
AUSTRALASIA
1:60M

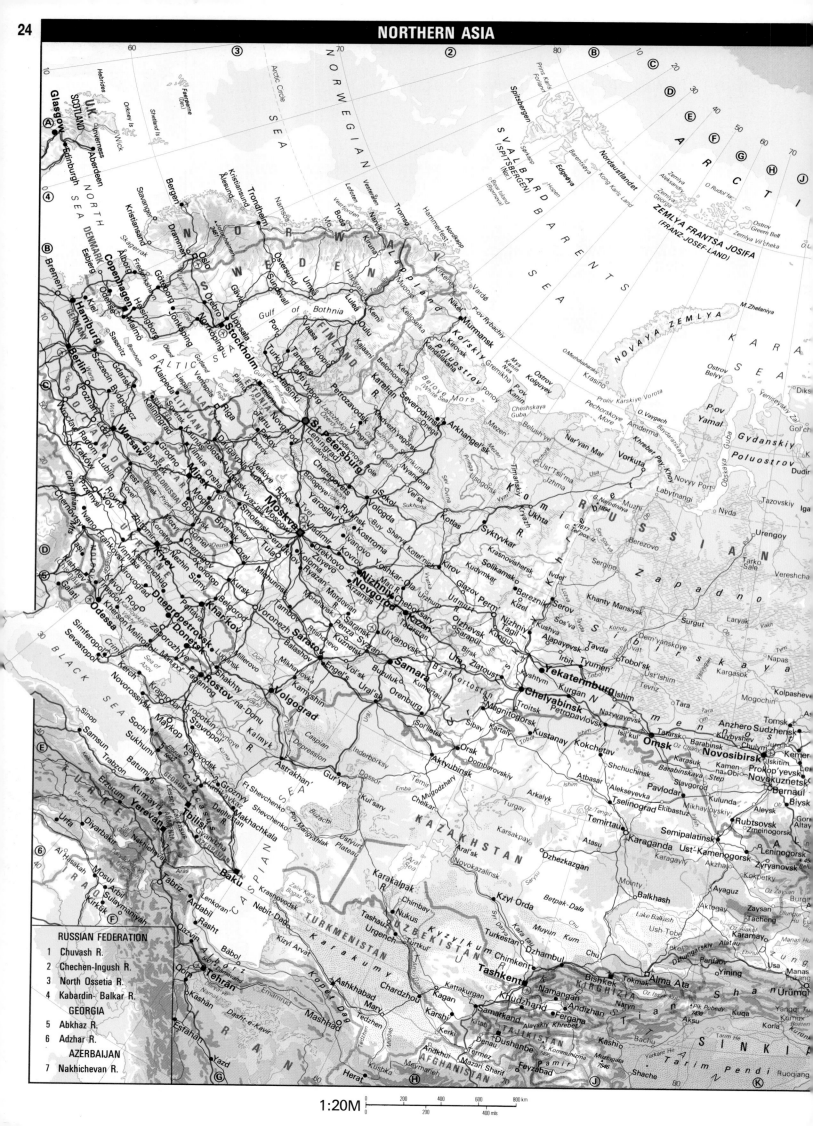

1:20M

Bering Str.
EAST SIBERIAN SEA
CHUKCHI SEA
BERING SEA
LAPTEV SEA
OCEAN
SEA OF OKHOTSK
SEA OF JAPAN
YELLOW SEA
Korea Bay
Bo Hai
Wrangel I.
NOVOSIBIRSKYE OSTROVA (NEW SIBERIAN ISLANDS)
SEVERNAYA ZEMLYA (NORTH LAND)
Ostrov Komsomolets
Ostrov Bol'shevik
Mys Chelyushin
Ostrov Kotel'nyy
Poluostrov Taymyr
Gory Byrranga
Gory Putorana
Chukotskiy Khrebet
Anadyrskoye Ploskogor'ye
Kolymskoye Nagor'ye
Koryakskoye Nagor'ye
KAMCHATKA
Sredinnyy Khrebet
Petropavlovsk-Kamchatskiy
Khrebet Cherskogo
Verkhoyanskiy Khrebet
Khrebet Orulgan
Khrebet Dzhugdzhur
Aldanskoye Nagor'ye
Stanovoy Khrebet
Patomskoye Nagor'ye
Severo Baykal'skoye Nagor'ye
Sredne Sibirskoye Ploskogor'ye
SIBERIA
RUSSIAN FEDERATION
SAKHALIN
Kuril Islands
HOKKAIDO
JAPAN
HONSHU
SHIKOKU
KYUSHU
NORTH KOREA
SOUTH KOREA
MANCHURIA
MONGOLIA
INNER MONGOLIA
GOBI
CHINA
Ordos
Yakutsk
Magadan
Okhotsk
Anadyr'
Pevek
Tiksi
Khatanga
Norilsk
Mirnyy
Lensk
Bratsk
Irkutsk
Angarsk
Ulan Ude
Chita
Krasnoyarsk
Kansk
Abakan
Kyzyl
Blagoveshchensk
Khabarovsk
Komsomol'sk-na-Amure
Vladivostok
Nakhodka
Yuzhno-Sakhalinsk
Sapporo
Asahikawa
Hakodate
Aomori
Sendai
Tōkyō
Yokohama
Nagoya
Kyōto
Kōbe
Ōsaka
Hiroshima
Fukuoka
Kita-Kyūshū
Nagasaki
Kagoshima
Ulaanbaatar
Harbin
Changchun
Jilin
Qiqihar
Shenyang
Fushun
Anshan
Dalian
P'yŏngyang
Seoul
Inch'ŏn
Taegu
Pusan
Kwangju
Beijing (Peking)
Tianjin (Tientsin)
Shijiazhuang
Jinan
Qingdao
Taiyuan
Baotou
Hohhot
Datong
Zhangjiakou
Yinchuan
Lanzhou
Xuzhou
Lianyungang
Hami
Yumen
GREAT WALL

RUSSIAN FEDERATION

KAMCHATKA

SEA OF OKHOTSK

Kuril'skiye Ostrova (Kuril Islands)

SAKHALIN

HOKKAIDŌ
Sapporo

SEA OF JAPAN

Tōkyō
Yokohama
Nagoya
Kyōto
Ōsaka
Kōbe
Kyūshū
Fukuoka

NORTH KOREA
P'yŏngyang

SOUTH KOREA
Seoul (Sŏul)
Inch'ŏn
Taegu
Pusan

Harbin
Changchun
Shenyang
Dalian
Beijing (Peking)
Tianjin (Tientsin)
Jinan

YELLOW SEA

Shanghai

EAST CHINA SEA

TAIWAN (FORMOSA)
Taipei
Kaohsiung

RYUKYU ISLANDS
Okinawa
Naha

Tropic of Cancer

PACIFIC OCEAN

MONGOLIA
Ulaanbaatar (Ulan Bator)

INNER MONGOLIA AUT. REG.

SINKIANG AUT. REG.
Ürümqi

Ordos

Lanzhou

C H I N A

Chengdu
Chongqing
Wuhan
Guangzhou (Canton)
HONG KONG (U.K.)
Macau (Port.)

Kowloon

TIBET AUT. REG.

BURMA

INDIA

Hanoi

R U S S I A N   F E D E R A T I O N
Novosibirsk
Krasnoyarsk
Irkutsk
Chita
Khabarovsk
Vladivostok
Komsomol'sk-na-Amure
Petropavlovsk-Kamchatskiy
Yuzhno-Sakhalinsk

1:20M

| 0 | 200 | 400 | 600 | 800 km |
| 0 | 200 | 400 | mls |

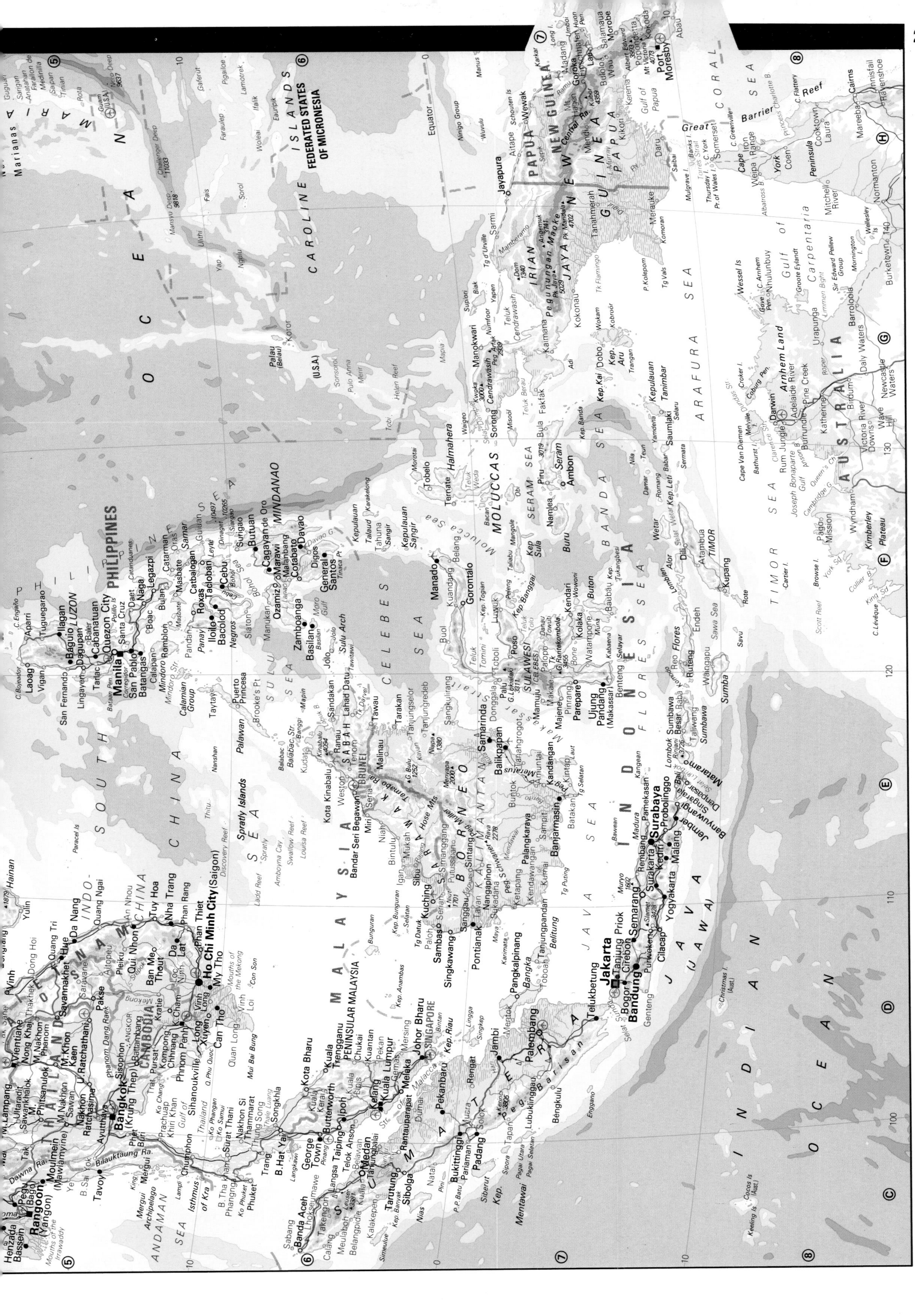

PHILIPPINES
LUZON
MINDANAO
Manila
Quezon City
Cebu
Davao
Zamboanga
Samar
Leyte
Negros
Panay
Mindoro
Palawan
SOUTH CHINA SEA
SULU SEA
CELEBES SEA
MOLUCCAS
SERAM SEA
BANDA SEA
FLORES SEA
JAVA SEA
ARAFURA SEA
TIMOR SEA
CORAL SEA
PACIFIC OCEAN
INDIAN OCEAN
ANDAMAN SEA
Gulf of Thailand
MALAYSIA
PENINSULAR MALAYSIA
SABAH
SARAWAK
BRUNEI
BORNEO
KALIMANTAN
INDONESIA
SULAWESI (CELEBES)
JAVA (JAWA)
SUMATERA
IRIAN JAYA
PAPUA NEW GUINEA
NEW GUINEA
AUSTRALIA
THAILAND
CAMBODIA
VIETNAM
INDOCHINA
FEDERATED STATES OF MICRONESIA
CAROLINE ISLANDS
Marianas
Guam (U.S.A.)
Palau (Belau) (U.S.A.)
Bangkok (Krung Thep)
Rangoon (Yangon)
Ho Chi Minh City (Saigon)
Phnom Penh
Vientiane
Kuala Lumpur
SINGAPORE
Jakarta
Bandung
Surabaya
Semarang
Yogyakarta
Medan
Palembang
Padang
Pekanbaru
Jambi
Pontianak
Kuching
Banjarmasin
Balikpapan
Samarinda
Kota Kinabalu
Bandar Seri Begawan
Ujung Pandang (Makassar)
Manado
Ambon
Jayapura
Port Moresby
Lae
Madang
Wewak
Darwin
Cairns
Equator
Timor
Kupang
Flores
Sumba
Sumbawa
Lombok
Bali
Halmahera
Seram
Buru
Gulf of Carpentaria
Gulf of Papua
Great Barrier Reef
Cape York Peninsula
Arnhem Land
Hainan
Mouths of the Mekong
Spratly Islands
Christmas I. (Aust.)
Cocos Is (Aust.)
Mentawai
Bangka
Belitung
Kep. Riau
Strait of Malacca

1:5M

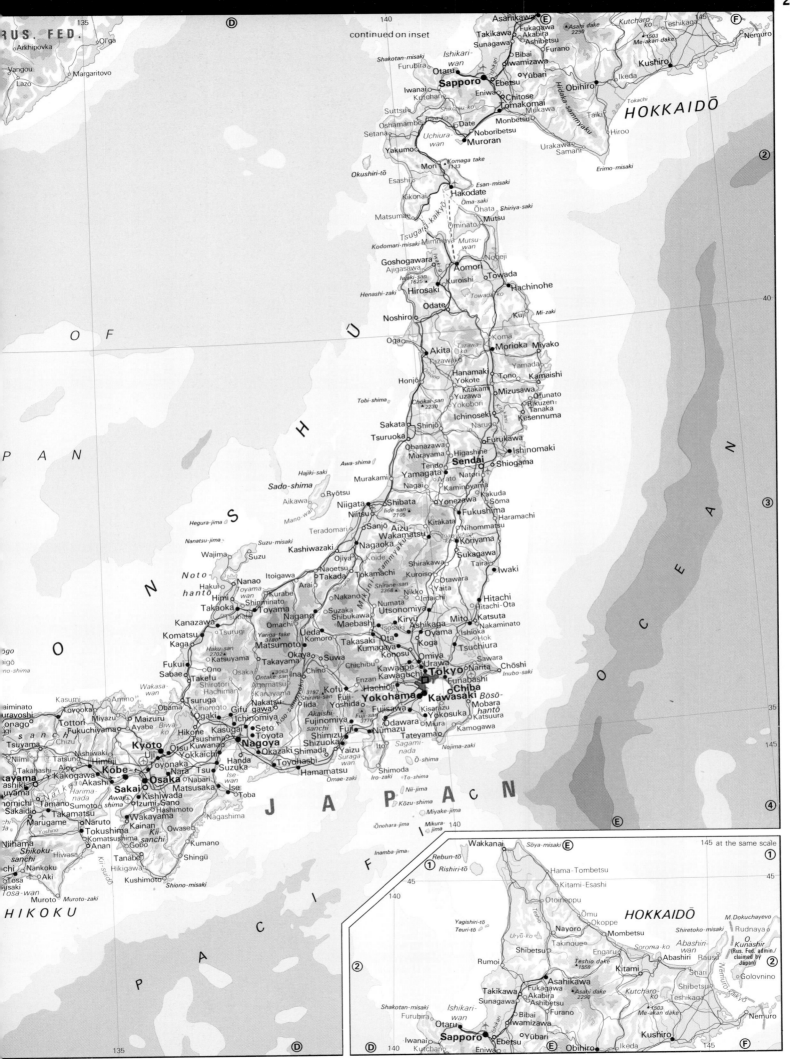

RUS. FED.
Arkhipovka
Vangou
Lazo
Margaritovo
Ol'ga

continued on inset

Asahikawa
Takikawa
Sunagawa
Fukagawa
Akabira
Ashibetsu
Furano
Bibai
Iwamizawa
Yubari
Chitose
Eniwa
Ebetsu
Sapporo
Iwanai
Kutchan
Suttsu
Shikotsu-ko
Tomakomai
Mukawa
Oshamambe
Setana
Uchiura-wan
Date
Monbetsu
Noboribetsu
Muroran
Yakumo
Komaga take
1133
Mori
Okushiri-tō
Esashi
Hakodate
Kikonai
Matsumae
Ōma-saki
Ōhata
Shiriya-saki
Mutsu
Ōminato
Tsugaru-kaikyō
Kodomari-misaki
Mimmaya
Mutsu-wan
Nobeji
Goshogawara
Ajigasawa
Iwaki-san
1625
Aomori
Towada
Hirosaki
Kuroishi
Hachinohe
Henashi-zaki
Towada-ko
Odate
Kuji
Mi-zaki
Noshiro
Oga
Koma
Akita
Tazawa-ko
Morioka
Miyako
Tazawako
Yamada
Hanamaki
Kamaishi
Honjō
Yokote
Kitakami
Tobi-shima
Yuzawa
Mizusawa
Ōfunato
Chokai-san
Yokobori
Rikuzen
2230
Ichinoseki
Tanaka
Kesennuma
Sakata
Shinjō
Tsuruoka
Naruto
Obanazawa
Furukawa
Murayama
Higashine
Ishinomaki
Awa-shima
Tendo
Shiogama
Murakami
Yamagata
Sendai
Natori
Hajiki-saki
Kaminoyama
Sado-shima
Nagai
Aikawa
Yonezawa
Kakuda
Ryōtsu
Sōma
Shibata
Fukushima
Niigata
Haramachi
Niitsu
Iide san
Kitakata
2105
Nihommatsu
Teradomari
Sanjō
Aizu
Kōriyama
Wakamatsu
Nagaoka
Koide
Sukagawa
Ojiya
Shirakawa
Kuroiso
Taira
Kashiwazaki
Naoetsu
Tokamachi
Iwaki
Itoigawa
Takada
Mikuni sammyaku
Shirane-san
Otawara
Yaita
Arai
Nakano
2368
Nikko
Hitachi
Nanatsu-jima
Numata
Imaichi
Hitachi-Ota
Haku-san
Suzu
Utsonomiya
Katsuta
Nanao
Shimminato
Toyama
Suzaka
Shibukawa
Mito
Nakaminato
Himi
Toyama-wan
Nagano
Maebashi
Oyama
Ishioka
Takaoka
Kurabe
Omachi
Kiryū
Ashikaga
Hok
Kanazawa
Tsubata
Yariga-take
Ueda
Komoro
Ota
Koga
Tsuchiura
Komatsu
Tsurugi
3180
Matsumoto
Takasaki
Konosu
Omiya
Sawara
Kaga
Haku-san
Okaya
Kumagaya
Chichibu
Kawagoe
Narita
Chōshi
Fukui
2702
Suwa
Urawa
Inubo-saki
Sabae
Ono
Takayama
Ina
Kawaguchi
Tokyo
Takefu
Shirotori
Nakatsu-
Enzan
Kawasaki
Funabashi
Hachiman
gawa
Kofu
Hachioji
Chiba
Tsuruga
Kinomoto
Gifu
3063
Fuji-
Yokohama
Kawasaki
Bōsō-
Obama
Ontake-san
Kanayama
Yoshida
Kisarazu
Mobara
Wakasa-
gawa
3192
Fuji-san
Fujisawa
Yokosuka
hantō
Kasumi
wan
Ichinomiya
Akaishi
3776
Odawara
Miura
Katsuura
Maizuru
Hikone
sanchi
Fujinomiya
Numazu
Tateyama
Tottori
Ayabe
Ōtsu
Kuwana
Iida
Fuji
Kamogawa
Fukuchiyama
Seto
Kiso
Shimizu
Toyota
Yaizu
Ito
Sagami-
Tsuyama
Chizu
Biwa-
Yokkaichi
Shimada
Shizuoka
nada
sanchi
Kyōto
ko
Nagoya
Okazaki
Shimada
Nojima-zaki
Miyazu
Nabari
Toyohashi
Nishiwaki
Toyonaka
Nara
Suzuka
Hamamatsu
Ō-shima
Himeji
Kobe
Handa
Shimoda
Takasago
Uji
Matsusaka
Omae-zaki
Iro-zaki
To-shima
Kakogawa
Akashi
Izumi-Sano
Ise
Suragu
Nii-jima
kayama
Osaka
Nabari
wan
Toba
Sakai
Kishiwada
Awaji-
Ise-
Shimoda
ashiku
Harima-
shima
wan
nomichi
nada
Izumi
Sumoto
Matsusaka
Kōzu-shima
Tamano
Hashimoto
Miyake-jima
Sakaido
Wakayama
Naruto
Kainan
Nagashima
Niihama
Tokushima
Kii
Ōnohara-jima
Mikura-
chi
Anan
Komatsushima
Gobo
Kumano
sanchi
jima
Tosa
Aki
Hiwasa
Yoshino
Kushimoto
Inamba-jima
HIKOKU
Nankoku
Tanabe
Shingū
Muroto
Muroto-zaki
Shiono-misaki

O F
O
F
P
A
N
O
F
O
N
O
S
H
Ū

J A P A N
P A C I F I C

O C E A N

HOKKAIDŌ
Kushiro
Ikeda
Obihiro
Hidaka-sammyaku
Taiki
Hiroo
Urakawa
Samani
Tokachi
Erimo-misaki

Kutcharo-ko
Teshikaga
Me-akan-dake
1503
2290
Asahi dake
Nemuro

(Inset map, lower right)

Wakkanai
Sōya-misaki
145 at the same scale
Rebun-tō
Rishiri-tō
Hama-Tombetsu
Kitami-Esashi
Yagishiri-tō
Ōmu
Okoppe
Teuri-tō
Nayoro
Mombetsu
Shiretoko-misaki
Rudnaya
Uryū-ko
Okoppe
M. Dokuchayevo
Rumoi
Takinoue
Engaru
Soroma-ko
Abashiri-
O.
Kunashir
wan
(Rus. Fed. admin./
Teshio dake
Kitami
Abashiri
claimed by Japan)
Takikawa
1558
Fukagawa
Shari
Golovnino
Asahikawa
Akabira
Asahi dake
Kutcharo-
Sunagawa
Ashibetsu
2290
ko
Shibetsu
Shakotan-misaki
Furano
Me-akan-dake
Teshikaga
Furubira
Bibai
Iwamizawa
1503
Ishikari-
Yubari
Nemuro
wan
Iwanai
Otaru
Bibai
Sapporo
Ebetsu
Ishikari
Iwanai
Eniwa
Obihiro
Kushiro
Kutchan

RUS. FED.
135
140
145
D
E
F
40
35
145
45
1
2
3
4

1:10M

0 100 200 300 400 km

0 100 200 mls

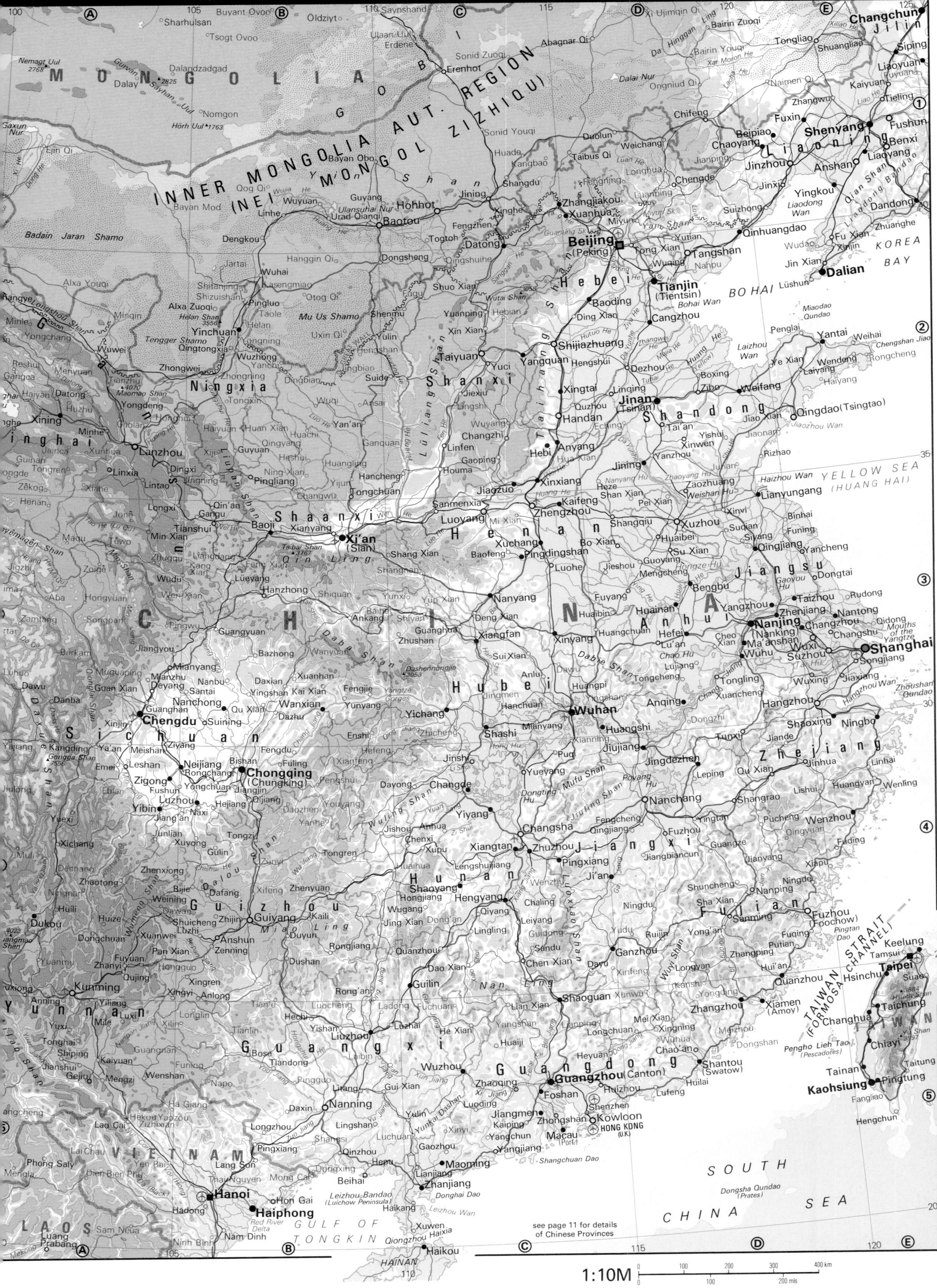

MONGOLIA

GOBI

INNER MONGOLIA AUT. REGION (NEI MONGOL ZIZHIQU)

Buyant Ovoo
Sharhulsan
Öldziyt
Tsogt Ovoo
Saynshand
Ulaan Uul
Erdene
Abagnar Qi
Xi Ujimqin Qi
Bairin Zuoqi
Da Hinggan Ling
Bairin Youqi
Xar Moron He
Tongliao
Shuangliao
Changchun
Jilin
Siping
Liaoyuan

Nemegt Uul 2768
Dalay
Suyhan-Uul
Nomgon
Hörh Uul 1763
Erenhot
Sonid Zuoqi
Sonid Youqi
Dalai Nur
Naimen Qi
Kaiyuan
Tieling
Fuyuan

Badain Jaran Shamo
Ejin Qi
Dalandzadgad
Qog alt
Wujia
Bayan Bod
Bayan Obo
Guyang
Hohhot
Jining
Shangdu
Huade
Kangbao
Taibus Qi
Longhua
Chifeng
Jianping
Ningcheng
Chengde
Beipiao
Chaoyang
Fuxin
Shenyang
Fushun
Benxi
Qian Shan

Baotou
Linhe
Wuyuan
Urad Qianqi
Ulansuhai Nur
Dengkou
Dongsheng
Fengzhen
Xinghe
Zhangjiakou
Xuanhua
Weichang
Luanping
Miyun
Guanting Sk
Beijing (Peking)
Tong Xian
Tangshan
Nanpu
Qinhuangdao
Wudao
Fu Xian
Yingkou
Liaoyang
Anshan
Liaodong Bandao
Dandong
Zhuanghe

Alxa Youqi
Hanggin Qi
Otog Qi
Togtoh
Qingshuihe
Datong
Shuo Xian
Yanqing
Hebian
Yang
Ding Xian
Baoding
Tianjin (Tientsin)
Wuqing
Bohai Wan
Cangzhou
Jin Xian
Lüshun
Dalian
KOREA BAY
BO HAI

Shitanjing
Shizuishan
Pingluo
Taole
Shenmu
Yulin
Hengshan
Jingbian
Suide
Xin Xian
Yuanping
Taiyuan
Yuci
Hengshui
Shijiazhuang
Yangquan
Xingtai
Linqing
Dezhou
Zhangwei
Boxing
Zibo
Weifang
Laizhou Wan
Yantai
Weihai
Chengshan Jiao
Rongcheng
Laiyang
Haiyang
Qingdao (Tsingtao)

Yinchuan
Helan Shan
Ningning
Wuzhong
Yanchi
Dingbian
Ansai
Yan'an
Jiexiu
Lingsh
Changzhi
Hebi
Anyang
Handan
Jinan (Tsinan)
Tai'an
Yishui
Xinwen
Jiaonan
Jiaozhou Wan

Ningxia
Zhongning
Qingtongxia
Zhongwei
Tongxin
Wuqi
Huanglin
Linfen
Houma
Hua Xian
Jining
Yanzhou
Weishan Hu
Rizhao
Haizhou Wan
YELLOW SEA (HUANG HAI)

Wuwei
Huan Xian
Huachi
Ganquan
Yijun
Hancheng
Gaoping
Jiaozuo
Xinxiang
Kaifeng
Heze
Shan Xian
Pei Xian
Xuzhou
Xinyi
Binhai
Lianyungang

Shaanxi
Baoji
Xianyang
Xi'an (Sian)
Qin Ling
Sanmenxia
Luoyang
Mi Xian
Zhengzhou
Shangqiu
Huaibei
Su Xian
Sudian
Siyang
Qingjiang
Yancheng
Funing

Henan
Xuchang
Baofeng
Pingdingshan
Luohe
Jieshou
Guoyang
Mengcheng
Bengbu
Gaoyou Hu
Gaoyou
Dongtai
Rudong

Shang Xian
Shangnan
Deng Xian
Nanyang
Fuyang
Huainan
Jiangsu
Yangzhou
Taizhou

Hanzhong
Shiquan
Yunxi
Yun Xian
Guanghua
Xiangfan
Sui Xian
Xinyang
Huangchuan
Anlu
Huanggang
Hefei
Lu'an
Chao Hu
Cheo Xian
Ma'anshan
Nanjing (Nanking)
Zhenjiang
Changzhou
Changshu
Wuxi
Suzhou
Wuxing
Shanghai
Songjiang
Jiaxing Wan
Zhoushan Qundao

Sichuan
Chengdu
Mianyang
Deyang
Nanbu
Daxian
Wanxian
Fengjie
Yunyang
Yichang
Shashi
Mianyang
Jingmen
Hanchuan
Wuhan
Huangshi
Anqing
Tongcheng
Wuhu
Tongling
Xuancheng
Hangzhou
Shaoxing
Ningbo

Mouths of the Yangtze
Qidong

Neijiang
Rongchang
Bishan
Chongqing (Chungking)
Fuling
Enshi
Hefeng
Jinshi
Li Shui
Pugi
Jiujiang
Jingdezhen
Leping
Qu Xian
Jinhua
Linhai
Huangyan
Wenling

Zigong
Yibin
Luzhou
Hejiang
Jiangjin
Qijiang
Pengshui
Dayong
Changde
Yueyang
Dongting Hu
Nanchang
Shangrao
Yingtan
Wenzhou
Fuding

Yunnan
Kunming
Xichang
Zhenxiong
Zhaotong
Bijie
Dafang
Xifeng
Zhenyuan
Tongren
Huaihua
Chenxi
Xupu
Yiyang
Changsha
Xiangtan
Zhuzhou
Jiangxi
Ji'an
Jianbiancun
Nanping
Ningde

Guizhou
Guiyang
Kaili
Duyun
Anshun
Zhenning
Rongjiang
Shaoyang
Hongjiang
Wugang
Jing Xian
Dong'an
Hunan
Hengyang
Qiyang
Leiyang
Lingling
Guidong
Sandu
Yudu
Ruijin
Yong'an
Sanming
Fuzhou (Foochow)
Pingtan Dao

Weining
Huize
Shuicheng
Zhijin
Lzhi
Quanzhou
Chen Xian
Dayu
Xinfeng
Yong'an
Zhangping
Yongchun
Putian
Quanzhou

Dao Xian
Guilin
Lian Xian
Shaoguan
Xunwu
Wuyi Shan
Longyan
Hui'an
Xiamen (Amoy)

Nan Ling

STRAIT (FORMOSA CHANNEL)
TAIWAN
Keelung
Tamsui
Taipei
Hsinchu
Suao

Gulin
Junlian
Xuyong
Tongzi
Zunyi
Dafang

Lianjiang
Liuzhou
He Xian
Huaiji
Mei Xian
Xingning
Wuhua
Meizhou
Changhua
Chiayi
Taichung

Guangxi
Nanning
Guigang
Gui Xian
Yulin
Luchuan
Qinzhou
Guangdong
Guangzhou (Canton)
Foshan
Shenzhen
Zhongshan
Kowloon
HONG KONG (U.K.)
Macau (Port.)
Shantou (Swatow)
Chao'an
Lufeng

Tainan
Kaohsiung
Pingtung
Fangliao
Hengchun

VIETNAM
LAOS
Hanoi
Haiphong
Red River Delta
Nam Dinh
Ninh Binh
Lang Son
Mong Cai
Beihai
Zhanjiang
Leizhou Bandao (Luichow Peninsula)
Donghai Dao
Haikou
HAINAN
Qiongshan Haixia

GULF OF TONGKIN
SOUTH CHINA SEA
Dongsha Qundao (Prates)
Shangchuan Dao

Zhaoqing
Jiangmen
Kaiping
Xinyi
Yangchun
Gaozhou
Maoming
Yangjiang

see page 11 for details of Chinese Provinces

1:10M

0 100 200 300 400 km
0 100 200 mls

BORNEO

Tajungselor
Tanjungredeb
Kelolokan
Kayal
Makassar Strait
Samarinda
Balikpapan
Banjarmasin
Kintap
Tg Selatan
Tanjung
Donggala
Palu
Poso
Toboli
Tolitoli
Gorontalo
Manado
Minahassa Peninsula
Teluk Tomini
Kep. Togian
Luwuk
Peleng
Kep. Banggai
Kep. Sula
Teluk Bone
Watampone
Pare-pare
Palopo
Kendari
Buton
Buru
SULAWESI (CELEBES)
Ujung Pandang (Makassar)
Bonthain
Kabaena
Selayar
Kep. Takabonerate
Kangean
Bali
Lombok
Mataram
Denpasar
Sumbawa
Raba
Sumba
Waingapu
Flores
Ende
Ruteng
Reo
Lomblen
Alor
Timor
Dili
Kupang
Rote
Savu
Lembata

MOLUCCAS
Morotai
Tubelo
Ternate
Halmahera
Belang
Molucca Sea
Weda
Teluk Weda
Waigeo
Kep. Asia
Kep. Ayu
Mapia
Selat Dampier
Sorong
Misool
Salawati
Batanta
Cendrawasih
Numfoor
Biak
Yapen
Manokwari
Teluk Cendrawasih
Sarmi
Jayapura

Seram Sea
Obi
Seram
Piru
Bula
Ambon (Amboina)
Namlea
Banda Sea
Kep. Gorong
Kep. Banda
Kep. Kai
Kep. Aru
Dobo
Kep. Tanimbar
Kep. Babar
Kep. Damar
Sermata
Kep. Leti
Wetar
Roma

IRIAN JAYA
INDONESIA
Pegunungan Maoke
Pk. Jaya 5029
Faktak
Kaimana
Kokonau
Tanahmerah
Dolak
Digul
Merauke
Tg Vals
Daru

PAPUA NEW GUINEA
Ninigo Is
Hermit Is
Admiralty Is
Mussau
Saint Matthias Group
New Hanover
Kavieng
Bismarck Archipelago
Manam
Bismarck Sea
Wewak
Aitape
Schouten Is
Sepik
Central Ra
Madang
Mt Wilhelm 4694
Mt Hagen
Mendi
Goroka
Mt Bismarck
Lae
Morobe
Bulolo
Kikori
Kerema
Gulf of Papua
Owen Stanley Ra
Port Moresby
Kupiano
Samarai
Popondetta
Kokoda
D Entrecasteaux Is
Trobriand Is
Mt St Mary 3667

Torres Strait
C. York
Somerset
Pr. of Wales I.
Saibai I.

INDIAN OCEAN
Java Trench

Timor Sea
Cartier I.
Scott Reef
C. Londonderry
Melville I.
Bathurst I.
Van Diemen G.
Clarence Str.
Darwin
Rum Jungle
Adelaide River
Burrundie
Pine Creek
Katherine
Daly
Roper
Groote Eylandt
Limmen Bight
Sir Edward Pellew Group
Cobourg Pen
Croker I.
Arnhem Land
C. Arnhem
Nhulunbuy
Wessel Is
Gulf of Carpentaria
Mornington
Wellesley Is

Arafura Sea

Cape York Peninsula
Weipa
Coen
Iron Range
C. Grenville
Princess Charlotte B.
Willis Group
Laura
Cooktown
Mitchell River
Mitchell
Normanton
Croydon
Forsayth
Gilbert
Palm Is
Ingham
Innisfail
Mt Bartle Frere 1611
Cairns
Ravenshoe
Coringa
Townsville
Charters Towers
Ayr
Bowen
Proserpine
Collinsville
Mackay
Sarina
Richmond
Hughenden
Burketown
Camooweal
Mount Isa
Cloncurry
Dajarra
Selwyn
Winton
QUEENSLAND
Barcaldine
Mount Morgan
Blackall
Rockhampton
Gladstone
Maryborough
Longreach
Emerald
Clermont
Windorah
Diamantina
Thomson
Barcoo
Charleville
Quilpie
Roma
Miles
Dalby
Toowoomba
Goondiwindi
St George
Cunnamulla
Warrego
Paroo

NORTHERN TERRITORY
Darwin
Pago Mission
Wyndham
Kununurra
L. Argyle
Victoria River Downs
Wave Hill
Newcastle Waters
Daly Waters
Birdum
Borroloola
Powell Creek
Barkly Tableland
Tennant Creek
Barrow Creek
Macdonnell Ranges
Mt Ziel 1510
Alice Springs
Finke
Simpson Desert
Petermann Ra
Mt Woodroffe 1440
Musgrave Ra
Mt Aloysius 887
Tomkinson Ra
Oodnadatta
Lake Eyre Basin
Birdsville
L. Eyre
Eyre Creek
Georgina
Diamantina

WESTERN AUSTRALIA
Broome
Lagrange
Eighty Mile Beach
Port Hedland
Shay Gap
De Grey
Marble Bar
Monte Bello Is
Dampier
Barrow I.
Roebourne
Fortescue
Nullagine
Wittenoom
Hamersley Ra
Mt Bruce 1226
Paraburdoo
Newman
Onslow
North West C.
Ashburton
Mt Augustus
Gibson Desert
L. Disappointment
I. Mackay
Gascoyne
Carnarvon
Shark B.
Dirk Hartog I.
Lyons
Barlee Ra
McLeod
L. Carnegie
Great Sandy Desert
Kimberley Plateau
Mt Ord 936
King Leopold Ra
Fitzroy Crossing
Hall's Creek
Sturt Ck
Derby
Collier B.
C. Lévêque
King Sound
Great Victoria Desert
L. Wells
Sandstone
Wiluna
Meekatharra
Cue
Mt Magnet
Leonora
Leinster
Houtman Abrolhos
Geraldton
Dongara
Northampton
Mullewa
Mt Barlee
L. Moore
Moora
Bullfinch
Southern Cross
Kalgoorlie
Coolgardie
Norseman
Rawlinna
Forrest
Nullarbor Plain
Ooldea
Eyre
Esperance
C. Pasley
Arch. of the Recherche
Perth
Fremantle
Pinjarra
Collie
Bunbury
C. Naturaliste
Busselton
Augusta
C. Leeuwin
Manjimup
Narrogin
Wagin
Katanning
Bluff Knoll 1710
C. Knob
Albany
Goomalling
Meredin
Corrigin
Northam
Bencubbin

SOUTH AUSTRALIA
Coober Pedy
Marree
Leigh Ck
L. Frome
Tarcoola
Woomera
L. Everard
Penong
St Mary Pk 1189
L. Torrens
Ceduna
L. Gairdner
Gawler Ranges
Iron Knob
Quorn
Port Augusta
Peterborough
Port Pirie
Whyalla
Wallaroo
Port Lincoln
Eyre Pen
Spencer Gulf
Flinders I.
Port Lincoln
Kangaroo I.
Investigator Str.
Elizabeth
Adelaide
Murray Bridge
Victor Harbour
Kingston
Naracoorte
Mount Gambier
Port MacDonnell
Great Australian Bight

NEW SOUTH WALES
Broken Hill
Milparinka
Wilcannia
Menindee
Ivanhoe
Bourke
Cobar
Darling
Walgett
Narrabri
Moree
Nyngan
Dubbo
Griffith
Hay
Balranald
Deniliquin
Wagga Wagga
Albury
Orange
Bathurst
Lithgow
Cessnock
Maitland
Newcastle
Gosford
Sydney
Wollongong
Goulburn
Canberra
A.C.T.
Mt Kosciusko 2230
Tamworth
Armidale
Glen Innes
Moree
Narrabri

VICTORIA
Mildura
Swan Hill
Echuca
Shepparton
Bendigo
Ballarat
Geelong
Melbourne
Colac
Morwell
Sale
Bairnsdale
Orbost
C. Howe
Horsham
Hamilton
Warrnambool
Portland
Port Fairy
Wonthaggi
Wilson's Prom.
Ararat
Murray

Bass Strait
King I.
Furneaux Group
Flinders I.
C. Barren

TASMANIA
C. Grim
Smithton
Burnie
Devonport
Launceston
Queenstown
Mt Ossa
St Mary's
Hobart
Geeveston
South West C.
South East C.

1:20M

0   200   400   600   800 km
0   200   400 mls

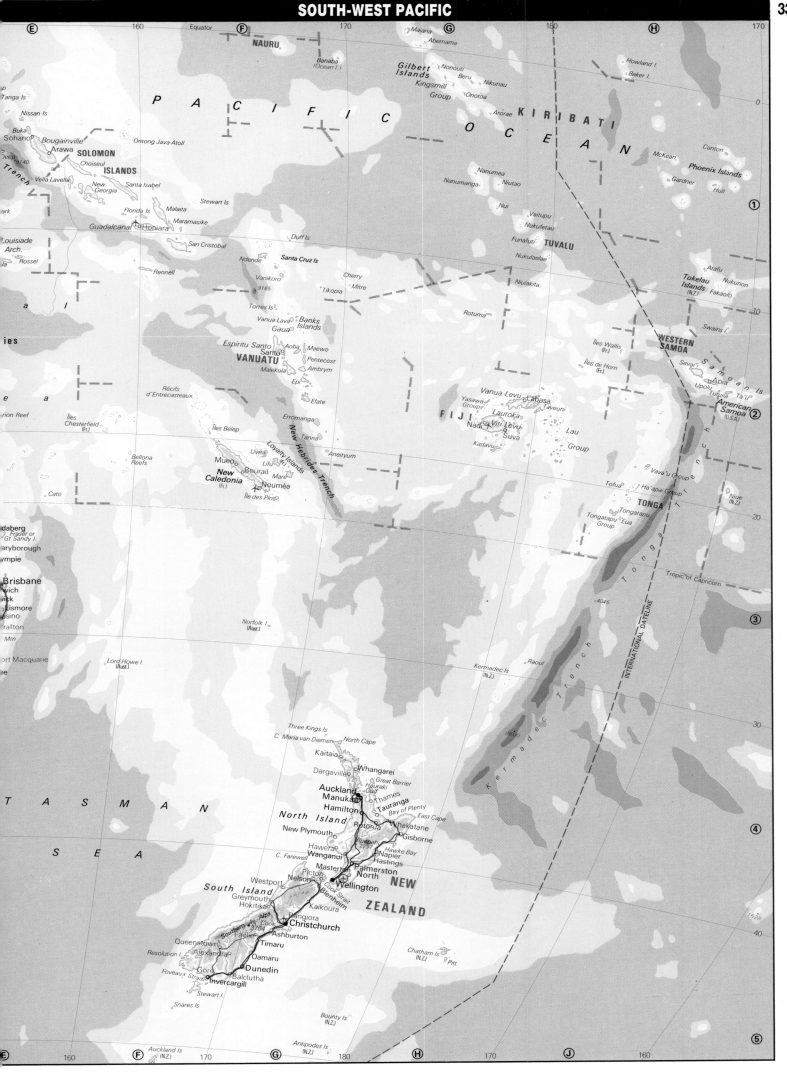

E 160 Equator F 170 G 180 H 170

NAURU

Banaba
(Ocean I.)

Maiana
Abemama

Gilbert
Islands
Kingsmill
Group

Nonouti
Beru
Nikunau
Onotoa

Howland I.
Baker I.

0

Tanga Is

Buka
Sohano
Arawa
SOLOMON
ISLANDS
Choiseul
Santa Isabel
Vella Lavella
New
Georgia
Florida Is
Malaita
Guadalcanal
Honiara
Maramasike
San Cristobal

Ontong Java Atoll

P   A   C   I   F   I   C

O   C   E   A   N

K   I   R   I   B   A   T   I

Arorae

McKean
Canton
Phoenix Islands
Gardner
Hull

①

Nanumea
Niutao
Nanumanga

Louisiade
Arch.

Rossel

Duff Is

Ndende
Santa Cruz Is

Vanikoro
9165

Cherry
Mitre

Nui
Vaitupu
Nukufetau

Funafuti TUVALU

Nukulaelae

Niulakita

Atafu
Nukunon
Tokelau
Islands
(N.Z.)
Fakaofo

⑩ 10

Swains I.

Torres Is
Tikopia

Rotuma

Îles Wallis
(Fr.)
Îles de Horn
(Fr.)

WESTERN
SAMOA

Savai'i
Apia
Upolu
Ta'u
Tutuila

American
Samoa
(U.S.A)

②

rion Reef

Îles
Chesterfield
(Fr.)

Bellona
Reefs

Cato

Vanua Lava
Gaua
Banks
Islands

Espiritu Santo
Santo
Aoba
Maewo
Pentecost
Ambrym
VANUATU
Malekula
Epi
Efate
Erromanga
Tanna
Aneityum

Récifs
d'Entrecasteaux

Îles Bélep

Uvéa
Lifu
Maré
Loyalty Islands

Mueo
Bourail
New
Caledonia
(Fr.)
Nouméa
Île des Pins

New Hebrides Trench

F   I   J   I

Yasawa
Group
Lautoka
Nadi
Viti Levu
Suva
Kadavu

Vanua Levu Labasa
Taveuni

Lau
Group

Vava'u Group

Tofua
Ha'apai Group

TONGA
Tongatapu
Tongatapu 'Eua
Group

Niue
(N.Z.)

③

Tropic of Capricorn

daberg
Fraser or
Gt Sandy I.
aryborough
ympie

Brisbane
wich
wick
Lismore
asino
rafton
Mtn

rt Macquarie
ee

Norfolk I.
(Aust.)

Lord Howe I.
(Aust.)

4045

Kermadec Trench

Tonga Trench

INTERNATIONAL DATELINE

③

Kermadec Is
(N.Z.)

Raoul

Three Kings Is
C. Maria van Diemen
North Cape

Kaitaia
Whangarei
Dargaville
Great Barrier
Auckland
Hauraki
Gulf
Thames
Manukau
Hamilton
Tauranga
Bay of Plenty
East Cape
North Island
Rotorua
Whakatane
New Plymouth
Ruapehu
2797
Gisborne
Hawera
Wanganui
Hawke Bay
Napier
C. Farewell
Masterton
Hastings
Picton
Palmerston
Nelson
North
Westport
Wellington
Greymouth
Blenheim
Cook Strait
Hokitika
Kaikoura
Alps
Rangiora
Southern Alps Cook
3764
Christchurch
Fairlie
Ashburton
Queenstown
Timaru
Resolution I.
Alexandra
Oamaru
Gore
Dunedin
Foveaux Strait
Balclutha
Invercargill
Stewart I.

T A S M A N

S E A

NEW

ZEALAND

Chatham Is
(N.Z.)
Pitt

④

30

40

1528

Snares Is

Bounty Is
(N.Z.)

Antipodes Is
(N.Z.)

⑤

E 160 F Auckland Is (N.Z.) 170 G 180 H 170 J 160

Auckland Is
(N.Z.)

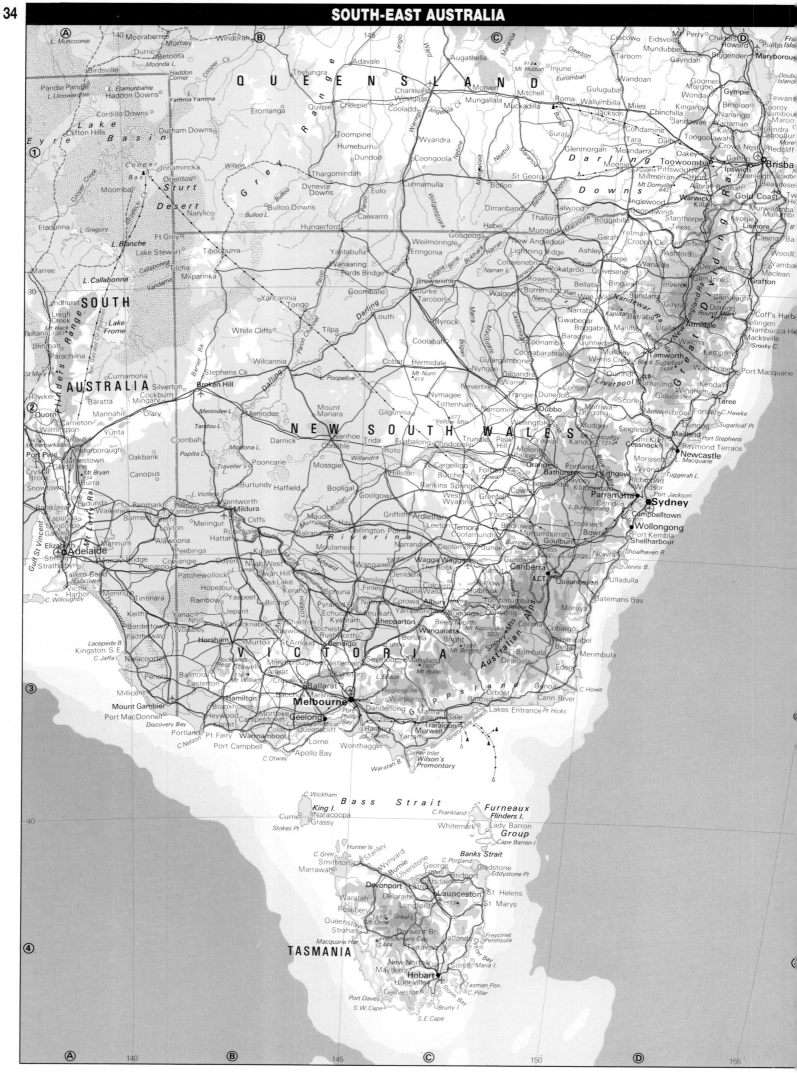

QUEENSLAND

SOUTH

AUSTRALIA

NEW SOUTH WALES

VICTORIA

Melbourne

Bass Strait

Furneaux Flinders I. Group

TASMANIA

Hobart

1:7.5M   100   200   300 km   50   100   150 mls

Three Kings Is
C. Maria
van Diemen
North
Cape
Rangaunu B.
Ninety Mile Beach
Doubtless B.

Ahipara B.
Tauroa Pt
Kaitaia
Bay of Islands
C.Brett
Russell
Kaikohe
Kawakawa
Hokianga Har.
Hikurangi
Hen & Chickens Is
Whangarei
Bream
B.
Dargaville
Little
Barrier I.
C.Colville
Great Barrier I.

Wellsford
Kaipara Har.
Hauraki
Gulf
Mercury Is
Mercury Bay
Manly
Takapuna
Coromandel
Peninsula
Auckland
Papatoetoe
Manukau
Papakura
Mayor I.
Pukekohe
Thames
Waiuku
Paeroa
Waihi

NORTH
Huntly
Te Aroha
Matakana I.
White I.
C. Runaway
Hicks
Bay
Glen Afton
Morrinsville
Tauranga
Bay of Plenty
East C.
Ngaruawahia
Hamilton
Cambridge
Te Puke
Whakatane
ISLAND
Te Awamutu
Rotorua
Opotiki
Kawhia
Putaruru
Kawerau
Taneatua
Otorohanga
Waitomo
Rotorua
Tokomaru
Bay
Te Kuiti
Mangakino
Tolaga
Bay
Mangakino
Murupara
Taupo
N. Taranaki Bight
Ohura
Taumarunui
Taupo
Waikaremoana
Gisborne
Waitara
Poverty Bay
New Plymouth
Inglewood
Mt
Ngauruhoe
2291
Mt
Makorako
1727
Tarawera
Mt Egmont
(Mt Taranaki)
2518
Stratford
Mt Ruapehu
2797
Ohakune
Waiouru
Wairoa
Hawke
Bay
Mahia Peninsula
C. Egmont
Eltham
Ohakune
Taradale
Napier
Portland I.
Opunake
Raetihi
Hastings
Hawera
Taihape
Havelock North
C. Kidnappers
S.Taranaki Bight
Patea
Wanganui
Marton
Waipukurau
Rangitikei
Feilding
Dannevirke
Palmerston N
Woodville
C.Turnagain
Herbertville
Foxton
Pahiatua
C. Farewell
Farewell Spit
Levin
Eketahuna
Rocks Pt
Collingwood
Golden
Bay
Separation Pt
C. Stephens
Otaki
Takaka
D'Urville I.
C.Jackson
Paraparaumu
Masterton
Tasman
Mts
Motueka
Tasman
Bay
Porirua
Carterton
Karamea
Bight
The Twins
1826
Motueka
Picton
Tawa
Upper Hutt
Wairarapa
Karamea
Nelson
Richmond
Wellington
Lower
Hutt
Seddonville
Richmond Ra.
Wairau
Blenheim
Mt Ross
983
Westport
Murchison
Palliser Bay
C. Campbell
C. Foulwind
Buller
L.Rotoroa
C. Palliser
Reefton
L.Rotoiti
Awatere
Victoria Ra.
Spenser Mts
Mt Travers
2338
Kaikoura
Ra.
Tapuaenuku
2885
Runanga
Grey
Brunner
Clarence
Kaikoura
Greymouth
Lewis Pass
Hanmer
Springs
Kaikoura Pen.
Hokitika
L. Sumner
Waiau
Ross
Arthurs
Pass
Culverden
Aorunui
Waiau
Cheviot
Franz Josef Gl
Pukeraki Ra.
Waipara
SOUTH
Abut Hd
Coleridge
Waimakariri
Rangiora
Pegasus
Bay
Waimakariri
Kaiapoi
Methven
Rakaia
Hornby
Christchurch
Mt Cook
3754
Lyttelton
ISLAND
Mt Sefton
3157
Hermitage
L.Tekapo
Canterbury
Lincoln
Banks
Peninsula
Jackson Hd
L.Coleridge
Akaroa
Cascade Pt
Pukaki
Geraldine
Plains
L. Ellesmere
Mt Aspiring
3027
Pollux
2542
Young Ra.
L. Tekapo
Temuka
Canterbury
Bight
Awarua Pt
Ohau
Pukaki
Ashburton
Milford Sd
Hawea
L.Benmore
Timaru
Milford Sd
Mt Pyramid
2326
Wanaka
L. Aviemore
George Sd
Horner
Tunnel
Arrowtown
Omarama
Kurow
Waimate
Caswell Sd
Wanaka
Hawkdun Ra.
Secretary
Fiordland
Queenstown
Cromwell
Waitaki
Doubtful
Sd
Te Anau
Wakatipu
Clyde
Ranfurly
Oamaru
Nat. Park
Te Anau
Alexandra
Breaksea Sd
Manapouri
Kingston
Hampden
Resolution
Sd
Mt Ward
1718
Manapouri
Roxburgh
Palmerston
Dusky
Sd
Lumsden
Waikouaiti
Ohai
Riversdale
Port Chalmers
Puysegur
Pt
Te
Waewae
Bay
Winton
Heriot
Mosgiel
Otago Peninsula
Tuatapere
Gore
Clutha
Lawrence
Dunedin
Mataura
Milton
Riverton
Edendale
Balclutha
Kaitangata
Invercargill
Owaka
Foveaux Strait
Bluff
Solander I.
Codfish I.
Oban
Stewart Island
Mt Allen
730
Paterson Inlet
Shelter Pt
Port Pegasus

TASMAN
SEA

PACIFIC

OCEAN

1:5M

0   50   100   150   200 km
0   50   100 mls

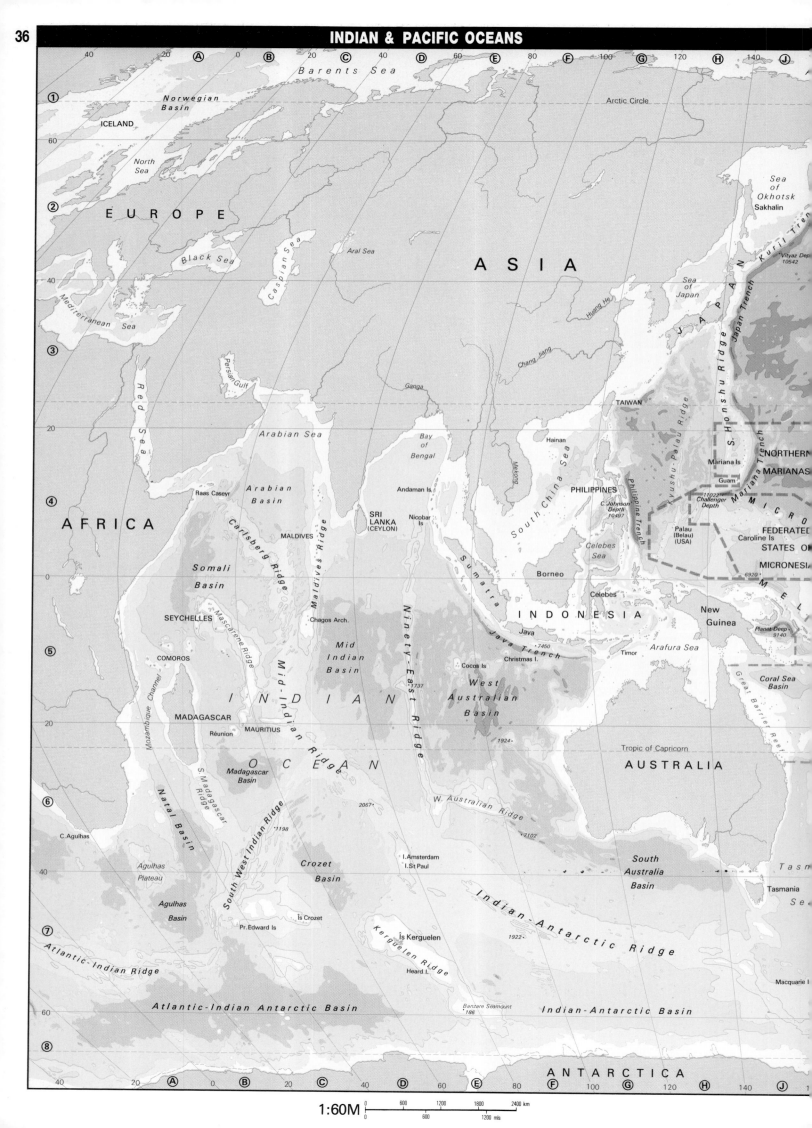

40 20 Ⓐ 0 Ⓑ 20 Ⓒ 40 Ⓓ 60 Ⓔ 80 Ⓕ 100 Ⓖ 120 Ⓗ 140 Ⓙ

Barents Sea

① Norwegian Basin

Arctic Circle

ICELAND

Sea of Okhotsk

60

North Sea

Sakhalin

② EUROPE

ASIA

Black Sea

Aral Sea

Caspian Sea

40

Sea of Japan

Mediterranean Sea

J A P A N

Kuril Trench

③ Persian Gulf

Chang Jiang

Huang He

*Vityaz Dep. 10542

Red Sea

Ganga

Japan Trench

Arabian Sea

TAIWAN

20

Bay of Bengal

Hainan

S. Honshu Ridge

Raas Caseyr

④ AFRICA

Arabian Basin

Andaman Is.

Mekong

South China Sea

PHILIPPINES

Mariana Is

NORTHERN

Philippine Trench

Guam

MARIANAS

SRI LANKA (CEYLON)

Nicobar Is

110221 Challenger Depth

Mariana Trench

Carlsberg Ridge

MALDIVES

C. Johnson Depth 10497

MICRO

Somali Basin

Maldives Ridge

Palau (Belau) (USA)

FEDERATED

SEYCHELLES

Chagos Arch.

Sumatra

Celebes Sea

Caroline Is

STATES OF

Mascarene Ridge

Borneo

MICRONESIA

0

COMOROS

Mid Indian Basin

Celebes

6920

ME

⑤ Madagascar

Java

INDONESIA

New Guinea

Planet Deep 9140

L

Java Trench

*7450

Mozambique Channel

I N D I A N

Ninety-East Ridge

MADAGASCAR

Mid-Indian Ridge

Christmas I.

Timor

Arafura Sea

Coral Sea Basin

Réunion

MAURITIUS

Cocos Is

*1737

West Australian Basin

Great Barrier Reef

20

S. Madagascar Ridge

O C E A N

*1924

Tropic of Capricorn

Natal Basin

Madagascar Basin

AUSTRALIA

⑥ C. Agulhas

W. Australian Ridge

2067•

South West Indian Ridge

*7102

Agulhas Plateau

*1198

I. Amsterdam

South Australia Basin

Tas

I. St Paul

40

Crozet Basin

Tasmania

Agulhas Basin

Îs Crozet

Sea

⑦ Pr. Edward Is

Kerguelen Ridge

Îs Kerguelen

1922•

Indian-Antarctic Ridge

Macquarie I

Atlantic-Indian Ridge

Heard I.

Banzare Seamount 186

60

Atlantic-Indian Antarctic Basin

Indian-Antarctic Basin

⑧

40 20 Ⓐ 0 Ⓑ 20 Ⓒ 40 Ⓓ 60 Ⓔ 80 Ⓕ 100 Ⓖ 120 Ⓗ 140 Ⓙ

A N T A R C T I C A

1:60M

0 600 1200 1800 2400 km
0 600 1200 mls

ic Ocean

GREENLAND

To enhance the ocean features,
the 3000m contour has been
added, and over 5000m is shown
by an extra tint.

ICELAND

①

Bering Sea

Hudson
Bay

C. Farewell

Labrador Basin

60

Aleutian Is

Atlantic

Aleutian Trench

Newfoundland

②

7822

Emperor Seamount Chain

Grand Banks

Ocean

NORTH

40

Mendocino Seascarp

AMERICA

North American

18

Murray Seascarp

Bermuda

③

104

Midway
Is

Basin
Van

1477

d - Pacific Mountains

Hawaiian
Islands

Tropic of Cancer

Gulf of
Mexico

C. Falso

CUBA

West
Indies

20

MARSHALL
ISLANDS

P
O
L

Clarion Fracture Zone

Is Revilla
Gigedo

Cayman Tr.

Middle America Trench

Caribbean Sea

④

Marshall
Is

A
C
I
F
I
C

East Pacific Rise

Cocos Ridge

SOUTH

NAURU

Line Is

Equator

Is Galápagos

0

KIRIBATI

Y
N

O
C
E
A
N

AMERICA

Phoenix Is

⑤

SOLOMON
ISLANDS

TUVALU

Is Marquises

East Pacific Ridge

6150

Tokelau

American
Samoa

French Polynesia

Peru Basin

S.W. Peru or
Nasca Ridge

Peru-Chile Trench

8066

NUATU

Wallis &
Futuna

Wrn
Samoa

Samoa
Is de la
Société
Tahiti

Is Tuamotu

FIJI

TONGA

Niue

Cook Is

S

Is Gambier

5537

20

New
Caledonia

Horizon Depth
10882

Tonga Trench

Is Tubuai

Pitcairn

A

1344

Sala y Gómez

S.Ambrosio

S.Félix

S. Fiji
Basin

Easter I.
(I. de Pascua)

⑥

Norfolk I. Ridge

Norfolk I.

10042

Kermadec Trench

INTERNATIONAL DATE LINE

Is Juan Fernández

N.Cape

rise

NEW
ZEALAND

South West
Pacific
Basin

Argentine
Basin

Chatham Is

⑦

New Zealand
Plateau

Pacific-Antarctic Ridge

Falkland Is

ckland Is

Campbell I.

N.Scotia Ridge

S.Georgia

6240

732

Scotia Sea

S.Sandwich Trench

South East Pacific Basin

Drake Passage

S.Sandwich Is

60

5486

S. Orkney Is

alleny Is

Scott Is

Antarctic
Peninsula

Weddell Sea

⑧

Antarctic Circle

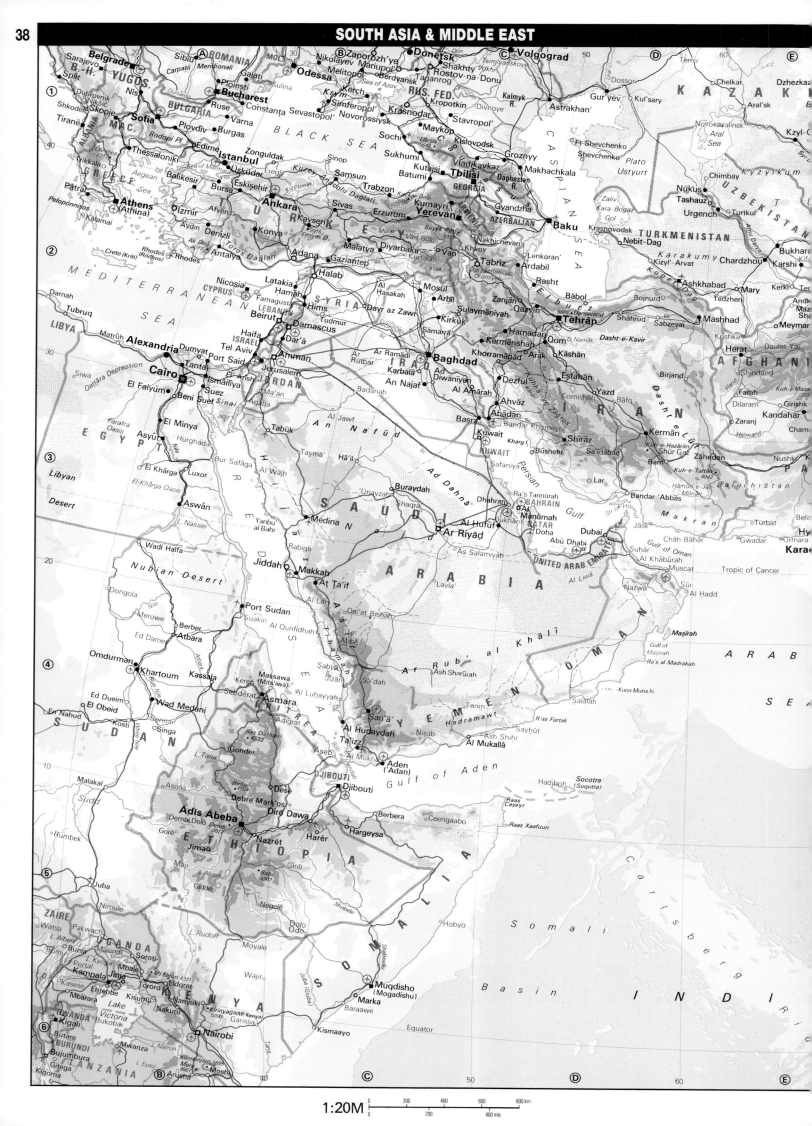

1:20M

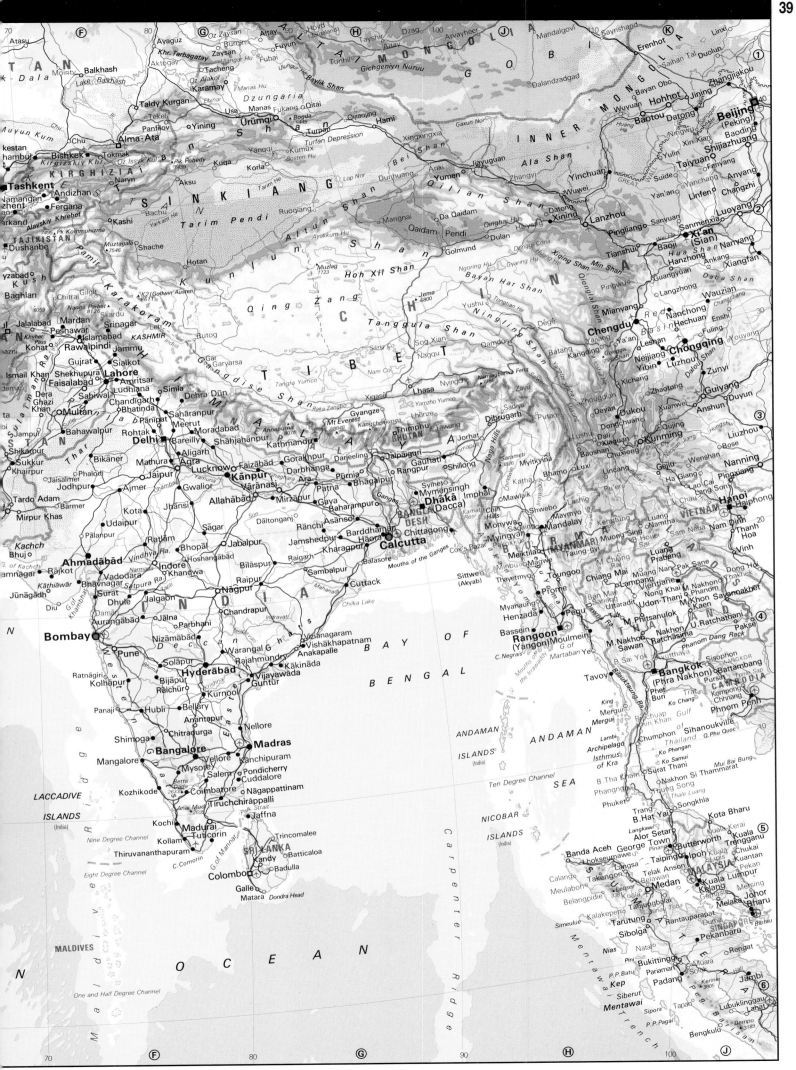

BLACK SEA

Istanbul
Ankara
TURKEY
Sea of Marmara

GREECE

Crete

CYPRUS
Nicosia
Limassol

Mediterranean Sea

SYRIA
Aleppo (Halab)
Latakia (Al Lādhiqīyah)
Hamāh
Hịms
Dayr az Zawr

Tripoli (Trâblous esh Shem)
Beirut (Beyrouth)
LEBANON
Damascus (Dimashq)

ISRAEL
Haifa
Tel Aviv-Yafo
Jerusalem
Ashdod
Gaza
Beersheba

JORDAN
Amman
Dead Sea

IRAQ

Alexandria (El Iskandarîya)
Cairo (El Qâhira)
El Gîza
Suez (El Suweis)
Port Said (Bûr Sa'îd)

EGYPT

SINAI

Libyan Plateau
Qattâra Depression

Gulf of Suez
Gulf of Aqaba
RED SEA

Luxor
Aswân
Khazzan an-Nasr (Lake Nasser)

SAUDI ARABIA
An Nafūd
Jabal Shammar

Medina (Al Madînah)

1:7.5 M
100   200   300 km
50   100   150 mls

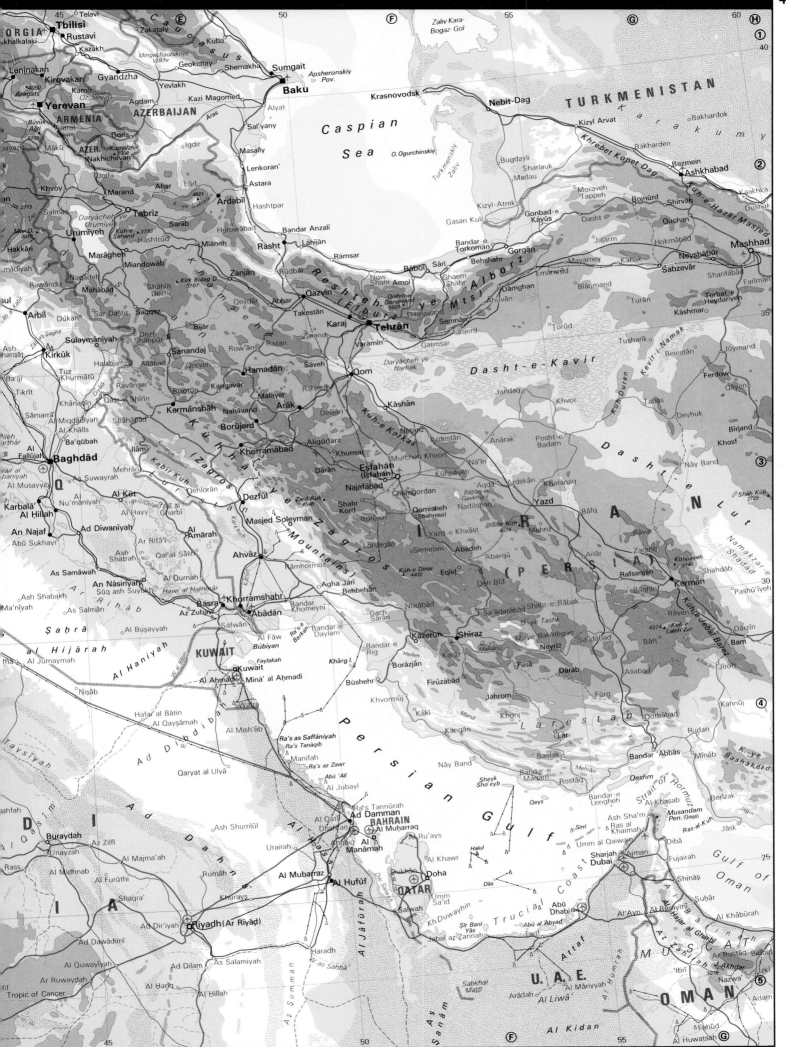

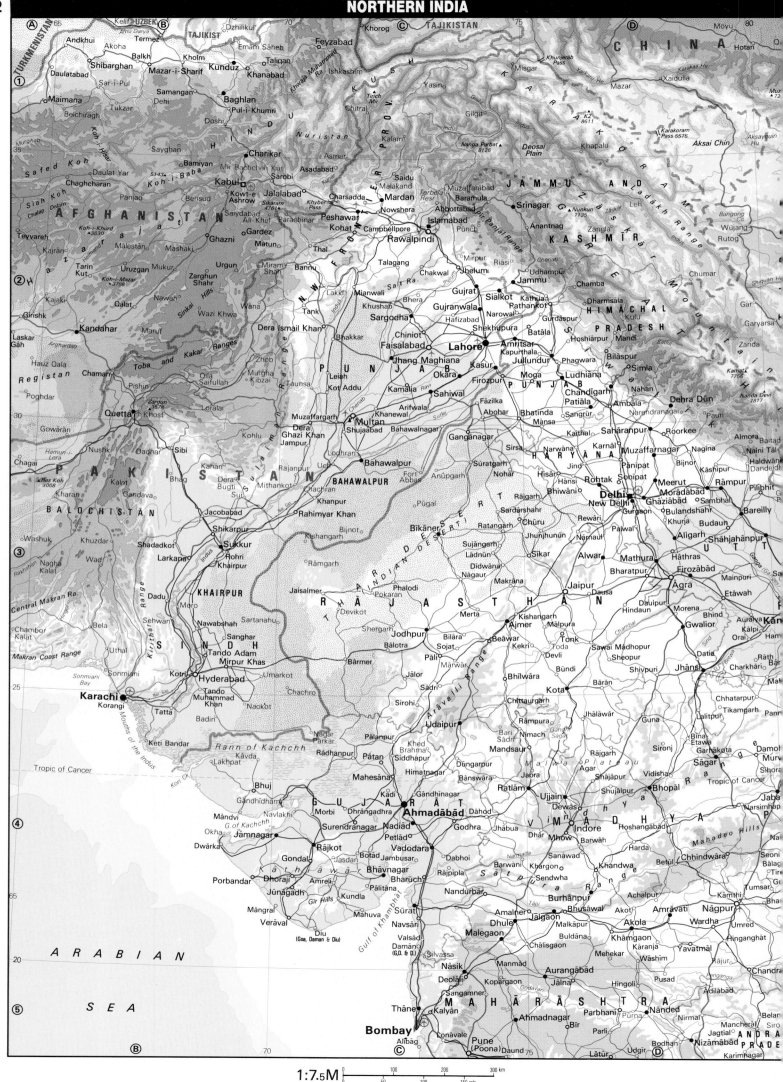

1:7.5M

| 0 | 100 | 200 | 300 km |
| 0 | 50 | 100 | 150 mls |

1:7.5M

CYPRUS

C.Kormakiti
Lapithos
Morphou
Karavostasi
Lefka
Khrysokhou Bay
C. Arnauti
Polis
Pedhoulas
Mt Olympus 1951
Troodos Range
Platres
Paphos (Pefos)
Episkopi
Akrotiri
Episkopi B
Akrotiri Bay
C.Zevgari
C. Gata
Kyrenia
Kythrea
Morphou
Nicosia
Dhali IDALION
Paleokhorio
Lefkara
Zyyi
Limassol
C.Kiti
Akanthou
Trikomo
Lefkoniko
ATTILA LINE
SALAMIS
Athna
Larnaca
Larnaca Bay
Yialousa
Leonarisso
Rizokaipaso
C.A.Andreas
C.Elea
Famagusta Bay
C.Greco
Famagusta

MEDITERRANEAN SEA

SYRIA

Al Bayḍiyah
Serai
Jisr ash Shughūr
Al Haffah
Silinfah
Latakia (Al Lādhiqīyah)
Al Qardahah
Jablah
'Arab al Mulk
Bāniyās
QAL'AT AL MARQAB
Ra's Ibn Hāni'
Az Zāwīyah
Ma'arrat an Nu'mān
Shathah
Khan at Tahtā' Shaykhūn
Şuqaylibīyah
(Orontes) Dayr Shumayyil
Hamāh
El Mīna
Tripoli (Trâblous)
Zghorta
Batroûn
Amioune
Jubail BYBLOS
Kartaba
Rhazir
Jounié
Beirut (Beyrouth)
Ba'abda
Aley
Damour
Beit ed Dine
Sidon (Saïda)
Jezzine
Mâchgharab
Rachaya
Tyre (Tyr,Sour)
Q.Shemona
Jouai'ya
Enn Nâqoûra
Nahariya
'Akko (Acre)
Haifa (Hefa)
'Atlit
Zikhron Ya'aqov
CAESAREA
Pardes Hanna
Hadera
Netanya
Herzliyya
Ramat Gan
Tel Aviv-Yafo (Jaffa)
Bat Yam
Rishon le Ziyon
Holon
Rehovot
Ashdod
Ashqelon
Qiryat Gat
Gaza
Gaza Strip
Khan Yunis
Rafah
Tartūs
Arwad
Duraykīsh
Şāfītā
An Nāşirah
Qal'at al Hiṣn (KRAK-DES CHEVALIERS)
Ḥamīdīyah
Tall Kalakh
Kleiá
Halba
El Hermel
Baṭroûn
Qoubayat
Ḥisyah
Jūsīyah
Yabrūd
An Nabk
Ba'albek
Laboue
Bcharre
Qornet es Saouda 3086
Deir el Ahmar
Zahle
Rayak
Bikfaya
Zabdani
'Ayn al Fijah
Damascus (Dimashq)
Qaţanā
Mt Hermon (Jebel esh Sheikh)
Marjayoun
Baniyas
Mas'adah
Al Quṇayṭirah
Al Kiswah
Dayr 'Alī
Nawa
As Sanamayn
Khushnīyah
Al Lajāh
Shaqqā
Izra'
Shahbā
Nazareth
Afula
Tiberias
Ma'agan
Deir Abu Sa'id
Irbid
Husn
Ajlūn
Mafraq
Jarash
Es Samrā'
Er Rummān
Salt
Suweilih
Zarqa
Amman
Jericho (Arīhā)
Jerusalem (El Quds) (Yerushalayim)
Bethlehem (Bayt Lahm)
Beit Jala
Hebron (El Khalil)
Beersheba (Be'er Sheva)
Madabā
Dead Sea (Bahr Lut)

ISRAEL

LEBANON

HIMS (Homs)

JORDAN

EGYPT

Dumyât (Damietta)
Kafr Sa'd
Fâriskûr
Port Said (Bûr Saïd)
Bûr Fu'ad
El Matariya
El Manzala
El Zarqa
El Mansûra
El Qantara
Ismâ'îlîya
Talata
Suez (El Suweis)
El Kûbri
El Shatt
Bûr Taufiq
Gulf of Suez

SINAI

El 'Arîsh
Români
Bîr el Duweidâr
Bîr Lahfân
Abu Aweigila
El Quseima
Qeziot
SHIVTA
AVEDAT
NIZANA
G.Libni 463
G.Maghâra 735
G.Halâl 892
G.Yi'allaq
G.Araif el Naqa 934
Har Ramon
Har Saggi
Mizpe Ramon
G.Umm Shaumer
Yotvata
Elat
Aqaba

Beer Ora
El Kuntilla
El Thamad
Ras Um Seisabân
J.el Harad 1274
Ras en Naqb

Negev

Revivim
Sede Boqer
Yeroham
Dimona
Oron
Hazeva
Ein Yahav

Ofaqim
Zeelim
Nevatim
Arad
Sedom

MOAB

Karak
Tafila
Shaubak
PETRA
Ma'an

1 : 2.5 M

0   25   50   75   100 km
0   25   50 mls

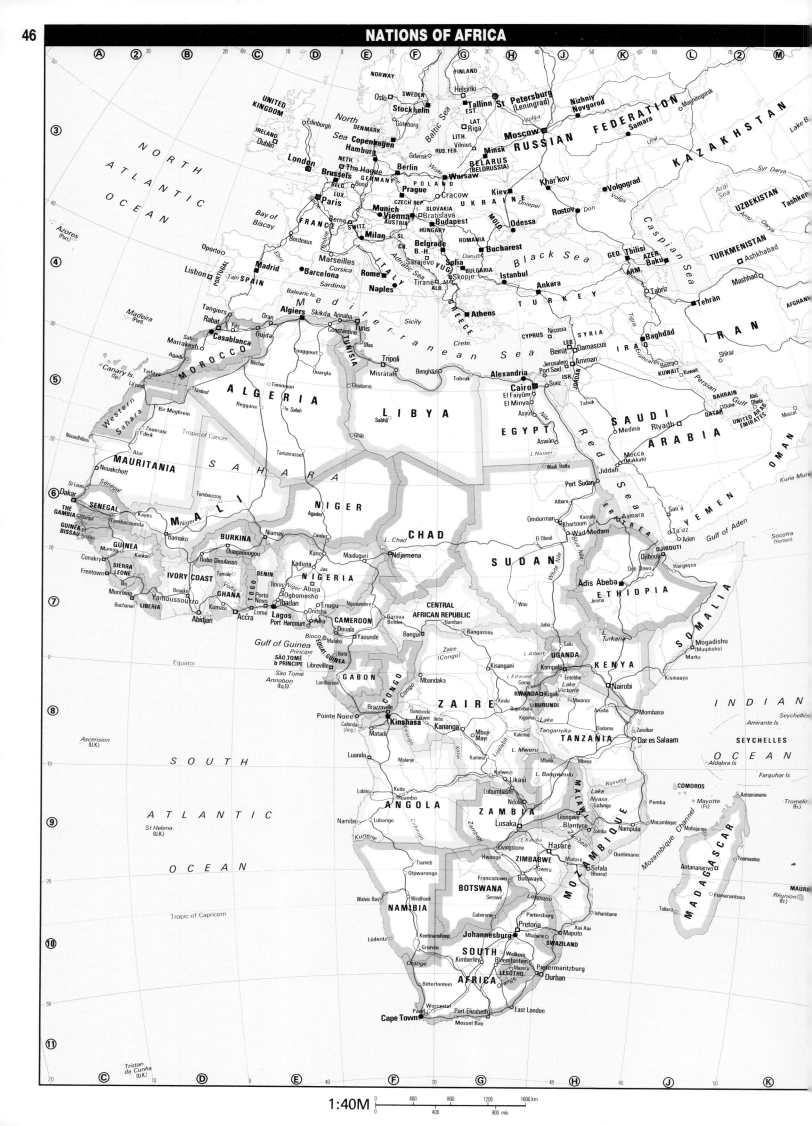

1:40M

| 400 | 800 | 1200 | 1600 km |
| 400 | 800 mls | | |

ZIMBABWE

BOTSWANA

NAMIBIA

SOUTH AFRICA

NORTHERN TRANSVAAL

EASTERN TRANSVAAL

SWAZILAND

KWAZULU

NATAL

LESOTHO

ORANGE FREE STATE

NORTH WEST

NORTHERN CAPE

EASTERN CAPE

WESTERN CAPE

Kalahari Desert

Central Kalahari Game Reserve

Gemsbok National Park

Kalahari Gemsbok Nat. Park

Tropic of Capricorn

Drakensberg

Great Karoo

Little Karoo

INDIAN OCEAN

ATLANTIC OCEAN

Pretoria
Johannesburg
Soweto
Randburg
Randfontein
Maputo
Durban
Amanzimtoti
Pietermaritzburg
Bloemfontein
Kimberley
Welkom
Cape Town
Port Elizabeth
East London
Windhoek
Gaborone

Cape of Good Hope
C. Agulhas

1:7.5M

0   100   200   300 km
0   50   100   150 mls

PORTUGAL · **SPAIN**

Lisbon (Lisboa) · Beja · Badajoz · Albacete · Ibiza · BALEARIC ISLANDS (Islas Baleares) · Sardinia (Sardegna) · Cagliari

Faro · Córdoba · Murcia · Alicante · Algiers (Alger) · Tizi Ouzou · Bejaïa (Bougie) · Skikda (Philippeville) · Annaba (Bône) · Béja · Bizer

Huelva · Sevilla (Seville) · Granada · Cartagena · Cherchell · Ech Cheliff · Blida · Constantine · Souk Ahras · El Kef · Maktar

Cádiz · Málaga · Almería · Mostaganem · Oran · Mascara · Sidi-bel-Abbès · Tiaret · Bou Saâda · M'sila · Sétif · Batna · Tébessa · Kairouan

Gibraltar (U.K.) · Ceuta (Sp) · Melilla (SP.) · Al Hoceima · Taza · Oujda · Tlemcen · Ksar El Boukhari · Djelfa · Aurès · Biskra · Kasserine · El Jem

MOROCCO · Tangier (Tanger) · Tetouan · Ksar-El-Kebir · Ouezzane · Kenitra · Rabat · Meknès · Fès · Taza · Ain Beni Mathar · Mecheria des · Ain Sefra · Ksour · Laghouat · Berriane · El Oued · Touggourt · **TUNISIA** · Tatouine

Casablanca (Dar-el-Beida) · El Jadida · Settat · Ben Slimane · Khenifra · Azrou · Midelt · Missour · Hauts Plateaux · Djebel · Chott · Gafsa · Gabès · Medenine

Safi · Marrakech · Beni Mellal · Tadla · Ifrane · Bou Arfa · Figuig · Atlas Saharien · Ghardaïa · El Golea · El Gassi · Ghadamis · Tozeur · Chott Melrhir

Essaouira · Haut Atlas · Toubkal 4165 · Ouarzazate · Jbel Sarhro · Béchar · Abadla · Grand Erg Occidental · Hassi Inifel

Agadir · Taroudannt · Anti Atlas · Zagora · Tata · Beni Abbès · Kerzaz · Timimoun · Plateau du Tademaït · Bordj Omar Driss · Hamada de Tinrhert · In Amenas

Tiznit · Bou Izakarn · Jbel Ouarkziz · Hamada du Dra · Tabelbala · **ALGERIA** · Adrar · In Belbel · In Salah · Ohanet · Ahert

Tan-Tan · Draa · Tindouf · Hamada Tounassine · Hassi Mdakane · Bj Flye Ste Marie · Reggane · Aoulef · Plaine du Tidikelt · Tin Fouye · In Amenas

Tarfaya · Hagunia · Erg Iguidi · El Eglab · Chenachèn · Arak · Tassili N'Ajjer · Tarat · Sarda

Laâyoune · Saguia el Hamra · El Farsia · Smara · Mcherrah · Erg Chech · Mts du Mouydir · In Ecker · Idelès · Djanet

C. Bojador · Erg Yetti · El Hank · El Mreiti · Troudenni · El Haricha · Tanezrouft · Asedjrad · Ouallen · Tropic of Cancer · Hoggar (Ahaggar) · Tahat 2918 · In Afaleleh · In Ezzane

Western Sahara · Tiris · Ausert · Aguenit · Bir Moghrein · Chegga · Aioun Abd el Malek · El Mzereb · Bidon 5 (Ruins) · Abalessa · Tamanrasset · In Ebeggi · Tin Tarabine · Ténéré du Tafassasset

Dakhla · B. de Rio de Oro · Zouerate · Fdérik · Tourine · Bir Zreigat · In Dagouber · El Guettâra · Silet · Mt Gréboun 1944 · In Guezzam

MAURITANIA · Atar · Ouadâne · Chinguetti · Oguilet Khenachich · El Khenachich · Taguenout Haggueret · Ardar · Tessalit · Aguelhok · Tassili du Hoggar · Iférouane · Timia

Nouadhibou · Ras Nouadhibou · Adrar · Soutouf · Tichla · Akjoujt · El Djouf · Araouane · Guir · Timetrine Monts · Tin Zaouaten · Talak · Air

Nouakchott · Tidjikja · Tichitt · Aklé Aouana · L. Faguibine · Tombouctou · Bourem · Kidal · Anéfis · Zeguerer · Vallée de l'Azaouak · Agadez · Erg du Ténéré

Rosso · Boutilimit · Tamchaket · Hodh · Aioun El Atrouss · Néma · Goundam · Niafounké · Gao · Ménaka · Tillia · Ingal · **NIGER**

St-Louis · Dagana · Kaédi · Kiffa · Timbédra · Niafounké · **MALI** · Ansongo · Bani Bangou · Tchin Tabaradene · Tahoua · Tanout · Tasker

Louga · Matam · Mbout · Nioro Du Sahel · Nara · Sokolo · Douentza · Gourma Rharous · Téra · Ualam · Birnin N'Konni · Illéla · Keita · Dakoro · Zinder · Gouré · Gudumaria

Dakar · Thiès · Diourbel · Bakel · Kidira · Diéma · Goumbou · **Massina** · Mopti · Bandiagara · Djibo · Dori · Tillabéri · Dogondoutchi · Dosso · Madaoua · Mayahi · Tessaoua · Maradi · Daura · Matameye

Rufisque · **SENEGAL** · Kaffrine · Kayes · Bafoulabé · Ke Macina · Djenné · Ouahigouya · Tougan · Kaya · Bogandé · Say · Kantchari · Niamey · Sokoto · Kaura Namoda · Yashi · Nguru · Gashua

Joal · Kaolack · Tambacounda · Kolokani · Kita · Banamba · Ségou · Tougan · Dédougou · Yako · Koupéla · Fada N'Gourma · Kandi · Birnin-Kebbi · Gusau · **NIGERIA** · Kano · Hadejia · Dam

THE GAMBIA · Banjul · Georgetown · Kéniéba · Bamako · Koulikoro · Kangaba · San · Nouna · Koudougou · Ouagadougou · Tenkodogo · Pama · Malanville · Yelwa · Zaria · Kaduna · Azare

Diouloulou · Bignona · Vélingara · Kédougou · **GUINEA** · Siguiri · Kangaba · Bougouni · Sikasso · Bobo Dioulasso · Boromo · **BURKINA** · Bawku · Kcontagora · Zungeru · Minna · Jos · Gombe · Núma

Ziguinchor · Sédhiou · Tougué · Dinguiraye · Kouroussa · Diébougou · Gaoua · Tumu · Bolgatanga · Mango · Bemberéké · Nikki · Bida · Abuja · Keffi · Wamba · Lafia · Gashaka · Gotel Mts

GUINEA-BISSAU · Bissau · Bolama · Gaoual · Fouta · Labé · Dabola · Dalaba · Kankan · Maninian · Tingrela · Gambaga · Djougou · Kouandé · Kainji Resr · Jebba · Ilorin · Oshogbo · Okene · Benue · Mokwa · Makurdi · Katsina Ala · Mamfé · Foumb

Arquipélago dos Bijagós · C. Verga · Boké · Fria · Kindia · **SIERRA LEONE** · Macenta · Odienné · Boundiali · Korhogo · Bassar · Parakou · Shaki · Lafiagi · Baro · Nasarawa · Ogoja · Wum · Bamenda · **CAMEROUN**

C. Sierra Leone · Freetown · Makeni · Kabala · Beyla · Kissidougou · Niakaramandougou · Ferkessédougou · Bouna · Bole · Tamale · Yendi · Bassar · Parakou · Bida · Ibadan · Oshogbo · Ife · Owo · Benin City · Onitsha · Abakaliki · Bafoussam

Moyamba · Mano · Kenema · Voinjama · **IVORY COAST** · Man · Séguéla · Bouaké · Bondoukou · Sunyani · **GHANA** · Atakpamé · Savalou · Savé · Oyo · Iwo · Ogbomosho · Abeokuta · Ijebu-Ode · Ondo · Enugu

Bonthe · Sherbro · Bo · Sanniquellie · Nzérékoré · Danané · Duékoué · Bouaflé · **(CÔTE D'IVOIRE)** · Katiola · Bouaké · Abengourou · Berekum · Mampong · Ho · Kpalimé · Pobé · Sakété · Lagos · Ikom · Bafoussam

LIBERIA · Bomi Hills · Gbarnga · Guiglo · Daloa · Yamoussoukro · Dimbokro · Agboville · Obuasi · Kumasi · Bibiani · Koforidua · Nsawam · Accra · Cotonou · Porto Novo · Benin City · Aba · Kumba · Nkongsamba

Robertsport · Monrovia · Buchanan · Chiehn · Mt Niete · Soubré · Bagnoa · Agboville · Enchi · Dunkwa · Oda · Winneba · Cape Coast · Lomé · Ouidah · Sapele · Warri · Owerri · Calabar · Mt Cameroun 4095 · Buéa · Douala

River Cess · Greenville · Lakota · Sassandra · Abidjan · Dabou · Grand Bassam · Sekondi · Takoradi · C. Three Points · **Bight of Benin** · Forcados · Mouths of the R. Niger · Port Harcourt · Bonny · Limbe · Edéa

Harper · Tabou · San Pédro · C. Palmas · **GULF OF GUINEA** · **Bight of Biafra** · Kribi · Ebolowa · Campo · Ambam

EQUATORIAL GUINEA · Bata · Ebebiyin · Cocobeach · Rio Benito · Medouneu · Evinayong · Kango · **GABON**

S. TOME & PRINCIPE · Principe · São Tomé · Libreville · Pte Pongara · Ndjolé

Pagalu (Equat. Guinea) · Pagalu

Azores (Açores) (Portugal) · Flores · Faial · Pico · São Jorge · Graciosa · Terceira · Angra Do Heroismo · São Miguel · Ponta Delgada · Formigas · Santa Maria · at the same scale

Madeira (Portugal) · Porto Santo · Funchal · Deserta Grande · Ilhas Selvagens (Port.)

Canary Islands (Islas Canarias) (Spain) · Santa Cruz De La Palma · La Palma · Gomera · Hierro · Tenerife · De Tenerife · Las Palmas De Gran Canaria · Gran Canaria · Fuerteventura · Pto Del Rosario · Arrecife · Lanzarote · C. Yubi

CAPE VERDE · Sto Antão · S Vincente · Sta Luzia · S Nicolau · Sal · Boa Vista · S Tiago · Maio · Fogo · Brava · Praia · at the same scale

MEDIT · Tropic of Cancer

1:15M · 0 · 100 · 200 · 300 · 400 · 600 km · 100 · 200 · 300 mls

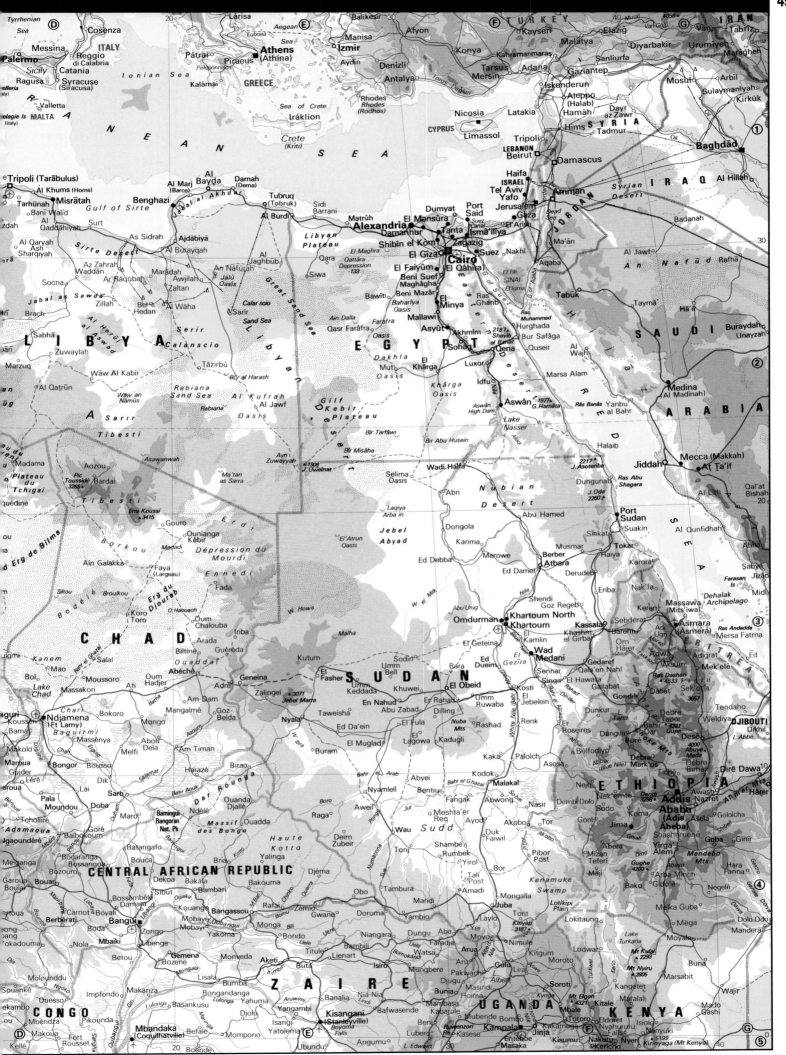

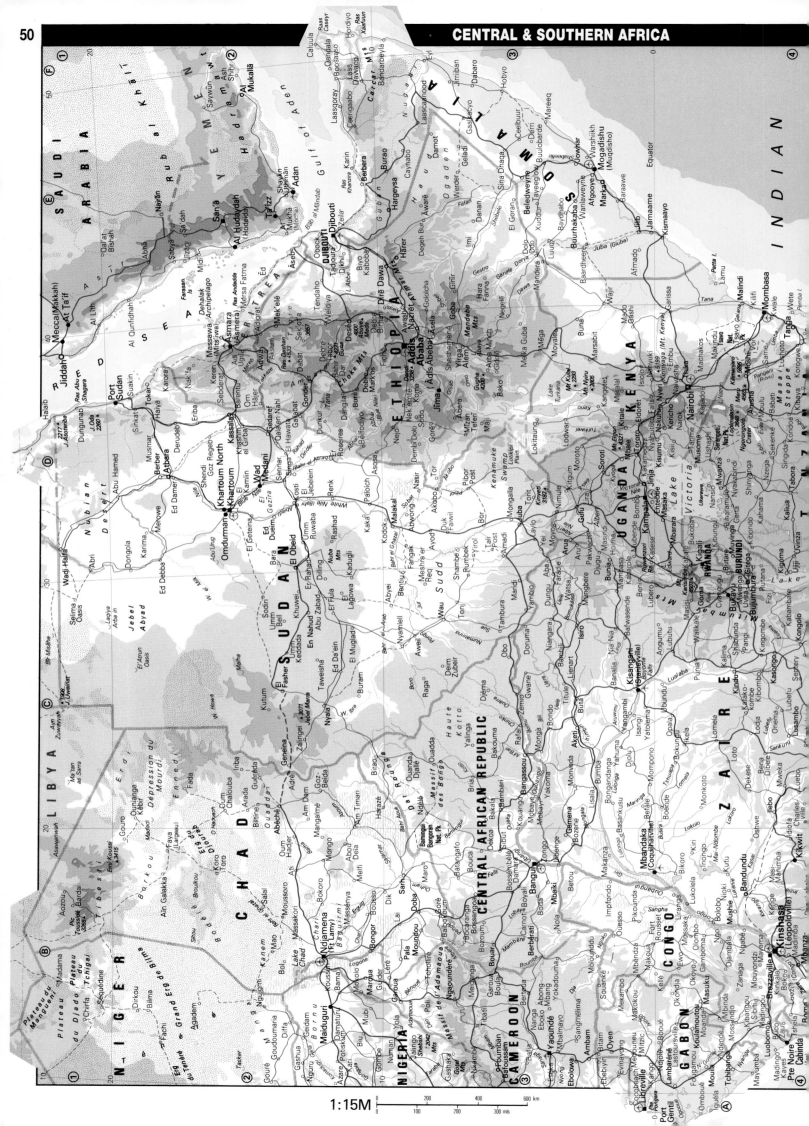

1:15M

200   400   600 km
100   200   300 mls

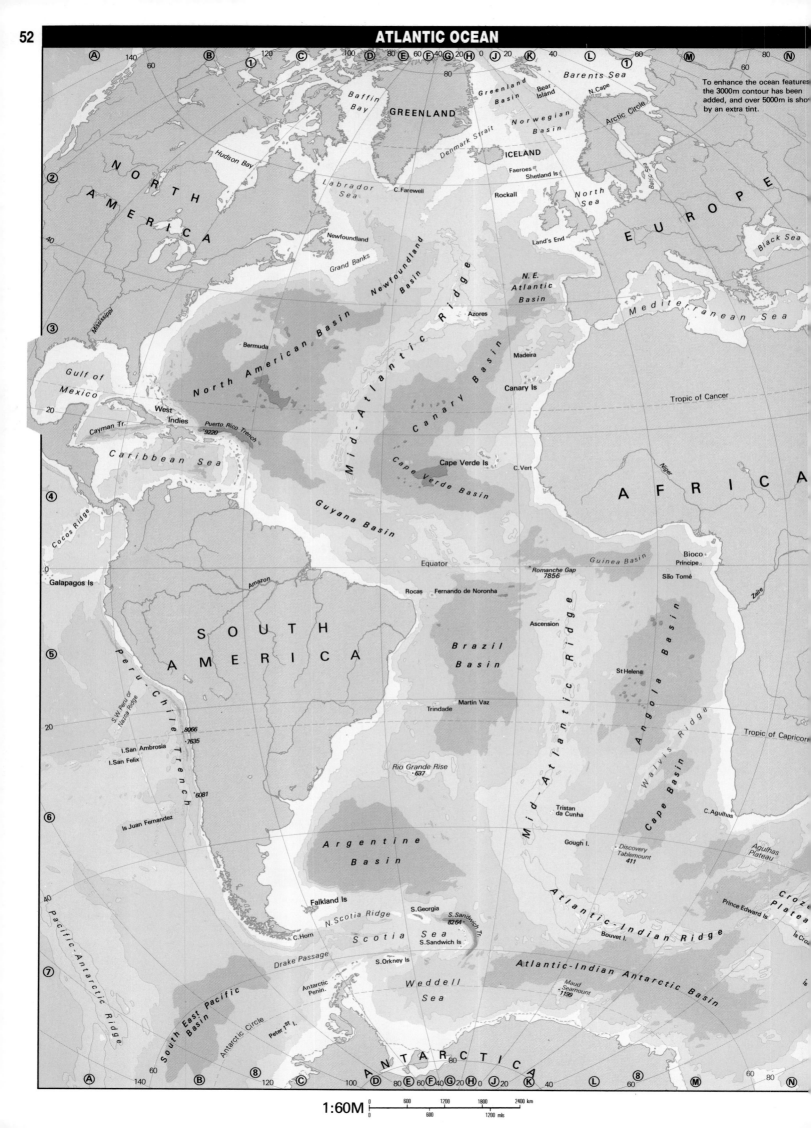

To enhance the ocean features
the 3000m contour has been
added, and over 5000m is show*
by an extra tint.

A 140 **B** 120 **C** 100 **D** 80 60 **F** 40 **G** 20 **H** 0 **J** 20 **K** 40 **L** 60 **M** 80 **N**

Baffin
Bay

GREENLAND

Greenland
Basin

Bear
Island

Barents Sea

N.Cape

Arctic Circle

② Hudson Bay

Denmark Strait

Norwegian
Basin

Labrador
Sea

ICELAND

Faeroes

Shetland Is

C.Farewell

North
Sea

Baltic Sea

Rockall

40

Land's End

EUROPE

Black Sea

Newfoundland

Grand Banks

Newfoundland
Basin

N. E.
Atlantic
Basin

Mediterranean Sea

③ Bermuda

Azores

North American Basin

Mid-Atlantic Ridge

Madeira

Canary Basin

Canary Is

Tropic of Cancer

Gulf of
Mexico

20

West
Indies

Puerto Rico Trench
·9220

Cape Verde Is

Cape Verde Basin

C.Vert

Cayman Tr.

Caribbean Sea

NORTH
AMERICA

Guyana Basin

AFRICA

Niger

④ Cocos Ridge

Galapagos Is

Guinea Basin

Bioco
Príncipe

0

Equator

Romanche Gap
7856

São Tomé

Amazon

Rocas Fernando de Noronha

Zaïre

SOUTH
AMERICA

Brazil
Basin

Ascension

St Helena

Angola Basin

⑤ Peru or Nazca Ridge

S.W.Peru or

Martin Vaz

Trindade

Mid-Atlantic Ridge

Walvis Ridge

Cape Basin

20 ·8066
·7635

I.San Ambrosia

I.San Felix

Peru-Chile Trench

Rio Grande Rise
·637

Tropic of Capricorn

·6081

Tristan
da Cunha

C.Agulhas

⑥ Is Juan Fernandez

Argentine

Basin

Gough I.

Discovery
Tablemount
411

Agulhas
Plateau

Falkland Is

S.Georgia

Atlantic-Indian Ridge

Croz
Platea

Prince Edward Is

40

N.Scotia Ridge

S.Sandwich Tr.
8264

Bouvet I.

Is Croz

Pacific-Antarctic Ridge

C.Horn

Scotia Sea

S.Sandwich Is

Drake Passage

S.Orkney Is

Atlantic-Indian Antarctic Basin

⑦ Antarctic
Penin.

Weddell
Sea

Maud
Seamount
1199

South East Pacific
Basin

Antarctic Circle

Peter 1st I.

80

ANTARCTICA

A 140 **B** ⑧ 120 **C** 100 **D** 80 **E** 60 **F** 40 **G** 20 **H** **J** 20 **K** 40 **L** 60 **M** 80 **N**

1:60M

0 600 1200 1800 2400 km
0 600 1200 mls

Arctic Ocean

Chukchi Sea

Bering Strait

Bering Sea

Beaufort Sea

GREENLAND (KALAALLIT NUNAAT) (Denmark)

Denmark Strait

ICELAND
Reykjavik

A L A S K A
Yukon
Prudhoe Bay
Inuvik
Fairbanks
Anchorage
Dawson
Whitehorse

Queen Elizabeth Islands

Banks I.
Victoria I.
Resolute
Devon I.
Ellesmere I.
Thule

Baffin Bay

Davis Strait

Gothab (Nuuk)

Labrador Sea

Aleutian Islands

Juneau
Alexander Arch.
Prince Rupert
Q. Charlotte Is
Vancouver I.

Dawson Creek
Prince George
Fraser

Great Bear L.
Yellowknife
Hay River
Great Slave L.
Uranium City
Athabasca
Peace

C A N A D A

Arctic Circle

Mackenzie

Southampton I.

Hudson Bay

Churchill
Inukjuak

Baffin I.

Hudson Strait

Scheffeville
Churchill Falls
Goose Bay

Newfoundland

Victoria
Vancouver
Seattle
Columbia
Portland
Spokane
Great Falls
Butte
Snake

Edmonton
Calgary
Medicine Hat
Saskatchewan
Saskatoon
Regina
Winnipeg
L. Winnipeg
Kenora

Thunder Bay
Fargo
Duluth
L. Superior
Sault Ste Marie
Sudbury

Québec
St Lawrence
Montréal
Ottawa
Toronto

Fredericton
Moncton
St. John
Halifax
Charlottetown
Anticosti I.
Sept Îles
Chibougamau
Moosonee
James Bay

St John's

San Francisco
Sacramento
Reno
Salt Lake City

U N I T E D   S T A T E S

Minneapolis
St Paul
Milwaukee
Chicago
L. Michigan
Detroit
L. Huron
L. Erie
Cleveland
Buffalo
L. Ontario
Boston

Omaha
Denver
Pueblo
Colorado
Arkansas

Kansas City
St Louis
Indianapolis
Cincinnati
Ohio

New York
Philadelphia
Baltimore
Washington
Newport News
Norfolk

O F   A M E R I C A

Los Angeles
San Bernardino
San Diego
Tijuana
Phoenix
Tucson

Wichita
Oklahoma City
Amarillo
Albuquerque

Nashville
Memphis
Birmingham
Jackson
Red
Mississippi

Atlanta

ATLANTIC OCEAN

Bermuda (U.K.)

El Paso
Ciudad Juárez
Hermosillo
Chihuahua

Fort Worth
Dallas
Austin
San Antonio

Baton Rouge
Mobile
Tallahassee
Charleston
Savannah
Jacksonville

Houston
New Orleans

Corpus Christi

M E X I C O

Gulf of Mexico

Tampa

Miami

Nassau

THE BAHAMAS

Sargasso Sea

Tropic of Cancer
Guadalupe (Mex.)
G. de California

Monterrey
Torreón
Durango
Mazatlán

Revilla Gigedo Is. (Mex.)

Tampico

Guadalajara
México
Veracruz
Mérida

Habana

CUBA

Guantánamo

DOMINICAN REP.
HAITI
Port-au-Prince
Santo Domingo
San Juan
Pto Rico (U.S.A.)

ANTIGUA & BARBUDA
ST KITTS-NEVIS
DOMINICA

JAMAICA
Kingston

PACIFIC OCEAN

Acapulco

BELIZE
Belmopan

GUATEMALA
Guatemala
S.Salvador
EL SALVADOR

HONDURAS
Tegucigalpa

NICARAGUA
Managua

CARIBBEAN SEA

Netherlands Antilles

ST LUCIA
ST VINCENT & THE GRENADINES
GRENADA
BAR-BADOS
TRINIDAD & TOBAGO

Clipperton (Fr.)

COSTA RICA
S.José

PANAMA
Panamá

Sta Marta
Barranquilla
Maracaibo
Caracas
Cd Guayana

VENEZUELA
Orinoco

I. del Coco (C.R)

Medellín
Bueraventura
Bogotá
Cali

COLOMBIA

Malpelo (Col.)

Equator

Galapagos Is (Ecu.)

Negro

Quito
ECUADOR

PERU

BRAZIL

1:35M

0 250 500 750 1000 1250 km

0 250 500 750 mls

1:15M

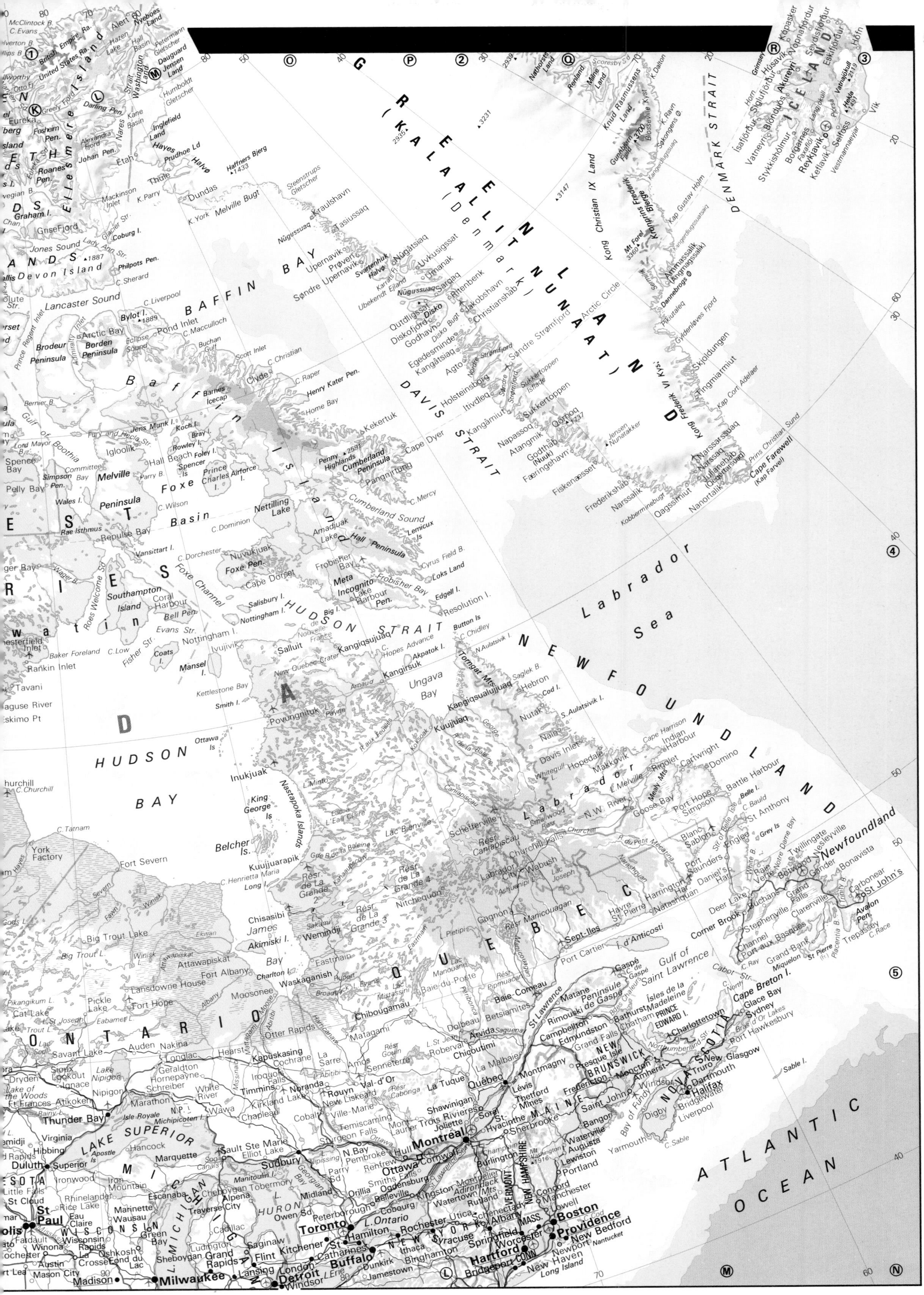

GREENLAND
(KALAALLIT NUNAAT)
(Denmark)
ICELAND
DENMARK STRAIT
BAFFIN BAY
Baffin Island
DAVIS STRAIT
Labrador Sea
HUDSON STRAIT
HUDSON BAY
James Bay
Foxe Basin
Ungava Bay
NEWFOUNDLAND
Newfoundland
Labrador
QUEBEC
ONTARIO
NEW BRUNSWICK
NOVA SCOTIA
PRINCE EDWARD I.
MAINE
VERMONT
NEW HAMPSHIRE
MASS.
CONN.
NEW YORK
MICHIGAN
WISCONSIN
LAKE SUPERIOR
L. HURON
L. MICHIGAN
L. Ontario
L. Erie
Gulf of Saint Lawrence
ATLANTIC OCEAN
Ellesmere Island
Devon Island
Lancaster Sound
Melville Peninsula
Southampton Island
Arctic Circle
Reykjavík
Nuuk
Godthåb
Montréal
Québec
Toronto
Ottawa
Boston
Providence
Hartford
Detroit
Buffalo
Milwaukee
St Paul
Duluth
Thunder Bay
Halifax
St John's
Sept-Îles
Schefferville
Labrador City
Churchill Falls
Goose Bay
Kuujjuaq
Thule
Sable I.
Cape Farewell
(Kap Farvel)

Names underlined indicate
Province/State capitals

1:12.5M

| 0 | 100 | 200 | 300 | 400 | 500 km |

| 0 | 100 | 200 | 300 mls |

SASKATCHEWAN

ALBERTA

BRITISH COLUMBIA

MONTANA

WYOMING

IDAHO

OREGON

WASHINGTON

Vancouver

Victoria

Seattle

Tacoma

Olympia

Portland

Salem

Eugene

Spokane

Helena

Billings

Great Falls

Butte

Bozeman

Missoula

Boise

Salt Lake City

Ogden

Yellowstone Nat. Park

Glacier Nat. Park

Olympic Nat. Park

Mount Rainier Nat. Park

ROCKY MOUNTAINS

BITTERROOT

Clearwater Mountains

Salmon River Mountains

Blue Mountains

COLUMBIA PLATEAU

Beaverhead Mts

Absaroka Range

Wind River Range

Teton Range

Harney Basin

High Desert

KLAMATH MOUNTAINS

Santa Rosa Ra.

Great Salt Lake

Great Salt Lake Desert

Columbia R.

Snake River Plain

Owyhee Mts

Steens Mtn

Black Rock Desert

1:5M

50   100   150   200 km

50   100 mils

CANADA

ALBERTA

SASKATCHEWAN

MANITOBA

MONTANA

NORTH DAKOTA

SOUTH DAKOTA

WYOMING

NEBRASKA

UTAH

COLORADO

KANSAS

ROCKY MOUNTAINS

Milk · Wild Horse · Consul · Govenlock · Climax · Val Marie · Rockglen · Willow Bunch · Radville · Carlyle · Souris · Melita · Boissevain

Cut Bank · Shelby · Chester · Gildford · Fresno Resr · Havre · Harlem · Opheim · Scobey · Plentywood · Fortuna · Portal · Mohall · Kenmare · Bottineau · Dunseith · Cando

Conrad · Teton · Big Sandy · Malta · Saco · Glasgow · Wolf Point · Poplar · Culbertson · Williston · Tioga · Stanley · Minot · Towner · Rugby

Choteau · Fairfield · Black Eagle · Fort Benton · Baldy Mtn 2116 · Milk · Missouri · Fort Peck · Fort Peck Reservoir · Sidney · Watford City · New Town · Lake Sakakawea · Garrison · Max · Drake · Harvey · Underwood · Carrington · Sheyenne

Helena · Great Falls · Cascade · Sun · Stanford · Royo · Jordan · Grassrange · Circle · Glendive · Wibaux · Beach · Badlands · Belfield · Halliday · Hebron · Mandan · Bismarck · Medina · Jamestown · Dawson · Napoleon

Three Forks · Townsend · White Sulphur Springs · Harlowtown · Lewistown · Roundup · Rosebud · Rock Springs · Yellowstone · Terry · Miles City · Baker · Marmarth · White Butte 1076 · Mott · Elgin · Sterling · Long L · Linton · Edgeley · Ellendale

Belgrade · Bozeman · Livingston · Big Timber · Columbus · Laurel · Billings · Hardin · Custer · Forsyth · Broadus · Volborg · Ekalaka · Bowman · Hettinger · Lemmon · McIntosh · McLaughlin · Mobridge · Aberdeen · Eureka · Ashley

Madison · Gallatin · Gardiner · Red Lodge · Granite Peak 3901 · Bridger · Bighorn · Lodge Grass · Tongue · Ashland · Powder · Hammond · Buffalo · Faith · Dupree · Moreau · La Plant · Eagle Butte · Gettysburg · Selby · Redfield

Electric Peak · Mt Washburn · West Yellowstone · Yellowstone Nat. Park · Shoshone · Lovell · Ranchester · Sheridan · Belle Fourche · Spearfish · Lead · Deadwood · Sundance · Enning · Moreau · Pierre · Blunt · Miller · Wessington Springs

Targhee Pass · Island Park · Shoshone · Powell · Shoshone · Cody · Greybull · Basin · Story · Clearmont · Moorcroft · Sturgis · Belle Fourche · Black Hills · Rapid City · Wall · Philip · Kadoka · Presho · Chamberlain · Plankinton

Grand Teton Nat. Park · Moran · Gros Ventre Range · Dubois · Thermopolis · Cloud Peak 4016 · Buffalo · Gillette · Osage · Newcastle · Custer · Nat. Pk · Hot Springs · Cheyenne · White · Murdo · Oacoma · Winner

Jackson · Absaroka Range · Owl Creek Mts · Worland · Kaycee · Mule Creek · Edgemont · Oelrichs · Pine Ridge · Wounded Knee · Martin · Mission · Gregory · Lake Andes · Bonesteel

Alpine · Afton · Daniel · Wind River Range · Boysen Resr · Riverton · Shoshoni · Midwest · Powder River · Wounded Knee · Chadron · Merriman · Valentine · Niobrara · Stuart · Ainsworth · Bassett

Cokeville · Kemmerer · Gannett Peak 4202 · Pinedale · Lander · Evansville · Shawnee · Lusk · Crawford · Rushville · Thedford · Dunning · Burwell · Ord · St Paul

Wyoming Peak 3480 · La Barge · Green · Sweetwater · Casper · Douglas · Guernsey · Alliance · Hyannis · Stapleton · Broken Bow · Ansley

Diamondville · Eden · Muddy Gap Pass · Pathfinder Resr · Lamont · Seminoe Resr · Medicine Bow · Wheatland · Fort Laramie · Lingle · Morrill · Scottsbluff · Bayard · Bridgeport · Broadwater · Oshkosh · Sutherland · North Platte · Gothenburg · Cozad · Lexington · Grand Island · Kearney

Reliance · Wamsutter · Rawlins · Elk Mtn 3400 · Saratoga · Rock River · Chugwater · Torrington · Gering · N Platte · L. McConaughy · Paxton · Big Springs · Maywood · Arapahoe · Holdrege

Rock Springs · Green River · Baggs · Bridger Peak 3662 · Medicine Bow Pk 3661 · Laramie · Foxpark · Pine Bluffs · Kimball · Sidney · Potter · Chappell · Ovid · Julesburg · McCook · Alma · Red Cloud

Evanston · Lyman · Manila · Flaming Gorge Resr · Medicine Bow Mts · Cheyenne · Wellington · Chadron · Republican

Kings Peak 4114 · Uinta Mts · Vernal · Roosevelt · Yampa · Craig · Hayden · Steamboat Springs · Fort Collins · Sterling · Holyoke · Imperial · Benkelman · Oberlin · Norton · Phillipsburg · Lebanon

Duchesne · Dinosaur · Rangely · Meeker · White · Kremmling · Rocky Mtn Nat. Park · Loveland · Estes Park · Greeley · Brush · Otis · Wray · Arapahoe

Price · Roan Plateau · Eagle · Granby · Longs Peak 4345 · Longmont · Fort Morgan · Culbertson · McCook

Green · Mack · Fruita · Grand Valley · Rifle · Minturn · Berthoud Pass · Boulder · Lafayette · Byers · Cope · Ankaree · St Francis · Colby

Grand Junction · Glenwood Springs · Loveland Pass · Idaho Springs · Denver · Lakewood · Aurora · Englewood · Littleton · Limon · Burlington · Goodland · Oakley · Saline · Smoky Hills

Palisade · Delta · Tennessee Pass · Leadville · Mt Evans 4349 · Castle Rock · Simla · Kit Carson · Cheyenne Wells · Weskan · Hill City · Stockton

Brendel · Arches N.P. · Moab · Uncompahgre Plateau · Montrose · Gunnison · Mt Elbert 4399 · Mt Harvard 4378 · Monarch Pass · Buena Vista · Manitou Springs · Colorado Springs · Kanorado · Wa Keeney · Russell · Hays

Canyonlands Nat. Pk · Mt Peale 3857 · Uravan · Dolores · Gunnison · Salida · Pikes Peak 4301 · Canon City · Florence · Pueblo · Boone · Ordway · Tribune · Scott City · Ness City · Hosington

Monticello · Abajo Mts · Dove Creek · Silverton · Mt Wilson 4342 · Ouray · Saguache · Monte Vista · Florence · Rocky Ford · Wiley · Jetmore · Larned · Kinsley · Lewis

Blanding · Bluff · Cortez · Mesa Verde N.P. · South Fork · Wolf Creek Pass · Alamosa · Blanca Peak 4364 · Walsenburg · Delhi · La Junta · Lakin · Garden City · Montezuma · Dodge City · Pratt · Greensburg

San Juan · Mexican Hat · Monument Valley · Durango · Pagosa Springs · Antonito · Sangre de Cristo Mts · Trinidad · Purgatoire · Springfield · Plains · Hugoton · Meade · Ashland · Medicine Lodge

Kayenta · Shiprock · Aztec · Bloomfield · Farmington · Chama · San Juan Mts · Tierra Amarilla · Raton · Liberal · Red Hills

Sangre de Cristo Mts · Sawatch Mts · Wind River Range · Bighorn Mts · Laramie Mts · Laramie

1:5M · 0 · 50 · 100 · 150 · 200 km · 50 · 100 mls

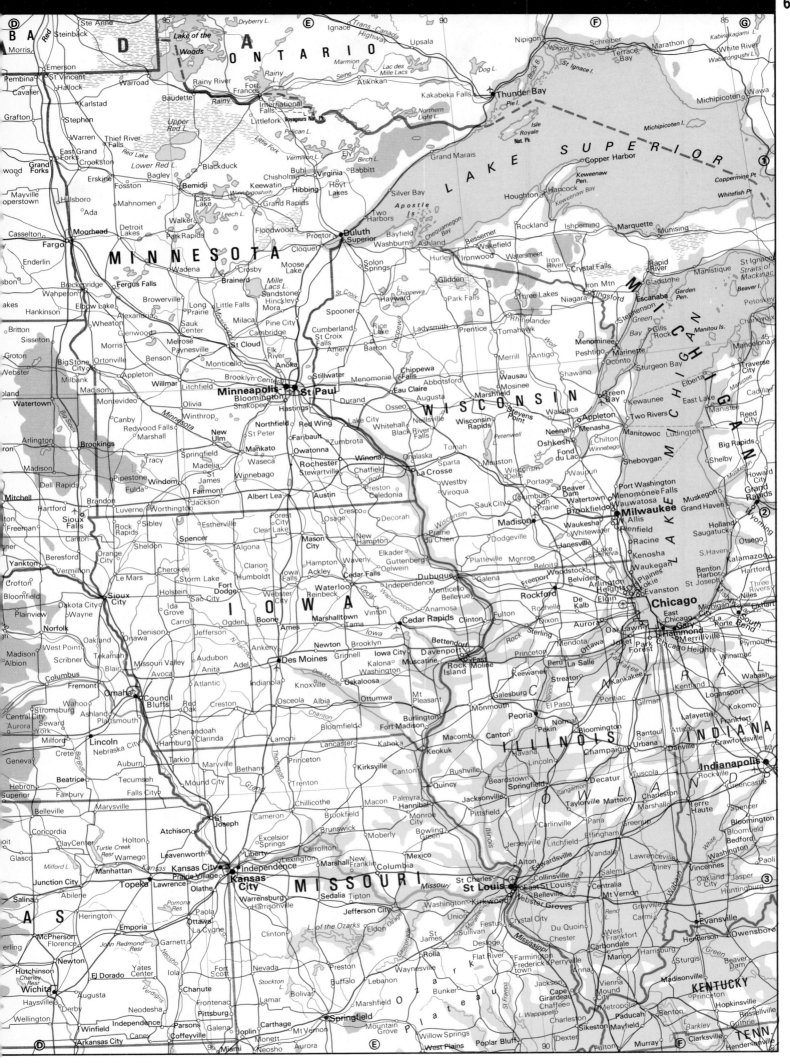

COLORADO

NEW MEXICO

TEXAS

KAN

O

CHIHUAHUA

COAHUILA

DURANGO

SINALOA

NUEVO LEON

MEXICO

PLATEAU

Llano Estacado

Sacramento Mts

San Andres Mts

Sangre de Cristo Mts

San Juan Mts

Zuni Mts

Edwards Plateau

Sierra Madre Occidental

Sierra Madre Oriental

Bolson de Mapimi

Red Hills

Wichita Mts

Monticello · Abajo Mts · Blanding · Bluff · Dove Creek · Silverton · Mt Wilson 4342 · Ouray (A) · Saguache · Monte Vista · South Fork · Wolf Creek Pass · Alamosa · Blanca Peak 4364 · Pueblo · Boone · Ordway · Rocky Ford · Fowler · John Martin Resr · Wiley (B) · Tribune · Scott City · Ness City · Great Bend

Cortez · Mesa Verde N.P. · Durango · Pagosa Springs · Chama · Antonito · Trinidad · Raton · Walsenburg · Delhi · La Junta · Las Animas · Lamar · Springfield · Syracuse · Lakin · Garden City · Jetmore · Larned · Kinsley · Lewis · Pratt

Shiprock · Aztec · Bloomfield · Farmington · Tierra Amarilla · Canjilon · Wheeler Peak 4011 · Taos · Springer · Cimarron · Des Moines · Clayton · Boise City · Hooker · Guymon · Texhoma · Stratford · Forgan · Fort Supply · Alva · Cherokee

Ganado · Tohatchi · Espanola · Los Alamos · Jemez Pueblo · Santa Fe · Watrous · Las Vegas · Mosquero · Dalhart · Hartley · Dumas · Spearman · Perryton · Woodward · Fairview · Seiling · Arnett

Gallup · Mentmore · Ft Wingate · Thoreau · Mt Taylor 3444 · Grants · Bernalillo · Albuquerque · Tucumcari · San Jon · Adrian · Canyon · Amarillo · Vega · Panhandle · Groom · Shamrock · Pampa · Borger · Stinnett · Canadian · Sayre · Clinton

Zuni · Laguna · Los Lunas · Moriarty · Newkirk · Santa Rosa · Vaughn · Ft Sumner · Clovis · Farwell · Friona · Tulia · Hereford · Memphis · Wellington · Mangum · Hollis · Altus · Lawton · Frederick

St Johns · Belen · Corona · Portales · Muleshoe · Earth · Plainview · Littlefield · Morton · Levelland · Floydada · Dickens · Guthrie · Quanah · Vernon · Childress · Paducah

Quemado · Magdalena · Polvadera · Socorro · San Antonio · South Baldy 3288 · Carrizozo · Roswell · Tatum · Brownfield · Lubbock · Tahoka · Post · Aspermont · Haskell · Stamford · Seymour · Olney · Jacksboro

Springerville · Alpine · Glenwood · Hillsboro · Truth or Consequences · Elephant Butte Resr · Salinas Peak · Tularosa · Hondo · Dexter · Lovington · Hobbs · Lamesa · Seminole · Andrews · Colorado City · Snyder · Anson · Breckenridge · Merkel

Gila · Silver City · Central · Bayard · Caballo Resr · Alamogordo · Mayhill · Artesia · L. McMillan · Eunice · Jal · Big Spring · Sweetwater · Abilene · Cisco · Stephenville

Tyrone · Lordsburg · San Andres Mts · Las Cruces · University Park · Anthony · Carlsbad Caverns N.P. · Carlsbad · Malaga · Sterling City · Coleman · Santa Anna · Comanche

Deming · Fairacres · Columbus · El Paso · Ciudad Juarez · Senecu · Guadalupe Pk 2667 · Guadalupe Mtns N.P. · Red Bluff L. · Kermit · Midland · Odessa · Carlsbad · San Angelo · Ballinger · Brownwood · Goldthwaite

Animas Peak 2597 · Fort Hancock · Sierra Blanca · Pecos · Toyah · Crane · Monahans · McCamey · Big Lake · Barnhart · Eden · Brady · Lampasas

Lag. de Guzman · Guadalupe · El Porvenir · Kent · Van Horn · Balmorhea · Fort Stockton · Sheffield · Ozona · Sonora · Mason · Llano · Fredericksburg

Lag de Sta Maria · Lucero · Eagle Peak · Mt Livermore 2554 · Fort Davis · Alpine · Marfa · Marathon · Sanderson · Rocksprings · Junction · Kerrville · Comfort · New Braunfels

Nueva Casas Grandes · Villa Ahumada · Valentine · Chinati Pk 2357 · Langtry · Leakey · Schertz · Alamo Heights · San Antonio

Galeana · San Antonio de Bravo · El Sueco · Gallego · Ojinaga · Presidio · Big Bend Nat. Park · Emory Pk 2389 · Manuel Benavides · Boquillas · Amistad Resr · Devils L. · Del Rio · Brackettville · Hondo · Uvalde · Medina L.

Buenaventura · Madera · Matachic · Aldama · Ciudad Guerrero · Chihuahua · Arquiles Serdan · Cuauhtemoc · Ciudad Acuna · Jimenez · San Carlos · El Moral · La Pryor · Crystal City · Pearsall · Pleasanton

Creel · Delicias · Eagle Pass · Piedras Negras · Zaragoza · Carrizo Springs · Dilley · Three Rivers · Cotulla

Saucillo · Presa de la Boquilla · Ciudad Camargo · Boquilla · San Juan · Allende · Va Union · Catarina · Encinal · Nueces

San Francisco del Oro · Hidalgo del Parral · Jimenez · Sierra Mojada · Nueva Rosita · Sabinas · Freer

Sta Barbara · Escalon · Lampazos · Nuevo Laredo · Laredo · Hebbronville · Falfurrias

Choix · Guasave · San Buenaventura · Monclova · Zapata · Falcon Resr · Rio Grande City · Edin · McA Mission

Sa de los Alamitos · Monterrey · Guadalupe · Sabinas Hidalgo · Reynosa

Rio Bravo del Norte · Rio Grande · Pecos · Conchos · Arkansas · Canadian · Washita · Red · Wichita · Colorado · Llano · N. Canadian · Prairie Dog Town Fork · Double Mtn Fork

1:5M   0 50 100 150 200 km   0 50 100 mils

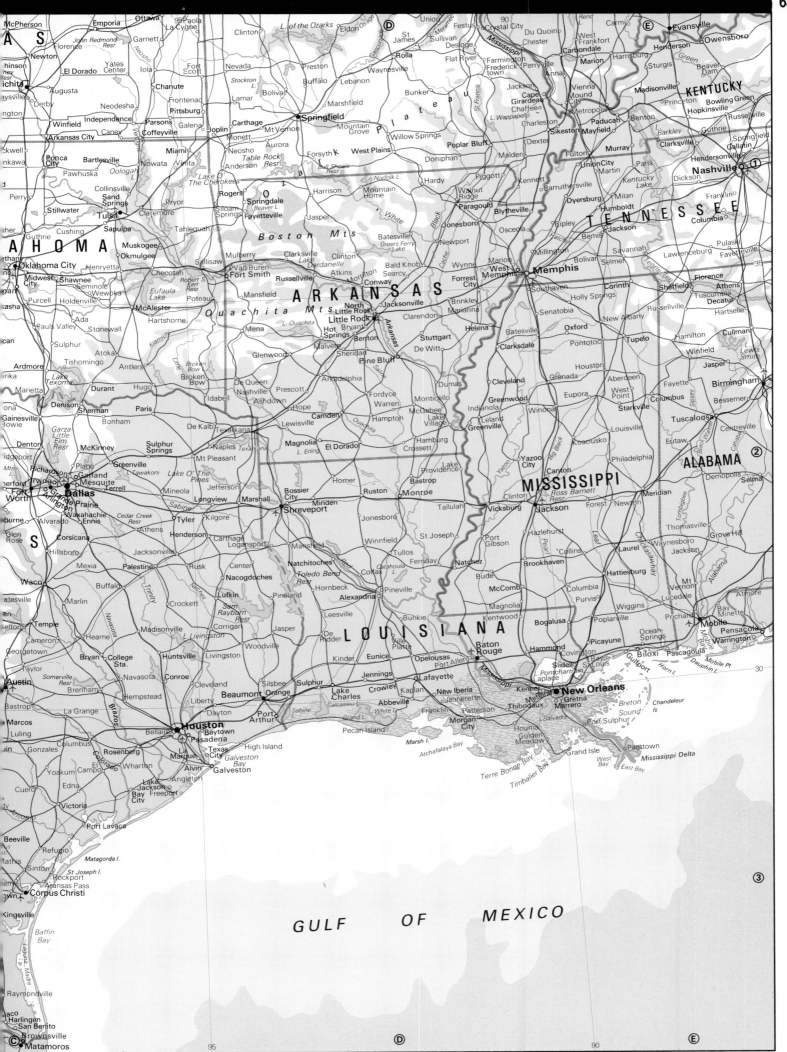

GULF OF MEXICO

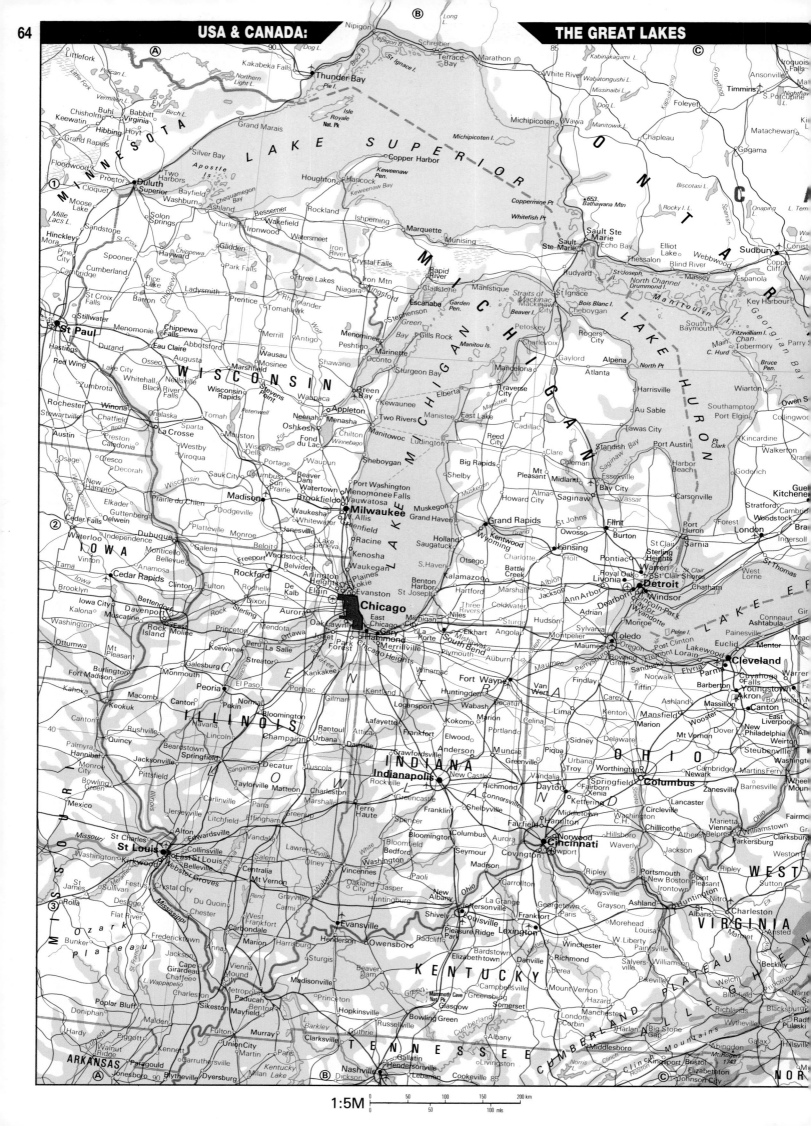

1:5M

0   50   100   150   200 km

0   50   100 mls

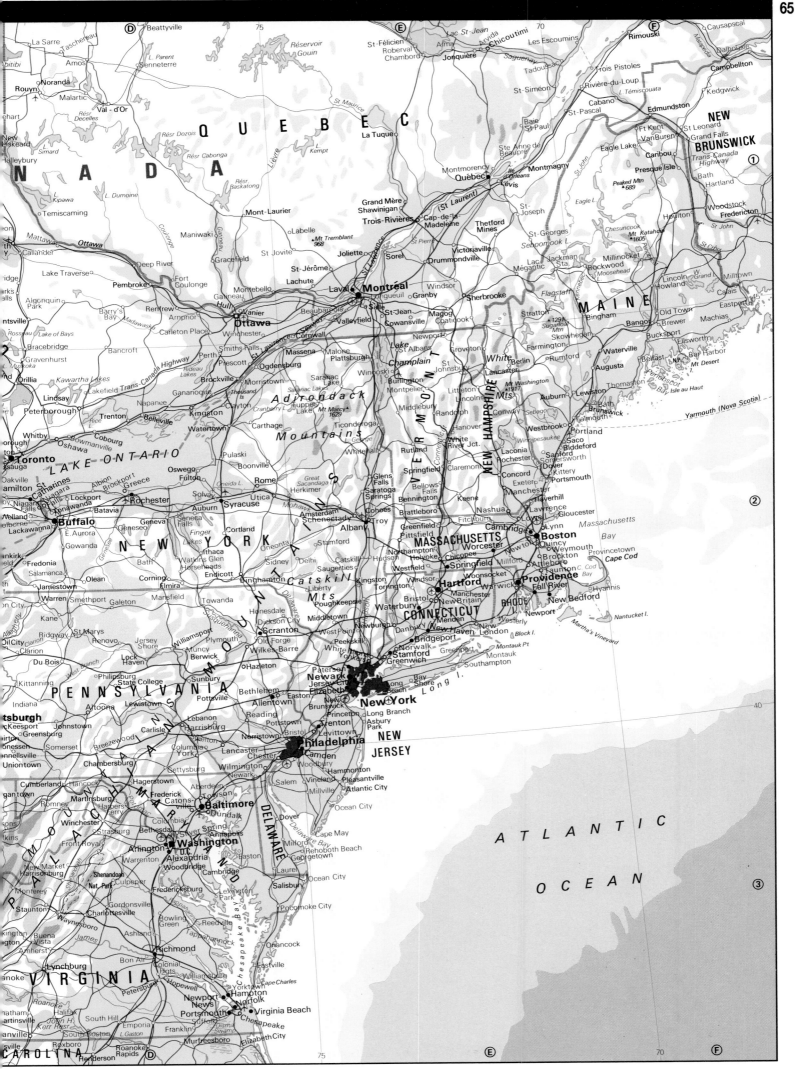

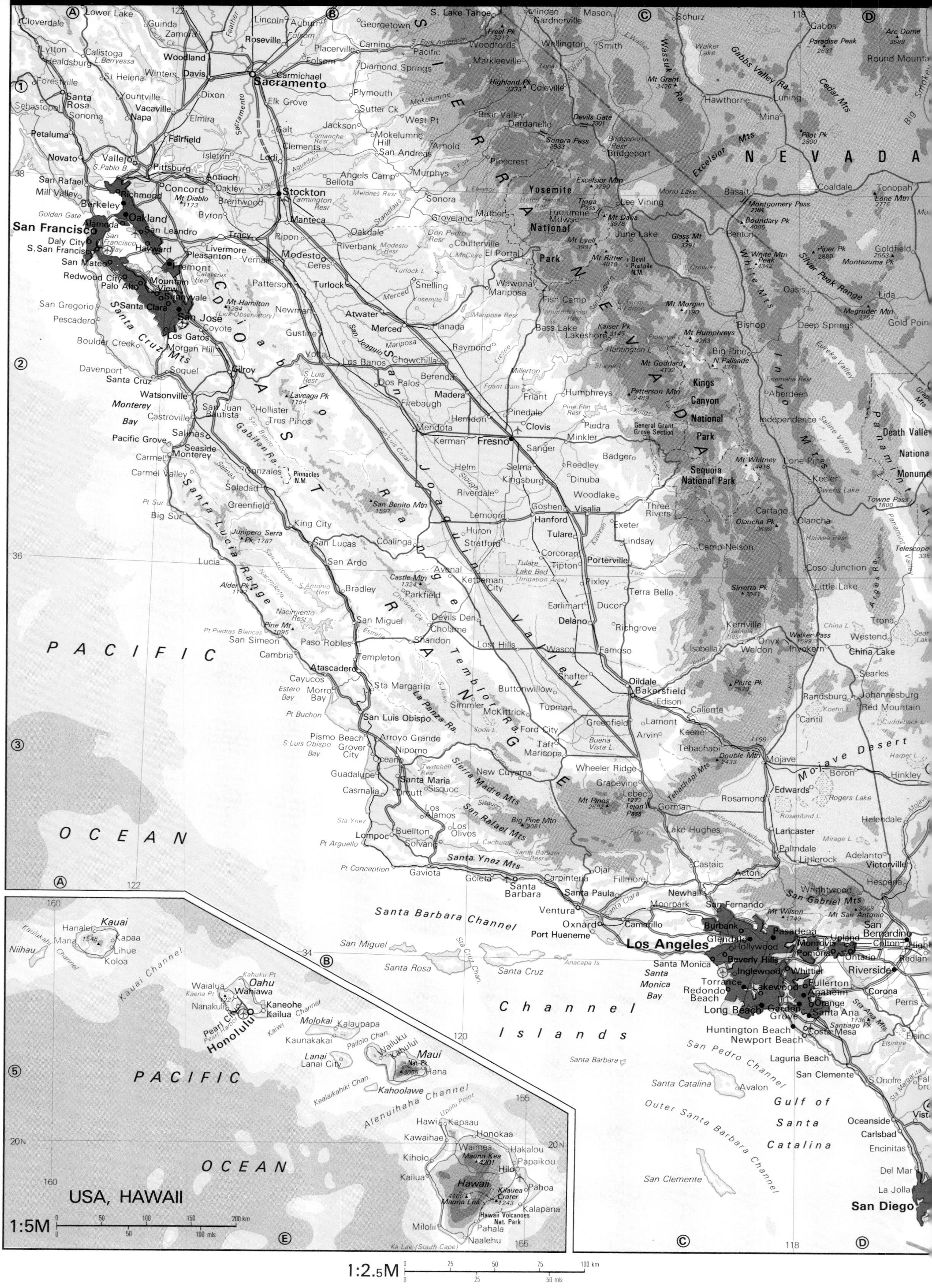
San Francisco
Oakland
Berkeley
Richmond
San Jose
Sacramento
Stockton
Modesto
Merced
Fresno
Visalia
Bakersfield
Los Angeles
Long Beach
Santa Ana
Anaheim
Pasadena
Riverside
San Diego
Santa Barbara
Ventura
Oxnard
San Luis Obispo
Santa Maria
Salinas
Monterey
Santa Cruz
Santa Rosa
Napa
Vallejo
Concord
Hayward
Fremont
Palo Alto
Santa Clara
Gilroy
Hollister
King City
Paso Robles
Lompoc
Tulare
Hanford
Porterville
Delano
Lancaster
Palmdale
Mojave
Victorville
Bishop
Lone Pine
Independence
Big Pine
Tonopah
Goldfield
Hawthorne
Bridgeport
S. Lake Tahoe
Yosemite National Park
Kings Canyon National Park
Sequoia National Park
Death Valley National Monument
Devil Postpile N.M.
Pinnacles N.M.
S I E R R A   N E V A D A
C O A S T   R A N G E S
San Joaquin Valley
Temblor Range
Santa Lucia Range
Santa Cruz Mts
Gabilan Ra.
Diablo Range
La Panza Ra.
Sierra Madre Mts
San Rafael Mts
Santa Ynez Mts
San Gabriel Mts
Tehachapi Mts
White Mts
Inyo Mts
Panamint Range
Wassuk Ra.
Excelsior Mts
Silver Peak Range
Mojave Desert
N E V A D A
Mt Whitney 4418
Mt Diablo 1173
Mt Hamilton 1284
Mt Pinos 2692
Mt San Antonio 3068
Mt Wilson 1740
Mt Dana 3978
Mt Lyell 3997
Mt Ritter 4010
White Mtn Peak 4342
Mt Humphreys 4263
Mt Goddard 4132
N. Palisade 4341
Montgomery Pass 2184
Boundary Pk 4005
Tioga Pass
Sonora Pass 2933
Devils Gate 2301
Walker Pass 1599
Tejon Pass
Towne Pass 1600
Mono Lake
Walker Lake
Owens Lake
Tulare Lake Bed (Irrigation Area)
Lake Isabella
P A C I F I C
O C E A N
Monterey Bay
Santa Barbara Channel
Channel Islands
San Miguel
Santa Rosa
Santa Cruz
Anacapa Is
Santa Barbara
Santa Catalina
San Clemente
Gulf of Santa Catalina
San Pedro Channel
Outer Santa Barbara Channel
Santa Monica Bay
Pt Conception
Pt Arguello
Pt Sur
Pt Buchon
Pt Piedras Blancas
Golden Gate
38
36
34
122
120
118
USA, HAWAII
Kauai
Niihau
Oahu
Molokai
Lanai
Maui
Kahoolawe
Hawaii
Honolulu
Pearl City
Wahiawa
Waialua
Kaneohe
Kailua
Lihue
Kapaa
Koloa
Hanalei
Kaunakakai
Kalaupapa
Lanai City
Wailuku
Kahului
Hana
Hilo
Kailua
Kapaau
Honokaa
Kawaihae
Waimea
Kiholo
Pahoa
Kalapana
Pahala
Naalehu
Milolii
Mauna Kea 4201
Mauna Loa 4169
Kilauea Crater 1243
Hawaii Volcanoes Nat. Park
Kauai Channel
Kaiwi Channel
Pailolo Chan.
Kealaikahiki Chan.
Alenuihaha Channel
Kaulakahi Channel
Ka Lae (South Cape)
Upolu Point
Kahuku Pt
Kaena Pt
P A C I F I C
O C E A N
160
155
20N
1:5M
0 50 100 150 200 km
0 50 100 mls
1:2.5M
0 25 50 75 100 km
0 25 50 mls

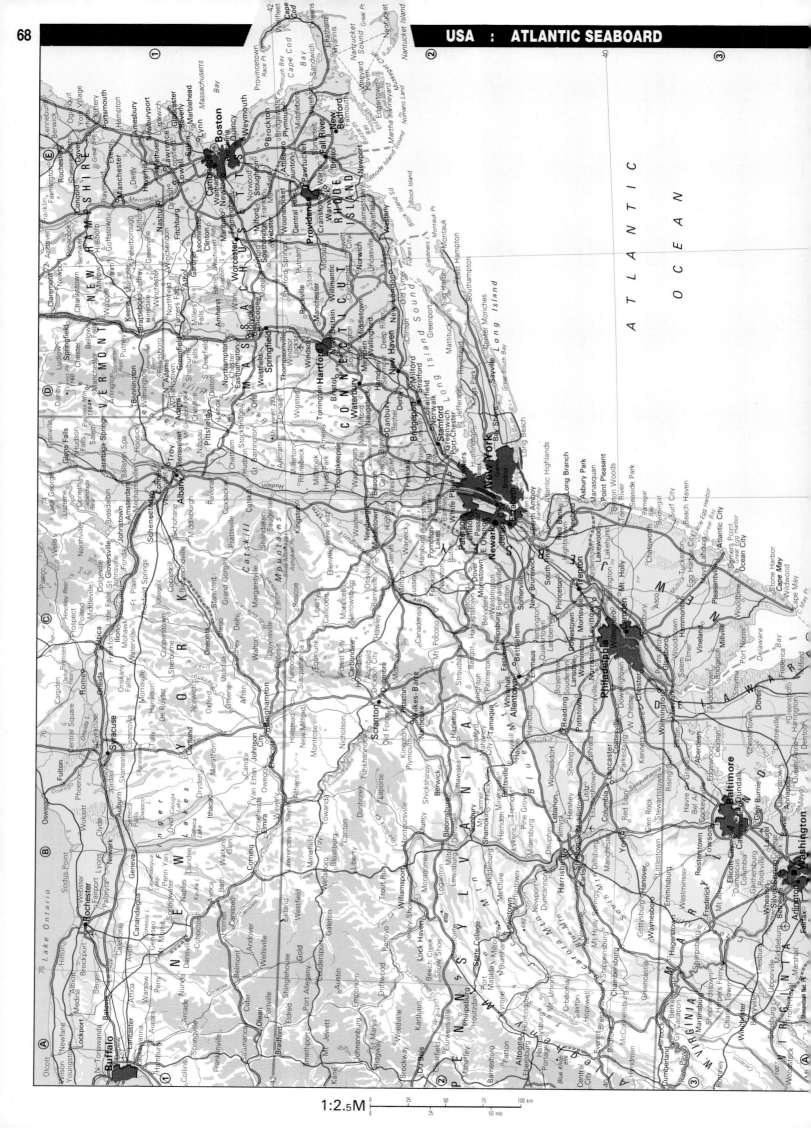

1:2.5M

TRINIDAD AND TOBAGO 1:2.5 M

DOMINICA 1:2.5 M

BARBADOS 1:2.5 M

ST LUCIA 1:2.5 M

ST VINCENT 1:2.5 M

GRENADA 1:2.5 M

1:2.5 M

JAMAICA 1:2.5 M

A T L A N T I C   O C E A N

PUERTO RICO TRENCH

Leeward Islands

Windward Islands

ANTIGUA & BARBUDA

ST KITTS & NEVIS

L E S S E R   A N T I L L E S

C A R I B B E A N   S E A

G R E A T E R   A N T I L L E S

THE BAHAMAS

C U B A

JAMAICA

HAITI

DOMINICAN REPUBLIC

H i s p a n i o l a

CAYMAN TRENCH

PUERTO RICO (U.S.A.)

FLORIDA

HONDURAS

NICARAGUA

COSTA RICA

PANAMA

COLOMBIA

V E N E Z U E L A

TRINIDAD AND TOBAGO

Gulf of Paria

1:10M

100   200   300   400 km

100   200 mls

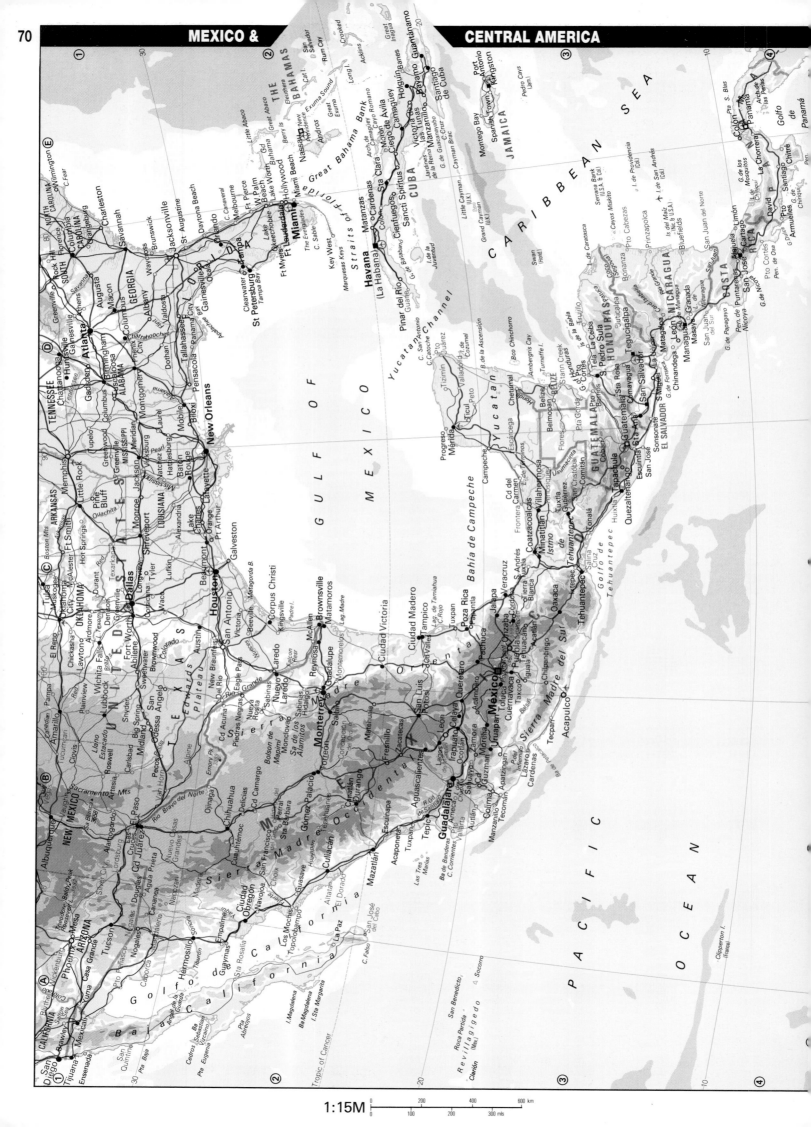

1:15M

A · B U.S.A. · C · D · E · F · G

① ② ③ ④ ⑤ ⑥ ⑦ ⑧ ⑨

Tropic of Cancer
Equator
Tropic of Capricorn

Gulf of Mexico

MEXICO
Mérida
BELIZE
Belmopan
GUATEMALA
Guatemala
HONDURAS
Tegucigalpa
S.Salvador
EL SALVADOR
NICARAGUA
Managua
COSTA RICA
S.José
Colón
Panamá
PANAMA

Miami
THE BAHAMAS
Habana
CUBA
Santiago de Cuba
Guantanamo
HAITI
JAMAICA
Kingston
Port au Prince
DOMINICAN REP.
Santiago
Santo Domingo
Pto Rico (U.S.A.)
San Juan

CARIBBEAN SEA
Neth. Antilles
Curaçao

ANTIGUA & BARBUDA
ST KITTS-NEVIS
Guadeloupe (Fr.)
DOMINICA
Martinique (Fr.)
ST LUCIA
ST VINCENT & THE GRENADINES
BARBADOS
GRENADA
Port of Spain
TRINIDAD & TOBAGO

I. del Coco (C.R.)
Malpelo (Col.)

Sta Marta
Barranquilla
Cartagena
Maracaibo
Barquisimeto
Caracas
Barcelona
Cd. Bolívar
Orinoco
Cd. Guayana

S.Cristóbal
VENEZUELA
GUYANA
Georgetown
Paramaribo
SURINAM
Cayenne
FR. GUIANA

Medellín
Manizales
Bogotá
Buenaventura
Cali
Popayán
S.Lorenzo
Pasto
COLOMBIA
Boa Vista
Branco
Negro

Galapagos Is (Ecu.)
Quito
ECUADOR
Guayaquil
Iquitos
Piura
Chiclayo
Trujillo
Chimbote
PERU
Marañón
Putumayo
Juruá
Purus
Ucayali
Amazon
Manaus
Santarém
Macapá
I. de Marajó
Belém
São Luís
Codó
Sobral
Teresina
Fortaleza
Natal
João Pessoa
Recife
Maceió
Aracajú

S.Pedro e S.Paulo (Braz.)
I. Fernando de Noronha (Braz.)
Rocas

Madeira
Tapajós
Xingu
Tocantins
Araguaia
BRAZIL

Callao
Lima
Huancayo
Cuzco
Pto Maldonado
Rio Branco
Pto Velho

SOUTH PACIFIC OCEAN

Arequipa
La Paz
Oruro
Cochabamba
Arica
Sucre
Sta Cruz
BOLIVIA
Corumbá
Cáceres
Cuiabá
Goiânia
Brasília
S.Francisco
Montes Claros
Corinto
Belo Horizonte
Vitória
Juazeiro
Alagoinhas
Salvador
Ilhéus

Iquique
Antofagasta
Salta
S.Miguel de Tucumán
S.Félix (Chile)

Campo Grande
Dourados
PARAGUAY
Concepción
Asunción
Foz do Iguaçu
Ribeirão Prêto
Campinas
Juiz de Fora
São Paulo
Santos
Rio de Janeiro
Campos
Paraná
Ponta Grossa
Curitiba
Florianópolis
Uruguay
Posadas
Resistencia
Salado

Juan Fernández Is. (Chile)
Córdoba
Santa Fe
Paraná
Mendoza
Viña del Mar
Valparaíso
Santiago
Rivera
Paysandú
Rio Grande
URUGUAY
Montevideo
Pto Alegre
Pelotas

CHILE
ARGENTINA

Talca
Rosario
Mar del Plata
R. de la Plata
Buenos Aires
Concepción
Colorado
Negro
Bahía Blanca
Temuco
Valdivia
Pto Montt

SOUTH ATLANTIC OCEAN

Chico
Cmd. Rivadavia
Deseado
G.San Jorge

Falkland Is (U.K.)
Stanley

Pto Natales
Rio Gallegos
Punta Arenas
Tierra del Fuego
Cape Horn

S.Georgia (U.K.)

S.Shetland Is (U.K.)
S.Orkney Is (U.K.)
ANTARCTICA

Trindade (Braz.)
S.Sandwich Is (U.K.)

1:35M

0 250 500 750 1000 1250 km
0 250 500 750 mls

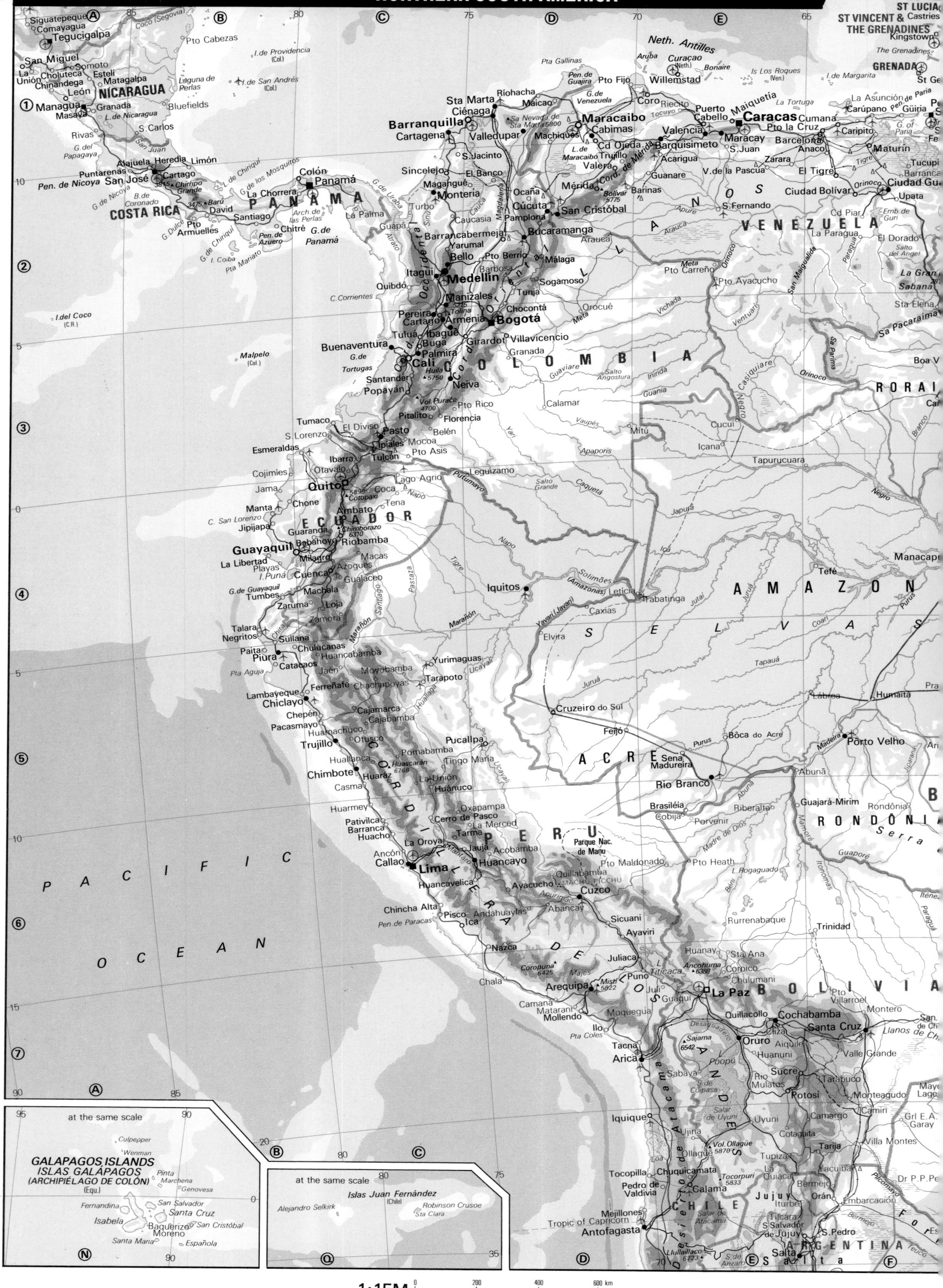

Roseau
(F) Fort-de-Franc
Martinique
(Fr.)
ST VINCENT &
THE GRENADINES
Kingstown
The Grenadines
GRENADA
St Ge

Siguatepeque (A) 85 (B) 80 (C) 75 (D) 70 (E) 65
Comayagua
Tegucigalpa
San Miguel
La
Unión Somoto
Chinandega Estelí
Matagalpa
León NICARAGUA
Managua Granada
Masaya L. de Nicaragua
Rivas S. Carlos
G. del Papagayo
Alajuela Heredia Limón
Puntarenas San José Cartago
Pen. de Nicoya
G. de Nicoya
COSTA RICA
Pto Armuelles
David
Santiago Chitré
Pen. de Azuero
PANAMA
Colón
Panamá
I. Coiba
Pta Mariato

Pto Cabezas
I. de Providencia (Col)
I. de San Andrés (Col)
Laguna de Perlas
Bluefields

I. del Coco (C.R.)

Malpelo (Col.)

Pta Gallinas
Pen. de Guajira
Ríohacha
Maicao
Sta Marta
Ciénaga
Barranquilla
Cartagena
Valledupar
S. Jacinto
Sincelejo El Banco
Magangué
Montería
Caucasia
Quibdó
Turbo
Barrancabermeja
Yarumal
Bello
Itagüí MEDELLIN
Manizales
Pereira
Cartago Armenia
Tuluá Ibagué
Buga
Buenaventura Palmira
CALI
Santander
Popayán
Tumaco Pasto
El Diviso Ipiales
S Lorenzo
Esmeraldas
Ibarra Tulcán
Otavalo
Cojimies
QUITO
Jama Chone Cotopaxi
Manta Ambato
Jipijapa Guaranda
Chimborazo
GUAYAQUIL Babahoyo Riobamba
La Libertad Milagro Macas
Playas I. Puná Cuenca Azogues
G. de Guayaquil Gualaceo
Tumbes Machala
Zaruma Loja
Talara Zamora
Negritos Sullana
Paita Chulucanas
Piura Catacaos
Pta Aguja Jaén
Lambayeque Ferreñafe
Chiclayo Chachapoyas
Chepén Cajamarca
Pacasmayo Celendín
Huamachuco
Trujillo Otusco
Huallanca Pomabamba
Chimbote Huaraz Huascarán 6768
Casma La Unión
Huarmey Huánuco
Oxapampa Cerro de Pasco
Barranca La Merced
Pativilca Tarma
Huacho La Oroya Jauja
Ancón Acobamba
Callao Huancayo
LIMA
Huancavelica
Chincha Alta Pisco Andahuaylas
Ica Ayacucho Abancay
Nazca
Chala
Arequipa Misti 5922
Camaná Moquegua
Matarani Mollendo
Ilo Pta Coles
Tacna
Arica

Rioacha
Aruba Curaçao Bonaire Is Los Roques (Ven)
G. de Venezuela Pto Fijo Coro
Maracaibo Cabimas
Machiques Cd Ojeda
L. de Maracaibo Trujillo
Ocaña Valera Mérida
Cúcuta Pamplona Barinas
Bucaramanga
Málaga
Sogamoso
Tunja
Chocontá
BOGOTÁ
Girardot Villavicencio
Granada
Neiva
Pitalito Florencia
Belén
Mocoa
Pto Asís
Leguizamo
Putumayo

COLOMBIA

Willemstad
Puerto Cabello
Maiquetía CARACAS
Valencia Maracay
Barquisimeto S. Juan
Acarigua Barcelona
Guanare V. de la Pascua
Guasdualito
VENEZUELA
San Fernando
Ciudad Bolívar
Upata
Cd Gu

La Asunción
Pampatar
Cumaná Carúpano
Pto la Cruz Güiria
Anaco Maturín
Zaraza El Tigre
Tucupita

LLANOS

Orinoco

Pto Carreño
Vichada
Orocué
Meta
Pto Ayacucho
Casiquiare
Orinoco
Inírida
Salto Angostura
Calamar Guainía
Guaviare
Vaupés
Mitú
Apaporis
Icana
Cucuí
Tapurucuara

RORAI

AMAZON
SELVAS
ACRE

Iquitos
Leticia
Tabatinga
Caxias
Elvira
Cruzeiro do Sul
Feijó
Bôca do Acre
Sena Madureira
Rio Branco
Abunã
Brasiléia
Cobija
Riberalta
Porvenir
Guajará-Mirim
Porto Velho
RONDÔNIA

Pucallpa
Tingo María
PERU
Pto Maldonado
Pto Heath
Parque Nac. de Manú
Quillabamba
MACHU PICCHU
Cuzco
Sicuani
Ayaviri
Juliaca
Puno L. Titicaca Ancohuma 6388
Huanay Sta Ana
Rurrenabaque Trinidad
La Paz
BOLIVIA
Oruro Cochabamba
Santa Cruz
Sajama 6542 Quillacollo
Huanuni Sucre
Potosí
Uyuni
Tupiza
Tarija
Villa Montes

Moyobamba
Tarapoto
Yurimaguas
Juruá
Purús
Madre de Dios
Beni
Mamoré

Iquique
Tocopilla
Pedro de Valdivia
Mejillones
Antofagasta
CHILE
Tropic of Capricorn
Calama Chuquicamata
Vol. Ollagüe 5870
Llullaillaco 6723
ARGENTINA
San Pedro
JUJUY
Salta

PACIFIC OCEAN

at the same scale
GALAPAGOS ISLANDS
ISLAS GALÁPAGOS
(ARCHIPIÉLAGO DE COLÓN) (Equ.)
Culpepper Wenman
Pinta Marchena Genovesa
Fernandina
Isabela Santa Cruz San Cristóbal
Baquerizo Moreno
Santa María Española

at the same scale
Islas Juan Fernández (Chile)
Alejandro Selkirk Robinson Crusoe
Sta Clara

1:15M
200 400 600 km
100 200 300 mls

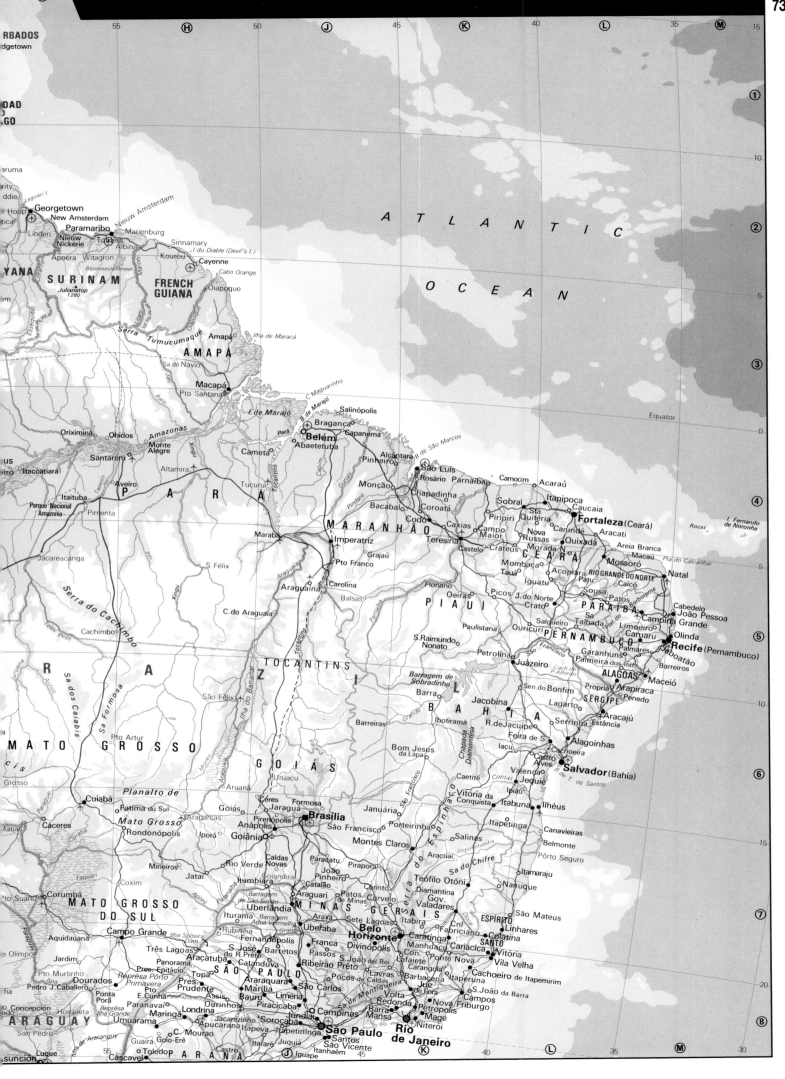

G   55   H   50   J   45   K   40   L   35   M   15

RBADOS
dgetown

① ② ③

ATLANTIC

OCEAN

10

5

Equator   0

DAD
GO

Georgetown
New Amsterdam
Paramaribo
Nieuw
Nickerie   Albina
Apoera   Witagron
Linden

Leguan I.
Hoop
ddie
tica

SURINAM
Julianatop
1280

Marienburg
Nieuw Amsterdam
Torres
Sinnamary
Kourou
Cayenne
I. du Diable (Devil's I.)

Blommesteinmeer

Serra Tumucumaque

FRENCH
GUIANA

Oiapoque

Cabo Orange

YANA   Amapá   Ilha de Maracá

e

AMAPÁ

Sa do Navio

Macapá
Pto Santana

C. Maguarinho

I. de Marajó   B de Marajó

Salinópolis

Oriximiná   Óbidos
Monte
Santarém   Alegre

Amazonas

Bragança
Belém   Capanema
Abaetetuba

Pará

Cametá
Pinheiro

Salgueiro

Alcântara   B. de São Marcos
São Luís
Rosário   Parnaíba
Monção   Chapadinha   Camocim   Acaraú

us
iro   Itacoatiara

Jacareacanga

Itaituba
Parque Nacional
Amazônia   Pimenta

PARÁ

Altamira

Tucuruí

Marabá

Imperatriz

Grajaú
Pto Franco

Carolina

MARANHÃO   Bacabal
Codó   Caxias

Coroatá

Sobral   Itapipoca
Piripiri   Sta   Caucaia
Campo   Quitéria   Fortaleza (Ceará)
Maior   Canindé   Aracati
Nova   Quixadá
Russas
Morada-N   Areia Branca

Teresina   Crateús   CEARÁ   Mossoró   Macau   Pta do Calcanhar

Castelo   Mombaça   Acopiara   RIO GRANDE DO NORTE   Natal
Tauá   Iguatu   Patu   Caicó
J. do Norte   Sousa   Garborema

Serra do Cachimbo

Teles Pires
Cachimbo

S. Félix

Araguaína

C. do Araguaia

Floriano   Picos
Oeiras

PIAUÍ   Crato   PARAÍBA   Campina   João Pessoa
S. Raimundo   Paulistana   Salgueiro   Sa   Grande   Cabedelo
Nonato   Ouricuri   Talhada   Limoeiro   Caruaru
Petrolina   PERNAMBUCO   Olinda   Recife (Pernambuco)
Juázeiro   Garanhuns   Palmares   Floatão
Cach. do   ALAGOAS   Barreiros
P. Afonso   Propriá   Arapiraca
Sen. do Bonfim   Maceió
Jacobina   Lagarto   SERGIPE   Penedo
Aracajú

I. Fernando
de Noronha

Rocas

① ② ③ ④ ⑤ ⑥ ⑦ ⑧

R   A   Z   I   L

TOCANTINS

MATO   GROSSO   Pto Artur

Sa dos Caiabis   Sa Formosa

São Félix

Barragem de
Sobradinho

B   A   H   I   A

Barra

Ibotirama   R. de Jacuípe   Serrinha   Estância
Barreiras   Iaçu   Feira de S.   Alagoinhas
Bom Jesus   Castro   Cachoeira
da Lapa   Valença   Alves
Jequié   B de T. os Santos   Salvador (Bahia)
Caetité   Ipiaú
Vitória da   Itabuna   Ilhéus
Conquista   Itapetinga

MATO   GROSSO

Cuiabá
Fátima du Sul
Mato Grosso
Cáceres   Rondonópolis

GOIÁS   Uruaçu

Planalto de

Aruanã

Céres
Goiás   Jaraguá   Formosa
Araçarás   Pirenópolis   Brasília   São Francisco
Anápolis   Goiânia   Porteirinha
Iporá   Montes Claros
Aquidauana

Caldas
Novas   Paracatu   Piropora   Salinas   Belmonte
Mineiros   Rio Verde   João   Pôrto Seguro
Jataí   Goiandira   Pinheiro   Arauaí   Canavieiras
Itumbiara   Catalão   Corinto   Itamaraju   Belmonte
Coxim   Aporé   Patos   Curvelo   Diamantina   Nanuque
de Minas   Araxá   Teófilo Otôni
Araguari   Itabira   São Mateus
Uberlândia   Sete Lagoas   Cnl   ESPÍRITO
Iturama   Uberaba   Gov.   Fabriciano   Linhares
Suárez   Corumbá   Ituiutaba   Valadares   Colatina
Rubinéia   MINAS   GERAIS   Manhuaçu   Cariacica   SANTO
Matias   Agua Vermelha   Caratinga   Ponte Nova   Vitória
Campo Grande   Ilha Solteira   Franca   Belo   Con.   Lafaiete   Vila Velha
Três Lagoas   Barragem   Passos   Horizonte   del Rei   Itaperuna
Olimpos   Jardim   de São Simão   Divinópolis   Cachoeiro de Itapemirim
Pres.   São José   Poços de Caldas   Pocos   Barbacena   Campos
Epitácio   do R. Preto   SÃO   Ribeirão Prêto   Lavras   Juiz   S.João da Barra
Pto Murtinho   Panorama   Catanduva   PAULO   de Fora   Nova
Pedro J. Caballero   Primavera   Aracatuba   Araraquara   Pocos de Caldas   Friburgo
Dourados   Pres.   Marília   São Carlos   Barra   Petrópolis
fia   Represa Pôrto   Prudente   Tupã   Limeira   Volta   Magé
Ponta   Assis   Bauru   Piracicaba   Redonda   Niterói
Porã   Apa   Paranavaí   Ourinhos   Campinas   Barra   Rio
Concepción   E. Cunha   Jacarezinho   Mansa   de Janeiro
Horqueta   Londrina   Jundiaí   Sorocaba   Santos
ARAGUAY   Maringá   Apucarana   Itapeva   Itapetininga   São Paulo
San Pedro   Umuarama   C. Mourão   Itararé   São Vicente
Luque   Guaíra   Gôio-Erê   Castro   Itanhaém
unción   Toledo   PARANÁ   Juquiá   Iguape

Corumbá
Pto Suárez

Cáceres

Aquidauana

MATO   GROSSO
DO   SUL

Campo Grande

Dourados

Ponta
Porã

55   50   45   40   35   30

1:15M

1:7.5M

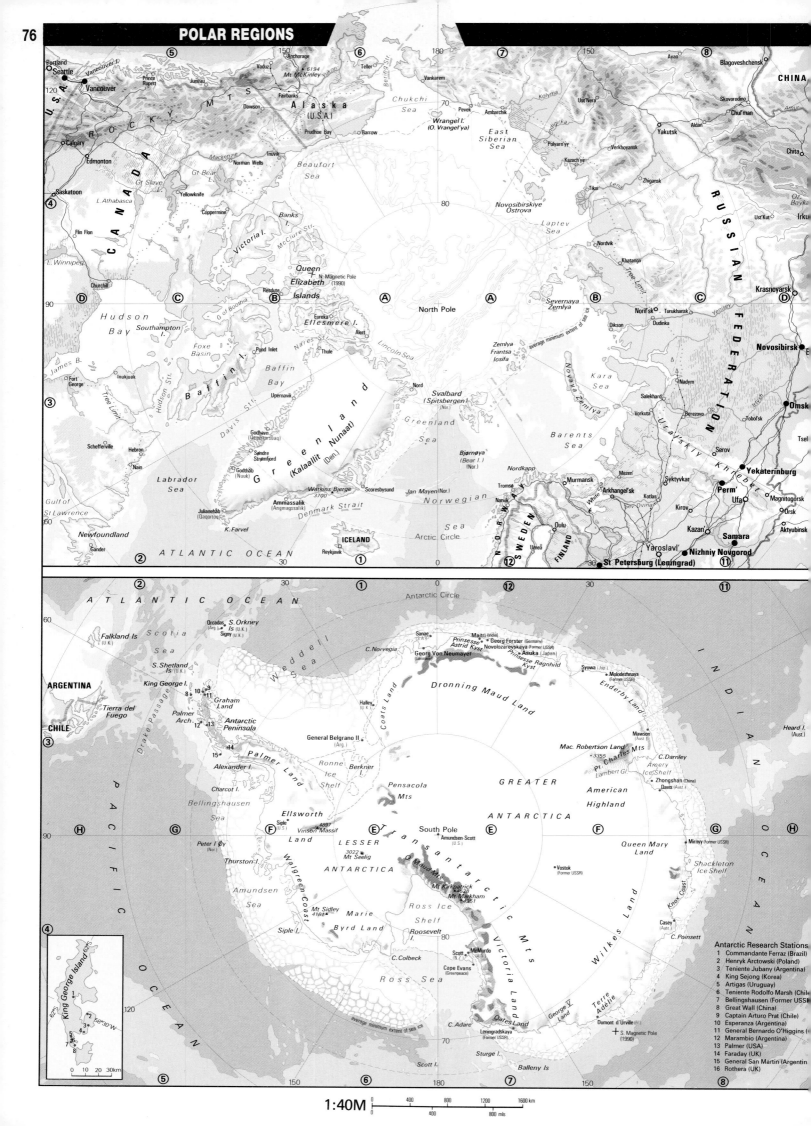

Introduction to the index

In the index, the first number refers to the page, and the following letter and number to the section of the map in which the index entry can be found.
For example, 14C2 **Paris** means that Paris can be found on page 14 where column C and row 2 meet.

Abbreviations used in the index

Arch	Archipelago
B	Bay
C	Cape
Chan	Channel
Gl	Glacier
I(s)	Island(s)
Lg	Lagoon
L	Lake
Mt(s)	Mountain(s)
P	Pass
Pass	Passage
Pen	Peninsula
Plat	Plateau
Pt	Point
Res	Reservoir
R	River
S	Sea
Sd	Sound
Str	Strait
UAE	United Arab Emirates
UK	United Kingdom
USA	United States of America
V	Valley

A

18B2 **Aachen** Germany
13C1 **Aalsmeer** Netherlands
13C2 **Aalst** Belgium
12K6 **Äänekoski** Finland
31A3 **Aba** China
48C4 **Aba** Nigeria
50D3 **Aba** Zaïre
41E3 **Abādān** Iran
41F3 **Abādeh** Iran
48B1 **Abadla** Algeria
75C2 **Abaeté** Brazil
75C2 **Abaeté** *R* Brazil
73J4 **Abaetetuba** Brazil
31D1 **Abagnar Qi** China
59E3 **Abajo Mts** USA
48C4 **Abakaliki** Nigeria
25L4 **Abakan** Russian Federation
48C3 **Abala** Niger
48C2 **Abalessa** Algeria
72D6 **Abancay** Peru
41F3 **Abarqū** Iran
29E2 **Abashiri** Japan
29E2 **Abashiri-wan** *B* Japan
27H7 **Abau** Papua New Guinea
50D3 **Abaya, L** Ethiopia
50D2 **Abbai** *R* Ethiopia/Sudan
50E2 **Abbe, L** Djibouti/Ethiopia
14C1 **Abbeville** France
63D3 **Abbeville** Louisiana, USA
67B2 **Abbeville** S Carolina, USA
58B1 **Abbotsford** Canada
64A2 **Abbotsford** USA
42C2 **Abbottabad** Pakistan
40D2 **'Abd al 'Azīz, Jebel** *Mt* Syria
20J5 **Abdulino** Russian Federation
50C2 **Abéché** Chad
48B4 **Abengourou** Ivory Coast
18B1 **Åbenrå** Denmark
48C4 **Abeokuta** Nigeria
50D3 **Abera** Ethiopia
7B3 **Aberaeron** Wales
7C4 **Aberdare** Wales
66C2 **Aberdeen** California, USA
65D3 **Aberdeen** Maryland, USA
63E2 **Aberdeen** Mississippi, USA
47C3 **Aberdeen** South Africa
8D3 **Aberdeen** Scotland
56D2 **Aberdeen** S Dakota, USA
56A2 **Aberdeen** Washington, USA
54J3 **Aberdeen L** Canada
7B3 **Aberdyfi** Wales
8D3 **Aberfeldy** Scotland
8C3 **Aberfoyle** Scotland
7C4 **Abergavenny** Wales
7B3 **Aberystwyth** Wales
20L2 **Abez'** Russian Federation
50E2 **Abhā** Saudi Arabia
41E2 **Abhar** Iran
48B4 **Abidjan** Ivory Coast
61D3 **Abilene** Kansas, USA
62C2 **Abilene** Texas, USA
7D4 **Abingdon** England
64C3 **Abingdon** USA
55K4 **Abitibi** *R* Canada
55L5 **Abitibi,L** Canada
21G7 **Abkhazian Republic** Georgia
42C2 **Abohar** India
48C4 **Abomey** Benin
50B3 **Abong Mbang** Cameroon
50B2 **Abou Deïa** Chad
8D3 **Aboyne** Scotland
41E4 **Abqaiq** Saudi Arabia
15A2 **Abrantes** Portugal
70A2 **Abreojos, Punta** *Pt* Mexico
50D1 **'Abri** Sudan
32A3 **Abrolhos** *I* Australia
75E2 **Abrolhos, Arquipélago dos** *Is* Brazil
56B2 **Absaroka Range** *Mts* USA
41F5 **Abū al Abyaḍ** *I* UAE
41E4 **Abū 'Alī** *I* Saudi Arabia
45D3 **Abu 'Amūd, Wadi** Jordan
45C3 **Abu 'Aweigîla** *Well* Egypt
41F5 **Abū Dhabi** UAE
45C3 **Ābū el Jurdhān** Jordan
50D2 **Abu Hamed** Sudan
48C4 **Abuja** Nigeria
45A3 **Abu Kebir Hihya** Egypt
72E5 **Abunã** Brazil
72E6 **Abunã** *R* Bolivia/Brazil
45C4 **Abu Rûtha, Gebel** *Mt* Egypt
41D3 **Abū Sukhayr** Iraq
45B3 **Abu Suweir** Egypt
45B4 **Abu Tarfa, Wadi** Egypt
35B2 **Abut Head** *C* New Zealand
40B4 **Abu Tig** Egypt
50D2 **Abu'Urug** *Well* Sudan
50D2 **Abuye Meda** *Mt* Ethiopia
50C2 **Abu Zabad** Sudan
50D3 **Abwong** Sudan
18B1 **Åby** Denmark
50C3 **Abyei** Sudan
65F2 **Acadia Nat Pk** USA
70B2 **Acámbaro** Mexico
69B5 **Acandí** Colombia
70B2 **Acaponeta** Mexico
70B3 **Acapulco** Mexico
73L4 **Acaraú** Brazil
72E2 **Acarigua** Venezuela
70C3 **Acatlán** Mexico
48B4 **Accra** Ghana
6C3 **Accrington** England
42D4 **Achalpur** India
74B6 **Achao** Chile
13E3 **Achern** Germany
9A3 **Achill Hd** *Pt* Irish Republic
10A3 **Achill I** Irish Republic
13E1 **Achim** Germany
25L4 **Achinsk** Russian Federation
16D3 **Acireale** Sicily, Italy
61E2 **Ackley** USA
69C2 **Acklins** *I* The Bahamas
72D6 **Acobamba** Peru
74B4 **Aconcagua** *Mt* Chile
73L5 **Acopiara** Brazil
Açores *Is* = **Azores**
A Coruña = **La Coruña**
Acre = **'Akko**
72D5 **Acre** *State* Brazil
66C3 **Acton** USA
63C2 **Ada** USA
15B1 **Adaja** *R* Spain
41G5 **Adam** Oman
50D3 **Adama** Ethiopia
75B3 **Adamantina** Brazil
50B3 **Adamaoua** *Region* Cameroon/Nigeria
50B3 **Adamaoua, Massif de l'** *Mts* Cameroon
68D1 **Adams** USA
44B4 **Adam's Bridge** India/Sri Lanka
56A2 **Adams,Mt** USA
44C4 **Adam's Peak** *Mt* Sri Lanka
'Adan = **Aden**
21F8 **Adana** Turkey
21E7 **Adapazarı** Turkey
76F7 **Adare,C** Antarctica
34B1 **Adavale** Australia
41E4 **Ad Dahnā'** *Region* Saudi Arabia
41F4 **Ad Dammam** Saudi Arabia
41D5 **Ad Dawādimī** Saudi Arabia
41E4 **Ad Dibdibah** *Region* Saudi Arabia
41E5 **Ad Dilam** Saudi Arabia
41E5 **Ad Dir'iyah** Saudi Arabia
50D3 **Addis Ababa** Ethiopia
41D3 **Ad Dīwanīyah** Iraq
40D3 **Ad Duwayd** Saudi Arabia
61E2 **Adel** USA
32C4 **Adelaide** Australia
67C4 **Adelaide** Bahamas
76G3 **Adelaide** *Base* Antarctica
54J3 **Adelaide Pen** Canada
27G8 **Adelaide River** Australia
66D3 **Adelanto** USA
38C4 **Aden** Yemen
38C4 **Aden,G of** Somalia/Yemen
48C3 **Aderbissinat** Niger
45D2 **Adhrā'** Syria
27G7 **Adi** *I* Indonesia
16C1 **Adige** *R* Italy
50D2 **Adigrat** Ethiopia
42D5 **Adilābād** India
58B2 **Adin** USA
65E2 **Adirondack Mts** USA
50D2 **Adi Ugrī** Eritrea
40C2 **Adıyaman** Turkey
17F1 **Adjud** Romania
54E4 **Admiralty I** USA
55K2 **Admiralty Inlet** *B* Canada
32D1 **Admiralty Is** Papua New Guinea
44B2 **Ādoni** India
14B3 **Adour** *R* France
48B2 **Adrar** Algeria
48C2 **Adrar** *Mts* Algeria
48A2 **Adrar** *Region* Mauritius
48A2 **Adrar Soutouf** *Region* Morocco
50C2 **Adré** Chad
49D2 **Adri** Libya
64C2 **Adrian** Michigan, USA
62B1 **Adrian** Texas, USA
16C2 **Adriatic S** Italy/Yugoslavia
50D2 **Adwa** Ethiopia
25P3 **Adycha** *R* Russian Federation
48B4 **Adzopé** Ivory Coast
20K2 **Adz'va** *R* Russian Federation
20K2 **Adz'vavom** Russian Federation
17E3 **Aegean Sea** Greece
38E2 **Afghanistan** *Republic* Asia
50E3 **Afgooye** Somalia
41D5 **'Afif** Saudi Arabia
48C4 **Afikpo** Nigeria
12G6 **Åfjord** Norway
48C1 **Aflou** Algeria
50E3 **Afmado** Somalia
48A3 **Afollé** *Region* Mauritius
68C1 **Afton** New York, USA
58D2 **Afton** Wyoming, USA
45C2 **Afula** Israel
21E8 **Afyon** Turkey
45A3 **Aga** Egypt
50B2 **Agadem** Niger
48C3 **Agadez** Niger
48B1 **Agadir** Morocco
42D4 **Agar** India
43G4 **Agartala** India
58B1 **Agassiz** Canada
48B4 **Agboville** Ivory Coast
40E1 **Agdam** Azerbaijan
29C3 **Agematsu** Japan
14C3 **Agen** France
41E3 **Agha Jārī** Iran
48B4 **Agnibilékrou** Ivory Coast
14C3 **Agout** *R* France
42D3 **Āgra** India
41D2 **Ağrı** Turkey
16D2 **Agri** *R* Italy
16C3 **Agrigento** Sicily, Italy
26H5 **Agrihan** *I* Marianas
17E3 **Agrínion** Greece
16C2 **Agropoli** Italy
20J4 **Agryz** Russian Federation
55N3 **Agto** Greenland
75B3 **Agua Clara** Brazil
69D3 **Aguadilla** Puerto Rico
70B1 **Agua Prieta** Mexico
75A3 **Aguaray Guazú** Paraguay
70B2 **Aguascalientes** Mexico
75D2 **Aguas Formosas** Brazil
75C2 **Agua Vermelha, Barragem** Brazil
15A1 **Agueda** Portugal
48C3 **Aguelhok** Mali
48A2 **Agüenit** *Well* Morocco
15B2 **Águilas** Spain
72B5 **Aguja, Puerta** Peru
36C7 **Agulhas Basin** Indian Ocean
51C7 **Agulhas,C** South Africa
36C6 **Agulhas Plat** Indian Ocean
Ahaggar = **Hoggar**
21H8 **Ahar** Iran
13D1 **Ahaus** Germany
35B1 **Ahipara B** New Zealand
13D2 **Ahlen** Germany
42C4 **Ahmadābād** India
44A2 **Ahmadnagar** India
50E3 **Ahmar Mts** Ethiopia
67C1 **Ahoskie** USA
13D2 **Ahr** *R* Germany
13D2 **Ahrgebirge** *Mts* Germany
12G7 **Åhus** Sweden
41F2 **Āhuvān** Iran
41E3 **Ahvāz** Iran
69A4 **Aiajuela** Costa Rica
14C3 **Aigoual, Mount** France
29C3 **Aikawa** Japan
67B2 **Aiken** USA
31A5 **Ailao Shan** *Upland* China
75D2 **Aimorés** Brazil
16B3 **Aïn Beïda** Algeria
48B1 **Aïn Beni Mathar** Morocco
49E2 **Aïn Dalla** *Well* Egypt
15C2 **Aïn el Hadjel** Algeria
50B2 **Aïn Galakka** Chad
15C2 **Aïn Oussera** Algeria
48B1 **Aïn Sefra** Algeria
40B4 **'Ain Sukhna** Egypt
60D2 **Ainsworth** USA
15B2 **Aïn Témouchent** Algeria
29B4 **Aioi** Japan
48B2 **Aïoun Abd el Malek** *Well* Mauritius
48B3 **Aïoun El Atrouss** Mauritius
72E7 **Aiquile** Bolivia
48C3 **Aïr** *Desert Region* Niger
8D4 **Airdrie** Scotland
13B2 **Aire** France
6D3 **Aire** *R* England
13C3 **Aire** *R* France
55L3 **Airforce I** Canada
54E3 **Aishihik** Canada
13B3 **Aisne** *Department* France
14C2 **Aisne** *R* France
27H7 **Aitape** Papua New Guinea
19F1 **Aiviekste** *R* Latvia
14D3 **Aix-en-Provence** France
14D2 **Aix-les-Bains** France
43F4 **Aiyar Res** India
17E3 **Aíyion** Greece
17E3 **Aíyna** *I* Greece
43G4 **Āīzawl** India
51B6 **Aizeb** *R* Namibia
29D3 **Aizu-Wakamatsu** Japan
16B2 **Ajaccio** Corsica, Italy
16B2 **Ajaccio, G d'** Corsica, Italy
49E1 **Ajdābiyā** Libya
29E2 **Ajigasawa** Japan
45C2 **Ajlūn** Jordan
41G4 **Ajman** UAE
42C3 **Ajmer** India
59D4 **Ajo** USA
15B1 **Ajo, Cabo de** *C* Spain
17F3 **Ak** *R* Turkey
29D2 **Akabira** Japan
29C3 **Akaishi-sanchi** *Mts* Japan
44B2 **Akalkot** India
45B1 **Akanthou** Cyprus
35B2 **Akaroa** New Zealand
29B4 **Akashi** Japan
21K5 **Akbulak** Russian Federation
40C2 **Akçakale** Turkey
48A2 **Akchar** *Watercourse* Mauritius
50C3 **Aketi** Zaïre
41D1 **Akhalkalaki** Georgia
40D1 **Akhalsikhe** Georgia
17E3 **Akharnái** Greece
49E1 **Akhdar, Jabal al** *Mts* Libya
41G5 **Akhdar, Jebel** *Mt* Oman
40A2 **Akhisar** Turkey
19F1 **Akhiste** Latvia
49F2 **Akhmîm** Egypt
21H6 **Akhtubinsk** Russian Federation
21E5 **Akhtyrka** Ukraine
29B4 **Aki** Japan
55K4 **Akimiski I** Canada
29E3 **Akita** Japan
48A3 **Akjoujt** Mauritius
45C2 **'Akko** Israel
54E3 **Aklavik** Canada
48B3 **Aklé Aouana** *Desert Region* Mauritius
50D3 **Akobo** Ethiopia
50D3 **Akobo** *R* Ethiopia/Sudan
42B1 **Akoha** Afghanistan
42D4 **Akola** India
42D4 **Akot** India
55M3 **Akpatok I** Canada
17E3 **Ákra Kafirévs** *C* Greece
17E4 **Ákra Líthinon** *C* Greece
17E3 **Ákra Maléa** *C* Greece
12A2 **Akranes** Iceland
17F3 **Ákra Sídheros** *C* Greece
17E3 **Ákra Spátha** *C* Greece
17E3 **Ákra Taínaron** *C* Greece
57E2 **Akron** USA
45B1 **Akrotiri** Cyprus
45B1 **Akrotiri B** Cyprus
42D1 **Aksai Chin** *Mts* China
21E8 **Aksaray** Turkey
21J5 **Aksay** Kazakhstan
42D1 **Aksayquin Hu** *L* China
40B2 **Akşehir** Turkey
40B2 **Akseki** Turkey
25N4 **Aksenovo Zilovskoye** Russian Federation
26E1 **Aksha** Russian Federation
39G1 **Aksu** China
50D2 **Aksum** Ethiopia
24J5 **Aktogay** Kazakhstan
21K6 **Aktumsyk** Kazakhstan
21K5 **Aktyubinsk** Kazakhstan
12B1 **Akureyri** Iceland
Akyab = **Sittwe**
24K5 **Akzhal** Kazakhstan
63E2 **Alabama** *R* USA
57E3 **Alabama** *State* USA
67A2 **Alabaster** USA
40C2 **Ala Dağları** *Mts* Turkey
21G7 **Alagir** Russian Federation
73L5 **Alagoas** *State* Brazil
73L6 **Alagoinhas** Brazil
15B1 **Alagón** Spain
41E4 **Al Ahmadi** Kuwait
70D3 **Alajuela** Costa Rica
54B3 **Alakanuk** USA
24K5 **Alakol, Ozero** *L* Kazakhstan/Russian Federation
12L5 **Alakurtti** Russian Federation
27H5 **Alamagan** *I* Pacific Ocean
41E3 **Al Amārah** Iraq
59B3 **Alameda** USA
59C3 **Alamo** USA
62A2 **Alamogordo** USA
62C3 **Alamo Heights** USA
62A1 **Alamosa** USA
12H6 **Åland** *I* Finland
21E8 **Alanya** Turkey
67B2 **Alapaha** *R* USA
42L4 **Alapayevsk** Russian Federation
15B2 **Alarcón, Embalse de** *Res* Spain
40A2 **Alaşehir** Turkey
26D3 **Ala Shan** *Mts* China
54C3 **Alaska** *State* USA
54D4 **Alaska,G of** USA
54C3 **Alaska Range** *Mts* USA
16B2 **Alassio** Italy
20H5 **Alatyr'** Russian Federation
34B2 **Alawoona** Australia
41G5 **Al'Ayn** UAE
39F2 **Alayskiy Khrebet** *Mts* Tajikistan
25R3 **Alazeya** *R* Russian Federation
14D3 **Alba** Italy
15B2 **Albacete** Spain
15A1 **Alba de Tormes** Spain
40D2 **Al Badi** Iraq
17E1 **Alba Iulia** Romania
17D2 **Albania** *Republic* Europe
32A4 **Albany** Australia
67B2 **Albany** Georgia, USA
64B3 **Albany** Kentucky, USA
65E2 **Albany** New York, USA
56A2 **Albany** Oregon, USA
55K4 **Albany** *R* Canada
15B1 **Albarracin, Sierra de** *Mts* Spain
41G5 **Al Bātinah** *Region* Oman
27H8 **Albatross B** Australia
49E1 **Al Bayḍa** Libya
45C1 **Al Baylūlīyah** Syria
67B1 **Albemarle** USA
67C1 **Albemarle Sd** USA
15B1 **Alberche** *R* Spain
13B2 **Albert** France
54G4 **Alberta** *Province* Canada
27H7 **Albert Edward** *Mt* Papua New Guinea
47C3 **Albertinia** South Africa
50D3 **Albert,L** Uganda/Zaïre
57D2 **Albert Lea** USA
50D3 **Albert Nile** *R* Uganda
58D1 **Alberton** USA
14D2 **Albertville** France
14C3 **Albi** France
61E2 **Albia** USA
73H2 **Albina** Surinam
64C2 **Albion** Michigan, USA
61D2 **Albion** Nebraska, USA
65D2 **Albion** New York, USA
40C4 **Al Bi'r** Saudi Arabia
15B2 **Alborán** *I* Spain
12G7 **Ålborg** Denmark
13E3 **Albstadt-Ebingen** Germany
40D3 **Al Bū Kamāl** Syria
56C3 **Albuquerque** USA
41G5 **Al Buraymī** Oman
49D1 **Al Burayqah** Libya
49E1 **Al Burdī** Libya
32D4 **Albury** Australia
41E3 **Al Buşayyah** Iraq
15B1 **Alcalá de Henares** Spain
16C3 **Alcamo** Sicily, Italy
15B1 **Alcañiz** Spain
73K4 **Alcântara** Brazil
15A2 **Alcántara, Embalse de** *Res* Spain
15B2 **Alcaraz** Spain

15B2 **Alcaraz, Sierra de** *Mts* Spain
15B2 **Alcázar de San Juan** Spain
15B2 **Alcira** Spain
75E2 **Alcobaça** Brazil
15B1 **Alcolea de Pinar** Spain
15B2 **Alcoy** Spain
15C2 **Alcudia** Spain
46J8 **Aldabra Is** Indian Ocean
62A3 **Aldama** Mexico
25O4 **Aldan** Russian Federation
25P4 **Aldan** *R* Russian Federation
25O4 **Aldanskoye Nagor'ye** *Upland* Russian Federation
7E3 **Aldeburgh** England
14B2 **Alderney** *I* Channel Islands
7D4 **Aldershot** England
48A3 **Aleg** Mauritius
75A2 **Alegre** *R* Brazil
74E3 **Alegrete** Brazil
25Q4 **Aleksandrovsk Sakhalinskiy** Russian Federation
24J4 **Alekseyevka** Kazakhstan
20F5 **Aleksin** Russian Federation
18D1 **Älem** Sweden
75D3 **Além Paraíba** Brazil
14C2 **Alençon** France
66E5 **Alenuihaha Chan** Hawaiian Islands
21F8 **Aleppo** Syria
55M1 **Alert** Canada
14C3 **Alès** France
16B2 **Alessandria** Italy
24B3 **Ålesund** Norway
54C4 **Aleutian Ra** *Mts* USA
37L2 **Aleutian Trench** Pacific Ocean
54E4 **Alexander Arch** USA
47B2 **Alexander Bay** South Africa
67A2 **Alexander City** USA
76G3 **Alexander I** Antarctica
35A3 **Alexandra** New Zealand
74J8 **Alexandra,C** South Georgia
55L2 **Alexandra Fjord** Canada
49E1 **Alexandria** Egypt
57D3 **Alexandria** Louisiana, USA
57D2 **Alexandria** Minnesota, USA
57F3 **Alexandria** Virginia, USA
17F2 **Alexandroúpolis** Greece
45C2 **Aley** Lebanon
24K4 **Aleysk** Russian Federation
41D3 **Al Fallūjah** Iraq
15B1 **Alfaro** Spain
17F2 **Alfatar** Bulgaria
41E4 **Al Fāw** Iraq
75C3 **Alfensas** Brazil
17E3 **Alfiós** *R* Greece
75D3 **Alfonso Cláudio** Brazil
8D3 **Alford** Scotland
75D3 **Alfredo Chaves** Brazil
7D3 **Alfreton** England
41E4 **Al Furūthi** Saudi Arabia
21K6 **Alga** Kazakhstan
15A2 **Algeciras** Spain
Alger = Algiers
48B2 **Algeria** *Republic* Africa
16B2 **Alghero** Sardinia, Italy
15C2 **Algiers** Algeria
61E2 **Algona** USA
65D1 **Algonquin Park** Canada
38D3 **Al Ḩadd** Oman
40D3 **Al Ḩadīthah** Iraq
40C3 **Al Ḩadīthah** Saudi Arabia
40D2 **Al Ḩaḑr** Iraq
45D1 **Al Haffah** Syria
41G5 **Al Ḩajar al Gharbī** *Mts* Oman
40C3 **Al Hamad** *Desert Region* Jordan/Saudi Arabia
41E4 **Al Haniyah** *Desert Region* Iraq
41E5 **Al Ḩariq** Saudi Arabia
40C3 **Al Harrah** *Desert Region* Saudi Arabia
49D2 **Al Harūj al Aswad** *Upland* Libya
41E4 **Al Hasa** *Region* Saudi Arabia
40D2 **Al Ḩasakah** Syria
40C4 **Al Hawjā'** Saudi Arabia
41E3 **Al Hayy** Iraq
45D2 **Al Hijānah** Syria
41D3 **Al Ḩillah** Iraq
41E5 **Al Ḩillah** Saudi Arabia
15B2 **Al Hoceima** Morocco
50E2 **Al Ḩudaydah** Yemen
41E4 **Al Hufūf** Saudi Arabia
41F5 **Al Humrah** *Region* UAE
41G5 **Al Huwatsah** Oman
41E2 **Alīābad** Iran
41G4 **Aliabad** Iran
17E2 **Aliákmon** *R* Greece
41E3 **Alī al Gharbī** Iraq
44A2 **Alībāg** India
15B2 **Alicante** Spain
56D4 **Alice** USA
16D3 **Alice, Punta** *Pt* Italy
32C3 **Alice Springs** Australia
16C3 **Alicudi** *I* Italy
42D3 **Aligarh** India
41E3 **Aligūdarz** Iran
42B2 **Ali-Khel** Afghanistan
17F3 **Alimniá** *I* Greece
43F3 **Alīpur Duār** India
64C2 **Aliquippa** USA
40C3 **Al' Isawiyah** Saudi Arabia
47D3 **Aliwal North** South Africa
49E2 **Al Jaghbūb** Libya
40D3 **Al Jālamīd** Saudi Arabia
49E2 **Al Jawf** Libya
40C4 **Al Jawf** Saudi Arabia
40D2 **Al Jazīrah** *Desert Region* Iraq/Syria
15A2 **Aljezur** Portugal
41E4 **Al Jubayl** Saudi Arabia
41D4 **Al Jumaymah** Saudi Arabia
45D4 **Al Kabid** *Desert* Jordan
41D4 **Al Kahfah** Saudi Arabia
41E4 **Al Kāmil** Oman
40D2 **Al Khābūr** *R* Syria
41G5 **Al Khābūrah** Oman
41D3 **Al Khālis** Iraq
41G4 **Al Khaşab** Oman
41F4 **Al Khawr** Qatar
49D1 **Al Khums** Libya
41F5 **Al Kidan** *Region* Saudi Arabia
45D2 **Al Kiswah** Syria
18A2 **Alkmaar** Netherlands
49E2 **Al Kufrah Oasis** Libya
41E3 **Al Kūt** Iraq
Al Lādhiqīyah = Latakia
43E3 **Allahābād** India
45D2 **Al Lajāh** *Mt* Syria
54C3 **Allakaket** USA
30B2 **Allanmyo** Burma
67B2 **Allatoona L** USA
47D1 **Alldays** South Africa
65D2 **Allegheny** *R* USA
57F3 **Allegheny Mts** USA
67B2 **Allendale** USA
6C2 **Allendale Town** England
9B2 **Allen, Lough** *L* Irish Republic
35A3 **Allen,Mt** New Zealand
65D2 **Allentown** USA
44B4 **Alleppey** India
14C2 **Aller** *R* France
60C2 **Alliance** USA
50E1 **Al Līth** Saudi Arabia
41F5 **Al Liwā'** *Region* UAE
8D3 **Alloa** Scotland
34D1 **Allora** Australia
65E1 **Alma** Canada
64C2 **Alma** Michigan, USA
60D2 **Alma** Nebraska, USA
39F1 **Alma Ata** Kazakhstan
15A2 **Almada** Portugal
41E4 **Al Majma'ah** Saudi Arabia
41F4 **Al Manāmah** Bahrain
41D3 **Al Ma'nīyah** Iraq
59B2 **Almanor,L** USA
15B2 **Almansa** Spain
41F5 **Al Māriyyah** UAE
49E1 **Al Marj** Libya
75C2 **Almas** *R* Brazil
15B1 **Almazán** Spain
13E2 **Alme** *R* Germany
13D1 **Almelo** Netherlands
75D2 **Almenara** Brazil
15A1 **Almendra, Embalse de** *Res* Spain
15B2 **Almería** Spain
15B2 **Almería, Golfo de** Spain
20J5 **Al'met'yevsk** Russian Federation
18C1 **Älmhult** Sweden
41D4 **Al Midhnab** Saudi Arabia
41E3 **Al Miqdādīyah** Iraq
17E3 **Almirós** Greece
41E4 **Al Mish'āb** Saudi Arabia
15A2 **Almodôvar** Portugal
42D3 **Almora** India
41E4 **Al Mubarraz** Saudi Arabia
40C4 **Al Mudawwara** Jordan
41F4 **Al Muḩarraq** Bahrain
38C4 **Al Mukallā** Yemen
50E2 **Al Mukhā** Yemen
41D3 **Al Musayyib** Iraq
40C4 **Al Muwaylih** Saudi Arabia
8C3 **Alness** Scotland
6D2 **Aln, R** England
41E3 **Al Nu'mānīyah** Iraq
6D2 **Alnwick** England
27F7 **Alor** *I* Indonesia
30C4 **Alor Setar** Malaysia
Alost = Aalst
32E2 **Alotau** Papua New Guinea
32B3 **Aloysius,Mt** Australia
64C1 **Alpena** USA
16C1 **Alpi Dolomitiche** *Mts* Italy
59E4 **Alpine** Arizona, USA
62B2 **Alpine** Texas, USA
58D2 **Alpine** Wyoming, USA
16B1 **Alps** *Mts* Europe
49D1 **Al Qaddāhiyah** Libya
45D1 **Al Qadmūs** Syria
40D3 **Al Qā'im** Iraq
40C4 **Al Qalībah** Saudi Arabia
40D2 **Al Qāmishlī** Syria
45D1 **Al Qardāḩah** Syria
49D1 **Al Qaryah Ash Sharqiyah** Libya
40C3 **Al Qaryatayn** Syria
41D4 **Al Qasīm** *Region* Saudi Arabia
41E4 **Al Qatīf** Saudi Arabia
49D2 **Al Qatrūn** Libya
41E4 **Al Qayşūmah** Saudi Arabia
15A2 **Alquera** *Res* Portugal/Spain
40C3 **Al Qunayţirah** Syria
50E2 **Al Qunfidhah** Saudi Arabia
41E3 **Al Qurnah** Iraq
45D1 **Al Quşayr** Syria
45D2 **Al Quţayfah** Syria
41E5 **Al Quwayīyah** Saudi Arabia
18B1 **Als** *I* Denmark
14D2 **Alsace** *Region* France
13D3 **Alsace, Plaine d'** France
18B2 **Alsfeld** Germany
6C2 **Alston** England
12J5 **Alta** Norway
74D4 **Alta Gracia** Argentina
69D5 **Altagracia de Orituco** Venezuela
26B2 **Altai** *Mts* Mongolia
67B2 **Altamaha** *R* USA
73H4 **Altamira** Brazil
16D2 **Altamura** Italy
26D1 **Altanbulag** Mongolia
70B2 **Altata** Mexico
24K5 **Altay** China
25L5 **Altay** Mongolia
24K4 **Altay** *Mts* Russian Federation
13D2 **Altenkirchen** Germany
75B2 **Alto Araguaia** Brazil
51D5 **Alto Molócue** Mozambique
7D4 **Alton** England
64A3 **Alton** USA
65D2 **Altoona** USA
75B2 **Alto Sucuriú** Brazil
7C3 **Altrincham** England
39G2 **Altun Shan** *Mts* China
58B2 **Alturas** USA
62C2 **Altus** USA
40C4 **Al'Ulā** Saudi Arabia
40C4 **Al Urayq** *Desert Region* Saudi Arabia
62C1 **Alva** USA
63C2 **Alvarado** USA
12G6 **Älvdalen** Sweden
63C3 **Alvin** USA
12J5 **Älvsbyn** Sweden
49D2 **Al Wāha** Libya
40C4 **Al Wajh** Saudi Arabia
42D3 **Alwar** India
40D3 **Al Widyān** *Desert Region* Iraq/Saudi Arabia
31A2 **Alxa Youqi** China
31B2 **Alxa Zuoqi** China
41E2 **Alyat** Azerbaijan
12J8 **Alytus** Lithuania
13E3 **Alzey** Germany
50D3 **Amadi** Sudan
41D2 **Amādīyah** Iraq
55L3 **Amadjuak L** Canada
12G7 **Åmål** Sweden
25N4 **Amalat** *R* Russian Federation
17E3 **Amaliás** Greece
42C4 **Amalner** India
75A3 **Amambaí** Brazil
75B3 **Amambaí** *R* Brazil
75A3 **Amamba, Serra** *Mts* Brazil/Paraguay
26F4 **Amami** *I* Japan
26F4 **Amami gunto** *Arch* Japan
73H3 **Amapá** Brazil
73H3 **Amapá** *State* Brazil
62B1 **Amarillo** USA
21F7 **Amasya** Turkey
73H4 **Amazonas** *R* Brazil
72E4 **Amazonas** *State* Brazil
42D2 **Ambāla** India
44C4 **Ambalangoda** Sri Lanka
51E6 **Ambalavao** Madagascar
50B3 **Ambam** Cameroon
51E5 **Ambanja** Madagascar
25S3 **Ambarchik** Russian Federation
72C4 **Ambato** Ecuador
51E5 **Ambato-Boeny** Madagascar
51E5 **Ambatolampy** Madagascar
51E5 **Ambatondrazaka** Madagascar
18C3 **Amberg** Germany
70D3 **Ambergris Cay** *I* Belize
43E4 **Ambikāpur** India
51E5 **Ambilobe** Madagascar
6C2 **Ambleside** England
51E6 **Amboasary** Madagascar
51E5 **Ambodifototra** Madagascar
51E6 **Ambohimahasoa** Madagascar
Amboina = Ambon
27F7 **Ambon** Indonesia
51E6 **Ambositra** Madagascar
51E6 **Ambovombe** Madagascar
27E6 **Amboyna Cay** *I* S China Sea
51E5 **Ambre, Montagne d'** *Mt* Madagascar
51B4 **Ambriz** Angola
33F2 **Ambrym** *I* Vanuatu
50C2 **Am Dam** Chad
20L2 **Amderma** Russian Federation
70B2 **Ameca** Mexico
18B2 **Ameland** *I* Netherlands
68D2 **Amenia** USA
58D2 **American Falls** USA
58D2 **American Falls Res** USA
59D2 **American Fork** USA
76F10 **American Highland** *Upland* Antarctica
37L5 **American Samoa** *Is* Pacific Ocean
67B2 **Americus** USA
18B2 **Amersfoort** Netherlands
47D2 **Amersfoort** South Africa
61E1 **Amery** USA
76G10 **Amery Ice Shelf** Antarctica
61E2 **Ames** USA
68E1 **Amesbury** USA
17E3 **Amfilokhía** Greece
17E3 **Amfissa** Greece
25P3 **Amga** Russian Federation
25P3 **Amgal** *R* Russian Federation
26G2 **Amgu** Russian Federation
26G1 **Amgun'** *R* Russian Federation
50D2 **Amhara** *Region* Ethiopia
55M5 **Amherst** Canada
68D1 **Amherst** Massachusetts, USA
65D3 **Amherst** Virginia, USA
44B3 **Amhūr** India
16C2 **Amiata, Monte** *Mt* Italy
14C2 **Amiens** France
29C3 **Amino** Japan
45C1 **Amioune** Lebanon
46K8 **Amirante Is** Indian Ocean
62B3 **Amistad Res** Mexico
43F3 **Amlekhganj** Nepal
7B3 **Amlwch** Wales
40C3 **Amman** Jordan
7C4 **Ammanford** Wales
12K6 **Ämmänsaari** Finland
55P3 **Ammassalik** Greenland
28A3 **Amnyong-dan** *C* N Korea
41F2 **Amol** Iran
17F3 **Amorgós** *I* Greece
55L5 **Amos** Canada
Amoy = Xiamen
51E6 **Ampanihy** Madagascar
75C3 **Amparo** Brazil
51E5 **Ampasimanolotra** Madagascar
15C1 **Amposta** Spain
42D4 **Amrāvati** India
42C4 **Amreli** India
42C2 **Amritsar** India
43K1 **Amroha** India
36E6 **Amsterdam** *I* Indian Ocean
18A2 **Amsterdam** Netherlands
47E2 **Amsterdam** South Africa
65E2 **Amsterdam** USA
50C2 **Am Timan** Chad
24H5 **Amu Darya** *R* Uzbekistan
55J2 **Amund Ringnes I** Canada
54F2 **Amundsen G** Canada
76E **Amundsen-Scott** *Base* Antarctica
76F4 **Amundsen Sea** Antarctica
27E7 **Amuntai** Indonesia
26F1 **Amur** *R* Russian Federation
25N2 **Anabar** *R* Russian Federation
66C4 **Anacapa Is** USA
72F2 **Anaco** Venezuela
56B2 **Anaconda** USA
58B1 **Anacortes** USA
62C1 **Anadarko** USA
25T3 **Anadyr'** Russian Federation
25T3 **Anadyr'** *R* Russian Federation
25U3 **Anadyrskiy Zaliv** *S* Russian Federation
25T3 **Anadyrskoya Ploskogor'ye** *Plat* Russian Federation
17F3 **Anáfi** *I* Greece
75D1 **Anagé** Brazil
40D3 **'Ānah** Iraq
59C4 **Anaheim** USA
44B3 **Anaimalai Hills** India
44C2 **Anakāpalle** India
51E5 **Analalava** Madagascar
27D6 **Anambas, Kepulauan** *Is* Indonesia
64A2 **Anamosa** USA
21E8 **Anamur** Turkey
29B4 **Anan** Japan
44B3 **Anantapur** India
42D2 **Anantnag** India
73J7 **Anápolis** Brazil
41G3 **Anār** Iran
41F3 **Anārak** Iran
27H5 **Anatahan** *I* Pacific Ocean
74D3 **Añatuya** Argentina
28B3 **Anbyŏn** N Korea
54D3 **Anchorage** USA
72E7 **Ancohuma** *Mt* Bolivia
72C6 **Ancón** Peru
16C2 **Ancona** Italy
68D1 **Ancram** USA
74B6 **Ancud** Chile
74B6 **Ancud, Golfo de** *G* Chile
13C4 **Ancy-le-Franc** France
72D6 **Andahuaylas** Peru
12F6 **Åndalsnes** Norway
15A2 **Andalucia** *Region* Spain
67A2 **Andalusia** USA
39H4 **Andaman Is** India
75D1 **Andaraí** Brazil
13C3 **Andelot** France
12H5 **Andenes** Norway
18B2 **Andernach** Germany
64B2 **Anderson** Indiana, USA
63D1 **Anderson** Missouri, USA
67B2 **Anderson** S Carolina, USA
54F3 **Anderson** *R* Canada
72C5 **Andes, Cordillera de los** *Mts* Peru
44B2 **Andhra Pradesh** *State* India
17E3 **Andikíthira** *I* Greece
24J5 **Andizhan** Uzbekistan
24H6 **Andkhui** Afghanistan
28B3 **Andong** S Korea
15C1 **Andorra** *Principality* SW Europe
15C1 **Andorra-La-Vella** Andorra
7D4 **Andover** England
68E1 **Andover** New Hampshire, USA
68B1 **Andover** New York, USA
75B3 **Andradina** Brazil
19G1 **Andreapol'** Russian Federation
40B2 **Andreas,C** Cyprus
62B2 **Andrews** USA
16D2 **Andria** Italy
17E3 **Ándros** *I* Greece
57F4 **Andros** *I* The Bahamas
67C4 **Andros Town** Bahamas
44A3 **Androth** *I* India
15B2 **Andújar** Spain
51B5 **Andulo** Angola
48C3 **Anéfis** Mali
48C4 **Aného** Togo
33F3 **Aneityum** *I* Vanuatu
25M4 **Angarsk** Russian Federation
20A3 **Ånge** Sweden
70A2 **Angel de la Guarda** *I* Mexico
12G7 **Ängelholm** Sweden
34C1 **Angellala Creek** *R* Australia
66B1 **Angels Camp** USA
27G7 **Angemuk** *Mt* Indonesia
14B2 **Angers** France
13B3 **Angerville** France
30C3 **Angkor** *Hist Site* Cambodia
10C3 **Anglesey** *I* Wales
63C3 **Angleton** USA
Angmagssalik = Ammassalik
51E5 **Angoche** Mozambique
74B5 **Angol** Chile
64C2 **Angola** Indiana, USA
51B5 **Angola** *Republic* Africa
52J5 **Angola Basin** Atlantic Ocean
14C2 **Angoulême** France
48A1 **Angra do Heroismo** Azores
75D3 **Angra dos Reis** Brazil
69E3 **Anguilla** *I* Caribbean Sea
69B2 **Anguilla Cays** *Is* Caribbean Sea
43F4 **Angul** India
50C4 **Angumu** Zaïre
18C1 **Anholt** *I* Denmark
31C4 **Anhua** China
26F2 **Anhui** China
31D3 **Anhui** *Province* China
75B2 **Anhumas** Brazil
28A3 **Anhŭng** S Korea
54C3 **Aniak** USA
75C2 **Anicuns** Brazil
62A1 **Animas** *R* USA
62A2 **Animas Peak** *Mt* USA

61E2 Anita USA
26H2 Aniva, Mys C Russian Federation
13B3 Anizy-le-Château France
14B2 Anjou Region France
51E5 Anjouan I Comoros
51E5 Anjozorobe Madagascar
28B3 Anju N Korea
31B3 Ankang China
21E8 Ankara Turkey
51E5 Ankaratra Mt Madagascar
51E6 Ankazoabo Madagascar
51E5 Ankazobe Madagascar
61E2 Ankeny USA
18C2 Anklam Germany
30D3 An Loc Vietnam
31B4 Anlong China
31C3 Anlu China
53B3 Anna USA
16B3 'Annaba Algeria
40C3 An Nabk Saudi Arabia
40C3 An Nabk Syria
40D4 An Nafūd Desert Saudi Arabia
49E2 An Nāfūrah Libya
41D3 An Najaf Iraq
8D4 Annan Scotland
65D3 Annapolis USA
43E3 Annapurna Mt Nepal
64C2 Ann Arbor USA
45D1 An Nāsirah Syria
41E3 An Nāsirīyah Iraq
14D2 Annecy France
30D3 An Nhon Vietnam
31A5 Anning China
67A2 Anniston USA
48C4 Annobon I Equatorial Guinea
14C2 Annonay France
69J1 Annotto Bay Jamaica
31D3 Anqing China
31B2 Ansai China
18C3 Ansbach Germany
69C3 Anse d'Hainault Haiti
31E1 Anshan China
31B4 Anshun China
60D2 Ansley USA
62C2 Anson USA
27F8 Anson B Australia
48C3 Ansongo Mali
64C1 Ansonville Canada
64C3 Ansted USA
21F8 Antakya Turkey
51F5 Antalaha Madagascar
21E8 Antalya Turkey
21E8 Antalya Körfezi B Turkey
51E5 Antananarivo Madagascar
76G1 Antarctic Circle Antarctica
76G3 Antarctic Pen Antarctica
15B2 Antequera Spain
62A2 Anthony USA
48B1 Anti-Atlas Mts Morocco
55M5 Anticosti, Î. de Canada
64B1 Antigo USA
69E3 Antigua I Caribbean Sea
Anti Lebanon = Sharqi, Jebel esh
59B3 Antioch USA
33G5 Antipodes Is New Zealand
63C2 Antlers USA
74B2 Antofagasta Chile
75C4 Antonina Brazil
62A1 Antonito USA
9C2 Antrim Northern Ireland
68E1 Antrim USA
9C2 Antrim County Northern Ireland
9C2 Antrim Hills Northern Ireland
51E5 Antsirabe Madagascar
51E5 Antsirañana Madagascar
51E5 Antsohiny Madagascar
28B2 Antu China
30D3 An Tuc Vietnam
13C2 Antwerp Belgium
Antwerpen = Antwerp
9C3 An Uaimh Irish Republic
28A3 Anui S Korea
42C3 Anūpgarh India
44C4 Anuradhapura Sri Lanka
Anvers = Antwerp
54B3 Anvik USA
25L5 Anxi China
31C2 Anyang China
31A3 A'nyêmaqên Shan Mts China
25S3 Anyuysk Russian Federation
24K4 Anzhero-Sudzhensk Russian Federation
16C2 Anzio Italy
33F2 Aoba I Vanuatu
29E2 Aomori Japan
16B1 Aosta Italy
48B3 Aouker Desert Region Mauritius
48C2 Aoulef Algeria
50B1 Aozou Chad
74E2 Apa R Brazil/Paraguay
57E4 Apalachee B USA
67B3 Apalachicola USA
67A3 Apalachicola B USA
72D3 Apaporis R Brazil/Colombia
75B3 Aparecida do Taboado Brazil
27F5 Aparri Philippines
17D1 Apatin Croatia
20E2 Apatity Russian Federation
70B3 Apatzingan Mexico
18B2 Apeldoorn Netherlands
33H2 Apia Western Samoa
75C3 Apiaí Brazil
73G2 Apoera Surinam
34B3 Apollo Bay Australia
67B3 Apopka,L USA
73H7 Aporé R Brazil
64A1 Apostle Is USA
57E3 Appalachian Mts USA
16C2 Appennino Abruzzese Mts Italy
16B2 Appennino Ligure Mts Italy
16D2 Appennino Lucano Mts Italy
16D2 Appennino Napoletano Mts Italy
16C2 Appennino Tosco-Emilliano Mts Italy
16C2 Appennino Umbro-Marchigiano Mts Italy
6C2 Appleby England
61D1 Appleton Minnesota, USA
64B2 Appleton Wisconsin, USA
21J7 Apsheronskiy Poluostrov Pen Azerbaijan
74F2 Apucarana Brazil
72E2 Apure R Venezuela
72D6 Apurimac R Peru
40C4 'Aqaba Jordan
40B4 'Aqaba,G of Egypt/Saudi Arabia
45C4 'Aqaba, Wadi el Egypt
41F3 'Aqdā Iran
73G8 Aqidauana Brazil
75A3 Aquidabán R Paraguay
74E2 Aquidauana Brazil
75A2 Aquidauana R Brazil
43E3 Ara India
67A2 Arab USA
45C1 'Arab al Mulk Syria
45C3 'Araba, Wadi Israel
36E4 Arabian Basin Indian Ocean
38E4 Arabian Sea SW Asia
45D2 'Arab, Jabal al Mt Syria
73L6 Aracajú Brazil
75A3 Aracanguy,Mts de Paraguay
73L4 Aracati Brazil
75D1 Aracatu Brazil
73H8 Araçatuba Brazil
15A2 Aracena Spain
73K7 Araçuaí Brazil
45C3 'Arad Israel
21C6 Arad Romania
50C2 Arada Chad
41F5 'Arādah UAE
32C1 Arafura S Indonesia/Australia
73H7 Aragarças Brazil
21G7 Aragats Mt Armenia
15B1 Aragon R Spain
15B1 Aragón Region Spain
75C1 Araguaçu Brazil
73H6 Araguaia R Brazil
73J5 Araguaína Brazil
73J7 Araguari Brazil
75C2 Araguari R Brazil
29C3 Arai Japan
45C3 Araif el Naqa, Gebel Mt Egypt
48C2 Arak Algeria
41E3 Arāk Iran
30A2 Arakan Yoma Mts Burma
44B3 Arakkonam India
24G5 Aral S Kazakhstan
24H5 Aral'sk Kazakhstan
15B1 Aranda de Duero Spain
10B2 Aran I Irish Republic
10B3 Aran Is Irish Republic
15B1 Aranjuez Spain
47B1 Aranos Namibia
63C3 Aransas Pass USA
28B4 Arao Japan
48B3 Araouane Mali
60D2 Arapahoe USA
74E4 Arapey R Uruguay
73L5 Arapiraca Brazil
75B3 Araporgas Brazil
74G3 Ararangua Brazil
73J8 Araraquara Brazil
75C3 Araras Brazil
32D4 Ararat Australia
41D2 Ararat Armenia
Ararat, Mt = Büyük Ağri Daği
75D3 Araruama, Lagoa de Brazil
40D3 Ar'ar, Wadi Watercourse Saudi Arabia
41D1 Aras R Turkey
41E2 Aras R Azerbaijan/Iran
29D3 Arato Japan
72E2 Arauca R Venezuela
72D2 Arauea Colombia
42C3 Arāvalli Range Mts India
33E1 Arawa Papua New Guinea
73J7 Araxá Brazil
21G8 Araxes R Iran
50D3 Arba Minch Ethiopia
16B3 Arbatax Sardinia, Italy
21G8 Arbīl Iraq
12H6 Arbrå Sweden
8D3 Arbroath Scotland
14B3 Arcachon France
68A1 Arcade USA
67B3 Arcadia USA
58B2 Arcata USA
66D1 Arc Dome Mt USA
20G3 Archangel Russian Federation
68C2 Archbald USA
59E3 Arches Nat Pk USA
13C3 Arcis-sur-Aube France
58D2 Arco USA
75C3 Arcos Brazil
15A2 Arcos de la Frontera Spain
55K2 Arctic Bay Canada
76C1 Arctic Circle
54E3 Arctic Red R Canada
54E3 Arctic Red River Canada
54D3 Arctic Village USA
76G2 Arctowski Base Antarctica
17F2 Arda R Bulgaria
21H8 Ardabīl Iran
21G7 Ardahan Turkey
12F6 Årdal Norway
48C2 Ardar des Iforas Upland Algeria/Mali
9C3 Ardee Irish Republic
41F3 Ardekān Iran
13C3 Ardennes Department France
18B2 Ardennes Region Belgium
41F3 Ardestāh Iran
40C3 Ardh es Suwwan Desert Region Jordan
15A2 Ardila R Portugal
34C2 Ardlethan Australia
56D3 Ardmore USA
8B3 Ardnamurchan Pt Scotland
13A2 Ardres France
8C3 Ardrishaig Scotland
8C4 Ardrossan Scotland
69D3 Arecibo Puerto Rico
73L4 Areia Branca Brazil
59B3 Arena,Pt USA
13D1 Arenberg Region Germany
12F7 Arendal Norway
72D7 Arequipa Peru
16C2 Arezzo Italy
16C2 Argenta Italy
14C2 Argentan France
13B3 Argenteuil France
71D7 Argentina Republic S America
52F7 Argentine Basin Atlantic Ocean
74B8 Argentino, Lago Argentina
14C2 Argenton-sur-Creuse France
17F2 Argeș R Romania
42B2 Arghardab R Afghanistan
17E3 Argolikós Kólpos G Greece
13C3 Argonne Region France
17E3 Árgos Greece
17E3 Argostólion Greece
66B3 Arguello,Pt USA
66D3 Argus Range Mts USA
32B2 Argyle,L Australia
8C3 Argyll Scotland
18C1 Århus Denmark
51C6 Ariamsvlei Namibia
48B3 Aribinda Burkina
74B1 Arica Chile
42C2 Arifwala Pakistan
Arihā = Jericho
60C3 Arikaree R USA
69L1 Arima Trinidad
75C2 Arinos Brazil
73G6 Arinos R Brazil
69L1 Aripo,Mt Trinidad
72F5 Aripuanã Brazil
72F5 Aripuanã R Brazil
8C3 Arisaig Scotland
45B3 'Arîsh, Wadi el Watercourse Egypt
56B3 Arizona State USA
12G7 Årjäng Sweden
25Q4 Arka Russian Federation
21G5 Arkadak Russian Federation
63D2 Arkadelphia USA
8C3 Arkaig, L Scotland
24H4 Arkalyk Kazakhstan
57D3 Arkansas R USA
57D3 Arkansas State USA
63C1 Arkansas City USA
29C2 Arkhipovka Russian Federation
25K2 Arkipelag Nordenshelda Arch Russian Federation
10B3 Arklow Irish Republic
15B1 Arlanzón R Spain
14C3 Arles France
61D2 Arlington S Dakota, USA
63C2 Arlington Texas, USA
65D3 Arlington Virginia, USA
58B1 Arlington Washington, USA
64B2 Arlington Heights USA
18B3 Arlon Belgium
Armageddon = Megiddo
9C2 Armagh Northern Ireland
9C2 Armagh County Northern Ireland
13B4 Armançon R France
21G7 Armavir Russian Federation
72C3 Armenia Colombia
21G7 Armenia Republic Europe
13B2 Armentières Belgium
32E4 Armidale Australia
55L3 Arnaud R Canada
40B2 Arnauti C Cyprus
62C1 Arnett USA
18B2 Arnhem Netherlands
32C2 Arnhem,C Australia
32C2 Arnhem Land Australia
66B1 Arnold USA
65D1 Arnprior Canada
13E2 Arnsberg Germany
47B2 Aroab Namibia
13E2 Arolsen Germany
33G1 Arorae I Kiribati
16B1 Arosa Switzerland
13B3 Arpajon France
75C1 Arraias Brazil
75C1 Arraias, Serra de Mts Brazil
41D3 Ar Ramādī Iraq
8C4 Arran, I of Scotland
40C2 Ar Raqqah Syria
49D2 Ar Rāqūbah Libya
14C1 Arras France
41D4 Ar Rass Saudi Arabia
45D1 Ar Rastan Syria
48A2 Arrecife Canary Islands
41E3 Ar Rifā'ī Iraq
41E3 Ar Rihāb Desert Region Iraq
Ar Riyād = Riyadh
8C3 Arrochar Scotland
75C1 Arrojado R Brazil
58C2 Arrowrock Res USA
35A2 Arrowtown New Zealand
66B3 Arroyo Grande USA
41F4 Ar Ru'ays Qatar
41G5 Ar Rustāq Oman
40D3 Ar Rutbah Iraq
41D5 Ar Ruwayḑah Saudi Arabia
44B3 Arsikere India
20H4 Arsk Russian Federation
17E3 Árta Greece
28C2 Artem Russian Federation
25L4 Artemovsk Russian Federation
25N4 Artemovskiy Russian Federation
56C3 Artesia USA
35B2 Arthurs P New Zealand
74E4 Artigas Uruguay
54H3 Artillery L Canada
14C1 Artois Region France
19F3 Artsiz Ukraine
76G2 Arturo Prat Base Antarctica
21G7 Artvin Turkey
50D3 Aru Zaïre
73H6 Aruanã Brazil
69C4 Aruba I Caribbean Sea
27G7 Aru, Kepulauan Arch Indonesia
43F3 Arun R Nepal
43G3 Arunāchal Pradesh Union Territory India
44B4 Aruppukkottai India
50D4 Arusha Tanzania
50C3 Aruwimi R Zaïre
60B3 Arvada USA
26D2 Arvayheer Mongolia
55L5 Arvida Canada
12H5 Arvidsjaur Sweden
12G7 Arvika Sweden
59C3 Arvin USA
45C1 Arwad I Syria
20G4 Arzamas Russian Federation
15B2 Arzew Algeria
42C2 Asadabad Afghanistan
29B4 Asahi R Japan
29E2 Asahi dake Mt Japan
29E2 Asahikawa Japan
28A3 Asan-man B S Korea
43F4 Asansol India
49D2 Asawanwah Well Libya
20L4 Asbest Russian Federation
47C2 Asbestos Mts South Africa
65E2 Asbury Park USA
52H5 Ascension I Atlantic Ocean
70D3 Ascensión, B de la Mexico
18B3 Aschaffenburg Germany
18C2 Aschersleben Germany
16C2 Ascoli Piceno Italy
50E2 Āseb Eritrea
48C2 Asedjrad Upland Algeria
50D3 Asela Ethiopia
12H6 Åsele Sweden
17E2 Asenovgrad Bulgaria
13C3 Asfeld France
20K4 Asha Russian Federation
7D3 Ashbourne England
67B2 Ashburn USA
33G5 Ashburton New Zealand
32A3 Ashburton R Australia
40B3 Ashdod Israel
63D2 Ashdown USA
67A1 Asheboro USA
57E3 Asheville USA
34D1 Ashford Australia
7E4 Ashford England
59D3 Ash Fork USA
29D2 Ashibetsu Japan
29D3 Ashikaga Japan
28B4 Ashizuri-misaki Pt Japan
24G6 Ashkhabad Turkmenistan
62C1 Ashland Kansas, USA
57E3 Ashland Kentucky, USA
60B1 Ashland Montana, USA
61D2 Ashland Nebraska, USA
64C2 Ashland Ohio, USA
56A2 Ashland Oregon, USA
65D3 Ashland Virginia, USA
61E1 Ashland Wisconsin, USA
34C1 Ashley Australia
60D1 Ashley USA
68C2 Ashokan Res USA
45C3 Ashqelon Israel
41D3 Ash Shabakh Iraq
41G4 Ash Sha'm UAE
41D2 Ash Sharqāţ Iraq
41E3 Ash Shaţrah Iraq
38C4 Ash Shiḩr Yemen
41E4 Ash Shumlūl Saudi Arabia
64C2 Ashtabula USA
55M4 Ashuanipi L Canada
21F8 Asi R Syria
15A2 Asilah Morocco
16B2 Asinara I Sardinia, Italy
24K4 Asino Russian Federation
50E1 Asīr Region Saudi Arabia
43E5 Aska India
40D2 Aşkale Turkey
12G7 Askersund Sweden
45B4 Asl Egypt
42C1 Asmar Afghanistan
50D2 Asmara Eritrea
Āsmera = Asmara
28B4 Aso Japan
50D2 Asosa Ethiopia
50D1 Asoteriba, Jebel Mt Sudan
62B2 Aspermont USA
35A2 Aspiring,Mt New Zealand
40C2 As Sabkhah Syria
41E5 As Salamiyah Saudi Arabia
40C2 As Salamīyah Syria
41D3 As Salmān Iraq
43G3 Assam State India
41E3 As Samāwah Iraq
41F5 Aş Şanām Region Saudi Arabia
45D2 Aş Şanamayn Syria
18B2 Assen Netherlands
18C1 Assens Denmark
49D1 As Sidrah Libya
54H5 Assiniboia Canada
54G4 Assiniboine,Mt Canada
73H8 Assis Brazil
40C3 As Sukhnah Syria
41E5 Aş Şumman Region Saudi Arabia
51E4 Assumption I Seychelles
40C3 As Suwaydā' Syria
41D3 Aş Şuwayrah Iraq
41E2 Astara Azerbaijan
16B2 Asti Italy
17F3 Astipálaia I Greece
15A1 Astorga Spain
56A2 Astoria USA
21H6 Astrakhan' Russian Federation
15A1 Asturias Region Spain
76F12 Asuka Base Antarctica
74E3 Asunción Paraguay
26H5 Asuncion I Marianas
50D3 Aswa R Uganda
40B5 Aswân Egypt
49F2 Aswân High Dam Egypt
49F2 Asyût Egypt
74C2 Atacama, Desierto de Desert Chile
33H1 Atafu I Tokelau Islands

45C3 **Atā'ita, Jebel el** *Mt* Jordan
48C4 **Atakpamé** Togo
27F7 **Atambua** Indonesia
55N3 **Atangmik** Greenland
45B4 **Ataqa, Gebel** *Mt* Egypt
48A2 **Atar** Mauritius
40C2 **Atatirk Baraji** *Res* Turkey
66B3 **Atascadero** USA
24J5 **Atasu** Kazakhstan
50D2 **Atbara** Sudan
24H4 **Atbasar** Kazakhstan
57D4 **Atchafalaya B** USA
57D3 **Atchison** USA
68C3 **Atco** USA
16C2 **Atessa** Italy
13B2 **Ath** Belgium
54G4 **Athabasca** Canada
54G4 **Athabasca** *R* Canada
54H4 **Athabasca,L** Canada
67A2 **Athens** Alabama, USA
57E3 **Athens** Georgia, USA
17E3 **Athens** Greece
64C3 **Athens** Ohio, USA
68B2 **Athens** Pennsylvania, USA
67B1 **Athens** Tennessee, USA
63C2 **Athens** Texas, USA
Athína = Athens
10B3 **Athlone** Irish Republic
45B1 **Athna** Cyprus
68D1 **Athol** USA
17E2 **Áthos** *Mt* Greece
9C3 **Athy** Irish Republic
50B2 **Ati** Chad
55J5 **Atikoken** Canada
25R3 **Atka** Russian Federation
21G5 **Atkarsk** Russian Federation
63D1 **Atkins** USA
57E3 **Atlanta** Georgia, USA
64C2 **Atlanta** Michigan, USA
61D2 **Atlantic** USA
57F3 **Atlantic City** USA
68C2 **Atlantic Highlands** USA
52H8 **Atlantic-Indian Antarctic Basin** Atlantic Ocean
52H7 **Atlantic Indian Ridge** Atlantic Ocean
Atlas Mts = Haut Atlas, Moyen Atlas
48C1 **Atlas Saharien** *Mts* Algeria
54E4 **Atlin** Canada
54E4 **Atlin L** Canada
45C2 **'Atlit** Israel
57E3 **Atmore** USA
51E6 **Atofinandrahana** Madagascar
63C2 **Atoka** USA
72C2 **Atrato** *R* Colombia
41F5 **Attaf** *Region* UAE
50E1 **Aṭ Ṭā'if** Saudi Arabia
45D2 **At Tall** Syria
67A2 **Attalla** USA
55K4 **Attawapiskat** Canada
55K4 **Attawapiskat** *R* Canada
41D3 **At Taysīyah** *Desert Region* Saudi Arabia
64B2 **Attica** Indiana, USA
68A1 **Attica** New York, USA
13C3 **Attigny** France
45B1 **Attila Line** Cyprus
65E2 **Attleboro** Massachusetts, USA
30D3 **Attopeu** Laos
40C4 **At Tubayq** *Upland* Saudi Arabia
12H7 **Atvidaberg** Sweden
66B2 **Atwater** USA
14D3 **Aubagne** France
13C3 **Aube** *Department* France
13C3 **Aube** *R* France
14C3 **Aubenas** France
67A2 **Auburn** Alabama, USA
59B3 **Auburn** California, USA
64B2 **Auburn** Indiana, USA
65E2 **Auburn** Maine, USA
61D2 **Auburn** Nebraska, USA
65D2 **Auburn** New York, USA
58B1 **Auburn** Washington, USA
14C3 **Auch** France
33G4 **Auckland** New Zealand
37K7 **Auckland Is** New Zealand
14C3 **Aude** *R* France
55K4 **Auden** Canada
61E2 **Audubon** USA
34C1 **Augathella** Australia
9C2 **Aughnacloy** Northern Ireland
47B2 **Aughrabies Falls** South Africa
18C3 **Augsburg** Germany
32A4 **Augusta** Australia
57E3 **Augusta** Georgia, USA
63C1 **Augusta** Kansas, USA
57G2 **Augusta** Maine, USA
58D1 **Augusta** Montana, USA
64A2 **Augusta** Wisconsin, USA
19E2 **Augustów** Poland
32A3 **Augustus,Mt** Australia
47B1 **Auob** *R* Namibia
42D3 **Auraiya** India
42D5 **Aurangābād** India
48C1 **Aurès** *Mts* Algeria
16B3 **Aurès, Mt de l'** Algeria
13D1 **Aurich** Germany
14C3 **Aurillac** France
56C3 **Aurora** Colorado, USA
64B2 **Aurora** Illinois, USA
64C3 **Aurora** Indiana, USA
63D1 **Aurora** Mississippi, USA
61D2 **Aurora** Nebraska, USA
47B2 **Aus** Namibia
64C2 **Au Sable** USA
48A2 **Ausert** *Well* Morocco
8D2 **Auskerry, I** Scotland
57D2 **Austin** Minnesota, USA
59C3 **Austin** Nevada, USA
68A2 **Austin** Pennsylvania, USA
56D3 **Austin** Texas, USA
32D4 **Australian Alps** *Mts* Australia
18C3 **Austria** *Federal Republic* Europe
70B3 **Autlán** Mexico
14C2 **Autun** France
14C2 **Auvergne** *Region* France
14C2 **Auxerre** France
13A2 **Auxi-le-Château** France
14C2 **Avallon** France
66C4 **Avalon** USA
55N5 **Avalon Pen** Canada
75C3 **Avaré** Brazil
13E1 **Ave** *R* Germany
45C3 **Avedat** *Hist Site* Israel
73G4 **Aveíro** Brazil
15A1 **Aveiro** Portugal
74E4 **Avellaneda** Argentina
16C2 **Avellino** Italy
66B3 **Avenal** USA
13B2 **Avesnes-sur-Helpe** France
12H6 **Avesta** Sweden
16C2 **Avezzano** Italy
8D3 **Aviemore** Scotland
35B2 **Aviemore,L** New Zealand
14C3 **Avignon** France
15B1 **Avila** Spain
15A1 **Avilés** Spain
61D2 **Avoca** Iowa, USA
68B1 **Avoca** New York, USA
34B3 **Avoca** *R* Australia
68B1 **Avon** USA
7C4 **Avon** *County* England
7D4 **Avon** *R* Dorset, England
7D3 **Avon** *R* Warwick, England
59D4 **Avondale** USA
7C4 **Avonmouth** Wales
67B3 **Avon Park** USA
13B3 **Avre** *R* France
17D2 **Avtovac** Bosnia-Herzegovina
45D2 **A'waj** *R* Syria
29D4 **Awaji-shima** *I* Japan
50E3 **Awarē** Ethiopia
35A2 **Awarua Pt** New Zealand
50E3 **Awash** Ethiopia
50E3 **Awash** *R* Ethiopia
29C3 **Awa-shima** *I* Japan
35B2 **Awatere** *R* New Zealand
49D2 **Awbārī** Libya
50C3 **Aweil** Sudan
8C3 **Awe, Loch** *L* Scotland
49E2 **Awjilah** Libya
55J1 **Axel Heiberg I** Canada
7C4 **Axminster** England
29C3 **Ayabe** Japan
74E5 **Ayacucho** Argentina
69C5 **Ayacucho** Colombia
72D6 **Ayacucho** Peru
24K5 **Ayaguz** Kazakhstan
39G2 **Ayakkum Hu** *L* China
15A2 **Ayamonte** Spain
25P4 **Ayan** Russian Federation
72D6 **Ayaviri** Peru
21D8 **Aydın** Turkey
17F3 **Áyios Evstrátios** *I* Greece
25N3 **Aykhal** Russian Federation
7D4 **Aylesbury** England
45D2 **'Ayn al Fijah** Syria
40D2 **Ayn Zālah** Iraq
49E2 **Ayn Zuwayyah** *Well* Libya
50D3 **Ayod** Sudan
32D2 **Ayr** Australia
8C4 **Ayr** Scotland
8C4 **Ayr** *R* Scotland
6B2 **Ayre,Pt of** Isle of Man, British Islands
17F2 **Aytos** Bulgaria
30C3 **Ayutthaya** Thailand
17F3 **Ayvacık** Turkey
17F3 **Ayvalık** Turkey
43E3 **Āzamgarh** India
48B3 **Azaouad** *Desert Region* Mali
48C3 **Azaouak, Vallée de l'** Niger
48D3 **Azare** Nigeria
40C2 **A'zāz** Syria
Azbine = Aïr
48A2 **Azeffal** *Watercourse* Mauritius
21H7 **Azerbaijan** *Republic* Europe
72C4 **Azogues** Ecuador
20H2 **Azopol'ye** Russian Federation
46B4 **Azores** *Is* Atlantic Ocean
50C2 **Azoum** *R* Chad
21F6 **Azov, S of** Russian Federation/Ukraine
48B1 **Azrou** Morocco
62A1 **Aztec** USA
72B2 **Azuero,Pen de** Panama
74E5 **Azul** Argentina
75B1 **Azul, Serra** *Mts* Brazil
16B3 **Azzaba** Algeria
45D2 **Az-Zabdānī** Syria
41G5 **Aẓ Ẓāhirah** *Mts* Oman
49D2 **Az Zahrah** Libya
40C3 **Az Zilaf** Syria
41D4 **Az Zilfī** Saudi Arabia
41E3 **Az Zubayr** Iraq

B

45C2 **Ba'abda** Lebanon
40C3 **Ba'albek** Lebanon
45C3 **Ba'al Hazor** *Mt* Israel
50E3 **Baardheere** Somalia
17F2 **Babadag** Romania
40A1 **Babaeski** Turkey
72C4 **Babahoyo** Ecuador
50E2 **Bāb al Mandab** *Str* Djibouti/Yemen
32B1 **Babar, Kepulauan** *I* Indonesia
50D4 **Babati** Tanzania
20F4 **Babayevo** Russian Federation
61E1 **Babbitt** USA
64C2 **Baberton** USA
54F4 **Babine L** Canada
32C1 **Babo** Indonesia
41F2 **Bābol** Iran
27F5 **Babuyan Is** Philippines
73J4 **Bacabal** Brazil
27F7 **Bacan** *I* Indonesia
21D6 **Bacău** Romania
30D1 **Bac Can** Vietnam
13D3 **Baccarat** France
34B3 **Bacchus Marsh** Australia
39F2 **Bachu** China
54J3 **Back** *R* Canada
30D1 **Bac Ninh** Vietnam
27F5 **Bacolod** Philippines
6C3 **Bacup** England
44B3 **Badagara** India
31A1 **Badain Jaran Shamo** *Desert* China
15A2 **Badajoz** Spain
15C1 **Badalona** Spain
40D3 **Badanah** Saudi Arabia
28B2 **Badaohe** China
13E3 **Bad Bergzabern** Germany
13D2 **Bad Ems** Germany
18B3 **Baden-Baden** Germany
13D3 **Badenviller** France
18B3 **Baden-Württemberg** *State* Germany
18C3 **Badgastein** Austria
66C2 **Badger** USA
18B2 **Bad-Godesberg** Germany
18B2 **Bad Hersfeld** Germany
13D2 **Bad Honnef** Germany
42B4 **Badin** Pakistan
16C1 **Bad Ischl** Austria
40C3 **Badiyat ash Sham** *Desert Region* Iraq/Jordan
18B3 **Bad-Kreuznach** Germany
60C1 **Badlands** *Region* USA
13E2 **Bad Lippspringe** Germany
13E2 **Bad Nauheim** Germany
13D2 **Bad Nevenahr-Ahrweiler** Germany
40C5 **Badr Ḥunayn** Saudi Arabia
13E2 **Bad Ryrmont** Germany
18C3 **Bad Tolz** Germany
44C4 **Badulla** Sri Lanka
13E2 **Bad Wildungen** Germany
13E3 **Bad Wimpfen** Germany
15B2 **Baena** Spain
48A3 **Bafatá** Guinea-Bissau
55L2 **Baffin B** Canada/Greenland
63C3 **Baffin B** USA
55L2 **Baffin I** Canada
50B3 **Bafia** Cameroon
48A3 **Bafing** *R* Mali
48A3 **Bafoulabé** Mali
50B3 **Bafoussam** Cameroon
41G3 **Bāfq** Iran
21F7 **Bafra Burun** *Pt* Turkey
41G4 **Bāft** Iran
50C3 **Bafwasende** Zaïre
43E3 **Bagaha** India
44B2 **Bāgalkot** India
51D4 **Bagamoyo** Tanzania
59D4 **Bagdad** USA
74F4 **Bagé** Brazil
60B2 **Baggs** USA
41D3 **Baghdād** Iraq
43F4 **Bagherhat** Bangladesh
41G3 **Bāghīn** Iran
42B1 **Baghlan** Afghanistan
61D1 **Bagley** USA
48B4 **Bagnoa** Ivory Coast
14C3 **Bagnols-sur-Cèze** France
Bago = Pegu
48B3 **Bagoé** *R* Mali
28A2 **Bag Tai** China
27F5 **Baguio** Philippines
43F3 **Bāhādurābād** Bangladesh
57F4 **Bahamas,The** *Is* Caribbean Sea
43F4 **Baharampur** India
40A4 **Bahariya Oasis** Egypt
42C3 **Bahawalnagar** Pakistan
42C3 **Bahawalpur** Pakistan
42C3 **Bahawalpur** *Division* Pakistan
Bahia = Salvador
73K6 **Bahia** *State* Brazil
74D5 **Bahía Blanca** Argentina
70D3 **Bahía, Islas de la** Honduras
56B4 **Bahia Kino** Mexico
74C6 **Bahias, Cabo dos** Argentina
50D2 **Bahir Dar** Ethiopia
45A3 **Bahra el Manzala** *L* Egypt
43E3 **Bahraich** India
38D3 **Bahrain** *Sheikhdom* Arabian Pen
41D3 **Bahr al Milh** *L* Iraq
50C3 **Bahr Aouk** *R* Chad/Central African Republic
Bahrat Lut = Dead Sea
Bahr el Abiad = White Nile
50C3 **Bahr el Arab** *Watercourse* Sudan
Bahr el Azraq = Blue Nile
50D3 **Bahr el Ghazal** *R* Sudan
50B2 **Bahr el Ghazal** *Watercourse* Chad
45A3 **Bahr Fâqûs** *R* Egypt
15A2 **Baia de Setúbal** *B* Portugal
51B5 **Baia dos Tigres** Angola
21C6 **Baia Mare** Romania
50B3 **Baïbokoum** Chad
26F2 **Baicheng** China
55M5 **Baie-Comeau** Canada
45C2 **Baie de St Georges** *B* Lebanon
55L4 **Baie-du-Poste** Canada
65E1 **Baie St Paul** Canada
55N5 **Baie-Verte** Canada
31B3 **Baihe** China
31C3 **Bai He** *R* China
41D3 **Ba'ījī** Iraq
25M4 **Baikal, L** Russian Federation
43E4 **Baikunthpur** India
Baile Atha Cliath = Dublin
17E2 **Băileşti** Romania
13B2 **Bailleul** France
31A3 **Baima** China
67B2 **Bainbridge** USA
54B3 **Baird Mts** USA
31D1 **Bairin Youqi** China
31D1 **Bairin Zuoqi** China
32D4 **Bairnsdale** Australia
43E3 **Baitadi** Nepal
28A2 **Baixingt** China
17D1 **Baja** Hungary
70A1 **Baja California** *Pen* Mexico
59C4 **Baja California** *State* Mexico
70A2 **Baja, Punta** *Pt* Mexico
20K5 **Bakal** Russian Federation
50C3 **Bakala** Central African Republic
48A3 **Bakel** Senegal
59C3 **Baker** California, USA
56C2 **Baker** Montana, USA
56B2 **Baker** Oregon, USA
55J3 **Baker Foreland** *Pt* Canada
54J3 **Baker L** Canada
54J3 **Baker Lake** Canada
56A2 **Baker,Mt** USA
56B3 **Bakersfield** USA
7D3 **Bakewell** England
41G2 **Bakharden** Turkmenistan
41G2 **Bakhardok** Turkmenistan
21E5 **Bakhmach** Ukraine
12C1 **Bakkaflói** *B* Iceland
50D3 **Bako** Ethiopia
50C3 **Bakouma** Central African Republic
21H7 **Baku** Azerbaijan
40B2 **Balâ** Turkey
7C3 **Bala** Wales
27E6 **Balabac** *I* Philippines
27E6 **Balabac Str** Malaysia/Philippines
43E4 **Bālaghāt** India
34A2 **Balaklava** Australia
21H5 **Balakovo** Russian Federation
43E4 **Balāngīr** India
21G5 **Balashov** Russian Federation
43F4 **Balasore** India
17D1 **Balaton** *L* Hungary
9C3 **Balbriggan** Irish Republic
74E5 **Balcarce** Argentina
17F2 **Balchik** Bulgaria
33F5 **Balclutha** New Zealand
63D1 **Bald Knob** USA
7D4 **Baldock** England
67B2 **Baldwin** USA
58E1 **Baldy Mt** USA
56C3 **Baldy Peak** *Mt* USA
15C2 **Balearic Is** Spain
75E2 **Baleia, Ponta da** *Pt* Brazil
55M4 **Baleine, Rivière de la** *R* Canada
27F5 **Baler** Philippines
20J4 **Balezino** Russian Federation
32A1 **Bali** *I* Indonesia
40A2 **Balıkesir** Turkey
40C2 **Balīkh** *R* Syria/Turkey
27E7 **Balikpapan** Indonesia
75B2 **Baliza** Brazil
42B1 **Balkh** Afghanistan
24J5 **Balkhash** Kazakhstan
24J5 **Balkhash, L** Kazakhstan
8C3 **Ballachulish** Scotland
8C4 **Ballantrae** Scotland
54G2 **Ballantyne Str** Canada
44B3 **Ballāpur** India
32D4 **Ballarat** Australia
8D3 **Ballater** Scotland
6B2 **Ballaugh** England
76G7 **Balleny Is** Antarctica
43E3 **Ballia** India
34D1 **Ballina** Australia
10B3 **Ballina** Irish Republic
62C2 **Ballinger** USA
9A4 **Ballinskelligis B** Irish Republic
13D4 **Ballon d'Alsace** *Mt* France
17D2 **Ballsh** Albania
68D1 **Ballston Spa** USA
9C2 **Ballycastle** Northern Ireland
9D2 **Ballyclare** Northern Ireland
9C4 **Ballycotton B** Irish Republic
9B3 **Ballyhaunis** Northern Ireland
9C2 **Ballymena** Northern Ireland
9C2 **Ballymoney** Northern Ireland
9C2 **Ballynahinch** Northern Ireland
9B2 **Ballyshannon** Irish Republic
9C3 **Ballyteige B** Irish Republic
34B3 **Balmoral** Australia
62B2 **Balmorhea** USA
42B3 **Balochistān** *Region* Pakistan
51B5 **Balombo** Angola
34C1 **Balonn** *R* Australia
42C3 **Bālotra** India
43E3 **Balrāmpur** India
32D4 **Balranald** Australia
73J5 **Balsas** Brazil
70B3 **Balsas** *R* Mexico
21D6 **Balta** Ukraine
12H7 **Baltic S** N Europe
40B3 **Baltîm** Egypt
57F3 **Baltimore** USA
43F3 **Bālurghāt** India
21J6 **Balykshi** Kazakhstan
41G4 **Bam** Iran
50B2 **Bama** Nigeria
48B3 **Bamako** Mali
50C3 **Bambari** Central African Republic
67B2 **Bamberg** USA
18C3 **Bamberg** Germany
50C3 **Bambili** Zaïre
75C3 **Bambuí** Brazil
50B3 **Bamenda** Cameroon
28A2 **Bamiancheng** China
50B3 **Bamingui** *R* Central African Republic
50B3 **Bamingui Bangoran National Park** Central African Republic
42B2 **Bamiyan** Afghanistan
33F1 **Banaba** *I* Kiribati
50C3 **Banalia** Zaïre
48B3 **Banamba** Mali
44E4 **Bananga** Nicobar Is, Indian Ocean
30C3 **Ban Aranyaprathet** Thailand
30C2 **Ban Ban** Laos
30C4 **Ban Betong** Thailand
9C2 **Banbridge** Northern Ireland
7D3 **Banbury** England
8D3 **Banchory** Scotland
70D3 **Banco Chinchorro** *Is* Mexico
65D1 **Bancroft** Canada
43E3 **Bānda** India
27C6 **Banda Aceh** Indonesia

27G7 **Banda, Kepulauan** *Arch* Indonesia
48B4 **Bandama** *R* Ivory Coast
41G4 **Bandar 'Abbās** Iran
21H8 **Bandar Anzalī** Iran
41F4 **Bandar-e Daylam** Iran
41F4 **Bandar-e Lengheh** Iran
41F4 **Bandar-e Māqām** Iran
41F4 **Bandar-e Rig** Iran
21J8 **Bandar-e Torkoman** Iran
41E3 **Bandar Khomeynī** Iran
27E6 **Bandar Seri Begawan** Brunei
27F7 **Banda S** Indonesia
75D3 **Bandeira** *Mt* Brazil
75B1 **Bandeirantes** Brazil
70B2 **Banderas, B de** Mexico
48B3 **Bandiagara** Mali
21D7 **Bandırma** Turkey
47D1 **Bandolier Kop** South Africa
50B4 **Bandundu** Zaïre
27D7 **Bandung** Indonesia
21H8 **Baneh** Iran
70E2 **Banes** Cuba
8D3 **Banff** Scotland
54G4 **Banff** *R* Canada
44B3 **Bangalore** India
50C3 **Bangassou** Central African Republic
32B1 **Banggai, Kepulauan** *I* Indonesia
27E6 **Banggi** *I* Malaysia
30D2 **Bang Hieng** *R* Laos
27D7 **Bangka** *I* Indonesia
30C3 **Bangkok** Thailand
30C3 **Bangkok, Bight of** *B* Thailand
39G3 **Bangladesh** *Republic* Asia
42D2 **Bangong Co** *L* China
57G2 **Bangor** Maine, USA
9D2 **Bangor** Northern Ireland
68C2 **Bangor** Pennsylvania, USA
7B3 **Bangor** Wales
30B3 **Bang Saphan Yai** Thailand
50B3 **Bangui** Central African Republic
51D5 **Bangweulu, L** Zambia
30C4 **Ban Hat Yai** Thailand
30C2 **Ban Hin Heup** Laos
30C1 **Ban Houei Sai** Laos
30B3 **Ban Hua Hin** Thailand
48B3 **Bani** *R* Mali
48C3 **Bani Bangou** Niger
49D1 **Banī Walīd** Libya
40C2 **Bāniyās** Syria
16D2 **Banja Luka** Bosnia-Herzegovina
27E7 **Banjarmasin** Indonesia
48A3 **Banjul** The Gambia
30B4 **Ban Kantang** Thailand
30D2 **Ban Khemmarat** Laos
30B4 **Ban Khok Kloi** Thailand
27H8 **Banks I** Australia
54E4 **Banks I** British Columbia, Canada
54F2 **Banks I** Northwest Territories, Canada
33F2 **Banks Is** Vanuatu
58C1 **Banks L** USA
35B2 **Banks Pen** New Zealand
34C4 **Banks Str** Australia
43F4 **Bankura** India
30B2 **Ban Mae Sariang** Thailand
30B2 **Ban Mae Sot** Thailand
43H4 **Banmauk** Burma
30D3 **Ban Me Thuot** Vietnam
9C3 **Bann** *R* Irish Republic
9C2 **Bann** *R* Northern Ireland
30B4 **Ban Na San** Thailand
42C2 **Bannu** Pakistan
30C2 **Ban Pak Neun** Laos
30C4 **Ban Pak Phanang** Thailand
30D3 **Ban Pu Kroy** Cambodia
30B3 **Ban Sai Yok** Thailand
30C3 **Ban Sattahip** Thailand
19D3 **Banská Bystrica** Slovakia
42C4 **Bānswāra** India
30B4 **Ban Tha Kham** Thailand
30D2 **Ban Thateng** Laos
30C2 **Ban Tha Tum** Thailand
10B3 **Bantry** Irish Republic
10A3 **Bantry** *B* Irish Republic
27C6 **Banyak, Kepulauan** *Is* Indonesia
30D3 **Ban Ya Soup** Vietnam
27E7 **Banyuwangi** Indonesia
36E7 **Banzare Seamount** Indian Ocean
31D2 **Baoding** China
31C3 **Baofeng** China
30C1 **Bao Ha** Vietnam
31B3 **Baoji** China
30D3 **Bao Loc** Vietnam
26C4 **Baoshan** China
31C1 **Baotou** China
44C2 **Bāpatla** India
13B2 **Bapaume** France
45C4 **Bāqir, Jebel** *Mt* Jordan
41D3 **Ba'qūbah** Iraq
17D2 **Bar** Montenegro, Yugoslavia
50D2 **Bara** Sudan
50E3 **Baraawe** Somalia
43E3 **Bāra Banki** India
28C2 **Barabash** Russian Federation
24J4 **Barabinsk** Kazakhstan/ Russian Federation
24J4 **Barabinskaya Step** *Steppe* Kazakhstan/ Russian Federation
15B1 **Baracaldo** Spain
69C2 **Baracoa** Cuba
45D2 **Baradá** *R* Syria
34C2 **Baradine** Australia
44A2 **Bārāmati** India
42C2 **Baramula** Pakistan
42D3 **Bārān** India
54E4 **Baranof I** USA
20D5 **Baranovichi** Belarus
34A2 **Baratta** Australia
43F3 **Barauni** India
73K8 **Barbacena** Brazil
69F4 **Barbados** *I* Caribbean Sea
15C1 **Barbastro** Spain
47E2 **Barberton** South Africa
14B2 **Barbezieux** France
72D2 **Barbosa** Colombia
69E3 **Barbuda** *I* Caribbean Sea
32D3 **Barcaldine** Australia
Barce = Al Marj
16D3 **Barcellona** Sicily, Italy
15C1 **Barcelona** Spain
72F1 **Barcelona** Venezuela
32D3 **Barcoo** *R* Australia
50B1 **Bardai** Chad
74C5 **Bardas Blancas** Argentina
43F4 **Barddhamān** India
19E3 **Bardejov** Slovakia
7B3 **Bardsey** *I* Wales
64B3 **Bardstown** USA
42D3 **Bareilly** India
Barentsovo More *S* = **Barents Sea**
24D2 **Barentsøya** *I* Svalbard
20F1 **Barents S** Russian Federation
50D2 **Barentu** Eritrea
14B2 **Barfleur, Pointe de** France
43E4 **Bargarh** India
25M4 **Barguzin** Russian Federation
25N4 **Barguzin** *R* Russian Federation
65F2 **Bar Harbor** USA
43F4 **Barhi** India
16D2 **Bari** Italy
15D2 **Barika** Algeria
72D2 **Barinas** Venezuela
43F4 **Baripāda** India
40B5 **Bârîs** Egypt
42C4 **Bari Sādri** India
43G4 **Barisal** Bangladesh
27D7 **Barisan, Pegunungan** *Mts* Indonesia
27E7 **Barito** *R* Indonesia
49D2 **Barjuj** *Watercourse* Libya
31A3 **Barkam** China
64B3 **Barkley,L** USA
47D3 **Barkly East** South Africa
32C2 **Barkly Tableland** *Mts* Australia
13C3 **Bar-le-Duc** France
32A3 **Barlee,L** Australia
32A3 **Barlee Range** *Mts* Australia
16D2 **Barletta** Italy
42C3 **Bārmer** India
34B2 **Barmera** Australia
7B3 **Barmouth** Wales
6D2 **Barnard Castle** England
24K4 **Barnaul** Russian Federation
68C3 **Barnegat** USA
68C3 **Barnegat B** USA
68A2 **Barnesboro** USA
55L2 **Barnes Icecap** Canada
67B2 **Barnesville** Georgia, USA
64C3 **Barnesville** Ohio, USA
62B2 **Barnhart** USA
7D3 **Barnsley** England
7B4 **Barnstaple** England
48C4 **Baro** Nigeria
43G3 **Barpeta** India
72E1 **Barquisimeto** Venezuela
13D3 **Barr** France
73K6 **Barra** Brazil
8B3 **Barra** *I* Scotland
34D2 **Barraba** Australia
75D1 **Barra da Estiva** Brazil
75A2 **Barra do Bugres** Brazil
75B2 **Barra do Garças** Brazil
75D3 **Barra do Piraí** Brazil
51D6 **Barra Falsa, Punta de** *Pt* Mozambique
73K6 **Barragem de Sobradinho** *Res* Brazil
15A2 **Barragem do Castelo do Bode** *Res* Portugal
15A2 **Barragem do Maranhão** *Res* Portugal
8B3 **Barra Head** *Pt* Scotland
73K8 **Barra Mansa** Brazil
72C6 **Barranca** Peru
72D2 **Barrancabermeja** Colombia
72F2 **Barrancas** Venezuela
74E3 **Barranqueras** Argentina
72D1 **Barranquilla** Colombia
8B3 **Barra,Sound of** *Chan* Scotland
68D1 **Barre** USA
73J6 **Barreiras** Brazil
15A2 **Barreiro** Portugal
73L5 **Barreiros** Brazil
32D5 **Barren,C** Australia
73J8 **Barretos** Brazil
65D2 **Barrie** Canada
34B2 **Barrier Range** *Mts* Australia
32E4 **Barrington,Mt** Australia
75C2 **Barro Alto** Brazil
27G8 **Barroloola** Australia
64A1 **Barron** USA
69N2 **Barrouallie** St Vincent
54C2 **Barrow** USA
9C3 **Barrow** *R* Irish Republic
32C3 **Barrow Creek** Australia
32A3 **Barrow I** Australia
6C2 **Barrow-in-Furness** England
54C2 **Barrow,Pt** USA
55J2 **Barrow Str** Canada
7C4 **Barry** Wales
65D1 **Barry's Bay** Canada
68C2 **Barryville** USA
44B2 **Barsi** India
13E1 **Barsinghausen** Germany
56B3 **Barstow** USA
14C2 **Bar-sur-Aube** France
13C3 **Bar-sur-Seine** France
73G2 **Bartica** Guyana
40B1 **Bartın** Turkey
32D2 **Bartle Frere,Mt** Australia
56D3 **Bartlesville** USA
60D2 **Bartlett** USA
51D6 **Bartolomeu Dias** Mozambique
6D3 **Barton-upon-Humber** England
19E2 **Bartoszyce** Poland
72B2 **Barú** *Mt* Panama
42D4 **Barwāh** India
42C4 **Barwāni** India
34C1 **Barwon** *R* Australia
20H5 **Barysh** Russian Federation
66C1 **Basalt** USA
50B3 **Basankusu** Zaïre
Basel = Basle
16D2 **Basento** *R* Italy
26F4 **Bashi Chan** Philippines/ Taiwan
20J5 **Bashkortostan** *Republic* Russian Federation
27F6 **Basilan** Philippines
27F6 **Basilan** *I* Philippines
7E4 **Basildon** England
58E2 **Basin** USA
7D4 **Basingstoke** England
56B2 **Basin Region** USA
65D1 **Baskatong, Réservoir** Canada
16B1 **Basle** Switzerland
41E3 **Basra** Iraq
13D3 **Bas-Rhin** *Department* France
30D3 **Bassac** *R* Cambodia
16C1 **Bassano** Italy
48C4 **Bassar** Togo
51D6 **Bassas da India** *I* Mozambique Channel
30A2 **Bassein** Burma
69E3 **Basse Terre** Guadeloupe
60D2 **Bassett** USA
48C4 **Bassila** Benin
66C2 **Bass Lake** USA
32D5 **Bass Str** Australia
13E1 **Bassum** Germany
12G7 **Båstad** Sweden
41F4 **Bastak** Iran
43E3 **Basti** India
16B2 **Bastia** Corsica, Italy
18B3 **Bastogne** Belgium
63D2 **Bastrop** Louisiana, USA
63C2 **Bastrop** Texas, USA
48C4 **Bata** Equatorial Guinea
27F5 **Bataan Pen** Philippines
69A2 **Batabanó, G de** Cuba
27E7 **Batakan** Indonesia
42D2 **Batāla** India
26C3 **Batang** China
50B3 **Batangafo** Central African Republic
27F5 **Batangas** Philippines
26F4 **Batan Is** Philippines
75C3 **Batatais** Brazil
65D2 **Batavia** USA
34D3 **Batemans Bay** Australia
67B2 **Batesburg** USA
63D1 **Batesville** Arkansas, USA
63E2 **Batesville** Mississippi, USA
65F1 **Bath** Canada
7C4 **Bath** England
65F2 **Bath** Maine, USA
65D2 **Bath** New York, USA
50B2 **Batha** *R* Chad
64C1 **Bathawana Mt** Canada
32D4 **Bathurst** Australia
55M5 **Bathurst** Canada
54F2 **Bathurst,C** Canada
32C2 **Bathurst I** Australia
54H2 **Bathurst I** Canada
54H3 **Bathurst Inlet** *B* Canada
48B4 **Batié** Burkina
41E4 **Bāţin, Wadi al** *Watercourse* Iraq
41F3 **Bāţlāq-e-Gavkhūnī** *Salt Flat* Iran
34C3 **Batlow** Australia
40D2 **Batman** Turkey
16B3 **Batna** Algeria
57D3 **Baton Rouge** USA
45C1 **Batroûn** Lebanon
30C3 **Battambang** Cambodia
44C4 **Batticaloa** Sri Lanka
44E4 **Batti Malv** *I* Nicobar Is, Indian Ocean
7E4 **Battle** England
57E2 **Battle Creek** USA
55N4 **Battle Harbour** Canada
58C2 **Battle Mountain** USA
21G7 **Batumi** Georgia
30C5 **Batu Pahat** Malaysia
45C2 **Bat Yam** Israel
32B1 **Baubau** Indonesia
48C3 **Bauchi** Nigeria
61E1 **Baudette** USA
55N4 **Bauld,C** Canada
25N4 **Baunt** Russian Federation
73J8 **Bauru** Brazil
75B2 **Baús** Brazil
18C2 **Bautzen** Germany
27E7 **Bawean** *I* Indonesia
49E2 **Bawîti** Egypt
48B3 **Bawku** Ghana
30B2 **Bawlake** Burma
34A2 **Bawlen** Australia
67B2 **Baxley** USA
70E2 **Bayamo** Cuba
43J2 **Bayana** India
26D2 **Bayandzürh** Mongolia
26C3 **Bayan Har Shan** *Mts* China
31A1 **Bayan Mod** China
31B1 **Bayan Obo** China
60C2 **Bayard** Nebraska, USA
62A2 **Bayard** New Mexico, USA
25N2 **Bayasgalant** Mongolia
40D1 **Bayburt** Turkey
57E2 **Bay City** Michigan, USA
63C3 **Bay City** Texas, USA
20M2 **Baydaratskaya Guba** *B* Russian Federation
50E3 **Baydhabo** Somalia
18C3 **Bayern** *State* Germany
14B2 **Bayeux** France
64A1 **Bayfield** USA
40C3 **Bāyir** Jordan
Baykal, Ozero *L* = **Baikal, L**
26D1 **Baykalskiy Khrebet** *Mts* Russian Federation
25L3 **Baykit** Russian Federation
25L5 **Baylik Shan** *Mts* China/ Mongolia
20K5 **Baymak** Russian Federation
63E2 **Bay Minette** USA
14B3 **Bayonne** France
18C3 **Bayreuth** Germany
63E2 **Bay St Louis** USA
65E2 **Bay Shore** USA
65D1 **Bays,L of** Canada
26B2 **Baytik Shan** *Mts* China
Bayt Lahm = Bethlehem
63D3 **Baytown** USA
15B2 **Baza** Spain
19F3 **Bazaliya** Ukraine
21H7 **Bazar-Dyuzi** *Mt* Azerbaijan
51D6 **Bazaruto, Ilha** Mozambique
14B3 **Bazas** France
31B3 **Bazhong** China
45D1 **Bcharre** Lebanon
60C1 **Beach** USA
68C3 **Beach Haven** USA
7E4 **Beachy Head** England
68D2 **Beacon** USA
51E5 **Bealanana** Madagascar
58D2 **Bear** *R* USA
64A2 **Beardstown** USA
24C2 **Bear I** Barents Sea
58D2 **Bear L** USA
66B1 **Bear Valley** USA
69C3 **Beata, Cabo** *C* Dominican Republic
69C3 **Beata, Isla** Dominican Republic
56D2 **Beatrice** USA
8D2 **Beatrice** *Oilfield* N Sea
54F4 **Beatton River** Canada
56B3 **Beatty** USA
65D1 **Beattyville** Canada
74E8 **Beauchene Is** Falkland Islands
34D1 **Beaudesert** Australia
67B2 **Beaufort** USA
54D2 **Beaufort S** Canada/USA
47C3 **Beaufort West** South Africa
65E1 **Beauharnois** Canada
8C3 **Beauly** Scotland
7B3 **Beaumaris** Wales
59C4 **Beaumont** California, USA
57D3 **Beaumont** Texas, USA
14C2 **Beaune** France
14C2 **Beauvais** France
54D3 **Beaver** USA
59D3 **Beaver** Utah, USA
54G4 **Beaver** *R* Canada
54D3 **Beaver Creek** Canada
64B3 **Beaver Dam** Kentucky, USA
64B2 **Beaver Dam** Wisconsin, USA
58D1 **Beaverhead Mts** USA
64B1 **Beaver I** USA
63D1 **Beaver L** USA
42C3 **Beāwar** India
75C3 **Bebedouro** Brazil
7E3 **Beccles** England
17E1 **Bečej** Serbia, Yugoslavia
48B1 **Béchar** Algeria
57E3 **Beckley** USA
13E2 **Beckum** Germany
6D2 **Bedale** England
13E1 **Bederkesa** Germany
7D3 **Bedford** England
64B3 **Bedford** Indiana, USA
68A3 **Bedford** Pennsylvania, USA
7D3 **Bedford** *County* England
69M2 **Bedford Pt** Grenada
68B2 **Beech Creek** USA
54D2 **Beechey Pt** USA
34C3 **Beechworth** Australia
34D1 **Beenleigh** Australia
45C3 **Beer Menuha** Israel
45C4 **Beer Ora** Israel
40B3 **Beersheba** Israel
Be'er Sheva = Beersheba
45C3 **Be'er Sheva** *R* Israel
56D4 **Beeville** USA
50C3 **Befale** Zaïre
51E5 **Befandriana** Madagascar
34C3 **Bega** Australia
Begicheva, Ostrov *I* = **Bol'shoy Begichev, Ostrov**
15C1 **Begur, C de** Spain
41F3 **Behbehān** Iran
41F2 **Behshahr** Iran
42B2 **Behsud** Afghanistan
26F2 **Bei'an** China
31B5 **Beihai** China
31D2 **Beijing** China
30E1 **Beiliu** China
31B4 **Beipan Jiang** *R* China
31E1 **Beipiao** China
Beira = Sofala
40C3 **Beirut** Lebanon
26C2 **Bei Shan** *Mts* China
47E1 **Beitbridge** Zimbabwe
45C2 **Beit ed Dīne** Lebanon
8C4 **Beith** Scotland
45C3 **Beit Jala** Israel
28A2 **Beizhen** China
15A2 **Beja** Portugal
16B3 **Béja** Tunisia
15C2 **Bejaïa** Algeria
15A1 **Béjar** Spain
41G3 **Bejestān** Iran
19E3 **Békéscsaba** Hungary
51E6 **Bekily** Madagascar
43E3 **Bela** India
42B3 **Bela** Pakistan
68B3 **Bel Air** USA
44B2 **Belampalli** India
27F6 **Belang** Indonesia
27C6 **Belangpidie** Indonesia
20D5 **Belarus** *Republic* Europe
Belau = Palau
75A3 **Béla Vista** Brazil/Paraguay
47E2 **Bela Vista** Mozambique
27C6 **Belawan** Indonesia
20K4 **Belaya** *R* Russian Federation
19G3 **Belaya Tserkov'** Ukraine
55J2 **Belcher Chan** Canada
55L4 **Belcher Is** Canada
42B1 **Belchiragh** Afghanistan
20J5 **Belebey** Russian Federation
50E3 **Beledweyne** Somalia
73J4 **Belém** Brazil
72C3 **Belén** Colombia
75A3 **Belén** Paraguay
56C3 **Belen** USA
33F2 **Bélep, Îles** Nouvelle Calédonie
16B3 **Belezma, Mts de** Algeria
9C2 **Belfast** Northern Ireland

47E2 **Belfast** South Africa
9C2 **Belfast Lough** *Estuary* Northern Ireland
60C1 **Belfield** USA
50D2 **Bēlfodiyo** Ethiopia
6D2 **Belford** England
14D2 **Belfort** France
44A2 **Belgaum** India
18A2 **Belgium** *Kingdom* NW Europe
21F5 **Belgorod** Russian Federation
21E6 **Belgorod Dnestrovskiy** Ukraine
58D1 **Belgrade** USA
17E2 **Belgrade** Serbia, Yugoslavia
49D2 **Bel Hedan** Libya
27D7 **Belitung** *I* Indonesia
70D3 **Belize** Belize
70D3 **Belize** *Republic* Central America
25P2 **Bel'kovskiy, Ostrov** *I* Russian Federation
14C2 **Bellac** France
54F4 **Bella Coola** Canada
63C3 **Bellaire** USA
44B2 **Bellary** India
34C1 **Bellata** Australia
68B2 **Bellefonte** USA
56C2 **Belle Fourche** USA
60C2 **Belle Fourche** *R* USA
14D2 **Bellegarde** France
13B4 **Bellegarde** France
67B3 **Belle Glade** USA
55N4 **Belle I** Canada
14B2 **Belle-Ile** *I* France
55N4 **Belle Isle,Str of** Canada
55L5 **Belleville** Canada
64B3 **Belleville** Illinois, USA
61D3 **Belleville** Kansas, USA
58D2 **Bellevue** Idaho, USA
64A2 **Bellevue** Iowa, USA
58B1 **Bellevue** Washington, USA
34D2 **Bellingen** Australia
6C2 **Bellingham** England
56A2 **Bellingham** USA
76G2 **Bellingshausen** *Base* Antarctica
76G3 **Bellingshausen S** Antarctica
16B1 **Bellinzona** Switzerland
72C2 **Bello** Colombia
33E3 **Bellona Reefs** Nouvelle Calédonie
66B1 **Bellota** USA
65E2 **Bellows Falls** USA
55K3 **Bell Pen** Canada
16C1 **Belluno** Italy
74D4 **Bell Ville** Argentina
68B1 **Belmont** USA
73L7 **Belmonte** Brazil
70D3 **Belmopan** Belize
26F1 **Belogorsk** Russian Federation
51E6 **Beloha** Madagascar
73K7 **Belo Horizonte** Brazil
61D3 **Beloit** Kansas, USA
57E2 **Beloit** Wisconsin, USA
20E3 **Belomorsk** Russian Federation
20K5 **Beloretsk** Russian Federation
Belorussia = Belarus
51E5 **Belo-Tsiribihina** Madagascar
Beloye More *S* **= White Sea**
20F3 **Beloye Ozero** *L* Russian Federation
20F3 **Belozersk** Russian Federation
7D3 **Belper** England
64C3 **Belpre** USA
34A2 **Beltana** Australia
63C2 **Belton** USA
19F3 **Bel'tsy** Moldavia
24K5 **Belukha** *Mt* Russian Federation
20H2 **Belush'ye** Russian Federation
64B2 **Belvidere** Illinois, USA
68C2 **Belvidere** New Jersey, USA
24J2 **Belyy, Ostrov** *I* Russian Federation
51B4 **Bembe** Angola
48C3 **Bembéréké** Benin
57D2 **Bemidji** USA
63E1 **Bemis** USA
50C4 **Bena Dibele** Zaïre
34C3 **Benalla** Australia
8C3 **Ben Attow** *Mt* Scotland
15A1 **Benavente** Spain
8B3 **Benbecula** *I* Scotland
32A4 **Bencubbin** Australia
56A2 **Bend** USA
8C3 **Ben Dearg** *Mt* Scotland
50E3 **Bendarbeyla** Somalia
19F3 **Bendery** Moldavia
32D4 **Bendigo** Australia
18C3 **Benešov** Czech Republic
16C2 **Benevento** Italy
39G4 **Bengal,B of** Asia
49D1 **Ben Gardane** Tunisia
31D3 **Bengbu** China
49E1 **Benghazi** Libya
27D7 **Bengkulu** Indonesia
51B5 **Benguela** Angola
40B3 **Benha** Egypt
8C2 **Ben Hope** *Mt* Scotland
50C3 **Beni** Zaïre
72E6 **Béni** *R* Bolivia
48B1 **Beni Abbès** Algeria
15C1 **Benicarló** Spain
15B2 **Benidorm** Spain
15C2 **Beni Mansour** Algeria
49F2 **Beni Mazâr** Egypt
48B1 **Beni Mellal** Morocco
48C4 **Benin** *Republic* Africa
48C4 **Benin City** Nigeria
15B2 **Beni-Saf** Algeria
49F2 **Beni Suef** Egypt
60C3 **Benkelman** USA
8C2 **Ben Kilbreck** *Mt* Scotland
10C2 **Ben Lawers** *Mt* Scotland
8D3 **Ben Macdui** *Mt* Scotland
8B3 **Ben More** Scotland
8C2 **Ben More Assynt** *Mt* Scotland
35B2 **Benmore,L** New Zealand
25R2 **Bennetta, Ostrov** *I* Russian Federation
8C3 **Ben Nevis** *Mt* Scotland
65E2 **Bennington** USA
45C2 **Bennt Jbail** Lebanon
50B3 **Bénoué** *R* Cameroon
13E3 **Bensheim** Germany
56B3 **Benson** Arizona, USA
61D1 **Benson** Minnesota, USA
27F7 **Benteng** Indonesia
50C3 **Bentiu** Sudan
75A2 **Bento Gomes** *R* Brazil
63D2 **Benton** Arkansas, USA
66C2 **Benton** California, USA
64B3 **Benton** Kentucky, USA
64B2 **Benton Harbor** USA
48C4 **Benue** *R* Nigeria
8C3 **Ben Wyvis** *Mt* Scotland
31E1 **Benxi** China
Beograd = Belgrade
43E4 **Beohāri** India
28C4 **Beppu** Japan
17D2 **Berat** Albania
27G7 **Berau, Teluk** *B* Indonesia
50D2 **Berber** Sudan
50E2 **Berbera** Somalia
50B3 **Berbérati** Central African Republic
19F3 **Berdichev** Ukraine
21F6 **Berdyansk** Ukraine
64C3 **Berea** USA
48B4 **Berekum** Ghana
66B2 **Berenda** USA
40C5 **Berenice** Egypt
54J4 **Berens** *R* Canada
54J4 **Berens River** Canada
61D2 **Beresford** USA
19E3 **Berettyóújfalu** Hungary
19E2 **Bereza** Belarus
19E3 **Berezhany** Ukraine
19F2 **Berezina** *R* Belarus
20G3 **Bereznik** Russian Federation
20K4 **Berezniki** Russian Federation
21E6 **Berezovka** Ukraine
20L3 **Berezovo** Russian Federation
40A2 **Bergama** Turkey
16B1 **Bergamo** Italy
12F6 **Bergen** Norway
68B1 **Bergen** USA
13C2 **Bergen op Zoom** Netherlands
14C3 **Bergerac** France
13D2 **Bergisch-Gladbach** Germany
44C2 **Berhampur** India
25S4 **Beringa, Ostrov** *I* Russian Federation
25T3 **Beringovskiy** Russian Federation
37K2 **Bering S** Russian Federation/USA
76C6 **Bering Str** Russian Federation/USA
41G4 **Berīzak** Iran
15B2 **Berja** Spain
13D1 **Berkel** *R* Germany/ Netherlands
56A3 **Berkeley** USA
68A3 **Berkeley Spring** USA
7D4 **Berkhamsted** England
76F2 **Berkner I** Antarctica
17E2 **Berkovitsa** Bulgaria
7D4 **Berkshire** *County* England
68D1 **Berkshire Hills** USA
18C2 **Berlin** Germany
18C2 **Berlin** *State* Germany
65E2 **Berlin** New Hampshire, USA
72F8 **Bermejo** Bolivia
74E3 **Bermejo** *R* Argentina
53M5 **Bermuda** *I* Atlantic Ocean
Bern = Berne
62A1 **Bernalillo** USA
75B4 **Bernardo de Irigoyen** Argentina
68C2 **Bernardsville** USA
18C2 **Bernburg** Germany
16B1 **Berne** Switzerland
8B3 **Berneray, I** Scotland
55K2 **Bernier B** Canada
18C3 **Berounka** *R* Czech Republic
34B2 **Berri** Australia
48C1 **Berriane** Algeria
14C2 **Berry** *Region* France
66A1 **Berryessa,L** USA
57F4 **Berry Is** The Bahamas
68B3 **Berryville** USA
47B2 **Berseba** Namibia
60B3 **Berthoud P** USA
50B3 **Bertoua** Cameroon
33G1 **Beru** *I* Kiribati
65D2 **Berwick** USA
6C2 **Berwick-upon-Tweed** England
7C3 **Berwyn Mts** Wales
51E5 **Besalampy** Madagascar
14D2 **Besançon** France
19E3 **Beskidy Zachodnie** *Mts* Poland
40C2 **Besni** Turkey
45C3 **Besor** *R* Israel
67A2 **Bessemer** Alabama, USA
64B1 **Bessemer** Michigan, USA
51E5 **Betafo** Madagascar
15A1 **Betanzos** Spain
45C3 **Bet Guvrin** Israel
47D2 **Bethal** South Africa
47B2 **Bethanie** Namibia
61E2 **Bethany** Missouri, USA
63C1 **Bethany** Oklahoma, USA
54B3 **Bethel** Alaska, USA
68D2 **Bethel** Connecticut, USA
64C2 **Bethel Park** USA
65D3 **Bethesda** USA
45C3 **Bethlehem** Israel
47D2 **Bethlehem** South Africa
65D2 **Bethlehem** USA
47D3 **Bethulie** South Africa
14C1 **Béthune** France
51E6 **Betioky** Madagascar
34B1 **Betoota** Australia
50B3 **Betou** Congo
39E1 **Betpak Dala** *Steppe* Kazakhstan
51E6 **Betroka** Madagascar
55M5 **Betsiamites** Canada
64A2 **Bettendorf** USA
43E3 **Bettiah** India
42D4 **Betūl** India
13C2 **Betuwe** *Region* Netherlands
42D3 **Betwa** *R* India
7C3 **Betws-y-coed** Wales
13D2 **Betzdorf** Germany
7D3 **Beverley** England
68E1 **Beverly** USA
66C3 **Beverly Hills** USA
7E4 **Bexhill** England
40B2 **Bey Dağları** Turkey
48B4 **Beyla** Guinea
44B3 **Beypore** India
Beyrouth = Beirut
40B2 **Beyşehir** Turkey
21E8 **Beyşehir Gölü** *L* Turkey
45C2 **Beyt Shean** Israel
20F4 **Bezhetsk** Russian Federation
14C3 **Béziers** France
41G2 **Bezmein** Turkmenistan
26D1 **Beznosova** Russian Federation
43F3 **Bhadgaon** Nepal
44C2 **Bhadrāchalam** India
43F4 **Bhadrakh** India
44B3 **Bhadra Res** India
44B3 **Bhadrāvati** India
42B3 **Bhag** Pakistan
43F3 **Bhāgalpur** India
42C2 **Bhakkar** Pakistan
42D4 **Bhandāra** India
42D3 **Bharatpur** India
42C4 **Bharūch** India
43F4 **Bhātiāpāra Ghat** Bangladesh
42C2 **Bhatinda** India
44A3 **Bhatkal** India
43F4 **Bhātpāra** India
42C4 **Bhāvnagar** India
43E5 **Bhawānipatna** India
42C2 **Bhera** Pakistan
43E3 **Bheri** *R* Nepal
43E4 **Bhilai** India
42C3 **Bhīlwāra** India
44C2 **Bhīmavaram** India
42D3 **Bhind** India
42D3 **Bhiwāni** India
44B2 **Bhongir** India
42D4 **Bhopāl** India
43F4 **Bhubaneshwar** India
42B4 **Bhuj** India
42D4 **Bhusāwal** India
39H3 **Bhutan** *Kingdom* Asia
27G7 **Biak** *I* Indonesia
19E2 **Biala Podlaska** Poland
18D2 **Białogard** Poland
19E2 **Bialystok** Poland
12A1 **Biargtangar** *C* Iceland
41G2 **Biārjmand** Iran
14B3 **Biarritz** France
40B4 **Biba** Egypt
29E2 **Bibai** Japan
51B5 **Bibala** Angola
18B3 **Biberach** Germany
48B4 **Bibiani** Ghana
17F1 **Bicaz** Romania
7D4 **Bicester** England
59D3 **Bicknell** USA
48C4 **Bida** Nigeria
44B2 **Bīdar** India
41G5 **Bidbid** Oman
65E2 **Biddeford** USA
7C6 **Bideford** England
7B4 **Bideford B** England
48C2 **Bidon 5** Algeria
19E2 **Biebrza** *R* Poland
16B1 **Biel** Switzerland
18D2 **Bielawa** Poland
18B2 **Bielefeld** Germany
16B1 **Biella** Italy
19E2 **Bielsk Podlaski** Poland
30D3 **Bien Hoa** Vietnam
55L4 **Bienville, Lac** Canada
16C2 **Biferno** *R* Italy
40A1 **Biga** Turkey
17F3 **Bigadiç** Turkey
58D1 **Big Belt Mts** USA
62B3 **Big Bend Nat Pk** USA
63E2 **Big Black** *R* USA
61D2 **Big Blue** *R* USA
67B3 **Big Cypress Swamp** USA
54D3 **Big Delta** USA
8D4 **Biggar** Scotland
54H4 **Biggar Kindersley** Canada
34D1 **Biggenden** Australia
7D3 **Biggleswade** England
58D1 **Big Hole** *R* USA
60B1 **Bighorn** *R* USA
60B1 **Bighorn L** USA
60B2 **Bighorn Mts** USA
48C4 **Bight of Benin** *B* W Africa
48C4 **Bight of Biafra** *B* Cameroon
55L3 **Big I** Canada
62B2 **Big Lake** USA
48A3 **Bignona** Senegal
59C3 **Big Pine** USA
67B4 **Big Pine Key** USA
66C3 **Big Pine Mt** USA
64B2 **Big Rapids** USA
54H4 **Big River** Canada
58D1 **Big Sandy** USA
61D2 **Big Sioux** *R* USA
66D1 **Big Smokey V** USA
56C3 **Big Spring** USA
60C2 **Big Springs** USA
61D1 **Big Stone City** USA
64C3 **Big Stone Gap** USA
66B2 **Big Sur** USA
58E1 **Big Timber** USA
55J4 **Big Trout L** Canada
55K4 **Big Trout Lake** Canada
16D2 **Bihać** Bosnia-Herzegovina
43F3 **Bihār** India
43F4 **Bihār** *State* India
50D4 **Biharamulo** Tanzania
21C6 **Bihor** *Mt* Romania
48A3 **Bijagós, Arquipélago dos** *Is* Guinea-Bissau
44B2 **Bijāpur** India
44C2 **Bijāpur** India
41E2 **Bījār** Iran
43E3 **Bijauri** Nepal
17D2 **Bijeljina** Bosnia-Herzegovina
31B4 **Bijie** China
42D3 **Bijnor** India
42C3 **Bijnot** Pakistan
42C3 **Bīkāner** India
45C2 **Bikfaya** Lebanon
26G2 **Bikin** Russian Federation
50B4 **Bikoro** Zaïre
Bilbo = Bilbao
42C3 **Bilāra** India
42D2 **Bilāspur** India
43E4 **Bilāspur** India
30B3 **Bilauktaung Range** *Mts* Burma/Thailand
15B1 **Bilbao** Spain
45A3 **Bilbeis** Egypt
18D3 **Bílé** *R* Czech Republic/ Slovakia
17D2 **Bileća** Bosnia-Herzegovina
40B1 **Bilecik** Turkey
50C3 **Bili** *R* Zaïre
25S3 **Bilibino** Russian Federation
56C2 **Billings** USA
50B2 **Bilma** Niger
57E3 **Biloxi** USA
50C2 **Biltine** Chad
67C3 **Bimini Is** Bahamas
42D4 **Bīna-Etawa** India
51D5 **Bindura** Zimbabwe
51C5 **Binga** Zimbabwe
51D5 **Binga, Mt** Mozambique/ Zimbabwe
34D1 **Bingara** Australia
18B3 **Bingen** Germany
65F1 **Bingham** USA
57F2 **Binghamton** USA
40D2 **Bingöl** Turkey
31D3 **Binhai** China
15C2 **Binibeca, Cabo** *C* Spain
27D6 **Bintan** *I* Indonesia
27E6 **Bintulu** Malaysia
74B5 **Bió Bió** *R* Chile
48C4 **Bioco** *I* Equatorial Guinea
44B2 **Bīr** India
49E2 **Bîr Abu Husein** *Well* Egypt
49E2 **Bi'r al Harash** *Well* Libya
50C2 **Birao** Central African Republic
43F3 **Biratnagar** Nepal
34B3 **Birchip** Australia
61E1 **Birch L** USA
54G4 **Birch Mts** Canada
55J4 **Bird** Canada
32C3 **Birdsville** Australia
32C2 **Birdum** Australia
45A4 **Bîr el 'Agramîya** *Well* Egypt
45B3 **Bîr el Duweidâr** *Well* Egypt
43E3 **Birganj** Nepal
45B3 **Bîr Gifgâfa** *Well* Egypt
45A4 **Bîr Gindali** *Well* Egypt
45B3 **Bîr Hasana** *Well* Egypt
75B3 **Birigui** Brazil
45D1 **Bīrīn** Syria
41G3 **Bīrjand** Iran
40B4 **Birkat Qârûn** *L* Egypt
13D3 **Birkenfeld** Germany
7C3 **Birkenhead** England
21D6 **Bîrlad** Romania
45B3 **Bîr Lahfân** *Well* Egypt
7C3 **Birmingham** England
57E3 **Birmingham** USA
49E2 **Bîr Misâha** *Well* Egypt
48A2 **Bir Moghrein** Mauritius
48C3 **Birnin-Kebbi** Nigeria
26G2 **Birobidzhan** Russian Federation
9C3 **Birr** Irish Republic
15C2 **Bir Rabalou** Algeria
34C1 **Birrie** *R* Australia
8D2 **Birsay** Scotland
20K4 **Birsk** Russian Federation
49E2 **Bîr Tarfâwi** *Well* Egypt
45B4 **Bîr Udelb** *Well* Egypt
25L4 **Biryusa** *R* Russian Federation
12J7 **Biržai** Lithuania
48B2 **Bir Zreigat** *Well* Mauritius
43K1 **Bisalpur** India
59E4 **Bisbee** USA
14A2 **Biscay,B of** France/Spain
67B3 **Biscayne B** USA
13D3 **Bischwiller** France
64C1 **Biscotasi L** Canada
31B4 **Bishan** China
39F1 **Bishkek** Kirgizia
56B3 **Bishop** USA
6D2 **Bishop Auckland** England
7C3 **Bishops Castle** England
7E4 **Bishop's Stortford** England
43E4 **Bishrāmpur** India
48C1 **Biskra** Algeria
56C2 **Bismarck** USA
32D1 **Bismarck Arch** Papua New Guinea
32D1 **Bismarck Range** *Mts* Papua New Guinea
32D1 **Bismarck S** Papua New Guinea
41E3 **Bīsotūn** Iran
48A3 **Bissau** Guinea-Bissau
57D1 **Bissett** Canada
54G4 **Bistcho L** Canada
17F1 **Bistrita** *R* Romania
50B3 **Bitam** Gabon
18B3 **Bitburg** Germany
13D3 **Bitche** France
40D2 **Bitlis** Turkey
17E2 **Bitola** Macedonia, Yugoslavia
18C2 **Bitterfeld** Germany
47B3 **Bitterfontein** South Africa
40B3 **Bitter Lakes** Egypt
56B2 **Bitteroot Range** *Mts* USA
48D3 **Biu** Nigeria
29D3 **Biwa-ko** *L* Japan
50E2 **Biyo Kaboba** Ethiopia
24K4 **Biysk** Russian Federation
16B3 **Bizerte** Tunisia
16D1 **Bjelovar** Croatia
48B2 **Bj Flye Ste Marie** Algeria
Bjørnøya *I* **= Bear I**
63D1 **Black** *R* USA

32D3 **Blackall** Australia
64B1 **Black B** Canada
6C3 **Blackburn** England
54D3 **Blackburn, Mt** USA
59D4 **Black Canyon City** USA
61E1 **Blackduck** USA
58D1 **Black Eagle** USA
58D2 **Blackfoot** USA
58D1 **Blackfoot** *R* USA
9B3 **Black Hd** *Pt* Irish Republic
54H5 **Black Hills** USA
8C3 **Black Isle** *Pen* Scotland
69Q2 **Blackman's** Barbados
59D3 **Black Mts** USA
7C4 **Black Mts** Wales
47B1 **Black Nosob** *R* Namibia
6C3 **Blackpool** England
69H1 **Black River** Jamaica
64A2 **Black River Falls** USA
56B2 **Black Rock Desert** USA
21D7 **Black S** Asia/Europe
64C3 **Blacksburg** USA
34D2 **Black Sugarloaf** *Mt* Australia
48B4 **Black Volta** *R* W Africa
63E2 **Black Warrior** *R* USA
7E4 **Blackwater** *R* England
10B3 **Blackwater** *R* Irish Republic
63C1 **Blackwell** USA
17E2 **Blagoevgrad** Bulgaria
25O4 **Blagoveshchensk** Russian Federation
58D1 **Blaikiston,Mt** Canada
58B1 **Blaine** USA
61D2 **Blair** USA
8D3 **Blair Atholl** Scotland
8D3 **Blairgowrie** Scotland
67C2 **Blakely** USA
74D5 **Blanca, Bahía** *B* Argentina
62A1 **Blanca Peak** *Mt* USA
16B3 **Blanc, C** Tunisia
34A1 **Blanche** *L* Australia
16B1 **Blanc, Mont** *Mt* France/Italy
56A2 **Blanco,C** USA
55N4 **Blanc Sablon** Canada
7C4 **Blandford Forum** England
59E3 **Blanding** USA
13B2 **Blankenberge** Belgium
69E4 **Blanquilla, Isla** Venezuela
51D5 **Blantyre** Malawi
9A3 **Blasket Sd** Irish Republic
14B2 **Blaye** France
34C2 **Blayney** Australia
33G5 **Blenheim** New Zealand
15C2 **Blida** Algeria
64C1 **Blind River** Canada
34A2 **Blinman** Australia
65E2 **Block I** USA
68E2 **Block Island Sd** USA
47D2 **Bloemfontein** South Africa
47D2 **Bloemhof** South Africa
47D2 **Bloemhof Dam** *Res* South Africa
73G3 **Blommesteinmeer** *L* Surinam
12A1 **Blönduós** Iceland
64B3 **Bloomfield** Indiana, USA
61E2 **Bloomfield** Iowa, USA
61D2 **Bloomfield** Nebraska,USA
62A1 **Bloomfield** New Mexico, USA
64B2 **Bloomington** Illinois, USA
64B3 **Bloomington** Indiana, USA
61E2 **Bloomington** Minnesota, USA
68B2 **Bloomsburg** USA
68B2 **Blossburg** USA
55Q3 **Blosseville Kyst** *Mts* Greenland
47D1 **Blouberg** *Mt* South Africa
18B3 **Bludenz** Austria
57E3 **Bluefield** USA
72B1 **Bluefields** Nicaragua
60D2 **Blue Hill** USA
68A2 **Blue Knob** *Mt* USA
69J1 **Blue Mountain Peak** *Mt* Jamaica
68B2 **Blue Mt** USA
34D2 **Blue Mts** Australia
56A2 **Blue Mts** USA
69J1 **Blue Mts, The** Jamaica
50D2 **Blue Nile** *R* Sudan
54G3 **Bluenose L** Canada
67C2 **Blue Ridge** USA
57E3 **Blue Ridge Mts** USA
9C2 **Blue Stack** *Mt* Irish Republic
35A3 **Bluff** New Zealand
59E3 **Bluff** USA
32A4 **Bluff Knoll** *Mt* Australia
74G3 **Blumenau** Brazil
60D2 **Blunt** USA
58B2 **Bly** USA
6D2 **Blyth** England
56B3 **Blythe** USA
57E3 **Blytheville** USA
48A4 **Bo** Sierra Leone
27F5 **Boac** Philippines
75D1 **Boa Nova** Brazil
64C2 **Boardman** USA
72F3 **Boa Vista** Brazil
48A4 **Boa Vista** *I* Cape Verde
30E1 **Bobai** China
44C2 **Bobbili** India
48B3 **Bobo Dioulasso** Burkina
19G2 **Bobrovica** Ukraine
20D5 **Bobruysk** Belarus
67B4 **Boca Chica Key** *I* USA
72E5 **Bôca do Acre** Brazil
75D2 **Bocaiúva** Brazil
50B3 **Bocaranga** Central African Republic
67B3 **Boca Raton** USA
19E3 **Bochnia** Poland
18B2 **Bocholt** Germany
13D2 **Bochum** Germany
51B5 **Bocoio** Angola
50B3 **Boda** Central African Republic
25N4 **Bodaybo** Russian Federation
59B3 **Bodega Head** *Pt* USA
50B2 **Bodélé** *Desert Region* Chad
12J5 **Boden** Sweden
9C3 **Boderg, L** Irish Republic
44B2 **Bodhan** India
44B3 **Bodināyakkanūr** India
7B4 **Bodmin** England
7B4 **Bodmin Moor** *Upland* England
12G5 **Bodø** Norway
17F3 **Bodrum** Turkey
50C4 **Boende** Zaïre
48A3 **Boffa** Guinea
30B2 **Bogale** Burma
63E2 **Bogalusa** USA
34C2 **Bogan** *R* Australia
48B3 **Bogande** Burkina
40C2 **Boğazlıyan** Turkey
20L4 **Bogdanovich** Russian Federation
26B2 **Bogda Shan** *Mt* China
47B2 **Bogenfels** Namibia
34D1 **Boggabilla** Australia
34C2 **Boggabri** Australia
7D4 **Bognor Regis** England
34C3 **Bogong** *Mt* Australia
27D7 **Bogor** Indonesia
25Q4 **Bogorodskoye** Russian Federation
20J4 **Bogorodskoye** Russian Federation
72D3 **Bogotá** Colombia
25K4 **Bogotol** Russian Federation
43F4 **Bogra** Bangladesh
31D2 **Bo Hai** *B* China
13B3 **Bohain-en-Vermandois** France
31D2 **Bohai Wan** *B* China
18C3 **Bohmer-wald** *Upland* Germany
27F6 **Bohol** *I* Philippines
27F6 **Bohol S** Philippines
75E1 **Boipeba, Ilha de** Brazil
75B2 **Bois** *R* Brazil
64C1 **Bois Blanc I** USA
56B2 **Boise** USA
62B1 **Boise City** USA
54F3 **Bois, Lac des** Canada
60C1 **Boissevain** Canada
48A2 **Bojador,C** Morocco
27F5 **Bojeador, C** Philippines
41G2 **Bojnūrd** Iran
48A3 **Boké** Guinea
34C1 **Bokhara** *R* Australia
12F7 **Boknafjord** *Inlet* Norway
50B4 **Boko** Congo
30C3 **Bokor** Cambodia
50B2 **Bokoro** Chad
50C4 **Bokungu** Zaïre
50B2 **Bol** Chad
48A3 **Bolama** Guinea-Bissau
14C2 **Bolbec** France
48B4 **Bole** Ghana
18D2 **Bolesławiec** Poland
48B3 **Bolgatanga** Ghana
21D6 **Bolgrad** Ukraine
63D1 **Bolivar** Missouri, USA
63E1 **Bolivar** Tennessee, USA
72D2 **Bolívar** *Mt* Venezuela
72E7 **Bolivia** *Republic* S America
12H6 **Bollnäs** Sweden
34C1 **Bollon** Australia
50B4 **Bolobo** Zaïre
16C2 **Bologna** Italy
20E4 **Bologoye** Russian Federation
26G1 **Bolon'** Russian Federation
26G2 **Bolon', Oz** *L* Russian Federation
16C2 **Bolsena, L di** Italy
25M2 **Bol'shevik, Ostrov** *I* Russian Federation
20J2 **Bol'shezemel'skaya Tundra** *Plain* Russian Federation
25S3 **Bol'shoy Anyuy** *R* Russian Federation
25N2 **Bol'shoy Begichev, Ostrov** *I* Russian Federation
21H5 **Bol'shoy Irgiz** *R* Russian Federation
28C2 **Bol'shoy Kamen** Russian Federation
25Q2 **Bol'shoy Lyakhovskiy, Ostrov** *I* Russian Federation
21H6 **Bol'shoy Uzen** *R* Kazakhstan
56C4 **Bolson de Mapimí** *Desert* Mexico
7C3 **Bolton** England
40B1 **Bolu** Turkey
12A1 **Bolungarvik** Iceland
9A4 **Bolus Hd** *Pt* Irish Republic
40B2 **Bolvadin** Turkey
16C1 **Bolzano** Italy
50B4 **Boma** Zaïre
32D4 **Bombala** Australia
44A2 **Bombay** India
51E5 **Bombetoka, Baie de** *B* Madagascar
50D3 **Bombo** Uganda
75C2 **Bom Despacho** Brazil
43G3 **Bomdila** India
48A4 **Bomi Hills** Liberia
73K6 **Bom Jesus da Lapa** Brazil
25O4 **Bomnak** Russian Federation
50C3 **Bomokāndi** *R* Zaïre
50C3 **Bomu** *R* Central African Republic/Zaïre
65D3 **Bon Air** USA
69D4 **Bonaire** *I* Caribbean Sea
70D3 **Bonanza** Nicaragua
55N5 **Bonavista** Canada
16C3 **Bon, C** Tunisia
50C3 **Bondo** Zaïre
48B4 **Bondoukou** Ivory Coast
Bône = 'Annaba
60D2 **Bonesteel** USA
73G3 **Bonfim** Guyana
50C3 **Bongandanga** Zaïre
50C3 **Bongo, Massif des** *Upland* Central African Republic
50B2 **Bongor** Chad
63C2 **Bonham** USA
16B2 **Bonifacio** Corsica, France
16B2 **Bonifacio,Str of** *Chan* Corsica, France/Sardinia, Italy
Bonin Is = Ogasawara Gunto
67B3 **Bonita Springs** USA
75A3 **Bonito** Brazil
18B2 **Bonn** Germany
58C1 **Bonners Ferry** USA
48C4 **Bonny** Nigeria
32A1 **Bonthain** Indonesia
48A4 **Bonthe** Sierra Leone
50E2 **Booaaso** Somalia
34B2 **Booligal** Australia
34D1 **Boonah** Australia
62B1 **Boone** Colorado, USA
61E2 **Boone** Iowa, USA
67B1 **Boone** North Carolina, USA
65D2 **Boonville** USA
34C2 **Boorowa** Australia
55J2 **Boothia,G of** Canada
55J2 **Boothia Pen** Canada
7C3 **Bootle** England
50B4 **Booué** Gabon
47C2 **Bophuthatswana** *Self governing homeland* South Africa
62B3 **Boquillas** Mexico
50D3 **Bor** Sudan
40B2 **Bor** Turkey
17E2 **Bor** Serbia, Yugoslavia
56B2 **Borah Peak** *Mt* USA
12G7 **Borås** Sweden
41F4 **Borāzjān** Iran
14B3 **Bordeaux** France
54G2 **Borden I** Canada
55K2 **Borden Pen** Canada
68C2 **Bordentown** USA
8D4 **Borders** *Region* Scotland
34B3 **Bordertown** Australia
15C2 **Bordj bou Arréidj** Algeria
48C2 **Bordj Omar Driss** Algeria
Borgå = Porvoo
55Q3 **Borgarnes** Iceland
56C3 **Borger** USA
12H7 **Borgholm** Sweden
19E3 **Borislav** Ukraine
21G5 **Borisoglebsk** Russian Federation
20D5 **Borisov** Belarus
21F5 **Borisovka** Russian Federation
75A4 **Borja** Paraguay
50B2 **Borkou** *Desert Region* Chad
13D1 **Borkum** *I* Germany
12H6 **Borlänge** Sweden
27E6 **Borneo** *I* Indonesia/Malaysia
12H7 **Bornholm** *I* Denmark
17F3 **Bornova** Turkey
48D3 **Bornu** *Region* Nigeria
50C3 **Boro** *R* Sudan
25P3 **Borogontsy** Russian Federation
48B3 **Boromo** Burkina
66D3 **Boron** USA
20E4 **Borovichi** Russian Federation
32C2 **Borroloola** Australia
17E1 **Borsa** Romania
41F3 **Borūjen** Iran
41E3 **Borūjerd** Iran
18D2 **Bory Tucholskie** *Region* Poland
19G2 **Borzna** Ukraine
25N4 **Borzya** Russian Federation
31B5 **Bose** China
47D2 **Boshof** South Africa
17D2 **Bosna** *R* Bosnia-Herzegovina
17D2 **Bosnia-Herzegovina** *Republic* Europe
29D3 **Bōsō-hantō** *B* Japan
Bosporus = Karadeniz Boğazi
15C2 **Bosquet** Algeria
50B3 **Bossangoa** Central African Republic
50B3 **Bossèmbélé** Central African Republic
63D2 **Bossier City** USA
24K5 **Bosten Hu** *L* China
7D3 **Boston** England
57F2 **Boston** USA
57D3 **Boston Mts** USA
42C4 **Botād** India
17E2 **Botevgrad** Bulgaria
47D2 **Bothaville** South Africa
20B3 **Bothnia,G of** Finland/Sweden
51C6 **Botletli** *R* Botswana
21D6 **Botoşani** Romania
51C6 **Botswana** *Republic* Africa
16D3 **Botte Donato** *Mt* Italy
60C1 **Bottineau** USA
13D2 **Bottrop** Germany
75C3 **Botucatu** Brazil
75D1 **Botuporã** Brazil
55N5 **Botwood** Canada
48B4 **Bouaké** Ivory Coast
50B3 **Bouar** Central African Republic
48B1 **Bouârfa** Morocco
50B3 **Bouca** Central African Republic
15C2 **Boufarik** Algeria
33E1 **Bougainville** *I* Papua New Guinea
16B3 **Bougaroun, C** Algeria
Bougie = Bejaïa
48B3 **Bougouni** Mali
15A2 **Bouhalla, Djebel** *Mt* Morocco
13C3 **Bouillon** France
15C2 **Bouïra** Algeria
48B2 **Bou Izakarn** Morocco
13D3 **Boulay-Moselle** France
56C2 **Boulder** Colorado, USA
58D1 **Boulder** Montana, USA
56B3 **Boulder City** USA
66A2 **Boulder Creek** USA
14C1 **Boulogne** France
50B3 **Boumba** *R* Cameroon/Central African Republic
48B4 **Bouna** Ivory Coast
56B3 **Boundary Peak** *Mt* USA
48B4 **Boundiali** Ivory Coast
58D2 **Bountiful** USA
33G5 **Bounty Is** New Zealand
33F3 **Bourail** New Caledonia
13C4 **Bourbonne-les-Bains** France
48B3 **Bourem** Mali
14D2 **Bourg** France
14D2 **Bourg de Péage** France
14C2 **Bourges** France
14C3 **Bourg-Madame** France
14C2 **Bourgogne** *Region* France
34C2 **Bourke** Australia
7D4 **Bournemouth** England
15C2 **Bou Saâda** Algeria
50B2 **Bousso** Chad
48A3 **Boutilimit** Mauritius
52J7 **Bouvet I** Atlantic Ocean
60C1 **Bowbells** USA
32D2 **Bowen** Australia
59E4 **Bowie** Arizona, USA
63C2 **Bowie** Texas, USA
6C3 **Bowland Fells** England
57E3 **Bowling Green** Kentucky, USA
63D1 **Bowling Green** Missouri, USA
64C2 **Bowling Green** Ohio, USA
65D3 **Bowling Green** Virginia, USA
60C1 **Bowman** USA
65D2 **Bowmanville** Canada
9C3 **Bowna, L** Irish Republic
34D2 **Bowral** Australia
31D3 **Bo Xian** China
31D2 **Boxing** China
40B1 **Boyabat** Turkey
50B3 **Boyali** Central African Republic
19G2 **Boyarka** Ukraine
54J4 **Boyd** Canada
68C2 **Boyertown** USA
10B3 **Boyle** Irish Republic
9C3 **Boyne** *R* Irish Republic
67B3 **Boynton Beach** USA
50C3 **Boyoma Falls** Zaïre
58E2 **Boysen Res** USA
17D1 **Bozanski Brod** Bosnia-Herzegovina/Croatia
17F3 **Bozca Ada** *I* Turkey
17F3 **Boz Dağları** *Mts* Turkey
56B2 **Bozeman** USA
Bozen = Bolzano
50B3 **Bozene** Zaïre
50B3 **Bozoum** Central African Republic
16D2 **Brač** *I* Croatia
8B3 **Bracadale, Loch** *Inlet* Scotland
16C2 **Bracciano, L di** Italy
65D1 **Bracebridge** Canada
49D2 **Brach** Libya
12H6 **Bräcke** Sweden
62B3 **Brackettville** USA
67B3 **Bradenton** USA
6D3 **Bradford** England
68A2 **Bradford** USA
66B3 **Bradley** USA
62C2 **Brady** USA
8E1 **Brae** Scotland
8D3 **Braemar** Scotland
15A1 **Braga** Portugal
73J4 **Bragança** Brazil
15A1 **Bragança** Portugal
75C3 **Bragança Paulista** Brazil
43G4 **Brahman-Baria** Bangladesh
43F4 **Brāhmani** *R* India
43G3 **Brahmaputra** *R* Bangladesh/India
21D6 **Brăila** Romania
57D2 **Brainerd** USA
7E4 **Braintree** England
47C3 **Brak** *R* South Africa
47D1 **Brak** *R* South Africa
13E1 **Brake** Germany
48A3 **Brakna** *Region* Mauritius
54F4 **Bralorne** Canada
65D2 **Brampton** Canada
6C2 **Brampton** England
13D1 **Bramsche** Germany
72F3 **Branco** *R* Brazil
51B6 **Brandberg** *Mt* Namibia
18C2 **Brandenburg** Germany
18C2 **Brandenburg** *State* Germany
47D2 **Brandfort** South Africa
56D2 **Brandon** Canada
61D2 **Brandon** USA
47C3 **Brandvlei** South Africa
18C2 **Brandýs-nad-Laben** Czech Republic
19D2 **Braniewo** Poland
57E2 **Brantford** Canada
34B3 **Branxholme** Australia
55M5 **Bras d'Or Lakes** Canada
72E6 **Brasiléia** Brazil
73J7 **Brasília** Brazil
75D2 **Brasília de Minas** Brazil
17F1 **Braşov** Romania
18D3 **Bratislava** Slovakia
25M4 **Bratsk** Russian Federation
19F3 **Bratslav** Ukraine
65E2 **Brattleboro** USA
18C2 **Braunschweig** Germany
48A4 **Brava** *I* Cape Verde
56B3 **Brawley** USA
9C3 **Bray** Irish Republic
55L3 **Bray I** Canada
13B3 **Bray-sur-Seine** France
71E5 **Brazil** *Republic* S America
52G5 **Brazil Basin** Atlantic Ocean
56D3 **Brazos** *R* USA
50B4 **Brazzaville** Congo
18C3 **Brdy** *Upland* Czech Republic
35A3 **Breaksea Sd** New Zealand
35B1 **Bream B** New Zealand
8D3 **Brechin** Scotland
13C2 **Brecht** Belgium
61D1 **Breckenridge** Minnesota, USA
62C2 **Breckenridge** Texas, USA
7E3 **Breckland** England
18D3 **Břeclav** Czech Republic
7C4 **Brecon** Wales
7C4 **Brecon Beacons** *Mts* Wales
7B3 **Brecon Beacons Nat Pk** Wales
18A2 **Breda** Netherlands

47C3 **Bredasdorp** South Africa
12H6 **Bredbyn** Sweden
20K5 **Bredy** Russian Federation
47B3 **Breede** *R* South Africa
65D2 **Breezewood** USA
12A1 **Breiethafjörethur** *B* Iceland
13D3 **Breisach** Germany
67A2 **Bremen** USA
18B2 **Bremen** Germany
18B2 **Bremerhaven** Germany
58B1 **Bremerton** USA
13E1 **Bremervörde** Germany
59E3 **Brendel** USA
63C2 **Brenham** USA
18C3 **Brenner** *P* Austria/Italy
66B2 **Brentwood** USA
16C1 **Brescia** Italy
Breslau = Wrocław
8E1 **Bressay** *I* Scotland
14B2 **Bressuire** France
14B2 **Brest** France
19E2 **Brest** Belarus
14B2 **Bretagne** *Region* France
13B3 **Breteuil** France
63E3 **Breton Sd** USA
68C2 **Breton Woods** USA
35B1 **Brett,C** New Zealand
67B1 **Brevard** USA
34C1 **Brewarrina** Australia
65F2 **Brewer** USA
68D2 **Brewster** New York, USA
58C1 **Brewster** Washington, USA
67A2 **Brewton** USA
47D2 **Breyten** South Africa
16D1 **Brežice** Slovenia
50C3 **Bria** Central African Republic
14D3 **Briançon** France
14C2 **Briare** France
7C4 **Bridgend** Wales
8C3 **Bridge of Orchy** Scotland
67A2 **Bridgeport** Alabama, USA
59C3 **Bridgeport** California, USA
65E2 **Bridgeport** Connecticut, USA
60C2 **Bridgeport** Nebraska, USA
63C2 **Bridgeport** Texas, USA
66C1 **Bridgeport Res** USA
58E1 **Bridger** USA
60B2 **Bridger Peak** USA
68C3 **Bridgeton** USA
69R3 **Bridgetown** Barbados
55M5 **Bridgewater** Canada
68E2 **Bridgewater** USA
7C4 **Bridgwater** England
7C4 **Bridgwater B** England
6D2 **Bridlington** England
6E3 **Bridlington Bay** England
34C4 **Bridport** Australia
7C4 **Bridport** England
13C3 **Brienne-le-Château** France
13C3 **Briey** France
16B1 **Brig** Switzerland
56B2 **Brigham City** USA
34C3 **Bright** Australia
7D4 **Brighton** England
75A3 **Brilhante** *R* Brazil
13E2 **Brilon** Germany
17D2 **Brindisi** Italy
63D2 **Brinkley** USA
33E3 **Brisbane** Australia
65E2 **Bristol** Connecticut, USA
7C4 **Bristol** England
65E2 **Bristol** Pennsylvania, USA
68E2 **Bristol** Rhode Island, USA
57E3 **Bristol** Tennessee, USA
64C3 **Bristol** USA
7B4 **Bristol Chan** England/Wales
54F4 **British Columbia** *Province* Canada
55K1 **British Empire Range** *Mts* Canada
54E3 **British Mts** Canada
47D2 **Brits** South Africa
47C3 **Britstown** South Africa
61D1 **Britton** USA
14C2 **Brive** France
7C4 **Brixham** England
18D3 **Brno** Czech Republic
67B2 **Broad** *R* USA
68C1 **Broadalbin** USA
55L4 **Broadback** *R* Canada
8B2 **Broad Bay** *Inlet* Scotland
8C3 **Broadford** Scotland
9B2 **Broad Haven, B** Irish Republic
7E4 **Broadstairs** England
60B1 **Broadus** USA
60C2 **Broadwater** USA
54H4 **Brochet** Canada
54G2 **Brock I** Canada
65D2 **Brockport** USA
68E1 **Brockton** USA
65D2 **Brockville** Canada
68A2 **Brockway** USA
55K2 **Brodeur Pen** Canada
8C4 **Brodick** Scotland
19D2 **Brodnica** Poland
21D5 **Brody** Ukraine
13D2 **Brokem Haltern** Germany
60D2 **Broken Bow** Nebraska, USA
63D2 **Broken Bow** Oklahoma, USA
63D2 **Broken Bow L** USA
32D4 **Broken Hill** Australia
7C3 **Bromsgrove** England
12G5 **Brønnøysund** Norway
68D2 **Bronx** *Borough* New York, USA
27E6 **Brooke's Pt** Philippines
61E3 **Brookfield** Missouri, USA
64B2 **Brookfield** Wisconsin, USA
57D3 **Brookhaven** USA
58B2 **Brookings** Oregon, USA
56D2 **Brookings** South Dakota, USA
68E1 **Brookline** USA
61E2 **Brooklyn** USA
68D2 **Brooklyn** *Borough* New York, USA
61E1 **Brooklyn Center** USA
54G4 **Brooks** Canada
54C3 **Brooks Range** *Mts* USA
67B3 **Brooksville** USA
34D1 **Brooloo** Australia
32B2 **Broome** Australia
8C3 **Broom, Loch** *Estuary* Scotland
8D2 **Brora** Scotland
58B2 **Brothers** USA
6C2 **Broughton** England
8D3 **Broughty Ferry** Scotland
50B2 **Broulkou** *Well* Chad
19G2 **Brovary** Ukraine
61E1 **Browerville** USA
62B2 **Brownfield** USA
56D4 **Brownsville** USA
56D3 **Brownwood** USA
27F8 **Browse I** Australia
13B2 **Bruay-en-Artois** France
32A3 **Bruce,Mt** Australia
64C1 **Bruce Pen** Canada
13E3 **Bruchsal** Germany
18D3 **Bruck an der Mur** Austria
Bruges = Brugge
13B2 **Brugge** Belgium
13D2 **Brühl** Germany
45B3 **Brûk, Wadi el** Egypt
75D1 **Brumado** Brazil
13D3 **Brumath** France
58C2 **Bruneau** USA
58C2 **Bruneau** *R* USA
27E6 **Brunei** *State* Borneo
16C1 **Brunico** Italy
35B2 **Brunner,L** New Zealand
13E1 **Brunsbüttel** Germany
57E3 **Brunswick** Georgia, USA
65F2 **Brunswick** Maine, USA
61E3 **Brunswick** Mississippi, USA
74B8 **Brunswick,Pen de** Chile
34C4 **Bruny I** Australia
20G3 **Brusenets** Russian Federation
60C2 **Brush** USA
69A3 **Brus Laguna** Honduras
Brüssel = Brussels
18A2 **Brussels** Belgium
Bruxelles = Brussels
13D3 **Bruyères** France
56D3 **Bryan** USA
34A2 **Bryan,Mt** Australia
20E5 **Bryansk** Russian Federation
63D2 **Bryant** USA
59D3 **Bryce Canyon Nat Pk** USA
18D2 **Brzeg** Poland
41E4 **Būbīyan** *I* Kuwait
50D4 **Bubu** *R* Tanzania
47E1 **Bubye** *R* Zimbabwe
72D2 **Bucaramanga** Colombia
8E3 **Buchan** *Oilfield* N Sea
48A4 **Buchanan** Liberia
62C2 **Buchanan,L** USA
8E3 **Buchan Deep** N Sea
55L2 **Buchan G** Canada
10C2 **Buchan Ness** *Pen* Scotland
55N5 **Buchans** Canada
17F2 **Bucharest** Romania
66B3 **Buchon,Pt** USA
13E1 **Bückeburg** Germany
59D4 **Buckeye** USA
8D3 **Buckhaven** Scotland
8D3 **Buckie** Scotland
7D3 **Buckingham** England
65F2 **Bucksport** USA
50B4 **Buco Zau** Congo
Bucureşti = Bucharest
19D3 **Budapest** Hungary
42D3 **Budaun** India
7B4 **Bude** England
63D2 **Bude** USA
21G7 **Budennovsk** Russian Federation
43J1 **Budhana** India
45B4 **Budhîya, Gebel** Egypt
13E2 **Büdingen** Germany
17D2 **Budva** Montenegro, Yugoslavia
48C4 **Buéa** Cameroon
66B3 **Buellton** USA
72C3 **Buenaventura** Colombia
62A3 **Buenaventura** Mexico
60B3 **Buena Vista** Colorado, USA
65D3 **Buena Vista** Virginia, USA
66C3 **Buena Vista L** USA
74E4 **Buenos Aires** Argentina
74E5 **Buenos Aires** *State* Argentina
74B7 **Buenos Aires, Lago** Argentina
63D1 **Buffalo** Mississipi, USA
57F2 **Buffalo** New York, USA
60C1 **Buffalo** S Dakota, USA
63C2 **Buffalo** Texas, USA
56C2 **Buffalo** Wyoming, USA
47E2 **Buffalo** *R* South Africa
58C1 **Buffalo Hump** *Mt* USA
54G3 **Buffalo L** Canada
54H4 **Buffalo Narrows** Canada
67B2 **Buford** USA
17F2 **Buftea** Romania
19E2 **Bug** *R* Poland/Ukraine
72C3 **Buga** Colombia
41F2 **Bugdayli** Turkmenistan
20H2 **Bugrino** Russian Federation
20J5 **Bugulma** Russian Federation
20J5 **Buguruslan** Russian Federation
40C2 **Buḩayrat al Asad** *Res* Syria
58D2 **Buhl** Idaho, USA
61E1 **Buhl** Minnesota, USA
7C3 **Builth Wells** Wales
50C4 **Bujumbura** Burundi
33E1 **Buka** *I* Papua New Guinea
51C4 **Bukama** Zaïre
50C4 **Bukavu** Zaïre
38E2 **Bukhara** Uzbekistan
27D7 **Bukittinggi** Indonesia
50D4 **Bukoba** Tanzania
27G7 **Bula** Indonesia
27F5 **Bulan** Philippines
42D3 **Bulandshahr** India
51C6 **Bulawayo** Zimbabwe
17F3 **Buldan** Turkey
42D4 **Buldāna** India
26D2 **Bulgan** Mongolia
17E2 **Bulgaria** *Republic* Europe
35B2 **Buller** *R* New Zealand
34C3 **Buller,Mt** Australia
32A4 **Bullfinch** Australia
34B1 **Bulloo** *R* Australia
34B1 **Bulloo Downs** Australia
34B1 **Bulloo L** Australia
63D1 **Bull Shoals Res** USA
32D1 **Bulolo** Papua New Guinea
47D2 **Bultfontein** South Africa
27E6 **Bulu, Gunung** *Mt* Indonesia
50C3 **Bumba** Zaïre
21D8 **Bu Menderes** *R* Turkey
30B2 **Bumphal Dam** Thailand
50D3 **Buna** Kenya
32A4 **Bunbury** Australia
9C2 **Buncrana** Irish Republic
33E3 **Bundaberg** Australia
34D2 **Bundarra** Australia
13E1 **Bünde** Germany
42D3 **Bündi** India
7E3 **Bungay** England
34C1 **Bungil** *R* Australia
51B4 **Bungo** Angola
28B4 **Bungo-suidō** *Str* Japan
27D6 **Bunguran** *I* Indonesia
27D6 **Bunguran, Kepulauan** *I* Indonesia
50D3 **Bunia** Zaïre
63D1 **Bunker** USA
63D2 **Bunkie** USA
67B3 **Bunnell** USA
27E7 **Buntok** Indonesia
27F6 **Buol** Indonesia
50C2 **Buram** Sudan
43E2 **Burang** China
50E3 **Burao** Somalia
45D2 **Burāq** Syria
41D4 **Buraydah** Saudi Arabia
59C4 **Burbank** USA
34C2 **Burcher** Australia
21E8 **Burdur** Turkey
50D2 **Burē** Ethiopia
7E3 **Bure** *R* England
26G1 **Bureinskiy Khrebet** *Mts* Russian Federation
26F2 **Bureya** Russian Federation
45B3 **Bûr Fu'ad** Egypt
18C2 **Burg** Germany
17F2 **Burgas** Bulgaria
67C2 **Burgaw** USA
47D3 **Burgersdorp** South Africa
15B1 **Burgos** Spain
13D1 **Burgsteinfurt** Germany
19D1 **Burgsvik** Sweden
17F3 **Burhaniye** Turkey
42D4 **Burhānpur** India
30C2 **Buriram** Thailand
75C2 **Buritis** Brazil
32C2 **Burketown** Australia
48B3 **Burkina** *Republic* W Africa
65D1 **Burk's Falls** Canada
56B2 **Burley** USA
60C3 **Burlington** Colorado, USA
57D2 **Burlington** Iowa, USA
68C2 **Burlington** New Jersey, USA
67C1 **Burlington** North Carolina, USA
57F2 **Burlington** Vermont, USA
58B1 **Burlington** Washington, USA
39H3 **Burma** *Republic* Asia
62C2 **Burnet** USA
58B2 **Burney** USA
68B2 **Burnham** USA
7E4 **Burnham-on-Crouch** England
32D5 **Burnie** Australia
6C3 **Burnley** England
58C2 **Burns** USA
54F4 **Burns Lake** Canada
24K5 **Burqin** China
34A2 **Burra** Australia
34D2 **Burragorang,L** Australia
8D2 **Burray** *I* Scotland
34C2 **Burren Junction** Australia
34C2 **Burrinjuck Res** Australia
62B3 **Burro, Serranías del** *Mts* Mexico
8C4 **Burrow Head** *Pt* Scotland
27G8 **Burrundie** Australia
21D7 **Bursa** Turkey
40B4 **Bur Safâga** Egypt
Bûr Saïd = Port Said
45B4 **Bûr Taufiq** Egypt
64C2 **Burton** USA
7D3 **Burton upon Trent** England
12J6 **Burtrask** Sweden
34B2 **Burtundy** Australia
27F7 **Buru** *I* Indonesia
50C4 **Burundi** *Republic* Africa
60D2 **Burwell** USA
7C3 **Bury** England
25N4 **Buryat Republic** Russian Federation
21J6 **Burynshik** Kazakhstan
7E3 **Bury St Edmunds** England
28A3 **Bushan** China
41F4 **Büshehr** Iran
9C2 **Bushmills** Northern Ireland
50B4 **Busira** *R* Zaïre
19E2 **Busko Zdrój** Poland
45D2 **Buşrá ash Shām** Syria
13D4 **Bussang** France
32A4 **Busselton** Australia
16B1 **Busto Arsizio** Italy
50C3 **Buta** Zaïre
50C4 **Butare** Rwanda
8C4 **Bute** *I* Scotland
26F2 **Butha Qi** China
65D2 **Butler** USA
32B1 **Buton** *I* Indonesia
48C4 **Butta** Togo
56B2 **Butte** USA
30C4 **Butterworth** Malaysia
47D3 **Butterworth** South Africa
10B2 **Butt of Lewis** *C* Scotland
55M3 **Button Is** Canada
66C3 **Buttonwillow** USA
27F6 **Butuan** Philippines
21G5 **Buturlinovka** Russian Federation
43E3 **Butwal** Nepal
13E2 **Butzbach** Germany
50E3 **Buulobarde** Somalia
50E3 **Buurhakaba** Somalia
7D3 **Buxton** England
20G4 **Buy** Russian Federation
31B1 **Buyant Ovoo** Mongolia
21H7 **Buynaksk** Russian Federation
25N5 **Buyr Nuur** *L* Mongolia
21G8 **Büyük Ağri Daği** *Mt* Turkey
40A2 **Büyük Menderes** *R* Turkey
17F1 **Buzău** Romania
17F1 **Buzău** *R* Romania
75D3 **Búzios, Ponta dos** *Pt* Brazil
20J5 **Buzuluk** Russian Federation
68E2 **Buzzards B** USA
17F2 **Byala** Bulgaria
17E2 **Byala Slatina** Bulgaria
54H2 **Byam Martin Channel** Canada
54H2 **Byam Martin I** Canada
45C1 **Byblos** *Hist site* Lebanon
19D2 **Bydgoszcz** Poland
60C3 **Byers** USA
12F7 **Bygland** Norway
19G2 **Bykhov** Belarus
55L2 **Bylot I** Canada
34C2 **Byrock** Australia
66B2 **Byron** USA
34D1 **Byron** *C* Australia
25P3 **Bytantay** *R* Russian Federation
19D2 **Bytom** Poland

C

74E3 **Caacupú** Paraguay
75A4 **Caaguazú** Paraguay
51B5 **Caála** Angola
75A4 **Caapucú** Paraguay
75B3 **Caarapó** Brazil
74E3 **Caazapá** Paraguay
15C1 **Caballería, Cabo de** *C* Spain
62A2 **Caballo Res** USA
27F5 **Cabanatuan** Philippines
65F1 **Cabano** Canada
73M5 **Cabedelo** Brazil
15A2 **Cabeza del Buey** Spain
72D1 **Cabimas** Venezuela
50B4 **Cabinda** Angola
50B4 **Cabinda** *Province* Angola
58C1 **Cabinet Mts** USA
75D3 **Cabo Frio** Brazil
55L5 **Cabonga,Réservoire** Canada
34D1 **Caboolture** Australia
51D5 **Cabora Bassa Dam** Mozambique
70A1 **Caborca** Mexico
55M5 **Cabot Str** Canada
15B2 **Cabra** Spain
75D2 **Cabral, Serra do** *Mts* Brazil
15A1 **Cabreira** *Mt* Portugal
15C2 **Cabrera** *I* Spain
15B2 **Cabriel** *R* Spain
17E2 **Čačak** Serbia, Yugoslavia
68A3 **Cacapon** *R* USA
73G7 **Cáceres** Brazil
15A2 **Cáceres** Spain
63D1 **Cache** *R* USA
66A1 **Cache Creek** *R* USA
58D2 **Cache Peak** *Mt* USA
74C3 **Cachi** Argentina
73G5 **Cachimbo** Brazil
73G5 **Cachimbo, Serra do** *Mts* Brazil
73L6 **Cachoeira** Brazil
75B2 **Cachoeira Alta** Brazil
73L5 **Cachoeira de Paulo Afonso** *Waterfall* Brazil
74F4 **Cachoeira do Sul** Brazil
73K8 **Cachoeiro de Itapemirim** Brazil
66C3 **Cachuma,L** USA
51B5 **Cacolo** Angola
51B5 **Caconda** Angola
62B1 **Cactus** USA
75B2 **Caçu** Brazil
75D1 **Caculé** Brazil
51B5 **Caculuvar** *R* Angola
19D3 **Čadca** Slovakia
7C3 **Cader Idris** *Mt* Wales
57E2 **Cadillac** USA
15A2 **Cádiz** Spain
15A2 **Cádiz, Golfo de** *G* Spain
14B2 **Caen** France
7B3 **Caernarfon** Wales
7B3 **Caernarfon B** Wales
7C4 **Caerphilly** Wales
45C2 **Caesarea** *Hist Site* Israel
75D1 **Caetité** Brazil
74C3 **Cafayate** Argentina
40B2 **Caga Tepe** *Mt* Turkey
27F6 **Cagayan de Oro** Philippines
16B3 **Cagliari** Sardinia, Italy
16B3 **Cagliari, G di** Sardinia, Italy
69D3 **Caguas** Puerto Rico
67A2 **Cahaba** *R* USA
9C3 **Cahir** Irish Republic
9C3 **Cahore Pt** Irish Republic
14C3 **Cahors** France
51D5 **Caia** Mozambique
73G6 **Caiabis, Serra dos** *Mts* Brazil
51C5 **Caianda** Angola
75B2 **Caiapó** *R* Brazil
75B2 **Caiapônia** Brazil
75B2 **Caiapó, Serra do** *Mts* Brazil
73L5 **Caicó** Brazil
69C2 **Caicos Is** Caribbean Sea
57F4 **Caicos Pass** The Bahamas
8D3 **Cairngorms** *Mts* Scotland
8C4 **Cairnryan** Scotland
32D2 **Cairns** Australia
40B3 **Cairo** Egypt
57E3 **Cairo** USA
8D2 **Caithness** Scotland
34B1 **Caiwarro** Australia
72C5 **Cajabamba** Peru
72C5 **Cajamarca** Peru
48C4 **Calabar** Nigeria
69D5 **Calabozo** Venezuela

17E2 **Calafat** Romania
74B8 **Calafate** Argentina
15B1 **Calahorra** Spain
14C1 **Calais** France
65F1 **Calais** USA
74C2 **Calama** Chile
72D3 **Calamar** Colombia
27E5 **Calamian Group** *Is* Philippines
51B4 **Calandula** Angola
27C6 **Calang** Indonesia
49E2 **Calanscio Sand Sea** Libya
27F5 **Calapan** Philippines
17F2 **Calarasi** Romania
15B1 **Calatayud** Spain
66B2 **Calaveras Res** USA
63D3 **Calcasieu L** USA
43F4 **Calcutta** India
15A2 **Caldas da Rainha** Portugal
73J7 **Caldas Novas** Brazil
74B3 **Caldera** Chile
56B2 **Caldwell** USA
47B3 **Caledon** South Africa
47D3 **Caledon** *R* South Africa
64A2 **Caledonia** Minnesota, USA
68B1 **Caledonia** New York, USA
74C7 **Caleta Olivia** Argentina
56B3 **Calexico** USA
54G4 **Calgary** Canada
67B2 **Calhoun** USA
67B2 **Calhoun Falls** USA
72C3 **Cali** Colombia
66C3 **Caliente** California, USA
56B3 **Caliente** Nevada, USA
62A1 **Caliente** New Mexico, USA
56A3 **California** *State* USA
66C3 **California Aqueduct** USA
70A1 **California, G de** Mexico
44B3 **Calimera,Pt** India
59C4 **Calipatria** USA
47C3 **Calitzdorp** South Africa
34B1 **Callabonna** *R* Australia
34A1 **Callabonna,L** Australia
65D1 **Callander** Canada
8C3 **Callander** Scotland
72C6 **Callao** Peru
68C2 **Callicoon** USA
67B3 **Caloosahatchee** *R* USA
34D1 **Caloundra** Australia
16C3 **Caltanissetta** Sicily, Italy
51B4 **Caluango** Angola
51B5 **Calulo** Angola
51B5 **Caluquembe** Angola
50F2 **Caluula** Somalia
16B2 **Calvi** Corsica, France
47B3 **Calvinia** South Africa
13E3 **Calw** Germany
75E1 **Camacari** Brazil
70E2 **Camagüey** Cuba
70E2 **Camagüey,Arch de** *Is* Cuba
75E1 **Camamu** Brazil
72D7 **Camaná** Peru
75B2 **Camapuã** Brazil
72E8 **Camargo** Bolivia
66C3 **Camarillo** USA
74C6 **Camarones** Argentina
58B1 **Camas** USA
51B4 **Camaxilo** Angola
51B4 **Cambatela** Angola
30C3 **Cambodia** *Republic* SE Asia
7B4 **Camborne** England
14C1 **Cambrai** France
66B3 **Cambria** USA
7C3 **Cambrian Mts** Wales
64C2 **Cambridge** Canada
7E3 **Cambridge** England
69H1 **Cambridge** Jamaica
65D3 **Cambridge** Maryland, USA
65E2 **Cambridge** Massachussets, USA
61E1 **Cambridge** Minnesota, USA
35C1 **Cambridge** New Zealand
64C2 **Cambridge** Ohio, USA
7D3 **Cambridge** *County* England
54H3 **Cambridge Bay** Canada
27F8 **Cambridge G** Australia
21F7 **Cam Burun** *Pt* Turkey
57D3 **Camden** Arkansas, USA
34D2 **Camden** Australia
65E3 **Camden** New Jersey, USA
68C1 **Camden** New York, USA
67B2 **Camden** South Carolina, USA
61E3 **Cameron** Missouri, USA
63C2 **Cameron** Texas, USA
54H2 **Cameron I** Canada
35A3 **Cameron Mts** New Zealand
50B3 **Cameroon** *Federal Republic* Africa
48C4 **Cameroun, Mt** Cameroon
73J4 **Cametá** Brazil
67B2 **Camilla** USA
66B1 **Camino** USA
72F8 **Camiri** Bolivia
51C4 **Camissombo** Angola
73K4 **Camocim** Brazil
32C2 **Camooweal** Australia
44E4 **Camorta** *I* Nicobar Is, Indian Ocean
74A7 **Campana** *I* Chile
47C2 **Campbell** South Africa
35B2 **Campbell,C** New Zealand
37K7 **Campbell I** New Zealand
54E3 **Campbell,Mt** Canada
42C2 **Campbellpore** Pakistan
54F5 **Campbell River** Canada
64B3 **Campbellsville** USA
55M5 **Campbellton** Canada
34D2 **Campbelltown** Australia
8C4 **Campbeltown** Scotland
70C3 **Campeche** Mexico
70C2 **Campeche, B de** Mexico
34B3 **Camperdown** Australia
73L5 **Campina Grande** Brazil
73J8 **Campinas** Brazil
75C2 **Campina Verde** Brazil
66C2 **Camp Nelson** USA
48C4 **Campo** Cameroon
16C2 **Campobasso** Italy
75C3 **Campo Belo** Brazil
75C2 **Campo Florido** Brazil
74D3 **Campo Gallo** Argentina
74F2 **Campo Grande** Brazil
73K4 **Campo Maior** Brazil
74F2 **Campo Mourão** Brazil
75D3 **Campos** Brazil
75C2 **Campos Altos** Brazil
59D4 **Camp Verde** USA
30D3 **Cam Ranh** Vietnam
54G4 **Camrose** Canada
51B5 **Camucuio** Angola
69K1 **Canaan** Tobago
68D1 **Canaan** USA
51B5 **Canacupa** Angola
53F3 **Canada** *Dominion* N America
74D4 **Cañada de Gómez** Argentina
68C2 **Canadensis** USA
62B1 **Canadian** USA
56C3 **Canadian** *R* USA
21D7 **Çanakkale** Turkey
68B1 **Canandaigua** USA
68B1 **Canandaigua L** USA
70A1 **Cananea** Mexico
75C4 **Cananeia** Brazil
Canarias, Islas = Canary Islands
52G3 **Canary Basin** Atlantic Ocean
48A2 **Canary Is** *Atlantic Ocean*
75C3 **Canastra, Serra da** *Mts* Brazil
70B2 **Canatlán** Mexico
57E4 **Canaveral,C** USA
73L7 **Canavieiras** Brazil
32D4 **Canberra** Australia
58B2 **Canby** California, USA
61D2 **Canby** Minnesota, USA
17F3 **Çandarlı Körfezi** *B* Turkey
68D2 **Candlewood,L** USA
60D1 **Cando** USA
68B1 **Candor** USA
74E4 **Canelones** Uruguay
63C1 **Caney** USA
51C5 **Cangamba** Angola
51C5 **Cangombe** Angola
31D2 **Cangzhou** China
55M4 **Caniapiscau** *R* Canada
55M4 **Caniapiscau, Réservoir** *Res* Canada
16C3 **Canicatti** Sicily, Italy
73L4 **Canindé** Brazil
68B1 **Canisteo** USA
68B1 **Canisteo** *R* USA
62A1 **Canjilon** USA
40B1 **Çankırı** Turkey
8B3 **Canna** *I* Scotland
44B3 **Cannanore** India
14D3 **Cannes** France
7C3 **Cannock** England
60C1 **Cannonball** *R* USA
34C3 **Cann River** Australia
74F3 **Canõas** Brazil
75B4 **Canoinhas** Brazil
60B3 **Canon City** USA
34B2 **Canopus** Australia
54H4 **Canora** Canada
34C2 **Canowindra** Australia
15B1 **Cantabria** *Region* Spain
14A3 **Cantabrica, Cord** *Mts* Spain
7E4 **Canterbury** England
35B2 **Canterbury Bight** *B* New Zealand
35B2 **Canterbury Plains** New Zealand
30D4 **Can Tho** Vietnam
66D3 **Cantil** USA
Canton = Guangzhou
63E2 **Canton** Mississippi, USA
64A2 **Canton** Missouri, USA
57E2 **Canton** Ohio, USA
68B2 **Canton** Pensylvania, USA
61D2 **Canton** S Dakota, USA
33H1 **Canton** *I* Phoenix Islands
75B3 **Cantu, Serra do** *Mts* Brazil
62B2 **Canyon** USA
58C2 **Canyon City** USA
58D1 **Canyon Ferry L** USA
59E3 **Canyonlands Nat Pk** USA
58B2 **Canyonville** USA
51C4 **Canzar** Angola
30D1 **Cao Bang** Vietnam
28B2 **Caoshi** China
73J4 **Capanema** Brazil
75C3 **Capão Bonito** Brazil
75D3 **Caparaó, Serra do** *Mts* Brazil
14B3 **Capbreton** France
16B2 **Cap Corse** *C* Corsica, France
14B2 **Cap de la Hague** *C* France
65E1 **Cap-de-la-Madeleine** Canada
15C2 **Capdepera** Spain
34C4 **Cape Barren I** Australia
52J6 **Cape Basin** Atlantic Ocean
55N5 **Cape Breton I** Canada
Cape, Cabo etc: see also individual cape names
48B4 **Cape Coast** Ghana
65E2 **Cape Cod B** USA
55M3 **Cape Dyer** Canada
76F7 **Cape Evans** *Base* Antarctica
67C2 **Cape Fear** *R* USA
63E1 **Cape Girardeau** USA
74C8 **Cape Horn** Chile
36H4 **Cape Johnson Depth** Pacific Ocean
75D2 **Capelinha** Brazil
54B3 **Cape Lisburne** USA
51B5 **Capelongo** Angola
65E3 **Cape May** USA
54F5 **Cape Mendocino** USA
51B4 **Capenda Camulemba** Angola
54F2 **Cape Parry** Canada
47B3 **Cape Town** South Africa
52G4 **Cape Verde** *Is* Atlantic Ocean
52G4 **Cape Verde Basin** Atlantic Ocean
32D2 **Cape York Pen** Australia
69C3 **Cap-Haïtien** Haiti
73J4 **Capim** *R* Brazil
75A3 **Capitán Bado** Paraguay
59E3 **Capitol Reef Nat Pk** USA
75A2 **Capivari** *R* Brazil
9C3 **Cappoquin** Irish Republic
69P2 **Cap Pt** St Lucia
16C2 **Capri** *I* Italy
51C5 **Caprivi Strip** *Region* Namibia
72D4 **Caquetá** *R* Colombia
17E2 **Caracal** Romania
72F3 **Caracaraí** Brazil
72E1 **Caracas** Venezuela
75A3 **Caracol** Brazil
75C3 **Caraguatatuba** Brazil
74B5 **Carahue** Chile
75D2 **Caraí** Brazil
75D3 **Carandaí** Brazil
75A2 **Carandazal** Brazil
73K8 **Carangola** Brazil
17E1 **Caransebeş** Romania
69A3 **Caratasca** Honduras
70D3 **Caratasca, L de** *Lg* Honduras
75D2 **Caratinga** Brazil
15B2 **Caravaca de la Cruz** Spain
75E2 **Caravelas** Brazil
16B3 **Carbonara, C** Sardinia, Italy
64B3 **Carbondale** Illinois, USA
68C2 **Carbondale** Pennsylvania, USA
55N5 **Carbonear** Canada
16B3 **Carbonia** Sardinia, Italy
54G4 **Carcajou** Canada
50E2 **Carcar Mts** Somalia
14C3 **Carcassonne** France
54E3 **Carcross** Canada
30C3 **Cardamomes, Chaîne des** *Mts* Cambodia
70D2 **Cardenas** Cuba
7C4 **Cardiff** Wales
7B3 **Cardigan** Wales
7B3 **Cardigan B** Wales
75C4 **Cardoso, Ilha do** Brazil
17E1 **Carei** Romania
73G4 **Careiro** Brazil
64C2 **Carey** USA
14B2 **Carhaix-Plouguer** France
74D5 **Carhué** Argentina
73K8 **Cariacica** Brazil
71C2 **Caribbean S** Central America
54J4 **Caribou** Canada
65F1 **Caribou** USA
54G4 **Caribou Mts** Alberta, Canada
54F4 **Caribou Mts** British Columbia, Canada
13C3 **Carignan** France
75D1 **Carinhanha** Brazil
75D1 **Carinhanha** *R* Brazil
72F1 **Caripito** Venezuela
65D1 **Carleton Place** Canada
47D2 **Carletonville** South Africa
58C2 **Carlin** USA
9C2 **Carlingford, L** Northern Ireland
64B3 **Carlinville** USA
6C2 **Carlisle** England
65D2 **Carlisle** USA
75D2 **Carlos Chagas** Brazil
9C3 **Carlow** Irish Republic
9C3 **Carlow** *County* Irish Republic
59C4 **Carlsbad** California, USA
56C3 **Carlsbad** New Mexico, USA
62B2 **Carlsbad Caverns Nat Pk** USA
36E4 **Carlsberg Ridge** Indian Ocean
54H5 **Carlyle** Canada
54E3 **Carmacks** Canada
7B4 **Carmarthen** Wales
7B4 **Carmarthen B** Wales
66B2 **Carmel** California, USA
68D2 **Carmel** New York, USA
7B3 **Carmel Hd** *Pt* Wales
45C2 **Carmel,Mt** Israel
66B2 **Carmel Valley** USA
56B4 **Carmen** *I* Mexico
74D6 **Carmen de Patagones** Argentina
64B3 **Carmi** USA
59B3 **Carmichael** USA
75C2 **Carmo do Paranaiba** Brazil
15A2 **Carmona** Spain
75E2 **Carnacá** Brazil
32A3 **Carnarvon** Australia
47C3 **Carnarvon** South Africa
9C2 **Carndonagh** Irish Republic
32B3 **Carnegie,L** Australia
44E4 **Car Nicobar** *I* Nicobar Is, Indian Ocean
50B3 **Carnot** Central African Republic
8D3 **Carnoustie** Scotland
9C3 **Carnsore Pt** Irish Republic
67B3 **Carol City** USA
73J5 **Carolina** Brazil
47E2 **Carolina** South Africa
67C2 **Carolina Beach** USA
27H6 **Caroline Is** Pacific Ocean
19F3 **Carpathian Mts** Romania
21C6 **Carpathians** *Mts* E Europe
32C2 **Carpentaria,G of** Australia
39H5 **Carpenter Ridge** Indian Ocean
14D3 **Carpentras** France
16C2 **Carpi** Italy
66C3 **Carpinteria** USA
67B3 **Carrabelle** USA
16C2 **Carrara** Italy
10B3 **Carrauntoohill** *Mt* Irish Republic
8C4 **Carrick** Scotland
9D2 **Carrickfergus** Northern Ireland
9C3 **Carrickmacross** Irish Republic
9C3 **Carrick-on-Suir** Irish Republic
34A2 **Carrieton** Australia
54J5 **Carrington** USA
15B1 **Carrión** *R* Spain
62C3 **Carrizo Springs** USA
62A2 **Carrizozo** USA
57D2 **Carroll** USA
67A2 **Carrollton** Georgia, USA
64B3 **Carrollton** Kentucky, USA
61E3 **Carrollton** Missouri, USA
9B2 **Carrowmore,L** *Irish Republic*
63E1 **Carruthersville** USA
21F7 **Carşamba** Turkey
21E8 **Carşamba** *R* Turkey
56B3 **Carson City** USA
64C2 **Carsonville** USA
8D4 **Carstairs** Scotland
69B4 **Cartagena** Colombia
15B2 **Cartagena** Spain
72C3 **Cartago** Colombia
70D4 **Cartago** Costa Rica
66C2 **Cartago** USA
35C2 **Carterton** New Zealand
63D1 **Carthage** Missouri, USA
65D2 **Carthage** New York, USA
63D2 **Carthage** Texas, USA
32B2 **Cartier I** Timor Sea
55N4 **Cartwright** Canada
73L5 **Caruaru** Brazil
72F1 **Carúpano** Venezuela
13B2 **Carvin** France
15A2 **Carvoeiro, Cabo** *C* Portugal
67C1 **Cary** USA
48B1 **Casablanca** Morocco
75C3 **Casa Branca** Brazil
56B3 **Casa Grande** USA
16B1 **Casale Monferrato** Italy
58D1 **Cascade** USA
35A2 **Cascade Pt** New Zealand
56A2 **Cascade Range** *Mts* USA
58C2 **Cascade Res** USA
74F2 **Cascavel** Brazil
16C2 **Caserta** Italy
76G9 **Casey** *Base* Antarctica
9C3 **Cashel** Irish Republic
33E3 **Casino** Australia
72C5 **Casma** Peru
66B3 **Casmalia** USA
15C1 **Caspe** Spain
56C2 **Casper** USA
21H6 **Caspian Depression** *Region* Kazakhstan
21H7 **Caspian S** Asia/Europe
65D3 **Cass** USA
51C5 **Cassamba** Angola
13B2 **Cassel** France
61D1 **Casselton** USA
54E3 **Cassiar Mts** Canada
75B2 **Cassilândia** Brazil
16C2 **Cassino** Italy
61E1 **Cass Lake** USA
66C3 **Castaic** USA
14D3 **Castellane** France
16C2 **Castello, Città di** Italy
15C1 **Castellón de la Plana** Spain
73K5 **Castelo** Brazil
15A2 **Castelo Branco** Portugal
14C3 **Castelsarrasin** France
16C3 **Castelvetrano** Sicily, Italy
34B3 **Casterton** Australia
15B2 **Castilla la Mancha** *Region* Spain
15B1 **Castilla y León** *Region* Spain
10B3 **Castlebar** Irish Republic
8B3 **Castlebay** Scotland
9C2 **Castleblayney** Irish Republic
59D3 **Castle Dale** USA
8D4 **Castle Douglas** Scotland
6D3 **Castleford** England
58C1 **Castlegar** Canada
34B3 **Castlemaine** Australia
66B3 **Castle Mt** USA
58D2 **Castle Peak** *Mt* USA
34C2 **Castlereagh** *R* Australia
60C3 **Castle Rock** USA
6B2 **Castletown** England
9B4 **Castletown Bere** Irish Republic
14C3 **Castres-sur-l'Agout** France
69P2 **Castries** St Lucia
74B6 **Castro** Argentina
74F2 **Castro** Brazil
73L6 **Castro Alves** Brazil
16D3 **Castrovillari** Italy
66B2 **Castroville** USA
35A2 **Caswell Sd** New Zealand
70E2 **Cat** *I* The Bahamas
72B5 **Catacaos** Peru
75D3 **Cataguases** Brazil
63D2 **Catahoula L** USA
75C2 **Catalão** Brazil
15C1 **Cataluña** *Region* Spain
74C3 **Catamarca** Argentina
74C3 **Catamarca** *State* Argentina
51D5 **Catandica** Mozambique
27F5 **Catanduanes** *I* Philippines
74G2 **Catanduva** Brazil
75B4 **Catanduvas** Brazil
16D3 **Catania** Sicily, Italy
16D3 **Catanzaro** Italy
62C3 **Catarina** USA
27F5 **Catarman** Philippines
69C5 **Catatumbo** *R* Venezuela
68B2 **Catawissa** USA
27F5 **Catbalogan** Philippines
16B2 **Cateraggio** Corsica, France
51B4 **Catete** Angola
47D3 **Cathcart** South Africa
48A3 **Catio** Guinea-Bissau
55J4 **Cat Lake** Canada
33E3 **Cato** *I* Australia
70D2 **Catoche,C** Mexico
68B3 **Catoctin Mt** USA
65D3 **Catonsville** USA
65E2 **Catskill** USA
65E2 **Catskill Mts** USA
72D2 **Cauca** *R* Colombia
73L4 **Caucaia** Brazil
72C2 **Caucasia** Colombia
21G7 **Caucasus** *Mts* Georgia
13B2 **Caudry** France
51B4 **Caungula** Angola
74B5 **Cauquenes** Chile
65F1 **Causapscal** Canada
44B3 **Cauvery** *R* India
14D3 **Cavaillon** France
75C1 **Cavalcante** Brazil
61D1 **Cavalier** USA
48B4 **Cavally** *R* Liberia
9C3 **Cavan** Irish Republic
9C3 **Cavan** *County* Irish Republic
72D4 **Caxias** Brazil

73K4 Caxias Brazil
74F3 Caxias do Sul Brazil
51B4 Caxito Angola
67B2 Cayce USA
40D1 Çayeli Turkey
73H3 Cayenne French Guiana
70E3 Cayman Brac I Cayman Is, Caribbean Sea
69A3 Cayman Is Caribbean Sea
69A3 Cayman Trench Caribbean Sea
50E3 Caynabo Somalia
70E2 Cayo Romano I Cuba
70D3 Cayos Miskito Is Nicaragua
69A2 Cay Sal I Caribbean Sea
66B3 Cayucos USA
68B1 Cayuga L USA
68C1 Cazenovia USA
51C5 Cazombo Angola
Ceará = Fortaleza
73K5 Ceará State Brazil
27F5 Cebu Philippines
27F5 Cebu I Philippines
68C3 Cecilton USA
16C2 Cecina Italy
61E2 Cedar R USA
56B3 Cedar City USA
63C2 Cedar Creek Res USA
61E2 Cedar Falls USA
54H4 Cedar L Canada
66D1 Cedar Mts USA
57D2 Cedar Rapids USA
67A2 Cedartown USA
70A2 Cedros I Mexico
56B4 Cedros, Isla de Mexico
32C4 Ceduna Australia
50E3 Ceelbuur Somalia
50E2 Ceerigaabo Somalia
16C3 Cefalù Sicily, Italy
19D3 Cegléd Hungary
51B5 Cela Angola
70B2 Celaya Mexico
Celebes = Sulawesi
27F6 Celebes S SE Asia
64C2 Celina USA
16D1 Celje Slovenia
18C2 Celle Germany
7A4 Celtic S British Islands
7B3 Cemmaes Hd Pt Wales
27G7 Cendrawasih Pen Indonesia
63D2 Center USA
67A1 Center Hill L USA
68D2 Center Moriches USA
67A2 Center Point USA
62A2 Central USA
8C3 Central Region Scotland
50B3 Central African Republic Africa
61D2 Central City Nebraska, USA
68A2 Central City Pennsylvania, USA
68E2 Central Falls USA
64B3 Centralia Illinois, USA
56A2 Centralia Washington, USA
47C1 Central Kalahari Game Res Botswana
42A3 Central Makran Ra Mts Pakistan
58B2 Central Point USA
27H7 Central Range Mts Papua New Guinea
68B1 Central Square USA
67A2 Centreville Alabama, USA
68B3 Centreville Maryland, USA
Ceram = Seram
Ceram Sea = Seram Sea
73J7 Ceres Brazil
47B3 Ceres South Africa
66B2 Ceres USA
14C2 Cergy-Pontoise France
16D2 Cerignola Italy
21D7 Cernavodă Romania
13D4 Cernay France
56C4 Cerralvo I Mexico
72C6 Cerro de Pasco Peru
69D3 Cerro de Punta Mt Puerto Rico
69C4 Cerron Mt Venezuela
74C5 Cerros Colorados, Embalse Res Argentina
16C2 Cesena Italy
20D4 Cēsis Latvia
18C3 České Budějovice Czech Republic
18D3 Českomoravská Vyosina Region Czech Republic
17F3 Çeşme Turkey
32E4 Cessnock Australia
16D2 Cetina R Croatia
15A2 Ceuta NW Africa
40C2 Ceyhan Turkey
40C2 Ceyhan R Turkey
40C2 Ceylanpınar Turkey
44C4 Ceylon I Indian Oc
Ceylon Republic = Sri Lanka
25L4 Chaa-Khol Russian Federation
14C2 Chaâteaudun France
13B4 Chablis France
72C5 Chachapoyas Peru
42C3 Chachran Pakistan
42C3 Chachro Pakistan
74D3 Chaco State Argentina
50B2 Chad Republic Africa
50B2 Chad, L C Africa
56C2 Chadron USA
28B3 Chaeryŏng N Korea
63E1 Chaffee USA
42A3 Chagai Pakistan
25P4 Chagda Russian Federation
42B2 Chaghcharan Afghanistan
36E5 Chagos Arch Indian Ocean
69L1 Chaguanas Trinidad
38E3 Chāh Bahār Iran
28A2 Ch'aho N Korea
30C2 Chai Badan Thailand
43F4 Chāībāsa India
30C2 Chaiyaphum Thailand
42C2 Chakwal Pakistan
72D7 Chala Peru
51D5 Chalabesa Zambia
42A2 Chalap Dalam Mts Afghanistan
57G2 Chaleurs, B des Canada
13C4 Chalindrey France
31C4 Chaling China
42D4 Chālisgaon India
27H5 Challenger Deep Pacific Ocean
13C3 Challerange France
58D2 Challis USA
13C3 Châlons-sur-Marne France
14C2 Chalon sur Saône France
28B2 Chaluhe China
18C3 Cham Germany
62A1 Chama USA
42B2 Chaman Pakistan
42D2 Chamba India
42D3 Chambal R India
60D2 Chamberlain USA
65D3 Chambersburg USA
14D2 Chambéry France
13B3 Chambly France
65E1 Chambord Canada
42A3 Chambor Kalat Pakistan
41F3 Chamgordan Iran
43E4 Chāmpa India
14C2 Champagne Region France
47D2 Champagne Castle Mt Lesotho
57E2 Champaign USA
43N2 Champaran District India
30D3 Champassak Laos
57F2 Champlain,L USA
44B3 Chāmrājnagar India
74B3 Chañaral Chile
54D3 Chandalar USA
54D3 Chandalar R USA
63E3 Chandeleur Is USA
42D2 Chandīgarh India
59D4 Chandler USA
43G4 Chandpur Bangladesh
42D5 Chandrapur India
47E1 Changane R Mozambique
51D5 Changara Mozambique
28B2 Changbai China
28B2 Changbai Shan Mts China
28B2 Changchun China
31C4 Changde China
28A3 Changdo N Korea
28A3 Changhai China
28A3 Changhang S Korea
28A3 Changhowan S Korea
26E4 Changhua Taiwan
28A4 Changhŭng S Korea
30D2 Changjiang China
31D3 Chang Jiang R China
28B2 Changjin N Korea
28A2 Changjin R N Korea
28A2 Changjin Res N Korea
28B3 Changnyŏn N Korea
31C4 Changsha China
31E3 Changshu China
31B2 Changwu China
28A3 Changyŏn N Korea
31C2 Changzhi China
31E3 Changzhou China
14B2 Channel Is British Isles
56B3 Channel Is USA
55N5 Channel Port-aux-Basques Canada
30C3 Chanthaburi Thailand
13B3 Chantilly France
55J3 Chantrey Inlet B Canada
63C1 Chanute USA
24J4 Chany, Ozero L Russian Federation
31D5 Chao'an China
31D3 Chao Hu L China
30C3 Chao Phraya R Thailand
15A2 Chaouen Morocco
31E1 Chaoyang China
73K6 Chapada Diamantina Mts Brazil
73K4 Chapadinha Brazil
70B2 Chapala, L de Mexico
21J5 Chapayevo Kazakhstan
74F3 Chapecó Brazil
7D3 Chapel-en-le-Frith England
67C1 Chapel Hill USA
69H1 Chapeltown Jamaica
55K5 Chapleau Canada
25U3 Chaplino, Mys C Russian Federation
20G5 Chaplygin Russian Federation
60C2 Chappell USA
76G3 Charcot I Antarctica
7C4 Chard England
38E2 Chardzhou Turkmenistan
14C2 Charente R France
50B2 Chari R Chad
50B2 Chari Baguirmi Region Chad
42B1 Charikar Afghanistan
61E2 Chariton R USA
73G2 Charity Guyana
42D3 Charkhāri India
13C2 Charleroi Belgium
57F3 Charles,C USA
64B3 Charleston Illinois, USA
63E1 Charleston Missouri, USA
57F3 Charleston S Carolina, USA
57E3 Charleston W Virginia, USA
59C3 Charleston Peak Mt USA
68B3 Charles Town USA
68D1 Charlestown USA
50C4 Charlesville Zaïre
32D3 Charleville Australia
14C2 Charleville-Mézières France
64B1 Charlevoix USA
64C2 Charlotte Michigan, USA
57E3 Charlotte N Carolina, USA
67B3 Charlotte Harbor B USA
57F3 Charlottesville USA
55M5 Charlottetown Canada
69K1 Charlotteville Tobago
34B3 Charlton Australia
57F1 Charlton I Canada
13D3 Charmes France
42C2 Charsadda Pakistan
32D3 Charters Towers Australia
14C2 Chartres France
74E5 Chascomús Argentina
28B2 Chasong N Korea
14B2 Châteaubriant France
14B2 Châteaulin France
13B4 Châteauneuf-sur-Loire France
14C2 Châteauroux France
13D3 Château-Salins France
14C2 Château-Thierry France
13C2 Châtelet Belgium
14C2 Châtellerault France
61E2 Chatfield USA
7F6 Chatham England
68E2 Chatham Massachusetts, USA
55M5 Chatham New Brunswick, Canada
68D1 Chatham New York, USA
64C2 Chatham Ontario, Canada
65D3 Chatham Virginia, USA
33H5 Chatham Is New Zealand
54E4 Chatham Str USA
14C2 Châtillon France
13B4 Châtillon-Coligny France
13C4 Châtillon-sur-Seine France
43E5 Chatrapur India
68C3 Chatsworth USA
67B2 Chattahoochee USA
67A2 Chattahoochee R USA
57E3 Chattanooga USA
30A1 Chauk Burma
43L2 Chauka R India
14D2 Chaumont France
13B3 Chauny France
30D3 Chau Phu Vietnam
44E4 Chaura I Nicobar Is, Indian Ocean
15A1 Chaves Portugal
20J4 Chaykovskiy Russian Federation
18C2 Cheb Czech Republic
20H4 Cheboksary Russian Federation
57E2 Cheboygan USA
19G2 Chechersk Belarus
28B3 Chech'on S Korea
63C1 Checotah USA
7C4 Cheddar England
30A2 Cheduba I Burma
34B1 Cheepie Australia
48B2 Chegga Mauritius
51D5 Chegutu Zimbabwe
58B1 Chehalis USA
28B4 Cheju S Korea
28B4 Cheju Do I S Korea
28B4 Cheju Haehyŏp Str S Korea
25P4 Chekunda Russian Federation
58B1 Chelan,L USA
21J8 Cheleken Turkmenistan
16B3 Chélia, Dj Mt Algeria
15C2 Cheliff R Algeria
38D1 Chelkar Kazakhstan
19E2 Chełm Poland
19D2 Chełmno Poland
7E4 Chelmsford England
7C4 Cheltenham England
20L4 Chelyabinsk Russian Federation
25M2 Chelyuskin, Mys C Russian Federation
51D5 Chemba Mozambique
18C2 Chemnitz Germ
68B1 Chemung R USA
42D2 Chenab R India/Pakistan
48B2 Chenachen Algeria
68C1 Chenango R USA
58C1 Cheney USA
63C1 Cheney Res USA
31D1 Chengde China
31A3 Chengdu China
31E2 Chengshan Jiao Pt China
28A3 Chengzitan China
31C4 Chenxi China
31C4 Chen Xian China
31D3 Cheo Xian China
72C5 Chepén Peru
7C4 Chepstow Wales
64A1 Chequamegon B USA
14C2 Cher R France
67C2 Cheraw USA
14B2 Cherbourg France
15C2 Cherchell Algeria
20K3 Cherdyn Russian Federation
25M4 Cheremkhovo Russian Federation
20F4 Cherepovets Russian Federation
21E6 Cherkassy Ukraine
21G7 Cherkessk Russian Federation
21E5 Chernigov Ukraine
19G2 Chernobyl Ukraine
21D6 Chernovtsy Ukraine
20K4 Chernushka Russian Federation
20C5 Chernyakhovsk Russian Federation
21H6 Chernyye Zemli Region Russian Federation
61D2 Cherokee Iowa, USA
62C1 Cherokee Oklahoma, USA
63D1 Cherokees,L o'the USA
43G3 Cherrapunji India
33F2 Cherry I Solomon Islands
25S3 Cherskiy Russian Federation
25Q3 Cherskogo, Khrebet Mts Russian Federation
20D5 Cherven' Belarus
19E2 Chervonograd Ukraine
65D3 Chesapeake USA
65D3 Chesapeake B USA
7D4 Chesham England
68D1 Cheshire USA
7C3 Cheshire County England
20H2 Chëshskaya Guba B Russian Federation
59B2 Chester California, USA
7C3 Chester England
64B3 Chester Illinois, USA
68D1 Chester Massachusets, USA
58D1 Chester Montana, USA
65D3 Chester Pennsylvania, USA
67B2 Chester S Carolina, USA
68D1 Chester Vermont, USA
68B3 Chester R USA
7D3 Chesterfield England
33E2 Chesterfield, Îles Nouvelle Calédonie
55J3 Chesterfield Inlet Canada
68B3 Chestertown USA
65F1 Chesuncook L USA
70D3 Chetumal Mexico
35B2 Cheviot New Zealand
10C2 Cheviots Hills England/Scotland
60C2 Cheyenne USA
60C2 Cheyenne R USA
60C3 Cheyenne Wells USA
43E3 Chhapra India
43G3 Chhātak Bangladesh
42D4 Chhatarpur India
42D4 Chhindwāra India
43F3 Chhukha Bhutan
51B5 Chiange Angola
30C2 Chiang Kham Thailand
30B2 Chiang Mai Thailand
31E5 Chiayi Taiwan
29E3 Chiba Japan
51B5 Chibia Angola
55L4 Chibougamau Canada
28B3 Chiburi-jima I Japan
47E1 Chibuto Mozambique
57E2 Chicago USA
64B2 Chicago Heights USA
54E4 Chichagof I USA
7D4 Chichester England
29C3 Chichibu Japan
26H4 Chichi-jima I Japan
57E3 Chickamauga L USA
63E2 Chickasawhay R USA
56D3 Chickasha USA
54D3 Chicken USA
72B5 Chiclayo Peru
56A3 Chico USA
74C6 Chico R Argentina
51D5 Chicoa Mozambique
65E2 Chicopee USA
55L5 Chicoutimi Canada
51D6 Chicualacuala Mozambique
44B3 Chidambaram India
55M3 Chidley,C Canada
67B3 Chiefland USA
48B4 Chiehn Liberia
51C4 Chiengi Zambia
13C3 Chiers R France
16C2 Chieti Italy
31D1 Chifeng China
73K7 Chifre, Serra do Mts Brazil
54C3 Chigmit Mts USA
47E1 Chigubo Mozambique
70B2 Chihuahua Mexico
62A3 Chihuahua State Mexico
44B3 Chik Ballāpur India
44B3 Chikmagalūr India
51D5 Chikwawa Malawi
30A1 Chi-kyaw Burma
44C2 Chilakalūrupet India
44B4 Chilaw Sri Lanka
34D1 Childers Australia
62B2 Childress USA
71C6 Chile Republic S America
51C5 Chililabombwe Zambia
43F5 Chilka L India
54F4 Chilko L Canada
74B5 Chillán Chile
61E3 Chillicothe Missouri, USA
64C3 Chillicothe Ohio, USA
43G3 Chilmari India
74B6 Chiloé, Isla de Chile
51D5 Chilongozi Zambia
58B2 Chiloquin USA
70C3 Chilpancingo Mexico
7D4 Chiltern Hills Upland England
64B2 Chilton USA
51D5 Chilumba Malawi
Chi-lung = Keelung
51D5 Chilwa, L Malawi
51D5 Chimanimani Zimbabwe
13C2 Chimay Belgium
24G5 Chimbay Uzbekistan
72C4 Chimborazo Mt Ecuador
72C5 Chimbote Peru
24H5 Chimkent Kazakhstan
51D5 Chimoio Mozambique
22F4 China Republic Asia
66D3 China L USA
66D3 China Lake USA
China, National Republic of = Taiwan
70D3 Chinandega Nicaragua
62B3 Chinati Peak Mt USA
72C6 Chincha Alta Peru
34D1 Chinchilla Australia
51D5 Chinde Mozambique
28A4 Chindo S Korea
43G4 Chindwin R Burma
51C5 Chingola Zambia
51B5 Chinguar Angola
48A2 Chinguetti Mauritius
28B3 Chinhae S Korea
51D5 Chinhoyi Zimbabwe
42C2 Chiniot Pakistan
28B3 Chinju S Korea
50C3 Chinko R Central African Republic
29C3 Chino Japan
51D5 Chinsali Zambia
16C1 Chioggia Italy
51D5 Chipata Zambia
51D6 Chipinge Zimbabwe
44A2 Chiplūn India
7C4 Chippenham England
64A1 Chippewa R USA
57D2 Chippewa Falls USA
64A1 Chippewa,L USA
7D4 Chipping Norton England
7C4 Chipping Sodbury England
72B4 Chira R Peru
44C2 Chīrāla India
51D6 Chiredzi Zimbabwe
50B1 Chirfa Niger
59E4 Chiricahua Peak Mt USA
70D4 Chiriquí, G de Panama
72B2 Chiriquí, Lago de Panama
17F2 Chirpan Bulgaria
72B2 Chirripó Grande Mt Costa Rica
51C5 Chirundu Zimbabwe
51C5 Chisamba Zambia
55L4 Chisasibi Canada

61E1 **Chisholm** USA
31B4 **Chishui He** *R* China
Chisimaio = Kismaayo
Chişinău = Kishinev
20H4 **Chistopol** Russian Federation
26E1 **Chita** Russian Federation
51B5 **Chitado** Angola
51B5 **Chitembo** Angola
29D2 **Chitose** Japan
44B3 **Chitradurga** India
42C1 **Chitral** Pakistan
72B2 **Chitré** Panama
43G4 **Chittagong** Bangladesh
42C4 **Chittaurgarh** India
44B3 **Chittoor** India
51C5 **Chiume** Angola
74D4 **Chivilcoy** Argentina
51D5 **Chivu** Zimbabwe
29B3 **Chizu** Japan
28A3 **Choch'iwŏn** S Korea
72D2 **Chocontá** Colombia
28A4 **Ch'o-do** *I* S Korea
74C5 **Choele Choel** Argentina
33E1 **Choiseul** *I* Solomon Islands
70B2 **Choix** Mexico
19D2 **Chojnice** Poland
29D3 **Chokai-san** *Mt* Japan
50D2 **Choke Mts** Ethiopia
25Q2 **Chokurdakh** Russian Federation
66B3 **Cholame** USA
66B3 **Cholame Creek** *R* USA
14B2 **Cholet** France
72A1 **Choluteca** Honduras
51C5 **Choma** Zambia
28A3 **Chŏmch'ŏn** S Korea
43F3 **Chomo Yummo** *Mt* China/India
18C2 **Chomutov** Czech Republic
25M3 **Chona** *R* Russian Federation
28B3 **Ch'ŏnan** S Korea
30C3 **Chon Buri** Thailand
28A2 **Chonchon** N Korea
72C4 **Chone** Ecuador
74B6 **Chones, Archipiélago de las** Chile
28A3 **Chongdo** S Korea
28B2 **Ch'ŏngjin** N Korea
28B3 **Chŏngju** N Korea
28B3 **Ch'ŏngju** S Korea
51B5 **Chongoroi** Angola
28A3 **Chongpyong** N Korea
31B4 **Chongqing** China
28A3 **Chŏngsŏn** S Korea
28B3 **Chŏngŭp** S Korea
28B3 **Ch'ŏnju** S Korea
43F3 **Cho Oyu** *Mt* China/Nepal
75B4 **Chopim** *R* Brazil
6C3 **Chorley** England
19F3 **Chortkov** Ukraine
28B3 **Ch'ŏrwŏn** S Korea
19D2 **Chorzów** Poland
28A2 **Chosan** N Korea
29E3 **Chōshi** Japan
18D2 **Choszczno** Poland
43E4 **Chotanāgpur** *Region* India
58D1 **Choteau** USA
48C1 **Chott ech Chergui** *L* Algeria
15C2 **Chott El Hodna** *L* Algeria
48C1 **Chott Melrhir** *L* Algeria
66B2 **Chowchilla** USA
25N5 **Choybalsan** Mongolia
7D4 **Christchurch** England
35B2 **Christchurch** New Zealand
47D2 **Christiana** South Africa
55M2 **Christian,C** Canada
55N3 **Christianshåb** Greenland
27D8 **Christmas I** Indian Ocean
24J5 **Chu** Kazakhstan
24J5 **Chu** *R* Kazakhstan
58D2 **Chubbuck** USA
74C6 **Chubut** *R* Argentina
74C6 **Chubut** *State* Argentina
20E4 **Chudovo** Russian Federation
54D3 **Chugach Mts** USA
28B3 **Chūgoku-sanchi** *Mts* Japan
60C2 **Chugwater** USA
74F4 **Chui** Uruguay
30C5 **Chukai** Malaysia
26G1 **Chukchagirskoye, Ozero** *L* Russian Federation
25T3 **Chukotskiy Khrebet** *Mts* Russian Federation
25U3 **Chukotskiy Poluostrov** *Pen* Russian Federation
30D2 **Chu Lai** Vietnam
59C4 **Chula Vista** USA
26F1 **Chulman** Russian Federation
72B5 **Chulucanas** Peru
72E7 **Chulumani** Bolivia
24K4 **Chulym** Russian Federation
25K4 **Chulym** *R* Russian Federation
25L4 **Chuma** *R* Russian Federation
42D2 **Chumar** India
25P4 **Chumikan** Russian Federation
30B3 **Chumphon** Thailand
28B3 **Ch'unch'ŏn** S Korea
43F4 **Chunchura** India
28B3 **Ch'ungju** S Korea
Chungking = Chongqing
28A4 **Ch'ungmu** S Korea
28B3 **Chŭngsan** N Korea
28A3 **Chungwa** N Korea
28C2 **Chunhua** China
51D4 **Chunya** Tanzania
25M3 **Chunya** *R* Russian Federation
28B2 **Chunyang** China
28A3 **Ch'unyang** S Korea
69L1 **Chupara Pt** Trinidad
74C2 **Chuquicamata** Chile
16B1 **Chur** Switzerland
43G4 **Churāchāndpur** India
25P3 **Churapcha** Russian Federation
55J4 **Churchill** Canada
55M4 **Churchill** *R* Labrador, Canada
55J4 **Churchill** *R* Manitoba, Canada
55J4 **Churchill,C** Canada
55M4 **Churchill Falls** Canada
54H4 **Churchill L** Canada
42C3 **Chūru** India
20K4 **Chusovoy** Russian Federation
20H4 **Chuvash Republic** Russian Federation
26D4 **Chuxiong** China
30D3 **Chu Yang Sin** *Mt* Vietnam
75B3 **Cianorte** Brazil
19E2 **Ciechanów** Poland
70E2 **Ciego de Ávila** Cuba
72D1 **Ciénaga** Colombia
70D2 **Cienfuegos** Cuba
19D3 **Cieszyn** Poland
15B2 **Cieza** Spain
40B2 **Cihanbeyli** Turkey
15B2 **Cijara, Embalse de** *Res* Spain
27D7 **Cilacap** Indonesia
62B1 **Cimarron** USA
62C1 **Cimarron** *R* USA
16C2 **Cimone, Monte** *Mt* Italy
17F1 **Cîmpina** Romania
15C1 **Cinca** *R* Spain
16D2 **Cincer** *Mt* Bosnia-Herzegovina
57E3 **Cincinnati** USA
17E1 **Cindrelu** *Mt* Romania
17F3 **Cine** *R* Turkey
13C2 **Ciney** Belgium
16B2 **Cinto, Monte** *Mt* Corsica, France
54D3 **Circle** Alaska, USA
60B1 **Circle** Montana, USA
64C3 **Circleville** USA
27D7 **Cirebon** Indonesia
7D4 **Cirencester** England
62C2 **Cisco** USA
70C3 **Citlaltepetl** *Vol* Mexico
47B3 **Citrusdal** South Africa
70B2 **Ciudad Acuña** Mexico
72F2 **Ciudad Bolívar** Venezuela
70B2 **Ciudad Camargo** Mexico
70C3 **Ciudad del Carmen** Mexico
15C2 **Ciudadela** Spain
72F2 **Ciudad Guayana** Venezuela
70B3 **Ciudad Guzman** Mexico
70B2 **Ciudad Juárez** Mexico
56C4 **Ciudad Lerdo** Mexico
70C2 **Ciudad Madero** Mexico
70B2 **Ciudad Obregon** Mexico
69C4 **Ciudad Ojeda** Venezuela
72F2 **Ciudad Piar** Venezuela
15B2 **Ciudad Real** Spain
15A1 **Ciudad Rodrigo** Spain
70C2 **Ciudad Valles** Mexico
70C2 **Ciudad Victoria** Mexico
16C2 **Civitavecchia** Italy
40D2 **Cizre** Turkey
7E4 **Clacton-on-Sea** England
54G4 **Claire,L** Canada
65D2 **Clairton** USA
67A2 **Clanton** USA
47B3 **Clanwilliam** South Africa
9C3 **Clara** Irish Republic
64C2 **Clare** USA
65E2 **Claremont** USA
63C1 **Claremore** USA
34D1 **Clarence** *R* Australia
35B2 **Clarence** *R* New Zealand
32C2 **Clarence Str** Australia
63D2 **Clarendon** USA
55N5 **Clarenville** Canada
54G4 **Claresholm** Canada
61D2 **Clarinda** USA
61E2 **Clarion** Iowa, USA
65D2 **Clarion** Pennsylvania, USA
70A3 **Clarión** *I* Mexico
65D2 **Clarion** *R* USA
37M4 **Clarion Fracture Zone** Pacific Ocean
57E3 **Clark Hill Res** USA
59C3 **Clark Mt** USA
64C2 **Clark,Pt** Canada
64C3 **Clarksburg** USA
57D3 **Clarksdale** USA
58C1 **Clarkston** USA
63D1 **Clarksville** Arkansas, USA
67A1 **Clarksville** Tennessee, USA
75B2 **Claro** *R* Brazil
74E5 **Claromecó** Argentina
61D3 **Clay Center** USA
8E2 **Claymore** *Oilfield* N Sea
56C3 **Clayton** New Mexico, USA
65D2 **Clayton** New York, USA
10B3 **Clear, C** Irish Republic
68A2 **Clearfield** Pennsylvania, USA
58D2 **Clearfield** Utah, USA
59B3 **Clear L** USA
61E2 **Clear Lake** USA
58B2 **Clear Lake Res** USA
60B2 **Clearmont** USA
57E4 **Clearwater** USA
58C1 **Clearwater Mts** USA
56D3 **Cleburne** USA
7D3 **Cleethorpes** England
6E2 **Cleeton** *Oilfield* N Sea
66B1 **Clements** USA
32D3 **Clermont** Australia
13B3 **Clermont** France
13C3 **Clermont-en-Argonne** France
14C2 **Clermont-Ferrand** France
13D2 **Clervaux** Luxembourg
63D2 **Cleveland** Mississippi, USA
57E2 **Cleveland** Ohio, USA
67B1 **Cleveland** Tennessee, USA
63C2 **Cleveland** Texas, USA
6D2 **Cleveland** *County* England
75B4 **Clevelândia** Brazil
58D1 **Cleveland,Mt** USA
10B3 **Clew B** Irish Republic
59E4 **Clifton** Arizona, USA
34D1 **Clifton** Australia
68C2 **Clifton** New Jersey, USA
34A1 **Clifton Hills** Australia
67B1 **Clinch** *R* USA
67B1 **Clinch Mts** USA
63D1 **Clinton** Arkansas, USA
54F4 **Clinton** Canada
68D2 **Clinton** Connecticut, USA
64A2 **Clinton** Iowa, USA
68E1 **Clinton** Massachusetts, USA
63D2 **Clinton** Mississippi, USA
63D1 **Clinton** Missouri, USA
67C2 **Clinton** N Carolina, USA
68C2 **Clinton** New Jersey, USA
62C1 **Clinton** Oklahoma, USA
54H3 **Clinton-Colden L** Canada
70B3 **Clipperton I** Pacific Ocean
6C3 **Clitheroe** England
72E7 **Cliza** Bolivia
9C3 **Clogher Hd** *Pt* Irish Republic
9B4 **Clonakilty B** Irish Republic
32D3 **Cloncurry** Australia
9C3 **Clones** Irish Republic
9C3 **Clonmel** Irish Republic
13E1 **Cloppenburg** Germany
57D2 **Cloquet** USA
75A4 **Clorinda** Argentina
60B2 **Cloud Peak** *Mt* USA
66A1 **Cloverdale** USA
66C2 **Clovis** California, USA
56C3 **Clovis** New Mexico, USA
21C6 **Cluj** Romania
17E1 **Cluj-Napoca** Romania
35A3 **Clutha** *R* New Zealand
7C3 **Clwyd** *County* Wales
7C3 **Clwyd** *R* Wales
55M2 **Clyde** Canada
35A3 **Clyde** New Zealand
6F1 **Clyde** *Oilfield* N Sea
68B1 **Clyde** USA
8C4 **Clyde** *R* Scotland
8C4 **Clydebank** Scotland
59C4 **Coachella** USA
62B3 **Coahuila** *State* Mexico
59C3 **Coaldale** USA
59B3 **Coalinga** USA
7D3 **Coalville** England
58D2 **Coalville** USA
75E1 **Coaraci** Brazil
72F5 **Coari** *R* Brazil
67A2 **Coastal Plain** USA
54E4 **Coast Mts** Canada
56A2 **Coast Ranges** *Mts* USA
8C4 **Coatbridge** Scotland
68C3 **Coatesville** USA
65E1 **Coaticook** Canada
55K3 **Coats I** Canada
76F1 **Coats Land** *Region* Antarctica
70C3 **Coatzacoalcas** Mexico
55L5 **Cobalt** Canada
70C3 **Cobán** Guatemala
32D4 **Cobar** Australia
34C3 **Cobargo** Australia
72E6 **Cobija** Bolivia
68C1 **Cobleskill** USA
55L5 **Cobourg** Canada
32C2 **Cobourg Pen** Australia
18C2 **Coburg** Germany
72C4 **Coca** Ecuador
75B1 **Cocalinho** Brazil
72E7 **Cochabamba** Bolivia
13D2 **Cochem** Germany
55K5 **Cochrane** Ontario, Canada
74B7 **Cochrane, Lago** Argentina/Chile
34B2 **Cockburn** Australia
6C2 **Cockermouth** England
68B3 **Cockeysville** USA
69H1 **Cockpit Country,The** Jamaica
47C3 **Cockscomb** *Mt* South Africa
70D3 **Coco** *R* Honduras/Nicaragua
67B3 **Cocoa** USA
48C4 **Cocobeach** Equatorial Guinea
44E3 **Coco Channel** Andaman Is/Burma
53K8 **Coco, Isla del** Costa Rica
75D1 **Côcos** Brazil
69L1 **Cocos B** Trinidad
27C8 **Cocos Is** Indian Ocean
37P4 **Cocos Ridge** Pacific Ocean
57F2 **Cod,C** USA
35A3 **Codfish I** New Zealand
55M4 **Cod I** Canada
15C1 **Codi, Sierra del** *Mts* Spain
73K4 **Codó** Brazil
56C2 **Cody** USA
27H8 **Coen** Australia
18B2 **Coesfeld** Germany
56B2 **Coeur d'Alene** USA
58C1 **Coeur d'Alene L** USA
13D1 **Coevorden** Netherlands
56D3 **Coffeyville** USA
34D2 **Coff's Harbour** Australia
47D3 **Cofimvaba** South Africa
16B2 **Coghinas, Lago del** Sardinia, Italy
14B2 **Cognac** France
68B1 **Cohocton** USA
68B1 **Cohocton** *R* USA
65E2 **Cohoes** USA
34B3 **Cohuna** Australia
72B2 **Coiba, Isla** Panama
74B7 **Coihaique** Chile
44B3 **Coimbatore** India
15A1 **Coimbra** Portugal
72B3 **Cojimies** Ecuador
58D2 **Cokeville** USA
32D4 **Colac** Australia
73K7 **Colatina** Brazil
76F6 **Colbeck,C** Antarctica
14B2 **Colby** USA
7E4 **Colchester** England
68D2 **Colchester** USA
8D4 **Coldstream** Scotland
64C2 **Coldwater** USA
58D1 **Coleman** Canada
64C2 **Coleman** Michigan, USA
62C2 **Coleman** Texas, USA
47D2 **Colenso** South Africa
9C2 **Coleraine** Northern Ireland
35B2 **Coleridge,L** New Zealand
47D3 **Colesberg** South Africa
72D7 **Coles, Puerta** Peru
66C1 **Coleville** USA
59B3 **Colfax** California, USA
63D2 **Colfax** Louisiana, USA
58C1 **Colfax** Washington, USA
74C7 **Colhué Huapí, Lago** Argentina
70B3 **Colima** Mexico
8B3 **Coll** *I* Scotland
34C1 **Collarenebri** Australia
67B2 **College Park** Georgia, USA
68B3 **College Park** Washington DC, USA
63C2 **College Station** USA
32A4 **Collie** Australia
32B2 **Collier B** Australia
13A2 **Collines de l'Artois** *Hills* France
13B3 **Collines de la Thiérache** *Hills* France
64C2 **Collingwood** Canada
35B2 **Collingwood** New Zealand
63E2 **Collins** Mississippi, USA
68A1 **Collins** New York, USA
54H2 **Collinson Pen** Canada
32D3 **Collinsville** Australia
64B3 **Collinsville** Illinois, USA
63C1 **Collinsville** Oklahoma, USA
14D2 **Colmar** France
6C3 **Colne** England
56B3 **Colnett, Cabo** *C* Mexico
18B2 **Cologne** Germany
75C3 **Colômbia** Brazil
65D3 **Colombia** USA
72D3 **Colombia** *Republic* S America
44B4 **Colombo** Sri Lanka
74E4 **Colón** Argentina
70D2 **Colon** Cuba
72C2 **Colón** Panama
Colón, Arch. de = Galapagos Islands
74E4 **Colonia** Uruguay
74C7 **Colonia Las Heras** Argentina
65D3 **Colonial Heights** USA
8B3 **Colonsay** *I* Scotland
69E5 **Coloradito** Venezuela
74D5 **Colorado** *R* Buenos Aires, Argentina
56D3 **Colorado** *R* Texas, USA
56B3 **Colorado** *R* Mexico/USA
56C3 **Colorado** *State* USA
62B2 **Colorado City** USA
56B3 **Colorado Plat** USA
56C3 **Colorado Springs** USA
68B3 **Columbia** Maryland, USA
63E2 **Columbia** Mississippi, USA
57D3 **Columbia** Missouri, USA
65D2 **Columbia** Pennsylvania, USA
57E3 **Columbia** S Carolina, USA
57E3 **Columbia** Tennessee, USA
56A2 **Columbia** *R* USA
58D1 **Columbia Falls** USA
54G4 **Columbia,Mt** Canada
58C1 **Columbia Plat** USA
47B3 **Columbine,C** South Africa
15C2 **Columbretes, Islas** Spain
57E3 **Columbus** Georgia, USA
64B3 **Columbus** Indiana, USA
57E3 **Columbus** Mississippi, USA
58E1 **Columbus** Montana, USA
56D2 **Columbus** Nebraska, USA
62A2 **Columbus** New Mexico, USA
57E2 **Columbus** Ohio, USA
63C3 **Columbus** Texas, USA
64B2 **Columbus** Wisconsin, USA
58C1 **Colville** USA
54C3 **Colville** *R* USA
35C1 **Colville,C** New Zealand
54F3 **Colville L** Canada
7C3 **Colwyn Bay** Wales
62C2 **Comanche** USA
66B1 **Comanche Res** USA
76G2 **Comandante Ferraz** *Base* Antarctica
70D3 **Comayagua** Honduras
13C4 **Combeaufontaine** France
9D2 **Comber** Northern Ireland
43G5 **Combermere B** Burma
9C3 **Comeragh Mts** Irish Republic
62C2 **Comfort** USA
43G4 **Comilla** Bangladesh
70C3 **Comitán** Mexico
13C3 **Commercy** France
55K3 **Committee B** Canada
16B1 **Como** Italy
74C7 **Comodoro Rivadavia** Argentina
16B1 **Como, L di** Italy
44B4 **Comorin,C** India
51E5 **Comoros** *Is, Republic* Indian Ocean
14C2 **Compiègne** France
75C3 **Comprida, Ilha** Brazil
15B2 **Comunidad Valenciana** *Region* Spain
43G3 **Cona** China
48A4 **Conakry** Guinea
14B2 **Concarneau** France
75E2 **Conceiçao da Barra** Brazil
73J5 **Conceição do Araguaia** Brazil
75D2 **Conceiçao do Mato Dentro** Brazil
74E4 **Concepción** Argentina
75A3 **Concepción** Brazil/Paraguay
74B5 **Concepción** Chile
74E2 **Concepción** Paraguay
70B2 **Concepción del Oro** Mexico
47A1 **Conception B** Namibia
56A3 **Conception,Pt** USA
75C3 **Conchas** Brazil
62B1 **Conchas L** USA
56C4 **Conchos** *R* Mexico
59B3 **Concord** California, USA
57F2 **Concord** New Hampshire, USA
67B1 **Concord** North Carolina, USA
74E4 **Concordia** Argentina
56D3 **Concordia** USA
58B1 **Concrete** USA

34D1 **Condamine** Australia
75D1 **Condeuba** Brazil
32D4 **Condobolin** Australia
58B1 **Condon** USA
13C2 **Condroz** *Mts* Belgium
67A2 **Conecuh** *R* USA
68B1 **Conesus L** USA
75A3 **Confuso** *R* Paraguay
7C3 **Congleton** England
46F8 **Congo** *R* W Africa
46F8 **Congo** *Republic* Africa
Congo,R = Zaire
64C1 **Coniston** Canada
64C2 **Conneaut** USA
65E2 **Connecticut** *R* USA
57F2 **Connecticut** *State* USA
65D2 **Connellsville** USA
64B3 **Connersville** USA
10B3 **Conn, Lough** *L* Irish Republic
34B2 **Conoble** Australia
58D1 **Conrad** USA
63C2 **Conroe** USA
75D3 **Conselheiro Lafaiete** Brazil
6D2 **Consett** England
30D4 **Con Son** *Is* Vietnam
21D7 **Constanţa** Romania
16B3 **Constantine** Algeria
74B5 **Constitución** Chile
58D2 **Contact** USA
73K6 **Contas** *R* Brazil
13C3 **Contrexéville** France
54H3 **Contwoyto L** Canada
57D3 **Conway** Arkansas, USA
65E2 **Conway** New Hampshire, USA
67C2 **Conway** South Carolina, USA
7C3 **Conwy** Wales
7C3 **Conwy** *R* Wales
32C3 **Coober Pedy** Australia
67A1 **Cookeville** USA
54C3 **Cook Inlet** *B* USA
37L5 **Cook Is** Pacific Ocean
35B2 **Cook,Mt** New Zealand
9C2 **Cookstown** Northern Ireland
33G5 **Cook Str** New Zealand
32D2 **Cooktown** Australia
34C2 **Coolabah** Australia
34C1 **Cooladdi** Australia
34C2 **Coolah** Australia
34C2 **Coolamon** Australia
32B4 **Coolgardie** Australia
59D4 **Coolidge** USA
34C3 **Cooma** Australia
34C2 **Coonabarabran** Australia
34C2 **Coonambie** Australia
34B2 **Coonbah** Australia
44A3 **Coondapoor** India
34C1 **Coongoola** Australia
44B3 **Coonoor** India
34B1 **Cooper Basin** Australia
32C3 **Cooper Creek** Australia
34B1 **Cooper Creek** *R* Australia
67C3 **Cooper's Town** Bahamas
68C1 **Cooperstown** New York, USA
61D1 **Cooperstown** North Dakota, USA
34A3 **Coorong,The** Australia
34D1 **Cooroy** Australia
58B2 **Coos B** USA
58B2 **Coos Bay** USA
32D4 **Cootamundra** Australia
9C2 **Cootehill** Irish Republic
60C3 **Cope** USA
18C1 **Copenhagen** Denmark
74B3 **Copiapó** Chile
54D3 **Copper Center** USA
64C1 **Copper Cliff** Canada
64B1 **Copper Harbor** USA
54G3 **Coppermine** Canada
54G3 **Coppermine** *R* Canada
64C1 **Coppermine Pt** Canada
Coquilhatville = Mbandaka
74B3 **Coquimbo** Chile
17E2 **Corabia** Romania
67B3 **Coral Gables** USA
55K3 **Coral Harbour** Canada
32E2 **Coral S** Australia/Papua New Guinea
36J5 **Coral Sea Basin** Pacific Ocean
32E2 **Coral Sea Island Territories** Australia
34B3 **Corangamite,L** Australia
73G3 **Corantijn** *R* Guyana/Surinam
13B3 **Corbeil-Essonnes** France
64C3 **Corbin** USA
6D2 **Corbridge** England
7D3 **Corby** England
66C2 **Corcoran** USA
74B6 **Corcovado, Golfo** *G* Chile
15A1 **Corcubion** Spain
57E3 **Cordele** USA
15A1 **Cordillera Cantabrica** *Mts* Spain
69C3 **Cordillera Central** *Mts* Dominican Republic/Haiti
75A4 **Cordillera de Caaguazú** Paraguay
70D3 **Cordillera Isabelia** *Mts* Nicaragua
72C2 **Cordillera Occidental** *Mts* Colombia
72C3 **Cordillera Oriental** *Mts* Colombia
34B1 **Cordillo Downs** Australia
74D4 **Córdoba** Argentina
70C3 **Córdoba** Mexico
15B2 **Córdoba** Spain
74D4 **Córdoba** *State* Argentina
54D3 **Cordova** USA
17D3 **Corfu** Greece
17D3 **Corfu** *I* Greece
75D1 **Coribe** Brazil
34D2 **Coricudgy,Mt** Australia
16D3 **Corigliano Calabro** Italy
32E2 **Coringa Is** Australia
17E3 **Corinth** Greece
57E3 **Corinth** Mississippi, USA
68D1 **Corinth** New York, USA
17E3 **Corinth, Gulf of** Greece
73K7 **Corinto** Brazil
10B3 **Cork** Irish Republic
40A1 **Çorlu** Turkey
73K7 **Cornel Fabriciano** Brazil
75B3 **Cornélio Procópio** Brazil
55N5 **Corner Brook** Canada
34C3 **Corner Inlet** *B* Australia
13D4 **Cornimont** France
65D2 **Corning** USA
16C2 **Corno, Monte** *Mt* Italy
55L5 **Cornwall** Canada
7B4 **Cornwall** *County* England
7B4 **Cornwall,C** England
54H2 **Cornwall I** Canada
55J2 **Cornwallis I** Canada
72E1 **Coro** Venezuela
73K4 **Coroatá** Brazil
72E7 **Coroico** Bolivia
75C2 **Coromandel** Brazil
44C3 **Coromandel Coast** India
35C1 **Coromandel Pen** New Zealand
35C1 **Coromandel Range** *Mts* New Zealand
66D4 **Corona** California, USA
62A2 **Corona** New Mexico, USA
72B2 **Coronado, B. de** Costa Rica
54G3 **Coronation G** Canada
74B5 **Coronel** Chile
75D2 **Coronel Fabriciano** Brazil
74E3 **Coronel Oviedo** Paraguay
74D5 **Coronel Pringles** Argentina
72D7 **Coropuna** *Mt* Peru
34C3 **Corowa** Australia
14D3 **Corps** France
56D4 **Corpus Christi** USA
63C3 **Corpus Christi,L** USA
9B3 **Corraun Pen** Irish Republic
27F5 **Corregidor** *I* Philippines
75D1 **Corrente** *R* Bahia, Brazil
75C1 **Corrente** *R* Goias, Brazil
75B2 **Corrente** *R* Mato Grosso, Brazil
75D1 **Correntina** Brazil
10B3 **Corrib, Lough** *L* Irish Republic
74E3 **Corrientes** Argentina
74E3 **Corrientes** *State* Argentina
72C2 **Corrientes, Cabo** *C* Colombia
70B2 **Corrientes, Cabo** *C* Mexico
63D2 **Corrigan** USA
32A4 **Corrigin** Australia
34C3 **Corryong** Australia
Corse = Corsica
8C4 **Corsewall Pt** Scotland
16B2 **Corsica** *I* Medit Sea
56D3 **Corsicana** USA
55O3 **Cort Adelaer, Kap** *C* Greenland
16B2 **Corte** Corsica, France
56C3 **Cortez** USA
16C1 **Cortina d'Ampezzo** Italy
65D2 **Cortland** USA
21G7 **Çoruh** *R* Turkey
21F7 **Çorum** Turkey
73G7 **Corumbá** Brazil
75C2 **Corumbá** *R* Brazil
75C2 **Corumbaiba** Brazil
58B2 **Corvallis** USA
48A1 **Corvo** *I* Azores
7C3 **Corwen** Wales
16D3 **Cosenza** Italy
51E5 **Cosmoledo Is** Seychelles
66D2 **Coso Junction** USA
15B2 **Costa Blanca** *Region* Spain
15C1 **Costa Brava** *Region* Spain
15B2 **Costa Calída** *Region* Spain
15B2 **Costa de Almería** *Region* Spain
15A2 **Costa de la Luz** *Region* Spain
15B2 **Costa del Sol** *Region* Spain
15C1 **Costa Dorada** *Region* Spain
66D4 **Costa Mesa** USA
70D3 **Costa Rica** *Republic* Central America
27F6 **Cotabato** Philippines
72E8 **Cotagaita** Bolivia
14D3 **Côte d'Azur** *Region* France
Côte D'Ivoire = Ivory Coast
13C4 **Côte-d'Or** *Department* France
13C3 **Côtes de Meuse** *Mts* France
7B4 **Cothi** *R* Wales
48C4 **Cotonou** Benin
72C4 **Cotopaxi** *Mt* Ecuador
7C4 **Cotswold Hills** *Upland* England
58B2 **Cottage Grove** USA
18C2 **Cottbus** Germany
59D4 **Cottonwood** USA
62C3 **Cotulla** USA
68A2 **Coudersport** USA
13B3 **Coulommiers** France
65D1 **Coulonge** *R* Canada
66B2 **Coulterville** USA
54B3 **Council** USA
56D2 **Council Bluffs** USA
8D3 **Coupar Angus** Scotland
19E1 **Courland Lagoon** *Lg* Lithuania/Russian Federation
Courtrai = Kortrijk
14B2 **Coutances** France
7D3 **Coventry** England
15A1 **Covilhã** Portugal
67B2 **Covington** Georgia, USA
64C3 **Covington** Kentucky, USA
63D2 **Covington** Louisiana, USA
65D3 **Covington** Virginia, USA
34C2 **Cowal,L** Australia
34B3 **Cowangie** Australia
65E1 **Cowansville** Canada
8D3 **Cowdenbeath** Scotland
34C3 **Cowes** Australia
7D4 **Cowes** England
58B1 **Cowichan L** Canada
58B1 **Cowlitz** *R* USA
34C2 **Cowra** Australia
73H7 **Coxim** Brazil
75B2 **Coxim** *R* Brazil
68D1 **Coxsackie** USA
43G4 **Cox's Bazar** Bangladesh
66B2 **Coyote** USA
60D2 **Cozad** USA
70D2 **Cozumel, Isla de** Mexico
34D1 **Cracow** Australia
19D2 **Cracow** Poland
47D3 **Cradock** South Africa
56C2 **Craig** USA
9C2 **Craigavon** Northern Ireland
18C3 **Crailsheim** Germany
17E2 **Craiova** Romania
65E2 **Cranberry L** USA
54G5 **Cranbrook** Canada
58C2 **Crane** Oregon, USA
62B2 **Crane** Texas, USA
68E2 **Cranston** USA
58B2 **Crater L** USA
58B2 **Crater Lake Nat Pk** USA
73K5 **Crateús** Brazil
73L5 **Crato** Brazil
60C2 **Crawford** USA
64B2 **Crawfordsville** USA
67B2 **Crawfordville** USA
7D4 **Crawley** England
58D1 **Crazy Mts** USA
7C4 **Crediton** England
54H4 **Cree L** Canada
13B3 **Creil** France
16C1 **Cremona** Italy
13B3 **Crépy-en-Valois** France
16C2 **Cres** *I* Croatia
58B2 **Crescent** USA
56A2 **Crescent City** USA
61E2 **Cresco** USA
61E2 **Creston** USA
67A2 **Crestview** USA
34B3 **Creswick** Australia
61D2 **Crete** USA
17E3 **Crete** *I* Greece
17E3 **Crete,S of** Greece
15C1 **Creus, Cabo de** *C* Spain
14C2 **Creuse** *R* France
7C3 **Crewe** England
8C3 **Crianlarich** Scotland
7B3 **Criccieth** Wales
74G3 **Criciuma** Brazil
8D3 **Crieff** Scotland
21E6 **Crimea** *Pen* Ukraine
75C2 **Cristalina** Brazil
75B1 **Cristalina** *R* Brazil
75C1 **Crixás** Brazil
75C1 **Crixás Acu** *R* Brazil
75B1 **Crixás Mirim** *R* Brazil
16D1 **Croatia** *Republic* Europe
63C2 **Crockett** USA
61D2 **Crofton** USA
32C2 **Croker I** Australia
8D3 **Cromarty** Scotland
7E3 **Cromer** England
35A3 **Cromwell** New Zealand
6D2 **Crook** England
57F4 **Crooked** *I* The Bahamas
56D2 **Crookston** USA
34C2 **Crookwell** Australia
34D1 **Croppa Creek** Australia
7C3 **Crosby** England
61E1 **Crosby** USA
47A1 **Cross,C** Namibia
57D3 **Crossett** USA
54E4 **Cross Sd** USA
67A1 **Crossville** USA
16D3 **Crotone** Italy
63D2 **Crowley** USA
66C2 **Crowley,L** USA
69K1 **Crown Pt** Tobago
34D1 **Crows Nest** Australia
32D2 **Croydon** Australia
7D4 **Croydon** England
36E6 **Crozet Basin** Indian Ocean
36D7 **Crozet, Îles** *Is* Indian Ocean
54F2 **Crozier Chan** Canada
74F3 **Cruz Alta** Brazil
69B3 **Cruz, Cabo** *C* Cuba
74D4 **Cruz del Eje** Argentina
75D3 **Cruzeiro** Brazil
72D5 **Cruzeiro do Sul** Brazil
34A2 **Crystal Brook** Australia
63D1 **Crystal City** Missouri, USA
62C3 **Crystal City** Texas, USA
64B1 **Crystal Falls** USA
51D5 **Cuamba** Mozambique
51C5 **Cuando** *R* Angola
51B5 **Cuangar** Angola
Cuango,R = Kwango,R
70B2 **Cuauhtémoc** Mexico
68A1 **Cuba** USA
70D2 **Cuba** *Republic* Caribbean Sea
51B5 **Cubango** *R* Angola
51B5 **Cuchi** Angola
51B5 **Cuchi** *R* Angola
7D4 **Cuckfield** England
72E3 **Cucuí** Brazil
72D2 **Cúcuta** Colombia
44B3 **Cuddalore** India
44B3 **Cuddapah** India
66D3 **Cuddeback L** USA
32A3 **Cue** Australia
72C4 **Cuenca** Ecuador
15B1 **Cuenca** Spain
70C3 **Cuernavaca** Mexico
63C3 **Cuero** USA
73G7 **Cuiabá** Brazil
75A1 **Cuiabá** *R* Brazil
75D2 **Cuieté** *R* Brazil
8B3 **Cuillin Hills** Scotland
51B4 **Cuilo** *R* Angola/Zaïre
51B5 **Cuito** *R* Angola
51B5 **Cuito Cuanavale** Angola
30D3 **Cu Lao Hon** *I* Vietnam
60C1 **Culbertson** Montana, USA
60C2 **Culbertson** Nebraska, USA
34C3 **Culcairn** Australia
34C1 **Culgoa** *R* Australia
70B2 **Culiacán** Mexico
67A2 **Cullman** USA
65D3 **Culpeper** USA
75B1 **Culuene** *R* Brazil
35B2 **Culverden** New Zealand
72F1 **Cumaná** Venezuela
57F3 **Cumberland** Maryland, USA
64A1 **Cumberland** Wisconsin, USA
57E3 **Cumberland** *R* USA
55M3 **Cumberland Pen** Canada
64C3 **Cumberland Plat** USA
55M3 **Cumberland Sd** Canada
8C4 **Cumbernauld** Scotland
6C2 **Cumbria** *County* England
59B3 **Cummings** USA
8C4 **Cumnock** Scotland
51B5 **Cunene** *R* Angola/Namibia
16B2 **Cuneo** Italy
32D3 **Cunnamulla** Australia
8D3 **Cupar** Scotland
17E2 **Čuprija** Serbia, Yugoslavia
69D4 **Curaçao** *I* Caribbean Sea
74B4 **Curicó** Chile
75B1 **Curisevo** *R* Brazil
74G3 **Curitiba** Brazil
34A2 **Curnamona** Australia
51B5 **Curoca** *R* Angola
73K7 **Curvelo** Brazil
68A2 **Curwensville** USA
63C1 **Cushing** USA
58E1 **Custer** Montana, USA
60C2 **Custer** S Dakota, USA
58D1 **Cut Bank** USA
67B2 **Cuthbert** USA
67B3 **Cutler Ridge** USA
43F4 **Cuttack** India
51B5 **Cuvelai** Angola
18B2 **Cuxhaven** Germany
64C2 **Cuyahoga Falls** USA
66C3 **Cuyama** *R* USA
72D6 **Cuzco** Peru
7C4 **Cwmbran** Wales
50C4 **Cyangugu** Zaïre
17E3 **Cyclades** *Is* Greece
40B3 **Cyprus** *Republic* Medit Sea
55M3 **Cyrus Field B** Canada
19C3 **Czech Republic** Europe
19D2 **Częstochowa** Poland

D

30C1 **Da** *R* Vietnam
26F2 **Da'an** China
45D3 **Dab'a** Jordan
45C3 **Dabab, Jebel ed** *Mt* Jordan
69C4 **Dabajuro** Venezuela
48B4 **Dabakala** Ivory Coast
50E3 **Dabaro** Somalia
31B3 **Daba Shan** *Mts* China
50D2 **Dabat** Ethiopia
42C4 **Dabhoi** India
31C3 **Dabie Shan** *U* China
48A3 **Dabola** Guinea
48B4 **Dabou** Ivory Coast
19D2 **Dabrowa Górn** Poland
Dacca = Dhākā
18C3 **Dachau** Germany
16C1 **Dachstein** *Mt* Austria
31A3 **Dada He** *R* China
67B3 **Dade City** USA
42B3 **Dadhar** Pakistan
42B3 **Dadu** Pakistan
26D3 **Dadu He** *R* China
27F5 **Daet** Philippines
31B4 **Dafang** China
30B2 **Daga** *R* Burma
48A3 **Dagana** Senegal
21H7 **Daghestan Republic** Russian Federation
27F5 **Dagupan** Philippines
43G3 **Dagzê** China
40B4 **Dahab** Egypt
25O5 **Da Hinggan Ling** *Mts* China
67B2 **Dahlonega** USA
42C4 **Dāhod** India
28A2 **Dahongqi** China
15C2 **Dahra** *Region* Algeria
21G8 **Dahuk** Iraq
28A2 **Dahushan** China
43E3 **Dailekh** Nepal
Dairen = Lüda
40B4 **Dairût** Egypt
26G4 **Daitō Is** Pacific Ocean
32C3 **Dajarra** Australia
48A3 **Dakar** Senegal
48A2 **Dakhla** Morocco
49E2 **Dakhla Oasis** Egypt
48C3 **Dakoro** Niger
61D2 **Dakota City** USA
17E2 **Dakovica** Serbia, Yugoslavia
17D1 **Dakovo** Croatia
20B3 **Dal** *R* Sweden
51C5 **Dala** Angola
48A3 **Dalaba** Guinea
31D1 **Dalai Nur** *L* China
26D2 **Dalandzadgad** Mongolia
30D3 **Da Lat** Vietnam
31A1 **Dalay** Mongolia
8D4 **Dalbeattie** Scotland
32E3 **Dalby** Australia
67A1 **Dale Hollow L** USA
12F7 **Dalen** Norway
6C2 **Dales,The** *Upland* England
67A2 **Daleville** USA
56C3 **Dalhart** USA
65F1 **Dalhousie** Canada
54E2 **Dalhousie,C** Canada
26D4 **Dali** China
31E2 **Dalian** China
8D4 **Dalkeith** Scotland
56D3 **Dallas** USA
58B1 **Dalles,The** USA
54E4 **Dall I** USA
43E4 **Dalli Rajhara** India
48C3 **Dallol** *Watercourse* Niger
8C3 **Dalmally** Scotland
16D2 **Dalmatia** *Region* Croatia
8C4 **Dalmellington** Scotland
26G2 **Dal'nerechensk** Russian Federation
48B4 **Daloa** Ivory Coast
31B4 **Dalou Shan** *Mts* China
8C4 **Dalry** Scotland
43E4 **Dāltenganj** India
6C2 **Dalton** England
67B2 **Dalton** Georgia, USA
68D1 **Dalton** Massachusetts, USA
55Q3 **Dalton, Kap** *C* Greenland

32C2 **Daly** *R* Australia
59B3 **Daly City** USA
32C2 **Daly Waters** Australia
42C4 **Damān** India
40B3 **Damanhûr** Egypt
32B1 **Damar** *I* Indonesia
50B3 **Damara** Central African Republic
32B1 **Damar, Kepulauan** *Is* Indonesia
40C3 **Damascus** Syria
68B3 **Damascus** USA
48D3 **Damaturu** Nigeria
41F2 **Damavand** Iran
51B4 **Damba** Angola
44C4 **Dambulla** Sri Lanka
41F2 **Damghan** Iran
Damietta = Dumyât
42D4 **Damoh** India
50E3 **Damot** Ethiopia
45C2 **Damour** Lebanon
32A3 **Dampier** Australia
45C3 **Danā** Jordan
66C2 **Dana,Mt** USA
48B4 **Danané** Liberia
30D2 **Da Nang** Vietnam
27C6 **Danau Toba** *L* Indonesia
27F7 **Danau Towuti** *L* Indonesia
31A3 **Danba** China
65E2 **Danbury** USA
68D1 **Danby** USA
43E3 **Dandeldhura** Nepal
44A2 **Dandeli** India
34C3 **Dandenong** Australia
28A2 **Dandong** China
47B3 **Danger Pt** *C* South Africa
50D2 **Dangila** Ethiopia
58D2 **Daniel** USA
55N4 **Daniel's Harbour** Canada
47C2 **Danielskuil** South Africa
55P3 **Dannebrogs Øy** *I* Greenland
35C2 **Dannevirke** New Zealand
68B1 **Dansville** USA
44C2 **Dantewāra** India
17F2 **Danube** *R* E Europe
57E2 **Danville** Illinois, USA
57E3 **Danville** Kentucky, USA
68B2 **Danville** Pennsylvania, USA
57F3 **Danville** Virginia, USA
Danzig = Gdańsk
31C4 **Dao Xian** China
31B4 **Daozhen** China
43H3 **Dapha Bum** *Mt* India
45B3 **Daphnae** *Hist Site* Egypt
26C3 **Da Qaidam** China
26F2 **Daqing** China
45D2 **Dar'a** Syria
40C3 **Dar'ā** Syria
41F4 **Dārāb** Iran
49D1 **Daraj** Libya
41F3 **Dārān** Iran
43F3 **Darbhanga** India
66C1 **Dardanelle** USA
63D1 **Dardanelle,L** USA
Dar-el-Beida = Casablanca
51D4 **Dar es Salaam** Tanzania
35B1 **Dargaville** New Zealand
67B2 **Darien** USA
69B5 **Darién, G of** Colombia/Panama
Darjeeling = Dārjiling
43F3 **Dārjiling** India
32D4 **Darling** *R* Australia
34C1 **Darling Downs** Australia
55L1 **Darling Pen** Canada
34B2 **Darlington** Australia
6D2 **Darlington** England
67C2 **Darlington** USA
18B3 **Darmstadt** Germany
49E1 **Darnah** Libya
34B2 **Darnick** Australia
54F3 **Darnley B** Canada
76G10 **Darnley,C** Antarctica
15B1 **Daroca** Spain
50C3 **Dar Rounga** *Region* Central African Republic
7C4 **Dart** *R* England
7C4 **Dartmoor** England
55M5 **Dartmouth** Canada
7C4 **Dartmouth** England
32D1 **Daru** Papua New Guinea
16D1 **Daruvar** Croatia
6C3 **Darwen** England
32C2 **Darwin** Australia
41F4 **Daryācheh-ye Bakhtegan** *L* Iran
41F4 **Daryācheh-ye Mahārlū** *L* Iran
41F3 **Daryācheh-ye Namak** *Salt Flat* Iran
21H8 **Daryācheh-ye Orūmīyeh** *L* Iran
41F4 **Daryācheh-ye Tashk** *L* Iran
41G4 **Dārzīn** Iran
41F4 **Dās** *I* UAE
31C3 **Dashennongjia** *Mt* China
41G2 **Dasht** Iran
41F3 **Dasht-e-Kavir** *Salt Desert* Iran
41G3 **Dasht-e Lut** *Salt Desert* Iran
29D2 **Date** Japan
42D3 **Datia** India
31A2 **Datong** China
31C1 **Datong** China
31A2 **Datong He** *R* China
27D6 **Datuk, Tanjung** *C* Indonesia
19E1 **Daugava** *R* Latvia
20D4 **Daugavpils** Latvia
55M1 **Dauguard Jensen Land** *Region* Canada
42A1 **Daulatabad** Afghanistan
42B2 **Daulat Yar** Afghanistan
42D3 **Daulpur** India
13D2 **Daun** Germany
44A2 **Daund** India
54H4 **Dauphin** Canada
68B2 **Dauphin** USA
14D3 **Dauphiné** *Region* France
63E2 **Dauphin I** USA
48C3 **Daura** Nigeria
42D3 **Dausa** India
44B3 **Dāvangere** India
27F6 **Davao** Philippines
27F6 **Davao G** Philippines
66A2 **Davenport** California, USA
57D2 **Davenport** Iowa, USA
7D3 **Daventry** England
72B2 **David** Panama
54D3 **Davidson Mts** USA
59B3 **Davis** USA
76G10 **Davis** *Base* Antarctica
55M4 **Davis Inlet** Canada
55N3 **Davis Str** Canada/Greenland
20K5 **Davlekanovo** Russian Federation
28A2 **Dawa** China
50E3 **Dawa** *R* Ethiopia
31A4 **Dawan** China
41F4 **Dawḩat Salwah** *B* Qatar/Saudi Arabia
30B2 **Dawna Range** *Mts* Burma/Thailand
54E3 **Dawson** Canada
67B2 **Dawson** Georgia, USA
60D1 **Dawson** N Dakota, USA
32D3 **Dawson** *R* Australia
54F4 **Dawson Creek** Canada
31A3 **Dawu** China
31C3 **Dawu** China
14B3 **Dax** France
31B3 **Daxian** China
31B5 **Daxin** China
31A3 **Daxue Shan** *Mts* China
31C4 **Dayong** China
45D2 **Dayr 'Alī** Syria
45D1 **Dayr 'Aṭīyah** Syria
40D2 **Dayr az Zawr** Syria
45D1 **Dayr Shumayyil** Syria
57E2 **Dayton** Ohio, USA
67A1 **Dayton** Tennessee, USA
63D3 **Dayton** Texas, USA
58C1 **Dayton** Washington, USA
57E4 **Daytona Beach** USA
31C4 **Dayu** China
31D2 **Da Yunhe** *R* China
58C2 **Dayville** USA
31B3 **Dazhu** China
47C3 **De Aar** South Africa
69C2 **Deadman's Cay** The Bahamas
40C3 **Dead S** Israel/Jordan
60C2 **Deadwood** USA
7E4 **Deal** England
47D2 **Dealesville** South Africa
64C2 **Dearborn** USA
54F3 **Dease Arm** *B* Canada
54E4 **Dease Lake** Canada
56B3 **Death V** USA
66D2 **Death Valley Nat Mon** USA
14C2 **Deauville** France
69L1 **Débé** Trinidad
19E2 **Dębica** Poland
19E2 **Dęblin** Poland
48B3 **Débo,L** Mali
50D3 **Debre Birhan** Ethiopia
19E3 **Debrecen** Hungary
50D2 **Debre Mark'os** Ethiopia
50D2 **Debre Tabor** Ethiopia
57E3 **Decatur** Alabama, USA
67B2 **Decatur** Georgia, USA
57E3 **Decatur** Illinois, USA
64C2 **Decatur** Indiana, USA
14C3 **Decazeville** France
65D1 **Decelles, Réservoir** Canada
47C1 **Deception** *R* Botswana
31A4 **Dechang** China
61E2 **Decorah** USA
48B3 **Dedougou** Burkina
51D5 **Dedza** Malawi
8C4 **Dee** *R* Dumfries and Galloway, Scotland
7C3 **Dee** *R* England/Wales
8D3 **Dee** *R* Grampian, Scotland
65D1 **Deep River** Canada
68D2 **Deep River** USA
66D2 **Deep Springs** USA
34D1 **Deepwater** Australia
55N5 **Deer Lake** Canada
56B2 **Deer Lodge** USA
58C2 **Deeth** USA
67A2 **De Funiak Springs** USA
26C3 **Dêgê** China
50E3 **Degeh Bur** Ethiopia
32A3 **De Grey** *R* Australia
50E2 **Dehalak Arch** *Is* Eritrea
41F3 **Deh Bīd** Iran
42B1 **Dehi** Afghanistan
48D1 **Dehibat** Tunisia
44B4 **Dehiwala-Mt Lavinia** Sri Lanka
41E3 **Dehlorān** Iran
42D2 **Dehra Dūn** India
43E4 **Dehri** India
50C3 **Deim Zubeir** Sudan
45C2 **Deir Abu Sa'id** Jordan
45D1 **Deir el Ahmar** Lebanon
21C6 **Dej** Romania
64B2 **De Kalb** Illinois, USA
63D2 **De Kalb** Texas, USA
25Q4 **De Kastri** Russian Federation
50C4 **Dekese** Zaïre
50B3 **Dekoa** Central African Republic
56B3 **Delano** USA
59D3 **Delano Peak** *Mt* USA
47D2 **Delareyville** South Africa
64C2 **Delaware** USA
65D2 **Delaware** *R* USA
57F3 **Delaware** *State* USA
57F3 **Delaware B** USA
34C3 **Delegate** Australia
13C1 **Delft** Netherlands
13D1 **Delfzijl** Netherlands
51E5 **Delgado, C** Mozambique
62B1 **Delhi** Colorado, USA
42D3 **Delhi** India
65E2 **Delhi** New York, USA
40B1 **Delice** Turkey
70B2 **Delicias** Mexico
41F3 **Delījān** Iran
61D2 **Dell Rapids** USA
15C2 **Dellys** Algeria
66D4 **Del Mar** USA
12F8 **Delmenhorst** Germany
25R2 **De-Longa, Ostrova** *Is* Russian Federation
54B3 **De Long Mts** USA
34C4 **Deloraine** Australia
54H5 **Deloraine** Canada
67B3 **Delray Beach** USA
56C4 **Del Rio** USA
56B3 **Delta** USA
68C1 **Delta Res** USA
50D3 **Dembī Dolo** Ethiopia
13C2 **Demer** *R* Belgium
19G1 **Demidov** Russian Federation
62A2 **Deming** USA
17F2 **Demirköy** Turkey
63E2 **Demopolis** USA
24H4 **Dem'yanskoye** Russian Federation
14C1 **Denain** France
39E2 **Denau** Uzbekistan
7C3 **Denbigh** Wales
13C2 **Dendermond** Belgium
50D3 **Dendi** *Mt* Ethiopia
13B2 **Dèndre** *R* Belgium
31B1 **Dengkou** China
31C3 **Deng Xian** China
Den Haag = The Hague
69H1 **Denham,Mt** Jamaica
18A2 **Den Helder** Netherlands
15C2 **Denia** Spain
32D4 **Deniliquin** Australia
58C2 **Denio** USA
61D2 **Denison** Iowa, USA
56D3 **Denison** Texas, USA
21D8 **Denizli** Turkey
12F7 **Denmark** *Kingdom* Europe
76C1 **Denmark Str** Greenland/Iceland
69P2 **Dennery** St Lucia
8D2 **Dennis Head** *Pt* Scotland
27E7 **Denpasar** Indonesia
68C3 **Denton** Maryland, USA
56D3 **Denton** Texas, USA
32E1 **D'Entrecasteaux Is** Papua New Guinea
56C3 **Denver** USA
50B3 **Déo** *R* Cameroon
48D4 **Déo** *R* Cameroon/Nigeria
43F4 **Deoghar** India
42C5 **Deolāli** India
43M2 **Deoria** *District* India
42D1 **Deosai Plain** India
68A1 **Depew** USA
68C1 **Deposit** USA
25P3 **Deputatskiy** Russian Federation
63D2 **De Queen** USA
42B3 **Dera Bugti** Pakistan
42C3 **Dera Ghazi Khan** Pakistan
42C2 **Dera Ismail Khan** Pakistan
21H7 **Derbent** Russian Federation
32B2 **Derby** Australia
68D2 **Derby** Connecticut, USA
7D3 **Derby** England
63C1 **Derby** Kansas, USA
7D3 **Derby** *County* England
21F5 **Dergachi** Ukraine
10B3 **Derg, Lough** *L* Irish Republic
63D2 **De Ridder** USA
Derna = Darnah
9C3 **Derravaragh, L** Irish Republic
50E3 **Derri** Somalia
68E1 **Derry** USA
50D2 **Derudeb** Sudan
47C3 **De Rust** South Africa
68C1 **De Ruyter** USA
6D3 **Derwent** *R* England
34C4 **Derwent Bridge** Australia
72E7 **Desaguadero** *R* Bolivia
59C4 **Descanso** Mexico
58B2 **Deschutes** *R* USA
50D2 **Desē** Ethiopia
74C7 **Deseado** Argentina
74C7 **Deseado** *R* Argentina
48A1 **Deserta Grande** *I* Madeira
59C4 **Desert Center** USA
59D2 **Desert Peak** *Mt* USA
63D1 **Desloge** USA
57D2 **Des Moines** Iowa, USA
62B1 **Des Moines** New Mexico, USA
61E2 **Des Moines** *R* USA
21E5 **Desna** *R* Russian Federation
74B8 **Desolación** *I* Chile
64B2 **Des Plaines** USA
18C2 **Dessau** Germany
54E3 **Destruction Bay** Canada
17E1 **Deta** Romania
51C5 **Dete** Zimbabwe
13E2 **Detmold** Germany
57E2 **Detroit** USA
61D1 **Detroit Lakes** USA
30D3 **Det Udom** Thailand
17E1 **Deva** Romania
18B2 **Deventer** Netherlands
8D3 **Deveron** *R* Scotland
42C3 **Devikot** India
66C2 **Devil Postpile Nat Mon** USA
66C3 **Devils Den** USA
66C1 **Devils Gate** *P* USA
6E1 **Devil's Hole** *Region* N Sea
Devil's Island = Diable, Isla du
60D1 **Devils L** N Dakota, USA
62B3 **Devils L** Texas, USA
56D2 **Devils Lake** USA
7D4 **Devizes** England
42D3 **Devli** India
17E2 **Devoll** *R* Albania
7B4 **Devon** *County* England
55J2 **Devon I** Canada
32D5 **Devonport** Australia
43G3 **Dewangiri** Bhutan
42D4 **Dewās** India
47D2 **Dewetsdorp** South Africa
57E3 **Dewey Res** USA
63D2 **De Witt** USA
6D3 **Dewsbury** England
63E1 **Dexter** Missouri, USA
62B2 **Dexter** New Mexico, USA
31A3 **Deyang** China
41G3 **Deyhuk** Iran
41E3 **Dezfūl** Iran
31D2 **Dezhou** China
41E2 **Dezh Shāhpūr** Iran
45D3 **Dhab'i, Wadi edh** Jordan
41F4 **Dhahran** Saudi Arabia
43G4 **Dhākā** Bangladesh
45B1 **Dhali** Cyprus
44B3 **Dhamavaram** India
43E4 **Dhamtari** India
43F4 **Dhanbād** India
43E3 **Dhangarhi** Nepal
43M1 **Dhang Range** *Mts* Nepal
43F3 **Dhankuta** Nepal
42D4 **Dhār** India
44B3 **Dharmapuri** India
42D2 **Dharmsāla** India
48B3 **Dhar Oualata** *Desert Region* Mauritius
43E3 **Dhaulagiri** *Mt* Nepal
43F4 **Dhenkānāl** India
45C3 **Dhībān** Jordan
17F3 **Dhíkti Óri** *Mt* Greece
Dhodhekánisos = Dodecanese
17E3 **Dhomokós** Greece
44B2 **Dhone** India
42C4 **Dhoraji** India
42C4 **Dhrāngadhra** India
43F3 **Dhuburi** India
42C4 **Dhule** India
73H2 **Diable, Isle du** French Guiana
66B2 **Diablo,Mt** USA
59B3 **Diablo Range** *Mts* USA
73K7 **Diamantina** Brazil
32D3 **Diamantina** *R* Australia
75A1 **Diamantino** Brazil
43F4 **Diamond Harbour** India
66B1 **Diamond Springs** USA
58D2 **Diamondville** USA
41G4 **Dibā** UAE
51C4 **Dibaya** Zaïre
43G3 **Dibrugarh** India
62B2 **Dickens** USA
56C2 **Dickinson** USA
67A1 **Dickson** USA
65D2 **Dickson City** USA
21G8 **Dicle** *R* Turkey
42C3 **Dīdwāna** India
47E2 **Die Berg** *Mt* South Africa
48B3 **Diébougou** Burkina
13E3 **Dieburg** Germany
74C9 **Diego Ramírez, Islas** Chile
Diégo Suarez = Antsirañana
13D3 **Diekirch** Luxembourg
48B3 **Diéma** Mali
30C1 **Dien Bien Phu** Vietnam
18B2 **Diepholz** Germany
14C2 **Dieppe** France
13C2 **Diest** Belgium
13D3 **Dieuze** France
48D3 **Diffa** Niger
43H3 **Digboi** India
55M5 **Digby** Canada
14D3 **Digne-les-B.** France
14C2 **Digoin** France
27F6 **Digos** Philippines
32C1 **Digul** *R* Indonesia
43G3 **Dihang** *R* China/India
Dijlah = Tigris
14C2 **Dijon** France
50B3 **Dik** Chad
50E2 **Dikhil** Djibouti
45A3 **Dîkirnis** Egypt
13B2 **Diksmuide** Belgium
24K2 **Dikson** Russian Federation
38E2 **Dilaram** Afghanistan
27F7 **Dili** Indonesia
30D3 **Di Linh** Vietnam
13E2 **Dillenburg** Germany
62C3 **Dilley** USA
50C2 **Dilling** Sudan
54C4 **Dillingham** USA
56B2 **Dillon** USA
68B2 **Dillsburg** USA
51C5 **Dilolo** Zaïre
43G3 **Dimāpur** India
Dimashq = Damascus
50C4 **Dimbelenge** Zaïre
48B4 **Dimbokro** Ivory Coast
17F2 **Dimitrovgrad** Bulgaria
20H5 **Dimitrovgrad** Russian Federation
45C3 **Dīmona** Israel
27F5 **Dinaget** *I* Philippines
43F3 **Dinajpur** India
14B2 **Dinan** France
13C2 **Dinant** Belgium
40B2 **Dinar** Turkey
50D2 **Dinder** *R* Sudan
44B3 **Dindigul** India
31B2 **Dingbian** China
43F3 **Dinggyê** China
10A3 **Dingle** Irish Republic
10A3 **Dingle B** Irish Republic
48A3 **Dinguiraye** Guinea
8C3 **Dingwall** Scotland
31A2 **Dingxi** China
31D2 **Ding Xian** China
30D1 **Dinh Lap** Vietnam
60B2 **Dinosaur** USA
66C2 **Dinuba** USA
48A3 **Diouloulou** Senegal
43G3 **Diphu** India
50E3 **Dirē Dawa** Ethiopia
32A3 **Dirk Hartog** *I* Australia
50B2 **Dirkou** Niger
34C1 **Dirranbandi** Australia
74J8 **Disappointment,C** South Georgia
58B1 **Disappointment,C** USA
32B3 **Disappointment,L** Australia
34B3 **Discovery B** Australia
27E5 **Discovery Reef** S China Sea
52J7 **Discovery Tablemount** Atlantic Ocean
40B4 **Dishna** Egypt
55N3 **Disko** *I* Greenland
55N3 **Disko Bugt** *B* Greenland
55N3 **Diskofjord** Greenland
65D3 **Dismal Swamp** USA
19F1 **Disna** *R* Belarus
67B3 **Disney World** USA
75C2 **Distrito Federal** Brazil
42C4 **Diu** India
73K8 **Divinópolis** Brazil
21G6 **Divnoye** Russian Federation
40C2 **Divriği** Turkey
66B1 **Dixon** California, USA
64B2 **Dixon** Illinois, USA
58D1 **Dixon** Montana, USA
54E4 **Dixon Entrance** *Sd* Canada/USA
41E3 **Diyālā** *R* Iraq

21G8 **Diyarbakır** Turkey
41E3 **Diz** *R* Iran
50B3 **Dja** *R* Cameroon
50B1 **Djado,Plat du** Niger
50B4 **Djambala** Congo
48C2 **Djanet** Algeria
48C1 **Djedi** *Watercourse* Algeria
48C1 **Djelfa** Algeria
50C3 **Djéma** Central African Republic
48B3 **Djenné** Mali
48B3 **Djibo** Burkina
50E2 **Djibouti** Djibouti
50E2 **Djibouti** *Republic* E Africa
50C3 **Djolu** Zaïre
48C4 **Djougou** Benin
50B2 **Djourab, Erg du** *Desert Region* Chad
50D3 **Djugu** Zaïre
12C2 **Djúpivogur** Iceland
15C2 **Djurdjura** *Mts* Algeria
25P2 **Dmitriya Lapteva, Proliv** *Str* Russian Federation
20F4 **Dmitrov** Russian Federation
Dnepr *R* Ukraine = **Dnieper**
21E6 **Dneprodzerzhinsk** Ukraine
21F6 **Dnepropetrovsk** Ukraine
20D5 **Dneprovskaya Nizmennost'** *Region* Belarus
21C6 **Dnestr** *R* Ukraine = **Dniester**
21E6 **Dnieper** *R* Ukraine
21C6 **Dniester** *R* Ukraine
20E4 **Dno** Russian Federation
50B3 **Doba** Chad
19E1 **Dobele** Latvia
32C1 **Dobo** Indonesia
17D2 **Doboj** Bosnia-Herzegovina
17F2 **Dobrich** Bulgaria
21E5 **Dobrush** Belarus
73K7 **Doce** *R* Brazil
74D2 **Doctor P P Peña** Paraguay
44B3 **Dod** India
44B3 **Doda Betta** *Mt* India
17F3 **Dodecanese** *Is* Greece
56C3 **Dodge City** USA
64A2 **Dodgeville** USA
50D4 **Dodoma** Tanzania
64B1 **Dog L** Canada
64C1 **Dog L** Canada
29B3 **Dōgo** *I* Japan
48C3 **Dogondoutchi** Niger
41D2 **Doğubayazit** Turkey
41F4 **Doha** Qatar
43G3 **Doilungdêqên** China
13D1 **Dokkum** Netherlands
29F2 **Dokuchayevo, Mys** *C* Russian Federation
32C1 **Dolak** *I* Indonesia
61D2 **Doland** USA
55L5 **Dolbeau** Canada
14D2 **Dole** France
7C3 **Dolgellau** Wales
68C1 **Dolgeville** USA
20K2 **Dolgiy, Ostrov** *I* Russian Federation
50E3 **Dolo Odo** Ethiopia
74E5 **Dolores** Argentina
60B3 **Dolores** *R* USA
54G3 **Dolphin and Union Str** Canada
74E8 **Dolphin,C** Falkland Islands
27G7 **Dom** *Mt* Indonesia
21K5 **Dombarovskiy** Russian Federation
12F6 **Dombås** Norway
13D3 **Dombasle-sur-Meurthe** France
17D1 **Dombóvár** Hungary
14B2 **Domfront** France
69E3 **Dominica** *I* Caribbean Sea
69C3 **Dominican Republic** Caribbean Sea
55L3 **Dominion,C** Canada
55N4 **Domino** Canada
26E1 **Domna** Russian Federation
16B1 **Domodossola** Italy
74B5 **Domuyo, Vol** Argentina
34D1 **Domville,Mt** Australia
8D3 **Don** *R* Scotland
21G6 **Don** *R* Russian Federation
9C2 **Donaghadee** Northern Ireland
Donau *R* Bulgaria = **Danube**
Donau *R* Austria/Germany = **Danube**
13E4 **Donaueschingen** Germany
18C3 **Donauwörth** Germany
15A2 **Don Benito** Spain
7D3 **Doncaster** England
51B4 **Dondo** Angola
51D5 **Dondo** Mozambique
44C4 **Dondra Head** *C* Sri Lanka
10B3 **Donegal** Irish Republic
9C2 **Donegal** *County* Irish Republic
10B3 **Donegal B** Irish Republic
9C2 **Donegal Mts** Irish Republic
9B3 **Donegal Pt** Irish Republic
21F6 **Donetsk** Ukraine
31C4 **Dong'an** China
32A3 **Dongara** Australia
31A4 **Dongchuan** China
30D2 **Dongfang** China
28B2 **Dongfeng** China
32A1 **Donggala** Indonesia
26C3 **Donggi Cona** *L* China
28A3 **Donggou** China
31C5 **Donghai Dao** *I* China
31A1 **Dong He** *R* China
30D2 **Dong Hoi** Vietnam
31C5 **Dong Jiang** *R* China
28A2 **Dongliao He** *R* China
28C2 **Dongning** China
50D2 **Dongola** Sudan
31D5 **Dongshan** China
26E4 **Dongsha Qundao** *I* China
31C2 **Dongsheng** China
31E3 **Dongtai** China
31C4 **Dongting Hu** *L* China
31B5 **Dongxing** China
31D3 **Dongzhi** China
63D1 **Doniphan** USA
16D2 **Donji Vakuf** Bosnia-Herzegovina
12G5 **Dönna** *I* Norway
59B3 **Donner P** USA
13D3 **Donnersberg** *Mt* Germany
47D2 **Donnybrook** South Africa
Donostia = San Sebastián
66B2 **Don Pedro Res** USA
8C4 **Doon, Loch** *L* Scotland
31A3 **Do Qu** *R* China
14D2 **Dorbirn** Austria
7C4 **Dorchester** England
55L3 **Dorchester,C** Canada
14C2 **Dordogne** *R* France
18A2 **Dordrecht** Netherlands
47D3 **Dordrecht** South Africa
68D1 **Dorest Peak** *Mt* USA
48B3 **Dori** Burkina
47B3 **Doring** *R* South Africa
7D4 **Dorking** England
13B3 **Dormans** France
18B3 **Dornbirn** Austria
8C3 **Dornoch** Scotland
8D3 **Dornoch Firth** *Estuary* Scotland
12H6 **Dorotea** Sweden
34D2 **Dorrigo** Australia
58B2 **Dorris** USA
7C4 **Dorset** *County* England
55L3 **Dorset, Cape** Canada
13D2 **Dorsten** Germany
18B2 **Dortmund** Germany
50C3 **Doruma** Zaïre
25N4 **Dosatuy** Russian Federation
42B1 **Doshi** Afghanistan
66B2 **Dos Palos** USA
48C3 **Dosso** Niger
24G5 **Dossor** Kazakhstan
57E3 **Dothan** USA
14C1 **Douai** France
50A3 **Douala** Cameroon
34D1 **Double Island Pt** Australia
62B2 **Double Mountain Fork** *R* USA
66C3 **Double Mt** USA
14D2 **Doubs** *R* France
35A3 **Doubtful Sd** New Zealand
48B3 **Douentza** Mali
56C3 **Douglas** Arizona, USA
67B2 **Douglas** Georgia, USA
6B2 **Douglas** Isle of Man, British Islands
47C2 **Douglas** South Africa
56C2 **Douglas** Wyoming, USA
67B1 **Douglas L** USA
13C2 **Doulevant-le-Château** France
13B2 **Doullens** France
75B2 **Dourada, Serra** *Mts* Brazil
75C1 **Dourada, Serra** *Mts* Brazil
73H8 **Dourados** Brazil
75B3 **Dourados** *R* Brazil
75B3 **Dourados, Serra dos** *Mts* Brazil
13B3 **Dourdan** France
15A1 **Douro** *R* Portugal
7D3 **Dove** *R* England
62A1 **Dove Creek** USA
65D3 **Dover** Delaware, USA
7E4 **Dover** England
65E2 **Dover** New Hampshire, USA
68C2 **Dover** New Jersey, USA
64C2 **Dover** Ohio, USA
7E4 **Dover,Str of** England/France
19G2 **Dovsk** Belarus
9C2 **Down** *County* Northern Ireland
68C3 **Downingtown** USA
9D2 **Downpatrick** Northern Ireland
68C1 **Downsville** USA
68C2 **Doylestown** USA
28B3 **Dōzen** *I* Japan
65D1 **Dozois, Réservoir** Canada
48A2 **Dr'aa** *Watercourse* Morocco
75B3 **Dracena** Brazil
13D1 **Drachten** Netherlands
68E1 **Dracut** USA
14D3 **Draguignan** France
60C1 **Drake** USA
51D6 **Drakensberg** *Mts* South Africa
47D2 **Drakensberg** *Mt* South Africa
52E7 **Drake Passage** Atlantic O/Pacific Ocean
17E2 **Dráma** Greece
12G7 **Drammen** Norway
12A1 **Drangajökull** *Ice cap* Iceland
16D1 **Drava** *R* Slovenia
13D1 **Drenthe** *Province* Netherlands
18C2 **Dresden** Germany
14C2 **Dreux** France
58C2 **Drewsey** USA
68A2 **Driftwood** USA
17E2 **Drin** *R* Albania
17D2 **Drina** *R* Bosnia-Herzegovina/Serbia, Yugoslavia
19F1 **Drissa** *R* Belarus
9C3 **Drogheda** Irish Republic
19E3 **Drogobych** Ukraine
9C3 **Droihead Nua** Irish Republic
7C3 **Droitwich** England
9C2 **Dromore** Northern Ireland
76F12 **Dronning Maud Land** *Region* Antarctica
54G4 **Drumheller** Canada
58D1 **Drummond** USA
64C1 **Drummond I** USA
65E1 **Drummondville** Canada
8C3 **Drumochter Pass** Scotland
19E2 **Druskininkai** Lithuania
25Q3 **Druzhina** Russian Federation
61E1 **Dryberry L** Canada
55J5 **Dryden** Canada
68B1 **Dryden** USA
69H1 **Dry Harbour Mts** Jamaica
30B3 **Duang** *I* Burma
40C4 **Dubā** Saudi Arabia
41G4 **Dubai** UAE
54H3 **Dubawnt** *R* Canada
54H3 **Dubawnt L** Canada
32D4 **Dubbo** Australia
9C3 **Dublin** Irish Republic
67B2 **Dublin** USA
9C3 **Dublin** *County* Irish Republic
20F4 **Dubna** Russian Federation
21D5 **Dubno** Ukraine
58D2 **Dubois** Idaho, USA
65D2 **Du Bois** USA
58E2 **Dubois** Wyoming, USA
19F3 **Dubossary** Moldavia
19F2 **Dubrovica** Ukraine
17D2 **Dubrovnik** Croatia
57D2 **Dubuque** USA
59D2 **Duchesne** USA
67A1 **Duck** *R* USA
66C3 **Ducor** USA
13D3 **Dudelange** Luxembourg
24K3 **Dudinka** Russian Federation
7C3 **Dudley** England
25L2 **Dudypta** *R* Russian Federation
48B4 **Duekoué** Ivory Coast
15B1 **Duero** *R* Spain
33F1 **Duff Is** Solomon Islands
8D3 **Dufftown** Scotland
16C2 **Dugi Otok** *I* Croatia
18B2 **Duisburg** Germany
47E1 **Duiwelskloof** South Africa
41E3 **Dūkan** Iraq
50D3 **Duk Faiwil** Sudan
41F4 **Dukhān** Qatar
31A4 **Dukou** China
26C3 **Dulan** China
70D4 **Dulce, Golfo** Costa Rica
43G4 **Dullabchara** India
13D2 **Dülmen** Germany
57D2 **Duluth** USA
7C4 **Dulverton** England
45D2 **Dūmā** Syria
27D6 **Dumai** Indonesia
56C3 **Dumas** USA
45D2 **Ḑumayr** Syria
8C4 **Dumbarton** Scotland
48B1 **Dumer Rbia** Morocco
8D4 **Dumfries** Scotland
8C4 **Dumfries and Galloway** *Region* Scotland
43F4 **Dumka** India
65D1 **Dumoine,L** Canada
76G8 **Dumont d'Urville** *Base* Antarctica
49F1 **Dumyat** Egypt
Dunărea *R* Romania = **Danube**
9C3 **Dunary Head** *Pt* Irish Republic
Dunav *R* Bulgaria = **Danube**
Dunav *R* Croatia/Serbia = **Danube**
28C2 **Dunay** Russian Federation
19F3 **Dunayevtsy** Ukraine
8D4 **Dunbar** Scotland
63C2 **Duncan** USA
68B2 **Duncannon** USA
44E3 **Duncan Pass** *Chan* Andaman Islands
8D2 **Duncansby Head** *Pt* Scotland
9C2 **Dundalk** Irish Republic
68B3 **Dundalk** USA
9C3 **Dundalk B** Irish Republic
55M2 **Dundas** Greenland
54G2 **Dundas Pen** Canada
27G8 **Dundas Str** Australia
47E2 **Dundee** South Africa
8D3 **Dundee** Scotland
68B1 **Dundee** USA
34B1 **Dundoo** Australia
9D2 **Dundrum B** Northern Ireland
43M2 **Dundwa Range** *Mts* Nepal
33G5 **Dunedin** New Zealand
67B3 **Dunedin** USA
34C2 **Dunedoo** Australia
8D3 **Dunfermline** Scotland
9C2 **Dungannon** Northern Ireland
42C4 **Dūngarpur** India
9C3 **Dungarvan** Irish Republic
7E4 **Dungeness** *Pen* England
34D2 **Dungog** Australia
50C3 **Dungu** Zaïre
50D1 **Dungunab** Sudan
28B2 **Dunhua** China
26C2 **Dunhuang** China
8D3 **Dunkeld** Scotland
Dunkerque = Dunkirk
13B2 **Dunkirk** France
57F2 **Dunkirk** USA
50D2 **Dunkur** Ethiopia
48B4 **Dunkwa** Ghana
10B3 **Dun Laoghaire** Irish Republic
9B4 **Dunmanus** Irish Republic
68C2 **Dunmore** USA
69B1 **Dunmore Town** The Bahamas
67C1 **Dunn** USA
8D2 **Dunnet Head** *Pt* Scotland
60C2 **Dunning** USA
8C4 **Dunoon** Scotland
8D4 **Duns** Scotland
60C1 **Dunseith** USA
58B2 **Dunsmuir** USA
35A2 **Dunstan Mts** New Zealand
13C3 **Dun-sur-Meuse** France
31D1 **Duolun** China
60C1 **Dupree** USA
64B3 **Du Quoin** USA
45C3 **Dura** Israel
14D3 **Durance** *R* France
64A2 **Durand** USA
70B2 **Durango** Mexico
15B1 **Durango** Spain
56C3 **Durango** USA
56D3 **Durant** USA
45D1 **Duraykīsh** Syria
74E4 **Durazno** Uruguay
47E2 **Durban** South Africa
13D2 **Duren** Germany
43E4 **Durg** India
43F4 **Durgapur** India
6D2 **Durham** England
57F3 **Durham** N Carolina, USA
68E1 **Durham** New Hampshire, USA
6D2 **Durham** *County* England
34B1 **Durham Downs** Australia
17D2 **Durmitor** *Mt* Montenegro, Yugoslavia
8C2 **Durness** Scotland
17D2 **Durrës** Albania
34B1 **Durrie** Australia
17F3 **Dursunbey** Turkey
35B2 **D'Urville I** New Zealand
41H2 **Dushak** Turkmenistan
31B4 **Dushan** China
39E2 **Dushanbe** Tajikistan
68B2 **Dushore** USA
35A3 **Dusky Sd** New Zealand
18B2 **Düsseldorf** Germany
59D3 **Dutton,Mt** USA
31B4 **Duyun** China
40B1 **Düzce** Turkey
20F2 **Dvinskaya Guba** *B* Russian Federation
42B4 **Dwārka** India
58C1 **Dworshak Res** USA
57E3 **Dyersburg** USA
7B3 **Dyfed** *County* Wales
21G7 **Dykh Tau** *Mt* Russian Federation
34B1 **Dynevor Downs** Australia
26C2 **Dzag** Mongolia
26E2 **Dzamīn Üüd** Mongolia
51E5 **Dzaoudzi** Mayotte, Indian Ocean
26C2 **Dzavhan Gol** *R* Mongolia
20G4 **Dzerzhinsk** Russian Federation
25O4 **Dzhalinda** Russian Federation
24J5 **Dzhambul** Kazakhstan
21E6 **Dzhankoy** Ukraine
24H5 **Dzhezkazgan** Kazakhstan
42B1 **Dzhilikul'** Tajikistan
25P4 **Dzhugdzhur, Khrebet** *Mts* Russian Federation
24J5 **Dzhungarskiy Alatau** *Mts* Kazakhstan
18D2 **Dzierzoniów** Poland
39G1 **Dzungaria Basin** China
25L5 **Dzüyl** Mongolia

E

55K4 **Eabamet L** Canada
60B3 **Eagle** Colorado, USA
60C1 **Eagle Butte** USA
58B2 **Eagle L** California, USA
65F1 **Eagle L** Maine, USA
65F1 **Eagle Lake** USA
63C2 **Eagle Mountain L** USA
56C4 **Eagle Pass** USA
62A2 **Eagle Peak** *Mt* USA
54E3 **Eagle Plain** Canada
59C3 **Earlimart** USA
8D3 **Earn** *R* Scotland
8C3 **Earn, Loch** *L* Scotland
59D4 **Earp** USA
62B2 **Earth** USA
6D2 **Easingwold** England
67B2 **Easley** USA
65D2 **East Aurora** USA
63E2 **East B** USA
7E4 **Eastbourne** England
68C1 **East Branch Delaware** *R* USA
33G4 **East C** New Zealand
64B2 **East Chicago** USA
26F3 **East China Sea** China/Japan
7E3 **East Dereham** England
37O6 **Easter I** Pacific Ocean
51C7 **Eastern Cape** *Province* South Africa
43E5 **Eastern Ghats** *Mts* India
51C6 **Eastern Transvaal** *Province* South Africa
74E8 **East Falkland** *Is* Falkland Islands
59C3 **Eastgate** USA
61D1 **East Grand Forks** USA
7D4 **East Grinstead** England
68D1 **Easthampton** USA
68D2 **East Hampton** USA
8C4 **East Kilbride** Scotland
64B2 **East Lake** USA
7D4 **Eastleigh** England
64C2 **East Liverpool** USA
47D3 **East London** South Africa
55L4 **Eastmain** Canada
55L4 **Eastmain** *R* Canada
67B2 **Eastman** USA
64A2 **East Moline** USA
65D3 **Easton** Maryland, USA
65D2 **Easton** Pennsylvania, USA
68C2 **East Orange** USA
37O5 **East Pacific Ridge** Pacific Ocean
37O4 **East Pacific Rise** Pacific Ocean
67B2 **East Point** USA
65F2 **Eastport** USA
7D3 **East Retford** England
67A1 **East Ridge** USA
57D3 **East St Louis** USA
25R2 **East Siberian S** Russian Federation
7E4 **East Sussex** *County* England
65D3 **Eastville** USA
66C1 **East Walker** *R* USA
67B2 **Eatonton** USA
61E2 **Eau Claire** USA
27H6 **Eauripik** *I* Pacific Ocean
7C4 **Ebbw Vale** Wales
50B3 **Ebebiyin** Equatorial Guinea
68A2 **Ebensburg** USA
13E3 **Eberbach** Germany
18C2 **Eberswalde** Germany
29D2 **Ebetsu** Japan
31A4 **Ebian** China
24K5 **Ebinur** *L* China

16D2 Eboli Italy
50B3 Ebolowa Cameroon
15B1 Ebro R Spain
40A1 Eceabat Turkey
15C2 Ech Cheliff Algeria
31D2 Eching China
58C1 Echo USA
54G3 Echo Bay Canada
13D3 Echternach Luxembourg
34B3 Echuca Australia
15A2 Ecija Spain
55K2 Eclipse Sd Canada
72C4 Ecuador Republic S America
50E2 Ed Eritrea
8D2 Eday I Scotland
50C2 Ed Da'ein Sudan
50D2 Ed Damer Sudan
50D2 Ed Debba Sudan
8C2 Eddrachillis B Scotland
50D2 Ed Dueim Sudan
34C4 Eddystone Pt Australia
13C1 Ede Netherlands
50A3 Edea Cameroon
34C3 Eden Australia
62C2 Eden Texas, USA
58E2 Eden Wyoming, USA
6C2 Eden R England
47D2 Edenburg South Africa
35A3 Edendale New Zealand
9C3 Edenderry Irish Republic
13D3 Edenkoben Germany
13E2 Eder R Germany
60D1 Edgeley USA
55M3 Edgell I Canada
60C2 Edgemont USA
24D2 Edgeøya I Svalbard, Norway
68B3 Edgewood USA
45C3 Edh Dhahiriya Israel
17E2 Edhessa Greece
62C3 Edinburg USA
8D3 Edinburgh Scotland
21D7 Edirne Turkey
66C3 Edison USA
67B2 Edisto R USA
58B1 Edmonds USA
54G4 Edmonton Canada
60D1 Edmore USA
55M5 Edmundston Canada
63C3 Edna USA
16C1 Edolo Italy
45C3 Edom Region Jordan
21D8 Edremit Turkey
17F3 Edremit Körfezi B Turkey
26C2 Edrengiyn Nuruu Mts Mongolia
54G4 Edson Canada
34B3 Edward R Australia
50C4 Edward,L Uganda/Zaïre
66D3 Edwards USA
56C3 Edwards Plat USA
64B3 Edwardsville USA
13B2 Eeklo Belgium
33F2 Efate I Vanuatu
57E3 Effingham USA
16C3 Egadi,I Sicily, Italy
59D3 Egan Range Mts USA
55N3 Egedesminde Greenland
54C4 Egegik USA
19E3 Eger Hungary
12F7 Egersund Norway
13E2 Eggegebirge Mts Germany
68C3 Egg Harbor City USA
54G2 Eglinton I Canada
35B1 Egmont,C New Zealand
35B1 Egmont,Mt New Zealand
6C2 Egremont England
40B2 Eğridir Gölü L Turkey
6D2 Egton England
75C1 Eguas R Brazil
25U3 Egvekinot Russian Federation
49E2 Egypt Republic Africa
15B1 Eibar Spain
34D1 Eidsvold Australia
13D2 Eifel Region Germany
8B3 Eigg I Scotland
39F5 Eight Degree Chan Indian Ocean
32B2 Eighty Mile Beach Australia
34C3 Eildon,L Australia
18B2 Eindhoven Netherlands
45C3 Ein Yahav Israel
18C2 Eisenach Germany
18C3 Eisenerz Austria
13D2 Eitorf Germany
31A1 Ejin qi China
60C1 Ekalaka USA
35C2 Eketahuna New Zealand
24J4 Ekibastuz Kazakhstan
25P4 Ekimchan Russian Federation
12H7 Eksjö Sweden
57E1 Ekwan R Canada
45A3 El Abbâsa Egypt
40A3 El'Alamein Egypt
47D2 Elands R South Africa
47C3 Elands Berg Mt South Africa
40B3 El'Arîsh Egypt
40B4 Elat Israel
50C2 El' Atrun Oasis Sudan
21F8 Elazığ Turkey
40C3 El Azraq Jordan
16C2 Elba I Italy
49F2 El Balyana Egypt
72D2 El Banco Colombia
17E2 Elbasan Albania
69D5 El Baúl Venezuela
18C2 Elbe R Germany
45D1 El Beqa'a R Lebanon
64B2 Elberta USA
56C3 Elbert,Mt USA
67B2 Elberton USA
14C2 Elbeuf France
40C2 Elbistan Turkey
19D2 Elblag Poland
74B6 El Bolsón Argentina
61D1 Elbow Lake USA
21G7 Elbrus Mt Russian Federation
Elburz Mts = Reshteh-ye Alborz
59C4 El Cajon USA
63C3 El Campo USA
59C4 El Centro USA
15B2 Elche Spain
74C5 El Chocón, Embalse Res Argentina
15B2 Elda Spain
25P3 El'dikan Russian Federation
72C3 El Diviso Colombia
48B2 El Djouf Desert Region Mauritius
63D1 Eldon USA
75B4 Eldorado Argentina
57D3 El Dorado Arkansas, USA
75C3 Eldorado Brazil
56D3 El Dorado Kansas, USA
70B2 El Dorado Mexico
62B2 Eldorado Texas, USA
72F2 El Dorado Venezuela
50D3 Eldoret Kenya
68A2 Eldred USA
45C1 Elea, C Cyprus
66C1 Eleanor,L USA
58D2 Electric Peak Mt USA
48B2 El Eglab Region Algeria
62A2 Elephant Butte Res USA
40D2 Eleşkirt Turkey
16B3 El Eulma Algeria
57F4 Eleuthera I The Bahamas
40B4 El Faiyûm Egypt
48B2 El Farsia Well Morocco
50C2 El Fasher Sudan
40B4 El Fashn Egypt
15A1 El Ferrol Spain
45B3 El Firdân Egypt
50C2 El Fula Sudan
48C1 El Gassi Algeria
50D2 El Geteina Sudan
50D2 El Gezîra Region Sudan
45C3 El Ghor V Israel/Jordan
57E2 Elgin Illinois, USA
60C1 Elgin N Dakota, USA
8D3 Elgin Scotland
40B3 El Gîza Egypt
48C1 El Golea Algeria
59D4 El Golfo de Santa Clara Mexico
50D3 Elgon,Mt Kenya/Uganda
50E3 El Goran Ethiopia
48B2 El Guettara Well Mali
48B2 El Hank Region Mauritius
48B2 El Haricha Desert Region Mali
40A4 El Harra Egypt
15C2 El Harrach Algeria
50D2 El Hawata Sudan
40B4 El'Igma Desert Region Egypt
Elisabethville = Lubumbashi
12K6 Elisenvaara Russian Federation
El Iskandarîya = Alexandria
21G6 Elista Russian Federation
32C4 Elizabeth Australia
65E2 Elizabeth USA
47B2 Elizabeth B Namibia
57F3 Elizabeth City USA
68E2 Elizabeth Is USA
67B1 Elizabethton Tennessee, USA
64B3 Elizabethtown Kentucky, USA
67C2 Elizabethtown N Carolina, USA
68B2 Elizabethtown Pennsylvania, USA
48B1 El Jadida Morocco
40C3 El Jafr Jordan
45D3 El Jafr L Jordan
50D2 El Jebelein Sudan
48D1 El Jem Tunisia
19E2 Ełk Poland
68C3 Elk R Maryland/Penn, USA
64C3 Elk R W Virginia, USA
61E2 Elkader USA
16B3 El Kala Algeria
50D2 El Kamlin Sudan
48C1 El Kef Tunisia
66B1 Elk Grove USA
El Khalil = Hebron Israel
45A3 El Khânka Egypt
40B4 El Khârga Egypt
40B4 El-Khârga Oasis Egypt
64B2 Elkhart USA
48B2 El Khenachich Desert Region Mali
61D2 Elkhorn R USA
17F2 Elkhovo Bulgaria
65D3 Elkins USA
68B2 Elkland USA
60B2 Elk Mt USA
58C1 Elko Canada
56B2 Elko USA
16B3 El Kroub Algeria
68C3 Elkton USA
45B3 El Kûbri Egypt
40B3 El Kuntilla Egypt
50C2 El Lagowa Sudan
54H2 Ellef Ringnes I Canada
60D1 Ellendale USA
59D3 Ellen,Mt USA
56A2 Ellensburg USA
68C2 Ellenville USA
55K2 Ellesmere I Canada
35B2 Ellesmere,L New Zealand
7C3 Ellesmere Port England
68B3 Ellicott City USA
47D3 Elliot South Africa
55K5 Elliot Lake Canada
58D2 Ellis USA
45C3 El Lisān Pen Jordan
47D1 Ellisras South Africa
65F2 Ellsworth USA
76F3 Ellsworth Land Region Antarctica
45A4 El Ma'âdi Egypt
49E1 El Maghra L Egypt
40B3 El Mahalla el Kubra Egypt
40B3 El Mansûra Egypt
45A3 El Manzala Egypt
45B3 El Matarîya Egypt
68C3 Elmer USA
48B3 El Mereié Desert Region Mali/Mauritius
16B3 El Milia Algeria
45C1 El Mîna Lebanon
40B4 El Minya Egypt
66B1 Elmira California, USA
57F2 Elmira New York, USA
59D4 El Mirage USA
62B3 El Moral Mexico
48B2 El Mreiti Well Mauritius
18B2 Elmshorn Germany
50C2 El Muglad Sudan
48B2 El Mzereb Well Mali
50D2 El Obeid Sudan
48C1 El Oued Algeria
59D4 Eloy USA
56C3 El Paso USA
59B3 El Portal USA
62A2 El Porvenir Mexico
15A2 El Puerto del Sta Maria Spain
El Qâhira = Cairo
45B3 El Qantara Egypt
El Quds = Jerusalem
45C3 El Quseima Egypt
45C4 El Quwetra Jordan
56D3 El Reno USA
54E3 Elsa Canada
45A4 El Saff Egypt
45B3 El Sâlhîya Egypt
70D3 El Salvador Republic Central America
59C4 El Sauzal Mexico
45B3 El Shallûfa Egypt
45B4 El Shatt Egypt
45A3 El Simbillâwein Egypt
66D4 Elsinore L USA
18C2 Elsterwerde Germany
62A3 El Sueco Mexico
El Suweis = Suez
45A4 El Tabbin Egypt
15A1 El Teleno Mt Spain
35B1 Eltham New Zealand
45C4 El Thamad Egypt
72F2 El Tigre Venezuela
40B4 El Tîh Desert Region Egypt
45B3 El Tîna Egypt
58C1 Eltopia USA
40B4 El Tûr Egypt
44C2 Elūru India
15A2 Elvas Portugal
72D5 Elvira Brazil
54H2 Elvira,C Canada
64B2 Elwood USA
7E3 Ely England
57D2 Ely Minnesota, USA
56B3 Ely Nevada, USA
64C2 Elyria USA
45A3 El Zarqa Egypt
41G2 Emāmrūd Iran
42B1 Emām Sāheb Afghanistan
18D1 Eman R Sweden
21K6 Emba Kazakhstan
21K6 Emba R Kazakhstan
Embalse de Ricobayo = Esla, Embalse
74D2 Embarcación Argentina
54G4 Embarras Portage Canada
50D4 Embu Kenya
18B2 Emden Germany
31A4 Emei China
32D3 Emerald Australia
54J5 Emerson Canada
58C2 Emigrant P USA
50B1 Emi Koussi Mt Chad
40B2 Emirdağ Turkey
68C2 Emmaus USA
18B2 Emmen Netherlands
13D3 Emmendingen Germany
13D2 Emmerich Germany
58C2 Emmett USA
68B3 Emmitsburg USA
56C4 Emory Peak Mt USA
70A2 Empalme Mexico
47E2 Empangeni South Africa
74E3 Empedrado Argentina
37K2 Emperor Seamount Chain Pacific Ocean
63C1 Emporia Kansas, USA
65D3 Emporia Virginia, USA
68A2 Emporium USA
18B2 Ems R Germany
28B2 Emu China
8C2 Enard B Scotland
74E3 Encarnación Paraguay
48B4 Enchi Ghana
62C3 Encinal USA
66D4 Encinitas USA
75D2 Encruzilhada Brazil
32B1 Endeh Indonesia
76G11 Enderby Land Region Antarctica
61D1 Enderlin USA
65D2 Endicott USA
54C3 Endicott Mts USA
16C3 Enfida Tunisia
67C1 Enfield USA
27F5 Engaño, C Philippines
29D2 Engaru Japan
45C3 En Gedi Israel
21H5 Engel's Russian Federation
27D7 Enggano I Indonesia
10C3 England UK
55N4 Englee Canada
67C1 Englehard USA
65D1 Englehart Canada
60C3 Englewood USA
10C3 English Channel England/France
63C1 Enid USA
29D2 Eniwa Japan
48B3 Enji Well Mauritius
13C1 Enkhuizen Netherlands
12H7 Enköping Sweden
16C3 Enna Sicily, Italy
50C2 En Nahud Sudan
50C2 Ennedi Desert Region Chad
9C3 Ennell, L Irish Republic
34C1 Enngonia Australia
60C2 Enning USA
10B3 Ennis Irish Republic
58D1 Ennis Montana, USA
63C2 Ennis Texas, USA
9C3 Enniscorthy Irish Republic
9C2 Enniskillen Northern Ireland
45C2 Enn Nâqoûra Lebanon
18C3 Enns R Austria
12F8 Enschede Netherlands
70A1 Ensenada Mexico
31B3 Enshi China
13D4 Ensisheim France
50D4 Entebbe Uganda
67A2 Enterprise Alabama, USA
58C1 Enterprise Oregon, USA
74E4 Entre Ríos State Argentina
48C4 Enugu Nigeria
13E3 Enz R Germany
29C3 Enzan Japan
14C2 Epernay France
40A2 Ephesus Turkey
59D3 Ephraim USA
68B2 Ephrata Pennsylvania, USA
58C1 Ephrata Washington, USA
33F2 Epi I Vanuatu
14D2 Épinal France
45B1 Episkopi Cyprus
45B1 Episkopi B Cyprus
7E4 Epping England
13E3 Eppingen Germany
7D4 Epsom England
47B1 Epukiro Namibia
41F3 Eqlid Iran
46D7 Equator
48C4 Equatorial Guinea Republic W Africa
68D1 Equinox Mt USA
68C2 Equinunk USA
13E3 Erbach Germany
13D3 Erbeskopf Mt Germany
41D2 Erciş Turkey
21F8 Erciyas Dağları Mt Turkey
28B2 Erdaobaihe China
28B2 Erdao Jiang R China
31C1 Erdene Mongolia
26D2 Erdenet Mongolia
50C2 Erdi Desert Region Chad
74F3 Erechim Brazil
40B1 Ereğli Turkey
40B2 Ereğli Turkey
26E2 Erenhot China
15B1 Eresma R Spain
13D2 Erft R Germany
18C2 Erfurt Germany
40C2 Ergani Turkey
48B2 Erg Chech Desert Region Algeria/Mali
48D3 Erg du Ténéré Desert Region Niger
40A1 Ergene R Turkey
48B2 Erg Iguidi Region Algeria/Mauritania
19F1 Ērgli Latvia
50B2 Erguig R Chad
25N4 Ergun' R China/Russian Federation
26E1 Ergun R China/Russian Federation
25O4 Ergun Zuoqi China
50D2 Eriba Sudan
8C2 Eriboll, Loch Inlet Scotland
8C3 Ericht, Loch L Scotland
57F2 Erie USA
57E2 Erie,L Canada/USA
29D2 Erimo-misaki C Japan
8B3 Eriskay I Scotland
50D2 Eritrea Republic Africa
13D2 Erkelenz Germany
18C3 Erlangen Germany
63D2 Erling,L USA
47D2 Ermelo South Africa
44B4 Ernākulam India
9C2 Erne, L Northern Ireland
44B3 Erode India
34B1 Eromanga Australia
47B1 Erongoberg Mt Namibia
48B1 Er Rachidia Morocco
50D2 Er Rahad Sudan
51D5 Errego Mozambique
10B2 Errigal Mt Irish Republic
10A3 Erris Head Pt Irish Republic
33F2 Erromanga I Vanuatu
50D2 Er Roseires Sudan
45C2 Er Rummān Jordan
61D1 Erskine USA
13D3 Erstein France
18C2 Erzgebirge Upland Germany
21F8 Erzincan Turkey
21G8 Erzurum Turkey
29D2 Esan-misaki C Japan
29D2 Esashi Japan
18B1 Esbjerg Denmark
59D3 Escalante USA
56C4 Escalón Mexico
57E2 Escanaba USA
70C3 Escárcega Mexico
13C3 Esch Luxembourg
59C4 Escondido USA
70B2 Escuinapa Mexico
70C3 Escuintla Guatemala
50B3 Eséka Cameroon
13D1 Esens Germany
14C3 Esera R Spain
15C1 Esera R Spain
41F3 Eşfahān Iran
47E2 Eshowe South Africa
45C3 Esh Sharā Upland Jordan
8D4 Esk R Scotland
35C1 Eskdale New Zealand
12C1 Eskifjörður Iceland
12H7 Eskilstuna Sweden
54E3 Eskimo Lakes Canada
55J3 Eskimo Point Canada
21E8 Eskişehir Turkey
15A1 Esla R Spain
15A1 Esla, Embalse del Res Spain
69B2 Esmeralda Cuba
74A7 Esmeralda I Chile
72C3 Esmeraldas Ecuador
14C3 Espalion France
64C1 Espanola Canada
62A1 Espanola USA
32B4 Esperance Australia
76G2 Esperanza Base Antarctica
15A2 Espichel, Cabo C Portugal
75D2 Espinhaço, Serra do Mts Brazil
75D2 Espírito Santo State Brazil
33F2 Espiritu Santo I Vanuatu
51D6 Espungabera Mozambique
74B6 Esquel Argentina
58B1 Esquimalt Canada
45D2 Es Samrā Jordan
48B1 Essaouira Morocco
18B2 Essen Germany
73G3 Essequibo R Guyana
7E4 Essex County England

64C2 **Essexville** USA
18B3 **Esslingen** Germany
13B3 **Essonne** *Department* France
13C3 **Essoyes** France
74D8 **Estados, Isla de los** Argentina
73L6 **Estância** Brazil
47D2 **Estcourt** South Africa
72A1 **Esteí** Nicaragua
13B3 **Esternay** France
66B3 **Estero B** USA
74D2 **Esteros** Paraguay
60B2 **Estes Park** USA
54H5 **Estevan** Canada
61E2 **Estherville** USA
67B2 **Estill** USA
13B3 **Estissac** France
20C4 **Estonia** *Republic* Europe
66B3 **Estrella** *R* USA
15A2 **Estremoz** Portugal
19D3 **Esztergom** Hungary
34A1 **Etadunna** Australia
55L2 **Etah** Canada
43K2 **Etah** India
13C3 **Etam** France
14C2 **Étampes** France
34A1 **Etamunbanie,L** Australia
42D3 **Etāwah** India
50D3 **Ethiopia** *Republic* Africa
8C3 **Etive, Loch** *Inlet* Scotland
16C3 **Etna** *Vol* Sicily, Italy
51B5 **Etosha Nat Pk** Namibia
51B5 **Etosha Pan** *Salt L* Namibia
67B2 **Etowah** *R* USA
13C3 **Ettelbruck** Luxembourg
33H3 **Eua** *I* Tonga
34C2 **Euabalong** Australia
17E3 **Euboea** *I* Greece
64C2 **Euclid** USA
34C3 **Eucumbene,L** Australia
34A2 **Eudunda** Australia
63C1 **Eufala L** USA
67A2 **Eufaula** USA
56A2 **Eugene** USA
70A2 **Eugenia, Punta** *Pt* Mexico
34C1 **Eulo** Australia
63D2 **Eunice** Louisiana, USA
62B2 **Eunice** New Mexico, USA
13D2 **Eupen** Germany
40D3 **Euphrates** *R* Iraq/Syria
63E2 **Eupora** USA
14C2 **Eure** *R* France
58B2 **Eureka** California, USA
55K1 **Eureka** Canada
58C1 **Eureka** Montana, USA
56B3 **Eureka** Nevada, USA
60D1 **Eureka** S Dakota, USA
59D3 **Eureka** Utah, USA
55K2 **Eureka Sd** Canada
66D2 **Eureka V** USA
34C3 **Euroa** Australia
34C1 **Eurombah** *R* Australia
51E6 **Europa** *I* Mozambique Channel
13C2 **Europoort** Netherlands
18B2 **Euskirchen** Germany
63E2 **Eutaw** USA
55K1 **Evans,C** Canada
55L4 **Evans,L** Canada
60B3 **Evans,Mt** Colorado, USA
58D1 **Evans,Mt** Montana, USA
55K3 **Evans Str** Canada
64B2 **Evanston** Illinois, USA
56B2 **Evanston** Wyoming, USA
57E3 **Evansville** Indiana, USA
60B2 **Evansville** Wyoming, USA
47D2 **Evaton** South Africa
32C4 **Everard,L** Australia
39G3 **Everest,Mt** China/Nepal
68A2 **Everett** Pennsylvania, USA
56A2 **Everett** Washington, USA
68D1 **Everett,Mt** USA
57E4 **Everglades,The** *Swamp* USA
67A2 **Evergreen** USA
7D3 **Evesham** England
50B3 **Evinayong** Equatorial Guinea
12F7 **Evje** Norway
15A2 **Évora** Portugal
14C2 **Evreux** France
Évvoia = Euboea
8C3 **Ewe, Loch** *Inlet* Scotland
50B4 **Ewo** Congo
66C1 **Excelsior Mt** USA
66C1 **Excelsior Mts** USA
61E3 **Excelsior Springs** USA
7C4 **Exe** *R* England
59C3 **Exeter** California, USA
7C4 **Exeter** England
65E2 **Exeter** New Hampshire, USA
7C4 **Exmoor** England
7C4 **Exmouth** England
15A2 **Extremadura** *Region* Spain
70E2 **Exuma Sd** The Bahamas
50D4 **Eyasi, L** Tanzania
8D4 **Eyemouth** Scotland
50E3 **Eyl** Somalia
32B4 **Eyre** Australia
32C3 **Eyre Creek** *R* Australia
32C3 **Eyre,L** Australia
32C4 **Eyre Pen** Australia
17F3 **Ezine** Turkey

F

54G3 **Faber L** Canada
12F7 **Fåborg** Denmark
16C2 **Fabriano** Italy
50B2 **Fachi** Niger
50C2 **Fada** Chad
48C3 **Fada N'Gourma** Burkina
25Q2 **Faddeyevskiy, Ostrov** *I* Russian Federation
16C2 **Faenza** Italy
55N3 **Færingehavn** Greenland
12D3 **Faeroes** *Is* N Atlantic Oc
50B3 **Fafa** *R* Central African Republic
50E3 **Fafan** *R* Ethiopia
17E1 **Făgăraş** Romania
13C2 **Fagnes** *Region* Belgium
48B3 **Faguibine,L** Mali
41G5 **Fahūd** Oman
48A1 **Faiol** *I* Azores
62A2 **Fairacres** USA
54D3 **Fairbanks** USA
64C3 **Fairborn** USA
56D2 **Fairbury** USA
68B3 **Fairfax** USA
59B3 **Fairfield** California, USA
68D2 **Fairfield** Connecticut, USA
58D2 **Fairfield** Idaho, USA
58D1 **Fairfield** Montana, USA
64C3 **Fairfield** Ohio, USA
9C2 **Fair Head** *Pt* Northern Ireland
10C2 **Fair Isle** *I* Scotland
35B2 **Fairlie** New Zealand
61E2 **Fairmont** Minnesota, USA
64C3 **Fairmont** W Virginia, USA
68B1 **Fairport** USA
62C1 **Fairview** USA
54E4 **Fairweather,Mt** USA
27H6 **Fais** *I* Pacific Ocean
42C2 **Faisalabad** Pakistan
60C1 **Faith** USA
8E1 **Faither,The** *Pen* Scotland
33H1 **Fakaofo** *I* Tokelau Islands
7E3 **Fakenham** England
32C1 **Fakfak** Indonesia
28A2 **Faku** China
43G4 **Falam** Burma
70C2 **Falcon Res** Mexico/USA
48A3 **Falémé** *R* Mali/Senegal/Guinea
62C3 **Falfurrias** USA
12G7 **Falkenberg** Sweden
8D4 **Falkirk** Scotland
74D8 **Falkland Is** *Dependency* S Atlantic
74E8 **Falkland Sd** Falkland Islands
12G7 **Falköping** Sweden
66D4 **Fallbrook** USA
56B3 **Fallon** USA
65E2 **Fall River** USA
60B2 **Fall River P** USA
61D2 **Falls City** USA
7B4 **Falmouth** England
69H1 **Falmouth** Jamaica
65E2 **Falmouth** Maine, USA
68E2 **Falmouth** Massachusetts, USA
7B4 **Falmouth Bay** England
47B3 **False B** South Africa
70A2 **Falso,C** Mexico
18C2 **Falster** *I* Denmark
17F1 **Fălticeni** Romania
12H6 **Falun** Sweden
40B2 **Famagusta** Cyprus
45B1 **Famagusta B** Cyprus
13C2 **Famenne** *Region* Belgium
66C3 **Famoso** USA
30B2 **Fang** Thailand
50D3 **Fangak** Sudan
31E5 **Fangliao** Taiwan
8C3 **Fannich, L** Scotland
16C2 **Fano** Italy
45A3 **Fâqûs** Egypt
76G3 **Faraday** *Base* Antarctica
50C3 **Faradje** Zaïre
51E6 **Farafangana** Madagascar
49E2 **Farafra Oasis** Egypt
38E2 **Farah** Afghanistan
27H5 **Farallon de Medinilla** *I* Pacific Ocean
26H4 **Farallon de Pajaros** *I* Marianas
48A3 **Faranah** Guinea
50E2 **Farasan Is** Saudi Arabia
27H6 **Faraulep** *I* Pacific Ocean
55J5 **Farbault** USA
7D4 **Fareham** England
55O4 **Farewell,C** Greenland
33G5 **Farewell,C** New Zealand
35B2 **Farewell Spit** *Pt* New Zealand
56D2 **Fargo** USA
45C2 **Fari'a** *R* Israel
57D2 **Faribault** USA
43F4 **Faridpur** Bangladesh
41G2 **Farīmān** Iran
45A3 **Fâriskûr** Egypt
65E2 **Farmington** Maine, USA
63D1 **Farmington** Missouri, USA
68E1 **Farmington** New Hampshire, USA
56C3 **Farmington** New Mexico, USA
58D2 **Farmington** Utah, USA
66B2 **Farmington Res** USA
6D2 **Farne Deep** N Sea
15A2 **Faro** Portugal
12H7 **Fårö** *I* Sweden
46K9 **Farquhar Is** Indian Ocean
8C3 **Farrar** *R* Scotland
64C2 **Farrell** USA
43K2 **Farrukhabad** *District* India
17E3 **Fársala** Greece
75B4 **Fartura, Serra de** *Mts* Brazil
62B2 **Farwell** USA
41F4 **Fasā** Iran
21D5 **Fastov** Ukraine
43K2 **Fatehgarh** India
43E3 **Fatehpur** India
73H7 **Fatima du Sul** Brazil
58C1 **Fauquier** Canada
47D2 **Fauresmith** South Africa
12H5 **Fauske** Norway
7E4 **Faversham** England
55K4 **Fawn** *R* Canada
12H6 **Fax** *R* Sweden
12A2 **Faxaflói** *B* Iceland
50B2 **Faya** Chad
63E2 **Fayette** USA
57D3 **Fayetteville** Arkansas, USA
57F3 **Fayetteville** N Carolina, USA
67A1 **Fayetteville** Tennessee, USA
45B3 **Fâyid** Egypt
41E4 **Faylakah** *I* Kuwait
42C2 **Fāzilka** India
48A2 **Fdérik** Mauritius
57F3 **Fear,C** USA
66B1 **Feather** *R* USA
59B3 **Feather Middle Fork** *R* USA
14C2 **Fécamp** France
18C2 **Fehmarn** *I* Germany
75D3 **Feia, Lagoa** Brazil
72D5 **Feijó** Brazil
31C5 **Feilai Xai Bei Jiang** *R* China
35C2 **Feilding** New Zealand
51D5 **Feira** Zambia
73L6 **Feira de Santan** Brazil
40C2 **Feke** Turkey
13D4 **Feldberg** *Mt* Germany
18B3 **Feldkirch** Austria
10D3 **Felixstowe** England
12G6 **Femund** *L* Norway
28A2 **Fengcheng** China
31B4 **Fengdu** China
31B3 **Fengjie** China
31D1 **Fengning** China
31B3 **Feng Xian** China
31C1 **Fengzhen** China
31C2 **Fen He** *R* China
51E5 **Fenoarivo Atsinanana** Madagascar
21F7 **Feodosiya** Ukraine
41G3 **Ferdow** Iran
13B3 **Fère-Champenoise** France
39F1 **Fergana** Uzbekistan
61D1 **Fergus Falls** USA
48B4 **Ferkessedougou** Ivory Coast
9C2 **Fermanagh** *County* Northern Ireland
67B2 **Fernandina Beach** USA
73M4 **Fernando de Noronha, Isla** Brazil
75B3 **Fernandópolis** Brazil
Fernando Poo *I* **=Bioko**
58B1 **Ferndale** USA
58C1 **Fernie** Canada
59C3 **Fernley** USA
16C2 **Ferrara** Italy
15B2 **Ferrat, Cap** *C* Algeria
72C5 **Ferreñafe** Peru
63D2 **Ferriday** USA
13B3 **Ferrières** France
48B1 **Fès** Morocco
63D1 **Festus** USA
17F2 **Feteşti** Romania
9C3 **Fethard** Irish Republic
40A2 **Fethiye** Turkey
21J7 **Fetisovo** Kazakhstan
8E1 **Fetlar** *I* Scotland
55L4 **Feuilles, Rivière aux** *R* Canada
24J6 **Feyzabad** Afghanistan
7C3 **Ffestiniog** Wales
51E6 **Fianarantsoa** Madagascar
50D3 **Fichē** Ethiopia
47D2 **Ficksburg** South Africa
45C3 **Fidan, Wadi** Jordan
17D2 **Fier** Albania
8D3 **Fife** *Region* Scotland
8D3 **Fife Ness** *Pen* Scotland
14C3 **Figeac** France
15A1 **Figueira da Foz** Portugal
Figueres = Figueras
15C1 **Figueras** Spain
48B1 **Figuig** Morocco
33G2 **Fiji** *Is* Pacific Ocean
15B2 **Filabres, Sierra de los** *Mts* Spain
73G8 **Filadelfia** Paraguay
6D2 **Filey** England
17E2 **Filiaşi** Romania
17E3 **Filiatrá** Greece
16C3 **Filicudi** *I* Italy
59C4 **Fillmore** California, USA
59D3 **Fillmore** Utah, USA
8C3 **Findhorn** *R* Scotland
57E2 **Findlay** USA
65D2 **Finger Lakes** USA
51D5 **Fingoè** Mozambique
21E8 **Finike** Turkey
15A1 **Finisterre, Cabo** *C* Spain
32C3 **Finke** *R* Australia
20C3 **Finland** *Republic* N Europe
12J7 **Finland,G of** N Europe
54F4 **Finlay** *R* Canada
54F4 **Finlay Forks** Canada
34C3 **Finley** Australia
9C2 **Finn** *R* Irish Republic
12H5 **Finnsnes** Norway
27H7 **Finschhafen** Papua New Guinea
12H7 **Finspång** Sweden
18C2 **Finsterwalde** Germany
9C2 **Fintona** Northern Ireland
35A3 **Fiordland Nat Pk** New Zealand
45C2 **Fiq** Syria
21F8 **Firat** *R* Turkey
66B2 **Firebaugh** USA
Firenze = Florence
42D3 **Firozābād** India
42C2 **Firozpur** India
8C4 **Firth of Clyde** *Estuary* Scotland
8D3 **Firth of Forth** *Estuary* Scotland
8B3 **Firth of Lorn** *Estuary* Scotland
10C2 **Firth of Tay** *Estuary* Scotland
41F4 **Firūzābād** Iran
47B2 **Fish** *R* Namibia
47C3 **Fish** *R* South Africa
66C2 **Fish Camp** USA
68D2 **Fishers I** USA
55K3 **Fisher Str** Canada
7B4 **Fishguard** Wales
55N3 **Fiskenæsset** Greenland
13B3 **Fismes** France
65E2 **Fitchburg** USA
8E2 **Fitful Head** *Pt* Scotland
67B2 **Fitzgerald** USA
32B2 **Fitzroy** *R* Australia
32B2 **Fitzroy Crossing** Australia
64C1 **Fitzwilliam I** Canada
Fiume = Rijeka
50C4 **Fizi** Zaïre
47D3 **Flagstaff** South Africa
56B3 **Flagstaff** USA
65E1 **Flagstaff L** USA
6D2 **Flamborough Head** *C* England
56C2 **Flaming Gorge Res** USA
27G7 **Flamingo, Teluk** *B* Indonesia
13B2 **Flandres, Plaine des** Belgium/France
8B2 **Flannan Isles** Scotland
56B2 **Flathead L** USA
63D1 **Flat River** USA
27H8 **Flattery,C** Australia
56A2 **Flattery,C** USA
6C3 **Fleetwood** England
12F7 **Flekkefjord** Norway
26H4 **Fleming Deep** Pacific Ocean
68C2 **Flemington** USA
18B2 **Flensburg** Germany
32C4 **Flinders** *I* Australia
32D5 **Flinders** *I* Australia
32D2 **Flinders** *R* Australia
32C4 **Flinders Range** *Mts* Australia
54H4 **Flin Flon** Canada
57E2 **Flint** USA
7C3 **Flint** Wales
57E3 **Flint** *R* USA
13B2 **Flixecourt** France
64A1 **Floodwood** USA
67A2 **Florala** USA
57E3 **Florence** Alabama, USA
59D4 **Florence** Arizona, USA
60B3 **Florence** Colorado, USA
16C2 **Florence** Italy
63C1 **Florence** Kansas, USA
58B2 **Florence** Oregon, USA
57F3 **Florence** S Carolina, USA
66C2 **Florence L** USA
72C3 **Florencia** Colombia
74C6 **Florentine Ameghino, Embalse** *Res* Argentina
13C3 **Florenville** Belgium
70D3 **Flores** Guatemala
48A1 **Flores** *I* Azores
32B1 **Flores** *I* Indonesia
27E7 **Flores S** Indonesia
73K5 **Floriano** Brazil
74G3 **Florianópolis** Brazil
74E4 **Florida** Uruguay
70D2 **Florida** *State* USA
67B3 **Florida B** USA
67B3 **Florida City** USA
33E1 **Florida Is** Solomon Islands
57E4 **Florida Keys** *Is* USA
57E4 **Florida,Strs of** USA
17E2 **Flórina** Greece
12F6 **Florø** Norway
62B2 **Floydada** USA
32D1 **Fly** *R* Papua New Guinea
17F1 **Focşani** Romania
16D2 **Foggia** Italy
48A4 **Fogo** *I* Cape Verde
14C3 **Foix** France
64C1 **Foleyet** Canada
55L3 **Foley I** Canada
16C2 **Foligno** Italy
7E4 **Folkestone** England
67B2 **Folkston** USA
16C2 **Follonica** Italy
66B1 **Folsom** USA
68C1 **Fonda** USA
54H4 **Fond-du-Lac** Canada
57E2 **Fond du Lac** USA
70D3 **Fonseca, G de** Honduras
14C2 **Fontainbleau** France
14B2 **Fontenay-le-Comte** France
17D1 **Fonyód** Hungary
Foochow = Fuzhou
54C3 **Foraker, Mt** USA
13D3 **Forbach** France
34C2 **Forbes** Australia
48C4 **Forcados** Nigeria
66C3 **Ford City** USA
12F6 **Førde** Norway
7D4 **Fordingbridge** England
34C1 **Fords Bridge** Australia
63D2 **Fordyce** USA
48A4 **Forécariah** Guinea
55P3 **Forel,Mt** Greenland
58D1 **Foremost** Canada
64C2 **Forest** Canada
63E2 **Forest** USA
61E2 **Forest City** Iowa, USA
68C2 **Forest City** Pennsylvania, USA
7C4 **Forest of Dean** England
67B2 **Forest Park** USA
66A1 **Forestville** USA
13B3 **Forêt d'Othe** France
8D3 **Forfar** Scotland
62B1 **Forgan** USA
58B1 **Forks** USA
16C2 **Forlì** Italy
7C3 **Formby** England
15C2 **Formentera** *I* Spain
15C1 **Formentor, Cabo** *C* Spain
16C2 **Formia** Italy
48A1 **Formigas** *I* Azores
Formosa = Taiwan
74E3 **Formosa** Argentina
73J7 **Formosa** Brazil
74D2 **Formosa** *State* Argentina
Formosa Channel = Taiwan Str
73G6 **Formosa, Serra** *Mts* Brazil
75C1 **Formoso** Brazil
75C1 **Formoso** *R* Brazil
8D3 **Forres** Scotland
32B4 **Forrest** Australia
57D3 **Forrest City** USA
32D2 **Forsayth** Australia
12J6 **Forssa** Finland
34D2 **Forster** Australia
63D1 **Forsyth** Missouri, USA
60B1 **Forsyth** Montana, USA
42C3 **Fort Abbas** Pakistan
55K4 **Fort Albany** Canada
73L4 **Fortaleza** Brazil
8C3 **Fort Augustus** Scotland
47D3 **Fort Beaufort** South Africa
58D1 **Fort Benton** USA
59B3 **Fort Bragg** USA
62C1 **Fort Cobb Res** USA
56C2 **Fort Collins** USA
65D1 **Fort Coulonge** Canada
62B2 **Fort Davis** USA
69E4 **Fort-de-France** Martinique
67A2 **Fort Deposit** USA

57D2 **Fort Dodge** USA
32A3 **Fortescue** *R* Australia
57D2 **Fort Frances** Canada
54F3 **Fort Franklin** Canada
54F3 **Fort Good Hope** Canada
34B1 **Fort Grey** Australia
8C3 **Forth** *R* Scotland
62A2 **Fort Hancock** USA
55K4 **Fort Hope** Canada
8F3 **Forties** *Oilfield* N Sea
65F1 **Fort Kent** USA
48C1 **Fort Lallemand** Algeria
Fort Lamy = Ndjamena
60C2 **Fort Laramie** USA
57E4 **Fort Lauderdale** USA
54F3 **Fort Liard** Canada
54G4 **Fort Mackay** Canada
54G5 **Fort Macleod** Canada
54G4 **Fort McMurray** Canada
54E3 **Fort McPherson** Canada
64A2 **Fort Madison** USA
56C2 **Fort Morgan** USA
57E4 **Fort Myers** USA
54F4 **Fort Nelson** Canada
54F3 **Fort Norman** Canada
67A2 **Fort Payne** USA
60B1 **Fort Peck** USA
56C2 **Fort Peck Res** USA
57E4 **Fort Pierce** USA
60C2 **Fort Pierre** USA
68C1 **Fort Plain** USA
54G3 **Fort Providence** Canada
54G3 **Fort Resolution** Canada
50B4 **Fort Rousset** Congo
54F4 **Fort St James** Canada
54F4 **Fort St John** Canada
63D1 **Fort Scott** USA
54E3 **Fort Selkirk** Canada
55K4 **Fort Severn** Canada
21J7 **Fort Shevchenko** Kazakhstan
54F3 **Fort Simpson** Canada
54G3 **Fort Smith** Canada
57D3 **Fort Smith** USA
54F3 **Fort Smith** *Region* Canada
56C3 **Fort Stockton** USA
62B2 **Fort Sumner** USA
62C1 **Fort Supply** USA
58B2 **Fortuna** California, USA
60C1 **Fortuna** N Dakota, USA
54G4 **Fort Vermilion** Canada
67A2 **Fort Walton Beach** USA
57E2 **Fort Wayne** USA
8C3 **Fort William** Scotland
62A1 **Fort Wingate** USA
56D3 **Fort Worth** USA
54D3 **Fort Yukon** USA
31C5 **Foshan** China
55K2 **Fosheim Pen** Canada
61D1 **Fosston** USA
50B4 **Fougamou** Gabon
14B2 **Fougères** France
8D1 **Foula** *I* Scotland
7E4 **Foulness I** England
35B2 **Foulwind,C** New Zealand
50B3 **Foumban** Cameroon
48B2 **Foum el Alba** *Region* Mali
14C1 **Fourmies** France
17F3 **Foúrnoi** *I* Greece
48A3 **Fouta Djallon** *Mts* Guinea
33F5 **Foveaux Str** New Zealand
7B4 **Fowey** England
62B1 **Fowler** USA
64B2 **Fox** *R* USA
55K3 **Foxe Basin** *G* Canada
55K3 **Foxe Chan** Canada
55L3 **Foxe Pen** Canada
60B2 **Foxpark** USA
35C2 **Foxton** New Zealand
10B2 **Foyle, Lough** *Estuary* Irish Republic/Northern Ireland
51B5 **Foz do Cuene** Angola
74F3 **Foz do Iguaçu** Brazil
68B2 **Frackville** USA
15C1 **Fraga** Spain
68E1 **Framingham** USA
73J8 **Franca** Brazil
14C2 **France** *Republic* Europe
14D2 **Franche Comté** *Region* France
47D1 **Francistown** Botswana
58E2 **Francs Peak** *Mt* USA
13E2 **Frankenberg** Germany
64B2 **Frankfort** Indiana, USA
57E3 **Frankfort** Kentucky, USA
68C1 **Frankfort** New York, USA
47D2 **Frankfort** South Africa
18B2 **Frankfurt am Main** Germany
18C2 **Frankfurt an-der-Oder** Germany
18C3 **Fränkischer Alb** *Upland* Germany
58D2 **Franklin** Idaho, USA
64B3 **Franklin** Indiana, USA
63D3 **Franklin** Louisiana, USA
68E1 **Franklin** Massachusetts, USA
67B1 **Franklin** N Carolina, USA
68E1 **Franklin** New Hampshire, USA
68C2 **Franklin** New Jersey, USA
65D2 **Franklin** Pennsylvania, USA
67A1 **Franklin** Tennessee, USA
65D3 **Franklin** Virginia, USA
54F2 **Franklin B** Canada
58C1 **Franklin D Roosevelt** *L* USA
54F3 **Franklin Mts** Canada
54J2 **Franklin Str** Canada
68A1 **Franklinville** USA
35B2 **Franz Josef Glacier** New Zealand
Franz-Josef-Land = Zemlya Frantsa Josifa
54F5 **Fraser** *R* Canada
47C3 **Fraserburg** South Africa
8D3 **Fraserburgh** Scotland
34D1 **Fraser I** Australia
68C3 **Frederica** USA
18B1 **Fredericia** Denmark
65D3 **Frederick** Maryland, USA
62C2 **Frederick** Oklahoma, USA
62C2 **Fredericksburg** Texas, USA
65D3 **Fredericksburg** Virginia, USA
64A3 **Fredericktown** USA
55M5 **Fredericton** Canada
55N3 **Frederikshåp** Greenland
12G7 **Frederikshavn** Denmark
65D2 **Fredonia** USA
12G7 **Fredrikstad** Norway
68C2 **Freehold** USA
66C1 **Freel Peak** *Mt* USA
61D2 **Freeman** USA
64B2 **Freeport** Illinois, USA
63C3 **Freeport** Texas, USA
69B1 **Freeport** The Bahamas
62C3 **Freer** USA
48A4 **Freetown** Sierra Leone
18B3 **Freiburg** Germany
13D3 **Freiburg im Breisgau** Germany
18C3 **Freistadt** Austria
32A4 **Fremantle** Australia
66B2 **Fremont** California, USA
61D2 **Fremont** Nebraska, USA
64C2 **Fremont** Ohio, USA
73H3 **French Guiana** *Dependency* S America
60B1 **Frenchman** *R* USA
34C4 **Frenchmans Cap** *Mt* Australia
37M5 **French Polynesia** *Is* Pacific Ocean
15C2 **Frenda** Algeria
70B2 **Fresnillo** Mexico
56B3 **Fresno** USA
66C2 **Fresno** *R* USA
58D1 **Fresno Res** USA
13E3 **Freudenstadt** Germany
13B2 **Frévent** France
34C4 **Freycinet Pen** Australia
48A3 **Fria** Guinea
66C2 **Friant** USA
66C2 **Friant Dam** USA
16B1 **Fribourg** Switzerland
13E2 **Friedberg** Germany
18B3 **Friedrichshafen** Germany
13C1 **Friesland** *Province* Netherlands
62C3 **Frio** *R* USA
75D3 **Frio, Cabo** *C* Brazil
62B2 **Friona** USA
55M3 **Frobisher B** Canada
55M3 **Frobisher Bay** Canada
54H4 **Frobisher L** Canada
21G6 **Frolovo** Russian Federation
7C4 **Frome** England
7C4 **Frome** *R* England
32C4 **Frome,L** Australia
63D1 **Frontenac** USA
70C3 **Frontera** Mexico
65D3 **Front Royal** USA
16C2 **Frosinone** Italy
60B3 **Fruita** USA
31C5 **Fuchuan** China
31E4 **Fuding** China
70B2 **Fuerte** *R* Mexico
75A3 **Fuerte Olimpo** Brazil
74E2 **Fuerte Olimpo** Paraguay
48A2 **Fuerteventura** *I* Canary Islands
31C2 **Fugu** China
26B2 **Fuhai** China
41G4 **Fujairah** UAE
29C3 **Fuji** Japan
31D4 **Fujian** *Province* China
26G2 **Fujin** China
29C3 **Fujinomiya** Japan
29D3 **Fuji-san** *Mt* Japan
29C3 **Fujisawa** Japan
29C3 **Fuji-Yoshida** Japan
29D2 **Fukagawa** Japan
24K5 **Fukang** China
29D3 **Fukuchiyama** Japan
28A4 **Fukue** Japan
28A4 **Fukue** *I* Japan
29D3 **Fukui** Japan
28C4 **Fukuoka** Japan
29E3 **Fukushima** Japan
29C4 **Fukuyama** Japan
61D2 **Fulda** USA
18B2 **Fulda** Germany
18B2 **Fulda** *R* Germany
31B4 **Fuling** China
69L1 **Fullarton** Trinidad
66D4 **Fullerton** USA
6F1 **Fulmar** *Oilfield* N Sea
64A2 **Fulton** Illinois, USA
64B3 **Fulton** Kentucky, USA
65D2 **Fulton** New York, USA
13C2 **Fumay** France
29D3 **Funabashi** Japan
33G1 **Funafuti** *I* Tuvalu
48A1 **Funchal** Madeira
75D2 **Fundão** Brazil
55M5 **Fundy,B of** Canada
51D6 **Funhalouro** Mozambique
31B5 **Funing** China
31D3 **Funing** China
48C3 **Funtua** Nigeria
31D4 **Fuqing** China
51D5 **Furancungo** Mozambique
29D2 **Furano** Japan
41G4 **Fūrg** Iran
75B2 **Furnas, Serra das** *Mts* Brazil
32D5 **Furneaux Group** *Is* Australia
13D1 **Furstenau** Germany
18C2 **Fürstenwalde** Germany
18C3 **Fürth** Germany
29D2 **Furubira** Japan
29E3 **Furukawa** Japan
55K3 **Fury and Hecla Str** Canada
28A2 **Fushun** China
31A4 **Fushun** Sichuan, China
28B2 **Fusong** China
18C3 **Füssen** Germany
31E2 **Fu Xian** China
31E1 **Fuxin** China
31D3 **Fuyang** China
31E1 **Fuyuan** Liaoning, China
31A4 **Fuyuan** Yunnan, China
26B2 **Fuyun** China
31D4 **Fuzhou** China
28A3 **Fuzhoucheng** China
18C1 **Fyn** *I* Denmark
8C3 **Fyne, Loch** *Inlet* Scotland

G

50E3 **Gaalkacyo** Somalia
59C3 **Gabbs** USA
66C1 **Gabbs Valley Range** *Mts* USA
51B5 **Gabela** Angola
48D1 **Gabès, G de** Tunisia
66B2 **Gabilan Range** *Mts* USA
50B4 **Gabon** *Republic* Africa
47D1 **Gaborone** Botswana
15A1 **Gabriel y Galán, Embalse** *Res* Spain
17F2 **Gabrovo** Bulgaria
41F3 **Gach Sārān** Iran
44B2 **Gadag** India
67A2 **Gadsden** Alabama, USA
59D4 **Gadsden** Arizona, USA
16C2 **Gaeta** Italy
27H6 **Gaferut** *I* Pacific Ocean
67B1 **Gaffney** USA
45A3 **Gafra, Wadi el** Egypt
48C1 **Gafsa** Tunisia
20E4 **Gagarin** Russian Federation
55M4 **Gagnon** Canada
21G7 **Gagra** Georgia
43F3 **Gaibanda** Bangladesh
74C6 **Gaimán** Argentina
67B3 **Gainesville** Florida, USA
67B2 **Gainesville** Georgia, USA
63C2 **Gainesville** Texas, USA
7D3 **Gainsborough** England
32C4 **Gairdner, L** Australia
8C3 **Gairloch** Scotland
68B3 **Gaithersburg** USA
28A2 **Gai Xian** China
44B2 **Gajendragarh** India
31D4 **Ga Jiang** *R* China
47C2 **Gakarosa** *Mt* South Africa
50D4 **Galana** *R* Kenya
72N **Galapagos Is** Pacific Ocean
Gálápagos, Islas = Galapagos Islands
8D4 **Galashiels** Scotland
17F1 **Galaţi** Romania
64C3 **Galax** USA
62A2 **Galeana** Mexico
54C3 **Galena** Alaska, USA
64A2 **Galena** Illinois, USA
63D1 **Galena** Kansas, USA
69L1 **Galeota Pt** Trinidad
69L1 **Galera Pt** Trinidad
64A2 **Galesburg** USA
68B2 **Galeton** USA
20G4 **Galich** Russian Federation
15A1 **Galicia** *Region* Spain
Galilee,S of = Tiberias,L
69J1 **Galina Pt** Jamaica
50D2 **Gallabat** Sudan
67A1 **Gallatin** USA
58D1 **Gallatin** *R* USA
44C4 **Galle** Sri Lanka
62A3 **Gallego** Mexico
15B1 **Gállego** *R* Spain
72D1 **Gallinas, Puerta** Colombia
Gallipoli = Gelibolu
17D2 **Gallipoli** Italy
20C2 **Gällivare** Sweden
8C4 **Galloway** *District* Scotland
8C4 **Galloway,Mull of** *C* Scotland
62A1 **Gallup** USA
66B1 **Galt** USA
9B3 **Galty Mts** Irish Republic
70C2 **Galveston** USA
57D4 **Galveston B** USA
10B3 **Galway** Irish Republic
10B3 **Galway B** Irish Republic
43F3 **Gamba** China
48B3 **Gambaga** Ghana
54B3 **Gambell** USA
48A3 **Gambia** *R* Senegal/The Gambia
48A3 **Gambia,The** *Republic* Africa
37N6 **Gambier, Îles** Pacific Ocean
50B4 **Gamboma** Congo
51B5 **Gambos** Angola
44C4 **Gampola** Sri Lanka
59E3 **Ganado** USA
50E3 **Ganale Dorya** *R* Ethiopia
65D2 **Gananoque** Canada
Gand = Gent
51B5 **Ganda** Angola
51C4 **Gandajika** Zaïre
43N2 **Gandak** *R* India/Nepal
43M2 **Gandak Dam** Nepal
42B3 **Gandava** Pakistan
55N5 **Gander** Canada
42B4 **Gāndhīdhām** India
42C4 **Gāndhīnagar** India
42D4 **Gāndhi Sāgar** *L* India
15B2 **Gandia** Spain
75E1 **Gandu** Brazil
Ganga *R* **=Ganges**
42C3 **Gangānagar** India
43G4 **Gangaw** Burma
31A2 **Gangca** China
39G2 **Gangdise Shan** *Mts* China
22F4 **Ganges** *R* India
43F4 **Ganges, Mouths of the** Bangladesh/India
28B2 **Gangou** China
43F3 **Gangtok** India
31B3 **Gangu** China
58E2 **Gannett Peak** *Mt* USA
31B2 **Ganquan** China
12K8 **Gantsevichi** Belarus
31D4 **Ganzhou** China
48C3 **Gao** Mali
31A2 **Gaolan** China
31C2 **Gaoping** China
48B3 **Gaoua** Burkina
48A3 **Gaoual** Guinea
31D3 **Gaoyou Hu** *L* China
31C5 **Gaozhou** China
14D3 **Gap** France
42D2 **Gar** China
9C3 **Gara,L** Irish Republic
34C1 **Garah** Australia
73L5 **Garanhuns** Brazil
59B2 **Garberville** USA
75C3 **Garça** Brazil
15A2 **Garcia de Sola, Embalse de** *Res* Spain
75B3 **Garcias** Brazil
16C1 **Garda, L di** Italy
62B1 **Garden City** USA
64B1 **Garden Pen** USA
42B2 **Gardez** Afghanistan
58D1 **Gardiner** USA
68D2 **Gardiners I** USA
68E1 **Gardner** USA
33H1 **Gardner** *I* Phoenix Islands
66C1 **Gardnerville** USA
16D2 **Gargano, Monte** *Mt* Italy
16D2 **Gargano, Prom. del** Italy
42D4 **Garhākota** India
43K1 **Garhmuktesar** India
20L4 **Gari** Russian Federation
47B3 **Garies** South Africa
50D4 **Garissa** Kenya
63C2 **Garland** USA
18C3 **Garmisch-Partenkirchen** Germany
41F2 **Garmsar** Iran
63C1 **Garnett** USA
56B2 **Garnett Peak** *Mt* USA
14C3 **Garonne** *R* France
49D4 **Garoua** Cameroon
49D4 **Garoua Boulai** Cameroon
60C1 **Garrison** USA
9D2 **Garron** *Pt* Northern Ireland
8C3 **Garry** *R* Scotland
54H3 **Garry L** Canada
43E4 **Garwa** India
64B2 **Gary** USA
39G2 **Garyarsa** China
63C2 **Garza-Little Elm** *Res* USA
41F2 **Gasan Kuli** Turkmenistan
14B3 **Gascogne** *Region* France
63D1 **Gasconade** *R* USA
32A3 **Gascoyne** *R* Australia
50B3 **Gashaka** Nigeria
48D3 **Gashua** Nigeria
57G2 **Gaspé** Canada
57G2 **Gaspé,C de** Canada
57G2 **Gaspé, Peninsule de** Canada
67B1 **Gastonia** USA
67C1 **Gaston,L** USA
45B1 **Gata, C** Cyprus
15B2 **Gata, Cabo de** *C* Spain
20D4 **Gatchina** Russian Federation
8C4 **Gatehouse of Fleet** Scotland
6D2 **Gateshead** England
63C2 **Gatesville** USA
13B3 **Gâtinais** *Region* France
65D1 **Gatineau** Canada
65D1 **Gatineau** *R* Canada
67B1 **Gatlinburg** USA
34D1 **Gatton** Australia
33F2 **Gaua** *I* Vanuatu
43G3 **Gauhāti** India
19E1 **Gauja** *R* Latvia
43E3 **Gauri Phanta** India
17E4 **Gávdhos** *I* Greece
75D1 **Gavião** *R* Brazil
66B3 **Gaviota** USA
12H6 **Gävle** Sweden
32C4 **Gawler Ranges** *Mts* Australia
31A1 **Gaxun Nur** *L* China
43E4 **Gaya** India
48C3 **Gaya** Niger
48C3 **Gaya** Nigeria
28B2 **Gaya He** *R* China
64C1 **Gaylord** USA
34D1 **Gayndah** Australia
20J3 **Gayny** Russian Federation
19F3 **Gaysin** Ukraine
40B3 **Gaza** Israel
40C2 **Gaziantep** Turkey
48B4 **Gbaringa** Liberia
48D1 **Gbbès** Tunisia
19D2 **Gdańsk** Poland
19D2 **Gdańsk,G of** Poland
12K7 **Gdov** Russian Federation
19D2 **Gdynia** Poland
45A4 **Gebel el Galâla el Baharîya** *Desert* Egypt
50D2 **Gedaref** Sudan
17F3 **Gediz** *R* Turkey
18C2 **Gedser** Denmark
13C2 **Geel** Belgium
34B3 **Geelong** Australia
34C4 **Geeveston** Australia
48D3 **Geidam** Nigeria
13D2 **Geilenkirchen** Germany
50D4 **Geita** Tanzania
31A5 **Gejiu** China
16C3 **Gela** Italy
50E3 **Geladī** Ethiopia
13D2 **Geldern** Germany
17F2 **Gelibolu** Turkey
40B2 **Gelidonya Burun** Turkey
13E2 **Gelnhausen** Germany
13D2 **Gelsenkirchen** Germany
12F8 **Gelting** Germany
30C5 **Gemas** Malaysia
13C2 **Gembloux** Belgium
50B3 **Gemena** Zaïre
40C2 **Gemerek** Turkey
40A1 **Gemlik** Turkey
16C1 **Gemona** Italy
47C2 **Gemsbok Nat Pk** Botswana
50C2 **Geneina** Sudan
74C5 **General Alvear** Argentina
76F2 **General Belgrano** *Base* Antarctica
76G2 **General Bernardo O'Higgins** *Base* Antarctica
74B7 **General Carrera, Lago** Chile
74D2 **General Eugenio A Garay** Paraguay
66C2 **General Grant Grove Section** *Region* USA
74C3 **General Manuel Belgrano** *Mt* Argentina
74D5 **General Pico** Argentina
74C5 **General Roca** Argentina
27F6 **General Santos** Philippines
65D2 **Genesee** *R* USA
65D2 **Geneseo** USA
61D2 **Geneva** Nebraska, USA
68B1 **Geneva** New York, USA
16B1 **Geneva** Switzerland
Geneva,L of = Léman, L
Genève = Geneva
15B2 **Genil** *R* Spain
16B2 **Gennargentu, Monti del** *Mt* Sardinia, Italy

34C3 **Genoa** Australia
16B2 **Genoa** Italy
Genova = Genoa
16B2 **Genova, G di** Italy
13B2 **Gent** Belgium
27D7 **Genteng** Indonesia
18C2 **Genthin** Germany
21H7 **Geokchay** Azerbaijan
47C3 **George** South Africa
55M4 **George** *R* Canada
34C2 **George,L** Australia
67B3 **George,L** Florida, USA
65E2 **George,L** New York, USA
35A2 **George Sd** New Zealand
34C4 **George Town** Australia
66B1 **Georgetown** California, USA
65D3 **Georgetown** Delaware, USA
73G2 **Georgetown** Guyana
64C3 **Georgetown** Kentucky, USA
30C4 **George Town** Malaysia
69N2 **Georgetown** St Vincent
67C2 **Georgetown** S Carolina, USA
63C2 **Georgetown** Texas, USA
48A3 **Georgetown** The Gambia
76G8 **George V Land** *Region* Antarctica
62C3 **George West** USA
21G7 **Georgia** *Republic* Europe
76F12 **Georg Forster** *Base* Antarctica
67B2 **Georgia** *State* USA
64C1 **Georgian B** Canada
54F5 **Georgia, Str of** Canada
32C3 **Georgina** *R* Australia
21F5 **Georgiu-Dezh** Russian Federation
21G7 **Georgiyevsk** Russian Federation
76F1 **Georg von Neumayer** *Base* Antarctica
18C2 **Gera** Germany
13B2 **Geraardsbergen** Belgium
75C1 **Geral de Goiás, Serra** *Mts* Brazil
35B2 **Geraldine** New Zealand
75C2 **Geral do Paraná, Serra** *Mts* Brazil
32A3 **Geraldton** Australia
57E2 **Geraldton** Canada
75D2 **Geral, Serra** *Mts* Bahia, Brazil
75B4 **Geral, Serra** *Mts* Paraná, Brazil
45C3 **Gerar** *R* Israel
13D3 **Gérardmer** France
54C3 **Gerdine,Mt** USA
30C4 **Gerik** Malaysia
60C2 **Gering** USA
21C6 **Gerlachovsky** *Mt* Poland
47D2 **Germiston** South Africa
13D2 **Gerolstein** Germany
15C1 **Gerona** Spain
13E2 **Geseke** Germany
50E3 **Gestro** *R* Ethiopia
15B1 **Getafe** Spain
68B3 **Gettysburg** Pennsylvania, USA
60D1 **Gettysburg** S Dakota, USA
41D2 **Gevaş** Turkey
17E2 **Gevgeliija** Macedonia, Yugoslavia
45D2 **Ghabāghib** Syria
45D3 **Ghadaf, Wadi el** Jordan
48C1 **Ghadamis** Libya
41F2 **Ghaem Shahr** Iran
43E3 **Ghāghara** *R* India
48B4 **Ghana** *Republic* Africa
47C1 **Ghanzi** Botswana
48C1 **Ghardaïa** Algeria
49D1 **Gharyān** Libya
49D2 **Ghāt** Libya
15B2 **Ghazaouet** Algeria
42D3 **Ghāziābād** India
42B2 **Ghazni** Afghanistan
17F1 **Gheorgheni** Romania
40D3 **Ghudāf, Wadi al** *Watercourse* Iraq
16D3 **Giarre** Sicily, Italy
60D2 **Gibbon** USA
47B2 **Gibeon** Namibia
15A2 **Gibraltar** *Colony* SW Europe
7E7 **Gibraltar** *Pt* England
15A2 **Gibraltar,Str of** Africa/Spain
32B3 **Gibson Desert** Australia
58B1 **Gibsons** Canada
44B2 **Giddalūr** India
45B3 **Giddi, Gebel el** *Mt* Egypt
45B3 **Giddi Pass** Egypt
50D3 **Gīdolē** Ethiopia
13B4 **Gien** France
18B2 **Giessen** Germany
8D4 **Gifford** Scotland
67B3 **Gifford** USA
29D3 **Gifu** Japan
8C4 **Gigha** *I* Scotland
16C2 **Giglio** *I* Italy
15A1 **Gijón** Spain
59D4 **Gila** *R* USA
59D4 **Gila Bend** USA
59D4 **Gila Bend Mts** USA
32D2 **Gilbert** *R* Australia
33G1 **Gilbert Is** Pacific Ocean
58D1 **Gildford** USA
51D5 **Gilé** Mozambique
45C2 **Gilead** *Region* Jordan
49E2 **Gilf Kebir Plat** Egypt
34C2 **Gilgandra** Australia
42C1 **Gilgit** Pakistan
42C1 **Gilgit** *R* Pakistan
34C2 **Gilgunnia** Australia
55J4 **Gillam** Canada
60B2 **Gillette** USA
7E4 **Gillingham** England
64B1 **Gills Rock** USA
64B2 **Gilman** USA
66B2 **Gilroy** USA
69P2 **Gimie, Mont** St Lucia
45B3 **Gineifa** Egypt
47E2 **Gingindlovu** South Africa
50E3 **Gīnīr** Ethiopia
17E3 **Gióna** *Mt* Greece
34C3 **Gippsland** *Mts* Australia
64C2 **Girard** USA
72D3 **Girardot** Colombia
8D3 **Girdle Ness** *Pen* Scotland
40C1 **Giresun** Turkey
40B4 **Girga** Egypt
42C4 **Gīr Hills** India
50B3 **Giri** *R* Zaïre
43F4 **Girīdīh** India
42A2 **Girishk** Afghanistan
13D4 **Giromagny** France
Girona = Gerona
14B2 **Gironde** *R* France
8C4 **Girvan** Scotland
35C1 **Gisborne** New Zealand
50C4 **Gitega** Burundi
Giuba,R = Juba,R
17F2 **Giurgiu** Romania
13C2 **Givet** France
25S3 **Gizhiga** Russian Federation
19E2 **Gizycko** Poland
17E2 **Gjirokastër** Albania
54J3 **Gjoatlaven** Canada
12G6 **Gjøvik** Norway
55M5 **Glace Bay** Canada
58B1 **Glacier Peak** *Mt* USA
55K2 **Glacier Str** Canada
32E3 **Gladstone** Queensland, Australia
34A2 **Gladstone** S Aust, Australia
34C4 **Gladstone** Tasmania, Australia
64B1 **Gladstone** USA
12A1 **Gláma** *Mt* Iceland
12G6 **Glåma** *R* Norway
13D3 **Glan** *R* Germany
61D3 **Glasco** USA
64B3 **Glasgow** Kentucky, USA
60B1 **Glasgow** Montana, USA
8C4 **Glasgow** Scotland
68C3 **Glassboro** USA
66C2 **Glass Mt** USA
7C4 **Glastonbury** England
20J4 **Glazov** Russian Federation
18D3 **Gleisdorf** Austria
35C1 **Glen Afton** New Zealand
9D2 **Glenarm** Northern Ireland
68B3 **Glen Burnie** USA
47E2 **Glencoe** South Africa
59D4 **Glendale** Arizona, USA
66C3 **Glendale** California, USA
60C1 **Glendive** USA
60C2 **Glendo Res** USA
9C2 **Glengad Hd** *Pt* Irish Republic
34D1 **Glen Innes** Australia
8C4 **Glenluce** Scotland
34C1 **Glenmorgan** Australia
34D2 **Glenreagh** Australia
68B3 **Glen Rock** USA
63C2 **Glen Rose** USA
8D3 **Glenrothes** Scotland
68D1 **Glens Falls** USA
63D2 **Glenwood** Arkansas, USA
61D1 **Glenwood** Minnesota, USA
62A2 **Glenwood** New Mexico, USA
60B3 **Glenwood Springs** USA
64A1 **Glidden** USA
12F6 **Glittertind** *Mt* Norway
19D2 **Gliwice** Poland
59D4 **Globe** USA
18D2 **Głogów** Poland
12G5 **Glomfjord** Norway
51E5 **Glorieuses, Isles** Madagascar
7C3 **Glossop** England
34D2 **Gloucester** Australia
7C4 **Gloucester** England
68E1 **Gloucester** USA
7C4 **Gloucester** *County* England
68C1 **Gloversville** USA
19F1 **Glubokoye** Belarus
13E1 **Glückstadt** Germany
21E5 **Glukhov** Ukraine
18D3 **Gmünd** Austria
18C3 **Gmunden** Austria
19D2 **Gniezno** Poland
44A2 **Goa, Daman and Diu** *Union Territory* India
47B2 **Goageb** Namibia
43G3 **Goālpāra** India
50D3 **Goba** Ethiopia
47B1 **Gobabis** Namibia
31B1 **Gobi** *Desert* China/Mongolia
29C4 **Gobo** Japan
19G1 **Gobza** *R* Russian Federation
47B1 **Gochas** Namibia
7D4 **Godalming** England
44C2 **Godāvari** *R* India
66C2 **Goddard,Mt** USA
64C2 **Goderich** Canada
55N3 **Godhavn** Greenland
42C4 **Godhra** India
57D1 **Gods L** Canada
55N3 **Godthåb** Greenland
Godwin Austen *Mt* **=K2**
68E1 **Goffstown** USA
64C1 **Gogama** Canada
13E1 **Gohfeld** Germany
75C2 **Goiandira** Brazil
75C2 **Goianésia** Brazil
75C2 **Goiânia** Brazil
75B2 **Goiás** Brazil
73J6 **Goiás** *State* Brazil
75B3 **Goio-Erê** Brazil
50D3 **Gojab** *R* Ethiopia
17F2 **Gökçeada** *I* Turkey
17F3 **Gökova Körfezi** *B* Turkey
21F8 **Goksu** *R* Turkey
40C2 **Göksun** Turkey
43G3 **Golāghāt** India
9B2 **Gola, I** Irish Republic
40C2 **Gölbaşı** Turkey
24K2 **Gol'chikha** Russian Federation
58C2 **Golconda** USA
68B2 **Gold** USA
58B2 **Gold Beach** USA
34D1 **Gold Coast** Australia
35B2 **Golden B** New Zealand
58B1 **Goldendale** USA
66A2 **Golden Gate** *Chan* USA
63D3 **Golden Meadow** USA
59C3 **Goldfield** USA
66D2 **Gold Point** USA
67C1 **Goldsboro** USA
62C2 **Goldthwaite** USA
18C2 **Goleniów** Poland
66C3 **Goleta** USA
26C3 **Golmud** China
50E3 **Gololcha** Ethiopia
29F2 **Golovnino** Russian Federation
50C4 **Goma** Zaïre
43L2 **Gomati** India
48D3 **Gombe** Nigeria
19G2 **Gomel** Belarus
48A2 **Gomera** *I* Canary Islands
70B2 **Gómez Palacio** Mexico
25O4 **Gonam** *R* Russian Federation
69C3 **Gonâve, Isla de la** Cuba
41G2 **Gonbad-e Kāvūs** Iran
43E3 **Gonda** India
42C4 **Gondal** India
50D2 **Gonder** Ethiopia
43E4 **Gondia** India
40A1 **Gönen** Turkey
17F3 **Gonen** *R* Turkey
31A4 **Gongga Shan** *Mt* China
31A2 **Gonghe** China
75D1 **Gongogi** *R* Brazil
48D3 **Gongola** *R* Nigeria
66B2 **Gonzales** California, USA
63C3 **Gonzales** Texas, USA
47B3 **Good Hope,C of** South Africa
58D2 **Gooding** USA
60C3 **Goodland** USA
34C1 **Goodooga** *R* Australia
7D3 **Goole** England
34C2 **Goolgowi** Australia
34A3 **Goolwa** Australia
32A4 **Goomalling** Australia
34C2 **Goombalie** Australia
34D1 **Goomeri** Australia
34D1 **Goondiwindi** Australia
55N4 **Goose Bay** Canada
67C2 **Goose Creek** USA
58B2 **Goose L** USA
44B2 **Gooty** India
32D1 **Goraka** Papua New Guinea
43E3 **Gorakhpur** India
20K3 **Gora Koyp** *Mt* Russian Federation
25M4 **Gora Munku Sardyk** *Mt* Mongolia/Russian Federation
20K3 **Gora Narodnaya** *Mt* Russian Federation
20L2 **Gora Pay-Yer** *Mt* Russian Federation
20K3 **Gora Telpos-Iz** *Mt*
17D2 **Goražde** Bosnia-Herzegovina
54D2 **Gordon** USA
65D3 **Gordonsville** USA
50B3 **Goré** Chad
50D3 **Gorē** Ethiopia
35A3 **Gore** New Zealand
25P4 **Gore Topko** *Mt* Russian Federation
9C3 **Gorey** Irish Republic
41F2 **Gorgān** Iran
13C2 **Gorinchem** Netherlands
41E2 **Goris** Armenia
16C1 **Gorizia** Italy
19G2 **Gorki** Belarus
20M2 **Gorki** Russian Federation
Gorki = Novgorod
20G4 **Gor'kovskoye Vodokhranilishche** *Res* Russian Federation
7E3 **Gorleston** England
18C2 **Görlitz** Germany
21F6 **Gorlovka** Ukraine
66C3 **Gorman** USA
17F2 **Gorna Orjahovica** Bulgaria
26B1 **Gorno-Altaysk** Russian Federation
26H2 **Gornozavodsk** Russian Federation
20K3 **Goro Denezhkin Kamen'** *Mt* Russian Federation
20G4 **Gorodets** Russian Federation
19G2 **Gorodnya** Ukraine
19F1 **Gorodok** Belarus
19E3 **Gorodok** Ukraine
19F3 **Gorodok** Ukraine
27H7 **Goroka** Papua New Guinea
51D5 **Gorongosa** Mozambique
27F6 **Gorontalo** Indonesia
20L4 **Goro Yurma** *Mt* Russian Federation
75D2 **Gorutuba** *R* Brazil
25M4 **Goryachinsk** Russian Federation
21J7 **Gory Akkyr** *Upland* Turkmenistan
25L2 **Gory Byrranga** *Mts* Russian Federation
19F3 **Goryn'** *R* Ukraine
25L3 **Gory Putorana** *Mts* Russian Federation
19E2 **Góry Świętokrzyskie** *Upland* Poland
12H8 **Gorzów Wielkopolski** Poland
66C2 **Goshen** USA
29E2 **Goshogawara** Japan
16D2 **Gospić** Croatia
7D4 **Gosport** England
17E2 **Gostivar** Macedonia, Yugoslavia
19D2 **Gostynin** Poland
12G7 **Göteborg** Sweden
50B3 **Gotel Mts** Nigeria
60C2 **Gothenburg** USA
12H7 **Gotland** *I* Sweden
28B4 **Gotō-rettō** *Is* Japan
12H7 **Gotska Sandön** *I* Sweden
28C4 **Gōtsu** Japan
18B2 **Göttingen** Germany
28A2 **Goubangzi** China
13C2 **Gouda** Netherlands
50B2 **Goudoumaria** Niger
52H7 **Gough I** Atlantic Ocean
55L5 **Gouin, Réservoire** Canada
34C2 **Goulburn** Australia
48B3 **Goumbou** Mali
48B3 **Goundam** Mali
50B2 **Gouré** Niger
48B3 **Gourma Rharous** Mali
50B2 **Gouro** Chad
58E1 **Govenlock** Canada
27G8 **Gove Pen** Australia
21C6 **Goverla** *Mt* Ukraine
75D2 **Governador Valadares** Brazil
43E4 **Govind Ballabh Paht Sāgar** *L* India
42B3 **Gowārān** Afghanistan
7B4 **Gower** Wales
74E3 **Goya** Argentina
50C2 **Goz-Beïda** Chad
16C3 **Gozo** *I* Malta
50D2 **Goz Regeb** Sudan
47C3 **Graaff-Reinet** South Africa
65D1 **Gracefield** Canada
69A4 **Gracias à Dios, Cabo** Honduras
34D1 **Grafton** Australia
61D1 **Grafton** N Dakota, USA
64C3 **Grafton** W Virginia, USA
54E4 **Graham I** Canada
59E4 **Graham,Mt** USA
47D3 **Grahamstown** South Africa
73J5 **Grajaú** Brazil
19E2 **Grajewo** Poland
17E2 **Grámmos** *Mt* Albania/Greece
8C3 **Grampian** *Mts* Scotland
8D3 **Grampian** *Region* Scotland
72D3 **Granada** Colombia
72A1 **Granada** Nicaragua
15B2 **Granada** Spain
65E1 **Granby** Canada
60B2 **Granby** USA
48A2 **Gran Canaria** *I* Canary Islands
74D3 **Gran Chaco** *Region* Argentina
64B2 **Grand** *R* Michigan, USA
61E2 **Grand** *R* Missouri, USA
69Q2 **Grand B** Dominica
57F4 **Grand Bahama** *I* The Bahamas
13D4 **Grand Ballon** *Mt* France
55N5 **Grand Bank** Canada
52F2 **Grand Banks** Atlantic Ocean
48B4 **Grand Bassam** Ivory Coast
59D3 **Grand Canyon** USA
59D3 **Grand Canyon Nat Pk** USA
69A3 **Grand Cayman** *I* Cayman Is, Caribbean Sea
58C1 **Grand Coulee** USA
73K6 **Grande** *R* Bahia, Brazil
75C2 **Grande** *R* Minas Gerais/São Paulo, Brazil
55L4 **Grande 2, Rēservoir de la** Canada
55L4 **Grande 3, Rēservoir de la** Canada
55L4 **Grande 4, Rēservoir de la** Canada
74C8 **Grande, Bahía** *B* Argentina
51E5 **Grande Comore** *I* Comoros
75D3 **Grande, Ilha** Brazil
63C2 **Grande Prairie** USA
50B2 **Grand Erg de Bilma** *Desert Region* Niger
48C1 **Grand Erg Occidental** *Desert* Algeria
48C2 **Grand Erg Oriental** *Desert* Algeria
55L4 **Grande Rivière de la Baleine** *R* Canada
58C1 **Grande Ronde** *R* USA
59D4 **Gran Desierto** USA
55M5 **Grand Falls** New Brunswick, Canada
55N5 **Grand Falls** Newfoundland, Canada
58C1 **Grand Forks** Canada
61D1 **Grand Forks** USA
68C1 **Grand Gorge** USA
64B2 **Grand Haven** USA
60D2 **Grand Island** USA
63E2 **Grand Isle** USA
60B3 **Grand Junction** USA
63D3 **Grand L** USA
64A1 **Grand Marais** USA
65E1 **Grand Mère** Canada
15A2 **Grândola** Portugal
54G4 **Grand Prairie** Canada
54J4 **Grand Rapids** Canada
64B2 **Grand Rapids** Michigan, USA
64A1 **Grand Rapids** Minnesota, USA
16B1 **Grand St Bernard, Col du** *P* Italy/Switzerland
56B2 **Grand Teton** *Mt* USA
58D2 **Grand Teton Nat Pk** USA
60B3 **Grand Valley** USA
58C1 **Grangeville** USA
58E1 **Granite Peak** *Mt* Montana, USA
59D2 **Granite Peak** *Mt* Utah, USA
15C1 **Granollérs** Spain
16B1 **Gran Paradiso** *Mt* Italy
7D3 **Grantham** England
66C1 **Grant,Mt** USA
8D3 **Grantown-on-Spey** Scotland
62A1 **Grants** USA
58B2 **Grants Pass** USA
14B2 **Granville** France
68D1 **Granville** USA
54H4 **Granville L** Canada
75D2 **Grão Mogol** Brazil
66C3 **Grapevine** USA
66D2 **Grapevine Mts** USA
47E1 **Graskop** South Africa
54G3 **Gras, Lac de** Canada
14D3 **Grasse** France
6D2 **Grassington** England
58E1 **Grassrange** USA
59B3 **Grass Valley** USA
74F4 **Gravatai** Brazil
54H5 **Gravelbourg** Canada

13B2 **Gravelines** France
51D6 **Gravelotte** South Africa
65D2 **Gravenhurst** Canada
58D1 **Grave Peak** *Mt* USA
34D1 **Gravesend** Australia
7E4 **Gravesend** England
58B1 **Grays Harbour** *B* USA
58D2 **Grays L** USA
64C3 **Grayson** USA
64B3 **Grayville** USA
18D3 **Graz** Austria
69H1 **Great** *R* Jamaica
57F4 **Great Abaco** *I* The Bahamas
32B4 **Great Australian Bight** *G* Australia
68E1 **Great B** New Hampshire, USA
68C3 **Great B** New Jersey, USA
70E2 **Great Bahama Bank** The Bahamas
35C1 **Great Barrier I** New Zealand
32D2 **Great Barrier Reef** *Is* Australia
68D1 **Great Barrington** USA
59C2 **Great Basin** USA
54F3 **Great Bear L** Canada
62C1 **Great Bend** USA
45B3 **Great Bitter L** Egypt
68A3 **Great Cacapon** USA
44E3 **Great Coco I** Burma
32D3 **Great Dividing Range** *Mts* Australia
6D2 **Great Driffield** England
68C3 **Great Egg Harbor** *B* USA
76F10 **Greater Antarctica** *Region* Antarctica
69B2 **Greater Antilles** *Is* Caribbean Sea
7D4 **Greater London** *Metropolitan County* England
7C3 **Greater Manchester** *Metropolitan County* England
70E2 **Great Exuma** *I* The Bahamas
58D1 **Great Falls** USA
47D3 **Great Fish** *R* South Africa
8C3 **Great Glen** *V* Scotland
43F3 **Great Himalayan Range** *Mts* Asia
57F4 **Great Inagua** *I* The Bahamas
47C3 **Great Karoo** *Mts* South Africa
47D3 **Great Kei** *R* South Africa
34C4 **Great L** Australia
7C3 **Great Malvern** England
51B6 **Great Namaland** *Region* Namibia
44E4 **Great Nicobar** *I* Indian Ocean
7C3 **Great Ormes Head** *C* Wales
68E2 **Great Pt** USA
57F4 **Great Ragged** *I* The Bahamas
51D4 **Great Ruaha** *R* Tanzania
65E2 **Great Sacandaga L** USA
58D2 **Great Salt L** USA
58D2 **Great Salt Lake Desert** USA
49E2 **Great Sand Sea** Egypt/Libya
32B3 **Great Sandy Desert** Australia
56A2 **Great Sandy Desert** USA
Great Sandy I = Fraser I
54G3 **Great Slave L** Canada
67B1 **Great Smoky Mts** USA
67B1 **Great Smoky Mts Nat Pk** USA
68D2 **Great South B** USA
47C3 **Great Tafelberg** *Mt* South Africa
32B3 **Great Victoria Desert** Australia
31B2 **Great Wall** China
7E3 **Great Yarmouth** England
48C2 **Gréboun, Mont** Niger
45C1 **Greco, C** Cyprus
15A1 **Gredos, Sierra de** *Mts* Spain
65D2 **Greece** USA
17E3 **Greece** *Republic* Europe
60C2 **Greeley** USA
55K1 **Greely Fjord** Canada
24H1 **Greem Bell, Ostrov** *I* Russian Federation
64B3 **Green** *R* Kentucky, USA
59D3 **Green** *R* Utah, USA
64B1 **Green B** USA
64B2 **Green Bay** USA
64B3 **Greencastle** Indiana, USA
68B3 **Greencastle** Pennsylvania, USA
68C1 **Greene** USA
67B1 **Greeneville** USA
66B2 **Greenfield** California, USA
66C3 **Greenfield** California, USA
68D1 **Greenfield** Massachusetts, USA
64B2 **Greenfield** Wisconsin, USA
55O2 **Greenland** *Dependency* N Atlantic Ocean
52F1 **Greenland** *I* Atlantic Ocean
52H1 **Greenland Basin** Greenland Sea
76B1 **Greenland Sea** Greenland
8D4 **Greenlaw** Scotland
8C4 **Greenock** Scotland
68D2 **Greenport** USA
59D3 **Green River** Utah, USA
58E2 **Green River** Wyoming, USA
68C3 **Greensboro** Maryland, USA
67C1 **Greensboro** N Carolina, USA
62C1 **Greensburg** Kansas, USA
64B3 **Greensburg** Kentucky, USA
65D2 **Greensburg** Pennsylvania, USA
8C3 **Greenstone Pt** Scotland
64B3 **Greenup** USA
59D4 **Green Valley** USA
67A2 **Greenville** Alabama, USA
48B4 **Greenville** Liberia
63D2 **Greenville** Mississippi, USA
67C1 **Greenville** N Carolina, USA
68E1 **Greenville** N Hampshire, USA
64C2 **Greenville** Ohio, USA
67B2 **Greenville** S Carolina, USA
63C2 **Greenville** Texas, USA
67B2 **Greenville** Florida, USA
27H8 **Greenville,C** Australia
7E4 **Greenwich** England
68D2 **Greenwich** USA
68C3 **Greenwood** Delaware, USA
63D2 **Greenwood** Mississippi, USA
67B2 **Greenwood** S Carolina, USA
63D1 **Greers Ferry L** USA
60D2 **Gregory** USA
34A1 **Gregory,L** Australia
32D2 **Gregory Range** *Mts* Australia
18C2 **Greifswald** Germany
20F2 **Gremikha** Russian Federation
18C1 **Grenå** Denmark
63E2 **Grenada** USA
69E4 **Grenada** *I* Caribbean Sea
69E4 **Grenadines,The** *Is* Caribbean Sea
34C2 **Grenfell** Australia
14D2 **Grenoble** France
69M2 **Grenville** Grenada
32D2 **Grenville,C** Australia
58B1 **Gresham** USA
63D3 **Gretna** USA
35B2 **Grey** *R* New Zealand
58E2 **Greybull** USA
55N4 **Grey Is** Canada
68D1 **Greylock,Mt** USA
35B2 **Greymouth** New Zealand
32D3 **Grey Range** *Mts* Australia
9C3 **Greystones** Irish Republic
47E2 **Greytown** South Africa
67B2 **Griffin** USA
34C2 **Griffith** Australia
32D5 **Grim,C** Australia
65D2 **Grimsby** Canada
7D3 **Grimsby** England
12B1 **Grimsey** *I* Iceland
12F7 **Grimstad** Norway
61E2 **Grinnell** USA
55J2 **Grinnell Pen** Canada
55K2 **Grise Fjord** Canada
20J3 **Griva** Russian Federation
12J7 **Grobina** Latvia
47D2 **Groblersdal** South Africa
19E2 **Grodno** Belarus
43E3 **Gromati** *R* India
13D1 **Gronan** Germany
18B2 **Groningen** Netherlands
13D1 **Groningen** *Province* Netherlands
62B1 **Groom** USA
47C3 **Groot** *R* South Africa
32C2 **Groote Eylandt** *I* Australia
51B5 **Grootfontein** Namibia
47B2 **Groot-Karasberge** *Mts* Namibia
47C1 **Groot Laagte** *R* Botswana/Namibia
47C2 **Groot Vloer** *Salt L* South Africa
69P2 **Gros Islet** St Lucia
13E2 **Grosser Feldberg** *Mt* Germany
16C2 **Grosseto** Italy
13E3 **Gross-Gerau** Germany
18C3 **Grossglockner** *Mt* Austria
58D2 **Gros Ventre Range** *Mts* USA
61D1 **Groton** USA
64C1 **Groundhog** *R* Canada
63E2 **Grove Hill** USA
66B2 **Groveland** USA
66B3 **Grover City** USA
65E2 **Groveton** USA
21H7 **Groznyy** Russian Federation
19D2 **Grudziądz** Poland
47B2 **Grünau** Namibia
8E2 **Grutness** Scotland
21G5 **Gryazi** Russian Federation
20G4 **Gryazovets** Russian Federation
74J8 **Grytviken** South Georgia
69B2 **Guacanayabo, G de** Cuba
75D3 **Guaçuí** Brazil
70B2 **Guadalajara** Mexico
15B1 **Guadalajara** Spain
33E1 **Guadalcanal** *I* Solomon Islands
15B2 **Guadalimar** *R* Spain
15B1 **Guadalope** *R* Spain
15B2 **Guadalqivir** *R* Spain
70B2 **Guadalupe** Mexico
66B3 **Guadalupe** USA
53G6 **Guadalupe** *I* Mexico
62C3 **Guadalupe** *R* USA
62B2 **Guadalupe Mtns Nat Pk** USA
62B2 **Guadalupe Peak** *Mt* USA
15A2 **Guadalupe, Sierra de** *Mts* Spain
15B1 **Guadarrama, Sierra de** *Mts* Spain
69E3 **Guadeloupe** *I* Caribbean Sea
15B2 **Guadian** *R* Spain
15A2 **Guadiana** *R* Portugal
15B2 **Guadiana** *R* Spain
15B2 **Guadix** Spain
75B3 **Guaíra** Brazil
72E6 **Guajará Mirim** Brazil
72D1 **Guajira,Pen de** Colombia
69C4 **Guajiri, Península de la** Colombia
72C4 **Gualaceo** Ecuador
27H5 **Guam** *I* Pacific Ocean
74D5 **Guaminí** Argentina
30C5 **Gua Musang** Malaysia
69A2 **Guanabacoa** Cuba
75D1 **Guanambi** Brazil
72E2 **Guanare** Venezuela
28B2 **Guandi** China
70D2 **Guane** Cuba
31C5 **Guangdong** *Province* China
31A3 **Guanghan** China
31C3 **Guanghua** China
31A4 **Guangmao Shan** *Mt* China
31A5 **Guangnan** China
31B5 **Guangxi** *Province* China
31B3 **Guangyuan** China
31D4 **Guangze** China
31C5 **Guangzhou** China
75D2 **Guanhães** Brazil
72E3 **Guania** *R* Colombia/Venezuela
69E5 **Guanipa** *R* Venezuela
69B2 **Guantánamo** Cuba
31D1 **Guanting Shuiku** *Res* China
31A3 **Guan Xian** China
72C2 **Guapá** Colombia
72F6 **Guaporé** *R* Bolivia/Brazil
72E7 **Guaquí** Bolivia
75D1 **Guará** *R* Brazil
72C4 **Guaranda** Ecuador
75B4 **Guarapuava** Brazil
75C4 **Guaraqueçaba** Brazil
15B1 **Guara, Sierra de** *Mts* Spain
75C3 **Guaratinguetá** Brazil
75C4 **Guaratuba, B** Brazil
15A1 **Guarda** Portugal
75C2 **Guarda Mor** Brazil
56C4 **Guasave** Mexico
70C3 **Guatemala** Guatemala
70C3 **Guatemala** *Republic* Central America
72D3 **Guaviare** *R* Colombia
75C3 **Guaxupé** Brazil
69L1 **Guayaguayare** Trinidad
72B4 **Guayaquil** Ecuador
72B4 **Guayaquil, Golfo de** Ecuador
70A2 **Guaymas** Mexico
51C5 **Guba** Zaïre
25P2 **Guba Buorkhaya** *B* Russian Federation
50E3 **Guban** *Region* Somalia
18C2 **Gubin** Poland
15B1 **Gudar, Sierra de** *Mts* Spain
44B3 **Gūdūr** India
13D4 **Guebwiller** France
16B3 **Guelma** Algeria
64C2 **Guelph** Canada
48A2 **Guelta Zemmur** Morocco
50C2 **Guéréda** Chad
14C2 **Guéret** France
60C2 **Guernsey** USA
14B2 **Guernsey** *I* Channel Islands
50D3 **Gughe** *Mt* Ethiopia
25O4 **Gugigu** China
27H5 **Guguan** *I* Pacific Ocean
49D4 **Guider** Cameroon
31C4 **Guidong** China
48B4 **Guiglo** Ivory Coast
47E1 **Guijá** Mozambique
31C5 **Gui Jiang** *R* China
7D4 **Guildford** England
31C4 **Guilin** China
31A2 **Guinan** China
66A1 **Guinda** USA
48A3 **Guinea** *Republic* Africa
52H4 **Guinea Basin** Atlantic Ocean
48A3 **Guinea-Bissau** *Republic* Africa
48C4 **Guinea,G of** W Africa
69A2 **Güines** Cuba
48B3 **Guir** *Well* Mali
75B2 **Guiratinga** Brazil
72F1 **Güiria** Venezuela
6D2 **Guisborough** England
13B3 **Guise** France
27F5 **Guiuan** Philippines
31B5 **Gui Xian** China
31B4 **Guiyang** China
31B4 **Guizhou** *Province* China
42C4 **Gujarāt** *State* India
42C2 **Gujranwala** Pakistan
42C2 **Gujrat** Pakistan
34C2 **Gulargambone** Australia
44B2 **Gulbarga** India
19F1 **Gulbene** Latvia
44B2 **Guledagudda** India
63E2 **Gulfport** USA
Gulf,The = Persian Gulf
34C2 **Gulgong** Australia
31B4 **Gulin** China
17F3 **Güllük Körfezi** *B* Turkey
50D3 **Gulu** Uganda
34C1 **Guluguba** Australia
48C3 **Gumel** Nigeria
43E4 **Gumla** India
13D2 **Gummersbach** Germany
40C1 **Gümüşhane** Turkey
42D4 **Guna** India
50D2 **Guna** *Mt* Ethiopia
34C3 **Gundagai** Australia
50B4 **Gungu** Zaïre
55Q3 **Gunnbjørn Fjeld** *Mt* Greenland
34D2 **Gunnedah** Australia
60B3 **Gunnison** USA
60B3 **Gunnison** *R* USA
44B2 **Guntakal** India
67A2 **Guntersville** USA
67A2 **Guntersville L** USA
44C2 **Guntūr** India
30C5 **Gunung Batu Puteh** *Mt* Malaysia
30C5 **Gunung Tahan** *Mt* Malaysia
51B5 **Gunza** Angola
31D3 **Guoyang** China
42D2 **Gurdāspur** India
42D3 **Gurgaon** India
72F2 **Guri, Embalse de** *Res* Venezuela
43E3 **Gurkha** Nepal
40C2 **Gürün** Turkey
73J4 **Gurupi** *R* Brazil
51D5 **Guruve** Zimbabwe
31A1 **Gurvan Sayhan Uul** *Upland* Mongolia
21J6 **Gur'yev** Kazakhstan
48C3 **Gusau** Nigeria
19E2 **Gusev** Russian Federation
28A3 **Gushan** China
20G4 **Gus' Khrustalnyy** Russian Federation
55P3 **Gustav Holm, Kap** *C* Greenland
54E4 **Gustavus** USA
66B2 **Gustine** USA
57E3 **Guston** USA
18B2 **Gütersloh** Germany
64B3 **Guthrie** Kentucky, USA
63C1 **Guthrie** Oklahoma, USA
62B2 **Guthrie** Texas, USA
61E2 **Guttenberg** USA
73G3 **Guyana** *Republic* S America
52F4 **Guyana Basin** Atlantic Ocean
31C1 **Guyang** China
14B3 **Guyenne** *Region* France
62B1 **Guymon** USA
34D2 **Guyra** Australia
31B2 **Guyuan** China
62A2 **Guzmán, Laguna** *L* Mexico
43G5 **Gwa** Burma
34C2 **Gwabegar** Australia
38E3 **Gwadar** Pakistan
42D3 **Gwalior** India
47D1 **Gwanda** Zimbabwe
50C3 **Gwane** Zaïre
7C4 **Gwent** *County* Wales
51C5 **Gweru** Zimbabwe
34C1 **Gwydir** *R* Australia
7C3 **Gwynedd** Wales
21H7 **Gyandzha** Azerbaijan
43F3 **Gyangzê** China
26C3 **Gyaring Hu** *L* China
24J2 **Gydanskiy Poluostrov** *Pen* Russian Federation
43F3 **Gyirong** China
55O3 **Gyldenløves Fjord** Greenland
34D1 **Gympie** Australia
19D3 **Gyöngyös** Hungary
19D3 **Györ** Hungary

H

33H2 **Ha'apai Group** *Is* Tonga
12K6 **Haapajärvi** Finland
20C4 **Haapsalu** Estonia
18A2 **Haarlem** Netherlands
13D2 **Haarstrang** *Region* Germany
Habana, La = Havana
43G4 **Habiganj** Bangladesh
29D4 **Hachijō-jima** *I* Japan
29C3 **Hachiman** Japan
29E2 **Hachinohe** Japan
29C3 **Hachioji** Japan
68C2 **Hackettstown** USA
34A2 **Hack** *Mt* Australia
8D4 **Haddington** Scotland
34B1 **Haddon Corner** Australia
34B1 **Haddon Downs** Australia
48D3 **Hadejia** Nigeria
48C3 **Hadejia** *R* Nigeria
45C2 **Hadera** Israel
18B1 **Haderslev** Denmark
38D4 **Hadīboh** Socotra
54H2 **Hadley B** Canada
28A3 **Hadong** S Korea
31B5 **Hadong** Vietnam
38C4 **Ḩaḑramawt** *Region* Yemen
18C1 **Hadsund** Denmark
28B3 **Haeju** N Korea
28A3 **Haeju-man** *B* N Korea
28A4 **Haenam** S Korea
41E4 **Hafar al Bātin** Saudi Arabia
55M2 **Haffners Bjerg** *Mt* Greenland
42C2 **Hafizabad** Pakistan
43G3 **Hāflong** India
12A2 **Hafnarfjörður** Iceland
18B2 **Hagen** Germany
68B3 **Hagerstown** USA
28B4 **Hagi** Japan
31A5 **Ha Giang** Vietnam
13D3 **Hagondange** France
13D3 **Haguenan** France
48A2 **Hagunia** *Well* Morocco
26H4 **Haha-jima** *I* Japan
26C3 **Hah Xil Hu** *L* China
28A2 **Haicheng** China
30D1 **Hai Duong** Vietnam
45C2 **Haifa** Israel
45C2 **Haifa,B of** Israel
31D2 **Hai He** *R* China
31C5 **Haikang** China
30E1 **Haikou** China
40D4 **Hā'il** Saudi Arabia
43G4 **Hailākāndi** India
25N5 **Hailar** China
28B2 **Hailong** China
26F2 **Hailun** China
12J5 **Hailuoto** *I* Finland
30D2 **Hainan** *I* China
54E4 **Haines** USA
54E3 **Haines Junction** Canada
18D3 **Hainfeld** Austria
31B5 **Haiphong** Vietnam
28A2 **Haisgai** China
69C3 **Haiti** *Republic* Caribbean Sea
66D2 **Haiwee Res** USA
50D2 **Haiya** Sudan
31A2 **Haiyan** China
31B2 **Haiyuan** China
19E3 **Hajdúböszörmény** Hungary
29C3 **Hajiki-saki** *Pt* Japan
43G4 **Haka** Burma
66E5 **Hakalau** Hawaiian Islands
41D2 **Hakkâri** Turkey
29E2 **Hakodate** Japan
29C3 **Hakui** Japan
29C3 **Haku-san** *Mt* Japan
Ḩalab = Aleppo
41E2 **Halabja** Iraq
50D1 **Halaib** Egypt
45B3 **Halāl, Gebel** *Mt* Egypt
45D1 **Halba** Lebanon
26C2 **Halban** Mongolia
18C2 **Halberstadt** Germany
12G7 **Halden** Norway
43F4 **Haldia** India
42D3 **Haldwāni** India

55M5 **Halifax** Canada
6D3 **Halifax** England
65D3 **Halifax** USA
45D1 **Halīmah, Jabal** *Mt* Lebanon/Syria
8D2 **Halkirk** Scotland
28A4 **Halla-san** *Mt* S Korea
55M1 **Hall Basin** *Sd* Canada/Greenland
55K3 **Hall Beach** Canada
13C2 **Halle** Belgium
18C2 **Halle** Germany
76F1 **Halley** *Base* Antarctica
65D1 **Halleybury** Canada
60C1 **Halliday** USA
12F6 **Hallingdal** *R* Norway
61D1 **Hallock** USA
55M3 **Hall Pen** Canada
32B2 **Hall's Creek** Australia
68C2 **Hallstead** USA
27F6 **Halmahera** *Is* Indonesia
12G7 **Halmstad** Sweden
16C3 **Halq el Qued** Tunisia
18B2 **Haltern** Germany
20C2 **Halti** *Mt* Finland/Norway
8D4 **Haltwhistle** England
41F4 **Halul** *I* Qatar
45C3 **Haluza** *Hist Site* Israel
28B4 **Hamada** Japan
48C2 **Hamada de Tinrhert** *Desert Region* Algeria
48B2 **Hamada du Dra** *Upland* Algeria
41E3 **Hamadān** Iran
48B2 **Hamada Tounassine** *Region* Algeria
21F8 **Ḩamāh** Syria
29C4 **Hamamatsu** Japan
12G6 **Hamar** Norway
40C5 **Hamâta, Gebel** *Mt* Egypt
29D1 **Hama-Tombetsu** Japan
44C4 **Hambantota** Sri Lanka
63D2 **Hamburg** Arkansas, USA
61D2 **Hamburg** Iowa, USA
68A1 **Hamburg** New York, USA
68C2 **Hamburg** Pennsylvania, USA
18B2 **Hamburg** Germany
68D2 **Hamden** USA
12J6 **Hämeenlinna** Finland
13E1 **Hameln** Germany
32A3 **Hamersley Range** *Mts* Australia
28B2 **Hamgyong Sanmaek** *Mts* N Korea
28B3 **Hamhŭng** N Korea
26C2 **Hami** China
45C1 **Ḩamīdīyah** Syria
63E2 **Hamilton** Alabama, USA
34B3 **Hamilton** Australia
65D2 **Hamilton** Canada
58D1 **Hamilton** Montana, USA
68C1 **Hamilton** New York, USA
35C1 **Hamilton** New Zealand
64C3 **Hamilton** Ohio, USA
8C4 **Hamilton** Scotland
66B2 **Hamilton,Mt** USA
12K6 **Hamina** Finland
43E3 **Hamīrpur** India
28A3 **Hamju** N Korea
18B2 **Hamm** Germany
49D2 **Hammādāh al Hamrā** *Upland* Libya
16C3 **Hammamet** Tunisia
16C3 **Hammamet, Golfe de** Tunisia
12H6 **Hammerdal** Sweden
12J4 **Hammerfest** Norway
64B2 **Hammond** Illinois, USA
63D2 **Hammond** Louisiana, USA
60C1 **Hammond** Montana, USA
68C3 **Hammonton** USA
35B3 **Hampden** New Zealand
7D4 **Hampshire** *County* England
63D2 **Hampton** Arkansas, USA
61E2 **Hampton** Iowa, USA
68E1 **Hampton** New Hampshire, USA
65D3 **Hampton** Virginia, USA
38D3 **Hāmūn-e-Jāz-Mūrīān** *L* Iran
42B3 **Hamun-i-Lora** *Salt L* Pakistan
28A3 **Han** *R* S Korea
66E5 **Hana** Hawaiian Islands
66E5 **Hanalei** Hawaiian Islands
29E3 **Hanamaki** Japan
13E2 **Hanau** Germany
31C2 **Hancheng** China
31C3 **Hanchuan** China
65D3 **Hancock** Maryland, USA
64B1 **Hancock** Michigan, USA
68C2 **Hancock** New York, USA
29C4 **Handa** Japan
8C2 **Handa, I** Scotland
31C2 **Handan** China
50D4 **Handeni** Tanzania
66C2 **Hanford** USA
31B2 **Hanggin Qi** China
12J7 **Hangö** Finland
31E3 **Hangzhou** China
31E3 **Hangzhou Wan** *B* China
61D1 **Hankinson** USA
59D3 **Hanksville** USA
35B2 **Hanmer Springs** New Zealand
54G4 **Hanna** Canada
61E3 **Hannibal** USA
18B2 **Hannover** Germany
12G7 **Hanöbukten** *B* Sweden
30D1 **Hanoi** Vietnam
47C3 **Hanover** South Africa
68B3 **Hanover** USA
74B8 **Hanover** *I* Chile
31C3 **Han Shui** *R* China
42D3 **Hānsi** India
26D2 **Hantay** Mongolia
31B3 **Hanzhong** China
43F4 **Hāora** India
12J5 **Haparanda** Sweden
28A3 **Hapch'on** S Korea
43G3 **Hāpoli** India
43J1 **Hapur** India
40C4 **Ḩaql** Saudi Arabia
41E5 **Ḩaradh** Saudi Arabia
45C4 **Harad, Jebel el** *Mt* Jordan
50E3 **Hara Fanna** Ethiopia
29D3 **Haramachi** Japan
51D5 **Harare** Zimbabwe
50C2 **Harazé** Chad
26F2 **Harbin** China
64C2 **Harbor Beach** USA
42D4 **Harda** India
12F6 **Hardangerfjord** *Inlet* Norway
13D1 **Härdenberg** Netherlands
13C1 **Harderwijk** Netherlands
60B1 **Hardin** USA
43L2 **Hardoi** India
13D3 **Hardt** *Region* Germany
63D1 **Hardy** USA
45C3 **Hareidin, Wadi** Egypt
50E3 **Harēr** Ethiopia
50E3 **Hargeysa** Somalia
45C3 **Har Hakippa** *Mt* Israel
26C3 **Harhu** *L* China
27D7 **Hari** *R* Indonesia
29B4 **Harima-nada** *B* Japan
64C3 **Harlan** USA
7B3 **Harlech** Wales
58E1 **Harlem** USA
7E3 **Harleston** England
18B2 **Harlingen** Netherlands
63C3 **Harlingen** USA
7E4 **Harlow** England
58E1 **Harlowtown** USA
45C2 **Har Meron** *Mt* Israel
58C2 **Harney Basin** USA
58C2 **Harney L** USA
12H6 **Härnösand** Sweden
48B4 **Harper** Liberia
66D3 **Harper L** USA
65D3 **Harpers Ferry** USA
13E1 **Harpstedt** Germany
45C3 **Har Ramon** *Mt* Israel
40C4 **Harrāt al 'Uwayrid** *Region* Saudi Arabia
40D5 **Ḩarrāt Kishb** *Region* Saudi Arabia
55L4 **Harricanaw** *R* Canada
67B1 **Harriman** USA
68D1 **Harriman Res** USA
68C3 **Harrington** USA
55N4 **Harrington Harbour** Canada
8B3 **Harris** *District* Scotland
64B3 **Harrisburg** Illinois, USA
68B2 **Harrisburg** Pennsylvania, USA
47D2 **Harrismith** South Africa
63D1 **Harrison** USA
65D3 **Harrisonburg** USA
55N4 **Harrison,C** Canada
61E3 **Harrisonville** USA
8B3 **Harris,Sound of** *Chan* Scotland
64C2 **Harrisville** USA
6D2 **Harrogate** England
45C3 **Har Saggi** *Mt* Israel
45D2 **Ḩarsīr, Wadī al** Syria
12H5 **Harstad** Norway
28A2 **Hartao** China
47C2 **Hartbees** *R* South Africa
12F6 **Hårteigen** *Mt* Norway
68D2 **Hartford** Connecticut, USA
64B2 **Hartford** Michigan, USA
61D2 **Hartford** S Dakota, USA
12G6 **Hartkjølen** *Mt* Norway
65F1 **Hartland** Canada
7B4 **Hartland** England
7B4 **Hartland Pt** England
6D2 **Hartlepool** England
62B1 **Hartley** USA
67A2 **Hartselle** USA
63C2 **Hartshorne** USA
67B2 **Hartwell Res** USA
47C2 **Hartz** *R* South Africa
45C3 **Hārūn, Jebel** *Mt* Jordan
25L5 **Har Us Nuur** *L* Mongolia
38E2 **Harut** *R* Afghanistan
60B3 **Harvard,Mt** USA
60C1 **Harvey** USA
7E4 **Harwich** England
42D3 **Haryāna** *State* India
45C3 **Hāsā** Jordan
45B3 **Hasana, Wadi** Egypt
45C3 **Hāsā, Wadi el** Jordan
45C2 **Hāsbaiya** Lebanon
13E1 **Hase** *R* Germany
13D1 **Haselünne** Germany
29C4 **Hashimoto** Japan
41E2 **Hashtpar** Iran
41E2 **Hashtrūd** Iran
62C2 **Haskell** USA
7D4 **Haslemere** England
44B3 **Hassan** India
18B2 **Hasselt** Belgium
48C2 **Hassi Inifel** Algeria
48B2 **Hassi Mdakane** *Well* Algeria
48C1 **Hassi Messaoud** Algeria
12G7 **Hässleholm** Sweden
34C3 **Hastings** Australia
7E4 **Hastings** England
61E2 **Hastings** Minnesota, USA
56D2 **Hastings** Nebraska, USA
35C1 **Hastings** New Zealand
63E1 **Hatchie** *R* USA
34B2 **Hatfield** Australia
42D3 **Hāthras** India
30D2 **Ha Tinh** Vietnam
34B2 **Hattah** Australia
57F3 **Hatteras,C** USA
63E2 **Hattiesburg** USA
19D3 **Hatvan** Hungary
30D3 **Hau Bon** Vietnam
50E3 **Haud** *Region* Ethiopia
12F7 **Haugesund** Norway
35C1 **Hauhungaroa Range** *Mts* New Zealand
35B1 **Hauraki G** New Zealand
35A3 **Hauroko,L** New Zealand
48B1 **Haut Atlas** *Mts* Morocco
50C3 **Haute Kotto** *Region* Central African Republic
13C3 **Haute-Marne** *Department* France
13D4 **Haute-Saône** *Department* France
13C2 **Hautes Fagnes** *Mts* Belgium/Germany
65F2 **Haut, Isle au** USA
13C2 **Hautmont** France
13D4 **Haut-Rhin** *Department* France
42A2 **Hauz Qala** Afghanistan
70D2 **Havana** Cuba
64A2 **Havana** USA
44B4 **Havankulam** Sri Lanka
59D4 **Havasu L** USA
67C2 **Havelock** USA
35C1 **Havelock North** New Zealand
7E3 **Haverhill** England
68E1 **Haverhill** USA
44B3 **Hāveri** India
68D2 **Haverstraw** USA
18D3 **Havlíčkův Brod** Czech Republic
58E1 **Havre** USA
68B3 **Havre de Grace** USA
55M4 **Havre-St-Pierre** Canada
17F2 **Havsa** Turkey
66E5 **Hawaii** *Is, State* Pacific Ocean
66E5 **Hawaii Volcanoes Nat Pk** Hawaiian Islands
35A2 **Hawea,L** New Zealand
35B1 **Hawera** New Zealand
66E5 **Hawi** Hawaiian Islands
8D4 **Hawick** Scotland
35A2 **Hawkdun Range** *Mts* New Zealand
35C1 **Hawke B** New Zealand
34D2 **Hawke,C** Australia
34A2 **Hawker** Australia
68C2 **Hawley** USA
30B1 **Hawng Luk** Burma
41D3 **Hawr al Habbaniyah** *L* Iraq
41E3 **Hawr al Hammár** *L* Iraq
40D3 **Ḩawrān, Wadi** *R* Iraq
66C1 **Hawthorne** USA
34B2 **Hay** Australia
7C3 **Hay** England
54G3 **Hay** *R* Canada
13C3 **Hayange** France
54B3 **Haycock** USA
59D4 **Hayden** Arizona, USA
60B2 **Hayden** Colorado, USA
55J4 **Hayes** *R* Canada
55M2 **Hayes Halvø** *Region* Greenland
54D3 **Hayes, Mt** USA
7B4 **Hayle** England
7D4 **Hayling** *I* England
68B3 **Haymarket** USA
54G3 **Hay River** Canada
60D3 **Hays** USA
63C1 **Haysville** USA
66A2 **Hayward** California, USA
64A1 **Hayward** Wisconsin, USA
7D4 **Haywards Heath** England
42A2 **Hazarajat** *Region* Afghanistan
64C3 **Hazard** USA
43F4 **Hazārībāg** India
13B2 **Hazebrouck** France
63D2 **Hazelhurst** USA
54F4 **Hazelton** Canada
54B3 **Hazen B** USA
55L1 **Hazen L** Canada
54G2 **Hazen Str** Canada
45C3 **Hazeva** Israel
68C2 **Hazleton** USA
66A1 **Healdsburg** USA
34C3 **Healesville** Australia
36E7 **Heard I** Indian Ocean
63C2 **Hearne** USA
57E2 **Hearst** Canada
60C1 **Heart** *R* USA
62C3 **Hebbronville** USA
31D2 **Hebei** *Province* China
34C1 **Hebel** Australia
58D2 **Heber City** USA
58D2 **Hebgen L** USA
31C2 **Hebi** China
31C2 **Hebian** China
55M4 **Hebron** Canada
45C3 **Hebron** Israel
60C1 **Hebron** N Dakota, USA
61D2 **Hebron** Nebraska, USA
54E4 **Hecate Str** Canada
31B5 **Hechi** China
13E3 **Hechingen** Germany
54G2 **Hecla and Griper B** Canada
35C2 **Hector,Mt** New Zealand
12G6 **Hede** Sweden
12H6 **Hedemora** Sweden
58C1 **He Devil Mt** USA
18B2 **Heerenveen** Netherlands
13C2 **Heerlen** Netherlands
Hefa = Haifa
31D3 **Hefei** China
31B4 **Hefeng** China
26G2 **Hegang** China
29C3 **Hegura-jima** *I* Japan
30B1 **Heho** Burma
45C3 **Heidan** *R* Jordan
18B2 **Heide** Germany
47C3 **Heidelberg** Cape Province, South Africa
47D2 **Heidelberg** Transvaal, South Africa
18B3 **Heidelberg** Germany
18C3 **Heidenheim** Germany
25O4 **Heihe** China
47D2 **Heilbron** South Africa
18B3 **Heilbronn** Germany
18C2 **Heiligenstadt** Germany
12K6 **Heinola** Finland
28A2 **Heishan** China
31B4 **Hejiang** China
55R3 **Hekla** *Mt* Iceland
30C1 **Hekou** Vietnam
31A5 **Hekou Yaozou Zizhixian** China
31B2 **Helan** China
31B2 **Helan Shan** *Mt* China
63D2 **Helena** Arkansas, USA
58D1 **Helena** Montana, USA
66D3 **Helendale** USA
27G6 **Helen Reef** Pacific Ocean
8C3 **Helensburgh** Scotland
45A3 **Heliopolis** Egypt
41F4 **Helleh** *R* Iran
15B2 **Hellín** Spain
58C1 **Hells Canyon** *R* USA
13D2 **Hellweg** *Region* Germany
66B2 **Helm** USA
38E2 **Helmand** *R* Afghanistan/Iran
47B2 **Helmeringhausen** Namibia
13C2 **Helmond** Netherlands
8D2 **Helmsdale** Scotland
51F5 **Helodrano Antongila** *B* Madagascar
28B2 **Helong** China
12G7 **Helsingborg** Sweden
Helsingfors = Helsinki
18C1 **Helsingør** Denmark
12J6 **Helsinki** Finland
7B4 **Helston** England
9C3 **Helvick Hd** *Pt* Irish Republic
40B4 **Helwân** Egypt
7D4 **Hemel Hempstead** England
63C2 **Hempstead** USA
12H7 **Hemse** Sweden
31A3 **Henan** China
31C3 **Henan** *Province* China
35B1 **Hen and Chickens Is** New Zealand
29C2 **Henashi-zaki** *C* Japan
64B3 **Henderson** Kentucky, USA
67C1 **Henderson** N Carolina, USA
59D3 **Henderson** Nevada, USA
63D2 **Henderson** Texas, USA
67B1 **Hendersonville** N Carolina, USA
67A1 **Hendersonville** Tennessee, USA
47D3 **Hendrik Verwoerd Dam** South Africa
31E5 **Hengchun** Taiwan
26C4 **Hengduan Shan** *Mts* China
18B2 **Hengelo** Netherlands
31B2 **Hengshan** China
31D2 **Hengshui** China
30D1 **Heng Xian** China
31C4 **Hengyang** China
30A4 **Henhoaha** Nicobar Is, India
7D4 **Henley-on-Thames** England
68C3 **Henlopen,C** USA
68E1 **Henniker** USA
62C2 **Henrietta** USA
55K4 **Henrietta Maria,C** Canada
59D3 **Henrieville** USA
63C1 **Henryetta** USA
55M3 **Henry Kater Pen** Canada
47A1 **Henties Bay** Namibia
26D2 **Hentiyn Nuruu** *Mts* Mongolia
30B2 **Henzada** Burma
31B5 **Hepu** China
38E2 **Herat** Afghanistan
54H4 **Herbert** Canada
35C2 **Herbertville** New Zealand
13E2 **Herborn** Germany
69A4 **Heredia** Costa Rica
7C3 **Hereford** England
62B2 **Hereford** USA
7C3 **Hereford & Worcester** *County* England
13C2 **Herentals** Belgium
13E1 **Herford** Germany
61D3 **Herington** USA
35A3 **Heriot** New Zealand
68C1 **Herkimer** USA
8E1 **Herma Ness** *Pen* Scotland
47B3 **Hermanus** South Africa
34C2 **Hermidale** Australia
35B2 **Hermitage** New Zealand
32D1 **Hermit Is** Papua New Guinea
45C2 **Hermon, Mt** Lebanon/Syria
70A2 **Hermosillo** Mexico
75B4 **Hernandarias** Paraguay
68B2 **Herndon** USA
66C2 **Herndon** USA
13D2 **Herne** Germany
7E4 **Herne Bay** England
18B1 **Herning** Denmark
41E2 **Herowābad** Iran
75A4 **Herradura** Argentina
15B2 **Herrera del Duque** Spain
68B2 **Hershey** USA
7D4 **Hertford** England
7D4 **Hertford** *County* England
45C2 **Herzliyya** Israel
13C2 **Hesbaye** Region, Belgium
13A2 **Hesdin** France
31B2 **Heshui** China
66D3 **Hesperia** USA
18B2 **Hessen** *State* Germany
66C2 **Hetch Hetchy Res** USA
60C1 **Hettinger** USA
48B1 **Heuts Plateaux** Algeria/Morocco
7E3 **Hewett** *Oilfield* N Sea
6C2 **Hexham** England
31C5 **He Xian** China
6C2 **Heysham** England
47D2 **Heystekrand** South Africa
31C5 **Heyuan** China
34B3 **Heywood** Australia
31D2 **Heze** China
67B3 **Hialeah** USA
61E1 **Hibbing** USA
67B1 **Hickory** USA
35C1 **Hicks Bay** New Zealand
34C3 **Hicks,Pt** Australia
63C2 **Hico** USA
29D2 **Hidaka-sammyaku** *Mts* Japan
70B2 **Hidalgo del Parral** Mexico
75C2 **Hidrolândia** Brazil
48A2 **Hierro** *I* Canary Islands
29D3 **Higashine** Japan
28B4 **Higashi-suidō** *Str* Japan
45B3 **Higâyib, Wadi el** Egypt
58B2 **High Desert** USA
63D3 **High Island** USA
66D3 **Highland** USA
8C3 **Highland** *Region* Scotland
8E2 **Highlander** *Oilfield* N Sea
66C1 **Highland Peak** *Mt* USA
68C2 **Highland Falls** USA
67B1 **High Point** USA
54G4 **High Prairie** Canada
54G4 **High River** Canada
67B3 **High Springs** USA
68C2 **Hightstown** USA
7D4 **High Wycombe** England
12J7 **Hiiumaa** *I* Estonia
40C4 **Hijaz** *Region* Saudi Arabia

29C4 **Hikigawa** Japan
59C3 **Hiko** USA
29C3 **Hikone** Japan
35B1 **Hikurangi** New Zealand
56C4 **Hildago del Parral** Mexico
18B2 **Hildesheim** Germany
69R2 **Hillaby,Mt** Barbados
60D3 **Hill City** USA
18C1 **Hillerød** Denmark
61D1 **Hillsboro** N Dakota, USA
68E1 **Hillsboro** New Hampshire, USA
62A2 **Hillsboro** New Mexico, USA
64C3 **Hillsboro** Ohio, USA
58B1 **Hillsboro** Oregon, USA
63C2 **Hillsboro** Texas, USA
34C2 **Hillston** Australia
64C3 **Hillsville** USA
8E1 **Hillswick** Scotland
66E5 **Hilo** Hawaiian Islands
6C2 **Hilpsford** *Pt* England
68B1 **Hilton** USA
40C2 **Hilvan** Turkey
18B2 **Hilversum** Netherlands
42D2 **Himāchal Pradesh** *State* India
Himalaya = Great Himalayan Range
39G3 **Himalaya** *Mts* Asia
43N1 **Himalchuli** *Mt* Nepal
42C4 **Himatnagar** India
29C4 **Himeji** Japan
29D3 **Himi** Japan
45D1 **Ḩimş** Syria
7D3 **Hinckley** England
61E1 **Hinckley** Minnesota, USA
68C1 **Hinckley Res** USA
42D3 **Hindaun** India
42B1 **Hindu Kush** *Mts* Afghanistan
44B3 **Hindupur** India
54G4 **Hines Creek** Canada
42D4 **Hinganghāt** India
42B3 **Hingol** *R* Pakistan
42D5 **Hingoli** India
66D3 **Hinkley** USA
12H5 **Hinnøya** *I* Norway
68D1 **Hinsdale** USA
62C1 **Hinton** USA
28A4 **Hirado** Japan
28A4 **Hirado-shima** *I* Japan
43E4 **Hirakud Res** India
40B2 **Hirfanli Baraji** *Res* Turkey
44B3 **Hirihar** India
29D2 **Hiroo** Japan
29E2 **Hirosaki** Japan
28C4 **Hiroshima** Japan
13C3 **Hirson** France
17F2 **Hîrşova** Romania
18B1 **Hirtshals** Denmark
42D3 **Hisār** India
69C3 **Hispaniola** *I* Caribbean Sea
45D1 **Ḩisyah** Syria
40D3 **Hīt** Iraq
29E3 **Hitachi** Japan
29D3 **Hitachi-Ota** Japan
7D4 **Hitchin** England
28C4 **Hitoyoshi** Japan
12F6 **Hitra** *I* Norway
29B4 **Hiuchi-nada** *B* Japan
29B4 **Hiwasa** Japan
45C3 **Hiyon** *R* Israel
18B1 **Hjørring** Denmark
30B1 **Hka** *R* Burma
48C4 **Ho** Ghana
30D1 **Hoa Binh** Vietnam
30D3 **Hoa Da** Vietnam
34C4 **Hobart** Australia
62C2 **Hobart** USA
62B2 **Hobbs** USA
18B1 **Hobro** Denmark
50E3 **Hobyo** Somalia
30D3 **Ho Chi Minh City** Vietnam
18C3 **Hochkonig** *Mt* Austria
28A2 **Hochon** N Korea
13E3 **Hockenheim** Germany
Hodeida = Al Ḩudaydah
17E1 **Hódmezö'hely** Hungary
15C2 **Hodna, Monts du** Algeria
18D3 **Hodonin** Czech Republic
13C2 **Hoek van Holland** Netherlands
28A3 **Hoengsŏng** S Korea
28B2 **Hoeryŏng** N Korea
28A3 **Hoeyang** N Korea
18C2 **Hof** Germany
55R3 **Höfn** Iceland
12B2 **Hofsjökull** *Mts* Iceland
28C4 **Hōfu** Japan
48C2 **Hoggar** *Upland* Algeria
13D2 **Hohe Acht** *Mt* Germany
13E2 **Hohes Gras** *Mts* Germany
31C1 **Hohhot** China
26C3 **Hoh Sai Hu** *L* China
39G2 **Hoh Xil Shan** *Mts* China
50D3 **Hoima** Uganda
43G3 **Hojāi** India
28B4 **Hojo** Japan
35B1 **Hokianga Harbour** *B* New Zealand
35B2 **Hokitika** New Zealand
26H2 **Hokkaidō** *I* Japan
41G2 **Hokmābād** Iran
29D3 **Hokota** Japan
7E3 **Holbeach** England
34C3 **Holbrook** Australia
59D4 **Holbrook** USA
59D3 **Holden** USA
63C1 **Holdenville** USA
60D2 **Holdrege** USA
44B3 **Hole Narsipur** India
69Q2 **Holetown** Barbados
69B2 **Holguín** Cuba
18D3 **Hollabrunn** Austria
64B2 **Holland** USA
68A2 **Hollidaysburg** USA
62C2 **Hollis** USA
66B2 **Hollister** USA
63E2 **Holly Springs** USA
66C3 **Hollywood** California, USA
67B3 **Hollywood** Florida, USA
54G2 **Holman Island** Canada
12J6 **Holmsund** Sweden
45C2 **Holon** Israel
18B1 **Holstebro** Denmark
61D2 **Holstein** USA
55N3 **Holsteinsborg** Greenland
67B1 **Holston** *R* USA
64C2 **Holt** USA
61D3 **Holton** USA
54C3 **Holy Cross** USA
7B3 **Holyhead** Wales
6D3 **Holy I** England
7B3 **Holy I** Wales
60C2 **Holyoke** Colorado, USA
68D1 **Holyoke** Massachusetts, USA
9D2 **Holywood** Northern Ireland
13E2 **Holzminden** Germany
43G4 **Homalin** Burma
13E2 **Homburg** Germany
55M3 **Home B** Canada
63D2 **Homer** Louisiana, USA
54C4 **Homer** USA
35A2 **Homer Tunnel** New Zealand
67B2 **Homerville** USA
67B3 **Homestead** USA
67A2 **Homewood** USA
44B2 **Homnābād** India
51D6 **Homoine** Mozambique
Homs = Al Khums
Homs = Ḩimş
47B3 **Hondeklip B** South Africa
62A2 **Hondo** New Mexico, USA
62C3 **Hondo** Texas, USA
70D3 **Hondo** *R* Mexico
70D3 **Honduras** *Republic* Central America
70D3 **Honduras,G of** Honduras
12G6 **Hønefoss** Norway
68C2 **Honesdale** USA
59B2 **Honey L** USA
Hong *R* **= Nui Con Voi**
30C1 **Hong** *R* Vietnam
30D1 **Hon Gai** Vietnam
28A3 **Hongchŏn** S Korea
31A4 **Hongguo** China
31C4 **Hong Hu** *L* China
31B2 **Honghui** China
31C4 **Hongjiang** China
31C5 **Hong Kong** *Colony* SE Asia
26E2 **Hongor** Mongolia
31B5 **Hongshui He** *R* China
28A3 **Hongsong** S Korea
28A3 **Hongwon** N Korea
31A3 **Hongyuan** China
31D3 **Hongze Hu** *L* China
33E1 **Honiara** Solomon Islands
7C4 **Honiton** England
29D3 **Honjō** Japan
30C4 **Hon Khoai** *I* Cambodia
30D3 **Hon Lan** *I* Vietnam
12K4 **Honnigsvåg** Norway
20D1 **Honningsvåg** Norway
66E5 **Honokaa** Hawaiian Islands
66E5 **Honolulu** Hawaiian Islands
30C4 **Hon Panjang** *I* Vietnam
26G3 **Honshū** *I* Japan
58B1 **Hood,Mt** USA
58B1 **Hood River** USA
13D1 **Hoogeveen** Netherlands
62B1 **Hooker** USA
9C3 **Hook Head** *C* Irish Republic
54E4 **Hoonah** USA
54B3 **Hooper Bay** USA
47D2 **Hoopstad** South Africa
18A2 **Hoorn** Netherlands
68D1 **Hoosick Falls** USA
56B3 **Hoover Dam** USA
63D2 **Hope** Arkansas, USA
55M4 **Hopedale** Canada
24D2 **Hopen** *I* Svalbard
55M3 **Hopes Advance,C** Canada
34B3 **Hopetoun** Australia
47C2 **Hopetown** South Africa
68A2 **Hopewell** Pennsylvania, USA
65D3 **Hopewell** Virginia, USA
64B3 **Hopkinsville** USA
58B1 **Hoquiam** USA
40D2 **Horasan** Turkey
13E3 **Horb** Germany
50E2 **Hordiyo** Somalia
31B1 **Hörh Uul** *Mt* Mongolia
37L6 **Horizon Depth** Pacific Ocean
41G4 **Hormuz,Str of** Oman/Iran
18D3 **Horn** Austria
55Q3 **Horn** *C* Iceland
12H5 **Hornavan** *L* Sweden
63D2 **Hornbeck** USA
58B2 **Hornbrook** USA
35B2 **Hornby** New Zealand
7D3 **Horncastle** England
68B1 **Hornell** USA
55K5 **Hornepayne** Canada
63E2 **Horn I** USA
33H2 **Horn, Îles de** Pacific Ocean
54F3 **Horn Mts** Canada
74C9 **Hornos, Cabo de** *C* Chile
6D3 **Hornsea** England
28A2 **Horqin Zuoyi Houqi** China
74E2 **Horqueta** Paraguay
68B1 **Horseheads** USA
18C1 **Horsens** Denmark
58B1 **Horseshoe Bay** Canada
58C2 **Horseshoe Bend** USA
34B3 **Horsham** Australia
7D4 **Horsham** England
12G7 **Horten** Norway
54F3 **Horton** *R* Canada
27E6 **Hose Mts** Borneo
42D4 **Hoshangābād** India
42D2 **Hoshiārpur** India
62C1 **Hosington** USA
44B2 **Hospet** India
74C9 **Hoste** *I* Chile
39F2 **Hotan** China
47C2 **Hotazel** South Africa
63D2 **Hot Springs** Arkansas, USA
60C2 **Hot Springs** S Dakota, USA
54G3 **Hottah L** Canada
69C3 **Hotte, Massif de la** *Mts* Haiti
47A2 **Hottentot Pt** Namibia
64B1 **Houghton** USA
65F1 **Houlton** USA
31C2 **Houma** China
63D3 **Houma** USA
8C3 **Hourn, Loch** *Inlet* Scotland
68D2 **Housatonic** *R* USA
63E2 **Houston** Mississippi, USA
63C3 **Houston** Texas, USA
32A3 **Houtman** *Is* Australia
68A2 **Houtzdale** USA
26C2 **Hovd** Mongolia
26D1 **Hövsgol Nuur** *L* Mongolia
34D1 **Howard** Australia
64B2 **Howard City** USA
50C2 **Howa, Wadi** *Watercourse* Chad/Sudan
34C3 **Howe,C** Australia
58B1 **Howe Sd** Canada
47E2 **Howick** South Africa
65F1 **Howland** USA
9C3 **Howth** Irish Republic
13E2 **Höxter** Germany
8D2 **Hoy** *I* Scotland
12F6 **Høyanger** Norway
61E1 **Hoyt Lakes** USA
18D2 **Hradec-Králové** Czech Republic
19D3 **Hranice** Czech Republic
19D3 **Hron** *R* Slovakia
31E5 **Hsinchu** Taiwan
30B1 **Hsipaw** Burma
31E5 **Hsüeh Shan** *Mt* Taiwan
47A1 **Huab** *R* Namibia
31B2 **Huachi** China
72C6 **Huacho** Peru
31C1 **Huade** China
28B2 **Huadian** China
31D3 **Huaibei** China
31D3 **Huaibin** China
28A2 **Huaide** China
28A2 **Huaidezhen** China
31D3 **Huai He** *R* China
31C4 **Huaihua** China
31C5 **Huaiji** China
31D3 **Huainan** China
59D3 **Hualapai Peak** *Mt* USA
26F4 **Hualien** Taiwan
72C5 **Huallaga** *R* Peru
72C5 **Huallanca** Peru
72C5 **Huamachuco** Peru
51B5 **Huambo** Angola
72E7 **Huanay** Bolivia
72C5 **Huancabamba** Peru
72C6 **Huancavelica** Peru
72C6 **Huancayo** Peru
31D3 **Huangchuan** China
Huang Hai = Yellow Sea
31D2 **Huang He** *R* China
31B2 **Huangling** China
30D2 **Huangliu** China
28B2 **Huangnihe** China
31C3 **Huangpi** China
31D3 **Huangshi** China
31D4 **Huangshan** China
31E4 **Huangyan** China
28B2 **Huanren** China
72C5 **Huānuco** Peru
74C1 **Huanuni** Bolivia
31B2 **Huan Xian** China
72C5 **Huaráz** Peru
72C6 **Huarmey** Peru
72C5 **Huascarán** *Mt* Peru
74B3 **Huasco** Chile
31C2 **Hua Xian** China
70B2 **Huayapan** *R* Mexico
31C3 **Hubei** *Province* China
44B2 **Hubli** India
28B2 **Huch'ang** N Korea
7D3 **Hucknell Torkard** England
7D3 **Huddersfield** England
13E1 **Hude** Germany
12H6 **Hudiksvall** Sweden
67B3 **Hudson** Florida, USA
64C2 **Hudson** Michigan, USA
68D1 **Hudson** New York, USA
68D1 **Hudson** *R* USA
55K4 **Hudson B** Canada
54H4 **Hudson Bay** Canada
68D1 **Hudson Falls** USA
55L3 **Hudson Str** Canada
30D2 **Hue** Vietnam
15A2 **Huelva** Spain
15B2 **Húercal Overa** Spain
15B1 **Huesca** Spain
32D3 **Hughenden** Australia
54C3 **Hughes** USA
43F4 **Hugli** *R* India
63C2 **Hugo** USA
62B1 **Hugoton** USA
31D4 **Hui'an** China
35C1 **Huiarau Range** *Mts* New Zealand
47B2 **Huib Hochplato** *Plat* Namibia
28B2 **Hŭich'ŏn** N Korea
72C3 **Huila** *Mt* Colombia
31D5 **Huilai** China
31A4 **Huili** China
28B2 **Huinan** China
70C3 **Huixtla** Mexico
31A4 **Huize** China
31C5 **Huizhou** China
40D4 **Ḩulayfah** Saudi Arabia
26G2 **Hulin** China
65D1 **Hull** Canada
6D3 **Hull** England
33H1 **Hull** *I* Phoenix Islands
18D1 **Hultsfred** Sweden
25N5 **Hulun Nur** *L* China
72F5 **Humaitá** Brazil
47C3 **Humansdorp** South Africa
7D3 **Humber** *R* England
6D3 **Humberside** *County* England
54H4 **Humboldt** Canada
61E2 **Humboldt** Iowa, USA
63E1 **Humboldt** Tennessee, USA
58C2 **Humboldt** *R* USA
58B2 **Humboldt B** USA
55M2 **Humboldt Gletscher** *Gl* Greenland
59C3 **Humboldt L** USA
34C1 **Humeburn** Australia
34C3 **Hume,L** Australia
13D1 **Hümmling** *Hill* Germany
51B5 **Humpata** Angola
66C2 **Humphreys** USA
66C2 **Humphreys,Mt** California, USA
59D3 **Humphreys Peak** *Mt* Arizona, USA
12A1 **Húnaflóri** *B* Iceland
31C4 **Hunan** *Province* China
28C2 **Hunchun** China
17E1 **Hunedoara** Romania
19D3 **Hungary** *Republic* Europe
34B1 **Hungerford** Australia
28B3 **Hŭngnam** N Korea
58D1 **Hungry Horse Res** USA
28B2 **Hunjiang** China
47B2 **Hunsberge** *Mts* Namibia
13D3 **Hunsrück** *Mts* Germany
7E3 **Hunstanton** England
13E1 **Hunte** *R* Germany
34D2 **Hunter** *R* Australia
34C4 **Hunter Is** Australia
64B3 **Huntingburg** USA
7D3 **Huntingdon** England
64B2 **Huntingdon** Indiana, USA
68A2 **Huntingdon** Pennsylvania, USA
64C3 **Huntington** USA
66C4 **Huntington Beach** USA
66C2 **Huntington L** USA
35C1 **Huntly** New Zealand
8D3 **Huntly** Scotland
54F3 **Hunt, Mt** Canada
67A2 **Huntsville** Alabama, USA
65D1 **Huntsville** Canada
63C2 **Huntsville** Texas, USA
30D2 **Huong Khe** Vietnam
27H7 **Huon Peninsula** Papua New Guinea
34C4 **Huonville** Australia
64C1 **Hurd,C** Canada
28A2 **Hure Qi** China
40B4 **Hurghada** Egypt
64A1 **Hurley** USA
66B2 **Huron** California, USA
61D2 **Huron** S Dakota, USA
64C1 **Huron,L** Canada/USA
35B2 **Hurunui** *R* New Zealand
12B1 **Húsavík** Iceland
17F1 **Huşi** Romania
12G7 **Huskvarna** Sweden
45C2 **Husn** Jordan
18B2 **Husum** Germany
56D3 **Hutchinson** USA
63C1 **Hutchinson** USA
34C1 **Hutton,Mt** Australia
31D2 **Hutuo He** *R* China
13C2 **Huy** Belgium
31A2 **Huzhu** China
16D2 **Hvar** *I* Croatia
28A2 **Hwadae** N Korea
51C5 **Hwange** Zimbabwe
51C5 **Hwange Nat Pk** Zimbabwe
28A2 **Hwapyong** N Korea
68E2 **Hyannis** Massachusetts, USA
60C2 **Hyannis** Nebraska, USA
26C2 **Hyargas Nuur** *L* Mongolia
54E4 **Hydaburg** USA
68D2 **Hyde Park** USA
44B2 **Hyderābād** India
42B3 **Hyderabad** Pakistan
14D3 **Hyères** France
14D3 **Hyères, Iles d'** *Is* France
28B2 **Hyesan** N Korea
68A3 **Hyndman** USA
56B2 **Hyndman Peak** *Mt* USA
20D3 **Hyrynsalmi** Finland
7E4 **Hythe** England
12J6 **Hyvinkää** Finland

I

73K6 **Iaçu** Brazil
17F2 **Ialomiţa** *R* Romania
17F1 **Iaşi** Romania
48C4 **Ibadan** Nigeria
72C3 **Ibagué** Colombia
17E2 **Ibar** *R* Montenegro/ Serbia, Yugoslavia
72C3 **Ibarra** Ecuador
13D1 **Ibbenbüren** Germany
75C2 **Ibiá** Brazil
75E1 **Ibicaraí** Brazil
74E3 **Ibicuí** *R* Brazil
74E4 **Ibicuy** Argentina
15C2 **Ibiza** Spain
15C2 **Ibiza** *I* Spain
51E5 **Ibo** Mozambique
73K6 **Ibotirama** Brazil
50C2 **Ibra, Wadi** *Watercourse* Sudan
41G5 **'Ibrī** Oman
72C6 **Ica** Peru
72E4 **Içá** *R* Brazil
72E3 **Içana** Brazil
12A1 **Iceland** *Republic* N Atlantic Ocean
25R4 **Icha** Russian Federation
44A2 **Ichalkaranji** India
29C3 **Ichinomiya** Japan
29E3 **Ichinosek** Japan
54B2 **Icy C** USA
63D2 **Idabell** USA
61D2 **Ida Grove** USA
58D2 **Idaho** State, USA
58C2 **Idaho City** USA
58D2 **Idaho Falls** USA
60B3 **Idaho Springs** USA
45B1 **Idalion** *Hist Site* Cyprus
58B2 **Idanha** USA
13D3 **Idar Oberstein** Germany
49D2 **Idehan Marzūg** *Desert* Libya
49D2 **Idehan Ubari** *Desert* Libya
48C2 **Idelès** Algeria
26C2 **Ideriym Gol** *R* Mongolia
40B5 **Idfu** Egypt
17E3 **Ídhi Óros** *Mt* Greece
17E3 **Ídhra** *I* Greece
50B4 **Idiofa** Zaïre
40C2 **Idlib** Syria
12K7 **Idritsa** Russian Federation
47D3 **Idutywa** South Africa
13B2 **Ieper** Belgium
17F3 **Ierápetra** Greece
25N4 **Iet Oktyob'ya** Russian Federation
51D4 **Ifakara** Tanzania
27H6 **Ifalik** *I* Pacific Ocean
51E6 **Ifanadiana** Madagascar
48C4 **Ife** Nigeria
48C3 **Iférouane** Niger
27E6 **Igan** Malaysia
75C3 **Igarapava** Brazil

24K3 Igarka Russian Federation
75A3 Igatimi Paraguay
41E2 Igdir Iran
12H6 Iggesund Sweden
16B3 Iglesias Sardinia, Italy
55K3 Igloolik Canada
57D2 Ignace Canada
40A1 Iğneada Burun *Pt* Turkey
48C1 Ignil-Izane Algeria
44E3 Ignoitijala Andaman Islands
17E3 Igoumenítsa Greece
20J4 Igra Russian Federation
20L3 Igrim Russian Federation
74F3 Iguaçu, Quedas do *Falls* Argentina/Brazil
70C3 Iguala Mexico
74G2 Iguape Brazil
75C3 Iguatama Brazil
75B3 Iguatemi Brazil
75A3 Iguatemi *R* Brazil
73L5 Iguatu Brazil
50A4 Iguéla Gabon
51E6 Ihosy Madagascar
29D3 Iida Japan
29C3 Iide-san *Mt* Japan
12K6 Iisalmi Finland
28B4 Iisuka Japan
48C4 Ijebu Nigeria
13C1 Ijmuiden Netherlands
13C1 Ijssel *R* Netherlands
18B2 Ijsselmeer *S* Netherlands
17F3 Ikaría *I* Greece
29E2 Ikeda Japan
50C4 Ikela Zaïre
17E2 Ikhtiman Bulgaria
28A4 Iki *I* Japan
51E5 Ikopa *R* Madagascar
27F5 Ilagan Philippines
41E3 Ilām Iran
26C1 Ilanskiy Russian Federation
50C4 Ilebo Zaïre
13B3 Île De France *Region* France
65E1 Ile d'Orleans Canada
21K5 Ilek *R* Russian Federation
7B4 Ilfracombe England
40B1 Ilgaz Dağları *Mts* Turkey
73H6 Ilha do Bananal *Region* Brazil
75D3 Ilha Grande, B de Brazil
73H8 Ilha Grande, Reprêsa Brazil/Paraguay
75B3 Ilha Solteira Dam Brazil
73L6 Ilhéus Brazil
54C4 Iliamna L USA
25M4 Ilim *R* Russian Fed
25M4 Ilimsk Russian Federation
25M4 Ilin *R* Russian Federation
26H2 Il'inskiy Russian Federation
17E3 Iliodhrómia *I* Greece
68C1 Ilion USA
6D3 Ilkley England
74B4 Illapel Chile
48C3 Illéla Niger
64A3 Illinois *R* USA
64B2 Illinois *State* USA
48C2 Illizi Algeria
20E4 Il'men, Ozero *L* Russian Federation
72D7 Ilo Peru
27F5 Iloilo Philippines
12L6 Ilomantsi Finland
48C4 Ilorin Nigeria
19G1 Il'yino Russian Federation
28B4 Imabari Japan
29C3 Imaichi Japan
12L5 Imandra, Ozero *L* Russian Federation
28A4 Imari Japan
20D3 Imatra Finland
74G3 Imbituba Brazil
75B4 Imbituva Brazil
50E3 Imi Ethiopia
28A3 Imjin *R* N Korea
58C2 Imlay USA
16C2 Imola Italy
73J5 Imperatriz Brazil
16B2 Imperia Italy
60C2 Imperial USA
59C4 Imperial V USA
50B3 Impfondo Congo
43G4 Imphāl India
29C3 Ina Japan
48C2 In Afaleleh *Well* Algeria
29C4 Inamba-jima *I* Japan
48C2 In Amenas Algeria
12K5 Inari Finland
12K5 Inarijärvi *L* Finland
29D3 Inawashiro-ko *L* Japan
48C2 In Belbel Algeria
21F7 Ince Burun *Pt* Turkey
40B2 Incekum Burun *Pt* Turkey
8C2 Inchnadamph Scotland
28B3 Inch'on S Korea
8B4 Indaal, Loch *Inlet* Scotland
48B2 In Dagouber *Well* Mali
75C2 Indaiá *R* Brazil
12H6 Indals *R* Sweden
66C2 Independence California, USA
61E2 Independence Iowa, USA
63C1 Independence Kansas, USA
61E3 Independence Missouri, USA
58C2 Independence Mts USA
21J6 Inderborskiy Kazakhstan
39F3 India *Federal Republic* Asia
65D2 Indiana USA
64B2 Indiana *State* USA
36F7 Indian-Antarctic Basin Indian Ocean
36F7 Indian-Antarctic Ridge Indian Ocean
64B3 Indianapolis USA
Indian Desert = Thar Desert
55N4 Indian Harbour Canada
36E5 Indian O
61E2 Indianola Iowa, USA
63D2 Indianola Mississippi, USA
75C2 Indianópolis Brazil
59C3 Indian Springs USA
20H2 Indiga Russian Federation
25Q3 Indigirka *R* Russian Federation
30D2 Indo-China *Region* SE Asia
27F7 Indonesia *Republic* SE Asia
42D4 Indore India
14C2 Indre *R* France
42B3 Indus *R* Pakistan
42B4 Indus, Mouths of the Pakistan
48C2 In Ebeggi *Well* Algeria
21E7 Inebolu Turkey
48C2 In Ecker Algeria
40A1 Inegöl Turkey
48D2 In Ezzane Algeria
47C3 Infantta, C South Africa
70B3 Infiernillo, Pico del *Mt* Mexico
48C3 Ingal Niger
64C2 Ingersoll Canada
32D2 Ingham Australia
55M2 Inglefield Land *Region* Greenland
35B1 Inglewood New Zealand
34D1 Inglewood Queensland, Australia
66C4 Inglewood USA
34B3 Inglewood Victoria, Australia
12B2 Ingólfshöfdi *I* Iceland
18C3 Ingolstadt Germany
43F4 Ingrāj Bāzār India
48C3 In Guezzam *Well* Algeria
47E2 Inhaca *I* Mozambique
47E2 Inhaca Pen Mozambique
51D6 Inhambane Mozambique
51D6 Inharrime Mozambique
75C2 Inhumas Brazil
72E3 Inirida *R* Colombia
9C2 Inishowen *District* Irish Republic
9C2 Inishtrahull Sd Irish Republic
34C1 Injune Australia
34B1 Innamincka Australia
8D4 Innerleithen Scotland
31B1 Inner Mongolia Aut. Region China
32D2 Innisfail Australia
18C3 Innsbruck Austria
50B4 Inongo Zaïre
19D2 Inowrocław Poland
48C2 In Salah Algeria
28A3 Insil S Korea
20L2 Inta Russian Federation
16B1 Interlaken Switzerland
33H3 International Date Line
61E1 International Falls USA
29D3 Inubo-saki *C* Japan
55L4 Inukjuak Canada
54E3 Inuvik Canada
54E3 Inuvik *Region* Canada
8C3 Inveraray Scotland
8D3 Inverbervie Scotland
35A3 Invercargill New Zealand
34D1 Inverell Australia
8C3 Invergordon Scotland
8C3 Inverness Scotland
8D3 Inverurie Scotland
32C4 Investigator Str Australia
26B1 Inya Russian Federation
25Q3 Inya *R* Russian Federation
51D5 Inyanga Zimbabwe
66D3 Inyokern USA
66C2 Inyo Mts USA
50B4 Inzia *R* Zaïre
17E3 Ioánnina Greece
63C1 Iola USA
8B3 Iona *I* Scotland
51B5 Iôna Nat Pk Angola
58C1 Ione USA
17E3 Ionian Is Greece
17D3 Ionian S Greece/Italy
Iónioi Nísoi *Is* = Ionian Islands
17F3 Íos *I* Greece
20J3 Iosser Russian Federation
61E2 Iowa *R* USA
61E2 Iowa *State* USA
64A2 Iowa City USA
61E2 Iowa Falls USA
75C2 Ipameri Brazil
75D2 Ipanema Brazil
21G6 Ipatovo Russian Federation
72C3 Ipiales Colombia
75E1 Ipiaú Brazil
75B4 Ipiranga Brazil
30C5 Ipoh Malaysia
73H7 Iporá Brazil
17F2 Ipsala Turkey
34D1 Ipswich Australia
7E3 Ipswich England
68E1 Ipswich USA
19G2 Iput *R* Russian Federation
75C3 Iquape Brazil
74B2 Iquique Chile
72D4 Iquitos Peru
17F3 Iráklion Greece
38D2 Iran *Republic* SW Asia
70B2 Irapuato Mexico
40D3 Iraq *Republic* SW Asia
75B4 Irati Brazil
49D2 Irāwan *Watercourse* Libya
45C2 Irbid Jordan
20L4 Irbit Russian Federation
10B3 Ireland, Republic of NW Europe
73G3 Ireng *R* Guyana
28B3 Iri S Korea
27G7 Irian Jaya *Province* Indonesia
50C2 Iriba Chad
51D4 Iringa Tanzania
26F4 Iriomote *I* Ryukyu Is, Japan
69A3 Iriona Honduras
73H5 Iriri *R* Brazil
10B3 Irish S England/Ire
25M4 Irkutsk Russian Federation
32C4 Iron Knob Australia
64B1 Iron Mountain USA
32D2 Iron Range Australia
64B1 Iron River USA
64C3 Irontown USA
64A1 Ironwood USA
57E2 Iroquois Falls Canada
29C4 Iro-zaki *C* Japan
30B2 Irrawaddy *R* Burma
30A2 Irrawaddy,Mouths of the Burma
24H4 Irtysh *R* Russian Federation
15B1 Irún Spain
8C4 Irvine Scotland
8C4 Irvine *R* Scotland
63C2 Irving USA
66C3 Isabella Res USA
54H2 Isachsen Canada
54H2 Isachsen,C Canada
55Q3 Ísafjörður Iceland
28C4 Isahaya Japan
50C3 Isangi Zaïre
8E1 Isbister Scotland
16C2 Ischia *I* Italy
29C4 Ise Japan
13D2 Iserlohn Germany
16C2 Isernia Italy
29C4 Ise-wan *B* Japan
Isfahan = Esfahan
26F4 Ishigaki *I* Ryukyu Is, Japan
29E2 Ishikari *R* Japan
29E2 Ishikari-wan *B* Japan
24H4 Ishim Russian Federation
24H4 Ishim *R* Kazakhstan
29E3 Ishinomaki Japan
29D3 Ishioka Japan
42C1 Ishkashim Afghanistan
64B1 Ishpeming USA
24J4 Isil'kul' Russian Federation
50D3 Isiolo Kenya
50C3 Isiro Zaïre
40C2 Iskenderun Turkey
40C2 Iskenderun Körfezi *B* Turkey
40B1 İskilip Turkey
24K4 Iskitim Russian Federation
17E2 Iskur *R* Bulgaria
42C2 Islamabad Pakistan
67B4 Islamorada USA
57D1 Island L Canada
9D2 Island Magee Northern Ireland
58D2 Island Park USA
35B1 Islands,B of New Zealand
Islas Baleares = Balearic Islands
Islas Malvinas = Falkland Islands
8B4 Islay *I* Scotland
14C2 Isle *R* France
Isle, Island, Isola etc : see also individual island names
7D4 Isle of Wight *County* England
64B1 Isle Royale Nat Pk USA
7A5 Isles of Scilly England
66B1 Isleton USA
40B3 Ismâ'ilîya Egypt
40B4 Isna Egypt
51E6 Isoanala Madagascar
51D5 Isoka Zambia
16D3 Isola de Correnti, C Sicily, Italy
29C3 Isosaki Japan
40B2 Isparta Turkey
45C2 Israel *Republic* SW Asia
15C2 Isser *R* Algeria
14C2 Issoire France
14C2 Issoudun France
39F1 Issyk Kul', Ozero *L* Kirgizia
40A1 İstanbul Turkey
17E3 Istiáia Greece
67B3 Istokpoga,L USA
16C1 Istra *Pen* Croatia
75C2 Itaberai Brazil
75D2 Itabira Brazil
75D3 Itabirito Brazil
75E1 Itabuna Brazil
75E1 Itacaré Brazil
73G4 Itacoatiara Brazil
75A3 Itacurubí del Rosario Paraguay
75C1 Itaguari *R* Brazil
72C2 Itagui Colombia
75B4 Itaipu, Reprêsa *Res* Brazil/Paraguay
73G4 Itaituba Brazil
74G3 Itajaí Brazil
75C3 Itajuba Brazil
16C2 Italy *Republic* Europe
75E2 Itamaraju Brazil
75D2 Itamarandiba Brazil
75D2 Itambacuri Brazil
75D2 Itambé Brazil
75D2 Itambé *Mt* Brazil
43G3 Itānagar India
75C3 Itanhaém Brazil
75D2 Itanhém Brazil
75D2 Itanhém *R* Brazil
75D2 Itaobím Brazil
75C1 Itapaci Brazil
75C3 Itapecerica Brazil
75D3 Itaperuna Brazil
73K7 Itapetinga Brazil
75C3 Itapetininga Brazil
75C3 Itapeva Brazil
73L4 Itapipoca Brazil
75C2 Itapuranga Brazil
74E3 Itaqui Brazil
75D2 Itarantim Brazil
75C3 Itararé Brazil
75C3 Itararé *R* Brazil
75D3 Itaúna Brazil
72F6 Iténez *R* Bolivia/Brazil
65D2 Ithaca USA
45D3 Ithrīyat, Jebel *Mt* Jordan
50C3 Itimbiri *R* Zaïre
75D2 Itinga Brazil
75A2 Itiquira *R* Brazil
55N3 Itivdleq Greenland
29C4 Ito Japan
29D3 Itoigawa Japan
72F6 Itonomas *R* Bolivia
75C3 Itu Brazil
75E1 Ituberá Brazil
75C2 Ituiutaba Brazil
75C2 Itumbiara Brazil
75B2 Iturama Brazil
74C2 Iturbe Argentina
26H2 Iturup *I* Russian Federation
18B2 Itzehoe Germany
25U3 Iul'tin Russian Federation
19F2 Ivacevichi Belarus
75B3 Ivai *R* Brazil
12K5 Ivalo Finland
17D2 Ivangrad Montenegro, Yugoslavia
34B2 Ivanhoe Australia
19E3 Ivano-Frankovsk Ukraine
20G4 Ivanovo Russian Federation
20L3 Ivdel' Russian Federation
50B3 Ivindo *R* Gabon
75B3 Ivinhema Brazil
75B3 Ivinhema *R* Brazil
51E6 Ivohibe Madagascar
51E5 Ivongo Soanierana Madagascar
48B4 Ivory Coast *Republic* Africa
16B1 Ivrea Italy
55L3 Ivujivik Canada
29E3 Iwaki Japan
29D2 Iwaki *R* Japan
29D2 Iwaki-san *Mt* Japan
28C4 Iwakuni Japan
29D2 Iwamizawa Japan
29E2 Iwanai Japan
48C4 Iwo Nigeria
26H4 Iwo Jima *I* Japan
70C3 Ixtepec Mexico
28B4 Iyo Japan
28B4 Iyo-nada *B* Japan
24G4 Izhevsk Russian Federation
20J2 Izhma Russian Federation
20J2 Izhma *R* Russian Federation
41G5 Izkī Oman
19F3 Izmail Ukraine
40A2 İzmir Turkey
17F3 İzmir Körfezi *B* Turkey
40A1 İzmit Turkey
40A1 İznik Turkey
17F2 Iznik Golü *L* Turkey
45D2 Izra' Syria
28A4 Izuhara Japan
29C4 Izumi-sano Japan
28B3 Izumo Japan

J

41F5 Jabal aẓ Ẓannah UAE
43E4 Jabalpur India
40D4 Jabal Shammar *Region* Saudi Arabia
45C1 Jablah Syria
18D2 Jablonec nad Nisou Czech Republic
73L5 Jaboatão Brazil
75C3 Jaboticabal Brazil
15B1 Jaca Spain
73G5 Jacareacanga Brazil
73H8 Jacarezinho Brazil
75C3 Jacarie Brazil
74C4 Jáchal Argentina
75B2 Jaciara Brazil
75D2 Jacinto Brazil
65E1 Jackman Station USA
62C2 Jacksboro USA
68B2 Jacks Mt USA
67A2 Jackson Alabama, USA
34C1 Jackson Australia
66B1 Jackson California, USA
64C2 Jackson Michigan, USA
61E2 Jackson Minnesota, USA
63D2 Jackson Mississippi, USA
64B3 Jackson Missouri, USA
64C3 Jackson Ohio, USA
63E2 Jackson Tennessee, USA
58D2 Jackson Wyoming, USA
35B2 Jackson,C New Zealand
35A2 Jackson Head *Pt* New Zealand
58D2 Jackson L USA
63D2 Jacksonville Arkansas, USA
67B2 Jacksonville Florida, USA
64A3 Jacksonville Illinois, USA
67C2 Jacksonville N Carolina, USA
63C2 Jacksonville Texas, USA
67B2 Jacksonville Beach USA
69C3 Jacmel Haiti
42B3 Jacobabad Pakistan
73K6 Jacobina Brazil
Jadotville = Likasi
72C5 Jaén Peru
15B2 Jaén Spain
Jaffa = Tel Aviv-Yafo
34A3 Jaffa,C Australia
44B4 Jaffna Sri Lanka
68D1 Jaffrey USA
43F4 Jagannathganj Ghat Bangladesh
44C2 Jagdalpur India
41G4 Jagin *R* Iran
44B2 Jagtial India
75E1 Jaguaquara Brazil
74F4 Jaguarão *R* Brazil/Uruguay
75C3 Jaguariaiva Brazil
21H8 Jahan Dāgh *Mt* Iran
41F4 Jahrom Iran
31A2 Jainca China
42D3 Jaipur India
42C3 Jaisalmer India
41G2 Jajarm Iran
16D2 Jajce Bosnia-Herzegovina
27D7 Jakarta Indonesia
55N3 Jakobshavn Greenland
12J6 Jakobstad Finland
62B2 Jal USA
42C2 Jalalabad Afghanistan
70C3 Jalapa Mexico
75B3 Jales Brazil
43F3 Jaleswar Nepal
42D4 Jalgaon India
48D4 Jalingo Nigeria
42D5 Jālna India
15B1 Jalón *R* Spain
49E2 Jalo Oasis Libya
42C3 Jālor India
43F3 Jalpāiguri India
49E2 Jālū Oasis Libya
72B4 Jama Ecuador
50E3 Jamaame Somalia
69B3 Jamaica *I* Caribbean Sea
69B3 Jamaica Chan Haiti/Jamaica
43F4 Jamalpur Bangladesh
27D7 Jambi Indonesia

42C4 **Jambusar** India
60D1 **James** *R* N Dakota, USA
65D3 **James** *R* Virginia, USA
55K4 **James B** Canada
34A2 **Jamestown** Australia
60D1 **Jamestown** N Dakota, USA
65D2 **Jamestown** New York, USA
68E2 **Jamestown** Rhode Island, USA
47D3 **Jamestown** South Africa
54J5 **Jamestown** USA
44B2 **Jamkhandi** India
42C2 **Jammu** India
42D2 **Jammu and Kashmīr** *State* India
42B4 **Jāmnagar** India
42C3 **Jampur** Pakistan
20C3 **Jämsä** Finland
43F4 **Jamshedpur** India
45D3 **Janab, Wadi el** Jordan
43F3 **Janakpur** Nepal
75D2 **Janaúba** Brazil
41F3 **Jandaq** Iran
34D1 **Jandowae** Australia
64B2 **Janesville** USA
76B1 **Jan Mayen** *I* Norwegian Sea
75D2 **Januária** Brazil
42D4 **Jaora** India
26G3 **Japan, S of** Japan
36J3 **Japan Trench** Pacific Ocean
72E4 **Japurá** *R* Brazil
40C2 **Jarābulus** Syria
75C2 **Jaraguá** Brazil
75B3 **Jaraguari** Brazil
15B1 **Jarama** *R* Spain
45C2 **Jarash** Jordan
75A3 **Jardim** Brazil
69B2 **Jardines de la Reina** *Is* Cuba
Jargalant = Hovd
73H3 **Jari** *R* Brazil
43G3 **Jaria Jhānjail** Bangladesh
13C3 **Jarny** France
18D2 **Jarocin** Poland
19E2 **Jarosław** Poland
12G6 **Järpen** Sweden
31B2 **Jartai** China
42C4 **Jasdan** India
48C4 **Jasikan** Ghana
41G4 **Jāsk** Iran
19E3 **Jasło** Poland
74D8 **Jason Is** Falkland Islands
63E2 **Jasper** Alabama, USA
63D1 **Jasper** Arkansas, USA
54G4 **Jasper** Canada
67B2 **Jasper** Florida, USA
64B3 **Jasper** Indiana, USA
63D2 **Jasper** Texas, USA
18D2 **Jastrowie** Poland
75B2 **Jataí** Brazil
15B2 **Játiva** Spain
75C3 **Jau** Brazil
72C6 **Jauja** Peru
43E3 **Jaunpur** India
44B3 **Javadi Hills** India
27D7 **Java,I** Indonesia
Javari *R* **= Yavari**
27D7 **Java S** Indonesia
32A2 **Java Trench** Indonesia
Jawa = Java
27G7 **Jaya, Pk** Indonesia
27H7 **Jayapura** Indonesia
45D2 **Jayrūd** Syria
63D3 **Jeanerette** USA
48C4 **Jebba** Nigeria
50C2 **Jebel Abyad** *Desert Region* Sudan
Jebel esh Sheikh = Hermon, Mt
8D4 **Jedburgh** Scotland
Jedda = Jiddah
19E2 **Jędrzejów** Poland
61E2 **Jefferson** Iowa, USA
63D2 **Jefferson** Texas, USA
58D1 **Jefferson** *R* USA
57D3 **Jefferson City** USA
56B3 **Jefferson,Mt** USA
64B3 **Jeffersonville** USA
45C3 **Jeib, Wadi el** Israel/Jordan
75A3 **Jejui-Guazú** *R* Paraguay
20D4 **Jekabpils** Latvia
18D2 **Jelena Góra** Poland
20C4 **Jelgava** Latvia
27E7 **Jember** Indonesia
62A1 **Jemez Pueblo** USA
18C2 **Jena** Germany
16B3 **Jendouba** Tunisia
45C2 **Jenin** Israel
63D2 **Jennings** USA
55O3 **Jensen Nunatakker** *Mt* Greenland
55K3 **Jens Munk** *I* Canada
34B3 **Jeparit** Australia
73L6 **Jequié** Brazil
75D2 **Jequitai** *R* Brazil
75D2 **Jequitinhonha** Brazil
73K7 **Jequitinhonha** *R* Brazil
48D1 **Jerba, I de** Tunisia
15A2 **Jerez de la Frontera** Spain
15A2 **Jerez de los Caballeros** Spain
45C3 **Jericho** Israel
34C3 **Jerilderie** Australia
58D2 **Jerome** USA
14B2 **Jersey** *I* Channel Islands
57F2 **Jersey City** USA
65D2 **Jersey Shore** USA
64A3 **Jerseyville** USA
40C3 **Jerusalem** Israel
34D3 **Jervis B** Australia
16C1 **Jesenice** Slovenia
18D2 **Jeseniky** *Upland* Czech Republic
43F4 **Jessore** Bangladesh
57E3 **Jesup** USA
62C1 **Jetmore** USA
13D1 **Jever** Germany
68E2 **Jewett City** USA
44C2 **Jeypore** India
17D2 **Jezerce** *Mt* Albania
19E2 **Jezioro Mamry** *L* Poland
19E2 **Jezioro Śniardwy** *L* Poland
45C2 **Jezzine** Lebanon
42C4 **Jhābua** India
42D4 **Jhālāwār** India
42C2 **Jhang Maghiana** Pakistan
42D3 **Jhānsi** India
43E4 **Jhārsuguda** India
42C2 **Jhelum** Pakistan
42C2 **Jhelum** *R* Pakistan
42D3 **Jhunjhunūn** India
31B3 **Jialing Jiang** *R* China
26G2 **Jiamusi** China
28B2 **Ji'an** China
31C4 **Ji'an** Jiangxi, China
31D4 **Jiande** China
31B4 **Jiang'an** China
31D4 **Jiangbiancun** China
31A5 **Jiangcheng** China
31C5 **Jiangmen** China
31D3 **Jiangsu** *Province* China
31C4 **Jiangxi** *Province* China
31A3 **Jiangyou** China
31D1 **Jianping** China
31A5 **Jianshui** China
31D4 **Jian Xi** *R* China
31D4 **Jianyang** China
28B2 **Jiaohe** China
31E2 **Jiaonan** China
31E2 **Jiao Xian** China
31E2 **Jiaozhou Wan** *B* China
31C2 **Jiaozuo** China
31E3 **Jiaxiang** China
26C3 **Jiayuguan** China
75C2 **Jibão, Serra do** *Mts* Brazil
50D1 **Jiddah** Saudi Arabia
31D3 **Jieshou** China
31C2 **Jiexiu** China
31A3 **Jigzhi** China
18D3 **Jihlava** Czech Republic
16B3 **Jijel** Algeria
50E3 **Jilib** Somalia
28B2 **Jilin** China
28B2 **Jilin** *Province* China
15B1 **Jiloca** *R* Spain
50D3 **Jima** Ethiopia
62B3 **Jiménez** Coahuila, Mexico
31D2 **Jinan** China
42D3 **Jind** India
31B2 **Jingbian** China
31D4 **Jingdezhen** China
30C1 **Jinghong** China
31C3 **Jingmen** China
31B2 **Jingning** China
31B4 **Jing Xian** China
28B2 **Jingyu** China
31D4 **Jinhua** China
31C1 **Jining** Inner Mongolia, China
31D2 **Jining** Shandong, China
50D3 **Jinja** Uganda
30C1 **Jinping** China
31A4 **Jinsha Jiang** *R* China
31C4 **Jinshi** China
31E1 **Jinxi** China
28A2 **Jin Xian** China
31E1 **Jinzhou** China
72F5 **Jiparaná** *R* Brazil
72B4 **Jipijapa** Ecuador
41G4 **Jīroft** Iran
50E3 **Jirriiban** Somalia
31B4 **Jishou** China
40C2 **Jisr ash Shughūr** Syria
17E2 **Jiu** *R* Romania
31D4 **Jiujiang** China
31C4 **Jiuling Shan** *Hills* China
31A4 **Jiulong** China
31D4 **Jiulong Jiang** *R* China
26G2 **Jixi** China
45C3 **Jīza** Jordan
50E2 **Jīzān** Saudi Arabia
48A3 **Joal** Senegal
75D2 **João Monlevade** Brazil
73M5 **João Pessoa** Brazil
73J7 **João Pinheiro** Brazil
42C3 **Jodhpur** India
12K6 **Joensuu** Finland
13C3 **Joeuf** France
43F3 **Jogbani** India
44A3 **Jog Falls** India
47D2 **Johannesburg** South Africa
59C3 **Johannesburg** USA
55L2 **Johan Pen** Canada
58C2 **John Day** USA
58B1 **John Day** *R* USA
57F3 **John H Kerr L** USA
65D3 **John H. Kerr Res** USA
62B1 **John Martin Res** USA
8D2 **John o'Groats** Scotland
63C1 **John Redmond Res** USA
68A2 **Johnsonburg** USA
68C1 **Johnson City** New York, USA
67B1 **Johnson City** Tennessee, USA
67B2 **Johnston** USA
69N2 **Johnston Pt** St Vincent
68C1 **Johnstown** New York, USA
65D2 **Johnstown** Pennsylvania, USA
30C5 **Johor Bharu** Malaysia
14C2 **Joigny** France
74G3 **Joinville** Brazil
13C3 **Joinville** France
20J5 **Jok** *R* Russian Federation
12H5 **Jokkmokk** Sweden
21H8 **Jolfa** Iran
57E2 **Joliet** USA
55L5 **Joliette** Canada
27F6 **Jolo** Philippines
27F6 **Jolo** *I* Philippines
39H2 **Joma** *Mt* China
19E1 **Jonava** Lithuania
31A3 **Jonê** China
57D3 **Jonesboro** Arkansas, USA
63D2 **Jonesboro** Louisiana, USA
55K2 **Jones Sd** Canada
19E1 **Joniškis** Lithuania
12G7 **Jönköping** Sweden
65E1 **Jonquière** Canada
57D3 **Joplin** USA
60B1 **Jordan** Montana, USA
68B1 **Jordan** New York, USA
40C3 **Jordan** *Kingdom* SW Asia
45C2 **Jordan** *R* Israel
58C2 **Jordan Valley** USA
75B4 **Jordão** *R* Brazil
43G3 **Jorhāt** India
20C2 **Jörn** Sweden
12F7 **Jørpeland** Norway
48C3 **Jos** Nigeria
32B2 **Joseph Bonaparte G** Australia
59D3 **Joseph City** USA
55M4 **Joseph, Lac** Canada
24B3 **Jotunheimen** *Mt* Norway
45C2 **Jouai'ya** Lebanon
45C2 **Jounié** Lebanon
43G3 **Jowai** India
50E3 **Jowhar** Somalia
54F5 **Juan de Fuca,Str of** Canada/USA
51E5 **Juan de Nova** *I* Mozambique Channel
72Q **Juan Fernández, Islas** Pacific Ocean
73K5 **Juàzeiro** Brazil
73L5 **Juàzeiro do Norte** Brazil
50D3 **Juba** Sudan
50E3 **Juba** *R* Somalia
45C1 **Jubail** Lebanon
76G2 **Jubany** *Base* Antarctica
40D4 **Jubbah** Saudi Arabia
15B2 **Júcar** *R* Spain
18C3 **Judenburg** Austria
13D1 **Juist** *I* Germany
73K8 **Juiz de Fora** Brazil
74C2 **Jujuy** *State* Argentina
60C2 **Julesburg** USA
72E7 **Juli** Peru
72D7 **Juliaca** Peru
73G3 **Julianatop** *Mt* Surinam
55O3 **Julianehåb** Greenland
13D2 **Jülich** Germany
42D2 **Jullundur** India
43E3 **Jumla** Nepal
45C3 **Jum Suwwāna** *Mt* Jordan
42C4 **Jūnāgadh** India
31D2 **Junan** China
62C2 **Junction** Texas, USA
59D3 **Junction** Utah, USA
56D3 **Junction City** USA
74G2 **Jundiaí** Brazil
54E4 **Juneau** USA
32D4 **Junee** Australia
66C2 **June Lake** USA
16B1 **Jungfrau** *Mt* Switzerland
68B2 **Juniata** *R* USA
74D4 **Junín** Argentina
66B2 **Junipero Serra Peak** *Mt* USA
31A4 **Junlian** China
75D2 **Juparanã, Lagoa** Brazil
74G2 **Juquiá** Brazil
50C3 **Jur** *R* Sudan
8C4 **Jura** *I* Scotland
14D2 **Jura** *Mts* France
8C3 **Jura,Sound of** *Chan* Scotland
45C3 **Jurf ed Darāwīsh** Jordan
24K4 **Jurga** Russian Federation
20C4 **Jūrmala** Latvia
72E4 **Juruá** *R* Brazil
73G6 **Juruena** *R* Brazil
45D1 **Jūsīyah** Syria
72E4 **Jutaí** *R* Brazil
70D3 **Juticalpa** Honduras
Jutland *Pen* **= Jylland**
69A2 **Juventud, Isla de la** Cuba
41G3 **Jūymand** Iran
18B1 **Jylland** *Pen* Denmark
12K6 **Jyväskyla** Finland

K

39F2 **K2** *Mt* China/India
41G2 **Kaakhka** Turkmenistan
47E2 **Kaapmuiden** South Africa
27F7 **Kabaena** Indonesia
32B1 **Kabaena** *I* Indonesia
48A4 **Kabala** Sierra Leone
50D4 **Kabale** Uganda
50C4 **Kabalo** Zaïre
50C4 **Kabambare** Zaïre
50D3 **Kabarole** Uganda
64C1 **Kabinakagami L** Canada
50C4 **Kabinda** Zaïre
45C1 **Kabīr** *R* Syria
41E3 **Kabir Kuh** *Mts* Iran
51C5 **Kabompo** Zambia
51C5 **Kabompo** *R* Zambia
51C4 **Kabongo** Zaïre
42B2 **Kabul** Afghanistan
42B4 **Kachchh,G of** India
20K4 **Kachkanar** Russian Federation
25M4 **Kachug** Russian Federation
30B3 **Kadan** *I* Burma
42C4 **Kadi** India
40B2 **Kadınhanı** Turkey
44B3 **Kadiri** India
21F6 **Kadiyevka** Ukraine
60C2 **Kadoka** USA
51C5 **Kadoma** Zimbabwe
50C2 **Kadugli** Sudan
48C3 **Kaduna** Nigeria
48C3 **Kaduna** *R* Nigeria
44B3 **Kadūr** India
43H3 **Kadusam** *Mt* China
20K3 **Kadzherom** Russian Federation
28A3 **Kaechon** N Korea
48A3 **Kaédi** Mauritius
66E5 **Kaena Pt** Hawaiian Islands
28B3 **Kaesŏng** N Korea
48C4 **Kafanchan** Nigeria
48A3 **Kaffrine** Senegal
45D1 **Kafr Behum** Syria
45A3 **Kafr Sa'd** Egypt
45A3 **Kafr Saqv** Egypt
45D1 **Kafrūn Bashūr** Syria
51C5 **Kafue** Zambia
51C5 **Kafue** *R* Zambia
51C5 **Kafue Nat Pk** Zambia
29D3 **Kaga** Japan
24H6 **Kagan** Uzbekistan
21G7 **Kağızman** Turkey
19F3 **Kagul** Moldavia
41G2 **Kāhak** Iran
50D4 **Kahama** Tanzania
42B3 **Kahan** Pakistan
51B4 **Kahemba** Zaïre
13E2 **Kahler Asten** *Mt* Germany
41G4 **Kahnūj** Iran
64A2 **Kahoka** USA
66E5 **Kahoolawe** *I* Hawaiian Islands
40C2 **Kahramanmaraş** Turkey
66E5 **Kahuku Pt** Hawaiian Islands
66E5 **Kahului** Hawaiian Islands
35B2 **Kaiapoi** New Zealand
59D3 **Kaibab Plat** USA
73G2 **Kaieteur Falls** Guyana
31C3 **Kaifeng** China
27G7 **Kai, Kepulauan** *Arch* Indonesia
35B1 **Kaikohe** New Zealand
33G5 **Kaikoura** New Zealand
35B2 **Kaikoura Pen** New Zealand
35B2 **Kaikoura Range** *Mts* New Zealand
31B4 **Kaili** China
28A2 **Kailu** China
66E5 **Kailua** Hawaii
66E5 **Kailua** Oahu, Hawaiian Islands
27G7 **Kaimana** Indonesia
35C1 **Kaimenawa Mts** New Zealand
29C4 **Kainan** Japan
48C3 **Kainji Res** Nigeria
35B1 **Kaipara Harbour** *B* New Zealand
31C5 **Kaiping** China
16C3 **Kairouan** Tunisia
66C2 **Kaiser Peak** *Mt* USA
14D2 **Kaiserslautern** Germany
28B2 **Kaishantun** China
19E2 **Kaisiadorys** Lithuania
35B1 **Kaitaia** New Zealand
35A3 **Kaitangata** New Zealand
42D3 **Kaithal** India
66E5 **Kaiwi Chan** Hawaiian Islands
31B3 **Kai Xian** China
28A2 **Kaiyuan** Liaoning, China
31A5 **Kaiyuan** Yunnan, China
12K6 **Kajaani** Finland
42B2 **Kajaki** Afghanistan
50D4 **Kajiado** Kenya
42B2 **Kajrān** Afghanistan
50D2 **Kaka** Sudan
64B1 **Kakabeka Falls** Canada
50D3 **Kakamega** Kenya
28B4 **Kake** Japan
21E6 **Kakhovskoye Vodokhranilishche** *Res* Ukraine
41F4 **Kākī** Iran
44C2 **Kākināda** India
29B4 **Kakogawa** Japan
54D2 **Kaktovik** USA
29D3 **Kakuda** Japan
16B3 **Kalaat Khasba** Tunisia
17E3 **Kalabáka** Greece
51C5 **Kalabo** Zambia
21G5 **Kalach** Russian Federation
21G6 **Kalach-na-Donu** Russian Federation
43G4 **Kaladan** *R* Burma/India
66E5 **Ka Lae** *C* Hawaiian Islands
51C6 **Kalahari Desert** Botswana
47C2 **Kalahari Gemsbok Nat Pk** South Africa
20C3 **Kalajoki** Finland
25N4 **Kalakan** Russian Federation
27C6 **Kalakepen** Indonesia
42C1 **Kalam** Pakistan
17E3 **Kalámai** Greece
57E2 **Kalamazoo** USA
66E5 **Kalapana** Hawaiian Islands
19F3 **Kalarash** Moldavia
42B3 **Kalat** Pakistan
66E5 **Kalaupapa** Hawaiian Islands
40B1 **Kalecik** Turkey
50C4 **Kalémié** Zaïre
20E2 **Kalevala** Russian Federation
43G4 **Kalewa** Burma
32B4 **Kalgoorlie** Australia
43E3 **Kali** *R* India/Nepal
50C4 **Kalima** Zaïre
27E7 **Kalimantan** *Terr* Indonesia
17F3 **Kálimnos** *I* Greece
43F3 **Kālimpang** India
43K1 **Kali Nadī** *R* India
12J8 **Kaliningrad** Russian Federation
21D5 **Kalinkovichi** Belarus
19F3 **Kalinovka** Ukraine
56B2 **Kalispell** USA
19D2 **Kalisz** Poland
50D4 **Kaliua** Tanzania
12J5 **Kalix** *R* Sweden
51B6 **Kalkfeld** Namibia
47C1 **Kalkfontein** Botswana
12K6 **Kallavesi** *L* Finland
17F3 **Kallonis Kólpos** *B* Greece
12H7 **Kalmar** Sweden
21H6 **Kalmyk Republic** Russian Federation
51C5 **Kalomo** Zambia
64A2 **Kalona** USA
44A3 **Kalpeni** *I* India
42D3 **Kālpi** India
20F5 **Kaluga** Russian Federation
12G7 **Kalundborg** Denmark
19E3 **Kalush** Ukraine
44A2 **Kalyān** India
44B3 **Kalyandurg** India
20F4 **Kalyazin** Russian Federation
20J3 **Kama** *R* Russian Federation
29E3 **Kamaishi** Japan
42C2 **Kamalia** Pakistan
51B5 **Kamanjab** Namibia
25O4 **Kamara** China
42D2 **Kamat** *Mt* China/India
44B4 **Kambam** India
20J4 **Kambarka** Russian Federation
48A4 **Kambia** Sierra Leone
25S4 **Kamchatka** *Pen* Russian Federation
19F3 **Kamenets Podolskiy** Ukraine
20G5 **Kamenka** Russian Federation

24K4 **Kamen-na-Obi** Russian Federation
25S3 **Kamenskoya** Russian Federation
20L4 **Kamensk-Ural'skiy** Russian Federation
47B3 **Kamieskroon** South Africa
54H3 **Kamilukuak L** Canada
51C4 **Kamina** Zaïre
55J3 **Kaminak L** Canada
29D3 **Kaminoyama** Japan
54F4 **Kamloops** Canada
41E1 **Kamo** Armenia
29D3 **Kamogawa** Japan
50D3 **Kampala** Uganda
30C5 **Kampar** Malaysia
18B2 **Kampen** Netherlands
30B2 **Kamphaeng Phet** Thailand
30C3 **Kampot** Cambodia
20K4 **Kamskoye Vodokhranilishche** *Res* Russian Federation
42D4 **Kāmthi** India
21H5 **Kamyshin** Russian Federation
20L4 **Kamyshlov** Russian Federation
55L4 **Kanaaupscow** *R* Canada
59D3 **Kanab** USA
50C4 **Kananga** Zaïre
20H4 **Kanash** Russian Federation
29C3 **Kanayama** Japan
29D3 **Kanazawa** Japan
44B3 **Kānchipuram** India
20E2 **Kandagan** Indonesia
42B2 **Kandahar** Afghanistan
20E2 **Kandalaksha** Russian Federation
12L5 **Kandalakshskaya Guba** *B* Russian Federation
13D3 **Kandel** *Mt* Germany
48C3 **Kandi** Benin
34C2 **Kandos** Australia
44C4 **Kandy** Sri Lanka
65D2 **Kane** USA
55L1 **Kane Basin** *B* Canada
50B2 **Kanem** *Desert Region* Chad
66E5 **Kaneohe** Hawaiian Islands
20F2 **Kanevka** Russian Federation
47C1 **Kang** Botswana
48B3 **Kangaba** Mali
40C2 **Kangal** Turkey
55N3 **Kangâmiut** Greenland
41F4 **Kangān** Iran
30C4 **Kangar** Malaysia
32C4 **Kangaroo I** Australia
55N3 **Kangâtsiaq** Greenland
41E3 **Kangavar** Iran
31C1 **Kangbao** China
39G3 **Kangchenjunga** *Mt* China/Nepal
31A4 **Kangding** China
32A1 **Kangean** *Is* Indonesia
55P3 **Kangerdlugssuaq** *B* Greenland
55P3 **Kangerdlugssuatsaiq** *B* Greenland
50D3 **Kangetet** Kenya
28B2 **Kanggye** N Korea
28B3 **Kanghwa** S Korea
55M4 **Kangiqsualujjuaq** Canada
55L3 **Kangiqsujuak** Canada
55L3 **Kangirsuk** Canada
28B3 **Kangnŭng** S Korea
50B3 **Kango** Gabon
28A2 **Kangping** China
26C4 **Kangto** *Mt* China/India
31B3 **Kang Xian** China
51C4 **Kaniama** Zaïre
44B2 **Kani Giri** India
20G2 **Kanin, Poluostrov** *Pen* Russian Federation
12J6 **Kankaanpää** Finland
64B2 **Kankakee** USA
64B2 **Kankakee** *R* USA
48B3 **Kankan** Guinea
43E4 **Kānker** India
67B1 **Kannapolis** USA
44B4 **Kanniyākumari** India
48C3 **Kano** Nigeria
60C3 **Kanorado** USA
43E3 **Kānpur** India
61D3 **Kansas** *R* USA
56D3 **Kansas** *State* USA
57D3 **Kansas City** USA
31D5 **Kanshi** China
25L4 **Kansk** Russian Federation
28A3 **Kansŏng** S Korea
48C3 **Kantchari** Burkina
48C4 **Kanté** Togo
43F4 **Kanthi** India
54C3 **Kantishna** USA
9B3 **Kanturk** Irish Republic
47D1 **Kanye** Botswana
26E4 **Kaohsiung** Taiwan
51B5 **Kaoka Veld** *Plain* Namibia
48A3 **Kaolack** Senegal
51C5 **Kaoma** Zambia
66E5 **Kapaa** Hawaiian Islands
66E5 **Kapaau** Hawaiian Islands
51C4 **Kapanga** Zaïre
12H7 **Kapellskär** Sweden
Kap Farvel = Farewell, C
51C5 **Kapiri** Zambia
63D2 **Kaplan** USA
18C3 **Kaplice** Czech Republic
30B4 **Kapoe** Thailand
51C4 **Kapona** Zaïre
17D1 **Kaposvár** Hungary
55L2 **Kap Parry** *C* Greenland
28A2 **Kapsan** N Korea
27E6 **Kapuas** *R* Indonesia
34A2 **Kapunda** Australia
42D2 **Kapurthala** India
55K5 **Kapuskasing** Canada
64C1 **Kapuskasing** *R* Canada
34D2 **Kaputar** *Mt* Australia
21H8 **Kapydzhik** *Mt* Armenia
28A3 **Kapyŏng** S Korea
21G8 **Kara** *R* Turkey
40B1 **Karabük** Turkey
17F2 **Karacabey** Turkey
42B4 **Karachi** Pakistan
44A2 **Karād** India
21F7 **Kara Dağları** *Mt* Turkey
21D7 **Karadeniz Boğazi** *Str* Turkey
26E1 **Karaftit** Russian Federation
24J5 **Karaganda** Kazakhstan
24J5 **Karagayly** Kazakhstan
25S4 **Karaginskiy, Ostrov** *I* Russian Federation
44B3 **Kāraikāl** India
41F2 **Karaj** Iran
40C3 **Karak** Jordan
24G5 **Karakalpak Republic** Uzbekistan
42D1 **Karakax He** *R* China
27F6 **Karakelong** *I* Indonesia
42D1 **Karakoram** *Mts* India
42D1 **Karakoram P** China/India
48A3 **Karakoro** *Watercourse* Mali/Mauritius
24G6 **Karakumy** *Desert* Turkmenistan
45C3 **Karama** Jordan
21E8 **Karaman** Turkey
24K5 **Karamay** China
35B2 **Karamea** New Zealand
35B2 **Karamea Bight** *B* New Zealand
42D4 **Kāranja** India
21E8 **Karanlik** *R* Turkey
40B2 **Karapınar** Turkey
24J2 **Kara S** Russian Federation
47B2 **Karasburg** Namibia
12K5 **Karasjok** Norway
24J4 **Karasuk** Russian Federation
40C2 **Karataş** Turkey
24H5 **Kara Tau** *Mts* Kazakhstan
30B3 **Karathuri** Burma
28B4 **Karatsu** Japan
24K2 **Karaul** Russian Federation
45B1 **Karavostasi** Cyprus
41F4 **Karāz** Iran
41D3 **Karbalā'** Iraq
19E3 **Karcag** Hungary
17E3 **Kardhítsa** Greece
20E3 **Karelian Republic** Russian Federation
44E3 **Karen** Andaman Islands
20K3 **Karepino** Russian Federation
12J5 **Karesvando** Sweden
48B2 **Karet** *Desert Region* Mauritius
24K4 **Kargasok** Russian Federation
20F3 **Kargopol'** Russian Federation
48D3 **Kari** Nigeria
51C5 **Kariba** Zimbabwe
51C5 **Kariba Dam** Zambia/Zimbabwe
51C5 **Kariba, L** Zambia/Zimbabwe
47B1 **Karibib** Namibia
50D2 **Karima** Sudan
27D7 **Karimata** *I* Indonesia
43G4 **Karīmganj** India
44B2 **Karīmnagar** India
50E2 **Karin** Somalia
12J6 **Karis** Finland
50C4 **Karisimbe** *Mt* Zaïre
17E3 **Káristos** Greece
44A3 **Kārkal** India
27H7 **Karkar** *I* Papua New Guinea
41E3 **Karkheh** *R* Iran
21E6 **Karkinitskiy Zaliv** *B* Ukraine
25L5 **Karlik Shan** *Mt* China
18D2 **Karlino** Poland
16D2 **Karlobag** Croatia
16D1 **Karlovac** Croatia
17E2 **Karlovo** Bulgaria
18C2 **Karlovy Vary** Czech Republic
12G7 **Karlshamn** Sweden
12G7 **Karlskoga** Sweden
12H7 **Karlskrona** Sweden
18B3 **Karlsruhe** Germany
12G7 **Karlstad** Sweden
61D1 **Karlstad** USA
54C4 **Karluk** USA
43G4 **Karnafuli Res** Bangladesh
42D3 **Karnāl** India
44A2 **Karnātaka** *State* India
17F2 **Karnobat** Bulgaria
51C5 **Karoi** Zimbabwe
51D4 **Karonga** Malawi
50D2 **Karora** Sudan
17F3 **Kárpathos** *I* Greece
55N2 **Karrats Fjord** Greenland
47C3 **Karree Berge** *Mts* South Africa
21G7 **Kars** Turkey
24H5 **Karsakpay** Kazakhstan
19F1 **Kārsava** Latvia
38E2 **Karshi** Uzbekistan
24G2 **Karskiye Vorota, Proliv** *Str* Russian Federation
12J6 **Karstula** Finland
45C1 **Kartaba** Lebanon
17F2 **Kartal** Turkey
20L5 **Kartaly** Russian Federation
68A2 **Karthaus** USA
41E3 **Kārūn** *R* Iran
19D3 **Karviná** Czech Republic
43E3 **Karwa** India
44A3 **Kārwār** India
26E1 **Karymskoye** Russian Federation
50B4 **Kasai** *R* Zaïre
51C5 **Kasaji** Zaïre
51D5 **Kasama** Zambia
51D4 **Kasanga** Tanzania
44A3 **Kāsaragod** India
54H3 **Kasba L** Canada
51C5 **Kasempa** Zambia
51C5 **Kasenga** Zaïre
50D3 **Kasese** Uganda
43K2 **Kasganj** India
41F3 **Kāshān** Iran
39F2 **Kashi** China
28B4 **Kashima** Japan
42D3 **Kāshipur** India
29D3 **Kashiwazaki** Japan
41G2 **Kāshmar** Iran
22E4 **Kashmir** *State* India
20G5 **Kasimov** Russian Federation
64B3 **Kaskaskia** *R* USA
12J6 **Kaskinen** Finland
20L4 **Kasli** Russian Federation
54G5 **Kaslo** Canada
50C4 **Kasongo** Zaïre
51B4 **Kasongo-Lunda** Zaïre
17F3 **Kásos** *I* Greece
21H6 **Kaspiyskiy** Russian Federation
50D2 **Kassala** Sudan
18B2 **Kassel** Germany
48C1 **Kasserine** Tunisia
51B5 **Kassinga** Angola
40B1 **Kastamonu** Turkey
17E3 **Kastélli** Greece
40A2 **Kastellorizon** *I* Greece
17E2 **Kastoría** Greece
17F3 **Kástron** Greece
29D3 **Kasugai** Japan
29B3 **Kasumi** Japan
51D5 **Kasungu** Malawi
42C2 **Kasur** Pakistan
51C5 **Kataba** Zambia
65F1 **Katahdin,Mt** USA
50C4 **Katako-kombe** Zaïre
54D3 **Katalla** USA
25Q4 **Katangli** Russian Federation
32A4 **Katanning** Australia
44E4 **Katchall** *I* Nicobar Is, Indian Ocean
17E2 **Kateríni** Greece
54E4 **Kates Needle** *Mt* Canada/USA
40B4 **Katharîna, Gebel** *Mt* Egypt
32C2 **Katherine** Australia
42C4 **Kāthiāwār** *Pen* India
45B3 **Kathib el Henu** *Hill* Egypt
43F3 **Kathmandu** Nepal
42D2 **Kathua** India
43F3 **Katihār** India
51C5 **Katima Mulilo** Namibia
48B4 **Katiola** Ivory Coast
54C4 **Katmai,Mt** USA
43E4 **Katni** India
34D2 **Katoomba** Australia
19D2 **Katowice** Poland
12H7 **Katrineholm** Sweden
8C3 **Katrine, Loch** *L* Scotland
48C3 **Katsina** Nigeria
48C4 **Katsina** *R* Cameroon/Nigeria
48C4 **Katsina Ala** Nigeria
29D3 **Katsuta** Japan
29D3 **Katsuura** Japan
29C3 **Katsuyama** Japan
24H6 **Kattakurgan** Uzbekistan
12G7 **Kattegat** *Str* Denmark/Sweden
13E3 **Katzenbuckel** *Mt* Germany
66E5 **Kauai** *I* Hawaiian Islands
66E5 **Kauai Chan** Hawaiian Islands
66E5 **Kaulakahi Chan** Hawaiian Islands
66E5 **Kaunakakai** Hawaiian Islands
20C5 **Kaunas** Lithuania
48C3 **Kaura Namoda** Nigeria
12J5 **Kautokeino** Norway
17E2 **Kavadarci** Macedonia, Yugoslavia
17D2 **Kavajë** Albania
44B3 **Kavali** India
17E2 **Kavála** Greece
42B4 **Kāvda** India
32E1 **Kavieng** Papua New Guinea
29C3 **Kawagoe** Japan
29C3 **Kawaguchi** Japan
66E5 **Kawaihae** Hawaiian Islands
35B1 **Kawakawa** New Zealand
51C4 **Kawambwa** Zambia
43E4 **Kawardha** India
65D2 **Kawartha Lakes** Canada
29D3 **Kawasaki** Japan
66C2 **Kaweah** *R* USA
35C1 **Kawerau** New Zealand
35B1 **Kawhia** New Zealand
48B3 **Kaya** Burkina
27E6 **Kayan** *R* Indonesia
44B4 **Kāyankulam** India
60B2 **Kaycee** USA
59D3 **Kayenta** USA
48A3 **Kayes** Mali
21F8 **Kayseri** Turkey
25P2 **Kazach'ye** Russian Federation
41E1 **Kazakh** Azerbaijan
24G5 **Kazakhstan** *Republic* Asia
20H4 **Kazan'** Russian Federation
17F2 **Kazanlŭk** Bulgaria
26H4 **Kazan Retto** *Is* Japan
19F3 **Kazatin** Ukraine
21G7 **Kazbek** *Mt* Georgia
41F4 **Kāzerūn** Iran
20J3 **Kazhim** Russian Federation
41E1 **Kazi Magomed** Azerbaijan
19E3 **Kazincbarcika** Hungary
20M3 **Kazym** *R* Russian Federation
20M3 **Kazymskaya** Russian Federation
17E3 **Kéa** *I* Greece
9C2 **Keady** Northern Ireland
66E5 **Kealaikahiki Chan** Hawaiian Islands
56D2 **Kearney** USA
59D4 **Kearny** USA
40C2 **Keban Baraji** *Res* Turkey
48A3 **Kébémer** Senegal
48C1 **Kebili** Tunisia
45D1 **Kebīr** *R* Lebanon/Syria
12H5 **Kebnekaise** *Mt* Sweden
19D3 **Kecskemét** Hungary
19E1 **Kedainiai** Lithuania
65F1 **Kedgwick** Canada
27E7 **Kediri** Indonesia
48A3 **Kédougou** Senegal
20J3 **Kedva** Russian Federation
54E3 **Keele Pk** *Mt* Canada
59C3 **Keeler** USA
27C8 **Keeling Is** Indian Ocean
26F4 **Keelung** Taiwan
66C3 **Keene** California, USA
65E2 **Keene** New Hampshire, USA
47B2 **Keetmanshoop** Namibia
64B2 **Keewanee** USA
64A1 **Keewatin** USA
55J3 **Keewatin** *Region* Canada
17E3 **Kefallinía** *I* Greece
45C2 **Kefar Sava** Israel
48C4 **Keffi** Nigeria
12A2 **Keflavík** Iceland
54G4 **Keg River** Canada
30B1 **Kehsi Mansam** Burma
48C3 **Keita** Niger
34B3 **Keith** Australia
8D3 **Keith** Scotland
54F3 **Keith Arm** *B* Canada
6C3 **Keithley** England
55M3 **Kekertuk** Canada
42D3 **Kekri** India
30C5 **Kelang** Malaysia
30C4 **Kelantan** *R* Malaysia
16C3 **Kelibia** Tunisia
42B1 **Kelif** Turkmenistan
40C1 **Kelkit** *R* Turkey
50B4 **Kellé** Congo
54F2 **Kellett,C** Canada
58C1 **Kellogg** USA
24D3 **Kelloselka** Finland
33B9 **Kells** Irish Republic
8C4 **Kells Range** *Hills* Scotland
19E1 **Kelme** Lithuania
54G5 **Kelowna** Canada
54F4 **Kelsey Bay** Canada
8D4 **Kelso** Scotland
58B1 **Kelso** USA
20E3 **Kem'** Russian Federation
20E3 **Kem'** *R* Russian Federation
48B3 **Ke Macina** Mali
24K4 **Kemerovo** Russian Federation
12J5 **Kemi** Finland
12K5 **Kemi** *R* Finland
12K5 **Kemijärvi** Finland
58D2 **Kemmerer** USA
13C2 **Kempen** *Region* Belgium
62C2 **Kemp,L** USA
69B2 **Kemps Bay** The Bahamas
34D2 **Kempsey** Australia
18C3 **Kempten** Germany
65E1 **Kempt,L** Canada
54C3 **Kenai** USA
54C3 **Kenai Pen** USA
50D3 **Kenamuke Swamp** Sudan
6C2 **Kendal** England
34D2 **Kendall** Australia
32B1 **Kendari** Indonesia
27E7 **Kendawangan** Indonesia
43F4 **Kendrāpāra** India
58C1 **Kendrick** USA
63C3 **Kenedy** USA
48A4 **Kenema** Sierra Leone
50B4 **Kenge** Zaïre
30B1 **Kengtung** Burma
47C2 **Kenhardt** South Africa
48A3 **Kéniéba** Mali
48B1 **Kenitra** Morocco
60C1 **Kenmare** USA
62B2 **Kenna** USA
65F1 **Kennebec** *R* USA
68E1 **Kennebunk** USA
63D3 **Kenner** USA
63E1 **Kennett** USA
68C3 **Kennett Square** USA
58C1 **Kennewick** USA
54F4 **Kenny Dam** Canada
55J5 **Kenora** Canada
57E2 **Kenosha** USA
62B2 **Kent** Texas, USA
58B1 **Kent** Washington, USA
7E4 **Kent** *County* England
64B2 **Kentland** USA
64C2 **Kenton** USA
54H3 **Kent Pen** Canada
64C3 **Kentucky** *R* USA
57E3 **Kentucky** *State* USA
57E3 **Kentucky L** USA
63D2 **Kentwood** Louisiana, USA
64B2 **Kentwood** Michigan, USA
50D3 **Kenya** *Republic* Africa
Kenya,Mt = Kirinyaga
64A2 **Keokuk** USA
43E4 **Keonchi** India
43F4 **Keonjhargarh** India
19D2 **Kępno** Poland
44B3 **Kerala** *State* India
34B3 **Kerang** Australia
12K6 **Kerava** Finland
21F6 **Kerch'** Ukraine
20J3 **Kerchem'ya** Russian Federation
32D1 **Kerema** Papua New Guinea
58C1 **Keremeos** Canada
50D2 **Keren** Eritrea
36E7 **Kerguelen** *Is* Indian Ocean
36E7 **Kerguelen Ridge** Indian Ocean
50D4 **Kericho** Kenya
27D7 **Kerinci** *Mt* Indonesia
50D3 **Kerio** *R* Kenya
48D1 **Kerkenna, Îles** Tunisia
38E2 **Kerki** Turkmenistan
Kérkira = Corfu
33H3 **Kermadec Is** Pacific Ocean
33H4 **Kermadec Trench** Pacific Ocean
41G3 **Kermān** Iran
66B2 **Kerman** USA
41E3 **Kermānshāh** Iran
62B2 **Kermit** USA
59C3 **Kern** *R* USA
66C3 **Kernville** USA
20J3 **Keros** Russian Federation
62C2 **Kerrville** USA
9B3 **Kerry Hd** Irish Republic
67B2 **Kershaw** USA
25N5 **Kerulen** *R* Mongolia
48B2 **Kerzaz** Algeria
17F2 **Keşan** Turkey
43N2 **Kesariya** India
29E3 **Kesennuma** Japan
21G7 **Kesir Dağları** *Mt* Turkey
12L5 **Kesten'ga** Russian Federation
6C2 **Keswick** England
48C4 **Kéta** Ghana
27E7 **Ketapang** Indonesia
54E4 **Ketchikan** USA

42B4 **Keti Bandar** Pakistan
19E2 **Kętrzyn** Poland
7D3 **Kettering** England
64C3 **Kettering** USA
58C1 **Kettle** *R* Canada
66C2 **Kettleman City** USA
58C1 **Kettle River Range** *Mts* USA
55L3 **Kettlestone B** Canada
68B1 **Keuka L** USA
41G3 **Kevir-i-Namak** *Salt Flat* Iran
64B2 **Kewaunee** USA
64B1 **Keweenaw B** USA
64B1 **Keweenaw Pen** USA
64C1 **Key Harbour** Canada
67B3 **Key Largo** USA
57E4 **Key West** USA
25M4 **Kezhma** Russian Federation
45D2 **Khabab** Syria
26G2 **Khabarovsk** Russian Federation
21G8 **Khabūr, al** *R* Syria
42B3 **Khairpur** Pakistan
42B3 **Khairpur** *Division* Pakistan
47C1 **Khakhea** Botswana
45B3 **Khalig el Tîna** *B* Egypt
38D4 **Khalīj Maşīrah** *G* Oman
17F3 **Khálki** *I* Greece
17E2 **Khalkidhíki** *Pen* Greece
17E3 **Khalkís** Greece
20L2 **Khal'mer-Yu** Russian Federation
20H4 **Khalturin** Russian Federation
42C4 **Khambhāt,G of** India
42D4 **Khāmgaon** India
30C2 **Kham Keut** Laos
44C2 **Khammam** India
45B3 **Khamsa** Egypt
41E2 **Khamseh** *Mts* Iran
30C2 **Khan** *R* Laos
42B1 **Khanabad** Afghanistan
41E3 **Khānaqīn** Iraq
42D4 **Khandwa** India
42C2 **Khanewal** Pakistan
45D3 **Khan ez Zabīb** Jordan
30D4 **Khanh Hung** Vietnam
17E3 **Khaniá** Greece
26G2 **Khanka, Ozero** *L* China/Russian Federation
Khankendy = Stepanakert
42C3 **Khanpur** Pakistan
45D1 **Khān Shaykhūn** Syria
24H3 **Khanty-Mansiysk** Russian Federation
45C3 **Khan Yunis** Israel
42D1 **Khapalu** India
26E2 **Khapcheranga** Russian Federation
21H6 **Kharabali** Russian Federation
43F4 **Kharagpur** India
42B3 **Kharan** Pakistan
41G4 **Khārān** *R* Iran
41F3 **Kharānaq** Iran
41F4 **Khārg** *I* Iran
49F2 **Khârga Oasis** Egypt
42D4 **Khargon** India
45B3 **Kharîm, Gebel** *Mt* Egypt
21F6 **Khar'kov** Ukraine
20F2 **Kharlovka** Russian Federation
17F2 **Kharmanli** Bulgaria
20G4 **Kharovsk** Russian Federation
50D2 **Khartoum** Sudan
50D2 **Khartoum North** Sudan
28C2 **Khasan** Russian Federation
50D2 **Khashm el Girba** Sudan
43G3 **Khasi-Jaintīa Hills** India
17F2 **Khaskovo** Bulgaria
25M2 **Khatanga** Russian Federation
25N2 **Khatangskiy Zaliv** *Estuary* Russian Federation
25T3 **Khatyrka** Russian Federation
30B3 **Khawsa** Burma
40C4 **Khaybar** Saudi Arabia
40B5 **Khazzan an-Nasr** *L* Egypt
30C2 **Khe Bo** Vietnam
42C4 **Khed Brahma** India
15C2 **Khemis** Algeria
16B3 **Khenchela** Algeria
48B1 **Khenifra** Morocco
43L1 **Kheri** *District* India
15D2 **Kherrata** Algeria
21E6 **Kherson** Ukraine
25N4 **Khilok** Russian Federation
17F3 **Khíos** Greece
17F3 **Khíos** *I* Greece
21D6 **Khmel'nitskiy** Ukraine
19E3 **Khodorov** Ukraine
42B1 **Kholm** Afghanistan
19G1 **Kholm** Russian Federation
47B1 **Khomas Hochland** *Mts* Namibia
30D3 **Khong** Laos
41F4 **Khonj** Iran
26G2 **Khor** Russian Federation
41F5 **Khōr Duwayhin** *B* UAE
42C1 **Khorog** Tajikistan
41E3 **Khorramābad** Iran
41E3 **Khorramshahr** Iran
41G3 **Khosf** Iran
42B2 **Khost** Pakistan
21D6 **Khotin** Ukraine
21D5 **Khoyniki** Belarus
41G2 **Khrebet Kopet Dag** *Mts* Iran/Turkmenistan
20L2 **Khrebet Pay-khoy** *Mts* Russian Federation
45B1 **Khrysokhou B** Cyprus
39E1 **Khudzhand** Tajikistan
20L3 **Khulga** *R* Russian Federation
43F4 **Khulna** Bangladesh
42D1 **Khunjerāb P** China/India
41F3 **Khunsar** Iran
41E4 **Khurays** Saudi Arabia
43F4 **Khurda** India
42D3 **Khurja** India
42C2 **Khushab** Pakistan
45C2 **Khushnīyah** Syria
45D4 **Khush Shah, Wadi el** Jordan
19E3 **Khust** Ukraine
50C2 **Khuwei** Sudan
42B3 **Khuzdar** Pakistan
21H5 **Khvalynsk** Russian Federation
41G3 **Khvor** Iran
41F4 **Khvormūj** Iran
21G8 **Khvoy** Iran
42C1 **Khwaja Muhammad Ra** *Mts* Afghanistan
42C2 **Khyber P** Afghanistan/Pakistan
51C4 **Kiambi** Zaïre
63C2 **Kiamichi** *R* USA
50B4 **Kibangou** Congo
50D4 **Kibaya** Tanzania
50C4 **Kibombo** Zaïre
50D4 **Kibondo** Tanzania
50D4 **Kibungu** Rwanda
17E2 **Kicevo** Macedonia, Yugoslavia
54G4 **Kicking Horse P** Canada
48C3 **Kidal** Mali
7C3 **Kidderminster** England
48A3 **Kidira** Senegal
35C1 **Kidnappers,C** New Zealand
18C2 **Kiel** Germany
19E2 **Kielce** Poland
6C2 **Kielder Res** England
18C2 **Kieler Bucht** *B* Germany
21E5 **Kiev** Ukraine
38E2 **Kifab** Uzbekistan
48A3 **Kiffa** Mauritius
50D4 **Kigali** Rwanda
50C4 **Kigoma** Tanzania
66E5 **Kiholo** Hawaiian Islands
29C4 **Kii-sanchi** *Mts* Japan
29C4 **Kii-suidō** *Str* Japan
25R4 **Kikhchik** Russian Federation
17E1 **Kikinda** Serbia, Yugoslavia
Kikládhes = Cyclades
32D1 **Kikon** Papua New Guinea
29D2 **Kikonai** Japan
27H7 **Kikori** Papua New Guinea
50B4 **Kikwit** Zaïre
66E5 **Kilauea Crater** *Vol* Hawaiian Islands
8C4 **Kilbrannan Sd** Scotland
54C3 **Kilbuck Mts** USA
28B2 **Kilchu** N Korea
34D1 **Kilcoy** Australia
9C3 **Kildare** Irish Republic
9C3 **Kildare** *County* Irish Republic
63D2 **Kilgore** USA
50E4 **Kilifi** Kenya
50D4 **Kilimanjaro** *Mt* Tanzania
51D4 **Kilindoni** Tanzania
40C2 **Kilis** Turkey
19F3 **Kiliya** Ukraine
9D2 **Kilkeel** Northern Ireland
9C3 **Kilkenny** Irish Republic
9C3 **Kilkenny** *County* Irish Republic
17E2 **Kilkís** Greece
34D1 **Killarney** Australia
10B3 **Killarney** Irish Republic
63C2 **Killeen** USA
8C3 **Killin** Scotland
17E3 **Killíni** *Mt* Greece
9B3 **Killorglin** Irish Republic
9D2 **Killyleagh** Northern Ireland
8C4 **Kilmarnock** Scotland
20J4 **Kil'mez** Russian Federation
9C3 **Kilmichael Pt** Irish Republic
51D4 **Kilosa** Tanzania
10B3 **Kilrush** Irish Republic
8C4 **Kilsyth** Scotland
51C4 **Kilwa** Zaïre
51D4 **Kilwa Kisiwani** Tanzania
51D4 **Kilwa Kivinje** Tanzania
60C2 **Kimball** USA
54G5 **Kimberley** Canada
47C2 **Kimberley** South Africa
32B2 **Kimberley Plat** Australia
28B2 **Kimch'aek** N Korea
28B3 **Kimch'ŏn** S Korea
28A3 **Kimhae** S Korea
17E3 **Kími** Greece
28A3 **Kimje** S Korea
20F4 **Kimry** Russian Federation
28A3 **Kimwha** N Korea
27E6 **Kinabalu** *Mt* Malaysia
8D2 **Kinbrace** Scotland
64C2 **Kincardine** Canada
63D2 **Kinder** USA
48A3 **Kindia** Guinea
50C4 **Kindu** Zaïre
20J5 **Kinel'** Russian Federation
20G4 **Kineshma** Russian Federation
34D1 **Kingaroy** Australia
59B3 **King City** USA
54F4 **Kingcome Inlet** Canada
63C1 **Kingfisher** USA
76H4 **King George I** Antarctica
55L4 **King George Is** Canada
32D5 **King I** Australia
32B2 **King Leopold Range** *Mts* Australia
56B3 **Kingman** USA
50C4 **Kingombe** Zaïre
66C2 **Kingsburg** USA
59C3 **Kings Canyon Nat Pk** USA
32B2 **King Sd** Australia
64B1 **Kingsford** USA
67B2 **Kingsland** USA
7E3 **King's Lynn** England
33G1 **Kingsmill Group** *Is* Kiribati
68D2 **Kings Park** USA
56B2 **Kings Peak** *Mt* USA
67B1 **Kingsport** USA
32C4 **Kingston** Australia
55L5 **Kingston** Canada
70E3 **Kingston** Jamaica
65E2 **Kingston** New York, USA
35A3 **Kingston** New Zealand
68C2 **Kingston** Pennsylvania, USA
69N2 **Kingstown** St Vincent
56D4 **Kingsville** USA
7C3 **Kington** England
8C3 **Kingussie** Scotland
54J3 **King William I** Canada
47D3 **King William's Town** South Africa
50B4 **Kinkala** Congo
12G7 **Kinna** Sweden
8D3 **Kinnairds Head** *Pt* Scotland
29C3 **Kinomoto** Japan
8D3 **Kinross** Scotland
50B4 **Kinshasa** Zaïre
62C1 **Kinsley** USA
67C1 **Kinston** USA
27E7 **Kintap** Indonesia
8C4 **Kintyre** *Pen* Scotland
50D3 **Kinyeti** *Mt* Sudan
17E3 **Kiparissía** Greece
17E3 **Kiparissiakós Kólpos** *G* Greece
65D1 **Kipawa,L** Canada
51D4 **Kipili** Tanzania
9C3 **Kippure** *Mt* Irish Republic
51C5 **Kipushi** Zaïre
25M4 **Kirensk** Russian Federation
24J5 **Kirghizia** *Republic* Asia
39F1 **Kirgizskiy Khrebet** *Mts* Kirgizia
50B4 **Kiri** Zaïre
33G1 **Kiribati** *Is, Republic* Pacific Ocean
40B2 **Kırıkkale** Turkey
50D4 **Kirinyaga, Mt** Kenya
20E4 **Kirishi** Russian Federation
42B3 **Kirithar Range** *Mts* Pakistan
17F3 **Kirkağaç** Turkey
21H8 **Kirk Bulāg Dāgh** *Mt* Iran
6C2 **Kirkby** England
8D3 **Kirkcaldy** Scotland
8C4 **Kirkcudbright** Scotland
12K5 **Kirkenes** Norway
6C3 **Kirkham** England
55K5 **Kirkland Lake** Canada
40A1 **Kırklareli** Turkey
6C2 **Kirkoswald** England
76E7 **Kirkpatrick,Mt** Antarctica
57D2 **Kirksville** USA
41D2 **Kirkūk** Iraq
8D2 **Kirkwall** Scotland
47D3 **Kirkwood** South Africa
61E3 **Kirkwood** USA
20E5 **Kirov** Russian Federation
20H4 **Kirov** Russian Federation
41D1 **Kirovakan** Armenia
20K4 **Kirovgrad** Russian Federation
21E6 **Kirovograd** Ukraine
20E2 **Kirovsk** Russian Federation
25R4 **Kirovskiy** Kamchatka, Russian Federation
8D3 **Kirriemuir** Scotland
20J4 **Kirs** Russian Federation
40B2 **Kırşehir** Turkey
18C2 **Kiruna** Sweden
29C3 **Kiryū** Japan
50C3 **Kisangani** Zaïre
29C3 **Kisarazu** Japan
43F3 **Kishanganj** India
42C3 **Kishangarh** India
19F3 **Kishinev** Moldavia
29C4 **Kishiwada** Japan
50D4 **Kisii** Kenya
51D4 **Kisiju** Tanzania
17D1 **Kiskunfélegyháza** Hungary
19D3 **Kiskunhalas** Hungary
21G7 **Kislovodsk** Russian Federation
50E4 **Kismaayo** Somalia
29C3 **Kiso-sammyaku** *Mts* Japan
48B4 **Kissidougou** Guinea
67B3 **Kissimmee,L** USA
50D4 **Kisumu** Kenya
19E3 **Kisvárda** Hungary
48B3 **Kita** Mali
24H6 **Kitab** Uzbekistan
29D3 **Kitakami** Japan
29D3 **Kitakami** *R* Japan
29D3 **Kitakata** Japan
28C4 **Kita-Kyūshū** Japan
50D3 **Kitale** Kenya
26H4 **Kitalo** *I* Japan
29E2 **Kitami** Japan
29D2 **Kitami-Esashi** Japan
60C3 **Kit Carson** USA
55K5 **Kitchener** Canada
50D3 **Kitgum** Uganda
17E3 **Kíthira** *I* Greece
17E3 **Kíthnos** *I* Greece
45B1 **Kiti, C** Cyprus
54G2 **Kitikmeot** *Region* Canada
54F4 **Kitimat** Canada
12K5 **Kitinen** *R* Finland
28B4 **Kitsuki** Japan
65D2 **Kittanning** USA
65E2 **Kittery** USA
12J5 **Kittilä** Finland
67C1 **Kitty Hawk** USA
51D4 **Kitunda** Tanzania
51C5 **Kitwe** Zambia
18C3 **Kitzbühel** Austria
18C3 **Kitzingen** Germany
50C4 **Kiumbi** Zaïre
54B3 **Kivalina** USA
19F2 **Kivercy** Ukraine
50C4 **Kivu,L** Rwanda/Zaïre
54B3 **Kiwalik** USA
Kiyev = Kiev
19G2 **Kiyevskoye Vodokhranilishche** *Res* Ukraine
20K4 **Kizel** Russian Federation
20G3 **Kizema** Russian Federation
40C2 **Kizil** *R* Turkey
38D2 **Kizyl'-Arvat** Turkmenistan
21J8 **Kizyl-Atrek** Turkmenistan
18C2 **Kladno** Czech Republic
18C3 **Klagenfurt** Austria
20C4 **Klaipēda** Lithuania
58B2 **Klamath** *R* USA
56A2 **Klamath Falls** USA
58B2 **Klamath Mts** USA
18C3 **Klatovy** Czech Republic
45C1 **Kleiat** Lebanon
47B2 **Kleinsee** South Africa
47D2 **Klerksdorp** South Africa
19G2 **Kletnya** Russian Federation
13D2 **Kleve** Germany
19G2 **Klimovichi** Belarus
20F4 **Klin** Russian Federation
19D1 **Klintehamn** Sweden
21E5 **Klintsy** Russian Federation
47C3 **Klipplaat** South Africa
16D2 **Ključ** Bosnia-Herzegovina
18D2 **Kłodzko** Poland
54D3 **Klondike Plat** Canada/USA
18D3 **Klosterneuburg** Austria
19D2 **Kluczbork** Poland
6D2 **Knaresborough** England
7C3 **Knighton** Wales
16D2 **Knin** Croatia
32A4 **Knob,C** Australia
9B3 **Knockmealdown Mts** Irish Republic
13B2 **Knokke-Heist** Belgium
76G9 **Knox Coast** Antarctica
61E2 **Knoxville** Iowa, USA
57E3 **Knoxville** Tennessee, USA
55Q3 **Knud Rasmussens Land** *Region* Greenland
7C3 **Knutsford** England
47C3 **Knysna** South Africa
55O3 **Kobberminebugt** *B* Greenland
29D4 **Kōbe** Japan
København = Copenhagen
18B2 **Koblenz** Germany
19E2 **Kobrin** Belarus
27G7 **Kobroör** *I* Indonesia
54B3 **Kobuk** *R* USA
17E2 **Kočani** Macedonia, Yugoslavia
28B3 **Kochang** S Korea
28B3 **Koch'ang** S Korea
30C3 **Ko Chang** *I* Thailand
43F3 **Koch Bihār** India
55L3 **Koch I** Canada
44B4 **Kochi** India
29C4 **Kōchi** Japan
54C4 **Kodiak** USA
54C4 **Kodiak I** USA
44B3 **Kodikkarai** India
50D3 **Kodok** Sudan
29D2 **Kodomari-misaki** *C* Japan
19F3 **Kodyma** Ukraine
66D3 **Koehn L** USA
47B2 **Koes** Namibia
47D2 **Koffiefontein** South Africa
48B4 **Koforidua** Ghana
29D3 **Kofu** Japan
29C3 **Koga** Japan
12G7 **Køge** Denmark
42C2 **Kohat** Pakistan
42B2 **Koh-i-Baba** *Mts* Afghanistan
42B1 **Koh-i-Hisar** *Mts* Afghanistan
42B2 **Koh-i-Khurd** *Mt* Afghanistan
43G3 **Kohīma** India
42B2 **Koh-i-Mazar** *Mt* Afghanistan
42B3 **Kohlu** Pakistan
20D4 **Kohtla Järve** Estonia
28A4 **Kohung** S Korea
28A4 **Kohyon** S Korea
29C3 **Koide** Japan
30A4 **Koihoa** Nicobar Is, India
28A2 **Koin** N Korea
28B4 **Koje Dŏ** *I* S Korea
29C2 **Ko-jima** *I* Japan
24H4 **Kokchetav** Kazakhstan
12J6 **Kokemäki** *L* Finland
12J6 **Kokkola** Finland
32D1 **Kokoda** Papua New Guinea
64B2 **Kokomo** USA
27G7 **Kokonau** Indonesia
26B2 **Kokpekty** Kazakhstan
28A3 **Koksan** N Korea
55M4 **Koksoak** *R* Canada
28A3 **Koksŏng** S Korea
47D3 **Kokstad** South Africa
30C3 **Ko Kut** *I* Thailand
20E2 **Kola** Russian Federation
27F7 **Kolaka** Indonesia
30B4 **Ko Lanta** *I* Thailand
44B3 **Kolār** India
44B3 **Kolār Gold Fields** India
48A3 **Kolda** Senegal
12F7 **Kolding** Denmark
20H2 **Kolguyev, Ostrov** *I* Russian Federation
44A2 **Kolhāpur** India
18D2 **Kolín** Czech Republic
44B4 **Kollam** India
Köln = Cologne
19D2 **Koło** Poland
66E5 **Koloa** Hawaiian Islands
18D2 **Kołobrzeg** Poland
48B3 **Kolokani** Mali
20F4 **Kolomna** Russian Federation
21D6 **Kolomyya** Ukraine
25R4 **Kolpakovskiy** Russian Federation
24K4 **Kolpashevo** Russian Federation
17F3 **Kólpos Merabéllou** *B* Greece
17E2 **Kólpos Singitikós** *G* Greece
17E2 **Kólpos Strimonikós** *G* Greece
17E2 **Kólpos Toronaíos** *G* Greece
20F2 **Kol'skiy Poluostrov** *Pen* Russian Federation
20K2 **Kolva** *R* Russian Federation
12G6 **Kolvereid** Norway
51C5 **Kolwezi** Zaïre
25R3 **Kolyma** *R* Russian Federation
25R3 **Kolymskaya Nizmennost'** *Lowland* Russian Federation
25S3 **Kolymskoye Nagor'ye** *Mts* Russian Federation
17E2 **Kom** *Mt* Bulgaria/Serbia, Yugoslavia
50D3 **Koma** Ethiopia
29D3 **Koma** Japan

48D3 **Komadugu Gana** *R* Nigeria
29D2 **Komaga take** *Mt* Japan
25S4 **Komandorskiye Ostrova** *Is* Russian Federation
19D3 **Komárno** Slovakia
47E2 **Komati** *R* South Africa/ Swaziland
47E2 **Komati Poort** South Africa
29D3 **Komatsu** Japan
29B4 **Komatsushima** Japan
20J3 **Komi Republic** Russian Federation
26B1 **Kommunar** Russian Federation
27E7 **Komodo** *I* Indonesia
27G7 **Komoran** *I* Indonesia
29C3 **Komoro** Japan
17F2 **Komotiní** Greece
47C3 **Kompasberg** *Mt* South Africa
30D3 **Kompong Cham** Cambodia
30C3 **Kompong Chhnang** Cambodia
30C3 **Kompong Som = Sihanoukville**
30D3 **Kompong Thom** Cambodia
30D3 **Kompong Trabek** Cambodia
19F3 **Komrat** Moldavia
47C3 **Komsberg** *Mts* South Africa
25L1 **Komsomolets, Ostrov** *I* Russian Federation
20L2 **Komsomol'skiy** Russian Federation
25P4 **Komsomol'sk na Amure** Russian Federation
24H4 **Konda** *R* Russian Federation
43E5 **Kondagaon** India
50D4 **Kondoa** Tanzania
20E3 **Kondopoga** Russian Federation
44B2 **Kondukūr** India
20F3 **Konevo** Russian Federation
55P3 **Kong Christian IX Land** *Region* Greenland
55O3 **Kong Frederik VI Kyst** *Region* Greenland
28A3 **Kongju** S Korea
24D2 **Kong Karls Land** *Is* Svalbard
50C4 **Kongolo** Zaïre
12F7 **Kongsberg** Norway
12G6 **Kongsvinger** Norway
Königsberg = Kaliningrad
19D2 **Konin** Poland
17D2 **Konjic** Bosnia-Herzegovina
20G3 **Konosha** Russian Federation
29C3 **Konosu** Japan
21E5 **Konotop** Ukraine
19E2 **Końskie** Poland
18B3 **Konstanz** Germany
48C3 **Kontagora** Nigeria
30D3 **Kontum** Vietnam
21E8 **Konya** Turkey
58C1 **Kootenay L** Canada
42C5 **Kopargaon** India
55R3 **Kópasker** Iceland
12A2 **Kópavogur** Iceland
16C1 **Koper** Slovenia
38D2 **Kopet Dag** *Mts* Iran/ Turkmenistan
20L4 **Kopeysk** Russian Federation
30C4 **Ko Phangan** *I* Thailand
30B4 **Ko Phuket** *I* Thailand
12H7 **Köping** Sweden
28A3 **Kopo-ri** S Korea
44B2 **Koppal** India
16D1 **Koprivnica** Croatia
42B4 **Korangi** Pakistan
44C2 **Koraput** India
43E4 **Korba** India
18B2 **Korbach** Germany
17E2 **Korçë** Albania
16D2 **Korčula** *I* Croatia
31E2 **Korea B** China/Korea
28B2 **Korea, North** *Republic* Asia
28B3 **Korea, South** *Republic* Asia
26F3 **Korea Strait** Japan/Korea
19F2 **Korec** Ukraine
25S3 **Korf** Russian Federation
40B1 **Körğlu Tepesi** *Mt* Turkey
48B4 **Korhogo** Ivory Coast
42B4 **Kori Creek** India
Kórinthos = Corinth
29E3 **Kōriyama** Japan
20L5 **Korkino** Russian Federation
25R3 **Korkodon** Russian Federation
25R3 **Korkodon** *R* Russian Federation
40B2 **Korkuteli** Turkey
39G1 **Korla** China
45B1 **Kormakiti, C** Cyprus
16D2 **Kornat** *I* Croatia
21E7 **Köroğlu Tepesi** *Mt* Turkey
50D4 **Korogwe** Tanzania
34B3 **Koroit** Australia
27G6 **Koror** Palau, Pacific Ocean
19E3 **Körös** *R* Hungary
21D5 **Korosten** Ukraine
19F2 **Korostyshev** Ukraine
50B2 **Koro Toro** Chad
26H2 **Korsakov** Russian Federation
12G7 **Korsør** Denmark
20J3 **Kortkeros** Russian Federation
18A2 **Kortrijk** Belgium
25S3 **Koryakskoye Nagor'ye** *Mts* Russian Federation
28A3 **Koryong** S Korea
17F3 **Kós** *I* Greece
30C4 **Ko Samui** *I* Thailand
28A3 **Kosan** N Korea
19D2 **Kościerzyna** Poland
63E2 **Kosciusko** USA
32D4 **Kosciusko** *Mt* Australia
43J2 **Kosi** India
43K1 **Kosi** *R* India
19E3 **Košice** Slovakia
20J2 **Kosma** *R* Russian Federation
28B3 **Kosŏng** N Korea
17E2 **Kosovo** *Region* Serbia, Yugoslavia
17E2 **Kosovska Mitrovica** Serbia, Yugoslavia
48B4 **Kossou** *L* Ivory Coast
47D2 **Koster** South Africa
50D2 **Kosti** Sudan
19F2 **Kostopol'** Ukraine
20G4 **Kostroma** Russian Federation
18C2 **Kostrzyn** Poland
20K2 **Kos'yu** *R* Russian Federation
12H8 **Koszalin** Poland
42D3 **Kota** India
30C4 **Kota Baharu** Malaysia
42C2 **Kot Addu** Pakistan
27E6 **Kota Kinabalu** Malaysia
44C2 **Kotapad** India
20H4 **Kotel'nich** Russian Federation
21G6 **Kotel'nikovo** Russian Federation
25P2 **Kotel'nyy, Ostrov** *I* Russian Federation
12K6 **Kotka** Finland
20H3 **Kotlas** Russian Federation
54B3 **Kotlik** USA
17D2 **Kotor** Montenegro, Yugoslavia
21D6 **Kotovsk** Ukraine
42B3 **Kotri** Pakistan
44C2 **Kottagūdem** India
44B4 **Kottayam** India
50C3 **Kotto** *R* Central African Republic
44B3 **Kottūru** India
25L3 **Kotuy** *R* Russian Federation
54B3 **Kotzebue** USA
54B3 **Kotzebue Sd** USA
48C3 **Kouandé** Benin
50C3 **Kouango** Central African Republic
48B3 **Koudougou** Burkina
47C3 **Kougaberge** *Mts* South Africa
50B4 **Koulamoutou** Gabon
48B3 **Koulikoro** Mali
48B3 **Koupéla** Burkina
73H2 **Kourou** French Guiana
48B3 **Kouroussa** Guinea
50B2 **Kousséri** Cameroon
12K6 **Kouvola** Finland
12L5 **Kovdor** Russian Federation
12L5 **Kovdozero, Ozero** *L* Russian Federation
19E2 **Kovel** Ukraine
Kovno = Kaunas
20G4 **Kovrov** Russian Federation
20G5 **Kovylkino** Russian Federation
20F3 **Kovzha** *R* Russian Federation
30C4 **Ko Way** *I* Thailand
31C5 **Kowloon** Hong Kong
28A3 **Kowŏn** N Korea
42B2 **Kowt-e-Ashrow** Afghanistan
40A2 **Köycegğiz** Turkey
20G2 **Koyda** Russian Federation
44A2 **Koyna Res** India
20H3 **Koynas** Russian Federation
54C3 **Koyukuk** USA
40C2 **Kozan** Turkey
17E2 **Kozańi** Greece
44B3 **Kozhikode** India
20K2 **Kozhim** Russian Federation
20H4 **Koz'modemyansk** Russian Federation
29C4 **Kōzu-shima** *I* Japan
48C4 **Kpalimé** Togo
47D3 **Kraai** *R* South Africa
12F7 **Kragerø** Norway
17E2 **Kragujevac** Serbia, Yugoslavia
30B3 **Kra,Isthmus of** Burma/ Malaysia
45D1 **Krak des Chevaliers** *Hist Site* Syria
Kraków = Cracow Poland
17E2 **Kraljevo** Serbia, Yugoslavia
21F6 **Kramatorsk** Ukraine
12H6 **Kramfors** Sweden
16C1 **Kranj** Slovenia
20H3 **Krasavino** Russian Federation
20J1 **Krasino** Russian Federation
28C2 **Kraskino** Russian Federation
19E2 **Kraśnik** Poland
21H5 **Krasnoarmeysk** Russian Federation
21F6 **Krasnodar** Russian Federation
20K4 **Krasnokamsk** Russian Federation
20L4 **Krasnotur'insk** Russian Federation
20K4 **Krasnoufimsk** Russian Federation
20K5 **Krasnousol'skiy** Russian Federation
20K3 **Krasnovishersk** Russian Federation
21J7 **Krasnovodsk** Turkmenistan
25L4 **Krasnoyarsk** Russian Federation
19E2 **Krasnystaw** Poland
21H5 **Krasnyy Kut** Russian Federation
21F6 **Krasnyy Luch** Ukraine
21H6 **Krasnyy Yar** Russian Federation
30D3 **Kratie** Cambodia
55N2 **Kraulshavn** Greenland
18B2 **Krefeld** Germany
21E6 **Kremenchug** Ukraine
21E6 **Kremenchugskoye Vodokhranilische** *Res* Ukraine
19F2 **Kremenets** Ukraine
60B2 **Kremming** USA
48C4 **Kribi** Cameroon
20E5 **Krichev** Belarus
44B2 **Krishna** *R* India
44B3 **Krishnagiri** India
43F4 **Krishnanagar** India
12F7 **Kristiansand** Norway
12G7 **Kristianstad** Sweden
24B3 **Kristiansund** Norway
12J6 **Kristiinankaupunki** Finland
12G7 **Kristinehamn** Sweden
Kríti = Crete
21E6 **Krivoy Rog** Ukraine
16C1 **Krk** *I* Croatia
47D1 **Krokodil** *R* South Africa
25S4 **Kronotskaya Sopka** *Mt* Russian Federation
25S4 **Kronotskiy, Mys** *C* Russian Federation
55P3 **Kronprins Frederik Bjerge** *Mts* Greenland
12K7 **Kronshtadt** Russian Federation
47D2 **Kroonstad** South Africa
21G6 **Kropotkin** Russian Federation
47E1 **Kruger Nat Pk** South Africa
47D2 **Krugersdorp** South Africa
17D2 **Kruje** Albania
Krung Thep = Bangkok
19F2 **Krupki** Belarus
17E2 **Kruševac** Serbia, Yugoslavia
12K7 **Krustpils** Latvia
Krym = Crimea
21F7 **Krymsk** Russian Federation
18D2 **Krzyz** Poland
15C2 **Ksar El Boukhari** Algeria
15A2 **Ksar-el-Kebir** Morocco
48C1 **Ksour, Mts des** Algeria
27C6 **Kuala** Indonesia
30C5 **Kuala Dungun** Malaysia
30C4 **Kuala Kerai** Malaysia
30C5 **Kuala Kubu Baharu** Malaysia
30C5 **Kuala Lipis** Malaysia
30C5 **Kuala Lumpur** Malaysia
30C4 **Kuala Trengganu** Malaysia
27F6 **Kuandang** Indonesia
28A2 **Kuandian** China
30C5 **Kuantan** Malaysia
21H7 **Kuba** Azerbaijan
27H7 **Kubor** *Mt* Papua New Guinea
27E6 **Kuching** Malaysia
27E6 **Kudat** Malaysia
20J4 **Kudymkar** Russian Federation
18C3 **Kufstein** Austria
41G3 **Kuh Duren** *Upland* Iran
41F3 **Kūh-e Dinar** *Mt* Iran
41G2 **Kūh-e-Hazār Masjed** *Mts* Iran
41G4 **Kūh-e Jebāl Barez** *Mts* Iran
41F3 **Kūh-e Karkas** *Mts* Iran
41G4 **Kūh-e Laleh Zar** *Mt* Iran
41E2 **Kūh-e Sahand** *Mt* Iran
38E3 **Kuh-e-Taftān** *Mt* Iran
21H9 **Kūhhaye Alvand** *Mts* Iran
21H8 **Kūhhaye Sabalan** *Mts* Iran
41E3 **Kūhhā-ye Zāgros** *Mts* Iran
12K6 **Kuhmo** Finland
41F3 **Kūhpāyeh** Iran
41G3 **Kūhpāyeh** *Mt* Iran
41G4 **Kūh-ye Bashākerd** *Mts* Iran
41E2 **Kūh-ye Sabalan** *Mt* Iran
47B2 **Kuibis** Namibia
47B1 **Kuiseb** *R* Namibia
51B5 **Kuito** Angola
28A3 **Kujang** N Korea
29E2 **Kuji** Japan
28B4 **Kuju-san** *Mt* Japan
17E2 **Kukës** Albania
30C5 **Kukup** Malaysia
41G4 **Kūl** *R* Iran
17F3 **Kula** Turkey
21K6 **Kulakshi** Kazakhstan
50D3 **Kulal,Mt** Kenya
17E2 **Kulata** Bulgaria
20C4 **Kuldīga** Latvia
20G2 **Kulov** *R* Russian Federation
21J6 **Kul'sary** Kazakhstan
42D2 **Kulu** India
40B2 **Kulu** Turkey
24J4 **Kulunda** Russian Federation
34B2 **Kulwin** Australia
21H7 **Kuma** *R* Russian Federation
29C3 **Kumagaya** Japan
27E7 **Kumai** Indonesia
21L5 **Kumak** Russian Federation
28C4 **Kumamoto** Japan
29C4 **Kumano** Japan
17E2 **Kumanovo** Macedonia, Yugoslavia
48B4 **Kumasi** Ghana
21G7 **Kumayri** Armenia
48C4 **Kumba** Cameroon
44B3 **Kumbakonam** India
28A3 **Kümch'ŏn** N Korea
20K5 **Kumertau** Russian Federation
28A3 **Kumgang** N Korea
12H7 **Kumla** Sweden
28A4 **Kümnyŏng** S Korea
28A4 **Kümo-do** *I* S Korea
44A3 **Kumta** India
39G1 **Kumüx** China
28B3 **Kumwha** S Korea
42C2 **Kunar** *R* Afghanistan
29F2 **Kunashir, Ostrov** *I* Russian Federation
12K7 **Kunda** Estonia
42C4 **Kundla** India
42B1 **Kunduz** Afghanistan
Kunene *R* **= Cunene R**
12G7 **Kungsbacka** Sweden
20K4 **Kungur** Russian Federation
30B1 **Kunhing** Burma
39G2 **Kunlun Shan** *Mts* China
31A4 **Kunming** China
20M3 **Kunovat** *R* Russian Federation
28B3 **Kunsan** S Korea
12K6 **Kuopio** Finland
16D1 **Kupa** *R* Bosnia-Herzegovina/Croatia
32B2 **Kupang** Indonesia
32D2 **Kupiano** Papua New Guinea
54E4 **Kupreanof I** USA
21F6 **Kupyansk** Ukraine
39G1 **Kuqa** China
21H8 **Kura** *R* Azerbaijan
29C3 **Kurabe** Japan
29C4 **Kurashiki** Japan
29B3 **Kurayoshi** Japan
41E2 **Kurdistan** *Region* Iran
17F2 **Kürdzhali** Bulgaria
28C4 **Kure** Japan
20C4 **Kuressaare** Estonia
25L3 **Kureyka** *R* Russian Federation
24H4 **Kurgan** Russian Federation
12J6 **Kurikka** Finland
25Q5 **Kuril Is** Russian Federation
Kuril'skiye Ostrova *Is* **= Kuril Islands**
36J2 **Kuril Trench** Pacific Ocean
21H8 **Kurinskaya Kosa** *Sand Spit* Azerbaijan
44B2 **Kurnool** India
29D2 **Kuroishi** Japan
29D3 **Kuroiso** Japan
35B2 **Kurow** New Zealand
34D2 **Kurri Kurri** Australia
21F5 **Kursk** Russian Federation
26B2 **Kuruktag** *R* China
47C2 **Kuruman** South Africa
47C2 **Kuruman** *R* South Africa
28C4 **Kurume** Japan
44C3 **Kurunegala** Sri Lanka
24K5 **Kuruntag** *R* China
20K3 **Kur'ya** Russian Federation
20K4 **Kusa** Russian Federation
17F3 **Kuşadası Körfezi** *B* Turkey
17F2 **Kus Golü** *L* Turkey
29D4 **Kushimoto** Japan
29E2 **Kushiro** Japan
38E2 **Kushka** Afghanistan
43F4 **Kushtia** Bangladesh
21J5 **Kushum** *R* Kazakhstan
20K4 **Kushva** Russian Federation
54B3 **Kuskokwim** *R* USA
54C3 **Kuskokwim Mts** USA
43E3 **Kusma** Nepal
28B3 **Kusŏng** N Korea
24H4 **Kustanay** Kazakhstan
27E7 **Kuta** *R* Indonesia
21D8 **Kütahya** Turkey
21G7 **Kutaisi** Georgia
29D2 **Kutchan** Japan
29E2 **Kutcharo-ko** *L* Japan
18D3 **Kutná Hora** Czech Republic
19D2 **Kutno** Poland
50B4 **Kutu** Zaïre
43G4 **Kutubdia I** Bangladesh
50C2 **Kutum** Sudan
55M4 **Kuujjuaq** Canada
55L4 **Kuujjuarapik** Canada
12K5 **Kuusamo** Finland
21K5 **Kuvandyk** Russian Federation
41E4 **Kuwait** Kuwait
38C3 **Kuwait** *Sheikhdom* SW Asia
29C3 **Kuwana** Japan
24J4 **Kuybyshev** Russian Federation
Kuybyshev = Samara
20H5 **Kuybyshevskoye Vodokhranilishche** *Res* Russian Federation
20E2 **Kuyto, Ozero** *L* Russian Federation
25M4 **Kuytun** Russian Federation
21F7 **Kuzey Anadolu Dağları** *Mts* Turkey
20F2 **Kuzomen** Russian Federation
20C2 **Kvænangen** *Sd* Norway
12G5 **Kvigtind** *Mt* Norway
20B2 **Kvikkjokk** Sweden
50D4 **Kwale** Kenya
28B3 **Kwangju** S Korea
50B4 **Kwango** *R* Zaïre
28A3 **Kwangyang** S Korea
28A2 **Kwanmo-bong** *Mt* N Korea
51D6 **KwaZulu Natal** *Province* South Africa
51C5 **Kwekwe** Zimbabwe
19D2 **Kwidzyn** Poland
54B4 **Kwigillingok** USA
27G7 **Kwoka** *Mt* Indonesia
34C3 **Kyabram** Australia
30B2 **Kyaikkami** Burma
30B2 **Kyaikto** Burma
26D1 **Kyakhta** Russian Federation
30B1 **Kyaukme** Burma
30B1 **Kyauk-padaung** Burma
30A2 **Kyaukpyu** Burma
20G2 **Kychema** Russian Federation
10B2 **Kyle of Lochalsh** Scotland
13D2 **Kyll** *R* Germany
34B3 **Kyneton** Australia
50D3 **Kyoga, L** Uganda
34D1 **Kyogle** Australia
28B3 **Kyŏngju** S Korea
28A3 **Kyongsang Sanmaek** *Mts* S Korea
28A2 **Kyŏngsŏng** N Korea
29D3 **Kyōto** Japan
45B1 **Kyrenia** Cyprus
20K3 **Kyrta** Russian Federation
20L4 **Kyshtym** Russian Federation
45B1 **Kythrea** Cyprus

28B4 **Kyūshū** *I* Japan
36H4 **Kyushu-Palau Ridge** Pacific Ocean
17E2 **Kyustendil** Bulgaria
25O2 **Kyusyur** Russian Federation
26C1 **Kyzyl** Russian Federation
24H5 **Kyzylkum** *Desert* Uzbekistan
24H5 **Kzyl Orda** Kazakhstan

L

50E3 **Laascaanood** Somalia
50E2 **Laas Dawaco** Somalia
13E2 **Laasphe** Germany
50E2 **Laasqoray** Somalia
72F1 **La Asunción** Venezuela
48A2 **Laâyoune** Morocco
58D2 **La Barge** USA
48A3 **Labé** Guinea
18D2 **Labe** *R* Czech Republic
65E1 **Labelle** Canada
67B3 **La Belle** USA
21G7 **Labinsk** Russian Federation
45D1 **Laboué** Lebanon
55M4 **Labrador** *Region* Canada
55M4 **Labrador City** Canada
55N4 **Labrador S** Canada/Greenland
72F5 **Lábrea** Brazil
27E6 **Labuk B** Malaysia
30A2 **Labutta** Burma
20M2 **Labytnangi** Russian Federation
13B2 **La Capelle** France
Laccadive Is = Lakshadweep
39F4 **Laccadive Is** India
70D3 **La Ceiba** Honduras
34A3 **Lacepede B** Australia
14C2 **La Châtre** France
45C3 **Lachish** *Hist Site* Israel
32D4 **Lachlan** *R* Australia
72C2 **La Chorrera** Panama
65E1 **Lachute** Canada
65D2 **Lackawanna** USA
54G4 **Lac la Biche** Canada
55L4 **Lac L'eau Claire** Canada
65E1 **Lac Mégantic** Canada
54G4 **Lacombe** Canada
65E2 **Laconia** USA
15A1 **La Coruña** Spain
57D2 **La Crosse** USA
63D1 **La Cygne** USA
42D2 **Ladākh Range** *Mts* India
27E6 **Ladd Reef** S China Sea
42C3 **Lādnūn** India
20E3 **Ladoga, L** Russian Federation
31B5 **Ladong** China
Ladozhskoye Oz *L* = **Ladoga, L**
55K2 **Lady Ann Str** Canada
34C4 **Lady Barron** Australia
47D2 **Ladybrand** South Africa
47D2 **Ladysmith** South Africa
64A1 **Ladysmith** USA
32D1 **Lae** Papua New Guinea
30C3 **Laem Ngop** Thailand
18C1 **Laesø** *I* Denmark
60B3 **Lafayette** Colorado, USA
57E2 **Lafayette** Indiana, USA
57D3 **Lafayette** Louisiana, USA
13B3 **La Fère** France
13B3 **La-Ferté-sous-Jouarre** France
48C4 **Lafia** Nigeria
48C4 **Lafiagi** Nigeria
14B2 **La Flèche** France
16B3 **La Galite** *I* Tunisia
18C1 **Lagan** *R* Sweden
73L6 **Lagarto** Brazil
8C3 **Laggan, L** Scotland
48C1 **Laghouat** Algeria
72C4 **Lago Agrio** Ecuador
48C4 **Lagos** Nigeria
15A2 **Lagos** Portugal
70B2 **Lagos de Moreno** Mexico
56B2 **La Grande** USA
32B2 **Lagrange** Australia
57E3 **La Grange** Georgia, USA
64B3 **La Grange** Kentucky, USA
67C1 **La Grange** N Carolina, USA
63C3 **La Grange** Texas, USA
72F2 **La Gran Sabana** *Mts* Venezuela
62A2 **Laguna** USA
59C4 **Laguna Beach** USA
56C4 **Laguna Seca** Mexico
28B2 **Lagusha** N Korea
27E6 **Lahad Datu** Malaysia
41F2 **Lāhījān** Iran
13D2 **Lahn** *R* Germany
13D2 **Lahnstein** Germany
42C2 **Lahore** Pakistan
13D3 **Lahr** Germany
12K6 **Lahti** Finland
50B3 **Lai** Chad
31B5 **Laibin** China
30C1 **Lai Chau** Vietnam
13C4 **Laignes** France
12J6 **Laihia** Finland
47C3 **Laingsburg** South Africa
8C2 **Lairg** Scotland
31E2 **Laiyang** China
31D2 **Laizhou Wan** *B* China
74B5 **Laja, Lago de la** Chile
74F3 **Lajes** Brazil
66D4 **La Jolla** USA
56C3 **La Junta** USA
60D2 **Lake Andes** USA
34C2 **Lake Cargelligo** Australia
57D3 **Lake Charles** USA
67B2 **Lake City** Florida, USA
61E2 **Lake City** Minnesota, USA
67C2 **Lake City** S Carolina, USA
6C2 **Lake District** *Region* England
66D4 **Lake Elsinore** USA
32C3 **Lake Eyre Basin** Australia
65D2 **Lakefield** Canada
64B2 **Lake Geneva** USA
68D1 **Lake George** USA
55M3 **Lake Harbour** Canada
59D4 **Lake Havasu City** USA
66C3 **Lake Hughes** USA
68C2 **Lakehurst** USA
66C3 **Lake Isabella** USA
63C3 **Lake Jackson** USA
67B3 **Lakeland** USA
55J5 **Lake of the Woods** Canada
58B1 **Lake Oswego** USA
12K7 **Lake Peipus** Estonia/Russian Federation
59B3 **Lakeport** USA
63D2 **Lake Providence** USA
35B2 **Lake Pukaki** New Zealand
34C3 **Lakes Entrance** Australia
66C2 **Lakeshore** USA
34B1 **Lake Stewart** Australia
65D1 **Lake Traverse** Canada
56A2 **Lakeview** USA
58B1 **Lakeview Mt** Canada
63D2 **Lake Village** USA
67B3 **Lake Wales** USA
66C4 **Lakewood** California, USA
60B3 **Lakewood** Colorado, USA
68C2 **Lakewood** New Jersey, USA
64C2 **Lakewood** Ohio, USA
67B3 **Lake Worth** USA
43E3 **Lakhīmpur** India
42B4 **Lakhpat** India
62B1 **Lakin** USA
42C2 **Lakki** Pakistan
17E3 **Lakonikós Kólpos** *G* Greece
48B4 **Lakota** Ivory Coast
12K4 **Laksefjord** *Inlet* Norway
12K4 **Lakselv** Norway
44A3 **Lakshadweep** *Is, Union Territory* India
72B4 **La Libertad** Ecuador
15A2 **La Linea** Spain
42D4 **Lalitpur** India
54H4 **La Loche** Canada
13C2 **La Louvière** Belgium
69A4 **La Luz** Nicaragua
55L5 **La Malbaie** Canada
56C3 **Lamar** Colorado, USA
63D1 **Lamar** Missouri, USA
63C3 **La Marque** USA
50B4 **Lambaréné** Gabon
72B5 **Lambayeque** Peru
76F10 **Lambert Glacier** Antarctica
47B3 **Lamberts Bay** South Africa
68C2 **Lambertville** USA
54F2 **Lambton,C** Canada
30C2 **Lam Chi** *R* Thailand
15A1 **Lamego** Portugal
72C6 **La Merced** Peru
62B2 **Lamesa** USA
59C4 **La Mesa** USA
17E3 **Lamía** Greece
8D4 **Lammermuir Hills** Scotland
12G7 **Lammhult** Sweden
61E2 **Lamoni** USA
66C3 **Lamont** California, USA
60B2 **Lamont** Wyoming, USA
27H6 **Lamotrek** *I* Pacific Ocean
13B4 **Lamotte-Beuvron** France
60D1 **La Moure** USA
62C2 **Lampasas** USA
7B3 **Lampeter** Wales
50E4 **Lamu** Kenya
66E5 **Lanai** *I* Hawaiian Islands
66E5 **Lanai City** Hawaiian Islands
27F6 **Lanao, L** Philippines
8D4 **Lanark** Scotland
30B3 **Lanbi** *I* Burma
30C1 **Lancang** *R* China
6C3 **Lancashire** *County* England
59C4 **Lancaster** California, USA
6C2 **Lancaster** England
61E2 **Lancaster** Missouri, USA
65E2 **Lancaster** New Hampshire, USA
68A1 **Lancaster** New York, USA
64C3 **Lancaster** Ohio, USA
57F3 **Lancaster** Pennsylvania, USA
67B2 **Lancaster** S Carolina, USA
55K2 **Lancaster Sd** Canada
13E3 **Landan** Germany
18C3 **Landeck** Austria
56C2 **Lander** USA
14B3 **Landes, Les** *Region* France
67B1 **Landrum** USA
18C3 **Landsberg** Germany
54F2 **Lands End** *C* Canada
7B4 **Land's End** *Pt* England
18C3 **Landshut** Germany
12G7 **Làndskrona** Sweden
67A2 **Lanett** USA
43E2 **La'nga Co** *L* China
60D1 **Langdon** USA
47C2 **Langeberg** *Mts* South Africa
18B2 **Langenhagen** Germany
13D1 **Langeoog** *I* Germany
8D4 **Langholm** Scotland
12A2 **Langjökull** *Mts* Iceland
30B4 **Langkawi** *I* Malaysia
34C1 **Langlo** *R* Australia
6B2 **Langness** *Pt* England
14B3 **Langon** France
14D2 **Langres** France
13C4 **Langres, Plateau de** France
27C6 **Langsa** Indonesia
26D2 **Lang Shan** *Mts* China
30D1 **Lang Son** Vietnam
62B3 **Langtry** USA
14C3 **Languedoc** *Region* France
74B5 **Lanin, Vol** Argentina
68C2 **Lansdale** USA
55K4 **Lansdowne House** Canada
68C2 **Lansford** USA
57E2 **Lansing** USA
48A2 **Lanzarote** *I* Canary Islands
31A2 **Lanzhou** China
27F5 **Laoag** Philippines
30C1 **Lao Cai** Vietnam
31D1 **Laoha He** *R* China
9C3 **Laois** *County* Irish Republic
28A2 **Laoling** China
13B3 **Laon** France
72C6 **La Oroya** Peru
30C2 **Laos** *Republic* SE Asia
75C4 **Lapa** Brazil
14C2 **Lapalisse** France
72C2 **La Palma** Panama
48A2 **La Palma** *I* Canary Islands
74C5 **La Pampa** *State* Argentina
66B3 **La Panza Range** *Mts* USA
72F2 **La Paragua** Venezuela
74E4 **La Paz** Argentina
72E7 **La Paz** Bolivia
70A2 **La Paz** Mexico
26H2 **La Perouse Str** Japan/Russian Federation
58B2 **La Pine** USA
45B1 **Lapithos** Cyprus
63D2 **Laplace** USA
60C1 **La Plant** USA
74E4 **La Plata** Argentina
64B2 **La Porte** USA
68B2 **Laporte** USA
12K6 **Lappeenranta** Finland
12H5 **Lappland** *Region* Finland/Sweden
62C3 **La Pryor** USA
25O2 **Laptev S** Russian Federation
12J6 **Lapua** Finland
56B4 **La Purísima** Mexico
50C1 **Laqiya Arbain** *Well* Sudan
74C2 **La Quiaca** Argentina
16C2 **L'Aquila** Italy
41F4 **Lār** Iran
15A2 **Larache** Morocco
56C2 **Laramie** USA
60B2 **Laramie Mts** USA
56C2 **Laramie Range** *Mts* USA
75B4 **Laranjeiras do Sul** Brazil
56D4 **Laredo** USA
41F4 **Larestan** *Region* Iran
Largeau = Faya
67B3 **Largo** USA
8C4 **Largs** Scotland
41E2 **Larī** Iran
74C3 **La Rioja** Argentina
15B1 **La Rioja** *Region* Spain
74C3 **La Rioja** *State* Argentina
17E3 **Lárisa** Greece
42B3 **Larkana** Pakistan
40B3 **Larnaca** Cyprus
45B1 **Larnaca B** Cyprus
9C2 **Larne** Northern Ireland
62C1 **Larned** USA
15A1 **La Robla** Spain
13C2 **La Roche-en-Ardenne** Belgium
14B2 **La Rochelle** France
14B2 **La Roche-sur-Yon** France
15B2 **La Roda** Spain
69D3 **La Romana** Dominican Republic
54H4 **La Ronge** Canada
12F7 **Larvik** Norway
24J3 **Laryak** Russian Federation
15B2 **La Sagra** *Mt* Spain
65E1 **La Salle** Canada
64B2 **La Salle** USA
62B1 **Las Animas** USA
55L5 **La Sarre** Canada
62A2 **Las Cruces** USA
69C3 **La Selle** *Mt* Haiti
31B2 **Lasengmiao** China
74B3 **La Serena** Chile
74E5 **Las Flores** Argentina
30B1 **Lashio** Burma
16D3 **La Sila** *Mts* Italy
41F2 **Lāsjerd** Iran
42A2 **Laskar Gāh** Afghanistan
15A2 **Las Marismas** *Marshland* Spain
48A2 **Las Palmas de Gran Canaria** Canary Islands
16B2 **La Spezia** Italy
74C6 **Las Plumas** Argentina
58B2 **Lassen Peak** *Mt* USA
58B2 **Lassen Volcanic Nat Pk** USA
50B4 **Lastoursville** Gabon
16D2 **Lastovo** *I* Croatia
70B2 **Las Tres Marias** *Is* Mexico
56B3 **Las Vegas** USA
40C2 **Latakia** Syria
16C2 **Latina** Italy
69D4 **La Tortuga, I** Venezuela
34C4 **Latrobe** Australia
45C3 **Latrun** Israel
55L5 **La Tuque** Canada
44B2 **Lātūr** India
20C4 **Latvia** *Republic* Europe
8D4 **Lauder** Scotland
18B2 **Lauenburg** Germany
33H2 **Lau Group** *Is* Fiji
32D5 **Launceston** Australia
7B4 **Launceston** England
74B6 **La Unión** Chile
70D3 **La Unión** El Salvador
72C5 **La Unión** Peru
32D2 **Laura** Australia
65D3 **Laurel** Delaware, USA
68B3 **Laurel** Maryland, USA
57E3 **Laurel** Mississippi, USA
58E1 **Laurel** Montana, USA
67B2 **Laurens** USA
67C2 **Laurinburg** USA
16B1 **Lausanne** Switzerland
27E7 **Laut** *I* Indonesia
74B7 **Lautaro** Chile
13E2 **Lauterbach** Germany
13D3 **Lauterecken** Germany
65E1 **Laval** Canada
14B2 **Laval** France
66B2 **Laveaga Peak** *Mt* USA
58E1 **Lavina** USA
13C3 **La Vôge** *Region* France
73K8 **Lavras** Brazil
54A3 **Lavrentiya** Russian Federation
47E2 **Lavumisa** Swaziland
30B1 **Lawksawk** Burma
61D3 **Lawrence** Kansas, USA
65E2 **Lawrence** Massachusetts, USA
35A3 **Lawrence** New Zealand
63E1 **Lawrenceburg** USA
64B3 **Lawrenceville** Illinois, USA
68B2 **Lawrenceville** Pennsylvania, USA
56D3 **Lawton** USA
40C4 **Lawz, Jebel al** *Mt* Saudi Arabia
6B2 **Laxey** England
38C3 **Layla'** Saudi Arabia
50D3 **Laylo** Sudan
70B3 **Lázaro Cardenas** Mexico
29C2 **Lazo** Russian Federation
56C2 **Lead** USA
60B3 **Leadville** USA
63E2 **Leaf** *R* USA
62C3 **Leakey** USA
7D5 **Leamington Spa, Royal** England
61E3 **Leavenworth** USA
19D2 **Łeba** Poland
60D3 **Lebanon** Kansas, USA
63D1 **Lebanon** Missouri, USA
58B2 **Lebanon** Oregon, USA
65D2 **Lebanon** Pennsylvania, USA
64B3 **Lebanon** Tennessee, USA
40C3 **Lebanon** *Republic* SW Asia
66C3 **Lebec** USA
51D6 **Lebombo Mts** Mozambique/South Africa/Swaziland
19D2 **Lębork** Poland
74B5 **Lebu** Chile
13B2 **Le Cateau** France
17D2 **Lecce** Italy
16B1 **Lecco** Italy
13D3 **Le Champ du Feu** *Mt* France
14C2 **Le Creusot** France
7C3 **Ledbury** England
43H3 **Ledo** India
68D1 **Lee** USA
61E1 **Leech L** USA
10C3 **Leeds** England
7C3 **Leek** England
18B2 **Leer** Germany
67B3 **Leesburg** Florida, USA
68B3 **Leesburg** Virginia, USA
63D2 **Leesville** USA
34C2 **Leeton** Australia
47C3 **Leeugamka** South Africa
18B2 **Leeuwarden** Netherlands
32A4 **Leeuwin,C** Australia
66C2 **Lee Vining** USA
69E3 **Leeward Is** Caribbean Sea
45B1 **Lefka** Cyprus
45B1 **Lefkara** Cyprus
45B1 **Lefkoniko** Cyprus
27F5 **Legazpi** Philippines
18D2 **Legnica** Poland
73G2 **Leguan Island** Guyana
72D4 **Leguizamo** Peru
42D2 **Leh** India
14C2 **Le Havre** France
59D2 **Lehi** USA
68C2 **Lehigh** *R* USA
68C2 **Lehighton** USA
13D3 **Le Hohneck** *Mt* France
42C2 **Leiah** Pakistan
18D3 **Leibnitz** Austria
7D3 **Leicester** England
7D3 **Leicester** *County* England
32C2 **Leichhardt** *R* Australia
18A2 **Leiden** Netherlands
13B2 **Leie** *R* Belgium
32C4 **Leigh Creek** Australia
7E4 **Leigh on Sea** England
7D4 **Leighton Buzzard** England
18B2 **Leine** *R* Germany
9C3 **Leinster** *Region* Irish Republic
18C2 **Leipzig** Germany
15A2 **Leiria** Portugal
12F7 **Leirvik** Norway
8D4 **Leith** Scotland
31C4 **Leiyang** China
31B5 **Leizhou Bandao** *Pen* China
31C5 **Leizhou Wan** *B* China
18A2 **Lek** *R* Netherlands
16B3 **Le Kef** Tunisia
63D2 **Leland** USA
17D2 **Lelija** *Mt* Bosnia-Herzegovina
16B1 **Léman, Lac** France/Switzerland
14C2 **Le Mans** France
61D2 **Le Mars** USA
13E1 **Lemgo** Germany
58D2 **Lemhi Range** *Mts* USA
55M3 **Lemieux Is** Canada
56C2 **Lemmon** USA
59D4 **Lemmon,Mt** USA
59C3 **Lemoore** USA
14C2 **Lempdes** France
43G4 **Lemro** *R* Burma
16D2 **Le Murge** *Region* Italy
25O3 **Lena** *R* Russian Federation
20E3 **Lendery** Russian Federation
13D1 **Lengerich** Germany
31C4 **Lengshuijiang** China
Leningrad = St Petersburg
76F7 **Leningradskaya** *Base* Antarctica
20J5 **Leninogorsk** Russian Federation
26B1 **Leninogorsk** Kazakhstan
24K4 **Leninsk-Kuznetskiy** Russian Federation
26G2 **Leninskoye** Russian Federation
21H8 **Lenkoran'** Azerbaijan
13E2 **Lenne** *R* Germany
67B1 **Lenoir** USA
68D1 **Lenox** USA
13B2 **Lens** France
25N3 **Lensk** Russian Federation
16C3 **Lentini** Sicily, Italy
30B3 **Lenya** *R* Burma
16C1 **Leoben** Austria
7C3 **Leominster** England
68E1 **Leominster** USA
70B2 **León** Mexico
72A1 **León** Nicaragua
15A1 **León** Spain
47B1 **Leonardville** Namibia

45C1 Leonarisso Cyprus
32B3 Leonora Australia
75D3 Leopoldina Brazil
Léopoldville = Kinshasa
20D5 Lepel Belarus
31D4 Leping China
14C2 Le Puy-en-Velay France
50B3 Léré Chad
47D2 Leribe Lesotho
15C1 Lérida Spain
17F3 Léros I Greece
68B1 Le Roy USA
10C1 Lerwick Scotland
69C3 Les Cayes Haiti
65F1 Les Escoumins Canada
31A4 Leshan China
17E2 Leskovac Serbia, Yugoslavia
47D2 Leslie South Africa
20J4 Lesnoy Russian Federation
25L4 Lesosibirsk Russian Federation
47D2 Lesotho Kingdom South Africa
26G2 Lesozavodsk Russian Federation
14B2 Les Sables-d'Olonne France
76E4 Lesser Antarctica Region Antarctica
69E3 Lesser Antilles Is Caribbean Sea
21G7 Lesser Caucasus Mts Azerbaijan/Georgia
17F3 Lésvos I Greece
18D2 Leszno Poland
47E1 Letaba R South Africa
43G4 Letha Range Mts Burma
54G5 Lethbridge Canada
73G3 Lethem Guyana
19F3 Letichev Ukraine
72E4 Letícia Colombia
32B1 Leti, Kepulauan I Indonesia
47D1 Letlhakeng Botswana
7E4 le Touquet-Paris-Plage France
30B2 Letpadan Burma
25N4 Let Oktyabr'ya Russian Federation
14C1 Le Tréport France
9C2 Letterkenny Irish Republic
27C6 Leuser Mt Indonesia
18A2 Leuven Belgium
17E3 Levádhia Greece
12G6 Levanger Norway
62B2 Levelland USA
8D3 Leven Scotland
8D3 Leven, Loch L Scotland
27F8 Lévèque,C Australia
13D2 Leverkusen Germany
19D3 Levice Slovakia
35C2 Levin New Zealand
55L5 Lévis Canada
65E2 Levittown USA
17E3 Lévka Óri Mt Greece
17E3 Levkás Greece
17E3 Levkás I Greece
32B2 Lévêque,C Australia
17F2 Levski Bulgaria
7E4 Lewes England
62C1 Lewis USA
10B2 Lewis I Scotland
68B2 Lewisburg USA
35B2 Lewis P New Zealand
56B2 Lewis Range Mts USA
67A2 Lewis Smith,L USA
56B2 Lewiston Idaho, USA
57F2 Lewiston Maine, USA
56C2 Lewistown Montana, USA
65D2 Lewistown Pennsylvania, USA
63D2 Lewisville USA
57E3 Lexington Kentucky, USA
61E3 Lexington Missouri, USA
67B1 Lexington N Carolina, USA
60D2 Lexington Nebraska, USA
65D3 Lexington Virginia, USA
65D3 Lexington Park USA
6D2 Leyburn England
27F5 Leyte I Philippines
17D2 Lezhe Albania
39H3 Lhasa China
43F3 Lhazê China
27C6 Lhokseumawe Indonesia
43G3 Lhozhag China
26C4 Lhunze China
Liancourt Rocks = Tok-do
28B2 Liangbingtai China
31B3 Liangdang China
31C5 Lianjiang China
31C5 Lianping China
31C5 Lian Xian China
31D3 Lianyungang China
31E1 Liaodong Bandao Pen China
31E1 Liaodong Wan B China
31E1 Liao He R China
28A2 Liaoning Province China
31E1 Liaoyang China
28A2 Liaoyangwopu China
31E1 Liaoyuan China
28A2 Liaozhong China
54F3 Liard R Canada
54F4 Liard River Canada
13C3 Liart France
45C2 Liban, Jebel Mts Lebanon
58C1 Libby USA
50B3 Libenge Zaïre
56C3 Liberal USA
18C2 Liberec Czech Republic
48A4 Liberia Republic Africa
61E3 Liberty Missouri, USA
65E2 Liberty New York, USA
68B2 Liberty Pennsylvania, USA
63D2 Liberty Texas, USA
45B3 Libni, Gebel Mt Egypt
14B3 Libourne France
48C4 Libreville Equatorial Guinea
49D2 Libya Republic Africa
49E2 Libyan Desert Egypt/Libya/Sudan
49E1 Libyan Plat Egypt
16C3 Licata Sicily, Italy
7D3 Lichfield England
51D5 Lichinga Mozambique
47D2 Lichtenburg South Africa
64C3 Licking R USA
66B2 Lick Observatory USA
16C2 Licosa, Punta Pt Italy
66D2 Lida USA
20D5 Lida Belarus
12G7 Lidköping Sweden
16C2 Lido di Ostia Italy
16B1 Liechtenstein Principality Europe
18B2 Liège Belgium
19E1 Lielupe R Latvia
50C3 Lienart Zaïre
18C3 Lienz Austria
12J7 Liepāja Latvia
13C2 Lier Belgium
65E1 Lièvre R Canada
18C3 Liezen Austria
9C3 Liffey R Irish Republic
9C2 Lifford Irish Republic
33F3 Lifu I Nouvelle Calédonie
34C1 Lightning Ridge Australia
13C3 Ligny-en-Barrois France
51D5 Ligonha R Mozambique
16B2 Ligurian S Italy
33E1 Lihir Group Is Papua New Guinea
66E5 Lihue Hawaiian Islands
51C5 Likasi Zaïre
14C1 Lille France
12G6 Lillehammer Norway
13B2 Lillers France
12G7 Lillestrøm Norway
51D5 Lilongwe Malawi
17D2 Lim R Montenegro/Serbia, Yugoslavia
72C6 Lima Peru
57E2 Lima USA
15A1 Lima R Portugal
58D2 Lima Res USA
40B3 Limassol Cyprus
9C2 Limavady Northern Ireland
48C4 Limbe Cameroon
51D5 Limbe Malawi
18B2 Limburg Germany
73J8 Limeira Brazil
10B3 Limerick Irish Republic
18B1 Limfjorden L Denmark
32C2 Limmen Bight B Australia
17F3 Límnos I Greece
73L5 Limoeiro Brazil
14C2 Limoges France
70D4 Limón Costa Rica
56C3 Limon USA
14C2 Limousin Region France
14C2 Limousin, Plateaux de France
47E1 Limpopo R Mozambique
74B5 Linares Chile
56D4 Linares Mexico
15B2 Linares Spain
26C4 Lincang China
74D4 Lincoln Argentina
7D3 Lincoln England
64B2 Lincoln Illinois, USA
65F1 Lincoln Maine, USA
56D2 Lincoln Nebraska, USA
65E2 Lincoln New Hampshire, USA
35B2 Lincoln New Zealand
7D3 Lincoln County England
58B2 Lincoln City USA
64C2 Lincoln Park USA
76A2 Lincoln Sea Greenland
16B2 L'Incudine Mt Corsica, France
18B3 Lindau Germany
73G2 Linden Guyana
12F7 Lindesnes C Norway
51D4 Lindi Tanzania
50C3 Lindi R Zaïre
47D2 Lindley South Africa
17F3 Lindos Greece
66C2 Lindsay California, USA
65D2 Lindsay Canada
60B1 Lindsay Montana, USA
37M4 Line Is Pacific Ocean
31C2 Linfen China
30D2 Lingao China
27F5 Lingayen Philippines
18B2 Lingen Germany
27D7 Lingga I Indonesia
60C2 Lingle USA
31C4 Lingling China
31B5 Lingshan China
31C2 Lingshi China
48A3 Linguère Senegal
31E4 Linhai Zhejiang, China
73L7 Linhares Brazil
31B1 Linhe China
28B2 Linjiang China
28A2 Linjiatai China
12H7 Linköping Sweden
8C3 Linnhe, Loch Inlet Scotland
31D2 Linqing China
75C3 Lins Brazil
31A2 Lintao China
60C1 Linton USA
26E2 Linxi China
31A2 Linxia China
18C3 Linz Austria
14C3 Lion, Golfe du G France
16C3 Lipari I Italy
16C3 Lipari, Isole Is Italy
21F5 Lipetsk Russian Federation
17E1 Lipova Romania
18B2 Lippe R Germany
13E2 Lippstadt Germany
50D3 Lira Uganda
50B4 Liranga Congo
50C3 Lisala Zaïre
Lisboa = Lisbon
15A2 Lisbon Portugal
61D1 Lisbon USA
9C2 Lisburn Northern Ireland
31D4 Lishui China
31C4 Li Shui R China
21F6 Lisichansk Ukraine
14C2 Lisieux France
21F5 Liski Russian Federation
13B3 L'Isle-Adam France
33E3 Lismore Australia
9C3 Lismore Irish Republic
31B5 Litang China
45C2 Lītāni R Lebanon
73H3 Litani R Surinam
64B3 Litchfield Illinois, USA
61E1 Litchfield Minnesota, USA
32E4 Lithgow Australia
20C4 Lithuania Republic Europe
68B2 Lititz USA
26G2 Litovko Russian Federation
63C2 Little R USA
57F4 Little Abaco I The Bahamas
44E3 Little Andaman I Andaman Islands
67C3 Little Bahama Bank Bahamas
35C1 Little Barrier I New Zealand
58D1 Little Belt Mts USA
45B3 Little Bitter L Egypt
70D3 Little Cayman I Cayman Is, Caribbean Sea
68C3 Little Egg Harbor B USA
61E1 Little Falls Minnesota, USA
68C1 Little Falls New York, USA
62B2 Littlefield USA
61E1 Littlefork USA
61E1 Little Fork R USA
8E2 Little Halibut Bank Sand-bank Scotland
7D4 Littlehampton England
69C2 Little Inagua I The Bahamas
47C3 Little Karoo Mts South Africa
66D3 Little Lake USA
60C1 Little Missouri R USA
30A4 Little Nicobar I Nicobar Is, India
57D3 Little Rock USA
66D3 Littlerock USA
68B3 Littlestown USA
60B3 Littleton Colorado, USA
65E2 Littleton New Hampshire, USA
28B2 Liuhe China
31B2 Liupan Shan Upland China
31B5 Liuzhou China
17E3 Livanátais Greece
19F1 Līvāni Latvia
67B2 Live Oak USA
59B3 Livermore USA
62B2 Livermore,Mt USA
55M5 Liverpool Canada
7C3 Liverpool England
54E2 Liverpool B Canada
7C3 Liverpool B England
55L2 Liverpool,C Canada
34D2 Liverpool Range Mts Australia
56B2 Livingston Montana, USA
67A1 Livingston Tennessee, USA
63D2 Livingston Texas, USA
8D4 Livingstone Scotland
51C5 Livingstone Zambia
63C2 Livingston,L USA
16D2 Livno Bosnia-Herzegovina
21F5 Livny Russian Federation
64C2 Livonia USA
16C2 Livorno Italy
75D1 Livramento do Brumado Brazil
51D4 Liwale Tanzania
7B5 Lizard Pt England
16C1 Ljubljana Slovenia
12G6 Ljungan R Sweden
12G7 Ljungby Sweden
12H6 Ljusdal Sweden
20B3 Ljusnan R Sweden
7C4 Llandeilo Wales
7C4 Llandovery Wales
7C3 Llandrindod Wells Wales
7C3 Llandudno Wales
7D4 Llanelli Wales
7C3 Llangollen Wales
62C2 Llano USA
62C2 Llano R USA
56C3 Llano Estacado Plat USA
72D2 Llanos Region Colombia/Venezuela
72F7 Llanos de Chiquitos Region Bolivia
7C4 Llantrisant Wales
7C3 Llanwrst Wales
Lleida = Lérida
15A2 Llerena Spain
7B3 Lleyn Pen Wales
54F4 Lloyd George,Mt Canada
54H4 Lloydminster Canada
74C2 Llullaillaco Mt Argentina/Chile
74C2 Loa R Chile
50B4 Loange R Zaïre
47D2 Lobatse Botswana
50B3 Lobaye R Central African Republic
51B5 Lobito Angola
8B3 Lochboisdale Scotland
8C3 Lochearnhead Scotland
14C2 Loches France
8C3 Lochgoilhead Scotland
8C2 Lochinver Scotland
8D4 Lochmaben Scotland
8B3 Lochmaddy Scotland
8D3 Lochnagar Mt Scotland
8C3 Loch Ness Scotland
58C1 Lochsa R USA
8C3 Lochy, Loch L Scotland
8D4 Lockerbie Scotland
65D2 Lock Haven USA
65D2 Lockport USA
30D3 Loc Ninh Vietnam
16D3 Locri Italy
45C3 Lod Israel
34B3 Loddon R Australia
20E3 Lodeynoye Pole Russian Federation
58E1 Lodge Grass USA
42C3 Lodhran Pakistan
16B1 Lodi Italy
59B3 Lodi USA
50C4 Lodja Zaïre
50D3 Lodwar Kenya
19D2 Łódź Poland
47B3 Loeriesfontein South Africa
12G5 Lofoten Is Norway
6D2 Loftus England
62B1 Logan New Mexico, USA
56B2 Logan Utah, USA
54D3 Logan,Mt Canada
64B2 Logansport Indiana, USA
15D3 Logansport Louisiana, USA
68B2 Loganton USA
50B2 Logone R Cameroon/Chad
15B1 Logroño Spain
43E4 Lohārdaga India
12J6 Lohja Finland
30B2 Loikaw Burma
12J6 Loimaa Finland
13B3 Loing R France
14C2 Loir R France
14C2 Loire R France
13B4 Loiret Department France
72C4 Loja Ecuador
15B2 Loja Spain
12K5 Lokan Tekojärvi Res Finland
13B2 Lokeren Belgium
27F7 Lokialaki, G Mt Indonesia
50D3 Lokitaung Kenya
19F1 Loknya Russian Federation
50C4 Lokolo R Zaïre
50C4 Lokoro R Zaïre
55M3 Loks Land I Canada
18C2 Lolland I Denmark
58D1 Lolo P USA
17E2 Lom Bulgaria
51C4 Lomami R Zaïre
48A4 Loma Mts Guinea/Sierra Leone
27F7 Lomblen I Indonesia
27E7 Lombok I Indonesia
48C4 Lomé Togo
50C4 Lomela Zaïre
50C4 Lomela R Zaïre
8C3 Lomond, Loch L Scotland
20D4 Lomonosov Russian Federation
59B4 Lompoc USA
19E2 Łomza Poland
44A2 Lonāvale India
74B5 Loncoche Chile
55K5 London Canada
7D4 London England
64C3 London USA
9C2 Londonderry Northern Ireland
9C2 Londonderry County Northern Ireland
74B9 Londonderry I Chile
32B2 Londonderry,C Australia
74C3 Londres Argentina
74F2 Londrina Brazil
66D1 Lone Mt USA
66C2 Lone Pine USA
27H7 Long I Papua New Guinea
57F4 Long I The Bahamas
25T2 Longa, Proliv Str Russian Federation
69H2 Long B Jamaica
67C2 Long B USA
56B3 Long Beach California, USA
65E2 Long Beach New York, USA
65E2 Long Branch USA
31D5 Longchuan China
58C2 Long Creek USA
7D3 Long Eaton England
34C4 Longford Australia
9C3 Longford Irish Republic
9C3 Longford County Irish Republic
8E3 Long Forties Region N Sea
28B2 Longgang Shan Mts China
31D1 Longhua China
57F4 Long I Bahamas
55L4 Long I Canada
32D1 Long I Papua New Guinea
57F2 Long I USA
68D2 Long Island Sd USA
28B2 Longjing China
64B1 Long L Canada
60C1 Long L USA
55K4 Longlac Canada
31B5 Longlin China
8C3 Long, Loch Inlet Scotland
7E3 Long Melford England
56C2 Longmont USA
13C3 Longny France
61E1 Long Prairie USA
32D3 Longreach Australia
31A2 Longshou Shan Upland China
60B2 Longs Peak Mt USA
7E3 Long Sutton England
6C2 Longtown England
65E1 Longueuil Canada
13C3 Longuyon France
57D3 Longview Texas, USA
56A2 Longview Washington, USA
14D2 Longwy France
31A3 Longxi China
30D3 Long Xuyen Vietnam
31D4 Longyan China
31B5 Longzhou China
13D1 Löningen Germany
74B5 Lonquimay Chile
14D2 Lons-le-Saunier France
7B4 Looe England
57F3 Lookout,C USA
50D4 Loolmalasin Mt Tanzania
25R4 Lopatka, Mys C Russian Federation
30C3 Lop Buri Thailand
26C2 Lop Nur L China
15A2 Lora del Rio Spain
57E2 Lorain USA
42B2 Loralai Pakistan
15B2 Lorca Spain
41F3 Lordegān Iran
33E4 Lord Howe I Australia
37K6 Lord Howe Rise Pacific Ocean
55J3 Lord Mayor B Canada
56C3 Lordsburg USA
75C3 Lorena Brazil
14B2 Lorient France

34B3 Lorne Australia
18B3 Lörrach Germany
13C3 Lorraine Region France
56C3 Los Alamos USA
66B3 Los Alamos USA
74B5 Los Angeles Chile
56B3 Los Angeles USA
66C3 Los Angeles Aqueduct USA
59B3 Los Banos USA
59B3 Los Gatos USA
16C2 Lošinj I Croatia
74B5 Los Lagos Chile
62A2 Los Lunas USA
70B2 Los Mochis Mexico
66B3 Los Olivos USA
72E1 Los Roques, Islas Venezuela
8D3 Lossie R Scotland
8D3 Lossiemouth Scotland
69E4 Los Testigos Is Venezuela
66C3 Lost Hills USA
58D1 Lost Trail P USA
74B4 Los Vilos Chile
14C3 Lot R France
8D4 Lothian Region Scotland
50D3 Lotikipi Plain Kenya/Sudan
50C4 Loto Zaïre
47D1 Lotsane R Botswana
12K5 Lotta R Finland/Russian Federation
14B2 Loudéac France
48A3 Louga Senegal
7D3 Loughborough England
54H2 Lougheed I Canada
64C3 Louisa USA
27E6 Louisa Reef S China Sea
33E2 Louisiade Arch Papua New Guinea
57D3 Louisiana State USA
47D1 Louis Trichardt South Africa
67B2 Louisville Georgia, USA
57E3 Louisville Kentucky, USA
63E2 Louisville Mississippi, USA
20E2 Loukhi Russian Federation
61D2 Loup R USA
14B3 Lourdes France
Lourenço Marques = Maputo
34C2 Louth Australia
7D3 Louth England
9C3 Louth County Irish Republic
Louvain = Leuven
14C2 Louviers France
20E4 Lovat R Russian Federation
17E2 Lovech Bulgaria
60B2 Loveland USA
60B3 Loveland P USA
58E2 Lovell USA
59C2 Lovelock USA
16C1 Lóvere Italy
62B2 Lovington USA
20F2 Lovozero Russian Federation
55K3 Low,C Canada
57F2 Lowell Massachusetts, USA
58B2 Lowell Oregon, USA
68E1 Lowell USA
58C1 Lower Arrow L Canada
35B2 Lower Hutt New Zealand
66A1 Lower Lake USA
61D1 Lower Red L USA
7E3 Lowestoft England
19D2 Łowicz Poland
34B2 Loxton Australia
47C3 Loxton South Africa
68B2 Loyalsock Creek R USA
33F3 Loyalty Is New Caledonia
17D2 Loznica Serbia, Yugoslavia
24H3 Lozva R Russian Federation
51C5 Luacano Angola
51C4 Luachimo Angola
50C4 Lualaba R Zaïre
51C5 Luampa Zambia
51C5 Luân Angola
31D3 Lu'an China
51B4 Luanda Angola
51B5 Luando R Angola
51C5 Luanginga R Angola
30C1 Luang Namtha Laos
30C2 Luang Prabang Laos
51B4 Luangue R Angola
51D5 Luangwa R Zambia
31D1 Luan He R China
31D1 Luanping China
51C5 Luanshya Zambia
51C5 Luapula R Zaïre
15A1 Luarca Spain
51B4 Lubalo Angola
19F2 L'uban Belarus
51B5 Lubango Angola
56C3 Lubbock USA
18C2 Lübeck Germany
50C4 Lubefu Zaïre
50C4 Lubefu R Zaïre
50C3 Lubero Zaïre
51C4 Lubilash R Zaïre
19E2 Lublin Poland
21E5 Lubny Ukraine
51C4 Lubudi Zaïre
51C4 Lubudi R Zaïre
27D7 Lubuklinggau Indonesia
51C5 Lubumbashi Zaïre
50C4 Lubutu Zaïre
75A1 Lucas Brazil
67C3 Lucaya Bahamas
16C2 Lucca Italy
8C4 Luce B Scotland
63E2 Lucedale USA
19D3 Lucenec Slovakia
Lucerne = Luzern
62A2 Lucero Mexico
31C5 Luchuan China
66B2 Lucia USA
18C2 Luckenwalde Germany
47C2 Luckhoff South Africa
43E3 Lucknow India
51C5 Lucusse Angola
13D2 Lüdenscheid Germany
47B2 Lüderitz Namibia
42D2 Ludhiana India
64B2 Ludington USA
59C4 Ludlow California, USA
7C3 Ludlow England
68D1 Ludlow Vermont, USA
17F2 Ludogorie Upland Bulgaria
67B2 Ludowici USA
17E1 Luduş Romania
12H6 Ludvika Sweden
18B3 Ludwigsburg Germany
18B3 Ludwigshafen Germany
18C2 Ludwigslust Germany
50C4 Luebo Zaïre
50C4 Luema R Zaïre
51C4 Luembe R Angola
51B5 Luena Angola
51C5 Luene R Angola
31B3 Lüeyang China
31D5 Lufeng China
57D3 Lufkin USA
20D4 Luga Russian Federation
20D4 Luga R Russian Federation
16B1 Lugano Switzerland
51D5 Lugela Mozambique
51D5 Lugenda R Mozambique
9C3 Lugnaquillia,Mt Irish Republic
15A1 Lugo Spain
17E1 Lugoj Romania
45D2 Luhfi, Wadi Jordan
31A3 Luhuo China
51B4 Lui R Angola
51C5 Luiana Angola
51C5 Luiana R Angola
Luichow Peninsula = Leizhou Bandao
20D2 Luiro R Finland
51C5 Luishia Zaïre
26C4 Luixi China
51C4 Luiza Zaïre
31D3 Lujiang China
50B4 Lukenie R Zaïre
59D4 Lukeville USA
50B4 Lukolela Zaïre
19E2 Łuków Poland
50C4 Lukuga R Zaïre
51C5 Lukulu Zambia
20C2 Lule R Sweden
12J5 Luleå Sweden
17F2 Lüleburgaz Turkey
31C2 Lüliang Shan Mts China
63C3 Luling USA
50C3 Lulonga R Zaïre
Luluabourg = Kananga
51C5 Lumbala Kaquengue Angola
57F3 Lumberton USA
20G2 Lumbovka Russian Federation
43G3 Lumding India
51C5 Lumeje Angola
35A3 Lumsden New Zealand
12G7 Lund Sweden
51D5 Lundazi Zambia
51D6 Lundi R Zimbabwe
7B4 Lundy I England
18C2 Lüneburg Germany
13D3 Lunéville France
51C5 Lunga R Zambia
43G4 Lunglei India
51B5 Lungue Bungo R Angola
19F2 Luninec Belarus
66C1 Luning USA
50B4 Luobomo Congo
31B5 Luocheng China
31C5 Luoding China
31C3 Luohe China
31C3 Luo He R Henan, China
31B2 Luo He R Shaanxi, China
31C4 Luoxiao Shan Hills China
31C3 Luoyang China
50B4 Luozi Zaïre
51C5 Lupane Zimbabwe
51D5 Lupilichi Mozambique
Lu Qu R = Tao He
74E3 Luque Paraguay
13D4 Lure France
9C2 Lurgan Northern Ireland
51D5 Lurio R Mozambique
41E3 Luristan Region Iran
51C5 Lusaka Zambia
50C4 Lusambo Zaïre
17D2 Lushnjë Albania
50D4 Lushoto Tanzania
26C4 Lushui China
31E2 Lüshun China
60C2 Lusk USA
7D4 Luton England
21D5 Lutsk Ukraine
50E3 Luuq Somalia
61D2 Luverne USA
51C4 Luvua R Zaïre
51D4 Luwegu R Tanzania
51D5 Luwingu Zambia
27F7 Luwuk Indonesia
14D2 Luxembourg Luxembourg
13D3 Luxembourg Grand Duchy NW Europe
13D4 Luxeuil-les-Bains France
31A5 Luxi China
49F2 Luxor Egypt
20H3 Luza Russian Federation
20H3 Luza R Russian Federation
16B1 Luzern Switzerland
68D1 Luzerne USA
31B5 Luzhai China
31B4 Luzhi China
31B4 Luzhou China
75C2 Luziânia Brazil
27F5 Luzon I Philippines
27F5 Luzon Str Philippines
19E3 L'vov Ukraine
8D2 Lybster Scotland
12H6 Lycksele Sweden
7E4 Lydd England
51C6 Lydenburg South Africa
56B3 Lyell,Mt USA
68B2 Lykens USA
58D2 Lyman USA
7C4 Lyme B England
7C4 Lyme Regis England
7D4 Lymington England
57F3 Lynchburg USA
34A2 Lyndhurst Australia
65E2 Lynn USA
67A2 Lynn Haven USA
54H4 Lynn Lake Canada
7C4 Lynton England
54H3 Lynx L Canada
14C2 Lyon France
67B2 Lyons Georgia, USA
68B1 Lyons New York, USA
32A3 Lyons R Australia
20K4 Lys'va Russian Federation
6C3 Lytham St Anne's England
35B2 Lyttelton New Zealand
66A1 Lytton USA
19F2 Lyubeshov Ukraine
20F4 Lyublino Russian Federation

M

30C1 Ma R Laos/Vietnam
45C2 Ma'agan Jordan
45C2 Ma'alot Tarshīhā Israel
40C3 Ma'ān Jordan
31D3 Ma'anshan China
45D1 Ma'arrat an Nu'mān Syria
13C2 Maas R Netherlands
13C2 Maaseik Belgium
18B2 Maastricht Netherlands
47E1 Mabalane Mozambique
73G2 Mabaruma Guyana
7E3 Mablethorpe England
51D6 Mabote Mozambique
19E2 Mabrita Belarus
75D3 Macaé Brazil
56D3 McAlester USA
56D4 McAllen USA
51D5 Macaloge Mozambique
73H3 Macapá Brazil
75D2 Macarani Brazil
72C4 Macas Ecuador
73L5 Macaú Brazil
31C5 Macau Dependency SE Asia
75D1 Macaúbas Brazil
50C3 M'Bari R Central African Republic
58C2 McCall USA
62B2 McCamey USA
58D2 McCammon USA
7C3 Macclesfield England
55K1 McClintock B Canada
54H2 McClintock Chan Canada
68B2 McClure USA
66B2 McClure,L USA
54G2 McClure Str Canada
63D2 McComb USA
60C2 McConaughy,L USA
68B3 McConnellsburg USA
56C2 McCook USA
55L2 Macculloch,C Canada
54F4 McDame Canada
58C2 McDermitt USA
58D1 McDonald Peak Mt USA
32C3 Macdonnell Ranges Mts Australia
8D3 MacDuff Scotland
15A1 Macedo de Cavaleiros Portugal
17E2 Macedonia Republic Europe
73L5 Maceió Brazil
48B4 Macenta Guinea
16C2 Macerata Italy
63D2 McGehee USA
59D3 McGill USA
54C3 McGrath USA
58D1 McGuire,Mt USA
75C3 Machado Brazil
51D6 Machaíla Mozambique
50D4 Machakos Kenya
72C4 Machala Ecuador
51D6 Machaze Mozambique
44B2 Mācherla India
45C2 Machgharab Lebanon
65F2 Machias USA
44C2 Machilīpatnam India
72D1 Machiques Venezuela
72D6 Machu-Picchu Hist Site Peru
7C3 Machynlleth Wales
51D6 Macia Mozambique
Macias Nguema I = Bioko
60C1 McIntosh USA
34C1 MacIntyre R Australia
60B3 Mack USA
32D3 Mackay Australia
58D2 Mackay USA
32B3 Mackay,L Australia
33H1 McKean I Phoenix Islands
65D2 McKeesport USA
54F3 Mackenzie R Canada
54E3 Mackenzie B Canada
54G2 Mackenzie King I Canada
54E3 Mackenzie Mts Canada
64C1 Mackinac,Str of USA
64C1 Mackinaw City USA
54C3 McKinley, Mt USA
63C2 McKinney USA
55L2 Mackinson Inlet B Canada
66C3 McKittrick USA
34D2 Macksville Australia
60C1 McLaughlin USA
34D1 Maclean Australia
47D3 Maclear South Africa
54G4 McLennan Canada
54G3 McLeod B Canada
32A3 McLeod,L Australia
58B2 McLoughlin,Mt USA
54E3 Macmillan R Canada
62B2 McMillan,L USA
58B1 McMinnville Oregon, USA
67A1 McMinnville Tennessee, USA
76F7 McMurdo Base Antarctica
59E4 McNary USA
64A2 Macomb USA
16B2 Macomer Sardinia, Italy
51D5 Macomia Mozambique
14C2 Mâcon France
57E3 Macon Georgia, USA
61E3 Macon Missouri, USA
51C5 Macondo Angola
63C1 McPherson USA
34C2 Macquarie R Australia
34C4 Macquarie Harbour B Australia
36J7 Macquarie Is Australia
34D2 Macquarie,L Australia
67B2 McRae USA
76F11 Mac Robertson Land Region Antarctica
54G3 McTavish Arm B Canada
54F3 McVicar Arm B Canada
45C3 Mādabā Jordan
50C2 Madadi Well Chad
46J9 Madagascar I Indian Ocean
36D6 Madagascar Basin Indian Ocean
50B1 Madama Niger
32D1 Madang Papua New Guinea
48C3 Madaoua Niger
43G4 Madaripur Bangladesh
41F2 Madau Turkmenistan
65D1 Madawaska R Canada
48A1 Madeira I Atlantic Ocean
72F5 Madeira R Brazil
19F2 M'adel Belarus
55M5 Madeleine Îles de la Canada
61E2 Madelia USA
70B2 Madera Mexico
59B3 Madera USA
44A2 Madgaon India
43F3 Madhubani India
43E4 Madhya Pradesh State India
44B3 Madikeri India
50B4 Madimba Zaïre
50B4 Madingo Kayes Congo
50B4 Madingou Congo
57E3 Madison Indiana, USA
61D1 Madison Minnesota, USA
61D2 Madison Nebraska, USA
61D2 Madison S Dakota, USA
57E2 Madison Wisconsin, USA
58D1 Madison R USA
64B3 Madisonville Kentucky, USA
63C2 Madisonville Texas, USA
50D3 Mado Gashi Kenya
44C3 Madras India
58B2 Madras USA
74A8 Madre de Dios I Chile
72E6 Madre de Dios R Bolivia
70C2 Madre, Laguna Mexico
63C3 Madre, Laguna USA
15B1 Madrid Spain
15B2 Madridejos Spain
27E7 Madura I Indonesia
44B4 Madurai India
29C3 Maebashi Japan
30B3 Mae Khlong R Thailand
30B4 Mae Luang R Thailand
30C2 Mae Nam Mun R Thailand
30B2 Mae Nam Ping R Thailand
28A3 Maengsan N Korea
51E5 Maevatanana Madagascar
33F2 Maewo I Vanuatu
47D2 Mafeteng Lesotho
34C3 Maffra Australia
51D4 Mafia I Tanzania
47D2 Mafikeng South Africa
74G3 Mafra Brazil
40C3 Mafraq Jordan
25R4 Magadan Russian Federation
74B8 Magallanes, Estrecho de Str Chile
72D2 Magangué Colombia
56B3 Magdalena Mexico
62A2 Magdalena USA
72D2 Magdalena R Colombia
70A2 Magdalena, Bahía Mexico
70A2 Magdalena, Isla Mexico
18C2 Magdeburg Germany
73K8 Magé Brazil
16B1 Maggiore, L Italy
40B4 Maghâgha Egypt
45B3 Maghâra, Gebel Mt Egypt
9C2 Maghera Northern Ireland
9C2 Magherafelt Northern Ireland
17D2 Maglie Italy
20K5 Magnitogorsk Russian Federation
63D2 Magnolia USA
51D5 Magoé Mozambique
65E1 Magog Canada
66D2 Magruder Mt USA
73J4 Maguarinho, Cabo C Brazil
47E2 Magude Mozambique
55J3 Maguse River Canada
Magway = Magwe
30B1 Magwe Burma
21H8 Mahābād Iran
43F3 Mahabharat Range Mts Nepal
44A2 Mahād India
42D4 Mahadeo Hills India
68A2 Mahaffey USA
51E5 Mahajamba, Baie de B Madagascar
51E5 Mahajanga Madagascar
47D1 Mahalapye Botswana
43E4 Mahānadi R India
51E5 Mahanoro Madagascar
68B2 Mahanoy City USA
44A2 Mahārāshtra State India
43E4 Māhāsamund India
30C2 Maha Sarakham Thailand
51E5 Mahavavy R Madagascar
44B2 Mahbūbnagar India
48D1 Mahdia Tunisia
44B3 Mahe India
51D4 Mahenge Tanzania
42C4 Mahesāna India
35C1 Mahia Pen New Zealand
61D1 Mahnomen USA
42D3 Mahoba India
15C2 Mahón Spain
48D1 Mahrès Tunisia
42C4 Mahuva India
72D1 Maicao Colombia
7D4 Maidenhead England
7E4 Maidstone England
50B2 Maiduguri Nigeria
43E4 Maihar India
43G4 Maijdi Bangladesh
43E4 Maikala Range Mts India
42A1 Maimana Afghanistan
64C1 Main Chan Canada
50B4 Mai-Ndombe, L Zaïre
57G2 Maine State, USA
8D2 Mainland I Scotland
42D3 Mainpuri India

51E5 Maintirano Madagascar
18B2 Mainz Germany
48A4 Maio I Cape Verde
74C4 Maipó, Vol Argentina/ Chile
72E1 Maiquetía Venezuela
43G3 Mairābāri India
43G4 Maiskhal I Bangladesh
32E4 Maitland New South Wales, Australia
76F12 Maitri Base Antarctica
70D3 Maíz, Isla del Caribbean Sea
29D3 Maizuru Japan
32A1 Majene Indonesia
72D7 Majes R Peru
50D3 Maji Ethiopia
31D2 Majia He R China
15C2 Majorca I Balearic Is, Spain
Majunga = Mahajanga
27E7 Makale Indonesia
43F3 Makalu Mt China/Nepal
50B3 Makanza Zaïre
20K2 Makarikha Russian Federation
16D2 Makarska Croatia
20G4 Makaryev Russian Federation
Makassar = Ujung Pandang
27E7 Makassar Str Indonesia
21J6 Makat Kazakhstan
48A4 Makeni Sierra Leone
13C1 Makerwaard Polder Netherlands
21F6 Makeyevka Ukraine
51C6 Makgadikgadi Salt Pan Botswana
21H7 Makhachkala Russian Federation
50D4 Makindu Kenya
Makkah = Mecca Saudi Arabia
55N4 Makkovik Canada
19E3 Makó Hungary
50B3 Makokou Gabon
35C1 Makorako,Mt New Zealand
50B3 Makoua Congo
42C3 Makrāna India
42A3 Makran Coast Range Mts Pakistan
16B3 Makthar Tunisia
21G8 Mākū Iran
50C4 Makumbi Zaïre
48C4 Makurdi Nigeria
44B3 Malabar Coast India
48C4 Malabo Equatorial Guinea
Malacca = Melaka
30C5 Malacca,Str of SE Asia
58D2 Malad City USA
72D2 Málaga Colombia
15B2 Málaga Spain
62B2 Malaga USA
51E6 Malaimbandy Madagascar
33F1 Malaita I Solomon Islands
50D3 Malakal Sudan
42C2 Malakand Pakistan
27F6 Malanbang Philippines
27E7 Malang Indonesia
51B4 Malanje Angola
48C3 Malanville Benin
25S3 Mal Anyuy R Russian Federation
12H7 Mälaren L Sweden
65D1 Malartic Canada
21F8 Malatya Turkey
51D5 Malawi Republic Africa
Malawi,L = Nyasa,L
41E3 Malāyer Iran
27D6 Malaysia Federation SE Asia
40D2 Malazgirt Turkey
19D2 Malbork Poland
18C2 Malchin Germany
63E1 Malden USA
39F5 Maldives Is Indian Ocean
36E4 Maldives Ridge Indian Ocean
7E4 Maldon England
74F4 Maldonado Uruguay
42C4 Malegaon India
18D3 Malé Karpaty Upland Slovakia
33F2 Malekula I Vanuatu
51D5 Malema Mozambique
20F3 Malen'ga Russian Federation
13B3 Malesherbes France
42B2 Mālestān Afghanistan
12H5 Malgomaj L Sweden
20B3 Malgomaj R Sweden
50C2 Malha Well Sudan
58C2 Malheur L USA
48B3 Mali Republic Africa
30B3 Mali Kyun I Burma
19F2 Malin Ukraine
27E6 Malinau Indonesia
50E4 Malindi Kenya
Malines = Mechelen
10B2 Malin Head Pt Irish Republic
42D4 Malkāpur India
17F2 Malkara Turkey
17F2 Malko Tŭrnovo Bulgaria
8C3 Mallaig Scotland
49F2 Mallawi Egypt
Mallorca I = Majorca
12G6 Malm Norway
12J5 Malmberget Sweden
13D2 Malmédy Germany
7C4 Malmesbury England
47B3 Malmesbury South Africa
12G7 Malmö Sweden
20J4 Malmyzh Russian Federation
65E2 Malone USA
47D2 Maloti Mts Lesotho
12F6 Måloy Norway
20J2 Malozemel'skaya Tundra Plain Russian Federation
71B3 Malpelo I Colombia
42D3 Mālpura India
58D2 Malta Idaho, USA
56C2 Malta Montana, USA
16C3 Malta I and Republic Medit Sea
16C3 Malta Chan Italy/Malta
47B1 Maltahöhe Namibia
6D2 Malton England
45D2 Ma'lūlā, Jabal Mt Syria
12G6 Malung Sweden
44A2 Mālvan India
63D2 Malvern USA
47E1 Malvérnia Mozambique
Malvinas, Islas = Falkland Islands
42D4 Malwa Plat India
25Q2 Malyy Lyakhovskiy, Ostrov I Russian Federation
25M2 Malyy Taymyr, Ostrov I Russian Federation
21H6 Malyy Uzen' R Kazakhstan
25N4 Mama Russian Federation
20J4 Mamadysh Russian Federation
50C3 Mambasa Zaïre
32C1 Mamberamo R Australia
27G7 Mamberamo R Indonesia
50B3 Mambéré R Central African Republic
48C4 Mamfé Cameroon
59D4 Mammoth USA
64B3 Mammoth Cave Nat Pk USA
66C2 Mammoth Pool Res USA
72E6 Mamoré R Bolivia/Brazil
48A3 Mamou Guinea
51E5 Mampikony Madagascar
48B4 Mampong Ghana
45C3 Mamshit Hist Site Israel
27E7 Mamuju Indonesia
47C1 Mamuno Botswana
48B4 Man Ivory Coast
66E5 Mana Hawaiian Islands
51E6 Manabo Madagascar
72F4 Manacapuru Brazil
15C2 Manacor Spain
27F6 Manado Indonesia
72A1 Managua Nicaragua
70D3 Managua, L de Nicaragua
51E6 Manakara Madagascar
32D1 Manam I Papua New Guinea
51E5 Mananara Madagascar
51E6 Mananjary Madagascar
35A3 Manapouri New Zealand
35A3 Manapouri,L New Zealand
39G1 Manas China
43G3 Manas R Bhutan
24K5 Manas Hu L China
43E3 Manaslu Mt Nepal
68C2 Manasquan USA
73G4 Manaus Brazil
21E8 Manavgat Turkey
40C2 Manbij Syria
6B2 Man,Calf of I Isle of Man, British Islands
64B2 Mancelona USA
44B2 Mancherāl India
65E2 Manchester Connecticut, USA
7C3 Manchester England
64C3 Manchester Kentucky, USA
57F2 Manchester New Hampshire, USA
68B2 Manchester Pennsylvania, USA
67A1 Manchester Tennessee, USA
68D1 Manchester Vermont, USA
26F2 Manchuria Division China
41F4 Mand R Iran
51D5 Manda Tanzania
75B3 Mandaguari Brazil
12F7 Mandal Norway
27G7 Mandala, Peak Mt Indonesia
30B1 Mandalay Burma
26D2 Mandalgovĭ Mongolia
56C2 Mandan USA
50E3 Mandera Ethiopia
69H1 Mandeville Jamaica
42D2 Mandi India
51D5 Mandimba Mozambique
75A2 Mandiore, Lagoa Brazil
43E4 Mandla India
51E5 Mandritsara Madagascar
42D4 Mandsaur India
17D2 Manduria Italy
42B4 Māndvi India
44B3 Mandya India
43E4 Manendragarh India
19F2 Manevichi Ukraine
40B4 Manfalût Egypt
16D2 Manfredonia Italy
75D1 Manga Brazil
50B2 Manga Desert Region Niger
35C1 Mangakino New Zealand
17F2 Mangalia Romania
50C2 Mangalmé Chad
44A3 Mangalore India
43H4 Mangin Range Mts Burma
26C3 Mangnai China
48C3 Mango Togo
51D5 Mangoche Malawi
51E6 Mangoky R Madagascar
27F7 Mangole I Indonesia
42B4 Māngral India
75B4 Mangueirinha Brazil
25O4 Mangui China
62C2 Mangum USA
21J7 Mangyshiak, Poluostrov Pen Kazakhstan
56D3 Manhattan USA
47E2 Manhica Mozambique
73K8 Manhuacu Brazil
51E5 Mania R Madagascar
51D5 Manica Mozambique
55M5 Manicouagan R Canada
55M5 Manicouagan, Réservoir Canada
41E4 Manifah Saudi Arabia
27F5 Manila Philippines
58E2 Manila USA
34D2 Manilla Australia
48B3 Maninian Ivory Coast
43G4 Manipur R Burma/India
43G4 Manipur State India
21D8 Manisa Turkey
10C3 Man,Isle of Irish Sea
64B2 Manistee USA
64B2 Manistee R USA
64B1 Manistique USA
54J4 Manitoba Province Canada
54J4 Manitoba,L Canada
60D1 Manitou Canada
64B1 Manitou Is USA
55K5 Manitoulin I Canada
60C3 Manitou Springs USA
64C1 Manitowik L Canada
64B2 Manitowoc USA
65D1 Maniwaki Canada
72C2 Manizales Colombia
51E6 Manja Madagascar
32A4 Manjimup Australia
44B2 Mānjra R India
57D2 Mankato USA
48B4 Mankono Ivory Coast
35B1 Manly New Zealand
42C4 Manmād India
34A2 Mannahill Australia
44B4 Mannar Sri Lanka
44B4 Mannār,G of India
44B3 Mannārgudi India
18B3 Mannheim Germany
67B2 Manning USA
34A2 Mannum Australia
48A4 Mano Sierra Leone
32C1 Manokwari Indonesia
51C4 Manono Zaïre
30B3 Manoron Burma
55L4 Manouane, Lac Canada
29C3 Mano-wan B Japan
28B2 Manp'o N Korea
42D2 Mānsa India
51C5 Mansa Zambia
55K3 Mansel I Canada
63D1 Mansfield Arkansas, USA
34C3 Mansfield Australia
7D3 Mansfield England
63D2 Mansfield Louisiana, USA
68E1 Mansfield Massachusetts, USA
57E2 Mansfield Ohio, USA
65D2 Mansfield Pennsylvania, USA
75B2 Manso R Brazil
27H5 Mansyu Deep Pacific Ocean
72B4 Manta Ecuador
28A2 Mantap-san Mt N Korea
72C6 Mantaro R Peru
66B2 Manteca USA
67C1 Manteo USA
14C2 Mantes France
59D3 Manti USA
75C3 Mantiqueira, Serra da Mts Brazil
16C1 Mantova Italy
12J6 Mäntta Finland
Mantua = Mantova
20G4 Manturovo Russian Federation
62B3 Manuel Benavides Mexico
75B3 Manuel Ribas Brazil
27F6 Manukan Philippines
33G4 Manukau New Zealand
27H7 Manus I Pacific Ocean
15B2 Manzanares Spain
70E2 Manzanillo Cuba
70B3 Manzanillo Mexico
25N5 Manzhouli China
45D3 Manzil Jordan
51D6 Manzini Swaziland
50B2 Mao Chad
27G7 Maoke, Pegunungan Mts Indonesia
31A2 Maomao Shan Mt China
31C5 Maoming China
51D6 Mapai Mozambique
43E2 Mapam Yumco L China
27G6 Mapia Is Pacific Ocean
27E6 Mapin I Philippines
54H5 Maple Creek Canada
47E1 Mapulanguene Mozambique
47E2 Maputo Mozambique
47E2 Maputo R Mozambique
47E2 Maputo, Baia de B Mozambique
Ma Qu = Huang He
31A3 Maqu China
43F3 Maquan He R China
50B4 Maquela do Zombo Angola
74C6 Maquinchao Argentina
73J5 Marabá Brazil
72D1 Maracaibo Venezuela
72D2 Maracaibo, Lago de Venezuela
73H3 Maracá, Ilha de I Brazil
75A3 Maracaju Brazil
75A3 Maracaju, Serra de Mts Brazil
75D1 Máracás Brazil
72E1 Maracay Venezuela
49D2 Marādah Libya
48C3 Maradi Niger
21H8 Marāgheh Iran
73J4 Marajó, Baia de B Brazil
73H4 Marajó, Ilha de I Brazil
28E5 Marakech Morocco
50D3 Maralal Kenya
33F1 Maramasike I Solomon Islands
Maramba = Livingstone
59D4 Marana USA
21H8 Marand Iran
75C1 Maranhão R Brazil
73J4 Maranhão State Brazil
34C1 Maranoa R Australia
72C4 Marañón R Peru
21F8 Maras Turkey
55K5 Marathon Canada
67B4 Marathon Florida, USA
68B1 Marathon New York, USA
62B2 Marathon Texas, USA
75E1 Maraú Brazil
27F6 Marawi Philippines
15B2 Marbella Spain
32A3 Marble Bar Australia
59D3 Marble Canyon USA
47D2 Marble Hall South Africa
68E1 Marblehead USA
18B2 Marburg Germany
Mar Cantabrico = Biscay, B of
51B5 Marca, Punta da Pt Angola
18B2 Marche Belgium
13C2 Marche-en-Famenne Belgium
15A2 Marchena Spain
74D4 Mar Chiquita, Lagoa L Argentina
67B3 Marco USA
65E2 Marcy,Mt USA
42C2 Mardan Pakistan
74E5 Mar del Plata Argentina
21G8 Mardin Turkey
33F3 Maré I New Caledonia
50D2 Mareb R Eritrea/Ethiopia
27H8 Mareeba Australia
8C3 Maree, Loch L Scotland
50E3 Mareeq Somalia
62B2 Marfa USA
68C1 Margaretville USA
69E4 Margarita, Isla Venezuela
72F1 Margarita, Islas de Venezuela
29C2 Margaritovo Russian Federation
7E4 Margate England
17E1 Marghita Romania
34C4 Maria I Australia
27H5 Marianas Is Pacific Ocean
36J4 Mariana Trench Pacific Ocean
43G3 Mariāni India
63D2 Marianna Arkansas, USA
67A2 Marianna Florida, USA
72B2 Mariato, Puerta Panama
57G4 Maria Van Diemen,C New Zealand
18D3 Mariazell Austria
16D1 Maribor Slovenia
47D1 Marico R Botswana/ South Africa
66C3 Maricopa USA
50C3 Maridi Sudan
76F5 Marie Byrd Land Region Antarctica
69E3 Marie Galante I Caribbean Sea
12H6 Mariehamn Finland
13C2 Mariembourg Belgium
73H2 Marienburg Surinam
47B1 Mariental Namibia
12G7 Mariestad Sweden
67B2 Marietta Georgia, USA
64C3 Marietta Ohio, USA
63C2 Marietta Oklahoma, USA
69Q2 Marigot Dominica
74G2 Marília Brazil
20C5 Marijampole Lithuania
51B4 Marimba Angola
57E2 Marinette USA
74F2 Maringá Brazil
50C3 Maringa R Zaïre
63D1 Marion Arkansas, USA
64B3 Marion Illinois, USA
57E2 Marion Indiana, USA
57E2 Marion Ohio, USA
67C2 Marion S Carolina, USA
57E3 Marion,L USA
33E2 Marion Reef Australia
59C3 Mariposa USA
66B2 Mariposa R USA
66B2 Mariposa Res USA
20H4 Mari Republic Russian Federation
21D7 Marista R Bulgaria
21F6 Mariupol' Ukraine
45C2 Marjayoun Lebanon
19F2 Marjina Gorki Belarus
45C3 Marka Jordan
50E3 Marka Somalia
18C1 Markaryd Sweden
7C3 Market Drayton England
7D3 Market Harborough England
6D3 Market Weighton England
76E7 Markham,Mt Antarctica
66C1 Markleeville USA
25T3 Markovo Russian Federation
68E1 Marlboro Massachusetts, USA
68D1 Marlboro New Hampshire, USA
32D3 Marlborough Australia
7D4 Marlborough England
13B3 Marle France
63C2 Marlin USA
68D1 Marlow USA
14C3 Marmande France
17F2 Marmara Adasi I Turkey
40A1 Marmara,S of Turkey
17F3 Marmaris Turkey
60C1 Marmarth USA
64C3 Marmet USA
61E1 Marmion L Canada
16C1 Marmolada Mt Italy
13C3 Marne Department France
13B3 Marne R France
50B3 Maro Chad
51E5 Maroantsetra Madagascar
51D5 Marondera Zimbabwe
73H3 Maroni R French Guiana
34D1 Maroochydore Australia
50B2 Maroua Cameroon
51E5 Marovoay Madagascar
57E4 Marquesas Keys Is USA
57E2 Marquette USA
37N5 Marquises, Îles Pacific Ocean
34C2 Marra R Australia
47E2 Marracuene Mozambique
50C2 Marra, Jebel Mt Sudan
48B1 Marrakech Morocco
32C3 Marree Australia
63D3 Marrero USA
51D5 Marromeu Mozambique
51D5 Marrupa Mozambique
40B4 Marsa Alam Egypt
50D3 Marsabit Kenya
16C3 Marsala Sicily, Italy
13E2 Marsberg Germany
14D3 Marseilles France
75D3 Mar, Serra do Mts Brazil
64B3 Marshall Illinois, USA
64C2 Marshall Michigan, USA
61D2 Marshall Minnesota, USA
61E3 Marshall Missouri, USA

57D3 **Marshall** Texas, USA
68B3 **Marshall** Virginia, USA
37K4 **Marshall Is** Pacific Ocean
61E2 **Marshalltown** USA
63D1 **Marshfield** Missouri, USA
64A2 **Marshfield** Wisconsin, USA
69B1 **Marsh Harbour** The Bahamas
63D3 **Marsh I** USA
30B2 **Martaban,G of** Burma
65E2 **Martha's Vineyard** *I* USA
14D2 **Martigny** Switzerland
14D3 **Martigues** France
19D3 **Martin** Slovakia
60C2 **Martin** S Dakota, USA
63E1 **Martin** Tennessee, USA
35C2 **Martinborough** New Zealand
69E4 **Martinique** *I* Caribbean Sea
67A2 **Martin,L** USA
65D3 **Martinsburg** USA
64C2 **Martins Ferry** USA
65D3 **Martinsville** USA
52G6 **Martin Vaz** *I* Atlantic Ocean
35C2 **Marton** New Zealand
15B2 **Martos** Spain
54G3 **Martre, Lac la** Canada
42B2 **Maruf** Afghanistan
29B4 **Marugame** Japan
59D3 **Marvine,Mt** USA
42C3 **Mārwār** India
24H6 **Mary** Turkmenistan
33E3 **Maryborough** Queensland, Australia
34B3 **Maryborough** Victoria, Australia
54F4 **Mary Henry,Mt** Canada
57F3 **Maryland** *State* USA
6C2 **Maryport** England
59B3 **Marysville** California, USA
61D3 **Marysville** Kansas, USA
58B1 **Marysville** Washington, USA
57D2 **Maryville** Iowa, USA
61D2 **Maryville** Missouri, USA
67B1 **Maryville** Tennessee, USA
49D2 **Marzuq** Libya
45A3 **Masabb Dumyât** *C* Egypt
Masada = Mezada
45C2 **Mas'adah** Syria
50D4 **Masai Steppe** *Upland* Tanzania
50D4 **Masaka** Uganda
41E2 **Masally** Azerbaijan
28B3 **Masan** S Korea
51D5 **Masasi** Tanzania
70D3 **Masaya** Nicaragua
27F5 **Masbate** Philippines
27F5 **Masbate** *I* Philippines
15C2 **Mascara** Algeria
36D5 **Mascarene Ridge** Indian Ocean
75E2 **Mascote** Brazil
47D2 **Maseru** Lesotho
42B2 **Mashaki** Afghanistan
41G2 **Mashhad** Iran
50B4 **Masi-Manimba** Zaïre
50D3 **Masindi** Uganda
38D3 **Maşīrah** *I* Oman
50C4 **Masisi** Zaïre
41E3 **Masjed Soleyman** Iran
51F5 **Masoala, C** Madagascar
66C1 **Mason** Nevada, USA
62C2 **Mason** Texas, USA
57D2 **Mason City** USA
Masqat = Muscat
16C2 **Massa** Italy
57F2 **Massachusetts** *State* USA
65E2 **Massachusetts B** USA
50B2 **Massakori** Chad
51D6 **Massangena** Mozambique
50D2 **Massawa** Eritrea
65E2 **Massena** USA
50B2 **Massénya** Chad
64C1 **Massey** Canada
14C2 **Massif Central** *Mts* France
51E6 **Massif de l'Isalo** *Upland* Madagascar
51E5 **Massif du Tsaratanana** *Mts* Madagascar
64C2 **Massillon** USA
48B3 **Massina** *Region* Mali
51D6 **Massinga** Mozambique
47E1 **Massingir** Mozambique
21J6 **Masteksay** Kazakhstan
33G5 **Masterton** New Zealand
28C4 **Masuda** Japan
50B4 **Masuku** Gabon
40C2 **Maşyāf** Syria
64C1 **Matachewan** Canada
62A3 **Matachie** Mexico
50B4 **Matadi** Zaïre
72A1 **Matagalpa** Nicaragua
55L5 **Matagami** Canada
56D4 **Matagorda B** USA
63C3 **Matagorda I** USA
35C1 **Matakana I** New Zealand
51B5 **Matala** Angola
44C4 **Matale** Sri Lanka
48A3 **Matam** Senegal
48C3 **Matameye** Niger
70C2 **Matamoros** Mexico
49E2 **Ma'tan as Sarra** *Well* Libya
55M5 **Matane** Canada
70D2 **Matanzas** Cuba
65F1 **Matapedia** *R* Canada
44C4 **Matara** Sri Lanka
32A1 **Mataram** Indonesia
72D7 **Matarani** Peru
75E1 **Mataripe** Brazil
15C1 **Mataró** Spain
47D3 **Matatiele** South Africa
35A3 **Mataura** New Zealand
70B2 **Matehuala** Mexico
69L1 **Matelot** Trinidad
16D2 **Matera** Italy
19E3 **Mátészalka** Hungary
16B3 **Mateur** Tunisia
66C2 **Mather** USA
64C1 **Matheson** Canada
63C3 **Mathis** USA
42D3 **Mathura** India
7D3 **Matlock** England
73G6 **Mato Grosso** *State* Brazil
73G7 **Mato Grosso do Sul** *State* Brazil
47E2 **Matola** Mozambique
49E1 **Matrûh** Egypt
28C3 **Matsue** Japan
29E2 **Matsumae** Japan
29D3 **Matsumoto** Japan
29D4 **Matsusaka** Japan
28C4 **Matsuyama** Japan
55K5 **Mattagami** *R* Canada
65D1 **Mattawa** Canada
16B1 **Matterhorn** *Mt* Italy/ Switzerland
58C2 **Matterhorn** *Mt* USA
69C2 **Matthew Town** The Bahamas
68D2 **Mattituck** USA
64B3 **Mattoon** USA
42B2 **Matun** Afghanistan
69L1 **Matura B** Trinidad
72F2 **Maturín** Venezuela
43E3 **Mau** India
51D5 **Maúa** Mozambique
14C1 **Maubeuge** France
34B2 **Maude** Australia
52J8 **Maud Seamount** Atlantic Ocean
26H4 **Maug Is** Marianas
66E5 **Maui** *I* Hawaiian Islands
64C2 **Maumee** USA
64C2 **Maumee** *R* USA
51C5 **Maun** Botswana
66E5 **Mauna Kea** *Vol* Hawaiian Islands
66E5 **Mauna Loa** *Vol* Hawaiian Islands
54F3 **Maunoir,L** Canada
14C2 **Mauriac** France
48A2 **Mauritania** *Republic* Africa
46K10 **Mauritius** *I* Indian Ocean
64A2 **Mauston** USA
51C5 **Mavinga** Angola
47E1 **Mavue** Mozambique
43G4 **Mawlaik** Burma
Mawlamyine = Moulmein
76G10 **Mawson** *Base* Antarctica
60C1 **Max** USA
47E1 **Maxaila** Mozambique
27D7 **Maya** *I* Indonesia
25P4 **Maya** *R* Russian Federation
40D2 **Mayādīn** Syria
57F4 **Mayaguana** *I* The Bahamas
69D3 **Mayagüez** Puerto Rico
48C3 **Mayahi** Niger
50B4 **Mayama** Congo
41G2 **Mayamey** Iran
8C4 **Maybole** Scotland
57F3 **May,C** USA
34C4 **Maydena** Australia
13D2 **Mayen** Germany
14B2 **Mayenne** France
59D4 **Mayer** USA
64B3 **Mayfield** USA
62A2 **Mayhill** USA
21G7 **Maykop** Russian Federation
30B1 **Maymyo** Burma
54E3 **Mayo** Canada
68B3 **Mayo** USA
15C2 **Mayor** *Mt* Spain
35C1 **Mayor I** New Zealand
74D1 **Mayor P Lagerenza** Paraguay
51E5 **Mayotte** *I* Indian Ocean
69H2 **May Pen** Jamaica
68C3 **May Point,C** USA
68C3 **Mays Landing** USA
64C3 **Maysville** USA
50B4 **Mayumba** Gabon
61D1 **Mayville** USA
60C2 **Maywood** USA
51C5 **Mazabuka** Zambia
42D1 **Mazar** China
45C3 **Mazār** Jordan
16C3 **Mazara del Vallo** Sicily, Italy
42B1 **Mazar-i-Sharif** Afghanistan
15B2 **Mazarrón, Golfo de** *G* Spain
70B2 **Mazatlán** Mexico
20C4 **Mazeikiai** Lithuania
45C3 **Mazra** Jordan
51D6 **Mbabane** Swaziland
50B3 **Mbaïki** Central African Republic
51D4 **Mbala** Zambia
51C6 **Mbalabala** Zimbabwe
50D3 **Mbale** Uganda
50B3 **Mbalmayo** Cameroon
50B3 **Mbam** *R* Cameroon
51D5 **Mbamba Bay** Tanzania
50B3 **Mbandaka** Zaïre
50B4 **Mbanza Congo** Angola
50B4 **Mbanza-Ngungu** Zaïre
50D4 **Mbarara** Uganda
50C3 **M'Bari,R** Central African Republic
50B3 **Mbèndza** Congo
50B3 **Mbére** *R* Cameroon/ Central African Republic/Chad
51D4 **Mbeya** Tanzania
50B4 **Mbinda** Congo
48A3 **Mbout** Mauritius
50C4 **Mbuji-Mayi** Zaïre
50D4 **Mbulu** Tanzania
48B2 **Mcherrah** *Region* Algeria
51D5 **Mchinji** Malawi
30D3 **Mdrak** Vietnam
62B1 **Meade** USA
56B3 **Mead,L** USA
54H4 **Meadow Lake** Canada
64C2 **Meadville** USA
29D2 **Me-akan dake** *Mt* Japan
55N4 **Mealy Mts** Canada
34C1 **Meandarra** Australia
54G4 **Meander River** Canada
9C3 **Meath** Irish Republic
14C2 **Meaux** France
50E1 **Mecca** Saudi Arabia
59C4 **Mecca** USA
68D1 **Mechanicville** USA
24G2 **Mechdusharskiy, O** *I* Russian Federation
18A2 **Mechelen** Belgium
48B1 **Mecheria** Algeria
18C2 **Meckenburg-Vorpommern** *State* Germany
18C2 **Mecklenburger Bucht** *B* Germany
51D5 **Meconta** Mozambique
51D5 **Mecuburi** Mozambique
51E5 **Mecufi** Mozambique
51D5 **Mecula** Mozambique
27C6 **Medan** Indonesia
74C7 **Médanosa, Puerta** *Pt* Argentina
15C2 **Médéa** Algeria
72C2 **Medellín** Colombia
13C1 **Medemblik** Netherlands
48D1 **Medenine** Tunisia
56A2 **Medford** USA
17F2 **Medgidia** Romania
17E1 **Mediaş** Romania
58C1 **Medical Lake** USA
60B2 **Medicine Bow** USA
60B2 **Medicine Bow Mts** USA
60B2 **Medicine Bow Peak** *Mt* USA
54G5 **Medicine Hat** Canada
62C1 **Medicine Lodge** USA
75D2 **Medina** Brazil
60D1 **Medina** N Dakota, USA
68A1 **Medina** New York, USA
40C5 **Medina** Saudi Arabia
15B1 **Medinaceli** Spain
15A1 **Medina del Campo** Spain
15A1 **Medina de Rioseco** Spain
62C3 **Medina L** USA
43F4 **Medinīpur** India
46E4 **Mediterranean S** Europe
16B3 **Medjerda** *R* Algeria/ Tunisia
16B3 **Medjerda, Mts de la** Algeria/Tunisia
21K5 **Mednogorsk** Russian Federation
25S4 **Mednyy, Ostrov** *I* Russian Federation
43H3 **Mêdog** China
50B3 **Medouneu** Gabon
21G5 **Medvedista** *R* Russian Federation
25S2 **Medvezh'i Ova** *Is* Russian Federation
20E3 **Medvezh'yegorsk** Russian Federation
32A3 **Meekatharra** Australia
60B2 **Meeker** USA
42D3 **Meerut** India
58E2 **Meeteetse** USA
50D3 **Mēga** Ethiopia
17E3 **Megalópolis** Greece
17E3 **Mégara** Greece
43G3 **Meghālaya** *State* India
43G4 **Meghna** *R* Bangladesh
45C2 **Megiddo** *Hist Site* Israel
42D4 **Mehekar** India
43M2 **Mehndawal** India
41F4 **Mehrān** *R* Iran
41F3 **Mehriz** Iran
75C2 **Meia Ponte** *R* Brazil
50B3 **Meiganga** Cameroon
30B1 **Meiktila** Burma
31A4 **Meishan** China
18C2 **Meissen** Germany
31D5 **Mei Xian** China
31D5 **Meizhou** China
72D8 **Mejillones** Chile
50B3 **Mekambo** Gabon
50D2 **Mek'elē** Ethiopia
48B1 **Meknès** Morocco
30D3 **Mekong** *R* Cambodia
30D4 **Mekong, Mouths of the** Vietnam
48C3 **Mekrou** *R* Benin
30C5 **Melaka** Malaysia
36J5 **Melanesia** *Region* Pacific Ocean
32D4 **Melbourne** Australia
57E4 **Melbourne** USA
56C4 **Melchor Muźguiz** Mexico
20K5 **Meleuz** Russian Federation
50B2 **Melfi** Chad
54H4 **Melfort** Canada
15B2 **Melilla** NW Africa
74B6 **Melimoyu** *Mt* Chile
60C1 **Melita** Canada
21F6 **Melitopol'** Ukraine
50D3 **Melka Guba** Ethiopia
13E1 **Melle** Germany
16B3 **Mellègue** *R* Algeria/ Tunisia
47E2 **Melmoth** South Africa
74F4 **Melo** Uruguay
75A3 **Melo** *R* Brazil
66B2 **Melones Res** USA
8D4 **Melrose** Scotland
61E1 **Melrose** USA
7D3 **Melton Mowbray** England
14C2 **Melun** France
54H4 **Melville** Canada
55M2 **Melville Bugt** *B* Greenland
69Q2 **Melville,C** Dominica
54F3 **Melville Hills** Canada
32C2 **Melville I** Australia
54G2 **Melville I** Canada
55N4 **Melville,L** Canada
55K3 **Melville Pen** Canada
51E5 **Memba** Mozambique
32A1 **Memboro** Indonesia
18C3 **Memmingen** Germany
57E3 **Memphis** Tennessee, USA
62B2 **Memphis** Texas, USA
63D2 **Mena** USA
19G2 **Mena** Ukraine
7B3 **Menai Str** Wales
48C3 **Ménaka** Mali
64B2 **Menasha** USA
27E7 **Mendawai** *R* Indonesia
14C3 **Mende** France
50D3 **Mendebo Mts** Ethiopia
32D1 **Mendi** Papua New Guinea
7C4 **Mendip Hills** *Upland* England
58B2 **Mendocino,C** USA
37M3 **Mendocino Seascarp** Pacific Ocean
66B2 **Mendota** California, USA
64B2 **Mendota** Illinois, USA
74C4 **Mendoza** Argentina
74C5 **Mendoza** *State* Argentina
17F3 **Menemen** Turkey
13B2 **Menen** Belgium
31D3 **Mengcheng** China
30B1 **Menghai** China
31A5 **Mengla** China
30B1 **Menglian** China
31A5 **Mengzi** China
32D4 **Menindee** Australia
34B2 **Menindee L** Australia
34A3 **Meningie** Australia
64B1 **Menominee** USA
64B2 **Menomonee Falls** USA
64A2 **Menomonie** USA
51B5 **Menongue** Angola
Menorca *I* **= Minorca**
27C7 **Mentawi, Kepulauan** *Is* Indonesia
62A1 **Mentmore** USA
27D7 **Mentok** Indonesia
64C2 **Mentor** USA
27E6 **Menyapa** *Mt* Indonesia
31A2 **Menyuan** China
16B3 **Menzel** Tunisia
20J4 **Menzelinsk** Russian Federation
13D1 **Meppel** Netherlands
18B2 **Meppen** Germany
15B1 **Mequinenza, Embalse de** *Res* Spain
63D1 **Meramec** *R* USA
16C1 **Merano** Italy
27E7 **Meratus, Pegunungan** *Mts* Indonesia
32D1 **Merauke** Indonesia
56A3 **Merced** USA
66B2 **Merced** *R* USA
74B4 **Mercedario** *Mt* Argentina
74E4 **Mercedes** Buenos Aires, Argentina
74E3 **Mercedes** Corrientes, Argentina
74C4 **Mercedes** San Luis, Argentina
74E4 **Mercedes** Uruguay
35C1 **Mercury B** New Zealand
35C1 **Mercury Is** New Zealand
54F2 **Mercy B** Canada
55M3 **Mercy,C** Canada
62B1 **Meredith,L** USA
30B3 **Mergui** Burma
30B3 **Mergui Arch** Burma
70D2 **Mérida** Mexico
15A2 **Mérida** Spain
72D2 **Mérida** Venezuela
72D2 **Mérida, Cordillera de** Venezuela
57E3 **Meridian** USA
34C3 **Merimbula** Australia
34B2 **Meringur** Australia
27G6 **Merir** *I* Pacific Ocean
62B2 **Merkel** USA
50D2 **Merowe** Sudan
32A4 **Merredin** Australia
8C4 **Merrick** *Mt* Scotland
64B1 **Merrill** USA
64B2 **Merrillville** USA
68E1 **Merrimack** *R* USA
60C2 **Merriman** USA
67B3 **Merritt Island** USA
34D2 **Merriwa** Australia
50E3 **Mersa Fatma** Eritrea
7E4 **Mersea** *I* England
15B2 **Mers el Kebir** Algeria
7C3 **Mersey** *R* England
7C3 **Merseyside** *Metropolitan County* England
21E8 **Mersin** Turkey
30C5 **Mersing** Malaysia
42C3 **Merta** India
7C4 **Merthyr Tydfil** Wales
15A2 **Mertola** Portugal
13B3 **Méru** France
50D4 **Meru** *Mt* Tanzania
21F7 **Merzifon** Turkey
13D3 **Merzig** Germany
56B3 **Mesa** USA
62A1 **Mesa Verde Nat Pk** USA
13E2 **Meschede** Germany
40D1 **Mescit Dağ** *Mt* Turkey
50C3 **Meshra'er Req** Sudan
17E3 **Mesolóngion** Greece
59D3 **Mesquite** Nevada, USA
63C2 **Mesquite** Texas, USA
51D5 **Messalo** *R* Mozambique
47D1 **Messina** South Africa
16D3 **Messina** Sicily, Italy
16D3 **Messina, Stretto de** *Str* Italy/Sicily
17E3 **Messíni** Greece
17E3 **Messiniakós Kólpos** *G* Greece
Mesta *R* **= Néstos**
17E2 **Mesta** *R* Bulgaria
16C1 **Mestre** Italy
72D3 **Meta** *R* Colombia/ Venezuela
20E4 **Meta** *R* Russian Federation
55M3 **Meta Incognita Pen** Canada
63D3 **Metairie** USA
58C1 **Metaline Falls** USA
74D3 **Metán** Argentina
51D5 **Metangula** Mozambique
16D2 **Metaponto** Italy
8D3 **Methil** Scotland
68E1 **Methuen** USA
35B2 **Methven** New Zealand
54E4 **Metlakatla** USA
64B3 **Metropolis** USA
44B3 **Mettūr** India
14D2 **Metz** France
27C6 **Meulaboh** Indonesia
13D3 **Meurthe** *R* France
13D3 **Meurthe-et-Moselle** *Department* France
13C3 **Meuse** *Department* France
13C2 **Meuse** *R* Belgium
14D2 **Meuse** *R* France
7D3 **Mexborough** England
63C2 **Mexia** USA
70A1 **Mexicali** Mexico
59E3 **Mexican Hat** USA
70C3 **México** Mexico
61E3 **Mexico** USA
70B2 **Mexico** *Federal Republic* Central America
70C2 **Mexico,G of** Central America
24H6 **Meymaneh** Afghanistan
45C3 **Mezada** *Hist Site* Israel

20G2 **Mezen'** Russian Federation
20H3 **Mezen'** *R* Russian Federation
14C3 **Mézenc, Mount** France
19G1 **Mezha** *R* Russian Federation
20J1 **Mezhdusharskiy, Ostrov** *I* Russian Federation
42D4 **Mhow** India
59D4 **Miami** Arizona, USA
57E4 **Miami** Florida, USA
63D1 **Miami** Oklahoma, USA
57E4 **Miami Beach** USA
21H8 **Miandowāb** Iran
51E5 **Miandrivazo** Madagascar
21H8 **Mīāneh** Iran
42C2 **Mianwali** Pakistan
31A3 **Mianyang** China
31C3 **Mianyang** China
31A3 **Mianzhu** China
31E2 **Miaodao Qundao** *Arch* China
31B4 **Miao Ling** *Upland* China
20L5 **Miass** Russian Federation
19E3 **Michalovce** Slovakia
58D1 **Michel** Canada
69D3 **Miches** Dominican Republic
57E2 **Michigan** *State* USA
64B2 **Michigan City** USA
57E2 **Michigan,L** USA
64C1 **Michipicoten** Canada
55K5 **Michipicoten I** Canada
17F2 **Michurin** Bulgaria
21G5 **Michurinsk** Russian Federation
36J4 **Micronesia, Fed. States of** *Is* Pacific Ocean
36J4 **Micronesia** *Region* Pacific Ocean
52F4 **Mid Atlantic Ridge** Atlantic Ocean
47C3 **Middelburg** Cape Province, South Africa
13B2 **Middelburg** Netherlands
47D2 **Middelburg** Transvaal, South Africa
58B2 **Middle Alkali L** USA
37O4 **Middle America Trench** Pacific Ocean
44E3 **Middle Andaman** *I* Indian Ocean
68E2 **Middleboro** USA
68B2 **Middleburg** Pennsylvania, USA
68B3 **Middleburg** Virginia, USA
68C1 **Middleburgh** USA
65E2 **Middlebury** USA
57E3 **Middlesboro** USA
6D2 **Middlesbrough** England
68D2 **Middletown** Connecticut, USA
68C3 **Middletown** Delaware, USA
65E2 **Middletown** New York, USA
64C3 **Middletown** Ohio, USA
68B2 **Middletown** Pennsylvania, USA
68C1 **Middleville** USA
7C3 **Middlewich** England
48B1 **Midelt** Morocco
7C4 **Mid Glamorgan** *County* Wales
50E2 **Mīdī** Yemen
36E5 **Mid Indian Basin** Indian Ocean
36E5 **Mid Indian Ridge** Indian Ocean
55L5 **Midland** Canada
64C2 **Midland** Michigan, USA
56C3 **Midland** Texas, USA
9B4 **Midleton** Irish Republic
51E6 **Midongy Atsimo** Madagascar
37K4 **Mid Pacific Mts** Pacific Ocean
58C2 **Midvale** USA
37L3 **Midway Is** Pacific Ocean
60B2 **Midwest** USA
63C1 **Midwest City** USA
40D2 **Midyat** Turkey
17E2 **Midžor** *Mt* Serbia, Yugoslavia
19E2 **Mielec** Poland
17F1 **Miercurea-Ciuc** Romania
15A1 **Mieres** Spain
68B2 **Mifflintown** USA
13B4 **Migennes** France
28B4 **Mihara** Japan
17E2 **Mikhaylovgrad** Bulgaria
21G5 **Mikhaylovka** Russian Federation
28C2 **Mikhaylovka** Russian Federation
24J4 **Mikhaylovskiy** Russian Federation
45C4 **Mikhrot Timna** Israel
12K6 **Mikkeli** Finland
17F3 **Míkonos** *I* Greece
18D3 **Mikulov** Czech Republic
51D4 **Mikumi** Tanzania
20J3 **Mikun** Russian Federation
29D3 **Mikuni-sammyaku** *Mts* Japan
29C4 **Mikura-jima** *I* Japan
61E1 **Milaca** USA
72C4 **Milagro** Ecuador
16B1 **Milan** Italy
63E1 **Milan** USA
51D5 **Milange** Mozambique
Milano = Milan
21D8 **Milas** Turkey
61D1 **Milbank** USA
32D4 **Mildura** Australia
31A5 **Mile** China
41D3 **Mileh Tharthār** *L* Iraq
32E3 **Miles** Australia
56C2 **Miles City** USA
16C2 **Miletto, Monte** *Mt* Italy
68D2 **Milford** Connecticut, USA
65D3 **Milford** Delaware, USA
61D2 **Milford** Nebraska, USA
68E1 **Milford** New Hampshire, USA
68C2 **Milford** Pennsylvania, USA
59D3 **Milford** Utah, USA
7B4 **Milford Haven** Wales
7B4 **Milford Haven** *Sd* Wales
61D3 **Milford L** USA
35A2 **Milford Sd** New Zealand
15C2 **Miliana** Algeria
54G4 **Milk** *R* Canada/USA
60B1 **Milk** *R* USA
25R4 **Mil'kovo** Russian Federation
50C2 **Milk, Wadi el** *Watercourse* Sudan
14C3 **Millau** France
68D2 **Millbrook** USA
67B2 **Milledgeville** USA
61E1 **Mille Lacs L** USA
61E1 **Mille Lacs, Lac des** Canada
60D2 **Miller** USA
21G6 **Millerovo** Russian Federation
68B2 **Millersburg** USA
68D1 **Millers Falls** USA
68D2 **Millerton** USA
66C2 **Millerton L** USA
65E2 **Millford** Massachusetts, USA
34B3 **Millicent** Australia
63E1 **Millington** USA
65F1 **Millinocket** USA
34D1 **Millmerran** Australia
6C2 **Millom** England
8C4 **Millport** Scotland
9B3 **Millstreet** Irish Republic
65F1 **Milltown** Canada
58D1 **Milltown** USA
66A2 **Mill Valley** USA
65E3 **Millville** USA
55Q2 **Milne Land** *I* Greenland
66E5 **Milolii** Hawaiian Islands
17E3 **Mílos** *I* Greece
32D3 **Milparinka** Australia
68B2 **Milroy** USA
67A2 **Milton** Florida, USA
35A3 **Milton** New Zealand
68B2 **Milton** Pennsylvania, USA
7D3 **Milton Keynes** England
57E2 **Milwaukee** USA
29D2 **Mimmaya** Japan
66C1 **Mina** USA
15C2 **Mina** *R* Algeria
41E4 **Mīnā' al Aḩmadī** Kuwait
41G4 **Mīnāb** Iran
74E4 **Minas** Uruguay
73J7 **Minas Gerais** *State* Brazil
75D2 **Minas Novas** Brazil
70C3 **Minatitlán** Mexico
30A1 **Minbu** Burma
30A1 **Minbya** Burma
8B3 **Minch,Little** *Sd* Scotland
8B2 **Minch,North** *Sd* Scotland
10B2 **Minch,The** *Sd* Scotland
27F6 **Mindanao** *I* Philippines
63D2 **Minden** Louisiana, USA
66C1 **Minden** Nevada, USA
18B2 **Minden** Germany
34B2 **Mindona L** Australia
27F5 **Mindoro** *I* Philippines
27F5 **Mindoro Str** Philippines
7C4 **Minehead** England
73H7 **Mineiros** Brazil
63C2 **Mineola** USA
62C2 **Mineral Wells** USA
68B2 **Minersville** USA
34B2 **Mingary** Australia
21H7 **Mingechaurskoye Vodokhranilische** *Res* Azerbaijan
8B3 **Mingulay, I** Scotland
31A2 **Minhe** China
44A4 **Minicoy** *I* India
31D4 **Min Jiang** *R* Fujian, China
31A4 **Min Jiang** *R* Sichuan, China
66C2 **Minkler** USA
34A2 **Minlaton** Australia
31A2 **Minle** China
48C4 **Minna** Nigeria
57D2 **Minneapolis** USA
54J4 **Minnedosa** Canada
61D2 **Minnesota** *R* USA
57D2 **Minnesota** *State* USA
15A1 **Miño** *R* Spain
15C1 **Minorca** *I* Spain
56C2 **Minot** USA
31A2 **Minqin** China
31A3 **Min Shan** *Upland* China
20D5 **Minsk** Belarus
19E2 **Mińsk Mazowiecki** Poland
54G2 **Minto Inlet** *B* Canada
55L4 **Minto,L** Canada
60B3 **Minturn** USA
26C1 **Minusinsk** Russian Federation
31A3 **Min Xian** China
45A3 **Minya el Qamn** Egypt
55N5 **Miquelon** *I* France
66D3 **Mirage L** USA
40D3 **Mīrah, Wadi al** *Watercourse* Iraq/Saudi Arabia
44A2 **Miraj** India
74E5 **Miramar** Argentina
42B2 **Miram Shah** Pakistan
75A3 **Miranda** Brazil
75A2 **Miranda** *R* Brazil
15B1 **Miranda de Ebro** Spain
75B3 **Mirante, Serra do** *Mts* Brazil
42B2 **Mīr Bachchen Kūt** Afghanistan
13C3 **Mirecourt** France
27E6 **Miri** Malaysia
48A3 **Mirik,C** Mauritius
74F4 **Mirim, Lagoa** *L* Brazil/Uruguay
25K3 **Mirnoye** Russian Federation
25N3 **Mirnyy** Russian Federation
76G9 **Mirnyy** *Base* Antarctica
19G3 **Mironovka** Ukraine
42C2 **Mirpur** Pakistan
42B3 **Mirpur Khas** Pakistan
17E3 **Mirtoan S** Greece
28B3 **Miryang** S Korea
43E3 **Mirzāpur** India
42C1 **Misgar** Pakistan
64B2 **Mishawaka** USA
28B4 **Mi-shima** *I* Japan
43H3 **Mishmi Hills** India
33E2 **Misima** *I* Papua New Guinea
74F3 **Misiones** *State* Argentina
19E3 **Miskolc** Hungary
45D2 **Mismīyah** Syria
27G7 **Misoöl** *I* Indonesia
49D1 **Misrātah** Libya
55K5 **Missinaibi** *R* Canada
64C1 **Missinaibi L** Canada
60C2 **Mission** S Dakota, USA
62C3 **Mission** Texas, USA
58B1 **Mission City** Canada
65D2 **Mississauga** Canada
57D3 **Mississippi** *R* USA
57D3 **Mississippi** *State* USA
63E3 **Mississippi Delta** USA
56B2 **Missoula** USA
48B1 **Missour** Morocco
57D3 **Missouri** *R* USA
57D3 **Missouri** *State* USA
61D2 **Missouri Valley** USA
57F1 **Mistassini,Lac** Canada
72D7 **Misti** *Mt* Peru
34C1 **Mitchell** Australia
56D2 **Mitchell** USA
32D2 **Mitchell** *R* Australia
57E3 **Mitchell,Mt** USA
27H8 **Mitchell River** Australia
45A3 **Mît el Nasâra** Egypt
45A3 **Mît Ghamr** Egypt
42C3 **Mithankot** Pakistan
17F3 **Mitilíni** Greece
45B3 **Mitla Pass** Egypt
29E3 **Mito** Japan
33G2 **Mitre** *I* Solomon Islands
Mits'iwa = Massawa
13D1 **Mittel Land Kanal** Germany
72D3 **Mitú** Colombia
51C4 **Mitumba, Chaine des** *Mts* Zaïre
50C4 **Mitumbar Mts** Zaïre
51C4 **Mitwaba** Zaïre
50B3 **Mitzic** Gabon
29C3 **Miura** Japan
31C3 **Mi Xian** China
26G3 **Miyake** *I* Japan
29C4 **Miyake-jima** *I* Japan
29E3 **Miyako** Japan
26F4 **Miyako** *I* Ryukyu Is, Japan
29C3 **Miyazu** Japan
28C4 **Miyoshi** Japan
31D1 **Miyun** China
31D1 **Miyun Shuiku** *Res* China
29D2 **Mi-zaki** *Pt* Japan
50D3 **Mīzan Teferī** Ethiopia
49D1 **Mizdah** Libya
17F1 **Mizil** Romania
43G4 **Mizo Hills** India
43G4 **Mizoram** *Union Territory* India
45C3 **Mizpe Ramon** Israel
29E3 **Mizusawa** Japan
12H7 **Mjölby** Sweden
51C5 **Mkushi** Zambia
47E2 **Mkuzi** South Africa
18C2 **Mladá Boleslav** Czech Republic
19E2 **Mława** Poland
17D2 **Mljet** *I* Croatia
47D2 **Mmabatho** South Africa
48A4 **Moa** *R* Sierra Leone
56C3 **Moab** USA
45C3 **Moab** *Region* Jordan
47E2 **Moamba** Mozambique
50B4 **Moanda** Congo
50B4 **Moanda** Gabon
9C3 **Moate** Irish Republic
51C4 **Moba** Zaïre
29D3 **Mobara** Japan
50C3 **Mobaye** Central African Republic
50C3 **Mobayi** Zaïre
57D3 **Moberly** USA
57E3 **Mobile** USA
57E3 **Mobile B** USA
63E2 **Mobile Pt** USA
56C2 **Mobridge** USA
51E5 **Moçambique** Mozambique
Moçâmedes = Namibe
30C1 **Moc Chau** Vietnam
Mocha = Al Mukhā
47D1 **Mochudi** Botswana
51E5 **Mocimboa da Praia** Mozambique
72C3 **Mocoa** Colombia
75C3 **Mococa** Brazil
51D5 **Mocuba** Mozambique
47D2 **Modder** *R* South Africa
16C2 **Modena** Italy
13D3 **Moder** *R* France
56A3 **Modesto** USA
66B2 **Modesto Res** USA
16C3 **Modica** Sicily,
18D3 **Mödling** Austria
8D4 **Moffat** Scotland
42D2 **Moga** India
50E3 **Mogadishu** Somalia
75C3 **Mogi das Cruzes** Brazil
19G2 **Mogilev** Belarus
21D6 **Mogilev Podol'skiy** Ukraine
75C3 **Mogi-Mirim** Brazil
51E5 **Mogincual** Mozambique
26E1 **Mogocha** Russian Federation
24K4 **Mogochin** Russian Federation
47D1 **Mogol** *R* South Africa
15A2 **Moguer** Spain
35C1 **Mohaka** *R* New Zealand
47D3 **Mohale's Hoek** Lesotho
60C1 **Mohall** USA
15C2 **Mohammadia** Algeria
43G4 **Mohanganj** Bangladesh
59D3 **Mohave,L** USA
68C1 **Mohawk** USA
65E2 **Mohawk** *R* USA
51E5 **Mohéli** *I* Comoros
51D4 **Mohoro** Tanzania
24J5 **Mointy** Kazakhstan
12G5 **Mo i Rana** Norway
14C3 **Moissac** France
59C3 **Mojave** USA
66D3 **Mojave** *R* USA
56B3 **Mojave Desert** USA
43F3 **Mokama** India
35B1 **Mokau** *R* New Zealand
66B1 **Mokelumne** *R* USA
66B1 **Mokelumne Aqueduct** USA
66B1 **Mokelumne Hill** USA
47D2 **Mokhotlong** Lesotho
16C3 **Moknine** Tunisia
43G3 **Mokokchūng** India
50B2 **Mokolo** Cameroon
28B4 **Mokp'o** S Korea
20G5 **Moksha** *R* Russian Federation
17E3 **Moláoi** Greece
7C3 **Mold** Wales
Moldavia = Moldova
12F6 **Molde** Norway
21D6 **Moldova** *Republic* Europe
17E1 **Moldoveanu** *Mt* Romania
47D1 **Molepolole** Botswana
13D3 **Molesheim** France
16D2 **Molfetta** Italy
72D7 **Mollendo** Peru
20D5 **Molodechno** Belarus
76G11 **Molodezhnaya** *Base* Antarctica
66E5 **Molokai** *I* Hawaiian Islands
20H4 **Moloma** *R* Russian Federation
34C2 **Molong** Australia
47C2 **Molopo** *R* Botswana/South Africa
50B3 **Molounddu** Cameroon
56D1 **Molson L** Canada
32B1 **Molucca S** Indonesia
27F7 **Moluccas** *Is* Indonesia
51D5 **Moma** Mozambique
73K5 **Mombaça** Brazil
50D4 **Mombasa** Kenya
29D2 **Mombetsu** Japan
75B2 **Mombuca, Serra da** *Mts* Brazil
50C3 **Mompono** Zaïre
18C2 **Mon** *I* Denmark
8B3 **Monach Is** Scotland
14D3 **Monaco** *Principality* Europe
8C3 **Monadhliath Mts** Scotland
9C2 **Monaghan** Irish Republic
9C2 **Monaghan** *County* Irish Republic
62B2 **Monahans** USA
69D3 **Mona Pass** Caribbean Sea
60B3 **Monarch P** USA
54G4 **Monashee Mts** Canada
10B3 **Monastereven** Irish Republic
16C3 **Monastir** Tunisia
29D2 **Monbetsu** Japan
73J4 **Monção** Brazil
12L5 **Monchegorsk** Russian Federation
18B2 **Mönchen-gladbach** Germany
70B2 **Monclova** Mexico
55M5 **Moncton** Canada
15A1 **Mondego** *R* Portugal
16B2 **Mondovi** Italy
69H1 **Moneague** Jamaica
65D2 **Monessen** USA
63D1 **Monett** USA
16C1 **Monfalcone** Italy
15A1 **Monforte de Lemos** Spain
50C3 **Monga** Zaïre
50C3 **Mongala** *R* Zaïre
50D3 **Mongalla** Sudan
30D1 **Mong Cai** Vietnam
50B2 **Mongo** Chad
26C2 **Mongolia** *Republic* Asia
51C5 **Mongu** Zambia
8D4 **Moniaive** Scotland
59C3 **Monitor Range** *Mts* USA
50C4 **Monkoto** Zaïre
64A2 **Monmouth** USA
7C4 **Monmouth** Wales
48C4 **Mono** *R* Benin/Togo
59C3 **Mono L** USA
17D2 **Monopoli** Italy
15B1 **Monreal del Campo** Spain
63D2 **Monroe** Louisiana, USA
64C2 **Monroe** Michigan, USA
67B2 **Monroe** N Carolina, USA
58B1 **Monroe** Washington, USA
64B2 **Monroe** Wisconsin, USA
61E3 **Monroe City** USA
48A4 **Monrovia** Liberia
66D3 **Monrovia** USA
18A2 **Mons** Belgium
68D1 **Monson** USA
18D1 **Mönsterås** Sweden
47C3 **Montagu** South Africa
54D4 **Montague I** USA
14B2 **Montaigu** France
16D3 **Montallo** *Mt* Italy
56B2 **Montana** *State* USA
15A1 **Montañas de León** *Mts* Spain
14C2 **Montargis** France
14C3 **Montauban** France
65E2 **Montauk** USA
65E2 **Montauk Pt** USA
13C4 **Montbard** France
14D2 **Montbéliard** France
Montblanc = Montblanch
16B1 **Mont Blanc** France/Italy
15C1 **Montblanch** Spain
14C2 **Montceau-les-Mines** France
16B1 **Mont Cenis, Col du** *P* France/Italy
15C1 **Montceny** *Mt* Spain
13C3 **Montcornet** France
14B3 **Mont-de-Marsan** France
14C2 **Montdidier** France
72F7 **Monteagudo** Bolivia
73H4 **Monte Alegre** Brazil
75D2 **Monte Azul** Brazil
65D1 **Montebello** Canada
32A3 **Monte Bello Is** Australia
14D3 **Monte Carlo** Monaco
75C2 **Monte Carmelo** Brazil
69C3 **Montecristi** Dominican Republic
16C2 **Montecristo** *I* Italy
69H1 **Montego Bay** Jamaica
14C3 **Montélimar** France
75A3 **Montelindo** *R* Paraguay
70C2 **Montemorelos** Mexico
15A2 **Montemor-o-Novo** Portugal

17D2 **Montenegro** *Republic* Yugoslavia
51D5 **Montepuez** Mozambique
13B3 **Montereau-Faut-Yonne** France
56A3 **Monterey** California, USA
65D3 **Monterey** Virginia, USA
56A3 **Monterey B** USA
72C2 **Montería** Colombia
72F7 **Montero** Bolivia
70B2 **Monterrey** Mexico
73K7 **Montes Claros** Brazil
15B2 **Montes de Toledo** *Mts* Spain
74E4 **Montevideo** Uruguay
61D2 **Montevideo** USA
62A1 **Monte Vista** USA
62B1 **Montezuma** USA
66D2 **Montezuma Peak** *Mt* USA
57E3 **Montgomery** Alabama, USA
68B2 **Montgomery** Pennsylvania, USA
7C3 **Montgomery** Wales
66C2 **Montgomery P** USA
13C3 **Monthermé** France
63D2 **Monticello** Arkansas, USA
64A2 **Monticello** Iowa, USA
61E1 **Monticello** Minnesota, USA
68C2 **Monticello** New York, USA
56C3 **Monticello** Utah, USA
13C3 **Montier-en-Der** France
55L5 **Mont-Laurier** Canada
14C2 **Montluçon** France
55L5 **Montmagny** Canada
13C3 **Montmédy** France
13B3 **Montmirail** France
Mont, Monte : see also individual mt. names
65E1 **Montmorency** Canada
15B2 **Montoro** Spain
68B2 **Montoursville** USA
58D2 **Montpelier** Idaho, USA
64C2 **Montpelier** Ohio, USA
57F2 **Montpelier** Vermont, USA
14C3 **Montpellier** France
55L5 **Montréal** Canada
14C1 **Montreuil** France
16B1 **Montreux** Switzerland
56C3 **Montrose** Colorado, USA
68C2 **Montrose** Pennsylvania, USA
10C2 **Montrose** Scotland
8F3 **Montrose** *Oilfield* N Sea
14B2 **Mont-St-Michel** France
69E3 **Montserrat** *I* Caribbean Sea
57F1 **Monts Otish** Canada
56B3 **Monument V** USA
50C3 **Monveda** Zaïre
30B1 **Monywa** Burma
16B1 **Monza** Italy
51C5 **Monze** Zambia
47E2 **Mooi** *R* South Africa
47D2 **Mooi River** South Africa
34B1 **Moomba** Australia
34D2 **Moonbi Range** *Mts* Australia
34B1 **Moonda L** Australia
34D1 **Moonie** Australia
34C1 **Moonie** *R* Australia
34A2 **Moonta** Australia
32A4 **Moora** Australia
34B1 **Mooraberree** Australia
60C2 **Moorcroft** USA
32A3 **Moore,L** Australia
8D4 **Moorfoot Hills** Scotland
56D2 **Moorhead** USA
66C3 **Moorpark** USA
47B3 **Moorreesburg** South Africa
55K4 **Moose** *R* Canada
65F1 **Moosehead L** USA
54H4 **Moose Jaw** Canada
61E1 **Moose Lake** USA
54H4 **Moosomin** Canada
55K4 **Moosonee** Canada
68E2 **Moosup** USA
51D5 **Mopeia** Mozambique
48B3 **Mopti** Mali
72D7 **Moquegua** Peru
12G6 **Mora** Sweden
61E1 **Mora** USA
42D3 **Morādābād** India
73L5 **Morada Nova** Brazil
75C2 **Morada Nova de Minas** Brazil
51E5 **Morafenobe** Madagascar
51E5 **Moramanga** Madagascar
58D2 **Moran** USA
69J2 **Morant Bay** Jamaica
69J2 **Morant Pt** Jamaica
8C3 **Morar, Loch** *L* Scotland
44B4 **Moratuwa** Sri Lanka
18D3 **Morava** *R* Austria/Czechoslovakia
17E2 **Morava** *R* Serbia, Yugoslavia
41G2 **Moraveh Tappeh** Iran
10C2 **Moray Firth** *Estuary* Scotland
42C4 **Morbi** India
41D2 **Mor Dağ** *Mt* Turkey
54J5 **Morden** Canada
20G5 **Mordovian Republic** Russian Federation
60C1 **Moreau** *R* USA
7C2 **Morecambe** England
7C2 **Morecambe B** England
32D3 **Moree** Australia
64C3 **Morehead** USA
67C2 **Morehead City** USA
70B3 **Morelia** Mexico
42D3 **Morena** India
15A2 **Morena, Sierra** *Mts* Spain
54E4 **Moresby I** Canada
34D1 **Moreton I** Australia
13B3 **Moreuil** France
63D3 **Morgan City** USA
66B2 **Morgan Hill** USA
66C2 **Morgan,Mt** USA
67B1 **Morganton** USA
65D3 **Morgantown** USA
47D2 **Morgenzon** South Africa
13D3 **Morhange** France
29E2 **Mori** Japan
69K1 **Moriah** Tobago
62A2 **Moriarty** USA
29E3 **Morioka** Japan
34D2 **Morisset** Australia
25N3 **Morkoka** *R* Russian Federation
14B2 **Morlaix** France
69Q2 **Morne Diablotin** *Mt* Dominica
34B1 **Morney** Australia
32C2 **Mornington** *I* Australia
42B3 **Moro** Pakistan
32D1 **Morobe** Papua New Guinea
48B1 **Morocco** *Kingdom* Africa
27F6 **Moro G** Philippines
51D4 **Morogoro** Tanzania
51E6 **Morombe** Madagascar
69B2 **Morón** Cuba
51E6 **Morondava** Madagascar
15A2 **Moron de la Frontera** Spain
51E5 **Moroni** Comoros
27F6 **Morotai** *I* Indonesia
50D3 **Moroto** Uganda
21G6 **Morozovsk** Russian Federation
6D2 **Morpeth** England
45B1 **Morphou** Cyprus
45B1 **Morphou B** Cyprus
60C2 **Morrill** USA
63D1 **Morrilton** USA
75C2 **Morrinhos** Brazil
35C1 **Morrinsville** New Zealand
61D1 **Morris** Canada
61D1 **Morris** USA
68C2 **Morristown** New Jersey, USA
65D2 **Morristown** New York, USA
67B1 **Morristown** Tennessee, USA
68C1 **Morrisville** New York, USA
68C2 **Morrisville** Pennsylvania, USA
66B3 **Morro Bay** USA
51D5 **Morrumbala** Mozambique
51D6 **Morrumbene** Mozambique
20G5 **Morshansk** Russian Federation
Mortes *R* **= Manso**
73H6 **Mortes** *R* Mato Grosso, Brazil
75D3 **Mortes** *R* Minas Gerais, Brazil
34B3 **Mortlake** Australia
62B2 **Morton** USA
69L1 **Moruga** Trinidad
34D3 **Moruya** Australia
34C1 **Morven** Australia
8C3 **Morvern** *Pen* Scotland
34C3 **Morwell** Australia
13E3 **Mosbach** Germany
30B3 **Moscos Is** Burma
58C1 **Moscow** Idaho, USA
68C2 **Moscow** Pennsylvania, USA
42F4 **Moscow** Russian Federation
18B2 **Mosel** *R* Germany
47C2 **Moselebe** *R* Botswana
13D3 **Moselle** *Department* France
13D3 **Moselle** *R* France
58C1 **Moses Lake** USA
35B3 **Mosgiel** New Zealand
50D4 **Moshi** Tanzania
64B2 **Mosinee** USA
12G5 **Mosjøen** Norway
25Q4 **Moskal'vo** Russian Federation
Moskva = Moscow
62B1 **Mosquero** USA
75D2 **Mosquito** *R* Brazil
72B2 **Mosquitos, Golfo de los** Panama
12G7 **Moss** Norway
50B4 **Mossaka** Congo
Mossâmedes = Namibe
47C3 **Mossel Bay** South Africa
50B4 **Mossendjo** Congo
34B2 **Mossgiel** Australia
73L5 **Mossoró** Brazil
18C2 **Most** Czech Republic
15C2 **Mostaganem** Algeria
17D2 **Mostar** Bosnia-Herzegovina
19E2 **Mosty** Belarus
41D2 **Mosul** Iraq
12H7 **Motala** Sweden
8D4 **Motherwell** Scotland
43E3 **Motihāri** India
15B2 **Motilla del Palancar** Spain
47D1 **Motloutse** *R* Botswana
15B2 **Motril** Spain
60C1 **Mott** USA
35B2 **Motueka** New Zealand
35B2 **Motueka** *R* New Zealand
50B4 **Mouila** Gabon
34B2 **Moulamein** Australia
54G2 **Mould Bay** Canada
69P2 **Moule à Chique, Cap** St Lucia
14C2 **Moulins** France
30B2 **Moulmein** Burma
48B1 **Moulouya** *R* Morocco
67B2 **Moultrie** USA
67C2 **Moultrie,L** USA
64B3 **Mound City** Illinois, USA
61D2 **Mound City** Missouri, USA
50B3 **Moundou** Chad
64C3 **Moundsville** USA
67A2 **Mountain Brook** USA
63D1 **Mountain Grove** USA
63D1 **Mountain Home** Arkansas, USA
58C2 **Mountain Home** Idaho, USA
66A2 **Mountain View** USA
54B3 **Mountain Village** USA
68B3 **Mount Airy** Maryland, USA
67B1 **Mount Airy** N Carolina, USA
47D3 **Mount Ayliff** South Africa
68B2 **Mount Carmel** USA
65F2 **Mount Desert I** USA
47D3 **Mount Fletcher** South Africa
34B3 **Mount Gambier** Australia
32D1 **Mount Hagen** Papua New Guinea
68C3 **Mount Holly** USA
68B2 **Mount Holly Springs** USA
32C3 **Mount Isa** Australia
68A3 **Mount Jackson** USA
68A2 **Mount Jewett** USA
34A2 **Mount Lofty Range** *Mts* Australia
32A3 **Mount Magnet** Australia
34B2 **Mount Manara** Australia
9C3 **Mountmellick** Irish Republic
32E3 **Mount Morgan** Australia
68B1 **Mount Morris** USA
34D1 **Mount Perry** Australia
63D2 **Mount Pleasant** Texas, USA
59D3 **Mount Pleasant** Utah, USA
68C2 **Mount Pocono** USA
58B1 **Mount Rainier Nat Pk** USA
7B4 **Mounts B** England
58B2 **Mount Shasta** USA
68B2 **Mount Union** USA
63E2 **Mount Vernon** Alabama, USA
64B3 **Mount Vernon** Illinois, USA
63D1 **Mount Vernon** Missouri, USA
58B1 **Mount Vernon** Washington, USA
50C2 **Mourdi, Dépression du** *Desert Region* Chad
9C2 **Mourne Mts** Northern Ireland
50B2 **Moussoro** Chad
48C2 **Mouydir, Mts du** Algeria
50B4 **Mouyondzi** Congo
13C3 **Mouzon** France
18D3 **M'óvár** Hungary
9C2 **Moville** Irish Republic
9B2 **Moy** *R* Irish Republic
50D3 **Moyale** Kenya
48A4 **Moyamba** Sierra Leone
48B1 **Moyen Atlas** *Mts* Morocco
47D3 **Moyeni** Lesotho
25M3 **Moyero** *R* Russian Federation
50D3 **Moyo** Uganda
72C5 **Moyobamba** Peru
42D1 **Moyu** China
51D6 **Mozambique** *Republic* Africa
51D6 **Mozambique Chan** Madagascar/Mozambique
20J4 **Mozhga** Russian Federation
12K8 **Mozyr'** Belarus
50D4 **Mpanda** Tanzania
51D5 **Mpika** Zambia
51D4 **Mporokosa** Zambia
51C5 **Mposhi** Zambia
48B4 **Mpraeso** Ghana
51D4 **Mpulungu** Zambia
50D4 **Mpwapwa** Tanzania
16C3 **M'saken** Tunisia
15C2 **M'Sila** Algeria
19G2 **Mstislavl'** Belarus
20F5 **Mtsensk** Russian Federation
47E2 **Mtubatuba** South Africa
51E5 **Mtwara** Tanzania
30C2 **Muang Chainat** Thailand
30C2 **Muang Chiang Rai** Thailand
30C2 **Muang Kalasin** Thailand
30C2 **Muang Khon Kaen** Thailand
30B2 **Muang Lampang** Thailand
30B2 **Muang Lamphun** Thailand
30C2 **Muang Loei** Thailand
30C2 **Muang Lom Sak** Thailand
30C2 **Muang Nakhon Phanom** Thailand
30B2 **Muang Nakhon Sawan** Thailand
30C2 **Muang Nan** Thailand
30C2 **Muang Phayao** Thailand
30C2 **Muang Phetchabun** Thailand
30C2 **Muang Phichit** Thailand
30C2 **Muang Phitsanulok** Thailand
30C2 **Muang Phrae** Thailand
30C2 **Muang Roi Et** Thailand
30C2 **Muang Sakon Nakhon** Thailand
30C3 **Muang Samut Prakan** Thailand
30C2 **Muang Uthai Thani** Thailand
30C2 **Muang Yasothon** Thailand
30C5 **Muar** Malaysia
27D7 **Muara** Indonesia
30A2 **Muaungmya** Burma
50D3 **Mubende** Uganda
49D3 **Mubi** Nigeria
45C3 **Mubrak, Jebel** *Mt* Jordan
51D5 **Muchinga Mts** Zambia
7C3 **Much Wenlock** England
8B3 **Muck** *I* Scotland
34C1 **Muckadilla** Australia
9B2 **Muckros Hd,** *Pt* Irish Republic
51C5 **Muconda** Angola
75E2 **Mucuri** Brazil
75D2 **Mucuri** *R* Brazil
51C5 **Mucusso** Angola
26F2 **Mudanjiang** China
60B2 **Muddy Gap P** USA
45D3 **Mudeisisat, Jebel** *Mt* Jordan
34C2 **Mudgee** Australia
66D2 **Mud L** USA
30B2 **Mudon** Burma
20F3 **Mud'yuga** Russian Federation
51D5 **Mueda** Mozambique
33F3 **Mueo** New Caledonia (Nouvelle Calédonie)
51C5 **Mufulira** Zambia
31C4 **Mufu Shan** *Hills* China
40C4 **Mughayra** Saudi Arabia
40A2 **Muğla** Turkey
21K5 **Mugodzhary** *Mts* Kazakhstan
43E3 **Mugu** Nepal
31A3 **Muguaping** China
40D3 **Muhaywir** Iraq
13E3 **Mühlacker** Germany
18C3 **Mühldorf** Germany
18C2 **Mühlhausen** Germany
12K6 **Muhos** Finland
30C4 **Mui Bai Bung** *C* Cambodia
9C3 **Muine Bheag** Irish Republic
45C3 **Mujib, Wadi** Jordan
51C5 **Mujimbeji** Zambia
19E3 **Mukachevo** Ukraine
27E6 **Mukah** Malaysia
29D2 **Mukawa** Japan
26H4 **Muko-jima** *I* Japan
43E3 **Muktinath** Nepal
42B2 **Mukur** Afghanistan
63D1 **Mulberry** USA
18C2 **Mulde** *R* Germany
60C2 **Mule Creek** USA
62B2 **Muleshoe** USA
27H8 **Mulgrave I** Australia
15B2 **Mulhacén** *Mt* Spain
13D2 **Mülheim** Germany
13D4 **Mulhouse** France
31A4 **Muli** China
8C3 **Mull** *I* Scotland
44C4 **Mullaittvu** Sri Lanka
34C2 **Mullaley** Australia
27E6 **Muller, Pegunungan** *Mts* Indonesia
9A2 **Mullet, The** *Pt* Irish Republic
32A3 **Mullewa** Australia
13D4 **Müllheim** Germany
68C3 **Mullica** *R* USA
9C3 **Mullingar** Irish Republic
8C4 **Mull of Kintyre** *Pt* Scotland
8B4 **Mull of Oa** *C* Scotland
34D1 **Mullumbimby** Australia
51C5 **Mulobezi** Zambia
42C2 **Multan** Pakistan
51C5 **Mumbwa** Zambia
21H6 **Mumra** Russian Federation
27F7 **Muna** Indonesia
München = Munich
28A3 **Munchŏn** N Korea
64B2 **Muncie** USA
34A1 **Muncoonie,L** Australia
68B2 **Muncy** USA
18B2 **Münden** Germany
34D1 **Mundubbera** Australia
34C1 **Mungallala** Australia
34C1 **Mungallala** *R* Australia
50C3 **Mungbere** Zaïre
43E4 **Mungeli** India
43F3 **Munger** India
34C1 **Mungindi** Australia
18C3 **Munich** Germany
64B1 **Munising** USA
74B8 **Muñoz Gamero,Pen** Chile
28A3 **Munsan** S Korea
13D3 **Munster** France
18B2 **Münster** Germany
13D2 **Münsterland** *Region* Germany
17E1 **Munţii Apuseni** *Mts* Romania
17E1 **Munţii Călimani** *Mts* Romania
17E1 **Munţii Carpaţii Meridionali** *Mts* Romania
17E1 **Munţii Rodnei** *Mts* Romania
17E1 **Munţii Zarandului** *Mts* Romania
40C2 **Munzur Silsilesi** *Mts* Turkey
30C1 **Muong Khoua** Laos
30D3 **Muong Man** Vietnam
30D2 **Muong Nong** Laos
30C1 **Muong Ou Neua** Laos
30C1 **Muong Sai** Laos
30C2 **Muong Sen** Vietnam
30C1 **Muong Sing** Laos
30C1 **Muong Son** Laos
12J5 **Muonio** Finland
12J5 **Muonio** *R* Finland/Sweden
28A3 **Muping** China
Muqdisho = Mogadishu
16C1 **Mur** *R* Austria
29D3 **Murakami** Japan
74B7 **Murallón** *Mt* Argentina/Chile
20H4 **Murashi** Russian Federation
40D2 **Murat** *R* Turkey
16B3 **Muravera** Sardinia, Italy
29D3 **Murayama** Japan
41F3 **Murcheh Khvort** Iran
35B2 **Murchison** New Zealand
32A3 **Murchison** *R* Australia
15B2 **Murcia** Spain
15B2 **Murcia** *Region* Spain
60C2 **Murdo** USA
17E1 **Mureş** *R* Romania
67C1 **Murfreesboro** N Carolina, USA
67A1 **Murfreesboro** Tennessee, USA
13E3 **Murg** *R* Germany
24H6 **Murgab** *R* Turkmenistan
42A1 **Murghab** *R* Afghanistan
42B2 **Murgha Kibzai** Pakistan
34D1 **Murgon** Australia
43F4 **Muri** India
75D3 **Muriaé** Brazil
51C4 **Muriege** Angola
20E2 **Murmansk** Russian Federation
20G4 **Murom** Russian Federation
29E2 **Muroran** Japan
15A1 **Muros** Spain
29C4 **Muroto** Japan
29B4 **Muroto-zaki** *C* Japan
58C2 **Murphy** Idaho, USA
67B1 **Murphy** N Carolina, USA
66B1 **Murphys** USA
64B3 **Murray** Kentucky, USA
58D2 **Murray** Utah, USA

34B2 **Murray** *R* Australia
34A3 **Murray Bridge** Australia
27H7 **Murray,L** Papua New Guinea
67B2 **Murray,L** USA
47C3 **Murraysburg** South Africa
37M3 **Murray Seacarp** Pacific Ocean
34B2 **Murrumbidgee** *R* Australia
34C2 **Murrumburrah** Australia
34D2 **Murrurundi** Australia
34B3 **Murtoa** Australia
28A2 **Muruin Sum** *R* China
35C1 **Murupara** New Zealand
43E4 **Murwāra** India
34D1 **Murwillimbah** Australia
27E7 **Muryo** *Mt* Indonesia
40D2 **Muş** Turkey
17E2 **Musala** *Mt* Bulgaria
28B2 **Musan** N Korea
41G4 **Musandam Pen** Oman
38D3 **Muscat** Oman
61E2 **Muscatine** USA
32C3 **Musgrave Range** *Mts* Australia
50B4 **Mushie** Zaïre
68E2 **Muskeget Chan** USA
64B2 **Muskegon** USA
64B2 **Muskegon** *R* USA
63C1 **Muskogee** USA
65D2 **Muskoka,L** Canada
50D2 **Musmar** Sudan
50D4 **Musoma** Tanzania
32D1 **Mussau** *I* Papua New Guinea
58E1 **Musselshell** *R* USA
51B5 **Mussende** Angola
14C3 **Mussidan** France
17F2 **Mustafa-Kemalpasa** Turkey
43E3 **Mustang** Nepal
74C7 **Musters, Lago** Argentina
28A2 **Musu-dan** *C* N Korea
34D2 **Muswellbrook** Australia
49E2 **Mut** Egypt
75E1 **Mutá, Ponta do** *Pt* Brazil
51D5 **Mutarara** Mozambique
51D5 **Mutare** Zimbabwe
20K2 **Mutnyy Materik** Russian Federation
51D5 **Mutoko** Zimbabwe
51E5 **Mutsamudu** Comoros
51C5 **Mutshatsha** Zaïre
29E2 **Mutsu** Japan
29E2 **Mutsu-wan** *B* Japan
75C1 **Mutunópolis** Brazil
31B2 **Mu Us Shamo** *Desert* China
51B4 **Muxima** Angola
25N4 **Muya** Russian Federation
20E3 **Muyezerskiy** Russian Federation
50D4 **Muyinga** Burundi
51C4 **Muyumba** Zaïre
39E1 **Muyun Kum** *Desert* Kazakhstan
42C2 **Muzaffarābad** Pakistan
42C2 **Muzaffargarh** Pakistan
42D3 **Muzaffarnagar** India
43F3 **Muzaffarpur** India
24H3 **Muzhi** Russian Federation
39G2 **Muzlag** *Mt* China
39F2 **Muztagala** *Mt* China
51D5 **Mvuma** Zimbabwe
50D4 **Mwanza** Tanzania
51C4 **Mwanza** Zaïre
50C4 **Mweka** Zaïre
51C4 **Mwene Ditu** Zaïre
51D6 **Mwenezi** Zimbabwe
47E1 **Mwenezi** *R* Zimbabwe
50C4 **Mwenga** Zaïre
51C4 **Mweru, L** Zaïre/Zambia
51C5 **Mwinilunga** Zambia
30B2 **Myanaung** Burma
Myanmar = Burma
18D3 **M'yaróvár** Hungary
30B1 **Myingyan** Burma
30B3 **Myinmoletkat** *Mt* Burma
30B3 **Myitta** Burma
43G4 **Mymensingh** Bangladesh
7C3 **Mynydd Eppynt** Wales
26G3 **Myojin** *I* Japan
28A2 **Myongchon** N Korea
28A2 **Myonggan** N Korea
12F6 **Myrdal** Norway
12B2 **Myrdalsjökull** *Mts* Iceland
67C2 **Myrtle Beach** USA
58B2 **Myrtle Creek** USA
12G7 **Mysen** Norway
20G2 **Mys Kanin Nos** *C* Russian Federation
19D3 **Myślenice** Poland
18C2 **Myśliborz** Poland
44B3 **Mysore** India
21E7 **Mys Sarych** *C* Ukraine
25U3 **Mys Shmidta** Russian Federation
20F2 **Mys Svyatoy Nos** *C* Russian Federation
68E2 **Mystic** USA
21J7 **Mys Tyub-Karagan** *Pt* Kazakhstan
24H2 **Mys Zhelaniya** *C* Russian Federation
30D3 **My Tho** Vietnam
58B2 **Mytle Point** USA
51D5 **Mzimba** Malawi
51D5 **Mzuzú** Malawi

N

66E5 **Naalehu** Hawaiian Islands
12J6 **Naantali** Finland
9C3 **Naas** Irish Republic
29C4 **Nabari** Japan
20J4 **Naberezhnyye Chelny** Russian Federation
16C3 **Nabeul** Tunisia
75A3 **Nabileque** *R* Brazil
45C2 **Nablus** Israel
51E5 **Nacala** Mozambique
58B1 **Naches** USA
51D5 **Nachingwea** Tanzania
66B3 **Nacimiento** *R* USA
66B3 **Nacimiento Res** USA
63D2 **Nacogdoches** USA
70B1 **Nacozari** Mexico
13E2 **Nadel** *Mt* Germany
42C4 **Nadiād** India
15B2 **Nador** Morocco
41F3 **Nadūshan** Iran
20E3 **Nadvoitsy** Russian Federation
19E3 **Nadvornaya** Ukraine
18C1 **Naestved** Denmark
49E2 **Nafoora** Libya
27F5 **Naga** Philippines
28B4 **Nagahama** Japan
43H3 **Naga Hills** India
29C3 **Nagai** Japan
43G3 **Nāgāland** *State* India
29D3 **Nagano** Japan
29D3 **Nagaoka** Japan
44B3 **Nāgappattinam** India
42C4 **Nagar Parkar** Pakistan
28B4 **Nagasaki** Japan
29C4 **Nagashima** Japan
28B4 **Nagato** Japan
42C3 **Nāgaur** India
44B4 **Nāgercoil** India
42B3 **Nagha Kalat** Pakistan
42D3 **Nagīna** India
13E3 **Nagold** Germany
29D3 **Nagoya** Japan
42D4 **Nāgpur** India
39H2 **Nagqu** China
18D3 **Nagykanizsa** Hungary
19D3 **Nagykörös** Hungary
26F4 **Naha** Okinawa, Japan
42D2 **Nāhan** India
54F3 **Nahanni Butte** Canada
45C2 **Nahariya** Israel
41E3 **Nahāvand** Iran
13D3 **Nahe** *R* Germany
31D2 **Nahpu** China
74B6 **Nahuel Haupí, Lago** Argentina
31E1 **Naimen Qi** China
55M4 **Nain** Canada
41F3 **Nā'īn** Iran
42D3 **Naini Tal** India
43E4 **Nainpur** India
8D3 **Nairn** Scotland
50D4 **Nairobi** Kenya
41F3 **Najafābād** Iran
40C4 **Najd** *Region* Saudi Arabia
28C2 **Najin** N Korea
50E2 **Najrān** Saudi Arabia
28A3 **Naju** S Korea
28A4 **Nakadori-jima** Japan
28B4 **Nakama** Japan
29E3 **Nakaminato** Japan
28B4 **Nakamura** Japan
29C3 **Nakano** Japan
29B3 **Nakano-shima** *I* Japan
28C4 **Nakatsu** Japan
29C3 **Nakatsu-gawa** Japan
50D2 **Nak'fa** Eritrea
21H8 **Nakhichevan** Azerbaijan
45B4 **Nakhl** Egypt
28C2 **Nakhodka** Russian Federation
30C3 **Nakhon Pathom** Thailand
30C3 **Nakhon Ratchasima** Thailand
30C4 **Nakhon Si Thammarat** Thailand
55K4 **Nakina** Ontario, Canada
54C4 **Naknek** USA
12G8 **Nakskov** Denmark
28A3 **Naktong** *R* S Korea
50D4 **Nakuru** Kenya
21G7 **Nal'chik** Russian Federation
44B2 **Nalgonda** India
44B2 **Nallamala Range** *Mts* India
49D1 **Nālūt** Libya
47E2 **Namaacha** Mozambique
24G6 **Namak** *L* Iran
41G3 **Namakzar-e Shadad** *Salt Flat* Iran
24J5 **Namangan** Uzbekistan
51D5 **Namapa** Mozambique
51B7 **Namaqualand** *Region* South Africa
34D1 **Nambour** Australia
34D2 **Nambucca Heads** Australia
30D4 **Nam Can** Vietnam
39H2 **Nam Co** *L* China
30D1 **Nam Dinh** Vietnam
51D5 **Nametil** Mozambique
47A1 **Namib Desert** Namibia
51B5 **Namibe** Angola
51B6 **Namibia** *Republic* Africa
27F7 **Namlea** Indonesia
43F3 **Namling** China
34C2 **Namoi** *R* Australia
58C2 **Nampa** USA
48B3 **Nampala** Mali
30C2 **Nam Phong** Thailand
28B3 **Namp'o** N Korea
51D5 **Nampula** Mozambique
12G6 **Namsos** Norway
30B1 **Namton** Burma
25O3 **Namtsy** Russian Federation
51D5 **Namuno** Mozambique
13C2 **Namur** Belgium
51B5 **Namutoni** Namibia
56A2 **Nanaimo** Canada
28B2 **Nanam** N Korea
34D1 **Nanango** Australia
29D3 **Nanao** Japan
29C3 **Nanatsu-jima** *I* Japan
31B3 **Nanbu** China
31D4 **Nanchang** China
31B3 **Nanchong** China
44E4 **Nancowry** *I* Nicobar Is, Indian Ocean
14D2 **Nancy** France
43E2 **Nanda Devi** *Mt* India
44B2 **Nānded** India
34D2 **Nandewar Range** *Mts* Australia
42C4 **Nandurbār** India
44B2 **Nandyāl** India
50B3 **Nanga Eboko** Cameroon
42C1 **Nanga Parbat** *Mt* Pakistan
27E7 **Nangapinon** Indonesia
13B3 **Nangis** France
28A2 **Nangnim** N Korea
28B2 **Nangnim Sanmaek** *Mts* N Korea
43G3 **Nang Xian** China
44B3 **Nanjangūd** India
31D3 **Nanjing** China
Nanking = Nanjing
29B4 **Nankoku** Japan
31C4 **Nan Ling** *Region* China
30D1 **Nanliu** *R* China
31B5 **Nanning** China
55O3 **Nanortalik** Greenland
31A5 **Nanpan Jiang** *R* China
43E3 **Nānpāra** India
31D4 **Nanping** China
28B2 **Nanping** China
55J1 **Nansen Sd** Canada
27E5 **Nanshan** *I* S China Sea
50D4 **Nansio** Tanzania
14B2 **Nantes** France
68C2 **Nanticoke** USA
31E3 **Nantong** China
68E2 **Nantucket** USA
68E2 **Nantucket I** USA
68E2 **Nantucket Sd** USA
7C3 **Nantwich** England
33G1 **Nanumanga** *I* Tuvalu
33G1 **Nanumea** *I* Tuvalu
75D2 **Nanuque** Brazil
31C3 **Nanyang** China
31D2 **Nanyang Hu** *L* China
50D3 **Nanyuki** Kenya
28A2 **Nanzamu** China
15C2 **Nao, Cabo de la** *C* Spain
29D3 **Naoetsu** Japan
42B4 **Naokot** Pakistan
66A1 **Napa** USA
65D2 **Napanee** Canada
24K4 **Napas** Russian Federation
55N3 **Napassoq** Greenland
30D2 **Nape** Laos
35C1 **Napier** New Zealand
67B3 **Naples** Florida, USA
16C2 **Naples** Italy
68B1 **Naples** New York, USA
63D2 **Naples** Texas, USA
31B5 **Napo** China
72D4 **Napo** *R* Ecuador/Peru
60D1 **Napoleon** USA
Napoli = Naples
41E2 **Naqadeh** Iran
45C3 **Naqb Ishtar** Jordan
29C4 **Nara** Japan
48B3 **Nara** Mali
32D4 **Naracoorte** Australia
44B2 **Narasarāopet** India
30C4 **Narathiwat** Thailand
43G4 **Narayanganj** Bangladesh
44B2 **Nārāyenpet** India
14C3 **Narbonne** France
30A3 **Narcondam** *I* Indian Ocean
42D2 **Narendranagar** India
55L2 **Nares Str** Canada
19E2 **Narew** *R* Poland
28B2 **Narhong** China
29D3 **Narita** Japan
42C4 **Narmada** *R* India
42D3 **Nārnaul** India
20F4 **Naro Fominsk** Russian Federation
50D4 **Narok** Kenya
19F2 **Narovl'a** Belarus
42C2 **Narowal** Pakistan
32D4 **Narrabri** Australia
34C1 **Narran** *R* Australia
34C2 **Narrandera** Australia
34C1 **Narran L** Australia
32A4 **Narrogin** Australia
34C2 **Narromine** Australia
64C3 **Narrows** USA
68C2 **Narrowsburg** USA
42D4 **Narsimhapur** India
44C2 **Narsīpatnam** India
55O3 **Narssalik** Greenland
55O3 **Narssaq** Greenland
55O3 **Narssarssuaq** Greenland
47B2 **Narubis** Namibia
29D3 **Narugo** Japan
29B4 **Naruto** Japan
20D4 **Narva** Russian Federation
12H5 **Narvik** Norway
42D3 **Narwāna** India
20J2 **Nar'yan Mar** Russian Federation
34B1 **Narylico** Australia
24J5 **Naryn** Kirgizia
48C4 **Nasarawa** Nigeria
52D6 **Nasca Ridge** Pacific Ocean
68E1 **Nashua** USA
63D2 **Nashville** Arkansas, USA
67A1 **Nashville** Tennessee, USA
17D1 **Našice** Croatia
42C4 **Nāsik** India
50D3 **Nasir** Sudan
69B1 **Nassau** The Bahamas
68D1 **Nassau** USA
49F2 **Nasser,L** Egypt
12G7 **Nässjö** Sweden
55L4 **Nastapoka Is** Canada
51C6 **Nata** Botswana
73L5 **Natal** Brazil
27C6 **Natal** Indonesia
36C6 **Natal Basin** Indian Ocean
41F3 **Natanz** Iran
55M4 **Natashquan** Canada
55M4 **Natashquan** *R* Canada
63D2 **Natchez** USA
63D2 **Natchitoches** USA
34C3 **Nathalia** Australia
55Q2 **Nathorsts Land** *Region* Greenland
59C4 **National City** USA
29D3 **Natori** Japan
50D4 **Natron, L** Tanzania
40A3 **Natrun, Wadi el** *Watercourse* Egypt
32A4 **Naturaliste,C** Australia
18C2 **Nauen** Germany
68D2 **Naugatuck** USA
18C2 **Naumburg** Germany
45C3 **Naur** Jordan
33F1 **Nauru** *I, Republic* Pacific Ocean
25M4 **Naushki** Russian Federation
47B2 **Naute Dam** *Res* Namibia
56C3 **Navajo Res** USA
15A2 **Navalmoral de la Mata** Spain
25T3 **Navarin, Mys** *C* Russian Federation
74C9 **Navarino** *I* Chile
15B1 **Navarra** *Province* Spain
63C2 **Navasota** USA
63C2 **Navasota** *R* USA
8C2 **Naver, L** Scotland
15A1 **Navia** *R* Spain
42C4 **Navlakhi** India
21E5 **Navlya** Russian Federation
70B2 **Navojoa** Mexico
17E3 **Návpaktos** Greece
17E3 **Návplion** Greece
42C4 **Navsāri** India
45D2 **Nawá** Syria
42B3 **Nawabshah** Pakistan
43F4 **Nawāda** India
42B2 **Nawah** Afghanistan
31B4 **Naxi** China
17F3 **Náxos** *I* Greece
41F4 **Nāy Band** Iran
41G3 **Nāy Band** Iran
29E2 **Nayoro** Japan
75E1 **Nazaré** Brazil
45C2 **Nazareth** Israel
72D6 **Nazca** Peru
40A2 **Nazilli** Turkey
25L4 **Nazimovo** Russian Federation
50D3 **Nazrēt** Ethiopia
41G5 **Nazwa'** Oman
24J4 **Nazyvayevsk** Russian Federation
51B4 **Ndalatando** Angola
50C3 **Ndélé** Central African Republic
50B4 **Ndendé** Gabon
33F2 **Ndende** *I* Solomon Islands
50B2 **Ndjamena** Chad
50B4 **Ndjolé** Gabon
51C5 **Ndola** Zambia
34C1 **Neabul** Australia
10B3 **Neagh, Lough** *L* Northern Ireland
17E3 **Neápolis** Greece
7C4 **Neath** Wales
34C1 **Nebine** *R* Australia
24G6 **Nebit Dag** Turkmenistan
56C2 **Nebraska** *State* USA
61D2 **Nebraska City** USA
16C3 **Nebrodi, Monti** *Mts* Sicily, Italy
63C2 **Neches** *R* USA
74E5 **Necochea** Argentina
43G3 **Nêdong** China
7E3 **Needham Market** England
59D4 **Needles** USA
7D4 **Needles** *Pt* England
64B2 **Neenah** USA
54J4 **Neepawa** Canada
13C2 **Neerpelt** Belgium
25M4 **Neftelensk** Russian Federation
50D3 **Negelē** Ethiopia
45C3 **Negev** *Desert* Israel
75A3 **Negla** *R* Paraguay
21C6 **Negolu** *Mt* Romania
44B4 **Negombo** Sri Lanka
30A2 **Negrais,C** Burma
72B4 **Negritos** Peru
72F4 **Negro** *R* Amazonas, Brazil
74D5 **Negro** *R* Argentina
74F4 **Negro** *R* Brazil/Uruguay
75A2 **Negro** *R* Mato Grosso do Sul, Brazil
75A3 **Negro** *R* Paraguay
15A2 **Negro, Cap** *C* Morocco
27F6 **Negros** *I* Philippines
17F2 **Negru Vodă** Romania
31B4 **Neijiang** China
64A2 **Neillsville** USA
Nei Monggol Zizhiqu = Inner Mongolia Aut. Region
72C3 **Neiva** Colombia
50D3 **Nejo** Ethiopia
50D3 **Nek'emte** Ethiopia
20E4 **Nelidovo** Russian Federation
61D2 **Neligh** USA
44B3 **Nellore** India
26G2 **Nel'ma** Russian Federation
54G5 **Nelson** Canada
6C3 **Nelson** England
35B2 **Nelson** New Zealand
34B3 **Nelson,C** Australia
47E2 **Nelspruit** South Africa
48B3 **Néma** Mauritius
31A1 **Nemagt Uul** *Mt* Mongolia
16B3 **Nementcha, Mts Des** Algeria
17F1 **Nemira** *Mt* Romania
13B3 **Nemours** France
19E1 **Nemunas** *R* Lithuania
29F2 **Nemuro** Japan
29F2 **Nemuro-kaikyō** *Str* Japan/Russian Federation
25O5 **Nen** *R* China
10B3 **Nenagh** Irish Republic
54D3 **Nenana** USA
7D3 **Nene** *R* England
26F2 **Nenjiang** China
63C1 **Neodesha** USA
63D1 **Neosho** USA
25M4 **Nepa** Russian Federation
39G3 **Nepal** *Kingdom* Asia
43E3 **Nepalganj** Nepal
59D3 **Nephi** USA
45C3 **Neqarot** *R* Israel
26E1 **Nerchinsk** Russian Federation
17D2 **Neretva** *R* Bosnia-Herzegovina/Croatia
27H5 **Nero Deep** Pacific Ocean
20G2 **Nes'** Russian Federation
12C1 **Neskaupstaður** Iceland
13B3 **Nesle** France
62C1 **Ness City** USA
8C3 **Ness, Loch** *L* Scotland
17E2 **Néstos** *R* Greece
45C2 **Netanya** Israel
68C2 **Netcong** USA
18B2 **Netherlands** *Kingdom* Europe
53M7 **Netherlands Antilles** *Is* Caribbean Sea
43G4 **Netrakona** Bangladesh
55L3 **Nettilling L** Canada
18C2 **Neubrandenburg** Germany
16B1 **Neuchâtel** Switzerland
13C3 **Neufchâteau** Belgium

13C3 **Neufchâteau** France
14C2 **Neufchâtel** France
18B2 **Neumünster** Germany
16D1 **Neunkirchen** Austria
13D3 **Neunkirchen** Germany
74C5 **Neuquén** Argentina
74C5 **Neuquén** *R* Argentina
74B5 **Neuquén** *State* Argentina
18C2 **Neuruppin** Germany
67C1 **Neuse** *R* USA
13D2 **Neuss** Germany
18C2 **Neustadt** Germany
13E3 **Neustadt an der Weinstrasse** Germany
13E1 **Neustadt a R** Germany
13E4 **Neustadt im Schwarzwald** Germany
18C2 **Neustrelitz** Germany
13E1 **Neuwerk** *I* Germany
13D2 **Neuwied** Germany
63D1 **Nevada** USA
56B3 **Nevada** *State* USA
15B2 **Nevada, Sierra** *Mts* Spain
45C3 **Nevatim** Israel
20D4 **Nevel'** Russian Federation
14C2 **Nevers** France
34C2 **Nevertire** Australia
Nevis = St Kitts-Nevis
40B2 **Nevşehir** Turkey
20L4 **Nev'yansk** Russian Federation
64C3 **New** *R* USA
51D5 **Newala** Tanzania
64B3 **New Albany** Indiana, USA
63E2 **New Albany** Mississippi, USA
73G2 **New Amsterdam** Guyana
34C1 **New Angledool** Australia
65D3 **Newark** Delaware, USA
57F2 **Newark** New Jersey, USA
68B1 **Newark** New York, USA
64C2 **Newark** Ohio, USA
7D3 **Newark-upon-Trent** England
65E2 **New Bedford** USA
58B1 **Newberg** USA
67C1 **New Bern** USA
67B2 **Newberry** USA
47C3 **New Bethesda** South Africa
69B2 **New Bight** The Bahamas
64C3 **New Boston** USA
62C3 **New Braunfels** USA
68D2 **New Britain** USA
32E1 **New Britain** *I* Papua New Guinea
32E1 **New Britain Trench** Papua New Guinea
68C2 **New Brunswick** USA
55M5 **New Brunswick** *Province* Canada
68C2 **Newburgh** USA
7D4 **Newbury** England
68E1 **Newburyport** USA
33F3 **New Caledonia** *I* SW Pacific Ocean
68D2 **New Canaan** USA
34D2 **Newcastle** Australia
64B3 **New Castle** Indiana, USA
9D2 **Newcastle** Northern Ireland
64C2 **New Castle** Pennsylvania, USA
47D2 **Newcastle** South Africa
60C2 **Newcastle** Wyoming, USA
8D4 **New Castleton** Scotland
7C3 **Newcastle under Lyme** England
6D2 **Newcastle upon Tyne** England
32C2 **Newcastle Waters** Australia
66C3 **New Cuyama** USA
42D3 **New Delhi** India
34D2 **New England Range** *Mts* Australia
68A1 **Newfane** USA
7D4 **New Forest,The** England
55N5 **Newfoundland** *I* Canada
55M4 **Newfoundland** *Province* Canada
52F2 **Newfoundland Basin** Atlantic Ocean
61E3 **New Franklin** USA
8C4 **New Galloway** Scotland
33E1 **New Georgia** *I* Solomon Islands
55M5 **New Glasgow** Canada
32D1 **New Guinea** *I* SE Asia
66C3 **Newhall** USA
57F2 **New Hampshire** *State* USA
61E2 **New Hampton** USA
47E2 **New Hanover** South Africa
32E1 **New Hanover** *I* Papua New Guinea
7E4 **Newhaven** England
65E2 **New Haven** USA
33F3 **New Hebrides Trench** Pacific Ocean
63D2 **New Iberia** USA
32E1 **New Ireland** *I* Papua New Guinea
57F2 **New Jersey** *State* USA
62B2 **Newkirk** USA
55L5 **New Liskeard** Canada
68D2 **New London** USA
32A3 **Newman** Australia
66B2 **Newman** USA
7E3 **Newmarket** England
65D3 **New Market** USA
58C2 **New Meadows** USA
56C3 **New Mexico** *State* USA
68D2 **New Milford** Connecticut, USA
68C2 **New Milford** Pennsylvania, USA
67B2 **Newnan** USA
34C4 **New Norfolk** Australia
57D3 **New Orleans** USA
68C2 **New Paltz** USA
64C2 **New Philadelphia** USA
35B1 **New Plymouth** New Zealand
63D1 **Newport** Arkansas, USA
7D4 **Newport** England
64C3 **Newport** Kentucky, USA
68D1 **Newport** New Hampshire, USA
58B2 **Newport** Oregon, USA
68B2 **Newport** Pennsylvania, USA
65E2 **Newport** Rhode Island, USA
65E2 **Newport** Vermont, USA
7C4 **Newport** Wales
58C1 **Newport** Washington, USA
66D4 **Newport Beach** USA
57F3 **Newport News** USA
69B1 **New Providence** *I* The Bahamas
7B4 **Newquay** England
7B3 **New Quay** Wales
55L3 **New Quebec Crater** Canada
7C3 **New Radnor** Wales
7E4 **New Romney** England
9C3 **New Ross** Irish Republic
9C2 **Newry** Northern Ireland
New Siberian Is = Novosibirskye Ostrova
67B3 **New Smyrna Beach** USA
32D4 **New South Wales** *State* Australia
61E2 **Newton** Iowa, USA
63C1 **Newton** Kansas, USA
68E1 **Newton** Massachusetts, USA
63E2 **Newton** Mississippi, USA
68C2 **Newton** New Jersey, USA
9D2 **Newtonabbey** Northern Ireland
7C4 **Newton Abbot** England
9C2 **Newton Stewart** Northern Ireland
8C4 **Newton Stewart** Scotland
60C1 **New Town** USA
7C3 **Newtown** Wales
9D2 **Newtownards** Northern Ireland
61E2 **New Ulm** USA
68B2 **Newville** USA
54F5 **New Westminster** Canada
57F2 **New York** USA
57F2 **New York** *State* USA
33G5 **New Zealand** *Dominion* SW Pacific Ocean
37K7 **New Zealand Plat** Pacific Ocean
20G4 **Neya** Russian Federation
41F4 **Neyrīz** Iran
41G2 **Neyshābūr** Iran
21E5 **Nezhin** Ukraine
50B4 **Ngabé** Congo
51C6 **Ngami, L** Botswana
49D4 **Ngaoundéré** Cameroon
30A1 **Ngape** Burma
35C1 **Ngaruawahia** New Zealand
35C1 **Ngaruroro** *R* New Zealand
35C1 **Ngauruhoe,Mt** New Zealand
50B4 **Ngo** Congo
30D2 **Ngoc Linh** *Mt* Vietnam
50B3 **Ngoko** *R* Cameroon/Central African Republic/Congo
26C3 **Ngoring Hu** *L* China
50D4 **Ngorongoro Crater** Tanzania
50B4 **N'Gounié** *R* Gabon
50B2 **Nguigmi** Niger
27G6 **Ngulu** *I* Pacific Ocean
48D3 **Nguru** Nigeria
30D3 **Nha Trang** Vietnam
75A2 **Nhecolândia** Brazil
34B3 **Nhill** Australia
47E2 **Nhlangano** Swaziland
30D2 **Nhommarath** Laos
32C2 **Nhulunbuy** Australia
48B3 **Niafounké** Mali
64B1 **Niagara** USA
65D2 **Niagara Falls** Canada
65D2 **Niagara Falls** USA
27E6 **Niah** Malaysia
48B4 **Niakaramandougou** Ivory Coast
48C3 **Niamey** Niger
50C3 **Niangara** Zaïre
50C3 **Nia Nia** Zaïre
27E6 **Niapa** *Mt* Indonesia
27C6 **Nias** *I* Indonesia
70D3 **Nicaragua** *Republic* Central America
70D3 **Nicaragua, L de** Nicaragua
16D3 **Nicastro** Italy
14D3 **Nice** France
69B1 **Nicholl's Town** The Bahamas
68C2 **Nicholson** USA
39H5 **Nicobar Is** India
45B1 **Nicosia** Cyprus
72A2 **Nicoya, Golfo de** Costa Rica
70D3 **Nicoya,Pen de** Costa Rica
6D2 **Nidd** *R* England
13E2 **Nidda** *R* Germany
19E2 **Nidzica** Poland
13D3 **Niederbronn** France
18B2 **Niedersachsen** *State* Germany
50C4 **Niemba** Zaïre
18B2 **Nienburg** Germany
13D2 **Niers** *R* Germany
48B4 **Niete,Mt** Liberia
73G2 **Nieuw Amsterdam** Surinam
73G2 **Nieuw Nickerie** Surinam
47B3 **Nieuwoudtville** South Africa
13B2 **Nieuwpoort** Belgium
40B2 **Niğde** Turkey
48B3 **Niger** *R* W Africa
48C3 **Niger** *Republic* Africa
48C4 **Nigeria** *Federal Republic* Africa
48C4 **Niger, Mouths of the** Nigeria
43L1 **Nighasan** India
64C1 **Nighthawk L** Canada
17E2 **Nigríta** Greece
29D3 **Nihommatsu** Japan
29D3 **Niigata** Japan
29C4 **Niihama** Japan
29C4 **Nii-jima** *I* Japan
29B4 **Niimi** Japan
29D3 **Niitsu** Japan
45C3 **Nijil** Jordan
18B2 **Nijmegen** Netherlands
20E2 **Nikel'** Russian Federation
48C4 **Nikki** Benin
29D3 **Nikko** Japan
21E6 **Nikolayev** Ukraine
21H6 **Nikolayevsk** Russian Federation
25Q4 **Nikolayevsk-na-Amure** Russian Federation
20H5 **Nikol'sk** Penza, Russian Federation
20H4 **Nikol'sk** Russian Federation
21E6 **Nikopol** Ukraine
40C1 **Niksar** Turkey
17D2 **Nikšić** Montenegro, Yugoslavia
33G1 **Nikunau** *I* Kiribati
27F7 **Nila** *I* Indonesia
38B3 **Nile** *R* NE Africa
64B2 **Niles** USA
44B3 **Nilgiri Hills** India
42C4 **Nimach** India
14C3 **Nîmes** France
34C3 **Nimmitabel** Australia
50D3 **Nimule** Sudan
39F5 **Nine Degree Chan** Indian Ocean
36F5 **Ninety-East Ridge** Indian Ocean
34C3 **Ninety Mile Beach** Australia
31D4 **Ningde** China
31D4 **Ningdu** China
26C3 **Ningjing Shan** *Mts* China
30D1 **Ningming** China
31A4 **Ningnan** China
31B2 **Ningxia** *Province* China
31B2 **Ning Xian** China
31B5 **Ninh Binh** Vietnam
32D1 **Ninigo Is** Papua New Guinea
75A3 **Nioaque** Brazil
60C2 **Niobrara** *R* USA
50B4 **Nioki** Zaïre
48B3 **Nioro du Sahel** Mali
14B2 **Niort** France
54H4 **Nipawin** Canada
55K5 **Nipigon** Canada
64B1 **Nipigon B** Canada
55K5 **Nipigon,L** Canada
64C1 **Nipissing,L** Canada
66B3 **Nipomo** USA
59C3 **Nipton** USA
75C1 **Niquelândia** Brazil
44B2 **Nirmal** India
43F3 **Nirmāli** India
17E2 **Niš** Serbia, Yugoslavia
38C4 **Nişāb** Yemen
26H4 **Nishino-shima** *I* Japan
28C3 **Nishino-shima** *I* Japan
28A4 **Nishi-suidō** *Str* S Korea
29B4 **Nishiwaki** Japan
33E1 **Nissan Is** Papua New Guinea
55L4 **Nitchequon** Canada
73K8 **Niterói** Brazil
8D4 **Nith** *R* Scotland
19D3 **Nitra** Slovakia
64C3 **Nitro** USA
33J2 **Niue** *I* Pacific Ocean
33G2 **Niulakita** *I* Tuvalu
27E6 **Niut** *Mt* Indonesia
33G1 **Niutao** *I* Tuvalu
28A2 **Niuzhuang** China
13C2 **Nivelles** Belgium
14C2 **Nivernais** *Region* France
12L5 **Nivskiy** Russian Federation
44B2 **Nizāmābād** India
45C3 **Nizana** *Hist Site* Israel
26C1 **Nizhneudinsk** Russian Federation
20K4 **Nizhniye Sergi** Russian Federation
20G5 **Nizhniy Lomov** Russian Federation
20G4 **Nizhniy Novgorod** Russian Federation
20J3 **Nizhniy Odes** Russian Federation
20K4 **Nizhniy Tagil** Russian Federation
25L3 **Nizhnyaya Tunguska** *R* Russian Federation
20G2 **Nizhnyaya Zolotitsa** Russian Federation
40C2 **Nizip** Turkey
12C1 **Njarðvik** Iceland
51C5 **Njoko** *R* Zambia
51D4 **Njombe** Tanzania
50B3 **Nkambé** Cameroon
51D5 **Nkhata Bay** Malawi
50B3 **Nkongsamba** Cameroon
48C3 **N'Konni** Niger
43G4 **Noakhali** Bangladesh
54B3 **Noatak** USA
54B3 **Noatak** *R* USA
28C4 **Nobeoka** Japan
29D2 **Noboribetsu** Japan
75A1 **Nobres** Brazil
63C2 **Nocona** USA
70A1 **Nogales** Sonora, Mexico
59D4 **Nogales** USA
28B4 **Nogata** Japan
13C3 **Nogent-en-Bassigny** France
13B3 **Nogent-sur-Seine** France
20F4 **Noginsk** Russian Federation
42C3 **Nohar** India
29D2 **Noheji** Japan
14B2 **Noirmoutier, Ile de** *I* France
47C1 **Nojane** Botswana
29C4 **Nojima-zaki** *C* Japan
50B3 **Nola** Central African Republic
20H4 **Nolinsk** Russian Federation
68E2 **Nomans Land** *I* USA
54B3 **Nome** USA
13D3 **Nomeny** France
31B1 **Nomgon** Mongolia
28A4 **Nomo-saki** *Pt* Japan
54H3 **Nonacho L** Canada
30C2 **Nong Khai** Thailand
47E2 **Nongoma** South Africa
33G1 **Nonouti** *I* Kiribati
28A3 **Nonsan** S Korea
13C1 **Noord Holland** *Province* Netherlands
47B2 **Noordoewer** Namibia
13C1 **Noordoost Polder** Netherlands
13C1 **Noordzeekanal** Netherlands
54B3 **Noorvik** USA
50B4 **Noqui** Angola
55L5 **Noranda** Canada
13B2 **Nord** *Department* France
24D2 **Nordaustlandet** *I* Svalbard
13D1 **Norden** Germany
13E1 **Nordenham** Germany
13D1 **Norderney** *I* Germany
12F6 **Nordfjord** *Inlet* Norway
12F8 **Nordfriesische** *Is* Germany
18C2 **Nordhausen** Germany
13D1 **Nordhorn** Germany
18B2 **Nordrhein Westfalen** *State* Germany
12J4 **Nordkapp** *C* Norway
55N3 **Nordre Strømfyord** *Fyord* Greenland
12G5 **Nord Storfjället** *Mt* Sweden
25N2 **Nordvik** Russian Federation
9C3 **Nore** *R* Irish Republic
61D2 **Norfolk** Nebraska, USA
65D3 **Norfolk** Virginia, USA
7E3 **Norfolk** *County* England
33F3 **Norfolk I** Pacific Ocean
37K6 **Norfolk I Ridge** Pacific Ocean
63D1 **Norfolk L** USA
25K3 **Noril'sk** Russian Federation
64B2 **Normal** USA
63C1 **Norman** USA
14B2 **Normandie** *Region* France
67B1 **Norman,L** USA
32D2 **Normanton** Australia
54F3 **Norman Wells** Canada
20B2 **Norra Storfjället** *Mt* Sweden
67B1 **Norris L** USA
65D2 **Norristown** USA
12H7 **Norrköping** Sweden
12H6 **Norrsundet** Sweden
12H7 **Norrtälje** Sweden
32B4 **Norseman** Australia
26F1 **Norsk** Russian Federation
75A1 **Nortelândia** Brazil
6D2 **Northallerton** England
32A4 **Northam** Australia
47D2 **Northam** South Africa
52E3 **North American Basin** Atlantic Ocean
32A3 **Northampton** Australia
7D3 **Northampton** England
65E2 **Northampton** USA
7D3 **Northampton** *County* England
44E3 **North Andaman** *I* Indian Ocean
54G3 **North Arm** *B* Canada
67B2 **North Augusta** USA
55M4 **North Aulatsivik** *I* Canada
54H4 **North Battleford** Canada
55L5 **North Bay** Canada
58B2 **North Bend** USA
8D3 **North Berwick** Scotland
68E1 **North Berwick** USA
55M5 **North,C** Canada
62B1 **North Canadian** *R* USA
57E3 **North Carolina** *State* USA
58B1 **North Cascades Nat Pk** USA
64C1 **North Chan** Canada
6B2 **North Chan** Ire/Scotland
56C2 **North Dakota** *State* USA
7E4 **North Downs** England
65D2 **North East** USA
52H2 **North East Atlantic Basin** Atlantic Ocean
54B3 **Northeast C** USA
51C6 **Northern Cape** *Province* South Africa
10B3 **Northern Ireland** UK
61E1 **Northern Light L** Canada/USA
27H5 **Northern Mariana Is** Pacific Ocean
69L1 **Northern Range** *Mts* Trinidad
32C2 **Northern Territory** Australia
51C6 **Northern Transvaal** *Province* South Africa
8D3 **North Esk** *R* Scotland
68D1 **Northfield** Massachusetts, USA
61E2 **Northfield** Minnesota, USA
7E4 **North Foreland** England
35B1 **North I** New Zealand
28B3 **North Korea** *Republic* SE Asia
North Land = Severnaya Zemlya
63D2 **North Little Rock** USA
60C2 **North Loup** *R* USA
76B4 **North Magnetic Pole** Canada
67B3 **North Miami** USA
67B3 **North Miami Beach** USA
66C2 **North Palisade** *Mt* USA
60C2 **North Platte** USA
56C2 **North Platte** *R* USA
76A **North Pole** Arctic
69R3 **North Pt** Barbados
64C1 **North Pt** USA
61E2 **North Raccoon** *R* USA
10B2 **North Rona** *I* Scotland
8D2 **North Ronaldsay** *I* Scotland
52F7 **North Scotia Ridge** Atlantic Ocean
10D2 **North Sea** NW Europe
44E3 **North Sentinel** *I* Andaman Islands
54D3 **North Slope** *Region* USA

34D1 North Stradbroke I Australia
68B1 North Syracuse USA
35B1 North Taranaki Bight *B* New Zealand
68A1 North Tonawanda USA
56C3 North Truchas Peak *Mt* USA
8B3 North Uist *I* Scotland
6C2 Northumberland *County* England
32E3 Northumberland Is Australia
55M5 Northumberland Str Canada
58B1 North Vancouver Canada
68C1 Northville USA
7E3 North Walsham England
54D3 Northway USA
51C6 North West *Province* South Africa
32A3 North West C Australia
42C2 North West Frontier Province Pakistan
55M4 North West River Canada
54G3 North West Territories Canada
61D1 Northwood USA
6D2 North York Moors England
6D2 North Yorkshire *County* England
60D3 Norton *R* USA
54B3 Norton Sd USA
76F1 Norvegia,C Antarctica
68D2 Norwalk Connecticut, USA
64C2 Norwalk Ohio, USA
12F6 Norway *Kingdom* Europe
54J4 Norway House Canada
55J2 Norwegian B Canada
52H1 Norwegian Basin Norwegian Sea
24B3 Norwegian S NW Europe
68D2 Norwich Connecticut, USA
7E3 Norwich England
68C1 Norwich New York, USA
68E1 Norwood Massachusetts, USA
64C3 Norwood Ohio, USA
17F2 Nos Emine *C* Bulgaria
29E2 Noshiro Japan
17F2 Nos Kaliakra *C* Bulgaria
47B1 Nosob *R* Namibia
20J2 Nosovaya Russian Federation
19G2 Nosovka Ukraine
8E1 Noss *I* Scotland
8D2 Noss Head, Pt Scotland
51E5 Nosy Barren *I* Madagascar
51E5 Nosy Bé *I* Madagascar
51F5 Nosy Boraha *I* Madagascar
51E6 Nosy Varika Madagascar
18D2 Notéc *R* Poland
54G4 Notikewin Canada
16D3 Noto Italy
12F7 Notodden Norway
29C3 Noto-hantō *Pen* Japan
55N5 Notre Dame B Canada
48C4 Notsé Togo
7D3 Nottingham England
7D3 Nottingham *County* England
55L3 Nottingham Canada
55L3 Nottingham Island Canada
48A2 Nouadhibou Mauritius
48A3 Nouakchott Mauritius
33F3 Nouméa New Caledonia
48B3 Nouna Burkina
8D2 Noup Head, Pt Scotland
47C3 Noupoort South Africa
55L3 Nouvelle-France, Cap de *C* Canada
75C2 Nova América Brazil
51B4 Nova Caipemba Angola
75B3 Nova Esperança Brazil
75D3 Nova Friburgo Brazil
51B5 Nova Gaia Angola
75C3 Nova Granada Brazil
75C3 Nova Horizonte Brazil
75D3 Nova Lima Brazil
Nova Lisboa = Huambo
75B3 Nova Londrina Brazil
51D6 Nova Mambone Mozambique
16B1 Novara Italy
75C1 Nova Roma Brazil
73K4 Nova Russas Brazil
55M5 Nova Scotia *Province* Canada
66A1 Novato USA
75D2 Nova Venécia Brazil
21E6 Novaya Kakhovka Ukraine
25R2 Novaya Sibir, Ostrov *I* Russian Federation
24G2 Novaya Zemlya *I* Russian Federation
17F2 Nova Zagora Bulgaria
19D3 Nové Zámky Slovakia
20E4 Novgorod Russian Federation
16B2 Novi Ligure Italy
17F2 Novi Pazar Bulgaria
17E2 Novi Pazar Serbia, Yugoslavia
17D1 Novi Sad Serbia, Yugoslavia
21K5 Novoalekseyevka Kazakhstan
21G5 Novoanninskiy Russian Federation
21F6 Novocherkassk Russian Federation
20G3 Novodvinsk Russian Federation
21D5 Novograd Volynskiy Ukraine
19F2 Novogrudok Belarus
74F3 Novo Hamburgo Brazil
24H5 Novokazalinsk Kazakhstan
24K4 Novokuznetsk Russian Federation
76F12 Novolazarevskaya *Base* Antarctica
16D1 Novo Mesto Slovenia
19G3 Novomirgorod Ukraine
20F5 Novomoskovsk Russian Federation
Novo Redondo = Sumbe
21F7 Novorossiysk Russian Federation
25M2 Novorybnoye Russian Federation
24K4 Novosibirsk Russian Federation
25P2 Novosibirskye Ostrova *Is* Russian Federation
21K5 Novotroitsk Russian Federation
21H5 Novo Uzensk Russian Federation
19E2 Novovolynsk Ukraine
20H4 Novo Vyatsk Russian Federation
21E5 Novozybkov Russian Federation
24J3 Novvy Port Russian Federation
19E2 Novy Dwór Mazowiecki Poland
20L4 Novyy Lyalya Russian Federation
20N2 Novyy Port Russian Federation
21J7 Novyy Uzen Kazakhstan
18D2 Nowa Sól Poland
63C1 Nowata USA
43G3 Nowgong India
34D2 Nowra Australia
41F2 Now Shahr Iran
42C2 Nowshera Pakistan
19E3 Nowy Sącz Poland
13B3 Noyon France
14B2 Nozay France
48B4 Nsawam Ghana
47E1 Nuanetsi Zimbabwe
50D2 Nuba Mts Sudan
50D1 Nubian Desert Sudan
56D4 Nueces *R* USA
54J3 Nueltin L Canada
28A2 Nü'erhe China
70B1 Nueva Casas Grandes Mexico
75A3 Nueva Germania Paraguay
69A2 Nueva Gerona Cuba
70B2 Nueva Rosita Mexico
69B2 Nuevitas Cuba
70B1 Nuevo Casas Grandes Mexico
70C2 Nuevo Laredo Mexico
50E3 Nugaal *Region* Somalia
55N2 Nûgâtsiaq Greenland
55N2 Nûgussuaq *I* Greenland
55N2 Nûgussuaq *Pen* Greenland
33G1 Nui *I* Tuvalu
31A5 Nui Con Voi *R* Vietnam
13C4 Nuits France
40D3 Nukhayb Iraq
33G1 Nukufetau *I* Tuvalu
33G1 Nukulaelae *I* Tuvalu
33H1 Nukunon *I* Tokelau Islands
24G5 Nukus Uzbekistan
54C3 Nulato USA
32B4 Nullarbor Plain Australia
48D4 Numan Nigeria
29C3 Numata Japan
50C3 Numatinna *R* Sudan
29D3 Numazu Japan
27G7 Numfoor *I* Indonesia
34C3 Numurkah Australia
68A1 Nunda USA
7D3 Nuneaton England
42D2 Nunkun *Mt* India
16B2 Nuoro Sicily, Italy
41F3 Nurābād Iran
34A2 Nuriootpa Australia
42C1 Nuristan *Region* Afghanistan
20J5 Nurlat Russian Federation
12K6 Nurmes Finland
18C3 Nürnberg Germany
34C2 Nurri,Mt Australia
40D2 Nusaybin Turkey
45D1 Nuşayrīyah, Jabalan *Mts* Syria
42B3 Nushki Pakistan
55M4 Nutak Canada
Nuuk = Godthåb
43E3 Nuwakot Nepal
44C4 Nuwara-Eliya Sri Lanka
47C3 Nuweveldreeks *Mts* South Africa
55L3 Nuyukjuak Canada
54C3 Nyac USA
68D2 Nyack USA
50D3 Nyahururu Falls Kenya
34B3 Nyah West Australia
26C3 Nyainqentanglha Shan *Mts* Tibet, China
50D4 Nyakabindi Tanzania
20L3 Nyaksimvol' Russian Federation
50C2 Nyala Sudan
43F3 Nyalam China
50C3 Nyamlell Sudan
51D6 Nyanda Zimbabwe
20G3 Nyandoma Russian Federation
50B4 Nyanga *R* Gabon
51D5 Nyasa, L Malawi/Mozambique
30B2 Nyaunglebin Burma
20K4 Nyazepetrovsk Russian Federation
12G7 Nyborg Denmark
12H7 Nybro Sweden
24J3 Nyda Russian Federation
55M1 Nyeboes Land *Region* Canada
50D4 Nyeri Kenya
51D5 Nyimba Zambia
39H2 Nyingchi China
19E3 Nyíregyháza Hungary
50D3 Nyiru,Mt Kenya
12J6 Nykarleby Finland
12F7 Nykøbing Denmark
12G8 Nykøbing Denmark
12H7 Nyköping Sweden
47D1 Nyl *R* South Africa
47D1 Nylstroom South Africa
34C2 Nymagee Australia
12H7 Nynäshamn Sweden
34C2 Nyngan Australia
50B3 Nyong *R* Cameroon
28A3 Nyongwol S Korea
28A3 Nyongwon N Korea
14D3 Nyons France
18D2 Nysa Poland
58C2 Nyssa USA
20H3 Nyukhcha Russian Federation
26F1 Nyukzha *R* Russian Federation
25N3 Nyurba Russian Federation
50D4 Nzega Tanzania
48B4 Nzérékoré Guinea
51B4 N'zeto Angola

O

60D2 Oacoma USA
60C2 Oahe,L *Res* USA
66E5 Oahu *I* Hawaiian Islands
34B2 Oakbank Australia
66B2 Oakdale USA
61D1 Oakes USA
34D1 Oakey Australia
59B3 Oakland California, USA
61D2 Oakland Nebraska, USA
58B2 Oakland Oregon, USA
64B3 Oakland City USA
64B2 Oak Lawn USA
66B2 Oakley California, USA
60C3 Oakley Kansas, USA
67B1 Oak Ridge USA
58B2 Oakridge USA
65D2 Oakville Canada
35B3 Oamaru New Zealand
66D2 Oasis California, USA
58D2 Oasis Nevada, USA
76F7 Oates Land *Region* Antarctica
34C4 Oatlands Australia
70C3 Oaxaca Mexico
24H3 Ob' *R* Russian Federation
29C3 Obama Japan
35A3 Oban New Zealand
8C3 Oban Scotland
29D3 Obanazawa Japan
13D2 Oberhausen Germany
60C3 Oberlin USA
13E3 Obernburg Germany
27F7 Obi *I* Indonesia
73G4 Obidos Brazil
29E2 Obihiro Japan
26G2 Obluch'ye Russian Federation
50C3 Obo Central African Republic
50E2 Obock Djibouti
18D2 Oborniki Poland
21F5 Oboyan' Russian Federation
58B2 O'Brien USA
21J5 Obshchiy Syrt *Mts* Russian Federation
24J3 Obskaya Guba *B* Russian Federation
48B4 Obuasi Ghana
67B3 Ocala USA
72D2 Ocaña Colombia
15B2 Ocaña Spain
65D3 Ocean City Maryland, USA
68C3 Ocean City New Jersey, USA
54F4 Ocean Falls Canada
Ocean I = Banaba
66B3 Oceano USA
66D4 Oceanside USA
63E2 Ocean Springs USA
20J4 Ocher Russian Federation
8D3 Ochil Hills Scotland
67B2 Ochlockonee *R* USA
69H1 Ocho Rios Jamaica
67B2 Ocmulgee *R* USA
67B2 Oconee *R* USA
64B2 Oconto USA
70B2 Ocotlán Mexico
48B4 Oda Ghana
28B3 Oda Japan
12B2 Ódáðahraun *Region* Iceland
28A2 Ŏdaejin N Korea
50D1 Oda, Jebel *Mt* Sudan
29E2 Odate Japan
29D3 Odawara Japan
12F6 Odda Norway
48C4 Ode Nigeria
63C3 Odem USA
15A2 Odemira Portugal
17F3 Ödemiş Turkey
47D2 Odendaalsrus South Africa
12G7 Odense Denmark
18C2 Oder *R* Germany/Poland
62B2 Odessa Texas, USA
21E6 Odessa Ukraine
58C1 Odessa Washington, USA
48B4 Odienné Ivory Coast
Odra = Oder
19D2 Odra *R* Poland
73K5 Oeiras Brazil
60C2 Oelrichs USA
61E2 Oelwein USA
16D2 Ofanto *R* Italy
45C3 Ofaqim Israel
9C3 Offaly *County* Irish Republic
13E2 Offenbach Germany
13D3 Offenburg Germany
29D3 Ofunato Japan
29D3 Oga Japan
50E3 Ogaden *Region* Ethiopia
29D3 Ōgaki Japan
60C2 Ogallala USA
26H4 Ogasawara Gunto *Is* Japan
48C4 Ogbomosho Nigeria
61E2 Ogden Iowa, USA
58D2 Ogden Utah, USA
65D2 Ogdensburg USA
67B2 Ogeechee *R* USA
54E3 Ogilvie Mts Canada
67B2 Oglethorpe,Mt USA
48C4 Ogoja Nigeria
19E1 Ogre Latvia
48B2 Oguilet Khenachich *Well* Mali
16D1 Ogulin Croatia
68E1 Ogunquit USA
21J8 Ogurchinskiy, Ostrov *I* Turkmenistan
35A3 Ohai New Zealand
35C1 Ohakune New Zealand
48C2 Ohanet Algeria
29D2 Ōhata Japan
35A2 Ohau,L New Zealand
74B7 O'Higgins, Lago Chile
64B3 Ohio *R* USA
57E2 Ohio *State* USA
13E2 Ohm *R* Germany
51B5 Ohopoho Namibia
18C2 Ohre *R* Czech Republic
17E2 Ohrid Macedonia, Yugoslavia
17E2 Ohridsko Jezero *L* Albania/Macedonia, Yugoslavia
35B1 Ohura New Zealand
73H3 Oiapoque French Guiana
65D2 Oil City USA
66C3 Oildale USA
13B3 Oise *Department* France
14C2 Oise *R* France
28C4 Ōita Japan
66C3 Ojai USA
70B2 Ojinaga Mexico
29C3 Ojiya Japan
74C3 Ojos del Salado *Mt* Argentina
20F5 Oka *R* Russian Federation
47B1 Okahandja Namibia
58C1 Okanagan Falls Canada
58C1 Okanogan USA
58C1 Okanogan *R* USA
58B1 Okanogan Range *Mts* Canada/USA
42C2 Okara Pakistan
47B1 Okasise Namibia
51B5 Okavango *R* Angola/Namibia
51C5 Okavango Delta *Marsh* Botswana
29D3 Okaya Japan
29C4 Okayama Japan
29C4 Okazaki Japan
67B3 Okeechobee USA
67B3 Okeechobee,L USA
67B2 Okefenokee Swamp USA
48C4 Okene Nigeria
42B4 Okha India
43F3 Okhaldunga Nepal
25Q4 Okhotsk Russian Federation
25Q4 Okhotsk, S of Russian Federation
26F4 Okinawa *I* Japan
26F4 Okinawa gunto *Arch* Japan
28C3 Oki-shotō *Is* Japan
28A2 Okkang-dong N Korea
56D3 Oklahoma *State* USA
63C1 Oklahoma City USA
63C1 Okmulgee USA
48C4 Okoja Nigeria
47B1 Okombahe Namibia
50B4 Okondja Gabon
29D2 Okoppe Japan
50B4 Okoyo Congo
48C4 Okpara *R* Benin/Nigeria
20A2 Okstindan *Mt* Norway
21K6 Oktyabr'sk Kazakhstan
20J5 Oktyabr'skiy Bashkirskaya, Russian Federation
26J1 Oktyabr'skiy Kamchatka, Russian Federation
20M3 Oktyabr'skoye Russian Federation
25L2 Oktyabrskoy Revolyutsii, Ostrov *I* Russian Federation
29D2 Okushiri-tō Japan
47C1 Okwa *R* Botswana
12B1 Olafsjorðr Iceland
66D2 Olancha USA
66C2 Olancha Peak *Mt* USA
12H7 Öland *I* Sweden
34B2 Olary Australia
61E3 Olathe USA
74D5 Olavarría Argentina
16B2 Olbia Sicily, Italy
68A1 Olcott USA
54E3 Old Crow Canada
18B2 Oldenburg Niedersachsen, Germany
18C2 Oldenburg Schleswig-Holstein, Germany
68C2 Old Forge USA
7C3 Oldham England
10B3 Old Head of Kinsale *C* Irish Republic
68D2 Old Lyme USA
8D3 Oldmeldrum Scotland
54G4 Olds Canada
65F2 Old Town USA
31B1 Öldziyt
68A1 Olean USA
25O4 Olekma *R* Russian Federation
25O3 Olekminsk Russian Federation
20E2 Olenegorsk Russian Federation
25N3 Olenek Russian Federation
25O2 Olenek *R* Russian Federation
19F2 Olevsk Ukraine
29D2 Ol'ga Russian Federation
47C3 Olifants *R* Cape Province, South Africa
47B1 Olifants *R* Namibia
47E1 Olifants *R* Transvaal, South Africa
47C2 Olifantshoek South Africa
17E2 Ólimbos *Mt* Greece
75C3 Olímpia Brazil
73M5 Olinda Brazil
74C4 Olivares *Mt* Argentina/Chile
75D3 Oliveira Brazil
61E2 Olivia USA
74C2 Ollagüe Chile
74C2 Ollagüe, Vol Bolivia
7D3 Ollerton England
64B3 Olney Illinois, USA
62C2 Olney Texas, USA

26E1 **Olochi** Russian Federation
12G7 **Olofström** Sweden
50B4 **Olombo** Congo
18D3 **Olomouc** Czech Republic
20E3 **Olonets** Russian Federation
14B3 **Oloron-Ste-Marie** France
26E1 **Olovyannaya** Russian Federation
13D2 **Olpe** Germany
19E2 **Olsztyn** Poland
16B1 **Olten** Switzerland
17E2 **Olt** *R* Romania
58B1 **Olympia** USA
58B1 **Olympic Nat Pk** USA
Olympus *Mt* = **Ólimbos**
45B1 **Olympus,Mt** Cyprus
58B1 **Olympus,Mt** USA
25T4 **Olyutorskiy, Mys** *C* Russian Federation
29C3 **Omachi** Japan
29C4 **Omae-zaki** *C* Japan
9C2 **Omagh** Northern Ireland
61D2 **Omaha** USA
58C1 **Omak** USA
38D4 **Oman** *Sultanate* Arabian Pen
38D3 **Oman,G of** UAE
47B1 **Omaruru** Namibia
47A1 **Omaruru** *R* Namibia
29D2 **Ōma-saki** *C* Japan
50A4 **Omboué** Gabon
50D2 **Omdurman** Sudan
50D2 **Om Häjer** Eritrea
29D2 **Ōminato** Japan
54F4 **Omineca Mts** Canada
29C3 **Omiya** Japan
54H2 **Ommanney B** Canada
50D3 **Omo** *R* Ethiopia
16B2 **Omodeo, L** Sardinia, Italy
25R3 **Omolon** *R* Russian Federation
25P3 **Omoloy** *R* Russian Federation
29D3 **Omono** *R* Japan
24J4 **Omsk** Russian Federation
29D2 **Ōmu** Japan
28C4 **Omura** Japan
47C1 **Omuramba Eiseb** *R* Botswana
28C4 **Ōmuta** Japan
20J4 **Omutninsk** Russian Federation
64A2 **Onalaska** USA
65D3 **Onancock** USA
43K1 **Onandausi** India
64C1 **Onaping L** Canada
61D2 **Onawa** USA
51B5 **Oncócua** Angola
51B5 **Ondangua** Namibia
19E3 **Ondava** *R* Slovakia
48C4 **Ondo** Nigeria
26E2 **Öndörhaan** Mongolia
39F5 **One and Half Degree Chan** Indian Ocean
42F3 **Onega** Russian Federation
20F3 **Onega** *R* Russian Federation
20F3 **Onega, L** Russian Federation
68C1 **Oneida** USA
68B1 **Oneida L** USA
60D2 **O'Neill** USA
26J2 **Onekotan** *I* Kuril Is, Russian Federation
50C4 **Onema** Zaïre
68C1 **Oneonta** USA
17F1 **Oneşti** Romania
20F3 **Onezhskaya Guba** *B* Russian Federation
Onezhskoye, Oz *L* = **Onega, L**
47C3 **Ongers** *R* South Africa
51B5 **Ongiva** Angola
28B3 **Ongjin** N Korea
31D1 **Ongniud Qi** China
44C2 **Ongole** India
51E6 **Onilahy** *R* Madagascar
48C4 **Onitsha** Nigeria
26D2 **Onjüül** Mongolia
29C3 **Ono** Japan
29C4 **Ōnohara-jima** *I* Japan
29C4 **Onomichi** Japan
33G1 **Onotoa** *I* Kiribati
32A3 **Onslow** Australia
67C2 **Onslow B** USA
29C3 **Ontake-san** *Mt* Japan
66D3 **Ontario** California, USA
58C2 **Ontario** Oregon, USA
55J4 **Ontario** *Province* Canada
65D2 **Ontario,L** Canada/USA
15B2 **Onteniente** Spain
33E1 **Ontong Java Atoll** Solomon Islands
28A3 **Onyang** S Korea
66C3 **Onyx** USA
32C3 **Oodnadatta** Australia
32C4 **Ooldea** Australia
63C1 **Oologah L** USA
13C1 **Oostelijk Flevoland** *Polder* Netherlands
13B2 **Oostende** Belgium
13B2 **Oosterschelde** *Estuary* Netherlands
44B3 **Ootacamund** India
25R4 **Opala** Russian Federation
50C4 **Opala** Zaïre
44C4 **Opanake** Sri Lanka
20H4 **Oparino** Russian Federation
19D3 **Opava** Czech Republic
67A2 **Opelika** USA
63D2 **Opelousas** USA
60B1 **Opheim** USA
19F1 **Opochka** Russian Federation
19D2 **Opole** Poland
15A1 **Oporto** Portugal
35C1 **Opotiki** New Zealand
67A2 **Opp** USA
12F6 **Oppdal** Norway
35B1 **Opunake** New Zealand
17E1 **Oradea** Romania
12B2 **Öræfajökull** *Mts* Iceland
42D3 **Orai** India
15B2 **Oran** Algeria
72F8 **Orán** Argentina
28A2 **Orang** N Korea
34C2 **Orange** Australia
66D4 **Orange** California, USA
14C3 **Orange** France
63D2 **Orange** Texas, USA
47B2 **Orange** *R* South Africa
67B2 **Orangeburg** USA
73H3 **Orange, Cabo** *C* Brazil
61D2 **Orange City** USA
47D2 **Orange Free State** *Province* South Africa
67B2 **Orange Park** USA
64C2 **Orangeville** Canada
18C2 **Oranienburg** Germany
47B2 **Oranjemund** Namibia
47D1 **Orapa** Botswana
27F5 **Oras** Philippines
17E1 **Orăştie** Romania
17E1 **Oraviţa** Romania
16C2 **Orbetello** Italy
68B2 **Orbisonia** USA
34C3 **Orbost** Australia
13B2 **Orchies** France
66B3 **Orcutt** USA
60D2 **Ord** USA
32B2 **Ord** *R* Australia
59D3 **Orderville** USA
32B2 **Ord,Mt** Australia
25M6 **Ordos** *Desert* China
40C1 **Ordu** Turkey
62B1 **Ordway** USA
12H7 **Örebro** Sweden
64C2 **Oregon** USA
56A2 **Oregon** *State* USA
58B1 **Oregon City** USA
12H6 **Öregrund** Sweden
20F4 **Orekhovo Zuyevo** Russian Federation
21F5 **Orel** Russian Federation
59D2 **Orem** USA
21J5 **Orenburg** Russian Federation
15A1 **Orense** Spain
18C1 **Oresund** *Str* Denmark/Sweden
35A3 **Oreti** *R* New Zealand
19F3 **Orgeyev** Moldavia
17F3 **Orhaneli** *R* Turkey
26D2 **Orhon Gol** *R* Mongolia
34B1 **Orientos** Australia
15B2 **Orihuela** Spain
65D2 **Orillia** Canada
72F2 **Orinoco** *R* Venezuela
68C1 **Oriskany Falls** USA
43E4 **Orissa** *State* India
16B3 **Oristano** Sicily, Italy
16B3 **Oristano, G. di** Sardinia, Italy
12K6 **Orivesi** *L* Finland
73G4 **Oriximiná** Brazil
70C3 **Orizaba** Mexico
75C2 **Orizona** Brazil
8D2 **Orkney** *Is, Region* Scotland
75C3 **Orlândia** Brazil
67B3 **Orlando** USA
14C2 **Orléanais** *Region* France
14C2 **Orléans** France
68E2 **Orleans** USA
25L4 **Orlik** Russian Federation
67B3 **Ormond Beach** USA
7C3 **Ormskirk** England
13C3 **Ornain** *R* France
14B2 **Orne** *R* France
12H6 **Örnsköldsvik** Sweden
28A2 **Oro** N Korea
72D3 **Orocué** Colombia
58C1 **Orofino** USA
45C3 **Oron** Israel
8B3 **Oronsay, I** Scotland
Orontes = **Asi**
19E3 **Orosháza** Hungary
25R3 **Orotukan** Russian Federation
59B3 **Oroville** California, USA
58C1 **Oroville** Washington, USA
19G2 **Orsha** Belarus
21K5 **Orsk** Russian Federation
12F6 **Ørsta** Norway
14B3 **Orthez** France
15A1 **Ortigueira** Spain
14E2 **Ortles** *Mt* Italy
69L1 **Ortoire** *R* Trinidad
61D1 **Ortonville** USA
25O3 **Orulgan, Khrebet** *Mts* Russian Federation
72E7 **Oruro** Bolivia
7E3 **Orwell** *R* England
20K4 **Osa** Russian Federation
61E2 **Osage** Iowa, USA
60C2 **Osage** Wyoming, USA
63D1 **Osage** *R* USA
29D4 **Ōsaka** Japan
70D4 **Osa,Pen de** Costa Rica
63E1 **Osceola** Arkansas, USA
61E2 **Osceola** Iowa, USA
58C2 **Osgood Mts** USA
29D2 **Oshamambe** Japan
65D2 **Oshawa** Canada
29D4 **Ō-shima** *I* Japan
60C2 **Oshkosh** Nebraska, USA
55K5 **Oshkosh** USA
64B2 **Oshkosh** Wisconsin, USA
21H8 **Oshnovīyeh** Iran
48C4 **Oshogbo** Nigeria
50B4 **Oshwe** Zaïre
17D1 **Osijek** Croatia
24K4 **Osinniki** Russian Federation
19F2 **Osipovichi** Belarus
61E2 **Oskaloosa** USA
20B4 **Oskarshamn** Sweden
12G6 **Oslo** Norway
40C2 **Osmaniye** Turkey
18B2 **Osnabrück** Germany
74B6 **Osorno** Chile
15B1 **Osorno** Spain
58C1 **Osoyoos** Canada
32D5 **Ossa,Mt** Australia
64A2 **Osseo** USA
68D2 **Ossining** USA
25S4 **Ossora** Russian Federation
20E4 **Ostashkov** Russian Federation
13E1 **Oste** *R* Germany
Ostend = **Oostende**
12G6 **Østerdalen** *V* Norway
13E1 **Osterholz-Scharmbeck** Germany
12G6 **Östersund** Sweden
13D1 **Ostfriesland** *Region* Germany
12H6 **Östhammär** Sweden
16C2 **Ostia** Italy
19D3 **Ostrava** Czech Republic
19D2 **Ostróda** Poland
19E2 **Ostrołęka** Poland
20D4 **Ostrov** Russian Federation
19D2 **Ostrów Wlkp** Poland
19E2 **Ostrowiec** Poland
19E2 **Ostrów Mazowiecka** Poland
15A2 **Osuna** Spain
65D2 **Oswego** USA
68B1 **Oswego** *R* USA
7C3 **Oswestry** England
19D3 **Oświęcim** Poland
29C3 **Ota** Japan
35B3 **Otago Pen** New Zealand
35C2 **Otaki** New Zealand
29E2 **Otaru** Japan
72C3 **Otavalo** Ecuador
51B5 **Otavi** Namibia
29D3 **Otawara** Japan
68C1 **Otego** USA
58C1 **Othello** USA
17E3 **Óthris** *Mt* Greece
60C2 **Otis** Colorado, USA
68D1 **Otis** Massachusetts, USA
68C2 **Otisville** USA
47B1 **Otjimbingwe** Namibia
51B6 **Otjiwarongo** Namibia
6D3 **Otley** England
31B2 **Otog Qi** China
29D2 **Otoineppu** Japan
35C1 **Otorohanga** New Zealand
12F7 **Otra** *R* Norway
17D2 **Otranto** Italy
17D2 **Otranto,Str of** *Chan* Albania/Italy
64B2 **Otsego** USA
68C1 **Otsego L** USA
29C3 **Ōtsu** Japan
12F6 **Otta** Norway
65D1 **Ottawa** Canada
64B2 **Ottawa** Illinois, USA
63C1 **Ottawa** Kansas, USA
65D1 **Ottawa** *R* Canada
55K4 **Ottawa Is** Canada
13E1 **Otterndorf** Germany
55K4 **Otter Rapids** Canada
55K1 **Otto Fjord** Canada
47D2 **Ottosdal** South Africa
64A2 **Ottumwa** USA
13D3 **Ottweiler** Germany
48C4 **Oturkpo** Nigeria
72C5 **Otusco** Peru
34B3 **Otway,C** Australia
19E2 **Otwock** Poland
30C1 **Ou** *R* Laos
63D2 **Ouachita** *R* USA
63D2 **Ouachita,L** USA
63D2 **Ouachita Mts** USA
48A2 **Ouadane** Mauritius
50C3 **Ouadda** Central African Republic
50C2 **Ouaddai** *Desert Region* Chad
48B3 **Ouagadougou** Burkina
48B3 **Ouahigouya** Burkina
50C3 **Ouaka** *R* Central African Republic
48C3 **Oualam** Niger
48C2 **Ouallen** Algeria
50C3 **Ouanda Djallé** Central African Republic
13B4 **Ouanne** *R* France
48A2 **Ouarane** *Region* Mauritius
48C1 **Ouargla** Algeria
48B2 **Ouarkziz, Jbel** *Mts* Morocco
50C3 **Ouarra** *R* Central African Republic
15C2 **Ouarsenis, Massif de l'** *Mts* Algeria
48B1 **Ouarzazate** Morocco
15C2 **Ouassel** *R* Algeria
50B3 **Oubangui** *R* Central African Republic/Congo/Zaïre
13B2 **Oudenaarde** Belgium
47C3 **Oudtshoorn** South Africa
15B2 **Oued Tlělat** Algeria
48B1 **Oued Zem** Morocco
40B4 **Ouena, Wadi** *Watercourse* Egypt
14A2 **Ouessant, Ile d'** *I* France
50B3 **Ouesso** Congo
48B1 **Ouezzane** Morocco
9C2 **Oughter, L** Irish Republic
50B3 **Ouham** *R* Chad
48C4 **Ouidah** Benin
48B1 **Oujda** Morocco
12J6 **Oulainen** Finland
15C3 **Ouled Nail, Monts des** Algeria
12K5 **Oulu** Finland
12K6 **Oulu** *R* Finland
12K6 **Oulujärvi** *L* Finland
50C2 **Oum Chalouba** Chad
16B3 **Oumel Bouaghi** Algeria
50B2 **Oum Hadjer** Chad
50C2 **Oum Haouach** *Watercourse* Chad
12K5 **Ounas** *R* Finland
20C2 **Ounastunturi** *Mt* Finland
50C2 **Ounianga Kebir** Chad
13D2 **Our** *R* Germany
62A1 **Ouray** USA
13C3 **Ource** *R* France
13B3 **Ourcq** *R* France
Ourense = **Orense**
73K5 **Ouricurí** Brazil
75C3 **Ourinhos** Brazil
75D3 **Ouro Prêto** Brazil
13C2 **Ourthe** *R* Belgium
7E3 **Ouse** *R* Norfolk, England
6D2 **Ouse** *R* N Yorks, England
10B2 **Outer Hebrides** *Is* Scotland
66C4 **Outer Santa Barbara** *Chan* USA
51B6 **Outjo** Namibia
12K6 **Outokumpu** Finland
34B3 **Ouyen** Australia
16B2 **Ovada** Italy
74B4 **Ovalle** Chile
51B5 **Ovamboland** *Region* Namibia
13D1 **Overijssel** *Province* Netherlands
59D3 **Overton** USA
12J5 **Övertorneå** Sweden
66D2 **Ovid** Colorado, USA
68B1 **Ovid** New York, USA
15A1 **Oviedo** Spain
12F6 **Øvre** Norway
21D5 **Ovruch** Ukraine
25O4 **Ovsyanka** Russian Federation
35A3 **Owaka** New Zealand
68B1 **Owasco L** USA
29C4 **Owase** Japan
61E2 **Owatonna** USA
68B1 **Owego** USA
66C2 **Owens** *R* USA
64B3 **Owensboro** USA
66D2 **Owens L** USA
64C2 **Owen Sound** Canada
32D1 **Owen Stanley Range** *Mts* Papua New Guinea
48C4 **Owerri** Nigeria
58E2 **Owl Creek Mts** USA
48C4 **Owo** Nigeria
64C2 **Owosso** USA
58C2 **Owyhee** USA
58C2 **Owyhee** *R* USA
58C2 **Owyhee Mts** USA
72C6 **Oxapampa** Peru
12H7 **Oxelösund** Sweden
7D3 **Oxford** England
68E1 **Oxford** Massachusetts, USA
63E2 **Oxford** Mississippi, USA
68C1 **Oxford** New York, USA
7D4 **Oxford** *County* England
66C3 **Oxnard** USA
29D3 **Oyama** Japan
50B3 **Oyen** Gabon
8C3 **Oykel** *R* Scotland
25Q3 **Oymyakon** Russian Federation
34C4 **Oyster B** Australia
27F6 **Ozamiz** Philippines
19F2 **Ozarichi** Belarus
67A2 **Ozark** USA
63D1 **Ozark Plat** USA
63D1 **Ozarks,L of the** USA
19E3 **Ózd** Hungary
62B2 **Ozona** USA
40D1 **Ozurgety** Georgia

P

47B3 **Paarl** South Africa
8B3 **Pabbay** *I* Scotland
19D2 **Pabianice** Poland
43F4 **Pabna** Bangladesh
19F1 **Pabrade** Lithuania
72F3 **Pacaraima, Serra** *Mts* Brazil/Venezuela
72C5 **Pacasmayo** Peru
70C2 **Pachuca** Mexico
66B1 **Pacific** USA
37N7 **Pacific-Antarctic Ridge** Pacific Ocean
66B2 **Pacific Grove** USA
37L4 **Pacific O**
75D2 **Pacuí** *R* Brazil
27D7 **Padang** Indonesia
20E3 **Padany** Russian Federation
18B2 **Paderborn** Germany
54J3 **Padlei** Canada
43G4 **Padma** *R* Bangladesh
16C1 **Padova** Italy
50B4 **Padrão, Ponta do** *Pt* Angola
56D4 **Padre I** USA
7B4 **Padstow** England
34B3 **Padthaway** Australia
Padua = **Padova**
64B3 **Paducah** Kentucky, USA
62B2 **Paducah** Texas, USA
12L5 **Padunskoye More** *L* Russian Federation
28A2 **Paegam** N Korea
35C1 **Paeroa** New Zealand
47E1 **Pafuri** Mozambique
16C2 **Pag** *I* Croatia
27D7 **Pagai Selatan** *I* Indonesia
27C7 **Pagai Utara** *I* Indonesia
27H5 **Pagan** *I* Pacific Ocean
59D3 **Page** USA
27F8 **Pago Mission** Australia
17F3 **Pagondhas** Greece
62A1 **Pagosa Springs** USA
66E5 **Pahala** Hawaiian Islands
35C2 **Pahiatua** New Zealand
66E5 **Pahoa** Hawaiian Islands
67B3 **Pahokee** USA
12K6 **Päijänne** *L* Finland
66E5 **Pailola Chan** Hawaiian Islands
64C2 **Painesville** USA
59D3 **Painted Desert** USA
64C3 **Paintsville** USA
8C4 **Paisley** Scotland
15B1 **País Vasco** *Region* Spain
72B5 **Paita** Peru
12J5 **Pajala** Sweden
38E3 **Pakistan** *Republic* Asia
30C2 **Pak Lay** Laos
43H4 **Pakokku** Burma
16D1 **Pakrac** Croatia
17D1 **Paks** Hungary
30C2 **Pak Sane** Laos
30D2 **Pakse** Laos
50D3 **Pakwach** Uganda
50B3 **Pala** Chad
16D2 **Palagruža** *I* Croatia
13B3 **Palaiseau** France
47D1 **Palala** *R* South Africa
44E3 **Palalankwe** Andaman Islands
25S4 **Palana** Russian Federation
27E7 **Palangkaraya** Indonesia
44B3 **Palani** India
42C4 **Pālanpur** India
47D1 **Palapye** Botswana
67B3 **Palatka** USA
36H4 **Palau** *USA Dependency* Pacific Ocean
30B3 **Palaw** Burma
27E6 **Palawan** *I* Philippines
44B4 **Palayankottai** India
12J7 **Paldiski** Estonia
27D7 **Palembang** Indonesia
15B1 **Palencia** Spain
45B1 **Paleokhorio** Cyprus
16C3 **Palermo** Sicily, Italy
63C2 **Palestine** USA

43G4 **Paletwa** Burma
44B3 **Pālghāt** India
42C3 **Pāli** India
60B3 **Palisade** USA
42C4 **Pālitāna** India
44B4 **Palk Str** India/Sri Lanka
21H5 **Pallasovka** Russian Federation
12J5 **Pallastunturi** *Mt* Finland
35B2 **Palliser B** New Zealand
35C2 **Palliser,C** New Zealand
51E5 **Palma** Mozambique
15C2 **Palma de Mallorca** Spain
73L5 **Palmares** Brazil
69A5 **Palmar Sur** Costa Rica
75B4 **Palmas** Brazil
48B4 **Palmas,C** Liberia
75D1 **Palmas de Monte Alto** Brazil
69B2 **Palma Soriano** Cuba
67B3 **Palm Bay** USA
67B3 **Palm Beach** USA
66C3 **Palmdale** USA
59C4 **Palm Desert** California, USA
75C4 **Palmeira** Brazil
73L5 **Palmeira dos Indos** Brazil
54D3 **Palmer** USA
76G3 **Palmer** *Base* Antarctica
76G3 **Palmer Arch** Antarctica
76F3 **Palmer Land** *Region* Antarctica
35B3 **Palmerston** New Zealand
35C2 **Palmerston North** New Zealand
68C2 **Palmerton** USA
67B3 **Palmetto** USA
16D3 **Palmi** Italy
72C3 **Palmira** Colombia
32D2 **Palm Is** Australia
59C4 **Palm Springs** USA
64A3 **Palmyra** Missouri, USA
68B1 **Palmyra** New York, USA
68B2 **Palmyra** Pennsylvania, USA
43F4 **Palmyras Pt** India
66A2 **Palo Alto** USA
27D6 **Paloh** Indonesia
50D2 **Paloích** Sudan
59C4 **Palomar Mt** USA
27F7 **Palopo** Indonesia
15B2 **Palos, Cabo de** *C* Spain
27E7 **Palu** Indonesia
40C2 **Palu** Turkey
42D3 **Palwal** India
48C3 **Pama** Burkina
27E7 **Pamekasan** Indonesia
14C3 **Pamiers** France
39F2 **Pamir** *Mts* Tajikistan
67C1 **Pamlico** *R* USA
67C1 **Pamlico Sd** USA
62B1 **Pampa** USA
74C4 **Pampa de la Salinas** *Plain* Argentina
74D5 **Pampas** *Plains* Argentina
72D2 **Pamplona** Colombia
15B1 **Pamplona** Spain
64B3 **Pana** USA
59D3 **Panaca** USA
17E2 **Panagyurishte** Bulgaria
44A2 **Panaji** India
72C2 **Panamá** Panama
72B2 **Panama** *Republic* Central America
69B5 **Panama Canal** Panama
67A2 **Panama City** USA
70E4 **Panamá, G de** Panama
59C3 **Panamint Range** *Mts* USA
66D2 **Panamint V** USA
27F5 **Panay** *I* Philippines
17E2 **Pancevo** Serbia, Yugoslavia
27F5 **Pandan** Philippines
44B2 **Pandharpur** India
34A1 **Pandie Pandie** Australia
19E1 **Panevežys** Lithuania
24K5 **Panfilov** Kazakhstan
30B1 **Pang** *R* Burma
50D4 **Pangani** Tanzania
50D4 **Pangani** *R* Tanzania
50C4 **Pangi** Zaïre
27D7 **Pangkalpinang** Indonesia
55M3 **Pangnirtung** Canada
30B1 **Pangtara** Burma
59D3 **Panguitch** USA
62B1 **Panhandle** USA
42D3 **Pānīpat** India
42B2 **Panjao** Afghanistan
28B3 **P'anmunjom** S Korea
43E4 **Panna** India
75B3 **Panorama** Brazil
28A2 **Panshan** China
28B2 **Panshi** China
75A2 **Pantanal de São Lourenço** *Swamp* Brazil
75A2 **Pantanal do Rio Negro** *Swamp* Brazil
75A2 **Pantanal do Taquari** *Swamp* Brazil
16C3 **Pantelleria** *I* Italy
31A4 **Pan Xian** China
16D3 **Paola** Italy
63D1 **Paola** USA
64B3 **Paoli** USA
18D3 **Pápa** Hungary
72A1 **Papagaya, Golfo del** Nicaragua
70D3 **Papagayo, G de** Costa Rica
66E5 **Papaikou** Hawaiian Islands
35B1 **Papakura** New Zealand
70C2 **Papantla** Mexico
8E1 **Papa Stour** *I* Scotland
35B1 **Papatoetoe** New Zealand
8D2 **Papa Westray** *I* Scotland
13D1 **Papenburg** Germany
45B1 **Paphos** Cyprus
8B4 **Paps of Jura** Scotland
32D1 **Papua,G of** Papua New Guinea
32D1 **Papua New Guinea** *Republic* SE Asia
30B2 **Papun** Burma
73J4 **Pará** *R* Brazil
73H4 **Pará** *State* Brazil
32A3 **Paraburdoo** Australia
72C6 **Paracas,Pen de** Peru
75C2 **Paracatu** Brazil
75C2 **Paracatu** *R* Brazil
30E2 **Paracel Is** SE Asia
34A2 **Parachilna** Australia
42C2 **Parachinar** Pakistan
17E2 **Paracin** Serbia, Yugoslavia
75D2 **Pará de Minas** Brazil
59B3 **Paradise** California, USA
59D3 **Paradise** Nevada, USA
66D1 **Paradise Peak** *Mt* USA
63D1 **Paragould** USA
72F6 **Paraguá** *R* Bolivia
72F2 **Paragua** *R* Venezuela
75D1 **Paraguaçu** *R* Brazil
73G7 **Paraguai** *R* Brazil
75A4 **Paraguarí** Paraguay
74E2 **Paraguay** *R* Paraguay
74E2 **Paraguay** *Republic* S America
75C3 **Paraíba** *R* Brazil
73L5 **Paraíba** *State* Brazil
75D3 **Paraíba do Sul** *R* Brazil
48C4 **Parakou** Benin
44B4 **Paramakkudi** India
73G2 **Paramaribo** Surinam
75D1 **Paramirim** Brazil
26J1 **Paramushir** *I* Russian Federation
74D4 **Paraná** Argentina
74E4 **Paraná** *R* Argentina
75B3 **Paraná** *R* Brazil
73J6 **Paranã** *R* Brazil
74F2 **Paraná** *State* Brazil
75C4 **Paranaguá** Brazil
75B2 **Paranaíba** Brazil
75B2 **Paranaíba** *R* Brazil
75B3 **Paranapanema** *R* Brazil
75C3 **Paranapiacaba, Serra do** *Mts* Brazil
75B3 **Paranavaí** Brazil
75D2 **Paraope** *R* Brazil
35B2 **Paraparaumu** New Zealand
75D1 **Paratinga** Brazil
44B2 **Parbhani** India
45C2 **Pardes Hanna** Israel
75E2 **Pardo** *R* Bahia, Brazil
75B3 **Pardo** *R* Mato Grosso do Sul, Brazil
75C2 **Pardo** *R* Minas Gerais, Brazil
75C3 **Pardo** *R* São Paulo, Brazil
18D2 **Pardubice** Czech Republic
26G4 **Parece Vela** *Reef* Pacific Ocean
75A1 **Parecis** Brazil
72F6 **Parecis, Serra dos** *Mts* Brazil
57F2 **Parent** Canada
65D1 **Parent,L** Canada
32A1 **Parepare** Indonesia
69E4 **Paria, G de** Trinidad/Venezuela
27D7 **Pariaman** Indonesia
69E4 **Paria, Peninsula de** Venezuela
72F3 **Parima, Serra** *Mts* Brazil
14C2 **Paris** France
64C3 **Paris** Kentucky, USA
63E1 **Paris** Tennessee, USA
63C2 **Paris** Texas, USA
59D4 **Parker** USA
64C3 **Parkersburg** USA
34C2 **Parkes** Australia
68C3 **Parkesburg** USA
64A1 **Park Falls** USA
66B3 **Parkfield** USA
64B2 **Park Forest** USA
61D1 **Park Rapids** USA
61D2 **Parkston** USA
58B1 **Parksville** Canada
58D2 **Park Valley** USA
44C2 **Parlākimidi** India
44B2 **Parli** India
16C2 **Parma** Italy
64C2 **Parma** USA
73K4 **Parnaiba** Brazil
73K4 **Parnaiba** *R* Brazil
17E3 **Párnon Óros** *Mts* Greece
20C4 **Pärnu** Estonia
43F3 **Paro** Bhutan
34B1 **Paroo** *R* Australia
34B2 **Paroo Channel** *R* Australia
17F3 **Páros** *I* Greece
59D3 **Parowan** USA
34D2 **Parramatta** Australia
56C4 **Parras** Mexico
55K3 **Parry B** Canada
54G2 **Parry Is** Canada
55L2 **Parry, Kap** *C* Canada
55L5 **Parry Sound** Canada
18C3 **Parsberg** Germany
54F4 **Parsnip** *R* Canada
63C1 **Parsons** Kansas, USA
65D3 **Parsons** West Virginia, USA
14B2 **Parthenay** France
16C3 **Partinico** Italy
28C2 **Partizansk** Russian Federation
9B3 **Partry** *Mts* Irish Republic
73H4 **Paru** *R* Brazil
44C2 **Parvatipuram** India
47D2 **Parys** South Africa
63C3 **Pasadena** Texas, USA
66C3 **Pasadena** USA
30B2 **Pasawing** Burma
63E2 **Pascagoula** USA
17F1 **Paşcani** Romania
58C1 **Pasco** USA
75E2 **Pascoal, Monte** Brazil
Pascua, Isla de = Easter I
13B2 **Pas-de-Calais** *Department* France
12G8 **Pasewalk** Germany
41G4 **Pashū'īyeh** Iran
32B4 **Pasley,C** Australia
74E3 **Paso de los Libres** Argentina
74E4 **Paso de los Toros** Uruguay
74B6 **Paso Limay** Argentina
66B3 **Paso Robles** USA
68C2 **Passaic** USA
18C3 **Passau** Germany
74F3 **Passo Fundo** Brazil
75C3 **Passos** Brazil
72C4 **Pastaza** *R* Peru
72C3 **Pasto** Colombia
19E1 **Pasvalys** Lithuania
74B8 **Patagonia** *Region* Argentina
42C4 **Pātan** India
43F3 **Patan** Nepal
43J1 **Patandi** India
34B3 **Patchewollock** Australia
35B1 **Patea** New Zealand
35B2 **Patea** *R* New Zealand
6D2 **Pateley Bridge** England
16C3 **Paterno** Sicily, Italy
68C2 **Paterson** USA
35A3 **Paterson Inlet** *B* New Zealand
42D2 **Pathankot** India
60B2 **Pathfinder Res** USA
42D2 **Patiāla** India
72C6 **Pativilca** Peru
17F3 **Pátmos** *I* Greece
43F3 **Patna** India
40D2 **Patnos** Turkey
25N4 **Patomskoye Nagor'ye** *Upland* Russian Federation
73L5 **Patos** Brazil
75C2 **Patos de Minas** Brazil
74F4 **Patos, Lagoa dos** *Lg* Brazil
17E3 **Pátrai** Greece
20L3 **Patrasuy** Russian Federation
75C2 **Patrocínio** Brazil
50E4 **Patta I** Kenya
30C4 **Pattani** Thailand
30C3 **Pattaya** Thailand
66B2 **Patterson** California, USA
63D3 **Patterson** Louisiana, USA
66C2 **Patterson Mt** USA
68A2 **Patton** USA
73L5 **Patu** Brazil
43G4 **Patuakhali** Bangladesh
70D3 **Patuca** *R* Honduras
14B3 **Pau** France
54F3 **Paulatuk** Canada
73K5 **Paulistana** Brazil
47E2 **Paulpietersburg** South Africa
63C2 **Pauls Valley** USA
30B2 **Paungde** Burma
42D2 **Pauri** India
75D2 **Pavão** Brazil
16B1 **Pavia** Italy
24J4 **Pavlodar** Kazakhstan
20K4 **Pavlovka** Russian Federation
20G4 **Pavlovo** Russian Federation
21G5 **Pavlovsk** Russian Federation
63C1 **Pawhuska** USA
68A3 **Paw Paw** USA
68E2 **Pawtucket** USA
60C2 **Paxton** USA
58C2 **Payette** USA
55L4 **Payne,L** Canada
61E1 **Paynesville** USA
74E4 **Paysandú** Uruguay
17E2 **Pazardzhik** Bulgaria
54G4 **Peace** *R* Canada
67B3 **Peace** *R* USA
54G4 **Peace River** Canada
59D3 **Peach Springs** USA
7D3 **Peak District Nat Pk** England
65F1 **Peaked Mt** USA
34C2 **Peak Hill** Australia
7D3 **Peak,The** *Mt* England
59E3 **Peale,Mt** USA
63D2 **Pearl** *R* USA
66E5 **Pearl City** Hawaiian Islands
66E5 **Pearl Harbor** Hawaiian Islands
62C3 **Pearsall** USA
47D3 **Pearston** South Africa
54H2 **Peary Chan** Canada
51D5 **Pebane** Mozambique
17E2 **Peć** Serbia, Yugoslavia
75D2 **Peçanha** Brazil
63D3 **Pecan Island** USA
12L5 **Pechenga** Russian Federation
20K2 **Pechora** Russian Federation
20J2 **Pechora** *R* Russian Federation
20J2 **Pechorskaya Guba** *G* Russian Federation
20J2 **Pechorskoye More** *S* Russian Federation
16D3 **Pecoraro** *Mt* Italy
62B2 **Pecos** USA
62B2 **Pecos** *R* USA
19D3 **Pécs** Hungary
45B1 **Pedhoulas** Cyprus
75D2 **Pedra Azul** Brazil
75C3 **Pedregulho** Brazil
69B3 **Pedro Cays** *Is* Caribbean Sea
74C2 **Pedro de Valdivia** Chile
75B2 **Pedro Gomes** Brazil
75A3 **Pedro Juan Caballero** Paraguay
44C4 **Pedro,Pt** Sri Lanka
34B2 **Peebinga** Australia
8D4 **Peebles** Scotland
67C2 **Pee Dee** *R* USA
68D2 **Peekskill** USA
6B2 **Peel** Isle of Man, British Islands
54E3 **Peel** *R* Canada
54J2 **Peel Sd** Canada
Pefos = Paphos
27G7 **Peg Arfak** *Mt* Indonesia
35B2 **Pegasus B** New Zealand
30B2 **Pegu** Burma
32C1 **Pegunungan Maoke** *Mts* Indonesia
30B2 **Pegu Yoma** *Mts* Burma
74D5 **Pehuajó** Argentina
Peipsi Järv = Lake Peipus
75B1 **Peixe** *R* Mato Grosso, Brazil
75B3 **Peixe** *R* São Paulo, Brazil
31D3 **Pei Xian** China
30C5 **Pekan** Malaysia
27D6 **Pekanbaru** Indonesia
64B2 **Pekin** USA
Peking = Beijing
30C5 **Pelabohan Kelang** Malaysia
14D3 **Pelat, Mont** France
17E1 **Peleaga** *Mt* Romania
25N4 **Peleduy** Russian Federation
64C2 **Pelee I** Canada
32B1 **Peleng** *I* Indonesia
61E1 **Pelican L** USA
47A1 **Pelican Pt** South Africa
17D2 **Pelješac** *Pen* Croatia
12J5 **Pello** Finland
55K3 **Pelly Bay** Canada
54E3 **Pelly Mts** Canada
74F4 **Pelotas** Brazil
74F3 **Pelotas** *R* Brazil
45B3 **Pelusium** *Hist Site* Egypt
14D2 **Pelvoux, Massif du** *Mts* France
20L3 **Pelym** *R* Russian Federation
51E5 **Pemba** Mozambique
51E5 **Pemba, Baiá de** *B* Mozambique
50D4 **Pemba I** Tanzania
61D1 **Pembina** USA
65D1 **Pembroke** Canada
67B2 **Pembroke** USA
7B4 **Pembroke** Wales
68E1 **Penacook** USA
75B3 **Penápolis** Brazil
15A2 **Peñarroya** Spain
15B1 **Peñarroya** *Mt* Spain
7C4 **Penarth** Wales
15A1 **Peñas, Cabo de** *C* Spain
74B7 **Penas, Golfo de** *G* Chile
15A1 **Peña Trevinca** *Mt* Spain
50B3 **Pende** *R* Central African Republic/Chad
58C1 **Pendleton** USA
58C1 **Pend Oreille** *R* USA
73L6 **Penedo** Brazil
42D5 **Penganga** *R* India
31D5 **Pengho Lieh Tao** *Is* Taiwan
31E2 **Penglai** China
31B4 **Pengshui** China
8D4 **Penicuik** Scotland
30C5 **Peninsular Malaysia** Malaysia
7D3 **Penistone** England
44B3 **Penner** *R* India
6C2 **Pennine Chain** *Mts* England
68C3 **Penns Grove** USA
57F2 **Pennsylvania** *State* USA
68B1 **Penn Yan** USA
55M3 **Penny Highlands** *Mts* Canada
65F1 **Penobscot** *R* USA
65F2 **Penobscot B** USA
34B3 **Penola** Australia
32C4 **Penong** Australia
69A5 **Penonomé** Panama
6C2 **Penrith** England
63E2 **Pensacola** USA
76E2 **Pensacola Mts** Antarctica
33F2 **Pentecost** *I* Vanuatu
54G5 **Penticton** Canada
8D2 **Pentland Firth** *Chan* Scotland
8D4 **Pentland Hills** Scotland
6C2 **Pen-y-ghent** *Mt* England
20H5 **Penza** Russian Federation
7B4 **Penzance** England
25S3 **Penzhina** *R* Russian Federation
25S3 **Penzhinskaya Guba** *B* Russian Federation
64B2 **Peoria** USA
30C5 **Perak** *R* Malaysia
75A3 **Perdido** *R* Brazil
72C3 **Pereira** Colombia
75B3 **Pereira Barreto** Brazil
21G6 **Perelazovskiy** Russian Federation
19G2 **Pereyaslav** Ukraine
74D4 **Pergamino** Argentina
40B2 **Perge** Turkey
55L4 **Péribonca** *R* Canada
14C2 **Périgueux** France
72C2 **Perlas, Archipiélago de las** Panama
69A4 **Perlas, Laguna de** Nicaragua
20K4 **Perm'** Russian Federation
Pernambuco = Recife
73L5 **Pernambuco** *State* Brazil
17E2 **Pernik** Bulgaria
13B3 **Péronne** France
14C3 **Perpignan** France
66D4 **Perris** USA
67B2 **Perry** Florida, USA
67B2 **Perry** Georgia, USA
68A1 **Perry** New York, USA
63C1 **Perry** Oklahoma, USA
54H3 **Perry River** Canada
64C2 **Perrysburg** USA
62B1 **Perryton** USA
63E1 **Perryville** Missouri, USA
Persia = Iran
38D3 **Persian Gulf** SW Asia
32A4 **Perth** Australia
65D2 **Perth** Canada
8D3 **Perth** Scotland
68C2 **Perth Amboy** USA
64B2 **Peru** USA
72D6 **Peru** *Republic* S America
37P5 **Peru Basin** Pacific Ocean
52E6 **Peru-Chile Trench** Pacific Ocean
16C2 **Perugia** Italy
16D2 **Perušic** Croatia
40D2 **Pervari** Turkey
20G5 **Pervomaysk** Russian Federation
21E6 **Pervomaysk** Ukraine
20K4 **Pervoural'sk** Russian Federation
16C2 **Pesaro** Italy
66A2 **Pescadero** USA
Pescadores = Pengho Lieh Tao
16C2 **Pescara** Italy
42C2 **Peshawar** Pakistan
17E2 **Peshkopi** Albania
64B1 **Peshtigo** USA
20F4 **Pestovo** Russian Federation
70B3 **Petacalco, B de** Mexico
45C2 **Petah Tiqwa** Israel
59B3 **Petaluma** USA
13C3 **Pétange** Luxembourg

51D5 **Petauke** Zambia
64B2 **Petenwell L** USA
34A2 **Peterborough** Australia
65D2 **Peterborough** Canada
7D3 **Peterborough** England
68E1 **Peterborough** USA
8E3 **Peterhead** Scotland
55M1 **Petermann Gletscher** *Gl* Greenland
32B3 **Petermann Range** *Mts* Australia
74B5 **Peteroa, Vol** Argentina/Chile
76G4 **Peter 1 Øy** *I* Antarctica
54E4 **Petersburg** USA
65D3 **Petersburg** Virginia, USA
7D4 **Petersfield** England
16B3 **Petite Kabylie** *Hills* Algeria
55M4 **Petit Mècatina, Rivière du** *R* Canada
42C4 **Petlād** India
70D2 **Peto** Mexico
64C1 **Petoskey** USA
45C3 **Petra** *Hist Site* Jordan
25N2 **Petra, Ostrova** *Is* Russian Federation
28C2 **Petra Velikogo, Zaliv** *B* Russian Federation
59E3 **Petrified Forest Nat Pk** USA
73K5 **Petrolina** Brazil
24H4 **Petropavlovsk** Kazakhstan
26J1 **Petropavlovsk-Kamchatskiy** Russian Federation
75D3 **Petrópolis** Brazil
21H5 **Petrovsk** Russian Federation
25M4 **Petrovsk Zabaykal'skiy** Russian Federation
20E3 **Petrozavodsk** Russian Federation
47D2 **Petrusburg** South Africa
47D2 **Petrus Steyn** South Africa
47C3 **Petrusville** South Africa
25T3 **Pevek** Russian Federation
20H2 **Peza** *R* Russian Federation
13E2 **Pfälzer Wald** *Region* Germany
18B3 **Pforzheim** Germany
42D2 **Phagwara** India
47E1 **Phalaborwa** South Africa
42C3 **Phalodī** India
13D3 **Phalsbourg** France
44A2 **Phaltan** India
30B4 **Phangnga** Thailand
30C3 **Phanom Dang** *Mts* Cambodia/Thailand
30D3 **Phan Rang** Vietnam
30D3 **Phan Thiet** Vietnam
62C3 **Pharr** USA
67C1 **Phelps L** USA
67A2 **Phenix City** USA
30B3 **Phet Buri** Thailand
30D3 **Phiafay** Laos
63E2 **Philadelphia** Mississippi, USA
68C2 **Philadelphia** Pennsylvania, USA
60C2 **Philip** USA
Philippeville = Skikda
13C2 **Philippeville** Belgium
27F5 **Philippine S** Pacific Ocean
27F5 **Philippines** *Republic* SE Asia
36H4 **Philippine Trench** Pacific Ocean
47D3 **Philippolis** South Africa
58D1 **Philipsburg** Montana, USA
65D2 **Philipsburg** Pennsylvania, USA
54D3 **Philip Smith Mts** USA
47C3 **Philipstown** South Africa
55K1 **Phillips B** Canada
60D3 **Phillipsburg** Kansas, USA
68C2 **Phillipsburg** New Jersey, USA
55K2 **Philpots Pen** Canada
30C3 **Phnom Penh** Cambodia
59D4 **Phoenix** Arizona, USA
68B1 **Phoenix** New York, USA
33H1 **Phoenix Is** Pacific Ocean
68C2 **Phoenixville** USA
30C1 **Phong Saly** Laos
30C3 **Phra Nakhon** Thailand
30C2 **Phu Bia** *Mt* Laos
30D3 **Phu Cuong** Vietnam
30B4 **Phuket** Thailand
43E4 **Phulbāni** India
30C2 **Phu Miang** *Mt* Thailand
30D2 **Phu Set** *Mt* Laos
30D1 **Phu Tho** Vietnam
30D4 **Phu Vinh** Vietnam
16B1 **Piacenza** Italy
34D1 **Pialba** Australia
34C2 **Pian** *R* Australia
16C2 **Pianosa** *I* Italy
16D2 **Pianosa** *I* Italy
19E2 **Piaseczno** Poland
75D1 **Piatã** Brazil
17F1 **Piatra-Neamţ** Romania
73K5 **Piauí** *State* Brazil
16C1 **Piave** *R* Italy
50D3 **Pibor** *R* Sudan
50D3 **Pibor Post** Sudan
13B3 **Picardie** *Region* France
63E2 **Picayune** USA
74B4 **Pichilemu** Chile
6D2 **Pickering** England
55J4 **Pickle Lake** Canada
48A1 **Pico** *I* Azores
69C5 **Pico Bolivar** *Mt* Venezuela
15A1 **Pico de Almanzor** *Mt* Spain
15C1 **Pico de Aneto** *Mt* Spain
69C3 **Pico Duarte** *Mt* Dominican Republic
73K5 **Picos** Brazil
15B1 **Picos de Europa** *Mt* Spain
34D2 **Picton** Australia
35B2 **Picton** New Zealand
50B1 **Pic Toussidé** *Mt* Chad
75C3 **Piedade** Brazil
66C2 **Piedra** USA
66B3 **Piedras Blancas,Pt** USA
70B2 **Piedras Negras** Mexico
64B1 **Pie I** Canada
12K6 **Pieksämäki** Finland
12K6 **Pielinen** *L* Finland
47D2 **Pienaar's River** South Africa
60C2 **Pierre** USA
19D3 **Pieštany** Slovakia
47E2 **Pietermaritzburg** South Africa
47D1 **Pietersburg** South Africa
47E2 **Piet Retief** South Africa
17F1 **Pietrosul** *Mt* Romania
27H6 **Pigailoe** *I* Pacific Ocean
63D1 **Piggott** USA
28A3 **Pihyŏn** N Korea
55J4 **Pikangikum L** Canada
60B3 **Pikes Peak** USA
47B3 **Piketberg** South Africa
64C3 **Pikeville** USA
55O3 **Pikiutaleq** Greenland
39F2 **Pik Kommunizma** *Mt* Tajikistan
50B3 **Pikounda** Congo
39G1 **Pik Pobedy** *Mt* China/Kirgizia
18D2 **Piła** Poland
74E3 **Pilar** Paraguay
74D2 **Pilcomayo** *R* Argentina/Bolivia/Paraguay
47E1 **Pilgrim's Rest** South Africa
42D3 **Pīlībhīt** India
19D2 **Pilica** *R* Poland
34C4 **Pillar,C** Australia
75C2 **Pilões, Serra dos** *Mts* Brazil
17E3 **Pílos** Greece
58C1 **Pilot Knob** *Mt* USA
66D1 **Pilot Peak** *Mt* USA
63E3 **Pilottown** USA
73G4 **Pimenta** Brazil
30C4 **Pinang** *I* Malaysia
69A2 **Pinar del Rio** Cuba
13C2 **Pinche** Belgium
73J4 **Pindaré** *R* Brazil
17E3 **Pindhos** *Mts* Greece
63D2 **Pine Bluff** USA
60C2 **Pine Bluffs** USA
61E1 **Pine City** USA
32C2 **Pine Creek** Australia
68B2 **Pine Creek** *R* USA
66C1 **Pinecrest** USA
66C2 **Pinedale** California, USA
58E2 **Pinedale** Wyoming, USA
66C2 **Pine Flat Res** USA
20G3 **Pinega** Russian Federation
20H3 **Pinega** *R* Russian Federation
68B2 **Pine Grove** USA
67B3 **Pine Hills** USA
67C1 **Pinehurst** USA
67B3 **Pine I** USA
63D2 **Pineland** USA
67B3 **Pinellas Park** USA
66B3 **Pine Mt** USA
54G3 **Pine Point** Canada
60C2 **Pine Ridge** USA
63D2 **Pines,L. o'the** USA
63D2 **Pineville** USA
31C3 **Pingdingshan** China
31B5 **Pingguo** China
31B2 **Pingliang** China
31B2 **Pingluo** China
31D4 **Pingtan Dao** *I* China
31E5 **Pingtung** Taiwan
31A3 **Pingwu** China
31B5 **Pingxiang** Guangxi, China
31C4 **Pingxiang** Jiangxi, China
73J4 **Pinheiro** Brazil
27C6 **Pini** *I* Indonesia
17E3 **Piniós** *R* Greece
32A4 **Pinjarra** Australia
66B2 **Pinnacles Nat. Mon.** USA
34B3 **Pinnaroo** Australia
Pinos,I de = Juventud, Isla de la
66C3 **Pinos,Mt** USA
59B3 **Pinos,Pt** USA
27E7 **Pinrang** Indonesia
33F3 **Pins, Île des** New Caledonia
21D5 **Pinsk** Belarus
20H3 **Pinyug** Russian Federation
59D3 **Pioche** USA
16C2 **Piombino** Italy
58D1 **Pioneer Mts** USA
25K2 **Pioner, Ostrov** *I* Russian Federation
20L3 **Pionerskiy** Russian Federation
19D2 **Piotrków Trybunalski** Poland
8F2 **Piper** *Oilfield* N Sea
66D2 **Piper Peak** *Mt* USA
61D2 **Pipestone** USA
57F2 **Pipmuacan, Rés** *Res* Canada
64C2 **Piqua** USA
75B4 **Piquiri** *R* Brazil
75C2 **Piracanjuba** Brazil
75C3 **Piracicaba** Brazil
75C3 **Piraçununga** Brazil
75C3 **Piraí do Sul** Brazil
17E3 **Piraiévs** Greece
75C3 **Pirajuí** Brazil
75B2 **Piranhas** Brazil
75D2 **Pirapora** Brazil
75C2 **Pirenópolis** Brazil
75C2 **Pires do Rio** Brazil
17E3 **Pírgos** Greece
14B3 **Pirineos** *Mts* France/Spain
73K4 **Piripiri** Brazil
13D3 **Pirmasens** Germany
17E2 **Pirot** Serbia, Yugoslavia
42C2 **Pīr Panjāl Range** *Mts* Pakistan
27F7 **Piru** Indonesia
66C3 **Piru Creek** *R* USA
16C2 **Pisa** Italy
72C6 **Pisco** Peru
68C1 **Piseco** USA
18C3 **Písek** Czech Republic
42B2 **Pishin** Pakistan
66B3 **Pismo Beach** USA
74C3 **Pissis** *Mt* Argentina
16C2 **Pistoia** Italy
15B1 **Pisuerga** *R* Spain
58B2 **Pit** *R* USA
72C3 **Pitalito** Colombia
37N6 **Pitcairn** *I* Pacific Ocean
12H5 **Pite** *R* Sweden
12J5 **Piteå** Sweden
17E2 **Piteşti** Romania
25L4 **Pit Gorodok** Russian Federation
13B3 **Pithiviers** France
20E3 **Pitkyaranta** Russian Federation
8D3 **Pitlochry** Scotland
20M2 **Pitlyar** Russian Federation
33H5 **Pitt** *I* New Zealand
54F4 **Pitt I** Canada
66B1 **Pittsburg** California, USA
63D1 **Pittsburg** Kansas, USA
65D2 **Pittsburgh** USA
64A3 **Pittsfield** Illinois, USA
68D1 **Pittsfield** Massachusetts, USA
68C2 **Pittston** USA
34D1 **Pittsworth** Australia
72B5 **Piura** Peru
66C3 **Piute Peak** *Mt* USA
43E3 **Piuthan** Nepal
66C3 **Pixley** USA
12B2 **Pjórsá** *R* Iceland
55N5 **Placentia B** Canada
66B1 **Placerville** USA
13C3 **Plaine Lorraine** *Region* France
62B1 **Plains** USA
61D2 **Plainview** Nebraska, USA
62B2 **Plainview** Texas, USA
66B2 **Planada** USA
73H7 **Planalto de Mato Grosso** *Plat* Brazil
73L5 **Planalto do Borborema** *Plat* Brazil
33E1 **Planet Deep** Papua New Guinea
60D2 **Plankinton** USA
63C2 **Plano** USA
67B3 **Plantation** USA
67B3 **Plant City** USA
15A1 **Plasencia** Spain
20L5 **Plast** Russian Federation
26G2 **Plastun** Russian Federation
74E5 **Plata, Río de la** Argentina/Uruguay
13D2 **Plateau Lorrain** France
69C5 **Plato** Colombia
45B1 **Platres** Cyprus
60D2 **Platte** USA
60C2 **Platte** *R* USA
64A2 **Platteville** USA
65E2 **Plattsburgh** USA
61D2 **Plattsmouth** USA
18C2 **Plauen** Germany
20F5 **Plavsk** Russian Federation
72B4 **Playas** Ecuador
66B2 **Pleasanton** California, USA
62C3 **Pleasanton** Texas, USA
68C3 **Pleasantville** USA
64B3 **Pleasure Ridge Park** USA
30D3 **Pleiku** Vietnam
35C1 **Plenty,B of** New Zealand
60C1 **Plentywood** USA
20G3 **Plesetsk** Russian Federation
19D2 **Pleszew** Poland
55L4 **Pletipi,L** Canada
17E2 **Pleven** Bulgaria
17D2 **Pljevlja** Montenegro, Yugoslavia
17D2 **Ploče** Bosnia-Herzegovina
19D2 **Płock** Poland
14B2 **Ploërmel** France
17F2 **Ploieşti** Romania
13D4 **Plombières-les-Bains** France
20C5 **Płońsk** Poland
17E2 **Plovdiv** Bulgaria
58C1 **Plummer** USA
51C6 **Plumtree** Zimbabwe
66B1 **Plymouth** California, USA
7B4 **Plymouth** England
64B2 **Plymouth** Indiana, USA
68E2 **Plymouth** Massachusetts, USA
68C2 **Plymouth** Pennsylvania, USA
68E2 **Plymouth B** USA
7B4 **Plymouth Sd** England
7C3 **Plynlimon** *Mt* Wales
18C3 **Plzeň** Czech Republic
18D2 **Pniewy** Poland
48B3 **Po** Burkina
16C2 **Po** *R* Italy
48C4 **Pobé** Benin
26H2 **Pobedino** Russian Federation
58D2 **Pocatello** USA
19G2 **Pochinok** Russian Federation
75D1 **Poções** Brazil
65D3 **Pocomoke City** USA
75A2 **Poconé** Brazil
75C3 **Poços de Caldas** Brazil
17D2 **Podgorica** Montenegro, Yugoslavia
25L3 **Podkamennaya Tunguska** *R* Russian Federation
20F4 **Podol'sk** Russian Federation
19F3 **Podol'skaya Vozvyshennost'** *Upland* Ukraine
20E3 **Podporozh'ye** Russian Federation
20G3 **Podyuga** Russian Federation
47B2 **Pofadder** South Africa
42A2 **Poghdar** Afghanistan
28B3 **P'ohang** S Korea
76G9 **Poinsett,C** Antarctica
34C2 **Point** Australia
69E3 **Pointe-à-Pitre** Guadeloupe
50B4 **Pointe Noire** Congo
34B3 **Point Fairy** Australia
69L1 **Point Fortin** Trinidad
54B3 **Point Hope** USA
54G3 **Point L** Canada
54B3 **Point Lay** USA
68C2 **Point Pleasant** New Jersey, USA
64C3 **Point Pleasant** W Virginia, USA
14C2 **Poitiers** France
14B2 **Poitou** *Region* France
13A3 **Poix** France
42C3 **Pokaran** India
34C1 **Pokataroo** Australia
43E3 **Pokhara** Nepal
25O3 **Pokrovsk** Russian Federation
59D3 **Polacca** USA
68C1 **Poland** USA
19D2 **Poland** *Republic* Europe
40B2 **Polatlı** Turkey
49D4 **Poli** Cameroon
16D3 **Policastro, G di** Italy
27F5 **Polillo Is** Philippines
25P4 **Poliny Osipenko** Russian Federation
45B1 **Polis** Cyprus
17E2 **Políyiros** Greece
44B3 **Pollāchi** India
16D3 **Pollino, Monte** *Mt* Italy
19F2 **Polonnye** Ukraine
19F1 **Polotsk** Belarus
58D1 **Polson** USA
21E6 **Poltava** Ukraine
16D1 **Pölten** Austria
20L3 **Polunochoye** Russian Federation
12L5 **Poluostrov Rybachiy** *Pen* Russian Federation
62A2 **Polvadera** USA
20E2 **Polyarnyy** Murmansk, Russian Federation
25Q2 **Polyarnyy** Yakutskaya, Russian Federation
20L2 **Polyarnyy Ural** *Mts* Russian Federation
37L4 **Polynesia** *Region* Pacific Ocean
72C5 **Pomabamba** Peru
75D3 **Pomba** *R* Brazil
9C2 **Pomeroy** Northern Ireland
66D3 **Pomona** USA
61D3 **Pomona Res** USA
67B3 **Pompano Beach** USA
68C2 **Pompton Lakes** USA
63C1 **Ponca City** USA
69D3 **Ponce** Puerto Rico
67B3 **Ponce de Leon B** USA
44B3 **Pondicherry** India
55L2 **Pond Inlet** Canada
15A1 **Ponferrada** Spain
48C4 **Pongara, Pte** Equatorial Guinea
50C3 **Pongo** *R* Sudan
47E2 **Pongola** *R* South Africa
44B3 **Ponnāni** India
43G4 **Ponnyadoung Range** *Mts* Burma
24F3 **Ponoy** Russian Federation
20G2 **Ponoy** *R* Russian Federation
14B2 **Pons** France
48A1 **Ponta Delgada** Azores
75B4 **Ponta Grossa** Brazil
75C3 **Pontal** Brazil
13C3 **Pont-à-Mousson** France
75A3 **Ponta Pora** Brazil
14D2 **Pontarlier** France
63D2 **Pontchartrain,L** USA
75A1 **Ponte de Pedra** Brazil
16C2 **Pontedera** Italy
7D3 **Pontefract** England
16B2 **Ponte Leccia** Corsica, France
15A1 **Pontevedra** Spain
64B2 **Pontiac** Illinois, USA
64C2 **Pontiac** Michigan, USA
27D7 **Pontianak** Indonesia
14B2 **Pontivy** France
13B3 **Pontoise** France
63E2 **Pontotoc** USA
13B3 **Pont-sur-Yonne** France
7C4 **Pontypool** Wales
7C4 **Pontypridd** Wales
16C2 **Ponziane, I** Italy
7D4 **Poole** England
Poona = Pune
34B2 **Pooncarie** Australia
34B2 **Poopelloe,L** Australia
72E7 **Poopó, Lago** Bolivia
54C3 **Poorman** USA
72C3 **Popayán** Colombia
13B2 **Poperinge** Belgium
34B2 **Popilta L** Australia
60B1 **Poplar** USA
63D1 **Poplar Bluff** USA
63E2 **Poplarville** USA
70C3 **Popocatepetl** *Vol* Mexico
50B4 **Popokabaka** Zaïre
27H7 **Popondetta** Papua New Guinea
17F2 **Popovo** Bulgaria
75C1 **Porangatu** Brazil
42B4 **Porbandar** India
75C1 **Porcos** *R* Brazil
54D3 **Porcupine** *R* Canada/USA
16C1 **Poreč** Croatia
75B3 **Porecatu** Brazil
12J6 **Pori** Finland
35B2 **Porirua** New Zealand
12H5 **Porjus** Sweden
69E4 **Porlamar** Venezuela
26H2 **Poronaysk** Russian Federation
20E3 **Porosozero** Russian Federation
12K4 **Porsangen** *Inlet* Norway
12F7 **Porsgrunn** Norway
9C2 **Portadown** Northern Ireland
9D2 **Portaferry** Northern Ireland
64B2 **Portage** USA
60C1 **Portal** USA
54F5 **Port Alberni** Canada
15A2 **Portalegre** Portugal
62B2 **Portales** USA
47D3 **Port Alfred** South Africa
54F4 **Port Alice** Canada
68A2 **Port Allegany** USA
63D2 **Port Allen** USA
58B1 **Port Angeles** USA
69B3 **Port Antonio** Jamaica
9C3 **Portarlington** Irish Republic
63D3 **Port Arthur** USA
8B4 **Port Askaig** Scotland
32C4 **Port Augusta** Australia
69C3 **Port-au-Prince** Haiti

64C2 Port Austin USA
44E3 Port Blair Andaman Islands
34B3 Port Campbell Australia
43F4 Port Canning India
55M5 Port Cartier Canada
35B3 Port Chalmers New Zealand
67B3 Port Charlotte USA
68D2 Port Chester USA
64C2 Port Clinton USA
65D2 Port Colborne Canada
34C4 Port Davey *B* Australia
69C3 Port-de-Paix Haiti
30C5 Port Dickson Malaysia
47E3 Port Edward South Africa
75D2 Porteirinha Brazil
64C2 Port Elgin Canada
47D3 Port Elizabeth South Africa
8B4 Port Ellen Scotland
6B2 Port Erin Isle of Man, British Islands
69N2 Porter Pt St Vincent
66C2 Porterville USA
32D4 Port Fairy Australia
50A4 Port Gentil Gabon
63D2 Port Gibson USA
58B1 Port Hammond Canada
48C4 Port Harcourt Nigeria
54F4 Port Hardy Canada
55M5 Port Hawkesbury Canada
7C4 Porthcawl Wales
32A3 Port Hedland Australia
7B3 Porthmadog Wales
55N4 Port Hope Simpson Canada
66C3 Port Hueneme USA
64C2 Port Huron USA
15A2 Portimão Portugal
34D2 Port Jackson *B* Australia
68D2 Port Jefferson USA
68C2 Port Jervis USA
34D2 Port Kembla Australia
7C4 Portland England
64C2 Portland Indiana, USA
65E2 Portland Maine, USA
34C2 Portland New South Wales, Australia
58B1 Portland Oregon, USA
34B3 Portland Victoria, Australia
69H2 Portland Bight *B* Jamaica
7C4 Portland Bill *Pt* England
34C4 Portland,C Australia
35C1 Portland I New Zealand
69H2 Portland Pt Jamaica
9C3 Port Laoise Irish Republic
63C3 Port Lavaca USA
32C4 Port Lincoln Australia
48A4 Port Loko Sierra Leone
51F6 Port Louis Mauritius
34B3 Port MacDonnell Australia
34D2 Port Macquarie Australia
68A2 Port Matilda USA
32D1 Port Moresby Papua New Guinea
47B2 Port Nolloth South Africa
68C3 Port Norris USA
Porto = Oporto
74F4 Pôrto Alegre Brazil
Porto Alexandre = Tombua
69A5 Porto Armuelles Panama
75A1 Pôrto Artur Brazil
75B3 Pôrto 15 de Novembro Brazil
75B1 Pôrto dos Meinacos Brazil
74F2 Pôrto E Cunha Brazil
75A2 Pôrto Esperança Brazil
16C2 Portoferraio Italy
69L1 Port of Spain Trinidad
75A2 Pôrto Jofre Brazil
75B3 Pôrto Mendez Brazil
75A3 Pôrto Murtinho Brazil
48C4 Porto Novo Benin
75B3 Pôrto Primavera, Represa *Res* Brazil
58B1 Port Orchard USA
58B2 Port Orford USA
75B3 Pôrto Santa Helena Brazil
48A1 Porto Santo *I* Madeira
75B3 Pôrto São José Brazil
73L7 Pôrto Seguro Brazil
16B2 Porto Torres Sardinia, Italy
75B4 Pôrto União Brazil
16B2 Porto Vecchio Corsica, France
72F5 Pôrto Velho Brazil
8C4 Portpatrick Scotland
35A3 Port Pegasus *B* New Zealand
34B3 Port Phillip B Australia
34A2 Port Pirie Australia
8B3 Portree Scotland
58B1 Port Renfrew Canada
69J2 Port Royal Jamaica
67B2 Port Royal Sd USA
9C2 Portrush Northern Ireland
45B3 Port Said Egypt
67A3 Port St Joe USA
47D3 Port St Johns South Africa
55N4 Port Saunders Canada
47E3 Port Shepstone South Africa
69Q2 Portsmouth Dominica
7D4 Portsmouth England
68E1 Portsmouth New Hampshire, USA
64C3 Portsmouth Ohio, USA
65D3 Portsmouth Virginia, USA
34D2 Port Stephens *B* Australia
9C2 Portstewart Northern Ireland
50D2 Port Sudan Sudan
63E3 Port Sulphur USA
12K5 Porttipahdan Tekojärvi *Res* Finland
15A2 Portugal *Republic* Europe
9B3 Portumna Irish Republic
68A1 Portville USA
64B2 Port Washington USA
30C5 Port Weld Malaysia
72E6 Porvenir Bolivia
12K6 Porvoo Finland
74E3 Posadas Argentina
15A2 Posadas Spain
41G3 Posht-e Badam Iran
27F7 Poso Indonesia
28A4 Posŏng S Korea
20M2 Pos Poluy Russian Federation
75C1 Posse Brazil
62B2 Post USA
19F1 Postavy Belarus
47C2 Postmasburg South Africa
16C1 Postojna Slovenia
28C2 Pos'yet Russian Federation
47D2 Potchefstroom South Africa
63D1 Poteau USA
16D2 Potenza Italy
47D1 Potgietersrus South Africa
62C3 Poth USA
21G7 Poti Georgia
48D3 Potiskum Nigeria
58C1 Potlatch USA
47C3 Potloer *Mt* South Africa
58C1 Pot Mt USA
65D3 Potomac *R* USA
72E7 Potosí Bolivia
74C3 Potrerillos Chile
18C2 Potsdam Germany
60C2 Potter USA
68C2 Pottstown USA
68B2 Pottsville USA
68D2 Poughkeepsie USA
75C3 Pouso Alegre Brazil
35C1 Poverty B New Zealand
20F3 Povonets Russian Federation
21G5 Povorino Russian Federation
55L4 Povungnituk Canada
60B1 Powder *R* USA
60B2 Powder River USA
58E2 Powell USA
32C2 Powell Creek Australia
59D3 Powell,L USA
54F5 Powell River Canada
7C3 Powys *County* Wales
75B2 Poxoréo Brazil
31D4 Poyang Hu *L* China
40C2 Pozantı Turkey
70C2 Poza Rica Mexico
18D2 Poznań Poland
74E2 Pozo Colorado Paraguay
16C2 Pozzuoli Italy
48B4 Pra *R* Ghana
30C3 Prachin Buri Thailand
30B3 Prachuap Khiri Khan Thailand
18D2 Praděd *Mt* Czech Republic
14C3 Pradelles France
75E2 Prado Brazil
18C2 Prague Czech Republic
Praha = Prague
48A4 Praia Cape Verde
75A1 Praia Rica Brazil
72F5 Prainha Brazil
62B2 Prairie Dog Town Fork *R* USA
64A2 Prairie du Chien USA
61E3 Prairie Village USA
30C3 Prakhon Chai Thailand
75C2 Prata Brazil
75C2 Prata *R* Brazil
Prates *I* = Dongsha Qundao
16C2 Prato Italy
68C1 Prattsville USA
67A2 Prattville USA
14B1 Prawle Pt England
25L4 Predivinsk Russian Federation
25Q3 Predporozhnyy Russian Federation
19E2 Pregolyu *R* Russian Federation
30D3 Prek Kak Cambodia
64A1 Prentice USA
18C2 Prenzlau Germany
44E3 Preparis I Burma
18D3 Přerov Czech Republic
59D4 Prescott Arizona, USA
63D2 Prescott Arkansas, USA
65D2 Prescott Canada
60C2 Presho USA
74D3 Presidencia Roque Sáenz Peña Argentina
75B3 Presidente Epitácio Brazil
75B2 Presidente Murtinho Brazil
75B3 Presidente Prudente Brazil
75B3 Presidente Venceslau Brazil
62B3 Presidio USA
19E3 Prešov Slovakia
65F1 Presque Isle USA
6C3 Preston England
56B2 Preston Idaho, USA
61E2 Preston Minnesota, USA
63D1 Preston Missouri, USA
8C4 Prestwick Scotland
73J8 Prêto Brazil
75C2 Prêto *R* Brazil
47D2 Pretoria South Africa
17E3 Préveza Greece
30D3 Prey Veng Cambodia
59D3 Price USA
63E2 Prichard USA
21E6 Prichernomorskaya Nizmennost' *Lowland* Ukraine
69M2 Prickly Pt Grenada
19F3 Pridneprovskaya Vozvyshennost' *Upland* Ukraine
19E1 Priekule Lithuania
47C2 Prieska South Africa
58C1 Priest L USA
58C1 Priest River USA
17E2 Prilep Albania/Macedonia, Yugoslavia/Greece
21E5 Priluki Ukraine
76G3 Primavera *Base* Antarctica
12K6 Primorsk Russian Federation
21F6 Primorsko-Akhtarsk Russian Federation
54H4 Prince Albert Canada
47C3 Prince Albert South Africa
54F2 Prince Albert,C Canada
54G2 Prince Albert Pen Canada
54G2 Prince Albert Sd Canada
55L3 Prince Charles I Canada
76F10 Prince Charles Mts Antarctica
55M5 Prince Edward I *Province* Canada
36C7 Prince Edward Is Indian Ocean
54F4 Prince George Canada
54H2 Prince Gustaf Adolf Sea Canada
27H8 Prince of Wales I Australia
54H2 Prince of Wales I Canada
54E4 Prince of Wales I USA
54G2 Prince of Wales Str Canada
54G2 Prince Patrick I Canada
55J2 Prince Regent Inlet *Str* Canada
54E4 Prince Rupert Canada
32D2 Princess Charlotte B Australia
69L1 Princes Town Trinidad
54F5 Princeton Canada
64B2 Princeton Illinois, USA
64B3 Princeton Kentucky, USA
61E2 Princeton Missouri, USA
68C2 Princeton New Jersey, USA
64C3 Princeton W Virginia, USA
54D3 Prince William Sd USA
48C4 Príncipe *I* Sao Tome & Principe
58B2 Prineville USA
55O3 Prins Christian Sund Greenland
76F12 Prinsesse Astrid Kyst *Region* Antarctica
76F12 Prinsesse Ragnhild Kyst *Region* Antarctica
24C2 Prins Karls Forland *I* Svalbard, Norway
70D3 Prinzapolca Nicaragua
20E3 Priozersk Russian Federation
19F2 Pripet *R* Belarus
Pripyat' *R* Belarus = Pripet
17E2 Prispansko Jezero *L* Albania/Macedonia, Yugoslavia/Greece
17E2 Priština Serbia, Yugoslavia
18C2 Pritzwalk Germany
20G5 Privolzhskaya Vozvyshennost' *Upland* Russian Federation
17E2 Prizren Serbia, Yugoslavia
27E7 Probolinggo Indonesia
61E1 Proctor USA
44B3 Proddatūr India
70D2 Progreso Mexico
58B2 Project City USA
21G7 Prokhladnyy Russian Federation
24K4 Prokop'yevsk Russian Federation
21G6 Proletarskaya Russian Federation
Prome = Pyè
75A2 Promissão Brazil
19G2 Pronya *R* Belarus
73L6 Propriá Brazil
32D3 Proserpine Australia
68C1 Prospect New York, USA
58B2 Prospect Oregon, USA
18D3 Prostějov Czech Republic
55N2 Prøven Greenland
14D3 Provence *Region* France
68E2 Providence USA
69A4 Providencia, Isla de Caribbean Sea
25U3 Provideniya Russian Federation
68E1 Provincetown USA
13B3 Provins France
59D2 Provo USA
54G4 Provost Canada
75B4 Prudentópolis Brazil
54D2 Prudhoe Bay USA
55M2 Prudhoe Land *Region* Greenland
19E2 Pruszkow Poland
19F3 Prut *R* Moldavia/Romania
21D6 Prutul *R* Romania
19E2 Pruzhany Belarus
63C1 Pryor USA
19E3 Przemyśl Poland
17F3 Psará *I* Greece
20D4 Pskov Russian Federation
19F2 Ptich *R* Belarus
17E2 Ptolemaïs Greece
28A3 Puan S Korea
72D5 Pucallpa Peru
31D4 Pucheng China
12K5 Pudasjärvi Finland
20F3 Pudozh Russian Federation
44B3 Pudukkottai India
70C3 Puebla Mexico
15A1 Puebla de Sanabria Spain
15A1 Puebla de Trives Spain
62B1 Pueblo USA
73L5 Puerta do Calcanhar *Pt* Brazil
47E2 Puerta do Oro *Pt* South Africa
75B3 Puerto Adela Brazil
74B7 Puerto Aisén Chile
70D4 Puerto Armuelles Panama
73G6 Puerto Artur Brazil
72C3 Puerto Asis Colombia
72E2 Puerto Ayacucho Venezuela
70D3 Puerto Barrios Guatemala
72D2 Puerto Berrio Colombia
72E1 Puerto Cabello Venezuela
70D3 Puerto Cabezas Nicaragua
72E2 Puerto Carreño Colombia
75A3 Puerto Casado Brazil
75A3 Puerto Cooper Brazil
70D4 Puerto Cortés Costa Rica
70D3 Puerto Cortés Honduras
48A2 Puerto del Rosario Canary Islands
73H8 Puerto E. Cunha Brazil
72D1 Puerto Fijo Venezuela
73J5 Puerto Franco Brazil
75A3 Puerto Guaraní Brazil
72E6 Puerto Heath Bolivia
70D2 Puerto Juárez Mexico
72F1 Puerto la Cruz Venezuela
15B2 Puertollano Spain
69C4 Puerto López Colombia
74D6 Puerto Madryn Argentina
72E6 Puerto Maldonado Peru
74B6 Puerto Montt Chile
73G8 Puerto Murtinho Brazil
74B8 Puerto Natales Chile
70A1 Puerto Peñasco Mexico
75A3 Puerto Pinasco Brazil
74D6 Puerto Pirámides Argentina
69C3 Puerto Plata Dominican Republic
74F3 Puerto Presidente Stroessner Brazil
27E6 Puerto Princesa Philippines
72C3 Puerto Rico Colombia
69D3 Puerto Rico *I* Caribbean Sea
69D3 Puerto Rico Trench Caribbean Sea
73H4 Puerto Santana Brazil
75A3 Puerto Sastre Brazil
74E1 Puerto Suárez Bolivia
70B2 Puerto Vallarta Mexico
74B6 Puerto Varas Chile
72F7 Puerto Villarroel Bolivia
21H5 Pugachev Russian Federation
42C3 Pūgal India
15C1 Puigcerdá Spain
28A2 Pujŏn N Korea
28A2 Pujŏn Res N Korea
35B2 Pukaki,L *L* New Zealand
28A2 Pukchin N Korea
28B2 Pukch'ŏng N Korea
35B1 Pukekohe New Zealand
35B2 Puketeraki Range *Mts* New Zealand
20G3 Puksoozero Russian Federation
16C2 Pula Croatia
65D2 Pulaski New York, USA
67A1 Pulaski Tennessee, USA
64C3 Pulaski Virginia, USA
27G7 Pulau Kolepom *I* Indonesia
27C7 Pulau Pulau Batu *Is* Indonesia
Pulau Pulau Macan - Kepulauan = Takabonerate
19E2 Puławy Poland
44C3 Pulicat L India
42B1 Pul-i-Khumri Afghanistan
44B4 Puliyangudi India
58C1 Pullman USA
27G6 Pulo Anna *I* Pacific Ocean
12L5 Pulozero Russian Federation
19E2 Pułtusk Poland
74C3 Puna de Atacama Argentina
72B4 Puná, Isla Ecuador
43F3 Punakha Bhutan
42C2 Pūnch Pakistan
47E1 Punda Milia South Africa
44A2 Pune India
28A2 Pungsan N Korea
28A2 Pungso N Korea
50C4 Punia Zaïre
74B4 Punitaqui Chile
42C2 Punjab *Province* Pakistan
42D2 Punjab *State* India
72D7 Puno Peru
74D5 Punta Alta Argentina
74B8 Punta Arenas Chile
59C4 Punta Banda, Cabo *C* Mexico
74F4 Punta del Este Uruguay
70D3 Punta Gorda Belize
67B3 Punta Gorda USA
72B1 Puntarenas Costa Rica
31C4 Puqi China
24J3 Pur *R* Russian Federation
72C3 Purace, Vol Colombia
63C1 Purcell USA
62B1 Purgatoire *R* USA
43F5 Puri India
44B2 Pūrna India
43F3 Pūrnia India
30C3 Pursat Cambodia
72F4 Purus *R* Brazil
63E2 Purvis USA
27D7 Purwokerto Indonesia
28B2 Puryŏng N Korea
42D5 Pusad India
28B3 Pusan S Korea
20E4 Pushkin Russian Federation
20F3 Pushlakhta Russian Federation
19F1 Pustoshka Russian Federation
43H3 Putao Burma
35C1 Putaruru New Zealand
31D4 Putian China
27E7 Puting, Tanjung *C* Indonesia
68E2 Putnam USA
68D1 Putney USA
44B4 Puttalam Sri Lanka
18C2 Puttgarden Germany
72C4 Putumayo *R* Colombia/Ecuador/Peru
27E6 Putussiban Indonesia
12K6 Puulavesi *L* Finland
58B1 Puyallup USA
35A3 Puysegur Pt New Zealand
51C4 Pweto Zaïre
7B3 Pwllheli Wales
51C6 PWV *Province* South Africa
20F3 Pyal'ma Russian Federation
20E2 Pyaozero, Ozero *L* Russian Federation
30B2 Pyapon Burma
25K2 Pyasina *R* Russian Federation

21G7 **Pyatigorsk** Russian Federation
43H5 **Pyè** Burma
12K6 **Pyhäselkä** *L* Finland
30B2 **Pyinmana** Burma
28A2 **Pyŏktong** N Korea
28A3 **Pyonggang** N Korea
28A3 **Pyŏnggok-dong** S Korea
28A3 **P'yŏngsan** N Korea
28A3 **P'yŏngt'aek** S Korea
28B3 **P'yŏngyang** N Korea
34B3 **Pyramid Hill** Australia
59C2 **Pyramid L** USA
35A2 **Pyramid,Mt** New Zealand
14B3 **Pyrénées** *Mts* France/Spain
19F1 **Pytalovo** Russian Federation
30B2 **Pyu** Burma

Q

45D4 **Qa'ash Shubyk, Wadi** Jordan
45C2 **Qabatiya** Israel
45D3 **Qā'el Hafīra** *Mud Flats* Jordan
45D3 **Qa'el Jinz** *Mud Flats* Jordan
55O3 **Qagssimiut** Greenland
26C3 **Qaidam Pendi** *Salt Flat* China
45D2 **Qa Khanna** *Salt Marsh* Jordan
50D2 **Qala'en Nahl** Sudan
42B2 **Qalat** Afghanistan
45D1 **Qal'at al Ḩişn** Syria
45C1 **Qal'at al Marqab** *Hist Site* Syria
50E2 **Qal'at Bīshah** Saudi Arabia
41E3 **Qal'at Sālih** Iraq
26C3 **Qamdo** Tibet, China
Qaqortoq = Julianehåb
50E2 **Qandala** Somalia
49E2 **Qara** Egypt
50E3 **Qardho** Somalia
21H8 **Qareh Dāgh** *Mts* Iran
41E4 **Qaryat al Ulyā** Saudi Arabia
45C3 **Qasr ed Deir, Jebel** *Mt* Jordan
45D3 **Qasr el Kharana** Jordan
41E3 **Qāşr e Shīrīn** Iran
49E2 **Qasr Farâfra** Egypt
45D2 **Qaṭanā** Syria
41F4 **Qatar** *Emirate* Arabian Pen
45C4 **Qatim, Jebel** *Mt* Jordan
45D3 **Qatrāna** Jordan
49E2 **Qattâra Depression** Egypt
41G3 **Qāyen** Iran
41F2 **Qazvīn** Iran
40B4 **Qena** Egypt
Qeqertarsuaq = Julianehåb
41E2 **Qeydār** Iran
41F4 **Qeys** *I* Iran
21H8 **Qezel Owzan** *R* Iran
45C3 **Qeziot** Israel
31B5 **Qian Jiang** *R* China
31E1 **Qian Shan** *Upland* China
31E3 **Qidong** China
31B4 **Qijiang** China
26C2 **Qijiaojing** China
42B2 **Qila Saifullah** Pakistan
31A2 **Qilian** China
26C3 **Qilian Shan** China
25L6 **Qilian Shan** *Mts* China
31B3 **Qin'an** China
31E2 **Qingdao** China
28A3 **Qingduizi** China
31A2 **Qinghai** *Province* China
26C3 **Qinghai Hu** *L* China
31D3 **Qingjiang** Jiangsu, China
31D4 **Qingjiang** Jiangxi, China
31B3 **Qing Jiang** *R* China
31C2 **Qingshuihe** China
31B2 **Qingshui He** *R* China
31B2 **Qingtongxia** China
31B2 **Qingyang** China
28A2 **Qingyuan** China
31D4 **Qingyuan** Zhejiang, China
39G2 **Qing Zang** *Upland* China
31B5 **Qingzhou** China
31D2 **Qinhuangdao** China
31B3 **Qin Ling** *Mts* China
30D1 **Qinzhou** China
30E2 **Qionghai** China
31A3 **Qionglai Shan** *Upland* China
30D1 **Qiongzhou Haixia** *Str* China
26F2 **Qiqihar** China
45C3 **Qīraîya, Wadi** Egypt
45C2 **Qiryat Ata** Israel
45C3 **Qiryat Gat** Israel
45C2 **Qiryat Shemona** Israel
45C2 **Qiryat Yam** Israel
45C2 **Qishon** *R* Israel
25K5 **Qitai** China
31C4 **Qiyang** China
31B1 **Qog Qi** China
41F2 **Qolleh-ye Damavand** *Mt* Iran
41F3 **Qom** Iran
41F3 **Qomisheh** Iran
Qomolangma Feng *Mt* **= Everest,Mt**
45D1 **Qornet es Saouda** *Mt* Lebanon
55N3 **Qôrnoq** Greenland
41E2 **Qorveh** Iran
41G4 **Qotbābad** Iran
21H8 **Qotur** *R* Iran
68D1 **Quabbin Res** USA
47C2 **Quaggablat** South Africa
13D1 **Quakenbrück** Germany
68C2 **Quakertown** USA
30C3 **Quam Phu Quoc** *I* Vietnam
62C2 **Quanah** USA
30D2 **Quang Ngai** Vietnam
30D2 **Quang Tri** Vietnam
30D4 **Quan Long** Vietnam
31D5 **Quanzhou** Fujian, China
31C4 **Quanzhou** Guangxi, China
54H4 **Qu' Appelle** *R* Canada
59D4 **Quartzsite** USA
41G2 **Quchan** Iran
34C3 **Queanbeyan** Australia
65E1 **Québec** Canada
55L4 **Quebec** *Province* Canada
75C2 **Quebra-Anzol** *R* Brazil
74F3 **Quedas do Iguaçu** *Falls* Argentina/Brazil
68C3 **Queen Anne** USA
54E4 **Queen Charlotte Is** Canada
54F4 **Queen Charlotte Sd** Canada
54F4 **Queen Charlotte Str** Canada
54H1 **Queen Elizabeth Is** Canada
76F9 **Queen Mary Land** *Region* Antarctica
54H3 **Queen Maud G** Canada
76E6 **Queen Maud Mts** Antarctica
68D2 **Queens** *Borough* New York, USA
27F8 **Queen's Ch** Australia
34B3 **Queenscliff** Australia
32D3 **Queensland** *State* Australia
34C4 **Queenstown** Australia
35A3 **Queenstown** New Zealand
47D3 **Queenstown** South Africa
68B3 **Queenstown** USA
51B4 **Quela** Angola
51D5 **Quelimane** Mozambique
62A2 **Quemado** USA
70B2 **Querétaro** Mexico
42B2 **Quetta** Pakistan
70C3 **Quezaltenango** Guatemala
27F5 **Quezon City** Philippines
51B5 **Quibala** Angola
51B4 **Quibaxe** Angola
72C2 **Quibdó** Colombia
14B2 **Quiberon** France
51B4 **Quicama Nat Pk** Angola
75A4 **Quiindy** Paraguay
72D6 **Quillabamba** Peru
72E7 **Quillacollo** Bolivia
14C3 **Quillan** France
54H4 **Quill Lakes** Canada
74B4 **Quillota** Chile
34B1 **Quilpie** Australia
51B4 **Quimbele** Angola
14B2 **Quimper** France
14B2 **Quimperlé** France
59B3 **Quincy** California, USA
64A3 **Quincy** Illinois, USA
68E1 **Quincy** Massachusetts, USA
30D3 **Qui Nhon** Vietnam
15B2 **Quintanar de la Orden** Spain
51B5 **Quirima** Angola
34D2 **Quirindi** Australia
51E5 **Quissanga** Mozambique
51D6 **Quissico** Mozambique
72C4 **Quito** Ecuador
73L4 **Quixadá** Brazil
31A4 **Qujing** China
47D3 **Qumbu** South Africa
32C4 **Quorn** Australia
40B4 **Qus** Egypt
40B4 **Quseir** Egypt
55N3 **Qutdligssat** Greenland
Quthing = Moyeni
31B3 **Qu Xian** Sichuan, China
31D4 **Qu Xian** Zhejiang, China
30D2 **Quynh Luu** Vietnam
31C2 **Quzhou** China
43G3 **Qūzū** China

R

12J6 **Raahe** Finland
8B3 **Raasay** *I* Scotland
8B3 **Raasay,Sound of** *Chan* Scotland
50F2 **Raas Caseyr** Somalia
16C2 **Rab** *I* Croatia
27E7 **Raba** Indonesia
18D3 **Rába** *R* Hungary
48B1 **Rabat** Morocco
32E1 **Rabaul** Papua New Guinea
45C3 **Rabba** Jordan
40C5 **Rābigh** Saudi Arabia
55N5 **Race,C** Canada
68E1 **Race Pt** USA
45C2 **Rachaya** Lebanon
18C3 **Rachel** *Mt* Germany
30D3 **Rach Gia** Vietnam
64B2 **Racine** USA
19F3 **Rădăuţi** Romania
64B3 **Radcliff** USA
64C3 **Radford** USA
42C4 **Radhanpur** India
69L1 **Radix,Pt** Trinidad
19E2 **Radom** Poland
19D2 **Radomsko** Poland
19F2 **Radomyshl'** Ukraine
18C3 **Radstad** Austria
19E1 **Radviliškis** Lithuania
54G3 **Rae** Canada
43E3 **Rāe Bareli** India
55K3 **Rae Isthmus** Canada
54G3 **Rae L** Canada
35C1 **Raetihi** New Zealand
74D4 **Rafaela** Argentina
45C3 **Rafah** Egypt
50C3 **Rafai** Central African Republic
41D3 **Rafhā** Saudi Arabia
41G3 **Rafsanjān** Iran
50C3 **Raga** Sudan
69Q2 **Ragged Pt** Barbados
16C3 **Ragusa** Sicily, Italy
50D2 **Rahad** *R* Sudan
42C3 **Rahimyar Khan** Pakistan
41F3 **Rāhjerd** Iran
44B2 **Rāichur** India
43E4 **Raigarh** India
34B3 **Rainbow** Australia
67A2 **Rainbow City** USA
58B1 **Rainier** USA
58B1 **Rainier,Mt** USA
61E1 **Rainy** *R* Canada/USA
55J5 **Rainy L** Canada
61E1 **Rainy L** Canada/USA
61E1 **Rainy River** Canada
43E4 **Raipur** India
44C2 **Rājahmundry** India
27E6 **Rajang** *R* Malaysia
42C3 **Rajanpur** Pakistan
44B4 **Rājapālaiyam** India
42C3 **Rājasthān** *State* India
42D4 **Rājgarh** Madhya Pradesh, India
42D3 **Rājgarh** Rājasthān, India
42C4 **Rājkot** India
43F4 **Rājmahāl Hills** India
43E4 **Raj Nāndgaon** India
42C4 **Rājpīpla** India
43F4 **Rajshahi** Bangladesh
42D4 **Rājur** India
35B2 **Rakaia** *R* New Zealand
39G3 **Raka Zangbo** *R* China
19E3 **Rakhov** Ukraine
42A3 **Rakhshan** *R* Pakistan
47C1 **Rakops** Botswana
19F2 **Rakov** Belarus
67C1 **Raleigh** USA
45C4 **Ram** Jordan
45C2 **Rama** Israel
75D1 **Ramalho, Serra do** *Mts* Brazil
45C3 **Ramallah** Israel
44B4 **Rāmanāthapuram** India
26H3 **Ramapo Deep** Pacific Ocean
45C2 **Ramat Gan** Israel
13D3 **Rambervillers** France
14C2 **Rambouillet** France
43F4 **Rāmgarh** Bihār, India
42C3 **Rāmgarh** Rājasthān, India
41E3 **Rāmhormoz** Iran
45C4 **Ram, Jebel** *Mt* Jordan
45C3 **Ramla** Israel
59C4 **Ramona** USA
42D3 **Rāmpur** India
42D4 **Rāmpura** India
43G5 **Ramree I** Burma
21J8 **Rāmsar** Iran
6B2 **Ramsey** Isle of Man, British Islands
68C2 **Ramsey** USA
7B4 **Ramsey I** Wales
7E4 **Ramsgate** England
45D2 **Ramtha** Jordan
32D1 **Ramu** *R* Papua New Guinea
27E6 **Ranau** Malaysia
74B4 **Rancagua** Chile
60B2 **Ranchester** USA
43F4 **Rānchi** India
43E4 **Rānchi Plat** India
74B6 **Ranco, Lago** Chile
47D2 **Randburg** South Africa
12F7 **Randers** Denmark
47D2 **Randfontein** South Africa
65E2 **Randolph** Vermont, USA
66D3 **Randsburg** USA
35B3 **Ranfurly** New Zealand
43G4 **Rangamati** Bangladesh
60B2 **Rangely** USA
35B2 **Rangiora** New Zealand
35C1 **Rangitaiki** *R* New Zealand
35B2 **Rangitata** *R* New Zealand
35C1 **Rangitikei** *R* New Zealand
30B2 **Rangoon** Burma
43F3 **Rangpur** Bangladesh
44B3 **Rānībennur** India
43F4 **Rānīganj** India
55J3 **Rankin Inlet** Canada
34C2 **Rankins Springs** Australia
8C3 **Rannoch, Loch** *L* Scotland
42B4 **Rann of Kachchh** *Flood Area* India
30B4 **Ranong** Thailand
27C6 **Rantauparapat** Indonesia
27F7 **Rantekombola, G** *Mt* Indonesia
64B2 **Rantoul** USA
75B1 **Ranuro** *R* Brazil
13D3 **Raon-l'Etape** France
33H3 **Raoul** *I* Pacific Ocean
16B2 **Rapallo** Italy
55M3 **Raper,C** Canada
60C2 **Rapid City** USA
64B1 **Rapid River** USA
65D3 **Rappahannock** *R* USA
43M2 **Rapti** *R* India
68C2 **Raritan B** USA
40C5 **Ras Abû Dâra** *C* Egypt
40C5 **Ra's Abu Madd** *C* Saudi Arabia
50D1 **Ras Abu Shagara** *C* Sudan
40D2 **Ra's al 'Ayn** Syria
41G4 **Ras al Khaimah** UAE
38D4 **Ra's al Madrakah** *C* Oman
50E2 **Ras Andadda** *C* Eritrea
41E4 **Ra's az Zawr** *C* Saudi Arabia
40C5 **Râs Banâs** *C* Egypt
45B3 **Râs Burûn** *C* Egypt
50D2 **Ras Dashan** *Mt* Ethiopia
41E3 **Ra's-e Barkan** *Pt* Iran
45A3 **Râs el Barr** *C* Egypt
16B3 **Ras El Hadid** Algeria
40A3 **Râs el Kenâyis** *Pt* Egypt
45C4 **Râs el Nafas** *Mt* Egypt
45B4 **Râs el Sudr** *C* Egypt
45C4 **Ras en Naqb** *Upland* Jordan
38D4 **Ra's Fartak** *C* Yemen
40B4 **Râs Ghârib** Egypt
50D2 **Rashad** Sudan
45C3 **Rashādīya** Jordan
40B3 **Rashîd** Egypt
41E2 **Rasht** Iran
45C1 **Ra's ibn Hāni'** *C* Syria
50E2 **Ras Khanzira** *C* Somalia
42B3 **Ras Koh** *Mt* Pakistan
45B4 **Râs Matarma** *C* Egypt
40B4 **Râs Muhammad** *C* Egypt
48A2 **Ras Nouadhibou** *C* Mauritius/Morocco
26J2 **Rasshua** *I* Kuril Is, Russian Federation
21G5 **Rasskazovo** Russian Federation
41E4 **Ra's Tanāqib** *C* Saudi Arabia
41F4 **Ra's Tannūrah** Saudi Arabia
18B3 **Rastatt** Germany
Ras Uarc = Tres Forcas, Cabo
45C4 **Ras Um Seisabān** *Mt* Jordan
50E2 **Ras Xaafuun** *C* Somalia
42C3 **Ratangarh** India
30B3 **Rat Buri** Thailand
42D3 **Rāth** India
18C2 **Rathenow** Germany
9C2 **Rathfriland** Northern Ireland
9C2 **Rathlin I** Northern Ireland
9C2 **Rathmelton** Irish Republic
45D4 **Ratiyah, Wadi** Jordan
42C4 **Ratlām** India
44A2 **Ratnāgiri** India
44C4 **Ratnapura** Sri Lanka
19E2 **Ratno** Ukraine
62B1 **Raton** USA
12H6 **Rättvik** Sweden
35C1 **Raukumara Range** *Mts* New Zealand
75D3 **Raul Soares** Brazil
12J6 **Rauma** Finland
43E4 **Raurkela** India
41E3 **Ravānsar** Iran
41G3 **Rāvar** Iran
19E2 **Rava Russkaya** Ukraine
68D1 **Ravena** USA
16C2 **Ravenna** Italy
18B3 **Ravensburg** Germany
32D2 **Ravenshoe** Australia
6E2 **Ravenspurn** *Oilfield* N Sea
42C2 **Ravi** *R* Pakistan
55Q3 **Ravn Kap** *C* Greenland
42C2 **Rawalpindi** Pakistan
41D2 **Rawāndiz** Iraq
18D2 **Rawicz** Poland
32B4 **Rawlinna** Australia
56C2 **Rawlins** USA
74D6 **Rawson** Argentina
6C3 **Rawtenstall** England
44B3 **Rāyadurg** India
44C2 **Rāyagada** India
45D2 **Rayak** Lebanon
55N5 **Ray,C** Canada
41G4 **Rāyen** Iran
66C2 **Raymond** California, USA
58D1 **Raymond** Canada
68E1 **Raymond** New Hampshire, USA
58B1 **Raymond** Washington, USA
34D2 **Raymond Terrace** Australia
63C3 **Raymondville** USA
41E2 **Razan** Iran
19G3 **Razdel'naya** Ukraine
28C2 **Razdol'noye** Russian Federation
17F2 **Razgrad** Bulgaria
17F2 **Razim** *L* Romania
7D4 **Reading** England
68C2 **Reading** USA
54G3 **Read Island** Canada
68D1 **Readsboro** USA
49E2 **Rebiana** *Well* Libya
49E2 **Rebiana Sand Sea** Libya
12L6 **Reboly** Russian Federation
29E1 **Rebun-tō** *I* Japan
32B4 **Recherche,Arch of the** *Is* Australia
19G2 **Rechitsa** Belarus
73M5 **Recife** Brazil
47D3 **Recife,C** South Africa
75E2 **Recifes da Pedra Grande** *Arch* Brazil
33F2 **Récifs d'Entrecasteaux** New Caledonia
13D2 **Recklinghausen** Germany
74E3 **Reconquista** Argentina
61D1 **Red** *R* Canada/USA
63D2 **Red** *R* USA
30C4 **Redang** *I* Malaysia
68C2 **Red Bank** New Jersey, USA
67A1 **Red Bank** Tennessee, USA
59B2 **Red Bluff** USA
62B2 **Red Bluff L** USA
6D2 **Redcar** England
34D1 **Redcliffe** Australia
34B2 **Red Cliffs** Australia
60D2 **Red Cloud** USA
54G4 **Red Deer** Canada
54G4 **Red Deer** *R* Canada
58B2 **Redding** USA
7D3 **Redditch** England
60D2 **Redfield** USA
7D4 **Redhill** England
62C1 **Red Hills** USA
57D2 **Red L** USA
55J4 **Red Lake** Canada
61D1 **Red Lake** *R* USA
66D3 **Redlands** USA
68B3 **Red Lion** USA
58E1 **Red Lodge** USA
58B2 **Redmond** USA
66D3 **Red Mountain** USA
61D2 **Red Oak** USA
14B2 **Redon** France
66C4 **Redondo Beach** USA
31B5 **Red River Delta** Vietnam
7B4 **Redruth** England
38B3 **Red Sea** Africa/Arabian Pen
54G4 **Redwater** Canada
61E2 **Red Wing** USA
66A2 **Redwood City** USA
61D2 **Redwood Falls** USA
64B2 **Reed City** USA
66C2 **Reedley** USA
58B2 **Reedsport** USA
65D3 **Reedville** USA
35B2 **Reefton** New Zealand
10B3 **Ree, Lough** *L* Irish Republic
6D2 **Reeth** England
40C2 **Refahiye** Turkey
63C3 **Refugio** USA
75E2 **Regência** Brazil
18C3 **Regensburg** Germany
48C2 **Reggane** Algeria
16D3 **Reggio di Calabria** Italy
16C2 **Reggio nell'Emilia** Italy
17E1 **Reghin** Romania
54H4 **Regina** Canada
42A2 **Registan** *Region* Afghanistan
47B1 **Rehoboth** Namibia
65D3 **Rehoboth Beach** USA
45C3 **Rehovot** Israel

67C1 **Reidsville** USA
7D4 **Reigate** England
14B2 **Ré, Ile de** *I* France
13B3 **Reims** France
74B8 **Reina Adelaida, Archipiélago de la** Chile
61E2 **Reinbeck** USA
54H4 **Reindeer L** Canada
15B1 **Reinosa** Spain
68B3 **Reisterstown** USA
47D2 **Reitz** South Africa
54H3 **Reliance** Canada
58E2 **Reliance** USA
15C2 **Relizane** Algeria
34A2 **Remarkable,Mt** Australia
27E7 **Rembang** Indonesia
13D3 **Remiremont** France
13D2 **Remscheid** Germany
68C1 **Remsen** USA
12G6 **Rena** Norway
64B3 **Rend L** USA
18B2 **Rendsburg** Germany
65D1 **Renfrew** Canada
8C4 **Renfrew** Scotland
27D7 **Rengat** Indonesia
19F3 **Reni** Ukraine
50D2 **Renk** Sudan
55Q2 **Renland** *Pen* Greenland
34B2 **Renmark** Australia
33F2 **Rennell** *I* Solomon Islands
14B2 **Rennes** France
59C3 **Reno** USA
16C2 **Reno** *R* Italy
68B2 **Renovo** USA
68D1 **Rensselaer** USA
58B1 **Renton** USA
27F7 **Reo** Indonesia
19G2 **Repki** Ukraine
75C3 **Reprêsa de Furnas** *Dam* Brazil
75C2 **Reprêsa Três Marias** *Dam* Brazil
58C1 **Republic** USA
60D2 **Republican** *R* USA
55K3 **Repulse Bay** Canada
41F2 **Reshteh-ye Alborz** *Mts* Iran
31A2 **Reshui** China
74E3 **Resistencia** Argentina
17E1 **Reşiţa** Romania
55J2 **Resolute** Canada
35A3 **Resolution I** New Zealand
55M3 **Resolution Island** Canada
47E2 **Ressano Garcia** Mozambique
13C3 **Rethel** France
17E3 **Réthimnon** Greece
36D6 **Réunion** *I* Indian Ocean
15C1 **Reus** Spain
18B3 **Reutlingen** Germany
20K4 **Revda** Russian Federation
54G4 **Revelstoke** Canada
13C3 **Revigny-sur-Ornain** France
70A3 **Revillagigedo** *Is* Mexico
37O4 **Revilla Gigedo, Islas** Pacific Ocean
13C3 **Revin** France
45C3 **Revivim** Israel
43E4 **Rewa** India
42D3 **Rewāri** India
58D2 **Rexburg** USA
12A2 **Reykjavik** Iceland
70C2 **Reynosa** Mexico
14B2 **Rezé** France
19F1 **Rezekne** Latvia
20L4 **Rezh** Russian Federation
7C3 **Rhayader** Wales
45C1 **Rhazīr** Lebanon
13E2 **Rheda Wiedenbrück** Germany
18B2 **Rhein** *R* W Europe
18B2 **Rheine** Germany
14D2 **Rheinland Pfalz** *Region* Germany
Rhine *R* **= Rhein**
68D2 **Rhinebeck** USA
64B1 **Rhinelander** USA
65E2 **Rhode Island** *State* USA
68E2 **Rhode Island Sd** USA
17F3 **Rhodes** Greece
17F3 **Rhodes** *I* Greece
47D1 **Rhodes Drift** *Ford* Botswana/South Africa
58D1 **Rhodes Peak** *Mt* USA
7C4 **Rhondda** Wales
14C3 **Rhône** *R* France
7C3 **Rhyl** Wales
73L6 **Riachão do Jacuipe** Brazil
75D1 **Riacho de Santana** Brazil
15A1 **Ria de Arosa** *B* Spain
15A1 **Ria de Betanzos** *B* Spain
15A1 **Ria de Corcubion** *B* Spain
15A1 **Ria de Lage** *B* Spain
15A1 **Ria de Sta Marta** *B* Spain
15A1 **Ria de Vigo** *B* Spain
42C2 **Riāsi** Pakistan
27D6 **Riau, Kepulauan** *Is* Indonesia
15A1 **Ribadeo** Spain
75B3 **Ribas do Rio Pardo** Brazil
51D5 **Ribauè** Mozambique
6C3 **Ribble** *R* England
75C3 **Ribeira** Brazil
75C3 **Ribeirão Prêto** Brazil
72E6 **Riberalta** Bolivia
65D2 **Rice L** Canada
64A1 **Rice Lake** USA
47E2 **Richard's Bay** South Africa
63C2 **Richardson** USA
54E3 **Richardson Mts** Canada
59D3 **Richfield** USA
68C1 **Richfield Springs** USA
66C3 **Richgrove** USA
58C1 **Richland** USA
64C3 **Richlands** USA
66A2 **Richmond** California, USA
47C3 **Richmond** Cape Province, South Africa
6D2 **Richmond** England
64C3 **Richmond** Kentucky, USA
47E2 **Richmond** Natal, South Africa
34D2 **Richmond** New South Wales, Australia
35B2 **Richmond** New Zealand
32D3 **Richmond** Queensland, Australia
65D3 **Richmond** Virginia, USA
35B2 **Richmond Range** *Mts* New Zealand
68C1 **Richmondville** USA
7D4 **Rickmansworth** England
65D2 **Rideau Lakes** Canada
67B2 **Ridgeland** USA
68A2 **Ridgway** USA
69D4 **Riecito** Venezuela
18C2 **Riesa** Germany
74B8 **Riesco** *I* Chile
47C2 **Riet** *R* South Africa
16C2 **Rieti** Italy
15B2 **Rif** *Mts* Morocco
48B1 **Rif** *R* Morocco
60B3 **Rifle** USA
19E1 **Riga** Latvia
11H2 **Riga,G of** Estonia/Latvia
Rīgas Jūrās Līcis = Gulf of Riga
58D2 **Rigby** USA
58C1 **Riggins** USA
55N4 **Rigolet** Canada
Riia Laht = Gulf of Riga
12J6 **Riihimaki** Finland
16C1 **Rijeka** Croatia
29D3 **Rikuzen-Tanaka** Japan
12H7 **Rimbo** Sweden
16C2 **Rimini** Italy
17F1 **Rîmnicu Sărat** Romania
17E1 **Rîmnicu Vîlcea** Romania
57G2 **Rimouski** Canada
12F7 **Ringkøbing** Denmark
27E7 **Rinjani** *Mt* Indonesia
8B4 **Rinns Point** Scotland
13E1 **Rinteln** Germany
72C4 **Riobamba** Ecuador
48C4 **Rio Benito** Equatorial Guinea
72E5 **Rio Branco** Brazil
75C4 **Rio Branco do Sul** Brazil
62C3 **Rio Bravo** Mexico
70B1 **Rio Bravo del Norte** *R* Mexico/USA
75B3 **Rio Brilhante** Brazil
75C3 **Rio Claro** Brazil
69L1 **Rio Claro** Trinidad
74D4 **Ríocuarto** Argentina
75D3 **Rio de Janeiro** Brazil
75D3 **Rio de Janeiro** *State* Brazil
48A2 **Rio de Oro, Bahia de** *B* Morocco
74C8 **Río Gallegos** Argentina
74C8 **Río Grande** Argentina
74F4 **Rio Grande** Brazil
69A4 **Rio Grande** Nicaragua
70B2 **Rio Grande** *R* Mexico/USA
70D3 **Rio Grande** *R* Nicaragua
62C3 **Rio Grande City** USA
70B2 **Rio Grande de Santiago** *R* Mexico
73L5 **Rio Grande do Norte** *State* Brazil
74F3 **Rio Grande Do Sul** *State* Brazil
52G6 **Rio Grande Rise** Atlantic Ocean
69C4 **Ríohacha** Colombia
14C2 **Riom** France
72E7 **Rio Mulatos** Bolivia
75C4 **Rio Negro** Brazil
74C5 **Río Negro** *State* Argentina
74E4 **Rio Negro, Embalse de** *Res* Uruguay
74F3 **Rio Pardo** Brazil
74B8 **Rio Turbio** Argentina
75B2 **Rio Verde** Brazil
75B2 **Rio Verde de Mato Grosso** Brazil
7D3 **Ripley** England
64C3 **Ripley** Ohio, USA
63E1 **Ripley** Tennessee, USA
64C3 **Ripley** West Virginia, USA
6D2 **Ripon** England
66B2 **Ripon** USA
29E1 **Rishiri-tō** *I* Japan
45C3 **Rishon le Zion** Israel
68B3 **Rising Sun** USA
12F7 **Risør** Norway
44E3 **Ritchie's Arch** *Is* Andaman Islands
55N2 **Ritenbenk** Greenland
66C2 **Ritter,Mt** USA
58C1 **Ritzville** USA
74B3 **Rivadavia** Chile
72A1 **Rivas** Nicaragua
74E4 **Rivera** Uruguay
66B2 **Riverbank** USA
48B4 **River Cess** Liberia
66C2 **Riverdale** USA
68D2 **Riverhead** USA
34B3 **Riverina** *Region* Australia
35A3 **Riversdale** New Zealand
47C3 **Riversdale** South Africa
66D4 **Riverside** USA
35A3 **Riverton** New Zealand
58E2 **Riverton** USA
67B3 **Riviera Beach** USA
65F1 **Riviére-du-Loup** Canada
28A2 **Riwon** N Korea
41E5 **Rīyadh** Saudi Arabia
40D1 **Rize** Turkey
31D2 **Rizhao** China
45C1 **Rizokaipaso** Cyprus
16D3 **Rizzuto, C** Italy
12F7 **Rjukan** Norway
8B2 **Roag, Loch** *Inlet* Scotland
55K2 **Roanes Pen** Canada
14C2 **Roanne** France
67A2 **Roanoke** Alabama, USA
65D3 **Roanoke** Virginia, USA
65D3 **Roanoke** *R* USA
67C1 **Roanoke Rapids** USA
59D3 **Roan Plat** USA
58D2 **Roberts** USA
59C3 **Roberts Creek Mt** USA
12J6 **Robertsfors** Sweden
63D1 **Robert S Kerr Res** USA
47B3 **Robertson** South Africa
48A4 **Robertsport** Liberia
55L5 **Roberval** Canada
6D2 **Robin Hood's Bay** England
34B2 **Robinvale** Australia
63C3 **Robstown** USA
15A2 **Roca, Cabo de** *C* Portugal
70A3 **Roca Partida** *I* Mexico
73M4 **Rocas** *I* Brazil
74F4 **Rocha** Uruguay
7C3 **Rochdale** England
75B2 **Rochedo** Brazil
14B2 **Rochefort** France
64B2 **Rochelle** USA
54G3 **Rocher River** Canada
34B3 **Rochester** Australia
55L5 **Rochester** Canada
7E4 **Rochester** England
61E2 **Rochester** Minnesota, USA
68E1 **Rochester** New Hampshire, USA
68B1 **Rochester** New York, USA
64B2 **Rock** *R* USA
52H2 **Rockall** *I* UK
64B2 **Rockford** USA
67B2 **Rock Hill** USA
67C2 **Rockingham** USA
64A2 **Rock Island** USA
64B1 **Rockland** Michigan, USA
34B3 **Rocklands Res** Australia
67B3 **Rockledge** USA
63C3 **Rockport** USA
61D2 **Rock Rapids** USA
60B2 **Rock River** USA
60B1 **Rock Springs** Montana, USA
62B2 **Rocksprings** Texas, USA
58E2 **Rock Springs** Wyoming, USA
35B2 **Rocks Pt** New Zealand
34C3 **Rock,The** Australia
68D2 **Rockville** Connecticut, USA
64B3 **Rockville** Indiana, USA
68B3 **Rockville** Maryland, USA
65F1 **Rockwood** USA
62B1 **Rocky Ford** USA
64C1 **Rocky Island L** Canada
67C1 **Rocky Mount** USA
60B2 **Rocky Mountain Nat Pk** USA
56B1 **Rocky Mts** Canada/USA
18C2 **Rødbyhavn** Denmark
14C3 **Rodez** France
Ródhos = Rhodes
16D2 **Rodi Garganico** Italy
17E2 **Rodopi Planina** *Mts* Bulgaria
32A3 **Roebourne** Australia
47D1 **Roedtan** South Africa
13D2 **Roer** *R* Netherlands
13C2 **Roermond** Netherlands
13B2 **Roeselare** Belgium
55K3 **Roes Welcome Sd** Canada
19F2 **Rogachev** Belarus
72E6 **Rogaguado, Lago** Bolivia
63D1 **Rogers** USA
64C1 **Rogers City** USA
66D3 **Rogers L** USA
64C3 **Rogers,Mt** USA
58D2 **Rogerson** USA
47B3 **Roggeveldberge** *Mts* South Africa
58B2 **Rogue** *R* USA
42B3 **Rohri** Pakistan
42D3 **Rohtak** India
19E1 **Roja** Latvia
70C2 **Rojo, Cabo** *C* Mexico
75B3 **Rolândia** Brazil
63D1 **Rolla** USA
58D1 **Rollins** USA
Roma = Rome
34C1 **Roma** Australia
67C2 **Romain,C** USA
17F1 **Roman** Romania
52H5 **Romanche Gap** Atlantic Ocean
27F7 **Romang** *I* Indonesia
21C6 **Romania** *Republic* E Europe
67B3 **Romano,C** USA
14D2 **Romans-sur-Isère** France
27F5 **Romblon** Philippines
67A2 **Rome** Georgia, USA
16C2 **Rome** Italy
68C1 **Rome** New York, USA
65D2 **Rome** USA
14C2 **Romilly-sur-Seine** France
65D3 **Romney** USA
21E5 **Romny** Ukraine
18B1 **Rømø** *I* Denmark
14C2 **Romorantin** France
8C3 **Rona, I** Scotland
8B3 **Ronay, I** Scotland
75B1 **Roncador, Serra do** *Mts* Brazil
15A2 **Ronda** Spain
15A2 **Ronda, Sierra de** *Mts* Spain
72F6 **Rondônia** Brazil
72F6 **Rondônia** *State* Brazil
75B2 **Rondonópolis** Brazil
31B4 **Rong'an** China
31B4 **Rongchang** China
31E2 **Rongcheng** China
54H4 **Ronge, Lac la** Canada
31B4 **Rongjiang** China
31B4 **Rong Jiang** *R* China
30A1 **Rongklang Range** *Mts* Burma
12G7 **Rønne** Denmark
12H7 **Ronneby** Sweden
76F2 **Ronne Ice Shelf** Antarctica
13B2 **Ronse** Belgium
13D1 **Roodeschool** Netherlands
56C3 **Roof Butte** *Mt* USA
42D3 **Roorkee** India
13C2 **Roosendaal** Netherlands
59D2 **Roosevelt** USA
76E6 **Roosevelt I** Antarctica
61E2 **Root** *R* USA
32C2 **Roper** *R* Australia
8D2 **Rora Head** *Pt* Scotland
72F2 **Roraima** *Mt* Brazil/Guyana/Venezuela
72F3 **Roraima** *State* Brazil
12G6 **Røros** Norway
12G6 **Rorvik** Norway
19G3 **Ros'** *R* Ukraine
69Q2 **Rosalie** Dominica
66C3 **Rosamond** USA
66C3 **Rosamond L** USA
74D4 **Rosario** Argentina
73K4 **Rosário** Brazil
75A3 **Rosario** Paraguay
75A1 **Rosário Oeste** Brazil
68C2 **Roscoe** USA
14B2 **Roscoff** France
10B3 **Roscommon** Irish Republic
9C3 **Roscrea** Irish Republic
69Q2 **Roseau** Dominica
34C4 **Rosebery** Australia
60B1 **Rosebud** USA
58B2 **Roseburg** USA
63C3 **Rosenberg** USA
18C3 **Rosenheim** Germany
54H4 **Rosetown** Canada
66B1 **Roseville** USA
12G7 **Roskilde** Denmark
20E5 **Roslavl'** Russian Federation
20G4 **Roslyatino** Russian Federation
17E2 **Roşorii de Vede** Romania
35B2 **Ross** New Zealand
16D3 **Rossano** Italy
10B3 **Rossan Pt** Irish Republic
63E2 **Ross Barnett Res** USA
65D1 **Rosseau L** Canada
33E2 **Rossel** *I* Papua New Guinea
76E6 **Ross Ice Shelf** Antarctica
58B1 **Ross L** USA
9C3 **Rosslare** Irish Republic
35C2 **Ross,Mt** New Zealand
48A3 **Rosso** Mauritius
16B2 **Rosso, C** Corsica, France
7C4 **Ross-on-Wye** England
21F5 **Rossosh** Russian Federation
54E3 **Ross River** Canada
76F6 **Ross S** Antarctica
41F4 **Rostāq** Iran
18C2 **Rostock** Germany
20F4 **Rostov** Russian Federation
21F6 **Rostov-na-Donu** Russian Federation
67B2 **Roswell** Georgia, USA
62B2 **Roswell** New Mexico, USA
27H5 **Rota** *I* Pacific Ocean
27F8 **Rote** *I* Indonesia
18B2 **Rotenburg** Niedersachsen, Germany
13E2 **Rothaar-Geb** *Region* Germany
6D2 **Rothbury** England
76G3 **Rothera** *Base* Antarctica
7D3 **Rotherham** England
8C4 **Rothesay** Scotland
8D3 **Rothes-on-Spey** Scotland
34C2 **Roto** Australia
35B2 **Rotoiti,L** New Zealand
35B2 **Rotoroa,L** New Zealand
35C1 **Rotorua** New Zealand
35C1 **Rotorua,L** New Zealand
13E3 **Rottenburg** Germany
18A2 **Rotterdam** Netherlands
13E3 **Rottweil** Germany
33G2 **Rotuma** *I* Fiji
13B2 **Roubaix** France
14C2 **Rouen** France
6E3 **Rough** *Oilfield* N Sea
Roulers = Roeselare
51F6 **Round I** Mauritius
66D1 **Round Mountain** USA
34D2 **Round Mt** Australia
58E1 **Roundup** USA
8D2 **Rousay** *I* Scotland
14C3 **Roussillon** *Region* France
47D3 **Rouxville** South Africa
65D1 **Rouyn** Canada
12K5 **Rovaniemi** Finland
16C1 **Rovereto** Italy
16C1 **Rovigo** Italy
16C1 **Rovinj** Croatia
19F2 **Rovno** Ukraine
41E2 **Row'ān** Iran
34C1 **Rowena** Australia
55L3 **Rowley I** Canada
32A2 **Rowley Shoals** Australia
27F5 **Roxas** Philippines
67C1 **Roxboro** USA
35A3 **Roxburgh** New Zealand
58E1 **Roy** USA
9C3 **Royal Canal** Irish Republic
64B1 **Royale, Isle** USA
7D3 **Royal Leamington Spa** England
64C2 **Royal Oak** USA
7E4 **Royal Tunbridge Wells** England
14B2 **Royan** France
13B3 **Roye** France
7D3 **Royston** England
19E3 **Rožňava** Slovakia
13B3 **Rozoy** France
21G5 **Rtishchevo** Russian Federation
7C3 **Ruabon** Wales
51D4 **Ruaha Nat Pk** Tanzania
35C1 **Ruahine Range** *Mts* New Zealand
35C1 **Ruapehu,Mt** New Zealand
38C4 **Rub' al Khālī** *Desert* Saudi Arabia
8B3 **Rubha Hunish** *C* Scotland
8C3 **Rubha Réidh** *Pt* Scotland
75B3 **Rubinéia** Brazil
24K4 **Rubtsovsk** Russian Federation
54C3 **Ruby** USA
59C2 **Ruby Mts** USA
41G4 **Rudan** Iran
43L2 **Rudanli** India
41E2 **Rūdbār** Iran
29F2 **Rudnaya** Russian Federation
26G2 **Rudnaya Pristan'** Russian Federation
19G2 **Rudnya** Russian Federation
17E2 **Rudoka Planina** *Mt* Macedonia, Yugoslavia
24G1 **Rudol'fa, Ostrov** *I* Russian Federation
31E3 **Rudong** China
64C1 **Rudyard** USA
14C2 **Ruffec** France
51D4 **Rufiji** *R* Tanzania
74D4 **Rufino** Argentina
48A3 **Rufisque** Senegal
51C5 **Rufunsa** Zambia

7D3 **Rugby** England
60C1 **Rugby** USA
12G8 **Rügen** *I* Germany
13D2 **Ruhr** *R* Germany
31D4 **Ruijin** China
17E2 **Rujen** *Mt* Bulgaria/Macedonia, Yugoslavia
51D4 **Rukwa, L** Tanzania
8B3 **Rum** *I* Scotland
17D1 **Ruma** Serbia, Yugoslavia
41E4 **Rumāh** Saudi Arabia
50C3 **Rumbek** Sudan
69C2 **Rum Cay** *I* The Bahamas
65E2 **Rumford** USA
32C2 **Rum Jungle** Australia
29D2 **Rumoi** Japan
51D5 **Rumphi** Malawi
35B2 **Runanga** New Zealand
35C1 **Runaway,C** New Zealand
7C3 **Runcorn** England
51B5 **Rundu** Namibia
51D4 **Rungwa** Tanzania
51D4 **Rungwa** *R* Tanzania
51D4 **Rungwe** *Mt* Tanzania
39G2 **Ruoqiang** China
26D2 **Ruo Shui** *R* China
17F1 **Rupea** Romania
58D2 **Rupert** USA
55L4 **Rupert** *R* Canada
13D2 **Rur** *R* Germany
72E6 **Rurrenabaque** Bolivia
51D5 **Rusape** Zimbabwe
17F2 **Ruse** Bulgaria
64A2 **Rushville** Illinois, USA
60C2 **Rushville** Nebraska, USA
34B3 **Rushworth** Australia
63C2 **Rusk** USA
67B3 **Ruskin** USA
35B1 **Russell** New Zealand
60D3 **Russell** USA
63E2 **Russellville** Alabama, USA
63D1 **Russellville** Arkansas, USA
64B3 **Russellville** Kentucky, USA
59B3 **Russian** *R* USA
20F4 **Russian Federation** *Republic* Asia/Europe
25L2 **Russkiy, Ostrov** *I* Russian Federation
41E1 **Rustavi** Georgia
47D2 **Rustenburg** South Africa
63D2 **Ruston** USA
50C4 **Rutana** Burundi
27F7 **Ruteng** Indonesia
47E1 **Rutenga** Zimbabwe
59C3 **Ruth** USA
13E2 **Rüthen** Germany
65E2 **Rutland** USA
44E3 **Rutland** *I* Andaman Islands
42D2 **Rutog** China
Ruvu = Pangani
51E5 **Ruvuma** *R* Mozambique/Tanzania
45D4 **Ruweila, Wadi** Jordan
50D3 **Ruwenzori Range** *Mts* Uganda/Zaïre
51D5 **Ruya** *R* Zimbabwe
19D3 **Ružomberok** Slovakia
50C4 **Rwanda** *Republic* Africa
8C4 **Ryan, L** Scotland
20F5 **Ryazan'** Russian Federation
20G5 **Ryazhsk** Russian Federation
20F4 **Rybinsk** Russian Federation
20F4 **Rybinskoye Vodokhranilishche** *Res* Russian Federation
19F3 **Rybnitsa** Moldavia
7D4 **Ryde** England
7E4 **Rye** England
58C2 **Rye Patch Res** USA
21E5 **Ryl'sk** Russian Federation
21H6 **Ryn Peski** *Desert* Kazakhstan
28A3 **Ryoju** S Korea
29D3 **Ryōtsu** Japan
19F3 **Ryskany** Moldavia
26F4 **Ryūkyū Is** Japan
19E2 **Rzeszów** Poland
20E4 **Rzhev** Russian Federation

S

41F3 **Sa'ādatābād** Iran
40B5 **Saad el Aali** *Dam* Egypt
18C2 **Saale** *R* Germany
13D3 **Saar** *R* Germany
13D3 **Saarbrücken** Germany
13D3 **Saarburg** Germany
12J7 **Saaremaa** *I* Estonia
13D3 **Saarland** *State* Germany
13D3 **Saarlouis** Germany
45B3 **Saba'a** Egypt
17D2 **Šabac** Serbia, Yugoslavia
15C1 **Sabadell** Spain
29C3 **Sabae** Japan
27E6 **Sabah** *State* Malaysia
69C4 **Sabanalarga** Colombia
27C6 **Sabang** Indonesia
44C2 **Sabari** *R* India
45C2 **Sabastiya** Israel
72E7 **Sabaya** Bolivia
40C3 **Sab'Bi'ār** Syria
45D2 **Sabhā** Jordan
49D2 **Sabhā** Libya
51D6 **Sabi** *R* Zimbabwe
47E2 **Sabie** *R* South Africa
70B2 **Sabinas** Mexico
70B2 **Sabinas Hidalgo** Mexico
63C2 **Sabine** *R* USA
63D3 **Sabine L** USA
41F5 **Sabkhat Maţţī** *Salt Marsh* UAE
45B3 **Sabkhet el Bardawîl** *Lg* Egypt
55M5 **Sable,C** Canada
67B3 **Sable,C** USA
55M5 **Sable I** Canada
50E2 **Şabyā** Saudi Arabia
41G2 **Sabzevār** Iran
58C1 **Sacajawea Peak** USA
68C1 **Sacandaga Res** USA
61E2 **Sac City** USA
57D1 **Sachigo** *R* Canada
28A3 **Sach'on** S Korea
18C2 **Sachsen** *State* Germany
18C2 **Sachsen-Anhalt** *State* Germany
54F2 **Sachs Harbour** Canada
65E2 **Saco** Maine, USA
60B1 **Saco** Montana, USA
66B1 **Sacramento** USA
66B1 **Sacramento** *R* USA
59B2 **Sacramento V** USA
62A2 **Sacramento Mts** USA
50E2 **Şa'dah** Yemen
17E2 **Sadanski** Bulgaria
43H3 **Sadiya** India
15A2 **Sado** *R* Portugal
29D3 **Sado-shima** *I* Japan
42C3 **Sādri** India
Safad = Zefat
42A2 **Safed Koh** *Mts* Afghanistan
12G7 **Säffle** Sweden
59E4 **Safford** USA
7E3 **Saffron Walden** England
40C3 **Safi** Jordan
48B1 **Safi** Morocco
45D1 **Şāfitā** Syria
19G1 **Safonovo** Russian Federation
20H2 **Safonovo** Russian Federation
41E3 **Safwān** Iraq
43F3 **Saga** China
28B4 **Saga** Japan
30B1 **Sagaing** Burma
29C4 **Sagami-nada** *B* Japan
42D4 **Sāgar** India
68D2 **Sag Harbor** USA
64C2 **Saginaw** USA
64C2 **Saginaw B** USA
55M4 **Saglek B** Canada
28A3 **Sagŏ-ri** S Korea
62A1 **Saguache** USA
69B2 **Sagua de Tánamo** Cuba
69B2 **Sagua la Grande** Cuba
57F2 **Saguenay** *R* Canada
48A2 **Saguia el Hamra** *Watercourse* Morocco
15B2 **Sagunto** Spain
45D3 **Sahāb** Jordan
15A1 **Sahagún** Spain
48C2 **Sahara** *Desert* N Africa
42D3 **Sahāranpur** India
43K1 **Sahaswan** India
45B4 **Saheira, Wadi el** Egypt
42C2 **Sahiwal** Pakistan
41D3 **Şaḩrā al Hijārah** *Desert Region* Iraq
40B4 **Sahra esh Sharqiya** *Desert Region* Egypt
70B2 **Sahuayo** Mexico
45D1 **Sahyūn** *Hist Site* Syria
32D1 **Saibai I** Australia
Saïda = Sidon
41G4 **Sa'īdābad** Iran
15B2 **Saïdia** Morocco
43F3 **Saidpur** Bangladesh
42C2 **Saidu** Pakistan
29B3 **Saigō** Japan
Saigon = Ho Chi Minh City
43G4 **Saiha** India
26E2 **Saihan Tal** China
29B4 **Saijo** Japan
28C4 **Saiki** Japan
12K6 **Saimaa** *L* Finland
8D4 **St Abb's Head** *Pt* Scotland
7D4 **St Albans** England
65E2 **St Albans** Vermont, USA
64C3 **St Albans** West Virginia, USA
7C4 **St Albans Head** *C* England
13B2 **St Amand-les-Eaux** France
14C2 **St Amand-Mont Rond** France
67A3 **St Andrew B** USA
8D3 **St Andrews** Scotland
67B2 **St Andrew Sd** USA
61D1 **Ste Anne** Canada
65E1 **Ste Anne de Beaupré** Canada
69H1 **St Ann's Bay** Jamaica
55N4 **St Anthony** Canada
58D2 **St Anthony** USA
34B3 **St Arnaud** Australia
51E6 **St Augustin, Baie de** *B* Madagascar
67B3 **St Augustine** USA
7B4 **St Austell** England
7B4 **St Austell Bay** England
13D3 **St-Avold** France
6C2 **St Bees Head** *Pt* England
7B4 **St Brides B** Wales
14B2 **St-Brieuc** France
65D2 **St Catharines** Canada
69M2 **St Catherine,Mt** Grenada
67B2 **St Catherines I** USA
7D4 **St Catherines Pt** England
14C2 **St-Chamond** France
58D2 **St Charles** Idaho, USA
61E3 **St Charles** Missouri, USA
64C2 **St Clair** USA
64C2 **St Clair,L** Canada/USA
64C2 **St Clair Shores** USA
14D2 **St Claude** France
61E1 **St Cloud** USA
69E3 **St Croix** *I* Caribbean Sea
65F1 **St Croix** *R* Canada/USA
64A1 **St Croix** *R* USA
64A1 **St Croix Falls** USA
7B4 **St Davids Head** *Pt* Wales
13B3 **St Denis** France
51F6 **St Denis** Réunion
13D3 **St-Dié** France
13C3 **St-Dizier** France
54D3 **St Elias, Mt** USA
54E3 **St Elias Mts** Canada
14B2 **Saintes** France
14C2 **St-Étienne** France
65E1 **St-Félicien** Canada
16B2 **St Florent, G de** Corsica, France
13B3 **St-Florentin** France
60C3 **St Francis** USA
63D1 **St Francis** *R* USA
47C3 **St Francis B** South Africa
47C3 **St Francis,C** South Africa
16B1 **St Gallen** Switzerland
14C3 **St-Gaudens** France
34C1 **St George** Australia
67B2 **St George** South Carolina, USA
59D3 **St George** Utah, USA
67B3 **St George I** Florida, USA
13E3 **St Georgen im Schwarzwald** Germany
58B2 **St George,Pt** USA
65E1 **St-Georges** Canada
69M2 **St George's** Grenada
7A4 **St George's Chan** Irish Republic/Wales
33E1 **St George's Chan** Papua New Guinea
16B1 **St Gotthard** *Pass* Switzerland
7B4 **St Govans Head** *Pt* Wales
66A1 **St Helena** USA
52H5 **St Helena** *I* Atlantic Ocean
47B3 **St Helena B** South Africa
67B2 **St Helena Sd** USA
34C4 **St Helens** Australia
7C3 **St Helens** England
58B1 **St Helens** USA
58B1 **St Helens,Mt** USA
14B2 **St Helier** Jersey, Channel Islands
13C2 **St-Hubert** Belgium
55L5 **St-Hyacinthe** Canada
64C1 **St Ignace** USA
64B1 **St Ignace I** Canada
7D3 **St Ives** Cambs, England
7B4 **St Ives** Cornwall, England
61E2 **St James** Minnesota, USA
63D1 **St James** Missouri, USA
54E4 **St James, C** Canada
65E1 **St-Jean** Canada
14B2 **St Jean-d'Angely** France
65E1 **St-Jean,L** Canada
65E1 **St-Jérôme** Canada
58C1 **St Joe** *R* USA
55M5 **Saint John** Canada
65F1 **St John** *R* Canada/USA
59E4 **St Johns** Arizona, USA
55N5 **St John's** Canada
64C2 **St Johns** Michigan, USA
67B3 **St Johns** *R* USA
65E2 **St Johnsbury** USA
6C2 **St John's Chapel** England
9D2 **St John's** *Pt* Northern Ireland
68C1 **St Johnsville** USA
65E1 **St-Joseph** Canada
63D2 **St Joseph** Louisiana, USA
64B2 **St Joseph** Michigan, USA
61E3 **St Joseph** Missouri, USA
69L1 **St Joseph** Trinidad
64C2 **St Joseph** *R* USA
64C1 **St Joseph I** Canada
63C3 **St Joseph I** USA
55J4 **St Joseph,L** Canada
14C2 **St-Junien** France
13B3 **St-Just-en-Chaussée** France
8A3 **St Kilda** *I* Scotland
69E3 **St Kitts-Nevis** *Is* Caribbean Sea
55M5 **St Lawrence** *R* Canada
55M5 **St Lawrence,G of** Canada
54B3 **St Lawrence I** USA
65D2 **St Lawrence Seaway** Canada/USA
65F1 **St Leonard** Canada
7E4 **St Leonards** England
14B2 **St-Lô** France
48A3 **St-Louis** Senegal
64A3 **St Louis** USA
13D4 **St-Loup-sur-Semouse** France
69E4 **St Lucia** *I* Caribbean Sea
47E2 **St Lucia,L** South Africa
8E1 **St Magnus B** Scotland
14B2 **St-Malo** France
14B2 **St-Malo, Golfe de** *B* France
13D3 **Ste-Marie-aux-Mines** France
58C1 **St Maries** USA
69E3 **St Martin** *I* Caribbean Sea
32D1 **St Mary,Mt** Papua New Guinea
34A2 **St Mary Peak** *Mt* Australia
34C4 **St Marys** Australia
65D2 **St Marys** USA
7A5 **St Marys** *I* England
67B2 **St Marys** *R* USA
32E1 **Saint Mathias Group** *Is* Papua New Guinea
65E1 **St Maurice** *R* Canada
13C3 **Ste-Menehould** France
54B3 **St Michael** USA
68B3 **St Michaels** USA
13C3 **St-Mihiel** France
16B1 **St Moritz** Switzerland
14B2 **St-Nazaire** France
7D3 **St Neots** England
13C2 **St-Niklaas** Belgium
13B2 **St-Omer** France
65F1 **St-Pascal** Canada
54G4 **St Paul** Canada
61E2 **St Paul** Minnesota, USA
60D2 **St Paul** Nebraska, USA
36E6 **St Paul** *I* Indian Ocean
48A4 **St Paul** *R* Liberia
61E2 **St Peter** USA
20E4 **St Petersburg** Russian Federation
67B3 **St Petersburg** USA
55N5 **St Pierre** *I* France
65E1 **St Pierre,L** Canada
13B2 **St-Pol-sur-Ternoise** France
18D3 **St Pölten** Austria
13B3 **St-Quentin** France
14D3 **St Raphaël** France
65F1 **St-Siméon** Canada
67B2 **St Simons I** USA
67B2 **St Stephen** USA
64C2 **St Thomas** Canada
14D3 **St Tropez** France
13C2 **St Truiden** Belgium
61D1 **St Vincent** USA
69E4 **St Vincent and The Grenadines** *Is* Caribbean Sea
34A2 **St Vincent,G** Australia
13D2 **St-Vith** Germany
13D3 **St Wendel** Germany
27H5 **Saipan** *I* Pacific Ocean
42B2 **Saiydabad** Afghanistan
72E7 **Sajama** *Mt* Bolivia
47C3 **Sak** *R* South Africa
29D4 **Sakai** Japan
29B4 **Sakaidi** Japan
28B3 **Sakaiminato** Japan
40D4 **Sakākah** Saudi Arabia
60C1 **Sakakawea,L** USA
57F1 **Sakami,L** Canada
51C5 **Sakania** Zaïre
51E6 **Sakaraha** Madagascar
21E7 **Sakarya** *R* Turkey
19E1 **Sakasleja** Latvia
29D3 **Sakata** Japan
48C4 **Sakété** Benin
26H1 **Sakhalin** *I* Russian Federation
26F4 **Sakishima guntō** *Is* Japan
47C3 **Sakrivier** South Africa
48A4 **Sal** *I* Cape Verde
21G6 **Sal** *R* Russian Federation
12H7 **Sala** Sweden
59C4 **Salada, Laguna** *L* Mexico
74D3 **Salado** *R* Sante Fe, Argentina
48B4 **Salaga** Ghana
30C3 **Sala Hintoun** Cambodia
50B2 **Salal** Chad
38D4 **Şalālah** Oman
15A1 **Salamanca** Spain
68A1 **Salamanca** USA
50B3 **Salamat** *R* Chad
27H7 **Salamaua** Papua New Guinea
45B1 **Salamis** *Hist Site* Cyprus
12H5 **Salangen** Norway
74C2 **Salar de Arizaro** *Salt Pan* Argentina
74C2 **Salar de Atacama** *Salt Pan* Chile
72E7 **Salar de Coipasa** *Salt Pan* Bolivia
72E8 **Salar de Uyuni** *Salt Pan* Bolivia
20K5 **Salavat** Russian Federation
32C1 **Salawati** *I* Indonesia
37O6 **Sala y Gómez** *I* Pacific Ocean
14C2 **Salbris** France
47B3 **Saldanha** South Africa
19E1 **Saldus** Latvia
34C3 **Sale** Australia
20M2 **Salekhard** Russian Federation
64B3 **Salem** Illinois, USA
44B3 **Salem** India
68E1 **Salem** Massachusetts, USA
68C3 **Salem** New Jersey, USA
68D1 **Salem** New York, USA
58B2 **Salem** Oregon, USA
64C3 **Salem** Virginia, USA
12G6 **Sälen** Sweden
16C2 **Salerno** Italy
7C3 **Salford** England
17D1 **Salgót** Hungary
19D3 **Salgótarján** Hungary
73L5 **Salgueiro** Brazil
60B3 **Salida** USA
17F3 **Salihli** Turkey
51D5 **Salima** Malawi
61D3 **Salina** Kansas, USA
59D3 **Salina** Utah, USA
16C3 **Salina** *I* Italy
70C3 **Salina Cruz** Mexico
75D2 **Salinas** Brazil
66B2 **Salinas** USA
66B2 **Salinas** *R* USA
15C2 **Salinas, Cabo de** *C* Spain
74D3 **Salinas Grandes** *Salt Pans* Argentina
62A2 **Salinas Peak** *Mt* USA
63D2 **Saline** *R* Arkansas, USA
60C3 **Saline** *R* Kansas, USA
69M2 **Salines,Pt** Grenada
66D2 **Saline V** USA
73J4 **Salinópolis** Brazil
Salisbury = Harare
7D4 **Salisbury** England
65D3 **Salisbury** Maryland, USA
67B1 **Salisbury** North Carolina, USA
55L3 **Salisbury I** Canada
7D4 **Salisbury Plain** England
45D2 **Şalkhad** Syria
12K5 **Salla** Finland
63D1 **Sallisaw** USA
55L3 **Salluit** Canada
43E3 **Sallyana** Nepal
41D2 **Salmas** Iran
12L6 **Salmi** Russian Federation
58C1 **Salmo** Canada
58D1 **Salmon** USA
58C1 **Salmon** *R* USA
54G4 **Salmon Arm** Canada
58C1 **Salmon River Mts** USA
12J6 **Salo** Finland
14D3 **Salon-de-Provence** France
Salonica = Thessaloníki
17E1 **Salonta** Romania
12K6 **Salpausselkä** *Region* Finland
21G6 **Sal'sk** Russian Federation
45C2 **Salt** Jordan
47C3 **Salt** *R* South Africa
59D4 **Salt** *R* USA
74C2 **Salta** Argentina
74C2 **Salta** *State* Argentina
7B4 **Saltash** England
9C3 **Saltee, I** Irish Republic
70B2 **Saltillo** Mexico
58D2 **Salt Lake City** USA
72D3 **Salto Angostura** *Waterfall* Colombia
75E2 **Salto da Divisa** Brazil
75B3 **Salto das Sete Quedas** Brazil
72F2 **Salto del Angel** *Waterfall* Venezuela
74E2 **Salto del Guaíra** *Waterfall* Brazil
72D4 **Salto Grande** *Waterfall* Colombia
59C4 **Salton S** USA
75B4 **Saltos do Iguaçu** *Waterfall* Argentina
74E4 **Salto Tacuarembó** Uruguay
42C2 **Salt Range** *Mts* Pakistan
69H2 **Salt River** Jamaica
67B2 **Saluda** USA

44C2 Sālūr India
73L6 Salvador Brazil
63D3 Salvador,L USA
41F5 Salwah Qatar
30B1 Salween R Burma
21H8 Sal'yany Azerbaijan
64C3 Salyersville USA
18C3 Salzburg Austria
18C2 Salzgitter Germany
18C2 Salzwedel Germany
26C1 Samagaltay Russian Federation
69D3 Samaná Dominican Republic
40C2 Samandağı Turkey
42B1 Samangan Afghanistan
29D2 Samani Japan
45A3 Samannûd Egypt
27F5 Samar I Philippines
20J5 Samara Russian Federation
32E2 Samarai Papua New Guinea
27E7 Samarinda Indonesia
38E2 Samarkand Uzbekistan
41D3 Sāmarrā' Iraq
43E4 Sambalpur India
27D6 Sambas Indonesia
51F5 Sambava Madagascar
42D3 Sambhal India
19E3 Sambor Ukraine
13B2 Sambre R France
28B3 Samch'ŏk S Korea
28A4 Samch'ŏnp'o S Korea
28A3 Samdŭng N Korea
50D4 Same Tanzania
51C5 Samfya Zambia
30B1 Samka Burma
30C1 Sam Neua Laos
33H2 Samoan Is Pacific Ocean
17F3 Sámos I Greece
17F2 Samothráki I Greece
27E7 Sampit Indonesia
63D2 Sam Rayburn Res USA
30C3 Samrong Cambodia
18C1 Samsø I Denmark
28A2 Samsu N Korea
40C1 Samsun Turkey
48B3 San Mali
30D3 San R Cambodia
19E2 San R Poland
50E2 San'ā Yemen
50B3 Sanaga R Cameroon
74C4 San Agustín Argentina
52D6 San Ambrosia, Isla Pacific Ocean
41E2 Sanandaj Iran
66B1 San Andreas USA
69A4 San Andres, Isla de Caribbean Sea
62A2 San Andres Mts USA
70C3 San Andrés Tuxtla Mexico
62B2 San Angelo USA
16B3 San Antioco Sardinia, Italy
16B3 San Antioco I Sardinia, Italy
56B4 San Antonia, Pt Mexico
74B4 San Antonio Chile
62A2 San Antonio New Mexico, USA
62C3 San Antonio Texas, USA
66B2 San Antonio R California, USA
63C3 San Antonio R Texas, USA
15C2 San Antonio Abad Spain
69A2 San Antonio, Cabo C Cuba
62B2 San Antonio de Bravo Mexico
69A2 San Antonio de los Banos Cuba
66D3 San Antonio,Mt USA
74D6 San Antonio Oeste Argentina
66B3 San Antonio Res USA
66B2 San Ardo USA
42D4 Sanāwad India
70A3 San Benedicto I Mexico
63C3 San Benito USA
66B2 San Benito R USA
66B2 San Benito Mt USA
66D3 San Bernardino USA
74B4 San Bernardo Chile
59C4 San Bernardo Mts USA
67A3 San Blas,C USA
70E4 San Blas, Puerta Pt Panama
74E3 San Borja Brazil
74B5 San Carlos Chile
72B1 San Carlos Nicaragua
59D4 San Carlos USA
74B6 San Carlos de Bariloche Argentina
20H4 Sanchursk Russian Federation
66D4 San Clemente USA
59C4 San Clemente I USA
70C3 San Cristóbal Mexico
72D2 San Cristóbal Venezuela
33F2 San Cristobal I Solomon Islands
70E2 Sancti Spíritus Cuba
14C2 Sancy, Puy de Mt France
47D1 Sand R South Africa
8C4 Sanda, I Scotland
27E6 Sandakan Malaysia
8D2 Sanday I Scotland
62B2 Sanderson USA
7E4 Sandgate England
59C4 San Diego USA
74C8 San Diego, Cabo Argentina
40B2 Sandıklı Turkey
43E3 Sandīla India
12F7 Sandnes Norway
12G5 Sandnessjøen Norway
51C4 Sandoa Zaïre
19E2 Sandomierz Poland
43G5 Sandoway Burma
7D4 Sandown England
12D3 Sandoy I Faeroes
58C1 Sandpoint USA
63C1 Sand Springs USA
32A3 Sandstone Australia
61E1 Sandstone USA
31C4 Sandu China
64C2 Sandusky USA
12H6 Sandviken Sweden
68E2 Sandwich USA
55J4 Sandy L Canada
75A3 San Estanislao Paraguay
56B3 San Felipe Baja Cal, Mexico
74B4 San Felipe Chile
69D4 San Felipe Venezuela
15C1 San Felíu de Guixols Spain
52D6 San Felix, Isla Pacific Ocean
74B4 San Fernando Chile
27F5 San Fernando Philippines
15A2 San Fernando Spain
69L2 San Fernando Trinidad
66C3 San Fernando USA
72E2 San Fernando Venezuela
67B3 Sanford Florida, USA
65E2 Sanford Maine, USA
67C1 Sanford N Carolina, USA
57E4 Sanford USA
54D3 Sanford, Mt USA
74D4 San Francisco Argentina
69C3 San Francisco Dominican Republic
66A2 San Francisco USA
66A2 San Francisco B USA
70B2 San Francisco del Oro Mexico
66D3 San Gabriel Mts USA
42C5 Sangamner India
64B3 Sangamon R USA
25O3 Sangar Russian Federation
44B2 Sangāreddi India
66C2 Sanger USA
31C2 Sanggan He R China
27E6 Sanggau Indonesia
50B3 Sangha R Congo
42B3 Sanghar Pakistan
27F6 Sangir I Indonesia
27F6 Sangir, Kepulauan Is Indonesia
30B3 Sangkhla Buri Thailand
27E6 Sangkulirang Indonesia
44A2 Sāngli India
50B3 Sangmélima Cameroon
56B3 San Gorgonio Mt USA
62A1 Sangre de Cristo Mts USA
66A2 San Gregorio USA
42D2 Sangrūr India
47E1 Sangutane R Mozambique
74E3 San Ignacio Argentina
72D2 San Jacinto Colombia
59C4 San Jacinto Peak Mt USA
28A2 Sanjiangkou China
29D3 Sanjō Japan
74H2 San João del Rei Brazil
66B2 San Joaquin R USA
66B2 San Joaquin Valley USA
62B1 San Jon USA
74C7 San Jorge, Golfo G Argentina
15C1 San Jorge, Golfo de G Spain
72B1 San José Costa Rica
70C3 San José Guatemala
66B2 San Jose USA
56B4 San José I Mexico
72F7 San José de Chiquitos Bolivia
56C4 San José del Cabo Mexico
74G2 San José do Rio Prêto Brazil
70B2 San Joseé del Cabo Mexico
28A3 Sanju S Korea
74C4 San Juan Argentina
69D3 San Juan Puerto Rico
69L1 San Juan Trinidad
72E2 San Juan Venezuela
69B2 San Juan Mt Cuba
66B3 San Juan R California, USA
70D3 San Juan R Costa Rica/Nicaragua
59D3 San Juan R Utah, USA
74C4 San Juan State Argentina
74E3 San Juan Bautista Paraguay
66B2 San Juan Bautista USA
70D3 San Juan del Norte Nicaragua
69D4 San Juan de los Cayos Venezuela
70D3 San Juan del Sur Nicaragua
58B1 San Juan Is USA
62A1 San Juan Mts USA
74C7 San Julián Argentina
50C4 Sankuru R Zaïre
66A2 San Leandro USA
40C2 Sanliurfa Turkey
72C3 San Lorenzo Colombia
72B4 San Lorenzo, Cabo C Ecuador
15B1 San Lorenzo de Escorial Spain
66B2 San Lucas USA
74C4 San Luis Argentina
59D4 San Luis USA
74C4 San Luis State Argentina
66B2 San Luis Canal USA
66B3 San Luis Obispo USA
66B3 San Luis Obispo B USA
70B2 San Luis Potosí Mexico
66B2 San Luis Res USA
16B3 Sanluri Sardinia, Italy
72E2 San Maigualida Mts Venezuela
63C3 San Marcos USA
76G3 San Martin Base Antarctica
74B7 San Martin, Lago Argentina/Chile
66A2 San Mateo USA
73G7 San Matías Bolivia
74D6 San Matías, Golfo G Argentina
31C3 Sanmenxia China
70D3 San Miguel El Salvador
66B3 San Miguel USA
66B3 San Miguel I USA
74C3 San Miguel de Tucumán Argentina
74F3 San Miguel d'Oeste Brazil
31D4 Sanming China
74D4 San Nicolas Argentina
56B3 San Nicolas I USA
47D2 Sannieshof South Africa
48B4 Sanniquellie Liberia
19E3 Sanok Poland
69B5 San Onofore Colombia
66D4 San Onofre USA
27F5 San Pablo Philippines
66A1 San Pablo B USA
48B4 San Pédro Ivory Coast
74D2 San Pedro Jujuy, Argentina
74E2 San Pedro Paraguay
59D4 San Pedro R USA
66C4 San Pedro Chan USA
56C4 San Pedro de los Colonias Mexico
70D3 San Pedro Sula Honduras
16B3 San Pietro I Sardinia, Italy
8D4 Sanquar Scotland
70A1 San Quintin Mexico
74C4 San Rafael Argentina
66A2 San Rafael USA
66C3 San Rafael Mts USA
16B2 San Remo Italy
62C2 San Saba R USA
71B2 San Salvador El Salvador
69C2 San Salvador I The Bahamas
74C2 San Salvador de Jujuy Argentina
15B1 San Sebastián Spain
16D2 San Severo Italy
66B3 San Simeon USA
72E7 Santa Ana Bolivia
70C3 Santa Ana Guatemala
66D4 Santa Ana USA
66D4 Santa Ana Mts USA
62C2 Santa Anna USA
70B2 Santa Barbara Mexico
66C3 Santa Barbara USA
66C4 Santa Barbara I USA
66B3 Santa Barbara Chan USA
66C3 Santa Barbara Res USA
66C4 Santa Catalina I USA
66C4 Santa Catalina,G of USA
74F3 Santa Catarina State Brazil
74G3 Santa Catarina, Isla de Brazil
69B2 Santa Clara Cuba
66B2 Santa Clara USA
66C3 Santa Clara R USA
74C8 Santa Cruz Argentina
72F7 Santa Cruz Bolivia
27F5 Santa Cruz Philippines
66A2 Santa Cruz USA
66C4 Santa Cruz I USA
59D4 Santa Cruz R USA
74B7 Santa Cruz State Argentina
75E2 Santa Cruz Cabrália Brazil
66C3 Santa Cruz Chan USA
48A2 Santa Cruz de la Palma Canary Islands
69B2 Santa Cruz del Sur Cuba
48A2 Santa Cruz de Tenerife Canary Islands
51C5 Santa Cruz do Cuando Angola
75C3 Santa Cruz do Rio Pardo Brazil
33F2 Santa Cruz Is Solomon Islands
66A2 Santa Cruz Mts USA
72F3 Santa Elena Venezuela
74D4 Santa Fe Argentina
62A1 Santa Fe USA
74D3 Santa Fe State Argentina
75B2 Santa Helena de Goiás Brazil
31B3 Santai China
74B8 Santa Inés I Chile
33E1 Santa Isabel I Solomon Islands
66B2 Santa Lucia Range Mts USA
48A4 Santa Luzia I Cape Verde
66B3 Santa Margarita USA
66D4 Santa Margarita R USA
70A2 Santa Margarita, Isla Mexico
74F3 Santa Maria Brazil
66B3 Santa Maria USA
48A1 Santa Maria I Azores
62A2 Santa María R Chihuahua, Mexico
47E2 Santa Maria, Cabo de C Mozambique
75D1 Santa Maria da Vitória Brazil
17D3 Santa Maria di Leuca, Capo C Italy
62A2 Santa María Laguna de L Mexico
69C4 Santa Marta Colombia
72D1 Santa Marta, Sierra Nevada de Mts Colombia
66C3 Santa Monica USA
66C4 Santa Monica B USA
75D1 Santana Brazil
74E4 Santana do Livramento Brazil
72C3 Santander Colombia
15B1 Santander Spain
15C2 Santañy Spain
66C3 Santa Paula USA
73K4 Santa Quitéria Brazil
73H4 Santarém Brazil
15A2 Santarém Portugal
75B2 Santa Rita do Araguaia Brazil
74D5 Santa Rosa Argentina
66A1 Santa Rosa California, USA
70D3 Santa Rosa Honduras
62B2 Santa Rosa New Mexico, USA
66B3 Santa Rosa I USA
70A2 Santa Rosalía Mexico
58C2 Santa Rosa Range Mts USA
73L5 Santa Talhada Brazil
75D2 Santa Teresa Brazil
16B2 Santa Teresa di Gallura Sardinia, Italy
66B3 Santa Ynez R USA
66B3 Santa Ynez Mts USA
67C2 Santee R USA
74B4 Santiago Chile
69C3 Santiago Dominican Republic
72B2 Santiago Panama
72C4 Santiago R Peru
15A1 Santiago de Compostela Spain
69B2 Santiago de Cuba Cuba
74D3 Santiago del Estero Argentina
74D3 Santiago del Estero State Argentina
66D4 Santiago Peak Mt USA
33F2 Santo Vanuatu
75C3 Santo Amaro, Ilha Brazil
75B3 Santo Anastatácio Brazil
74F3 Santo Angelo Brazil
48A4 Santo Antão I Cape Verde
75B3 Santo Antônio da Platina Brazil
75E1 Santo Antônio de Jesus Brazil
75A2 Santo Antônio do Leverger Brazil
69D3 Santo Domingo Dominican Republic
75C3 Santos Brazil
75D3 Santos Dumont Brazil
59C4 Santo Tomas Mexico
74E3 Santo Tomé Argentina
74B7 San Valentin Mt Chile
16C3 San Vito, C Sicily, Italy
28B2 Sanyuanpu China
51B4 Sanza Pomba Angola
75C3 São Carlos Brazil
75C1 São Domingos Brazil
73H5 São Félix Mato Grosso, Brazil
75D3 São Fidélis Brazil
75D2 São Francisco Brazil
73L5 São Francisco R Brazil
74G3 São Francisco do Sul Brazil
75C4 São Francisco, Ilha de Brazil
75C2 São Gotardo Brazil
51D4 Sao Hill Tanzania
75A2 São Jerônimo, Serra de Mts Brazil
75D3 São João da Barra Brazil
75C3 São João da Boa Vista Brazil
75C1 São João d'Aliança Brazil
75D2 São João da Ponte Brazil
75D3 São João del Rei Brazil
75D2 São João do Paraíso Brazil
75C3 São Joaquim da Barra Brazil
48A1 São Jorge I Azores
75C3 São José do Rio Prêto Brazil
75C3 São José dos Campos Brazil
75C4 São José dos Pinhais Brazil
75A2 São Lourenço R Brazil
73K4 São Luís Brazil
75C2 São Marcos R Brazil
73K4 São Marcos, Baia de B Brazil
75D2 São Maria do Suaçui Brazil
75E2 São Mateus Brazil
75D2 São Mateus R Brazil
48A1 São Miguel I Azores
75B1 São Miguel de Araguaia Brazil
14C2 Saône R France
48A4 São Nicolau I Cape Verde
75D1 São Onofre R Brazil
75C3 São Paulo Brazil
75B3 São Paulo State Brazil
71H3 São Pedro e São Paulo Is Atlantic Ocean
73K5 São Raimundo Nonato Brazil
75C2 São Romão Brazil
75C3 São Sebastia do Paraíso Brazil
75C3 São Sebastião, Ilha de Brazil
75B2 São Simão,Barragem de Brazil
75B2 São Simão Goias, Brazil
75C3 São Simão São Paulo, Brazil
48A4 São Tiago I Cape Verde
48C4 São Tomé I W Africa
48C4 Sao Tome and Principe Republic W Africa
75D3 São Tomé, Cabo de C Brazil
48B2 Saoura Watercourse Algeria
75A1 Saouriuiná R Brazil
75C3 São Vicente Brazil
15A2 São Vicente, Cabo de C Portugal
48A4 São Vincente I Cape Verde
17F2 Sápai Greece
48C4 Sapele Nigeria
29E2 Sapporo Japan
16D2 Sapri Italy
63C1 Sapulpa USA
41E2 Saqqez Iran
21H8 Sarāb Iran
17D2 Sarajevo Bosnia-Herzegovina
21K5 Saraktash Russian Federation
25K4 Sarala Russian Federation
65E2 Saranac Lake USA
17E3 Sarandë Albania
20L3 Saranpaul' Russian Federation
20H5 Saransk Russian Federation
20J4 Sarapul Russian Federation
67B3 Sarasota USA
17F1 Sărat Romania
19F3 Sarata Ukraine
60B2 Saratoga USA
68D1 Saratoga Springs USA

21H5 **Saratov** Russian Federation
21H5 **Saratovskoye Vodokhranilishche** *Res* Russian Federation
30D2 **Saravane** Laos
27E6 **Sarawak** *State* Malaysia
40A2 **Saraykoy** Turkey
49D2 **Sardalas** Libya
41E2 **Sar Dasht** Iran
Sardegna = Sardinia
16B2 **Sardinia** *I* Medit Sea
12H5 **Sarektjåkkå** *Mt* Sweden
42C2 **Sargodha** Pakistan
50B3 **Sarh** Chad
48B1 **Sarhro, Jbel** *Mt* Morocco
41F2 **Sārī** Iran
45C2 **Sarida** *R* Israel
27H5 **Sarigan** *I* Pacific Ocean
40D1 **Sarıkamış** Turkey
32D3 **Sarina** Australia
42B1 **Sar-i-Pul** Afghanistan
49E2 **Sarīr** Libya
49D2 **Sarir Tibesti** *Desert* Libya
28B3 **Sariwŏn** N Korea
14B2 **Sark** *I* Channel Islands
40C2 **Şarkışla** Turkey
27G7 **Sarmi** Indonesia
74C7 **Sarmiento** Argentina
12G6 **Särna** Sweden
64C2 **Sarnia** Canada
19F2 **Sarny** Ukraine
42B2 **Sarobi** Afghanistan
17E3 **Saronikós Kólpos** *G* Greece
17F2 **Saros Körfezi** *B* Turkey
20M2 **Saroto** Russian Federation
12G7 **Sarpsborg** Norway
55N2 **Sarqaq** Greenland
13D3 **Sarralbe** France
13D3 **Sarrebourg** France
13D3 **Sarreguemines** France
13D3 **Sarre-Union** France
15B1 **Sarrion** Spain
42B3 **Sartanahu** Pakistan
16B2 **Sartène** Corsica, France
14B2 **Sarthe** *R* France
45D1 **Sārūt** *R* Syria
21J6 **Sarykamys** Kazakhstan
24H5 **Sarysu** *R* Kazakhstan
43E4 **Sasarām** India
28B4 **Sasebo** Japan
54H4 **Saskatchewan** *Province* Canada
54H4 **Saskatchewan** *R* Canada
54H4 **Saskatoon** Canada
25N2 **Saskylakh** Russian Federation
47D2 **Sasolburg** South Africa
20G5 **Sasovo** Russian Federation
48B4 **Sassandra** Ivory Coast
48B4 **Sassandra** *R* Ivory Coast
16B2 **Sassari** Sardinia, Italy
18C2 **Sassnitz** Germany
28A4 **Sasuna** Japan
44A2 **Sātāra** India
54G2 **Satellite B** Canada
12H6 **Säter** Sweden
67B2 **Satilla** *R* USA
20K4 **Satka** Russian Federation
42D2 **Satluj** *R* India
43E4 **Satna** India
42C4 **Sātpura Range** *Mts* India
17E1 **Satu Mare** Romania
12B1 **Sauðárkrókur** Iceland
12F7 **Sauda** Norway
38C3 **Saudi Arabia** *Kingdom* Arabian Pen
13D3 **Sauer** *R* Germany/ Luxembourg
13D2 **Sauerland** *Region* Germany
64B2 **Saugatuck** USA
68D1 **Saugerties** USA
61E1 **Sauk Center** USA
64B2 **Sauk City** USA
64C1 **Sault Ste Marie** Canada
64C1 **Sault Ste Marie** USA
27G7 **Saumlaki** Indonesia
14B2 **Saumur** France
51C4 **Saurimo** Angola
69M2 **Sauteurs** Grenada
17D2 **Sava** *R* Serbia, Yugoslavia
33H2 **Savai'i** *I* Western Samoa
48C4 **Savalou** Benin
67B2 **Savannah** Georgia, USA
63E1 **Savannah** Tennessee, USA
67B2 **Savannah** *R* USA
30C2 **Savannakhet** Laos
69G1 **Savanna la Mar** Jamaica
55J4 **Savant Lake** Canada
48C4 **Savé** Benin
51D6 **Save** *R* Mozambique
41F3 **Sāveh** Iran
13D3 **Saverne** France
13B3 **Savigny** France
20G3 **Savinskiy** Russian Federation
14D2 **Savoie** *Region* France
16B2 **Savona** Italy
12K6 **Savonlinna** Finland
54A3 **Savoonga** USA
32B2 **Savu** *I* Indonesia
12K5 **Savukoski** Finland
27F7 **Savu S** Indonesia
30A1 **Saw** Burma
42D3 **Sawai Mādhopur** India
30C2 **Sawankhalok** Thailand
29D3 **Sawara** Japan
60B3 **Sawatch Mts** USA
49D2 **Sawdā', Jabal as** *Mts* Libya
58C2 **Sawtooth Range** *Mts* USA
27F8 **Sawu** *I* Indonesia
7E3 **Saxmundham** England
68A2 **Saxton** USA
48C3 **Say** Niger
42B1 **Sayghan** Afghanistan
38D4 **Sayḩūt** Yemen
21H6 **Saykhin** Kazakhstan
26D2 **Saynshand** Mongolia
62C1 **Sayre** Oklahoma, USA
68B2 **Sayre** Pennsylvania, USA
21J7 **Say-Utes** Kazakhstan
68D2 **Sayville** USA
18C3 **Sázava** *R* Czech Republic
15C2 **Sbisseb** *R* Algeria
6C2 **Scafell Pike** *Mt* England
8E1 **Scalloway** Scotland
8C3 **Scalpay, I** Scotland
8D2 **Scapa Flow** *Sd* Scotland
65D2 **Scarborough** Canada
6D2 **Scarborough** England
69K1 **Scarborough** Tobago
8B2 **Scarp** *I* Scotland
16B1 **Schaffhausen** Switzerland
18C3 **Schärding** Austria
13E1 **Scharhörn** *I* Germany
13D2 **Scharteberg** *Mt* Germany
55M4 **Schefferville** Canada
13B2 **Schelde** *R* Belgium
59D3 **Schell Creek Range** *Mts* USA
68D1 **Schenectady** USA
62C3 **Schertz** USA
13C2 **Schiedam** Netherlands
13D1 **Schiermonnikoog** *I* Netherlands
13D2 **Schleiden** Germany
18B2 **Schleswig** Germany
18B2 **Schleswig Holstein** *State* Germany
68C1 **Schoharie** USA
32D1 **Schouten Is** Papua New Guinea
13E3 **Schramberg** Germany
55K5 **Schreiber** Canada
9B4 **Schull** Irish Republic
59C3 **Schurz** USA
68C2 **Schuylkill** *R* USA
68B2 **Schuylkill Haven** USA
18B3 **Schwabische Alb** *Upland* Germany
27E7 **Schwaner, Pegunungan** *Mts* Indonesia
47B2 **Schwarzrand** *Mts* Namibia
13E3 **Schwarzwald** *Mts* Germany
18C2 **Schweinfurt** Germany
47D2 **Schweizer Reneke** South Africa
18C2 **Schwerin** Germany
16B1 **Schwyz** Switzerland
16C3 **Sciacca** Italy
7A5 **Scilly, Isles of** England
64C3 **Scioto** *R* USA
60B1 **Scobey** USA
34D2 **Scone** Australia
55Q2 **Scoresby Sd** Greenland
52F7 **Scotia Sea** Atlantic Ocean
8C3 **Scotland** U K
76F7 **Scott** *Base* Antarctica
47E3 **Scottburgh** South Africa
62B1 **Scott City** USA
76G6 **Scott I** Antarctica
55L2 **Scott Inlet** *B* Canada
58B2 **Scott,Mt** USA
32B2 **Scott Reef** Timor Sea
60C2 **Scottsbluff** USA
67A2 **Scottsboro** USA
34C4 **Scottsdale** Australia
59D4 **Scottsdale** USA
68C2 **Scranton** USA
61D2 **Scribner** USA
7D3 **Scunthorpe** England
Scutari = Shkodër
47C3 **Seacow** *R* South Africa
7E4 **Seaford** England
54J4 **Seal** *R* Canada
34B3 **Sea Lake** Australia
59D3 **Searchlight** USA
63D1 **Searcy** USA
66D3 **Searles** USA
66B2 **Seaside** California, USA
58B1 **Seaside** Oregon, USA
68C3 **Seaside Park** USA
58B1 **Seattle** USA
65E2 **Sebago L** USA
70A2 **Sebastian Vizcaino, B** Mexico
66A1 **Sebastopol** USA
50D2 **Sebderat** Eritrea
19F1 **Sebez** Russian Federation
65F1 **Seboomook L** USA
67B3 **Sebring** USA
35A3 **Secretary I** New Zealand
61E3 **Sedalia** USA
13C3 **Sedan** France
6C2 **Sedbergh** England
35B2 **Seddonville** New Zealand
45C3 **Sede Boqer** Israel
45C3 **Sederot** Israel
48A3 **Sédhiou** Senegal
45C3 **Sedom** Israel
59D4 **Sedona** USA
47B2 **Seeheim** Namibia
76E4 **Seelig,Mt** Antarctica
35B2 **Sefton,Mt** New Zealand
30C5 **Segamat** Malaysia
20E3 **Segezha** Russian Federation
15B2 **Segorbe** Spain
48B3 **Ségou** Mali
Segovia = Coco
15B1 **Segovia** Spain
15C1 **Segre** *R* Spain
48B4 **Séguéla** Ivory Coast
63C3 **Seguin** USA
15B2 **Segura** *R* Spain
15B2 **Segura, Sierra de** *Mts* Spain
42B3 **Sehwan** Pakistan
62C1 **Seiling** USA
13D3 **Seille** *R* France
12J6 **Seinäjoki** Finland
61E1 **Seine** *R* Canada
14C2 **Seine** *R* France
13B3 **Seine-et-Marne** *Department* France
50D4 **Sekenke** Tanzania
48B4 **Sekondi** Ghana
50D2 **Sek'ot'a** Ethiopia
58B1 **Selah** USA
27G7 **Selaru** *I* Indonesia
27D6 **Selatan** *I* Indonesia
27G7 **Selat Dampier** *Str* Indonesia
27E7 **Selat Lombok** *Chan* Indonesia
27D7 **Selat Sunda** *Str* Indonesia
27F7 **Selat Wetar** *Chan* Indonesia
54C3 **Selawik** USA
32B1 **Selayar** *I* Indonesia
6D3 **Selby** England
60C1 **Selby** USA
17F3 **Selçuk** Turkey
47D1 **Selebi Pikwe** Botswana
25Q3 **Selennyakh** *R* Russian Federation
13D3 **Selestat** France
55Q3 **Selfoss** Iceland
60C1 **Selfridge** USA
50C1 **Selima Oasis** Sudan
19G1 **Selizharovo** Russian Federation
54J4 **Selkirk** Canada
8D4 **Selkirk** Scotland
54G4 **Selkirk Mts** Canada/USA
67A2 **Selma** Alabama, USA
66C2 **Selma** California, USA
63E1 **Selmer** USA
15B2 **Selouane** Morocco
72D5 **Selvas** *Region* Brazil
48A2 **Selvagens, Ilhas** *Is* Atlantic Ocean
58C1 **Selway** *R* USA
32D3 **Selwyn** Australia
54E3 **Selwyn Mts** Canada
27E7 **Semarang** Indonesia
20G4 **Semenov** Russian Federation
21F5 **Semiluki** Russian Federation
60B2 **Seminoe Res** USA
63C1 **Seminole** Oklahoma, USA
62B2 **Seminole** Texas, USA
67B2 **Seminole,L** USA
24K4 **Semipalatinsk** Kazakhstan
41F3 **Semirom** Iran
41F2 **Semnān** Iran
13C3 **Semois** *R* Belgium
72E5 **Sena Madureira** Brazil
51C5 **Senanga** Zambia
63E2 **Senatobia** USA
29E3 **Sendai** Japan
42D4 **Sendwha** India
68B1 **Seneca Falls** USA
68B1 **Seneca L** USA
62A2 **Senecu** Mexico
48A3 **Sénégal** *R* Mauritius/ Senegal
48A3 **Senegal** *Republic* Africa
47D2 **Senekal** South Africa
73L6 **Senhor do Bonfim** Brazil
16C2 **Senigallia** Italy
16D2 **Senj** Croatia
26F4 **Senkaku Gunto** *Is* Japan
13B3 **Senlis** France
50D2 **Sennar** Sudan
55L5 **Senneterre** Canada
13D3 **Senones** France
13B3 **Sens** France
17D1 **Senta** Serbia, Yugoslavia
50C4 **Sentery** Zaïre
42D4 **Seoni** India
28B3 **Seoul** S Korea
35B2 **Separation Pt** New Zealand
75D3 **Sepetiba, B de** Brazil
27H7 **Sepik** *R* Papua New Guinea
28A3 **Sep'o** N Korea
30D2 **Sepone** Laos
75A2 **Sepotuba** *R* Brazil
55M4 **Sept-Iles** Canada
50B1 **Séquédine** Niger
66C2 **Sequoia Nat Pk** USA
45C1 **Serai** Syria
27F7 **Seram** *I* Indonesia
27F7 **Seram Sea** Indonesia
17D2 **Serbia** *Republic* Yugoslavia
21G5 **Serdobsk** Russian Federation
13B4 **Serein** *R* France
30C5 **Seremban** Malaysia
50D4 **Serengeti Nat Pk** Tanzania
51D5 **Serenje** Zambia
19F3 **Seret** *R* Ukraine
20H4 **Sergach** Russian Federation
28C2 **Sergeyevka** Russian Federation
24H3 **Sergino** Russian Federation
73L6 **Sergipe** *State* Brazil
20F4 **Segiyev Posad** Georgia
27E6 **Seria** Brunei
27E6 **Serian** Malaysia
17E3 **Sérifos** *I* Greece
49E2 **Serir Calanscio** *Desert* Libya
13C3 **Sermaize-les-Bains** France
32B1 **Sermata** *I* Indonesia
55P3 **Sermilik** *Fjord* Greenland
20J5 **Sernovodsk** Russian Federation
20L4 **Serov** Russian Federation
47D1 **Serowe** Botswana
15A2 **Serpa** Portugal
20F5 **Serpukhov** Russian Federation
15A1 **Serra da Estrela** *Mts* Portugal
73H3 **Serra do Navio** Brazil
17E2 **Sérrai** Greece
70D3 **Serrana Bank** *Is* Caribbean Sea
15B1 **Serraná de Cuenca** *Mts* Spain
75B2 **Serranópolis** Brazil
16B3 **Serrat, C** Tunisia
13B3 **Serre** *R* France
73L6 **Serrinha** Brazil
75D2 **Serro** Brazil
15C2 **Sersou, Plateau du** Algeria
75B3 **Sertanópolis** Brazil
31A3 **Sêrtar** China
47D1 **Serule** Botswana
51B5 **Sesfontein** Namibia
51C5 **Sesheke** Zambia
29D2 **Setana** Japan
14C3 **Sète** France
75D2 **Sete Lagoas** Brazil
15C2 **Sétif** Algeria
29C3 **Seto** Japan
28B4 **Seto Naikai** *S* Japan
48B1 **Settat** Morocco
6C2 **Settle** England
15A2 **Setúbal** Portugal
55J4 **Seul, Lac** Canada
21H7 **Sevan, Ozero** *L* Armenia
21E7 **Sevastopol'** Ukraine
7E4 **Sevenoaks** England
55K4 **Severn** *R* Canada
7C3 **Severn** *R* England
20G3 **Severnaya Dvina** *R* Russian Federation
25L1 **Severnaya Zemlya** *I* Russian Federation
20L3 **Severnyy Sos'va** *R* Russian Federation
20K3 **Severnyy Ural** *Mts* Russian Federation
25M4 **Severo Baykal'skoye Nagor'ye** *Mts* Russian Federation
21F6 **Severo Donets** *R* Ukraine
20F3 **Severodvinsk** Russian Federation
24H3 **Severo Sos'va** *R* Russian Federation
20L3 **Severoural'sk** Russian Federation
59D3 **Sevier** *R* USA
59D3 **Sevier Desert** USA
59D3 **Sevier L** USA
Sevilla = Seville
15A2 **Seville** Spain
17F2 **Sevlievo** Bulgaria
48A4 **Sewa** *R* Sierra Leone
61D2 **Seward** Nebraska, USA
54D3 **Seward** USA
54B3 **Seward Pen** USA
46K8 **Seychelles** *Is, Republic* Indian Ocean
40C2 **Seyhan** *R* Turkey
12C1 **Seyðisfjörður** Iceland
21F5 **Seym** *R* Russian Federation
25R3 **Seymchan** Russian Federation
34C3 **Seymour** Australia
68D2 **Seymour** Connecticut, USA
64B3 **Seymour** Indiana, USA
62C2 **Seymour** Texas, USA
13B3 **Sézanne** France
48D1 **Sfax** Tunisia
17F1 **Sfîntu Gheorghe** Romania
's-Gravenhage = The Hague
8C3 **Sgúrr na Lapaich,** *Mt* Scotland
31B3 **Shaanxi** *Province* China
50E3 **Shabeelle** *R* Ethiopia/ Somalia
50C4 **Shabunda** Zaïre
39F2 **Shache** China
76G9 **Shackleton Ice Shelf** Antarctica
42B3 **Shadadkot** Pakistan
41F3 **Shādhām** *R* Iran
66C3 **Shafter** USA
7C4 **Shaftesbury** England
28A2 **Shagang** China
74J8 **Shag Rocks** *Is* South Georgia
44B2 **Shāhābād** India
41E3 **Shāhābād** Iran
45D2 **Shahbā** Syria
41G3 **Shahdāb** Iran
43E4 **Shahdol** India
41E2 **Shāhīn Dezh** Iran
41G3 **Shāh Kūh** *Mt* Iran
41G3 **Shahr-e Bābak** Iran
Shahresa = Qomisheh
41F3 **Shahr Kord** Iran
21J8 **Shahsavār** Iran
20L3 **Shaim** Russian Federation
45C4 **Sha'īra, Gebel** *Mt* Egypt
40B5 **Sha'īt, Wadi** *Watercourse* Egypt
42D3 **Shājahānpur** India
42D4 **Shājāpur** India
21G6 **Shakhty** Russian Federation
20H4 **Shakhun'ya** Russian Federation
48C4 **Shaki** Nigeria
61E2 **Shakopee** USA
29D2 **Shakotan-misaki** *C* Japan
20K4 **Shamary** Russian Federation
50D3 **Shambe** Sudan
68B2 **Shamokin** USA
62B1 **Shamrock** USA
68C1 **Shandaken** USA
66B3 **Shandon** USA
31D2 **Shandong** *Province* China
31C5 **Shangchuan Dao** *I* China
31C1 **Shangdu** China
31E3 **Shanghai** China
31C3 **Shangnan** China
51C5 **Shangombo** Zambia
31D3 **Shangqiu** China
31D4 **Shangrao** China
31B5 **Shangsi** China
31C3 **Shang Xian** China
7D4 **Shanklin** England
9B3 **Shannon** *R* Irish Republic
28B2 **Shansonggang** China
26G1 **Shantarskiye Ostrova** *I* Russian Federation
31D5 **Shantou** China
31C2 **Shanxi** *Province* China
31D3 **Shan Xian** China
31C5 **Shaoguan** China
31E4 **Shaoxing** China
31C4 **Shaoyang** China
8D2 **Shapinsay** *I* Scotland
45D2 **Shaqqā** Syria
41E4 **Shaqra'** Saudi Arabia
31A1 **Sharhulsan** Mongolia
29D2 **Shari** Japan
41G2 **Sharifābād** Iran
41G4 **Sharjah** UAE
32A3 **Shark B** Australia
41G2 **Sharlauk** Turkmenistan
45C2 **Sharon,Plain of** Israel
68B3 **Sharpsburg** USA
40C3 **Sharqi, Jebel esh** *Mts* Lebanon/Syria
20H4 **Sharya** Russian Federation
50D3 **Shashamenē** Ethiopia
47D1 **Shashani** *R* Zimbabwe
47D1 **Shashe** *R* Botswana

31C3 Shashi China
58B2 Shasta L USA
58B2 Shasta,Mt USA
45D1 Shaṯḩah at Taḩtā Syria
41E3 Shaṭṭ al Gharraf R Iraq
45C3 Shaubak Jordan
66C2 Shaver L USA
68C2 Shawangunk Mt USA
64B2 Shawano USA
65E1 Shawinigan Canada
63C1 Shawnee Oklahoma, USA
60B2 Shawnee Wyoming, USA
31D4 Sha Xian China
32B3 Shay Gap Australia
45D2 Shaykh Miskīn Syria
50E2 Shaykh 'Uthmān Yemen
21F5 Shchigry Russian Federation
21E5 Shchors Ukraine
24J4 Shchuchinsk Kazakhstan
50E3 Shebele R Ethiopia
64B2 Sheboygan USA
50B3 Shebshi Mts Nigeria
9C3 Sheelin, L Irish Republic
9C2 Sheep Haven Estuary Irish Republic
7E4 Sheerness England
45C2 Shefar'am Israel
63E2 Sheffield Alabama, USA
7D3 Sheffield England
62B2 Sheffield Texas, USA
8C3 Sheil, Loch L Scotland
42C2 Shekhupura Pakistan
25T2 Shelagskiy, Mys C Russian Federation
68D1 Shelburne Falls USA
64B2 Shelby Michigan, USA
58D1 Shelby Montana, USA
67B1 Shelby N Carolina, USA
64B3 Shelbyville Indiana, USA
67A1 Shelbyville Tennessee, USA
61D2 Sheldon USA
54C4 Shelikof Str USA
58D2 Shelley USA
34D2 Shellharbour Australia
35A3 Shelter Pt New Zealand
58B1 Shelton USA
41E1 Shemakha Azerbaijan
61D2 Shenandoah USA
65D3 Shenandoah R USA
65D3 Shenandoah Nat Pk USA
48C4 Shendam Nigeria
50D2 Shendi Sudan
20G3 Shenkursk Russian Federation
31C2 Shenmu China
31E1 Shenyang China
31C5 Shenzhen China
42D3 Sheopur India
19F2 Shepetovka Ukraine
68B3 Shepherdstown USA
34C3 Shepparton Australia
7E4 Sheppey I England
55K2 Sherard,C Canada
7C4 Sherborne England
48A4 Sherbro I Sierra Leone
65E1 Sherbrooke Canada
68C1 Sherburne USA
42C3 Shergarh India
63D2 Sheridan Arkansas, USA
60B2 Sheridan Wyoming, USA
7E3 Sheringham England
63C2 Sherman USA
18B2 's-Hertogenbosch Netherlands
10C1 Shetland Is Scotland
21J7 Shevchenko Kazakhstan
60D1 Sheyenne USA
60D1 Sheyenne R USA
41F4 Sheyk Sho'eyb I Iran
8B3 Shiant, Sd of Scotland
26J2 Shiashkotan I Kuril Is, Russian Federation
42B1 Shibarghan Afghanistan
29D3 Shibata Japan
29D2 Shibetsu Japan
49F1 Shibîn el Kom Egypt
45A3 Shibîn el Qanâtir Egypt
29C3 Shibukawa Japan
68B2 Shickshinny USA
28A3 Shidao China
31C2 Shijiazhuang China
42B3 Shikarpur Pakistan
26G3 Shikoku I Japan
29B4 Shikoku-sanchi Mts Japan
26H2 Shikotan I Russian Federation
29D2 Shikotsu-ko L Japan
20G3 Shilega Russian Federation
43F3 Shiliguri India
26E1 Shilka Russian Federation
26E1 Shilka R Russian Federation
68C2 Shillington USA
43G3 Shillong India
20G5 Shilovo Russian Federation
28B4 Shimabara Japan
29C4 Shimada Japan
26F1 Shimanovsk Russian Federation
29D3 Shimizu Japan
29C4 Shimoda Japan
44B3 Shimoga India
28C4 Shimonoseki Japan
29C3 Shinano R Japan
41G5 Shināş Oman
38E2 Shindand Afghanistan
68A2 Shinglehouse USA
29D4 Shingū Japan
29D3 Shinjō Japan
8C2 Shin, Loch L Scotland
29D3 Shinminato Japan
45D1 Shinshār Syria
50D4 Shinyanga Tanzania
29E3 Shiogama Japan
29C4 Shiono-misaki C Japan
31A5 Shiping China
68B2 Shippensburg USA
62A1 Shiprock USA
31B3 Shiquan China
29D3 Shirakawa Japan
29C3 Shirane-san Mt Japan
41F4 Shīraz Iran
45A3 Shirbîn Egypt
29F2 Shiretoko-misaki C Japan
29D2 Shiriya-saki C Japan
41F3 Shīr Kūh Mt Iran
29C3 Shirotori Japan
41G2 Shirvān Iran
54B3 Shishmaref USA
31B2 Shitanjing China
64B3 Shively USA
42D3 Shivpuri India
45C3 Shivta Hist Site Israel
59D3 Shivwits Plat USA
51D5 Shiwa Ngandu Zambia
31C3 Shiyan China
31B2 Shizuishan China
29C3 Shizuoka Japan
17D2 Shkodër Albania
19G2 Shkov Belarus
25L1 Shmidta, Ostrov I Russian Federation
34D2 Shoalhaven R Australia
28B4 Shobara Japan
44B3 Shoranūr India
44B2 Shorāpur India
59C3 Shoshone California, USA
58D2 Shoshone Idaho, USA
58E2 Shoshone R USA
58D2 Shoshone L USA
59C3 Shoshone Mts USA
58E2 Shoshoni USA
21E5 Shostka Ukraine
59D4 Show Low USA
63D2 Shreveport USA
7C3 Shrewsbury England
7C3 Shropshire County England
31E1 Shuangliao China
28B2 Shuangyang China
26G2 Shuangyashan China
21K6 Shubar-Kuduk Kazakhstan
20N2 Shuga Russian Federation
31D2 Shu He R China
31A4 Shuicheng China
42C3 Shujaabad Pakistan
42D4 Shujālpur India
26C2 Shule He R China
17F2 Shumen Bulgaria
20H4 Shumerlya Russian Federation
31D4 Shuncheng China
54C3 Shungnak USA
31C2 Shuo Xian China
38D3 Shūr Gaz Iran
51C5 Shurugwi Zimbabwe
20G4 Shuya Russian Federation
30B1 Shwebo Burma
30B2 Shwegyin Burma
42A2 Siah Koh Mts Afghanistan
42C2 Sialkot Pakistan
Sian = Xi'an
27F6 Siargao I Philippines
27F6 Siaton Philippines
19E1 Šiauliai Lithuania
20K5 Sibay Russian Federation
47E2 Sibayi L South Africa
16D2 Šibenik Croatia
25L5 Siberia Russian Federation
27C7 Siberut I Indonesia
42B3 Sibi Pakistan
50B4 Sibiti Congo
50D4 Sibiti R Tanzania
17E1 Sibiu Romania
61D2 Sibley USA
27C6 Sibolga Indonesia
43G3 Sibsāgar India
27E6 Sibu Malaysia
50B3 Sibut Central African Republic
31A3 Sichuan Province China
Sicilia = Sicily
16C3 Sicilian Chan Italy/Tunisia
16C3 Sicily I Medit Sea
72D6 Sicuani Peru
42C4 Siddhapur India
44B2 Siddipet India
43E4 Sidhi India
49E1 Sidi Barrani Egypt
15B2 Sidi-bel-Abbès Algeria
48B1 Sidi Kacem Morocco
8D3 Sidlaw Hills Scotland
76F5 Sidley,Mt Antarctica
7C4 Sidmouth England
58B1 Sidney Canada
60C1 Sidney Montana, USA
60C2 Sidney Nebraska, USA
68C1 Sidney New York, USA
64C2 Sidney Ohio, USA
67B2 Sidney Lanier,L USA
45C2 Sidon Lebanon
75B3 Sidrolândia Brazil
19E2 Siedlce Poland
13D2 Sieg R Germany
13D2 Siegburg Germany
13D2 Siegen Germany
30C3 Siem Reap Cambodia
16C2 Siena Italy
19D2 Sierpc Poland
62A2 Sierra Blanca USA
70B2 Sierra de los Alamitos Mts Mexico
48A4 Sierra Leone Republic Africa
48A4 Sierra Leone,C Sierra Leone
70B3 Sierra Madre del Sur Mexico
66B3 Sierra Madre Mts USA
70B2 Sierra Madre Occidental Mts Mexico
70B2 Sierra Madre Oriental Mts Mexico
56C4 Sierra Mojada Mexico
59B3 Sierra Nevada Mts USA
59D4 Sierra Vista USA
75A3 Siete Puntas R Paraguay
17E3 Sífnos I Greece
15B2 Sig Algeria
20E2 Sig Russian Federation
19E3 Sighetu Marmaţiei Romania
17E1 Sighişoara Romania
12B1 Siglufjörður Iceland
72A1 Siguatepeque Honduras
15B1 Sigüenza Spain
48B3 Siguiri Guinea
30C3 Sihanoukville Cambodia
42D4 Sihora India
40D2 Siirt Turkey
43J1 Sikandarabad India
42D3 Sīkar India
42B2 Sikaram Mt Afghanistan
48B3 Sikasso Mali
63E1 Sikeston USA
26G2 Sikhote-Alin' Mts Russian Federation
17F3 Síkinos I Greece
17E3 Sikionía Greece
43F3 Sikkim State India
25O3 Siktyakh Russian Federation
15A1 Sil R Spain
43G4 Silchar India
48C2 Silet Algeria
43E3 Silgarhi Nepal
40B2 Silifke Turkey
45D1 Şilinfah Syria
39G2 Siling Co L China
17F2 Silistra Bulgaria
20A3 Siljan L Sweden
12F7 Silkeborg Denmark
6C2 Silloth England
63D1 Siloam Springs USA
63D2 Silsbee USA
50B2 Siltou Well Chad
19E1 Šilute Lithuania
40D2 Silvan Turkey
75C2 Silvania Brazil
42C4 Silvassa India
61E1 Silver Bay USA
59C3 Silver City Nevada, USA
62A2 Silver City New Mexico, USA
58B2 Silver Lake USA
66D2 Silver Peak Range Mts USA
68B3 Silver Spring USA
34B2 Silverton Australia
62A1 Silverton USA
27E6 Simanggang Malaysia
30C1 Simao China
65D1 Simard,L Canada
41E3 Simareh R Iran
17F3 Simav Turkey
17F3 Simav R Turkey
65D2 Simcoe,L Canada
27C6 Simeulue I Indonesia
21E7 Simferopol' Ukraine
17F3 Sími I Greece
43E3 Simikot Nepal
42D2 Simla India
60C3 Simla USA
13D2 Simmern Germany
66C3 Simmler USA
47B3 Simonstown South Africa
14D2 Simplon Mt Switzerland
16B1 Simplon Pass Italy/Switzerland
54C2 Simpson,C USA
32C3 Simpson Desert Australia
55K3 Simpson Pen Canada
12G7 Simrishamn Sweden
26J2 Simushir I Kuril Is, Russian Federation
50E3 Sina Dhaga Somalia
40B4 Sinai Pen Egypt
72C2 Sincelejo Colombia
67B2 Sinclair,L USA
75D1 Sincora, Serra do Mts Brazil
42D3 Sind R India
42B3 Sindh Province Pakistan
17F3 Sindirği Turkey
43F4 Sindri India
15A2 Sines Portugal
15A2 Sines, Cabo de C Portugal
50D2 Singa Sudan
30C5 Singapore Republic SE Asia
30C5 Singapore,Str of SE Asia
27E7 Singaraja Indonesia
13E4 Singen Germany
50D4 Singida Tanzania
43H3 Singkaling Hkamti Burma
27D6 Singkawang Indonesia
27D7 Singkep I Indonesia
34D2 Singleton Australia
30B1 Singu Burma
47E1 Singuédeze R Mozambique
28A3 Sin'gye N Korea
28A2 Sinhŭng N Korea
16B2 Siniscola Sardinia, Italy
40D2 Sinjár Iraq
42B2 Sinkai Hills Mts Afghanistan
50D2 Sinkat Sudan
39G1 Sinkiang Autonomous Region China
43K2 Sinkobabad India
73H2 Sinnamary French Guiana
45B4 Sinn Bishr, Gebel Mt Egypt
28A3 Sinnyong S Korea
40C1 Sinop Turkey
28A2 Sinpa N Korea
28A2 Sinp'o N Korea
28A3 Sinp'yong N Korea
17E1 Sîntana Romania
27E6 Sintang Indonesia
63C3 Sinton USA
15A2 Sintra Portugal
72C2 Sinú R Colombia
28A2 Sinŭiju N Korea
19D3 Siófok Hungary
16B1 Sion Switzerland
61D2 Sioux City USA
61D2 Sioux Falls USA
69L1 Siparia Trinidad
28A2 Siping China
76F3 Siple Base Antarctica
76F5 Siple I Antarctica
27C7 Sipora I Indonesia
63E2 Sipsey R USA
45B4 Sîq, Wadi el Egypt
44B3 Sira India
Siracusa = Syracuse
43F4 Sirajganj Bangladesh
41F5 Şīr Banī Yās I UAE
32C2 Sir Edward Pellew Group Is Australia
17F1 Siret R Romania
40C3 Sirhān, Wādi as V Jordan/Saudi Arabia
40D2 Şirnak Turkey
42C4 Sirohi India
44C2 Sironcha India
42D4 Sironj India
17E3 Síros I Greece
66C3 Sirretta Peak Mt USA
41F4 Sīrrī I Iran
42C3 Sirsa India
44A3 Sirsi India
49D1 Sirt Libya
49D1 Sirte Desert Libya
49D1 Sirte,G of Libya
21H9 Sirvan R Iran
16D1 Sisak Croatia
30C2 Sisaket Thailand
30C3 Sisophon Cambodia
66B3 Sisquoc USA
66C3 Sisquoc R USA
61D1 Sisseton USA
13B3 Sissonne France
14D3 Sisteron France
25L4 Sistig Khem Russian Federation
43E3 Sītāpur India
17F3 Sitía Greece
75C1 Sítio d'Abadia Brazil
54E4 Sitka USA
30B2 Sittang R Burma
13C2 Sittard Netherlands
43G4 Sittwe Burma
40C2 Sivas Turkey
40C2 Siverek Turkey
40B2 Sivrihisar Turkey
25S4 Sivuchiy, Mys C Russian Federation
49E2 Siwa Egypt
42D2 Siwalik Range Mts India
43E3 Siwalik Range Mts Nepal
20G3 Siya Russian Federation
31D3 Siyang China
18C1 Sjaelland I Denmark
12G7 Skagen Denmark
12F7 Skagerrak Str Denmark/Norway
58B1 Skagit R USA
58B1 Skagit Mt Canada
54E4 Skagway USA
68B1 Skaneateles USA
68B1 Skaneateles L USA
12G7 Skara Sweden
19E2 Skarzysko-Kamienna Poland
54F4 Skeena R Canada
54F4 Skeene Mts Canada
54D3 Skeenjek R USA
7E3 Skegness England
20B2 Skellefte R Sweden
12J6 Skellefteå Sweden
9C3 Skerries Irish Republic
17E3 Skíathos I Greece
54E4 Skidegate Canada
19E2 Skiemiewice Poland
12F7 Skien Norway
16B3 Skikda Algeria
6D3 Skipton England
17E3 Skíros I Greece
12F7 Skive Denmark
18B1 Skjern Denmark
55O3 Skjoldungen Greenland
64B2 Skokie USA
17E3 Skópelos I Greece
17E2 Skopje Macedonia, Yugoslavia
12G7 Skövde Sweden
25O4 Skovorodino Russian Federation
65F2 Skowhegan USA
47E1 Skukuza South Africa
54C3 Skwentna USA
18D2 Skwierzyna Poland
10B2 Skye I Scotland
12G7 Slagelse Denmark
27D7 Slamet Mt Indonesia
9C3 Slaney R Irish Republic
17E2 Slatina Romania
54G3 Slave R Canada
19G2 Slavgorod Belarus
24J4 Slavgorod Russian Federation
19F2 Slavuta Ukraine
21F6 Slavyansk Ukraine
18D2 Sławno Poland
7D3 Sleaford England
8C3 Sleat,Sound of Chan Scotland
54C3 Sleetmute USA
63E2 Slidell USA
68C2 Slide Mt USA
9B3 Slieve Aughty Mts Irish Republic
9C3 Slieve Bloom Mts Irish Republic
10B3 Sligo Irish Republic
10B3 Sligo B Irish Republic
17F2 Sliven Bulgaria
59C3 Sloan USA
17F2 Slobozia Romania
19F2 Slonim Belarus
7D4 Slough England
66B2 Slough R USA
19D3 Slovakia Republic Europe
16C1 Slovenia Republic Europe
18C2 Słubice Poland
19F2 Sluch' R Ukraine
18D2 Słupsk Poland
19F2 Slutsk Belarus
19F2 Slutsk R Belarus
10A3 Slyne Head Pt Irish Republic
25M4 Slyudyanka Russian Federation
55M4 Smallwood Res Canada
48A2 Smara Morocco
17E2 Smederevo Serbia, Yugoslavia
17E2 Smederevska Palanka Serbia, Yugoslavia
21E6 Smela Ukraine
68A2 Smethport USA
66C1 Smith USA
54F3 Smith Arm B Canada
54F4 Smithers Canada
67C1 Smithfield N Carolina, USA
47D3 Smithfield South Africa
58D2 Smithfield Utah, USA
55L3 Smith I Canada
65D2 Smiths Falls Canada
34C4 Smithton Australia
60C3 Smoky R USA
34D2 Smoky C Australia
60D3 Smoky Hills USA
58D2 Smoky Mts USA
12F6 Smøla I Norway
20E5 Smolensk Russian Federation
17E2 Smólikas Mt Greece
17E2 Smolyan Bulgaria

19F2 **Smorgon'** Belarus
Smyrna = Izmir
68C3 **Smyrna** Delaware, USA
67B2 **Smyrna** Georgia, USA
12B2 **Snæfell** *Mt* Iceland
6B2 **Snaefell** *Mt* Isle of Man, British Islands
58C1 **Snake** *R* USA
56B2 **Snake River Canyon** USA
58D2 **Snake River Plain** USA
33F5 **Snares Is** New Zealand
18B2 **Sneek** Netherlands
66B2 **Snelling** USA
18D2 **Sněžka** *Mt* Czech Republic/Poland
8B3 **Snizort, Loch** *Inlet* Scotland
12F6 **Snøhetta** *Mt* Norway
58B1 **Snohomish** USA
58B1 **Snoqualmie P** USA
30D3 **Snoul** Cambodia
7B3 **Snowdon** *Mt* Wales
7B3 **Snowdonia Nat Pk** Wales
54G3 **Snowdrift** Canada
59D4 **Snowflake** USA
54H4 **Snow Lake** Canada
68B2 **Snow Shoe** USA
34A2 **Snowtown** Australia
58D2 **Snowville** USA
34C3 **Snowy Mts** Australia
62B2 **Snyder** USA
28B4 **Soan Kundo** *Is* S Korea
8B3 **Soay, I** Scotland
28A3 **Sobaek Sanmaek** *Mts* S Korea
50D3 **Sobat** *R* Sudan
73K4 **Sobral** Brazil
19E2 **Sochaczew** Poland
21F7 **Sochi** Russian Federation
28A3 **Sŏch'on** S Korea
37M5 **Société, Îles de la** Pacific Ocean
49D2 **Socna** Libya
62A2 **Socorro** USA
70A3 **Socorro** *I* Mexico
38D4 **Socotra** *I* Yemen
66C3 **Soda L** USA
12K5 **Sodankylä** Finland
58D2 **Soda Springs** USA
50D3 **Soddo** Ethiopia
12H6 **Söderhamn** Sweden
12H7 **Södertälje** Sweden
50C2 **Sodiri** Sudan
50D3 **Sodo** Ethiopia
68B1 **Sodus Point** USA
13E2 **Soest** Germany
51D5 **Sofala** Mozambique
17E2 **Sofia** Bulgaria
Sofiya = Sofia
20E2 **Sofporog** Russian Federation
26H4 **Sofu Gan** *I* Japan
72D2 **Sogamoso** Colombia
12F6 **Sognefjorden** *Inlet* Norway
28A4 **Sŏgwi-ri** S Korea
39H2 **Sog Xian** China
40B4 **Sohâg** Egypt
33E1 **Sohano** Papua New Guinea
13B2 **Soignies** Belgium
13B3 **Soissons** France
42C3 **Sojat** India
28A3 **Sokcho** S Korea
40A2 **Söke** Turkey
19E2 **Sokołka** Poland
48C4 **Sokodé** Togo
20G4 **Sokol** Russian Federation
48B3 **Sokolo** Mali
55Q3 **Søkongens Øy** *I* Greenland
48C3 **Sokoto** Nigeria
48C3 **Sokoto** *R* Nigeria
35A3 **Solander I** New Zealand
44B2 **Solāpur** India
69C4 **Soledad** Colombia
66B2 **Soledad** USA
7D4 **Solent** *Sd* England
13B2 **Solesmes** France
19F2 **Soligorsk** Belarus
20K4 **Solikamsk** Russian Federation
21J5 **Sol'Iletsk** Russian Federation
72D4 **Solimões** Peru
13D2 **Solingen** Germany
47B1 **Solitaire** Namibia
12H6 **Sollefteå** Sweden
27D7 **Solok** Indonesia
33E1 **Solomon Is** Pacific Ocean
64A1 **Solon Springs** USA
20F2 **Solovetskiye, Ostrova** *I* Russian Federation
12F8 **Soltau** Germany
66B3 **Solvang** USA
68B1 **Solvay** USA
8D4 **Solway Firth** *Estuary* England/Scotland
51C5 **Solwezi** Zambia
29D3 **Sōma** Japan
17F3 **Soma** Turkey
38C5 **Somalia** *Republic* E Africa
36D4 **Somali Basin** Indian Ocean
17D1 **Sombor** Serbia, Yugoslavia
44E4 **Sombrero Chan** Nicobar Is, Indian Ocean
32D2 **Somerset** Australia
64C3 **Somerset** Kentucky, USA
68E2 **Somerset** Massachusetts, USA
65D2 **Somerset** Pennsylvania, USA
7C4 **Somerset** *County* England
47D3 **Somerset East** South Africa
55J2 **Somerset I** Canada
68D1 **Somerset Res** USA
68C3 **Somers Point** USA
68E1 **Somersworth** USA
68C2 **Somerville** USA
63C2 **Somerville Res** USA
17E1 **Someş** *R* Romania
13B3 **Somme** *Department* France
13B3 **Somme** *R* France
13C3 **Sommesous** France
72A1 **Somoto** Nicaragua
43E4 **Son** *R* India
28A3 **Sŏnch'ŏn** N Korea
47D3 **Sondags** *R* South Africa
12F8 **Sønderborg** Denmark
55N3 **Søndre Strømfjord** Greenland
55N2 **Søndre Upernavik** Greenland
14D2 **Sondrio** Italy
30D3 **Song Ba** *R* Vietnam
30D3 **Song Cau** Vietnam
28A3 **Sŏngch'on** N Korea
51D5 **Songea** Tanzania
28A2 **Songgan** N Korea
26F2 **Songhua** *R* China
31E3 **Songjiang** China
28A3 **Songjŏng** S Korea
30C4 **Songkhla** Thailand
30C5 **Sông Pahang** *R* Malaysia
31A3 **Songpan** China
28A4 **Sŏngsan-ni** S Korea
31C1 **Sonid Youqi** China
42D3 **Sonīpat** India
30C1 **Son La** Vietnam
42B3 **Sonmiani** Pakistan
42B3 **Sonmiani Bay** Pakistan
59D4 **Sonoita** Mexico
66A1 **Sonoma** USA
66B2 **Sonora** California, USA
62B2 **Sonora** Texas, USA
70A2 **Sonora** *R* Mexico
59D4 **Sonora** *State* Mexico
56B3 **Sonoran Desert** USA
66C1 **Sonora P** USA
70D3 **Sonsonate** El Salvador
27G6 **Sonsorol** *I* Pacific Ocean
57E2 **Soo Canals** Canada/USA
19D2 **Sopot** Poland
18D3 **Sopron** Hungary
66B2 **Soquel** USA
16C2 **Sora** Italy
45C3 **Sored** *R* Israel
65E1 **Sorel** Canada
34C4 **Sorell** Australia
40C2 **Sorgun** Turkey
15B1 **Soria** Spain
24C2 **Sørkapp** *I* Barents Sea
12J5 **Sørkjosen** Norway
21J6 **Sor Mertvyy Kultuk** *Plain* Kazakhstan
75C3 **Sorocaba** Brazil
20J5 **Sorochinsk** Moldavia
19F3 **Soroki** Russian Federation
27H6 **Sorol** *I* Pacific Ocean
29D2 **Soroma-ko** *L* Japan
27G7 **Sorong** Indonesia
50D3 **Soroti** Uganda
12J4 **Sørøya** *I* Norway
16C2 **Sorrento** Italy
12K5 **Sorsatunturi** *Mt* Finland
12H5 **Sorsele** Sweden
20E3 **Sortavala** Russian Federation
28B3 **Sŏsan** S Korea
19D2 **Sosnowiec** Poland
20L4 **Sos'va** Russian Federation
50B3 **Souanké** Congo
48B4 **Soubré** Ivory Coast
68C2 **Souderton** USA
69P2 **Soufrière** St Lucia
69N2 **Soufrière** *Mt* St Vincent
14C3 **Souillac** France
16B3 **Souk Ahras** Algeria
Sŏul = Seoul
15C2 **Soummam** *R* Algeria
Sour = Tyre
47D2 **Sources,Mt aux** Lesotho
60C1 **Souris** Manitoba, Canada
60C1 **Souris** *R* Canada/USA
73L5 **Sousa** Brazil
16C3 **Sousse** Tunisia
51C7 **South Africa** *Republic* Africa
68C2 **S Amboy** USA
64C2 **Southampton** Canada
7D4 **Southampton** England
68D2 **Southampton** USA
55K3 **Southampton I** Canada
44E3 **South Andaman** *I* Indian Ocean
55M4 **South Aulatsivik I** Canada
32C3 **South Australia** *State* Australia
36H6 **South Australian Basin** Indian Ocean
63E2 **Southaven** USA
62A2 **South Baldy** *Mt* USA
67B3 **South Bay** USA
64C1 **South Baymouth** Canada
64B2 **South Bend** Indiana, USA
58B1 **South Bend** Washington, USA
65D3 **South Boston** USA
68E1 **Southbridge** USA
South Cape = Ka Lae
57E3 **South Carolina** *State* USA
27E5 **South China S** SE Asia
56C2 **South Dakota** *State* USA
68D1 **South Deerfield** USA
7D4 **South Downs** England
34C4 **South East C** Australia
37O7 **South East Pacific Basin** Pacific Ocean
54H4 **Southend** Canada
7E4 **Southend-on-Sea** England
35A2 **Southern Alps** *Mts* New Zealand
32A4 **Southern Cross** Australia
54J4 **Southern Indian L** Canada
67C1 **Southern Pines** USA
69H2 **Southfield** Jamaica
37K6 **South Fiji Basin** Pacific Ocean
7E4 **South Foreland** *Pt* England
62A1 **South Fork** USA
66B1 **South Fork** *R* California, USA
66B1 **South Fork American** *R* USA
66C3 **South Fork Kern** *R* USA
71G9 **South Georgia** *I* S Atlantic Ocean
7C4 **South Glamorgan** *County* Wales
64B2 **South Haven** USA
54J3 **South Henik L** Canada
65D3 **South Hill** USA
36J3 **South Honshu Ridge** Pacific Ocean
35A2 **South I** New Zealand
68D2 **Southington** USA
28B3 **South Korea** *Republic* S Korea
59B3 **South Lake Tahoe** USA
36D6 **South Madagascar Ridge** Indian Ocean
76G8 **South Magnetic Pole** Antarctica
67B3 **South Miami** USA
68B3 **South Mt** USA
54F3 **South Nahanni** *R* Canada
69G1 **South Negril Pt** Jamaica
52F8 **South Orkney Is** Atlantic Ocean
71B5 **South Pacific O**
60C2 **South Platte** *R* USA
76E **South Pole** Antarctica
64C1 **South Porcupine** Canada
7C3 **Southport** England
69Q2 **South Pt** Barbados
68C2 **South River** USA
8D2 **South Ronaldsay** *I* Scotland
52G7 **South Sandwich Trench** Atlantic Ocean
66A2 **South San Francisco** USA
54H4 **South Saskatchewan** *R* Canada
6D2 **South Shields** England
35B1 **South Taranaki Bight** *B* New Zealand
8B3 **South Uist** *I* Scotland
South West Africa = Namibia
32D5 **South West C** Australia
36D6 **South West Indian Ridge** Indian Ocean
37M6 **South West Pacific Basin** Pacific Ocean
52D5 **South West Peru Ridge** Pacific Ocean
7E3 **Southwold** England
7D3 **South Yorkshire** *County* England
47D1 **Soutpansberg** *Mts* South Africa
19E1 **Sovetsk** Russian Federation
20H4 **Sovetsk** Russian Federation
26G2 **Sovetskaya Gavan'** Russian Federation
20L3 **Sovetskiy** Russian Federation
47D2 **Soweto** South Africa
29D1 **Sōya-misaki** *C* Japan
51B4 **Soyo Congo** Angola
19G2 **Sozh** *R* Belarus
13C2 **Spa** Belgium
15 **Spain** *Kingdom* SW Europe
Spalato = Split
7D3 **Spalding** England
64C1 **Spanish** *R* Canada
59D2 **Spanish Fork** USA
69J1 **Spanish Town** Jamaica
59C3 **Sparks** USA
64A2 **Sparta** USA
67B2 **Spartanburg** USA
17E3 **Spartí** Greece
16D3 **Spartivento, C** Italy
26G2 **Spassk Dal'niy** Russian Federation
60C2 **Spearfish** USA
62B1 **Spearman** USA
69R2 **Speightstown** Barbados
54D3 **Spenard** USA
55J3 **Spence Bay** Canada
64B3 **Spencer** Indiana, USA
61D2 **Spencer** Iowa, USA
32C4 **Spencer G** Australia
55L3 **Spencer Is** Canada
35B2 **Spenser Mts** New Zealand
9C2 **Sperrin Mts** Northern Ireland
8D3 **Spey** *R* Scotland
18B3 **Speyer** Germany
69K1 **Speyside** Tobago
58C1 **Spirit Lake** USA
54G4 **Spirit River** Canada
24C2 **Spitsbergen** *I* Svalbard, Norway
Spitsbergen *Is* **= Svalbard**
18C3 **Spittal** Austria
13D1 **Spjekeroog** *I* Germany
12F6 **Spjelkavik** Norway
16D2 **Split** Croatia
58C1 **Spokane** USA
64A1 **Spooner** USA
Sporádhes *Is* **= Dodecanese**
27E6 **Spratly** *I* S China Sea
27E6 **Spratly Is** S China Sea
58C2 **Spray** USA
18C2 **Spree** *R* Germany
47B2 **Springbok** South Africa
63D1 **Springdale** USA
62B1 **Springer** USA
59E4 **Springerville** USA
62B1 **Springfield** Colorado, USA
64B3 **Springfield** Illinois, USA
68D1 **Springfield** Massachusetts, USA
61E2 **Springfield** Minnesota, USA
63D1 **Springfield** Missouri, USA
64C3 **Springfield** Ohio, USA
58B2 **Springfield** Oregon, USA
67A1 **Springfield** Tennessee, USA
65E2 **Springfield** Vermont, USA
47D3 **Springfontein** South Africa
59C3 **Spring Mts** USA
47D2 **Springs** South Africa
68A1 **Springville** New York, USA
59D2 **Springville** Utah, USA
68B1 **Springwater** USA
58D2 **Spruce Mt** USA
7E3 **Spurn Head** *C* England
58B1 **Spuzzum** Canada
16D3 **Squillace, G di** Italy
25S4 **Sredinnyy Khrebet** *Mts* Russian Federation
25R3 **Srednekolymsk** Russian Federation
20F5 **Sredne-Russkaya Vozvyshennost'** *Upland* Russian Federation
25M3 **Sredne Sibirskoye Ploskogorye** *Tableland* Russian Federation
20K4 **Sredniy Ural** *Mts* Russian Federation
30D3 **Srepok** *R* Cambodia
26E1 **Sretensk** Russian Federation
30C3 **Sre Umbell** Cambodia
44C2 **Srīkākulam** India
44B3 **Sri Kālahasti** India
39G5 **Sri Lanka** *Republic* S Asia
42C2 **Srīnagar** Pakistan
44A2 **Srīvardhan** India
18D2 **Środa Wlk.** Poland
8C2 **Stack Skerry** *I* Scotland
13E1 **Stade** Germany
13E1 **Stadthagen** Germany
8B3 **Staffa** *I* Scotland
7C3 **Stafford** England
7C3 **Stafford** *County* England
68D2 **Stafford Springs** USA
Stalingrad = Volgograd
47B3 **Stallberg** *Mt* South Africa
55J1 **Stallworthy,C** Canada
19E2 **Stalowa Wola** Poland
68D2 **Stamford** Connecticut, USA
7D3 **Stamford** England
68C1 **Stamford** New York, USA
62C2 **Stamford** Texas, USA
47B1 **Stampriet** Namibia
47D2 **Standerton** South Africa
64C2 **Standish** USA
58D1 **Stanford** USA
47E2 **Stanger** South Africa
6C2 **Stanhope** England
66B2 **Stanislaus** *R* USA
17E2 **Stanke Dimitrov** Bulgaria
34C4 **Stanley** Australia
74E8 **Stanley** Falkland Islands
58D2 **Stanley** Idaho, USA
60C1 **Stanley** N Dakota, USA
44B3 **Stanley Res** India
Stanleyville = Kisangani
70D3 **Stann Creek** Belize
26F1 **Stanovoy Khrebet** *Mts* Russian Federation
34D1 **Stanthorpe** Australia
8A3 **Stanton Banks** *Sand-bank* Scotland
60C2 **Stapleton** USA
19E2 **Starachowice** Poland
17E2 **Stara Planiná** *Mts* Bulgaria
20E4 **Staraya Russa** Russian Federation
17F2 **Stara Zagora** Bulgaria
18D2 **Stargard Szczecinski** Poland
63E2 **Starkville** USA
18C3 **Starnberg** Germany
19D2 **Starogard Gdański** Poland
19F3 **Starokonstantinov** Ukraine
7C4 **Start Pt** England
21F5 **Staryy Oskol** Russian Federation
68B2 **State College** USA
68C2 **Staten I** USA
67B2 **Statesboro** USA
67B1 **Statesville** USA
65D3 **Staunton** USA
12F7 **Stavanger** Norway
13C2 **Stavelot** Belgium
13C1 **Stavoren** Netherlands
21G6 **Stavropol'** Russian Federation
34B3 **Stawell** Australia
58B2 **Stayton** USA
60B2 **Steamboat Springs** USA
68B2 **Steelton** USA
58C2 **Steens Mt** USA
55N2 **Steenstrups Gletscher** *Gl* Greenland
13D1 **Steenwijk** Netherlands
54H2 **Stefansson I** Canada
47E2 **Stegi** Swaziland
61D1 **Steinbach** Canada
12G6 **Steinkjer** Norway
47B2 **Steinkopf** South Africa
47C2 **Stella** South Africa
47B3 **Stellenbosch** South Africa
13C3 **Stenay** France
18C2 **Stendal** Germany
21H8 **Stepanakert** Azerbaijan
61D1 **Stephen** USA
35B2 **Stephens,C** New Zealand
34B2 **Stephens Creek** Australia
64B1 **Stephenson** USA
55N5 **Stephenville** Canada
62C2 **Stephenville** USA
47D3 **Sterkstroom** South Africa
60C2 **Sterling** Colorado, USA
64B2 **Sterling** Illinois, USA
62C1 **Sterling** Kansas, USA
60C1 **Sterling** N Dakota, USA
62B2 **Sterling City** USA
64C2 **Sterling Heights** USA
20K5 **Sterlitamak** Russian Federation
54G4 **Stettler** Canada
64C2 **Steubenville** USA
7D4 **Stevenage** England
64B2 **Stevens Point** USA
54D3 **Stevens Village** USA
54F4 **Stewart** Canada
59C3 **Stewart** USA
54E3 **Stewart** *R* Canada
35A3 **Stewart I** New Zealand
33F1 **Stewart Is** Solomon Islands
8C4 **Stewarton** Scotland
54E3 **Stewart River** Canada
68B3 **Stewartstown** USA
61E2 **Stewartville** USA
47D3 **Steynsburg** South Africa
18C3 **Steyr** Austria
47C3 **Steytlerville** South Africa

54F4 **Stikine** *R* Canada
61E1 **Stillwater** Minnesota, USA
63C1 **Stillwater** Oklahoma, USA
59C3 **Stillwater Range** *Mts* USA
62B1 **Stinnett** USA
34A2 **Stirling** Australia
8D3 **Stirling** Scotland
12G6 **Stjørdal** Norway
13E4 **Stockach** Germany
68D1 **Stockbridge** USA
18D3 **Stockerau** Austria
12H7 **Stockholm** Sweden
7C3 **Stockport** England
66B2 **Stockton** California, USA
6D2 **Stockton** England
60D3 **Stockton** Kansas, USA
63D1 **Stockton L** USA
7C3 **Stoke-on-Trent** England
12G5 **Stokmarknes** Norway
25P2 **Stolbovoy, Ostrov** *I* Russian Federation
12K8 **Stolbtsy** Russian Federation
19F2 **Stolin** Belarus
7C3 **Stone** England
68C3 **Stone Harbor** USA
8D3 **Stonehaven** Scotland
63C2 **Stonewall** USA
7D3 **Stony Stratford** England
12H5 **Storavan** *L* Sweden
12G6 **Støren** Norway
34C4 **Storm B** Australia
61D2 **Storm Lake** USA
8B2 **Stornoway** Scotland
19F3 **Storozhinets** Ukraine
68D2 **Storrs** USA
12G6 **Storsjön** *L* Sweden
12H5 **Storuman** Sweden
60B2 **Story** USA
68E1 **Stoughton** USA
7E4 **Stour** *R* England
7C3 **Stourbridge** England
7C3 **Stourport** England
7E3 **Stowmarket** England
9C2 **Strabane** Northern Ireland
34C4 **Strahan** Australia
18C2 **Stralsund** Germany
47B3 **Strand** South Africa
12F6 **Stranda** Norway
9D2 **Strangford Lough** *L* Irish Republic
12H7 **Strängnäs** Sweden
8C4 **Stranraer** Scotland
14D2 **Strasbourg** France
65D3 **Strasburg** USA
66C2 **Stratford** California, USA
64C2 **Stratford** Canada
68D2 **Stratford** Connecticut, USA
35B1 **Stratford** New Zealand
62B1 **Stratford** Texas, USA
7D3 **Stratford-on-Avon** England
34A3 **Strathalbyn** Australia
8C4 **Strathclyde** *Region* Scotland
65E1 **Stratton** USA
64B2 **Streator** USA
8D2 **Stroma, I** Scotland
16D3 **Stromboli** *I* Italy
8D2 **Stromness** Scotland
61D2 **Stromsburg** USA
12H6 **Stromsund** Sweden
12G6 **Ströms Vattudal** *L* Sweden
8D2 **Stronsay** *I* Scotland
7C4 **Stroud** England
68C2 **Stroudsburg** USA
17E2 **Struma** *R* Bulgaria
7B3 **Strumble Head** *Pt* Wales
17E2 **Strumica** Macedonia, Yugoslavia
19E3 **Stryy** Ukraine
19E3 **Stryy** *R* Ukraine
34B1 **Strzelecki Creek** *R* Australia
67B3 **Stuart** Florida, USA
60D2 **Stuart** Nebraska, USA
54F4 **Stuart L** Canada
12G8 **Stubice** Poland
30D3 **Stung Sen** *R* Cambodia
30D3 **Stung Treng** Cambodia
16B2 **Stura** *R* Italy
76G7 **Sturge I** Antarctica
64B2 **Sturgeon Bay** USA
65D1 **Sturgeon Falls** Canada
64B3 **Sturgis** Kentucky, USA
64B2 **Sturgis** Michigan, USA
60C2 **Sturgis** S Dakota, USA
32B2 **Sturt Creek** *R* Australia
34B1 **Sturt Desert** Australia
47D3 **Stutterheim** South Africa
63D2 **Stuttgart** USA
18B3 **Stuttgart** Germany
12A1 **Stykkishólmur** Iceland
19F2 **Styr'** *R* Ukraine
75D2 **Suaçuí Grande** *R* Brazil
50D2 **Suakin** Sudan
28A3 **Suan** N Korea
31E5 **Suao** Taiwan
17D1 **Subotica** Serbia, Yugoslavia
21D6 **Suceava** Romania
72E7 **Sucre** Bolivia
75B2 **Sucuriú** *R* Brazil
50C2 **Sudan** *Republic* Africa
64C1 **Sudbury** Canada
7E3 **Sudbury** England
50C3 **Sudd** *Swamp* Sudan
73G2 **Suddie** Guyana
45B4 **Sudr** Egypt
50C3 **Sue** *R* Sudan
40B4 **Suez** Egypt
40B3 **Suez Canal** Egypt
40B4 **Suez,G of** Egypt
68C2 **Suffern** USA
65D3 **Suffolk** USA
7E3 **Suffolk** *County* England
65E2 **Sugarloaf Mt** USA
34D2 **Sugarloaf Pt** Australia
25R3 **Sugoy** *R* Russian Federation
41G5 **Suḩār** Oman
26D1 **Sühbaatar** Mongolia
42B3 **Sui** Pakistan
31C2 **Suide** China
28C2 **Suifen He** *R* China
26F2 **Suihua** China
31B3 **Suining** China
13C3 **Suippes** France
10B3 **Suir** *R* Irish Republic
31C3 **Sui Xian** China
31E1 **Suizhong** China
42C3 **Sujāngarh** India
27D7 **Sukadana** Indonesia
29E3 **Sukagawa** Japan
26C3 **Sukai Hu** *L* China
28B3 **Sukch'ŏn** N Korea
20F5 **Sukhinichi** Russian Federation
20G4 **Sukhona** *R* Russian Federation
21G7 **Sukhumi** Georgia
55N3 **Sukkertoppen** Greenland
55N3 **Sukkertoppen Isflade** *Ice field* Greenland
12L6 **Sukkozero** Russian Federation
42B3 **Sukkur** Pakistan
44C2 **Sukma** India
51B6 **Sukses** Namibia
28B4 **Sukumo** Japan
21F5 **Sula** *R* Russian Federation
42B3 **Sulaiman Range** *Mts* Pakistan
32B1 **Sula, Kepulauan** *I* Indonesia
8B2 **Sula Sgeir** *I* Scotland
27E7 **Sulawesi** *Is* Indonesia
41E2 **Sulaymānīyah** Iraq
8C2 **Sule Skerry** *I* Scotland
17F1 **Sulina** Romania
13E1 **Sulingen** Germany
12H5 **Sulitjelma** Norway
72B4 **Sullana** Peru
63D1 **Sullivan** USA
13B4 **Sully-sur-Loire** France
16C2 **Sulmona** Italy
63D2 **Sulphur** Louisiana, USA
63C2 **Sulphur** Oklahoma, USA
63C2 **Sulphur Springs** USA
21E8 **Sultan Dağları** *Mts* Turkey
43E3 **Sultānpur** India
27F6 **Sulu Arch** *Is* Philippines
27E6 **Sulu S** Philippines
13E3 **Sulz** Germany
74D3 **Sumampa** Argentina
27C6 **Sumatera** *I* Indonesia
27E8 **Sumba** *I* Indonesia
27E7 **Sumbawa** *I* Indonesia
27E7 **Sumbawa Besar** Indonesia
51D4 **Sumbawanga** Tanzania
51B5 **Sumbe** Angola
8E2 **Sumburgh Head** *Pt* Scotland
43N2 **Sumesar Ra** *Mts* Nepal
21H7 **Sumgait** Azerbaijan
26H3 **Sumisu** *I* Japan
54F4 **Summit Lake** Canada
59C3 **Summit Mt** USA
35B2 **Sumner,L** New Zealand
29B4 **Sumoto** Japan
67B2 **Sumter** USA
21E5 **Sumy** Ukraine
58D1 **Sun** *R* USA
29D2 **Sunagawa** Japan
28A3 **Sunan** N Korea
8C3 **Sunart, Loch** *Inlet* Scotland
68B2 **Sunbury** USA
28B3 **Sunch'ŏn** N Korea
28B4 **Sunch'ŏn** S Korea
60C2 **Sundance** USA
43E4 **Sundargarh** India
43F4 **Sunderbans** *Swamp* Bangladesh/India
6D2 **Sunderland** England
65D1 **Sundridge** Canada
12H6 **Sundsvall** Sweden
58C1 **Sunnyside** USA
59B3 **Sunnyvale** USA
64B2 **Sun Prairie** USA
25N3 **Suntar** Russian Federation
58D2 **Sun Valley** USA
48B4 **Sunyani** Ghana
20E3 **Suojarvi** Russian Federation
28B4 **Suō-nada** *B* Japan
12K6 **Suonenjoki** Finland
43F3 **Supaul** India
59D4 **Superior** Arizona, USA
61D2 **Superior** Nebraska, USA
64A1 **Superior** Wisconsin, USA
64B1 **Superior,L** Canada/USA
30C3 **Suphan Buri** Thailand
40D2 **Süphan Dağ** *Mt* Turkey
27G7 **Supiori** *I* Indonesia
41E3 **Sūq ash Suyūkh** Iraq
45D1 **Şuqaylibīyah** Syria
31D3 **Suqian** China
Suqutra = Socotra
38D3 **Sūr** Oman
20H5 **Sura** *R* Russian Federation
27E7 **Surabaya** Indonesia
29C4 **Suraga-wan** *B* Japan
27E7 **Surakarta** Indonesia
45D1 **Şūrān** Syria
34C1 **Surat** Australia
42C4 **Sūrat** India
42C3 **Sūratgarh** India
30B4 **Surat Thani** Thailand
42C4 **Surendranagar** India
68C3 **Surf City** USA
24J3 **Surgut** Russian Federation
44B2 **Suriāpet** India
27F6 **Surigao** Philippines
30C3 **Surin** Thailand
73G3 **Surinam** *Republic* S America
66B2 **Sur,Pt** USA
7D4 **Surrey** *County* England
49D1 **Surt** Libya
12A2 **Surtsey** *I* Iceland
16B1 **Susa** Italy
28B4 **Susa** Japan
29B4 **Susaki** Japan
59B2 **Susanville** USA
68C2 **Susquehanna** USA
68B3 **Susquehanna** *R* USA
68C2 **Sussex** USA
7D4 **Sussex West** England
47C3 **Sutherland** South Africa
60C2 **Sutherland** USA
42C2 **Sutlej** *R* Pakistan
59B3 **Sutter Creek** USA
64C3 **Sutton** USA
29D2 **Suttsu** Japan
29D3 **Suwa** Japan
19E2 **Suwałki** Poland
67B3 **Suwannee** *R* USA
45C2 **Suweilih** Jordan
28B3 **Suwŏn** S Korea
31D3 **Su Xian** China
29C3 **Suzaka** Japan
31E3 **Suzhou** China
29D3 **Suzu** Japan
29C4 **Suzuka** Japan
29C3 **Suzu-misaki** *C* Japan
24C2 **Svalbard** *Is* Barents Sea
19E3 **Svalyava** Ukraine
55N2 **Svartenhuk Halvø** *Region* Greenland
12G5 **Svartisen** *Mt* Norway
30D3 **Svay Rieng** Cambodia
12G6 **Sveg** Sweden
12G7 **Svendborg** Denmark
Sverdlovsk = Yekaterinburg
55J1 **Sverdrup Chan** Canada
54H2 **Sverdrup Is** Canada
26G2 **Svetlaya** Russian Federation
19E2 **Svetlogorsk** Russian Federation
12K6 **Svetogorsk** Russian Federation
17E2 **Svetozarevo** Serbia, Yugoslavia
17F2 **Svilengrad** Bulgaria
19F2 **Svir'** Belarus
20E3 **Svir'** *R* Russian Federation
18D3 **Švitavy** Czech Republic
26F1 **Svobodnyy** Russian Federation
12G5 **Svolvær** Norway
7E3 **Swaffam** England
33E3 **Swain Reefs** Australia
67B2 **Swainsboro** USA
33H2 **Swains I** American Samoa
47B1 **Swakop** *R* Namibia
47A1 **Swakopmund** Namibia
6D2 **Swale** *R* England
27E6 **Swallow Reef** S China Sea
44B3 **Swāmihalli** India
70D3 **Swan** *I* Honduras
7D4 **Swanage** England
34B3 **Swan Hill** Australia
69A3 **Swan I** Caribbean Sea
54H4 **Swan River** Canada
7C4 **Swansea** Wales
7C4 **Swansea B** Wales
47C3 **Swartberge** *Mts* South Africa
47D2 **Swartruggens** South Africa
Swatow = Shantou
47E2 **Swaziland** *Kingdom* South Africa
12G7 **Sweden** *Kingdom* N Europe
58B2 **Sweet Home** USA
62B2 **Sweetwater** USA
60B2 **Sweetwater** *R* USA
47C3 **Swellendam** South Africa
18D2 **Świdnica** Poland
18D2 **Świdwin** Poland
18D2 **Świebodzin** Poland
19D2 **Świecie** Poland
54H4 **Swift Current** Canada
9C2 **Swilly, Lough** *Estuary* Irish Republic
7D4 **Swindon** England
18C2 **Świnoujście** Poland
14D2 **Switzerland** Europe
9C3 **Swords** Irish Republic
43M1 **Syang** Nepal
9A3 **Sybil Pt** Irish Republic
34D2 **Sydney** Australia
20H3 **Syktyvkar** Russian Federation
67A2 **Sylacauga** USA
12G6 **Sylarna** *Mt* Sweden
43G4 **Sylhet** Bangladesh
18B1 **Sylt** *I* Germany
64C2 **Sylvania** USA
76G11 **Syowa** *Base* Antarctica
16D3 **Syracuse** Italy
62B1 **Syracuse** Kansas, USA
68B1 **Syracuse** New York, USA
65D2 **Syracuse** USA
24H5 **Syr Darya** *R* Kazakhstan
40C2 **Syria** *Republic* SW Asia
20L4 **Sysert'** Russian Federation
20H5 **Syzran'** Russian Federation
18C2 **Szczecin** Poland
18D2 **Szczecinek** Poland
19E2 **Szczytno** Poland
19E3 **Szeged** Hungary
19D3 **Székesfehérvar** Hungary
19D3 **Szekszárd** Hungary
19D3 **Szolnok** Hungary
18D3 **Szombathely** Hungary
18D2 **Szprotawa** Poland

T

47D3 **Tabankulu** South Africa
32E1 **Tabar Is** Papua New Guinea
16B3 **Tabarka** Tunisia
41G3 **Tabas** Iran
72E4 **Tabatinga** Brazil
48B2 **Tabelbala** Algeria
30C3 **Tabeng** Cambodia
54G5 **Taber** Canada
47B3 **Table Mt** South Africa
63D1 **Table Rock Res** USA
18C3 **Tábor** Czech Republic
50D4 **Tabora** Tanzania
20L4 **Tabory** Russian Federation
48B4 **Tabou** Ivory Coast
41E2 **Tabrīz** Iran
40C4 **Tabūk** Saudi Arabia
39G1 **Tacheng** China
27F5 **Tacloban** Philippines
72D7 **Tacna** Peru
59D4 **Tacna** USA
56A2 **Tacoma** USA
68D1 **Taconic Range** USA
75A3 **Tacuatí** Paraguay
48C2 **Tademait, Plateau du** Algeria
50E2 **Tadjoura** Djibouti
65F1 **Tadoussac** Canada
44B3 **Tādpatri** India
28B3 **Taebaek Sanmaek** *Mts* N Korea/S Korea
28B3 **T'aech'ŏn** N Korea
28A3 **Taech'on** S Korea
28A3 **Taedasa-Do** N Korea
28A3 **Taedong** *R* N Korea
28A3 **Taegang-got** *Pen* N Korea
28B3 **Taegu** S Korea
28A2 **Taehung** N Korea
28B3 **Taejŏn** S Korea
15B1 **Tafalla** Spain
48C2 **Tafasaset** *Watercourse* Algeria
7C4 **Taff** *R* Wales
45C3 **Tafila** Jordan
66C3 **Taft** USA
21F6 **Taganrog** Russian Federation
48A3 **Tagant** *Region* Mauritius
48B2 **Taguenout Hagguerete** *Well* Mali
33E2 **Tagula** *I* Papua New Guinea
Tagus = Tejo
48C2 **Tahat** *Mt* Algeria
37M5 **Tahiti** *I* Pacific Ocean
63C1 **Tahlequah** USA
59B3 **Tahoe City** USA
59B3 **Tahoe,L** USA
62B2 **Tahoka** USA
48C3 **Tahoua** Niger
40B4 **Tahta** Egypt
27F6 **Tahuna** Indonesia
31D2 **Tai'an** China
28A2 **Tai'an** China
31B3 **Taibai Shan** *Mt* China
31D1 **Taibus Qi** China
31E5 **Taichung** Taiwan
35B3 **Taieri** *R* New Zealand
31C2 **Taihang Shan** *Upland* China
35C1 **Taihape** New Zealand
31E3 **Tai Hu** *L* China
29D2 **Taiki** Japan
34A3 **Tailem Bend** Australia
8C3 **Tain** Scotland
31E5 **Tainan** Taiwan
75D2 **Taiobeiras** Brazil
31E5 **Taipei** Taiwan
30C5 **Taiping** Malaysia
29D3 **Taira** Japan
28B3 **Taisha** Japan
74B7 **Taitao,Pen de** Chile
31E5 **Taitung** Taiwan
12K5 **Taivalkoski** Finland
26F4 **Taiwan** *Republic* China
31D5 **Taiwan Str** China/Taiwan
45C3 **Taiyiba** Jordan
31C2 **Taiyuan** China
31D3 **Taizhou** China
50E2 **Ta'izz** Yemen
39E2 **Tajikistan** *Republic* Asia
15B1 **Tajo** *R* Spain
30B2 **Tak** Thailand
32B1 **Takabonerate, Kepulauan** *Is* Indonesia
29D3 **Takada** Japan
29B4 **Takahashi** Japan
35B2 **Takaka** New Zealand
29C4 **Takamatsu** Japan
29D3 **Takaoka** Japan
35B1 **Takapuna** New Zealand
29D3 **Takasaki** Japan
29C3 **Takayama** Japan
29D3 **Takefu** Japan
27C6 **Takengon** Indonesia
30C3 **Takeo** Cambodia
28B4 **Takeo** Japan
Take-shima = Tok-do
41E2 **Takestān** Iran
28B4 **Taketa** Japan
29D2 **Takikawa** Japan
29D2 **Takinoue** Japan
54G3 **Takiyvak L** Canada
50D2 **Takkaze** *R* Eritrea/Ethiopia
48B4 **Takoradi** Ghana
42C2 **Talagang** Pakistan
44B4 **Talaimannar** Sri Lanka
48C3 **Talak** *Desert Region* Niger
72B4 **Talara** Peru
32E1 **Talasea** Papua New Guinea
45B3 **Talata** Egypt
27F6 **Talaud, Kepulauan** *Is* Indonesia
15B2 **Talavera de la Reina** Spain
74B5 **Talca** Chile
74B5 **Talcahuano** Chile
43F4 **Tālcher** India
39F1 **Taldy Kurgan** Kazakhstan
27F7 **Taliabu** *I* Indonesia
42B1 **Taligan** Afghanistan
50D3 **Tali Post** Sudan
27E7 **Taliwang** Indonesia
54D3 **Talkeetna** USA
45A3 **Talkha** Egypt
67A2 **Talladega** USA
40D2 **Tall 'Afar** Iraq
67B2 **Tallahassee** USA
45D1 **Tall Bīsah** Syria
20C4 **Tallinn** Estonia
40C3 **Tall Kalakh** Syria
63D2 **Tallulah** USA
26B1 **Tal'menka** Russian Federation
21E6 **Tal'noye** Ukraine
19E2 **Talpaki** Russian Federation
74B3 **Taltal** Chile
34C1 **Talwood** Australia
61E2 **Tama** USA
27E6 **Tamabo Ra** *Mts* Borneo
48B4 **Tamale** Ghana
29C4 **Tamano** Japan
48C2 **Tamanrasset** Algeria
48C2 **Tamanrasset** *Watercourse* Algeria
68C2 **Tamaqua** USA
7B4 **Tamar** *R* England
Tamatave = Toamasina
48A3 **Tambacounda** Senegal

21G5 Tambov Russian Federation
15A1 Tambre R Spain
50C3 Tambura Sudan
48A3 Tamchaket Mauritius
15A1 Tamega R Portugal
70C2 Tamiahua, L de Lg Mexico
44B3 Tamil Nādu State India
17E1 Tamiş R Romania
30D2 Tam Ky Vietnam
67B3 Tampa USA
67B3 Tampa B USA
12J6 Tampere Finland
70C2 Tampico Mexico
26E2 Tamsagbulag Mongolia
31E4 Tamsui Taiwan
43G4 Tamu Burma
34D2 Tamworth Australia
7D3 Tamworth England
20D1 Tana Norway
12K5 Tana R Finland/Norway
50E4 Tana R Kenya
29C4 Tanabe Japan
12K4 Tanafjord Inlet Norway
27E7 Tanahgrogot Indonesia
27G7 Tanahmerah Indonesia
50D2 Tana, L Ethiopia
54C3 Tanana USA
54C3 Tanana R USA
Tananarive = Antananarivo
28B2 Tanch'ŏn N Korea
74E5 Tandil Argentina
27G7 Tandjung d'Urville C Indonesia
27G7 Tandjung Vals C Indonesia
42B3 Tando Adam Pakistan
42B3 Tando Muhammad Khan Pakistan
34B2 Tandou L Australia
44B2 Tāndūr India
35C1 Taneatua New Zealand
30B2 Tanen Range Mts Burma/Thailand
48B2 Tanezrouft Desert Region Algeria
50D4 Tanga Tanzania
33E1 Tanga Is Papua New Guinea
50C4 Tanganyika,L Tanzania/Zaïre
Tanger = Tangiers
39H2 Tanggula Shan Mts China
15A2 Tangiers Morocco
28A3 Tangjin S Korea
39G2 Tangra Yumco L China
31D2 Tangshan China
26D1 Tanguy Russian Federation
27G7 Tanimbar, Kepulauan Arch Indonesia
51E6 Tanjona Ankaboa C Madagascar
51E5 Tanjona Anorontany C Madagascar
51E5 Tanjona Bobaomby C Madagascar
51E5 Tanjona Vilanandro C Madagascar
51E6 Tanjona Vohimena C Madagascar
27C6 Tanjungbalai Indonesia
27D7 Tanjungpandan Indonesia
27D7 Tanjung Priok Indonesia
27E6 Tanjungredeb Indonesia
32A1 Tanjung Selatan Pt Indonesia
27E6 Tanjungselor Indonesia
32C1 Tanjung Vals Pt Indonesia
42C2 Tank Pakistan
33F2 Tanna I Vanuatu
26C1 Tannu Ola Mts Russian Federation
48B4 Tano R Ghana
48C3 Tanout Niger
43E3 Tansing Nepal
49F1 Tanta Egypt
48A2 Tan-Tan Morocco
54B3 Tanunak USA
28A3 Tanyang S Korea
50D4 Tanzania Republic Africa
31A3 Tao He R China
31B2 Taole China
62A1 Taos USA
48B1 Taourirt Morocco
20D4 Tapa Estonia
70C3 Tapachula Mexico
73G4 Tapajós R Brazil
27D7 Tapan Indonesia
35A3 Tapanui New Zealand
72E5 Tapauá R Brazil
42D4 Tāpi R India
43F3 Taplejung Nepal
65D3 Tappahannock USA
35B2 Tapuaenuku Mt New Zealand
75C3 Tapuaritinga Brazil
72F4 Tapurucuara Brazil
75B2 Taquaral, Serra do Mts Brazil
75B2 Taquari R Brazil
34D1 Tara Australia
24J4 Tara Russian Federation
24J4 Tara R Russian Federation
17D2 Tara R Bosnia-Herzegovina
48D4 Taraba R Nigeria
72F7 Tarabuco Bolivia
Tarābulus = Tripoli (Libya)
35C1 Taradale New Zealand
27E6 Tarakan Indonesia
Taranaki, Mt = Egmont, Mt
15B1 Tarancón Spain
8B3 Taransay I Scotland
16D2 Taranto Italy
16D2 Taranto, G di Italy
72C5 Tarapoto Peru
14C2 Tarare France
35C2 Tararua Range Mts New Zealand
20H2 Tarasovo Russian Federation
48C2 Tarat Algeria
35C1 Tarawera New Zealand
15B1 Tarazona Spain
39G1 Tarbagatay, Khrebet Mts Russian Federation
8D3 Tarbat Ness Pen Scotland
42C2 Tarbela Res Pakistan
8C4 Tarbert Strathclyde, Scotland
8B3 Tarbert Western Isles, Scotland
14B3 Tarbes France
67C1 Tarboro USA
32C4 Tarcoola Australia
34C2 Tarcoon Australia
34D2 Taree Australia
48A2 Tarfaya Morocco
58D2 Targhee P USA
49D1 Tarhūnah Libya
41F5 Tarīf UAE
72F8 Tarija Bolivia
44B3 Tarikere India
38C4 Tarīm Yemen
50D4 Tarime Tanzania
39G1 Tarim He R China
39G2 Tarim Pendi Basin China
42B2 Tarin Kut Afghanistan
47D3 Tarkastad South Africa
61D2 Tarkio USA
27F5 Tarlac Philippines
72C6 Tarma Peru
14C3 Tarn R France
19E2 Tarnobrzeg Poland
19E3 Tarnów Poland
16B2 Taro R Italy
32D3 Taroom Australia
48B1 Taroudannt Morocco
15C1 Tarragona Spain
34C4 Tarraleah Australia
15C1 Tarrasa Spain
68D2 Tarrytown USA
40B2 Tarsus Turkey
8E2 Tartan Oilfield N Sea
26H2 Tartarskiy Proliv Str Russian Federation
20D4 Tartu Estonia
40C3 Tartūs Syria
75D2 Tarumirim Brazil
27C6 Tarutung Indonesia
16C1 Tarvisio Italy
65D1 Taschereau Canada
38D1 Tashauz Turkmenistan
43G3 Tashigang Bhutan
39E1 Tashkent Uzbekistan
24K4 Tashtagol Russian Federation
25K4 Tashtyp Russian Federation
45C2 Tasīl Syria
55N2 Tasiussaq Greenland
50B2 Tasker Well Niger
35B2 Tasman B New Zealand
32D5 Tasmania I Australia
35B2 Tasman Mts New Zealand
34C4 Tasman Pen Australia
33E4 Tasman S Australia/New Zealand
40C1 Taşova Turkey
48C2 Tassili du Hoggar Desert Region Algeria
48C2 Tassili N'jjer Desert Region Algeria
48B2 Tata Morocco
19D3 Tatabánya Hungary
48D1 Tataouine Tunisia
24J4 Tatarsk Russian Federation
20J4 Tatarstan Republic Russian Federation
29C3 Tateyama Japan
54G3 Tathlina L Canada
55J4 Tatnam, Cape Canada
19D3 Tatry Mts Poland/Slovakia
29B4 Tatsuno Japan
42B4 Tatta Pakistan
75C3 Tatuí Brazil
62B2 Tatum USA
40D2 Tatvan Turkey
33H2 Ta'u I American Samoa
73K5 Tauá Brazil
75C3 Taubaté Brazil
13E2 Taufstein Mt Germany
35C1 Taumarunui New Zealand
47C2 Taung South Africa
30B2 Taungdwingyi Burma
30B1 Taung-gyi Burma
30A2 Taungup Burma
42C2 Taunsa Pakistan
7C4 Taunton England
68E2 Taunton USA
40B2 Taunus Mts Turkey
13E2 Taunus Region Germany
35C1 Taupo New Zealand
35C1 Taupo,L New Zealand
19E1 Taurage Lithuania
35C1 Tauranga New Zealand
35C1 Tauranga Harbour B New Zealand
35B1 Tauroa Pt New Zealand
40B2 Taurus Mts Turkey
55J3 Tavani Canada
24H4 Tavda Russian Federation
24H4 Tavda R Russian Federation
33H2 Taveuni I Fiji
15A2 Tavira Portugal
7B4 Tavistock England
30B3 Tavoy Burma
30B3 Tavoy Pt Burma
40A2 Tavşanlı Turkey
7C4 Taw R England
35B2 Tawa New Zealand
63C2 Tawakoni,L USA
64C2 Tawas City USA
27E6 Tawau Malaysia
50C2 Taweisha Sudan
27F6 Tawitawi I Philippines
70C3 Taxco Mexico
8D3 Tay R Scotland
27E7 Tayan Indonesia
50E3 Tayeeglow Somalia
8C3 Tay, Loch L Scotland
64C2 Taylor Michigan, USA
63C2 Taylor Texas, USA
54B3 Taylor USA
62A1 Taylor,Mt USA
64B3 Taylorville USA
40C4 Taymā' Saudi Arabia
25L3 Taymura R Russian Federation
25M2 Taymyr, Ozero L Russian Federation
25L2 Taymyr, Poluostrov Pen Russian Federation
30D3 Tay Ninh Vietnam
25L4 Tayshet Russian Federation
26C2 Tayshir Mongolia
8D3 Tayside Region Scotland
27E5 Taytay Philippines
48B1 Taza Morocco
29D3 Tazawako Japan
29D3 Tazawa-ko L Japan
49E2 Tāzirbū Libya
24J3 Tazovskiy Russian Federation
21G7 Tbilisi Georgia
50B4 Tchibanga Gabon
50B1 Tchigai,Plat du Niger
48C3 Tchin Tabaradene Niger
50B3 Tcholliré Cameroon
19D2 Tczew Poland
35A3 Te Anau New Zealand
35A3 Te Anua,L New Zealand
35C1 Te Aroha New Zealand
35C1 Te Awamutu New Zealand
16B3 Tébessa Algeria
16B3 Tébessa, Mts De Algeria/Tunisia
16B3 Téboursouk Tunisia
59C4 Tecate Mexico
20L4 Techa R Russian Federation
70B3 Tecomán Mexico
70B3 Tecpan Mexico
17F1 Tecuci Romania
61D2 Tecumseh USA
24H6 Tedzhen Turkmenistan
24H6 Tedzhen R Turkmenistan
6D2 Tees R England
72F4 Tefé Brazil
70D3 Tegucigalpa Honduras
66C3 Tehachapi USA
66C3 Tehachapi Mts USA
59C3 Tehachapi P USA
54J3 Tehek L Canada
41F2 Tehrān Iran
70C3 Tehuacán Mexico
70C3 Tehuantepec Mexico
70C3 Tehuantepec, G de Mexico
70C3 Tehuantepec, Istmo de isthmus Mexico
7B3 Teifi R Wales
7C4 Teignmouth England
15A2 Tejo R Portugal
66C3 Tejon P USA
61D2 Tekamah USA
35B2 Tekapo,L New Zealand
39F1 Tekeli Kazakhstan
40A1 Tekirdağ Turkey
17F2 Tekir Dağları Mts Turkey
43G4 Teknaf Bangladesh
35C1 Te Kuiti New Zealand
70D3 Tela Honduras
21H7 Telavi Georgia
45C2 Tel Aviv Yafo Israel
54E4 Telegraph Creek Canada
74C5 Telén Argentina
59C3 Telescope Peak Mt USA
73G5 Teles Pires R Brazil
7C3 Telford England
25K4 Teli Russian Federation
45C3 Tell el Meise Mt Jordan
54B3 Teller USA
44B3 Tellicherry India
30C5 Telok Anson Malaysia
20K3 Tel'pos-iz, Gory Mt Russian Federation
19E1 Telšiai Lithuania
27D7 Telukbetung Indonesia
27F7 Teluk Bone B Indonesia
27G7 Teluk Cendrawasih B Indonesia
27E6 Teluk Darvel B Malaysia
27F7 Teluk Tolo B Indonesia
27F6 Teluk Tomini B Indonesia
27F6 Teluk Weda B Indonesia
64C1 Temagami,L Canada
69E5 Temblador Venezuela
66B3 Temblor Range Mts USA
7C3 Teme R England
30C5 Temerloh Malaysia
24G5 Temir Kazakhstan
24J4 Temirtau Kazakhstan
65D1 Temiscaming Canada
65F1 Témiscouata,L Canada
34C2 Temora Australia
59D4 Tempe USA
63C2 Temple USA
9C3 Templemore Irish Republic
66B3 Templeton USA
74B5 Temuco Chile
35B2 Temuka New Zealand
72C4 Tena Ecuador
44C2 Tenāli India
30B3 Tenasserim Burma
7B4 Tenby Wales
50E3 Tendaho Ethiopia
16B2 Tende, Colle de P France/Italy
44E4 Ten Degree Chan Indian Ocean
29E3 Tendo Japan
50B2 Ténéré, Erg du Desert Region Niger
48A2 Tenerife I Canary Islands
15C2 Ténès Algeria
30B1 Teng R Burma
31A2 Tengger Shamo Desert China
24H4 Tengiz, Ozero L Kazakhstan
76G2 Teniente Rodolfo Marsh Base Antarctica
44B4 Tenkāsi India
51C5 Tenke Zaïre
48B3 Tenkodogo Burkina
32C2 Tennant Creek Australia
63E1 Tennessee R USA
57E3 Tennessee State USA
60B3 Tennessee P USA
27E6 Tenom Malaysia
70C3 Tenosique Mexico
34D1 Tenterfield Australia
67B3 Ten Thousand Is USA
75D2 Teófilo Otôni Brazil
70B2 Tepehuanes Mexico
70B2 Tepic Mexico
18C2 Teplice Czech Republic
35C1 Te Puke New Zealand
15C1 Ter R Spain
48C3 Téra Niger
29C3 Teradomari Japan
16C2 Teramo Italy
48A1 Terceira I Azores
19F3 Terebovlya Ukraine
75B3 Terenos Brazil
73K5 Teresina Brazil
75D3 Teresópolis Brazil
44E4 Teressa I Nicobar Is, Indian Ocean
40C1 Terme Turkey
38E2 Termez Uzbekistan
70C3 Términos, L de Lg Mexico
16C2 Termoli Italy
27F6 Ternate Indonesia
16C2 Terni Italy
19F3 Ternopol Ukraine
26H2 Terpeniya, Zaliv B Russian Federation
66C3 Terra Bella USA
64B1 Terrace Bay Canada
16C2 Terracina Italy
51C6 Terrafirma South Africa
76G8 Terre Adélie Region Antarctica
63D3 Terre Bonne B USA
64B3 Terre Haute USA
63C2 Terrell USA
60B1 Terry USA
18B2 Terschelling I Netherlands
15B1 Teruel Spain
54C2 Teshekpuk Lake USA
29D2 Teshikaga Japan
29E2 Teshio R Japan
29D2 Teshio dake Mt Japan
25L5 Tesiyn Gol R Mongolia
54E3 Teslin Canada
75B2 Tesouro Brazil
48C2 Tessalit Mali
48C3 Tessaoua Niger
7D4 Test R England
51D5 Tete Mozambique
19F2 Teterev R Ukraine
58D1 Teton R USA
58D2 Teton Range Mts USA
48B1 Tetouan Morocco
20H5 Tetyushi Russian Federation
72F8 Teuco R Argentina
74D2 Teuco R Paraguay
16B3 Teulada, C Sardinia, Italy
27F7 Teun I Indonesia
29D2 Teuri-tō I Japan
13E1 Teutoburger Wald Hills Germany
16C2 Tevere R Italy
8D4 Teviot R Scotland
24J4 Tevriz Russian Federation
35A3 Te Waewae B New Zealand
34D1 Tewantin Australia
7C3 Tewkesbury England
31A3 Têwo China
63D2 Texarkana USA
63D2 Texarkana,L USA
34D1 Texas Australia
56C3 Texas State USA
63D3 Texas City USA
18A2 Texel I Netherlands
62B1 Texhoma USA
63C2 Texoma,L USA
47D2 Teyateyaneng Lesotho
42A2 Teyvareh Afghanistan
43G3 Tezpur India
30C1 Tha R Laos
47D2 Thabana Ntlenyana Mt Lesotho
47D2 Thaba Putsoa Mt Lesotho
47D1 Thabazimbi South Africa
30B3 Thagyettaw Burma
30D1 Thai Binh Vietnam
30C2 Thailand Kingdom SE Asia
30C3 Thailand,G of Thailand
30D1 Thai Nguyen Vietnam
30D2 Thakhek Laos
42C2 Thal Pakistan
30C4 Thale Luang L Thailand
34C1 Thallon Australia
35C1 Thames New Zealand
7E4 Thames R England
21G8 Thamhar, Wadi ath R Iraq
44A2 Thāne India
30D2 Thanh Hoa Vietnam
44B3 Thanjāvūr India
13D4 Thann France
42C3 Thar Desert India
34B1 Thargomindah Australia
17E2 Thásos I Greece
30B2 Thaton Burma
30A2 Thayetmyo Burma
7E3 The Broads England
54F5 The Dalles USA
60C2 Thedford USA
48A3 The Gambia Republic W Africa
41F4 The Gulf SW Asia
18A2 The Hague Netherlands
54H3 Thelon R Canada
7E4 The Naze Pt England
32E3 Theodore Australia
59D4 Theodore Roosevelt L USA
72F6 Theodore Roosevelt, R Brazil
54H4 The Pas Canada
17E2 Thermaïkós Kólpos G Greece
58E2 Thermopolis USA
54F2 Thesiger B Canada
64C1 Thessalon Canada
17E2 Thessaloníki Greece
7E3 Thetford England
65E1 Thetford Mines Canada
47D2 Theunissen South Africa
63D3 Thibodaux USA
54J4 Thicket Portage Canada
61D1 Thief River Falls USA
58B2 Thielsen,Mt USA
14C2 Thiers France
48A3 Thiès Senegal
50D4 Thika Kenya
43F3 Thimphu Bhutan
14D2 Thionville France
17F3 Thíra I Greece

6D2 **Thirsk** England
44B4 **Thiruvananthapuram** India
12F7 **Thisted** Denmark
27E5 **Thitu** S China Sea
17E3 **Thívai** Greece
14C2 **Thiviers** France
66C2 **Thomas A Edison,L** USA
67B2 **Thomaston** Georgia, USA
65F2 **Thomaston** Maine, USA
9C3 **Thomastown** Irish Republic
63E2 **Thomasville** Alabama, USA
67B2 **Thomasville** Georgia, USA
67C1 **Thomasville** N Carolina, USA
55J2 **Thom Bay** Canada
54J4 **Thompson** Canada
61E2 **Thompson** *R* USA
58C1 **Thompson Falls** USA
54G3 **Thompson Landing** Canada
68D2 **Thompsonville** USA
67B2 **Thomson** USA
32D3 **Thomson** *R* Australia
30C3 **Thon Buri** Thailand
30B2 **Thongwa** Burma
62A1 **Thoreau** USA
6D2 **Thornaby** England
7D3 **Thorne** England
8D4 **Thornhill** Scotland
14B2 **Thouars** France
65D2 **Thousand Is** Canada/USA
58D1 **Three Forks** USA
64B1 **Three Lakes** USA
30B2 **Three Pagodas P** Thailand
48B4 **Three Points, C** Ghana
66C2 **Three Rivers** California, USA
64B2 **Three Rivers** Michigan, USA
62C3 **Three Rivers** Texas, USA
58B2 **Three Sisters** *Mt* USA
55M2 **Thule** Greenland
16B1 **Thun** Switzerland
64B1 **Thunder Bay** Canada
30B4 **Thung Song** Thailand
18C2 **Thüringen** *State* Germany
18C2 **Thüringer Wald** *Upland* Germany
9C3 **Thurles** Irish Republic
8D2 **Thurso** Scotland
76F4 **Thurston I** Antarctica
34B1 **Thylungra** Australia
31B5 **Tiandong** China
31B5 **Tian'e** China
31D2 **Tianjin** China
31B5 **Tianlin** China
28B2 **Tianqiaoling** China
24J5 **Tian Shan** *Mts* China/Kirgizia
31B3 **Tianshui** China
31A2 **Tianzhu** China
15C2 **Tiaret** Algeria
75B3 **Tibagi** *R* Brazil
48D4 **Tibati** Cameroon
45C2 **Tiberias** Israel
45C2 **Tiberias,L** Israel
Tiber,R = Tevere,R
58D1 **Tiber Res** USA
50B1 **Tibesti** *Mountain Region* Chad
39G2 **Tibet** *Autonomous Region* China
34B1 **Tibooburra** Australia
43E3 **Tibrikot** Nepal
70A2 **Tiburón** *I* Mexico
48B3 **Tichitt** Mauritius
48A2 **Tichla** Morocco
65E2 **Ticonderoga** USA
70D2 **Ticul** Mexico
48C2 **Tidikelt, Plaine du** *Desert Region* Algeria
48A3 **Tidjikja** Mauritius
48A3 **Tidra, Isla** Mauritius
13C2 **Tiel** Netherlands
28A2 **Tieling** China
13B2 **Tielt** Belgium
13C2 **Tienen** Belgium
13E4 **Tiengen** Germany
Tientsin = Tianjin
12H6 **Tierp** Sweden
62A1 **Tierra Amarilla** USA
70C3 **Tierra Blanca** Mexico
71C9 **Tierra del Fuego** *I* Argentina/Chile
74C8 **Tierra del Fuego** *Territory* Argentina
74C8 **Tierra del Fuego, Isla Grande de** Argentina/Chile
75C3 **Tietê** Brazil
75B3 **Tiete** *R* Brazil
64C2 **Tiffin** USA
67B2 **Tifton** USA
25R4 **Tigil** Russian Federation
72C4 **Tigre** *R* Peru
72F2 **Tigre** *R* Venezuela
50D2 **Tigre** *Region* Ethiopia
41E3 **Tigris** *R* Iraq
45B4 **Tīh, Gebel el** *Upland* Egypt
59C4 **Tijuana** Mexico
42D4 **Tikamgarh** India
21G6 **Tikhoretsk** Russian Federation
20E4 **Tikhvin** Russian Federation
33F2 **Tikopia** *I* Solomon Islands
41D3 **Tikrīt** Iraq
25O2 **Tiksi** Russian Federation
13C2 **Tilburg** Netherlands
7E4 **Tilbury** England
74C2 **Tilcara** Argentina
34B1 **Tilcha** Australia
48C3 **Tilemis, Vallée du** Mali
43K2 **Tilhar** India
30A1 **Tilin** Burma
48C3 **Tillabéri** Niger
58B1 **Tillamook** USA
44E4 **Tillanchong** *I* Nicobar Is, Indian Ocean
48C3 **Tillia** Niger
6D2 **Till, R** England
17F3 **Tílos** *I* Greece
34B2 **Tilpa** Australia
8D3 **Tilt** *R* Scotland
20H2 **Timanskiy Kryazh** *Mts* Russian Federation
35B2 **Timaru** New Zealand
21F6 **Timashevsk** Russian Federation
17E3 **Timbákion** Greece
63D3 **Timbalier B** USA
48B3 **Timbédra** Mauritius
Timbuktu = Tombouctou
48B3 **Timétrine Monts** *Mts* Mali
48C3 **Timia** Niger
17E1 **Timiş** *R* Romania
48C2 **Timimoun** Algeria
17E1 **Timişoara** Romania
64C1 **Timmins** Canada
32B1 **Timor** *I* Indonesia
32B2 **Timor S** Australia/Indonesia
45B3 **Timsâh,L** Egypt
67A1 **Tims Ford L** USA
27F6 **Tinaca Pt** Philippines
69D5 **Tinaco** Venezuela
44B3 **Tindivanam** India
48B2 **Tindouf** Algeria
66C2 **Tinemaha Res** USA
48B2 **Tinfouchy** Algeria
48C2 **Tin Fouye** Algeria
55O3 **Tingmiarmiut** Greenland
72C5 **Tingo María** Peru
48B3 **Tingrela** Ivory Coast
43F3 **Tingri** China
75E1 **Tinharé, Ilha de** Brazil
27H5 **Tinian** Pacific Ocean
74C3 **Tinogasta** Argentina
17F3 **Tínos** *I* Greece
43H3 **Tinsukia** India
7B4 **Tintagel Head** *Pt* England
48C2 **Tin Tarabine** *Watercourse* Algeria
34B3 **Tintinara** Australia
48C2 **Tin Zaouaten** Algeria
60C1 **Tioga** USA
68B2 **Tioga** *R* USA
66C2 **Tioga P** USA
30C5 **Tioman** *I* Malaysia
68B1 **Tioughnioga** *R* USA
10B3 **Tipperary** Irish Republic
9C3 **Tipperary** *County* Irish Republic
66C2 **Tipton** California, USA
61E3 **Tipton** Missouri, USA
44B3 **Tiptūr** India
17D2 **Tiranë** Albania
19F3 **Tiraspol** Moldavia
45A3 **Tir'at el Ismâilîya** *Canal* Egypt
17F3 **Tire** Turkey
40C1 **Tirebolu** Turkey
8B3 **Tiree** *I* Scotland
17F2 **Tîrgovişte** Romania
17E1 **Tîrgu Jiu** Romania
17E1 **Tîrgu Mureş** Romania
42C1 **Tirich Mir** *Mt* Pakistan
48A2 **Tiris** *Region* Morocco
20K5 **Tirlyanskiy** Russian Federation
17E1 **Tîrnăveni** Romania
17E3 **Tírnavos** Greece
42D4 **Tirodi** India
16B2 **Tirso** *R* Sardinia, Italy
44B4 **Tiruchchendūr** India
44B3 **Tiruchchirāppalli** India
44B4 **Tirunelveli** India
44B3 **Tirupati** India
44B3 **Tiruppattūr** India
44B3 **Tiruppur** India
44B3 **Tiruvannāmalai** India
63C2 **Tishomingo** USA
45D2 **Tisīyah** Syria
19E3 **Tisza** *R* Hungary
72E7 **Titicaca, Lago** Bolivia/Peru
43E4 **Titlagarh** India
17E2 **Titov Veles** Macedonia, Yugoslavia
50C3 **Titule** Zaïre
67B3 **Titusville** USA
8B2 **Tiumpan Head** *Pt* Scotland
7C4 **Tiverton** England
16C2 **Tivoli** Italy
70D2 **Tizimín** Mexico
15C2 **Tizi Ouzou** Algeria
48B2 **Tiznit** Morocco
48B1 **Tlemcen** Algeria
51E5 **Toamasina** Madagascar
29C4 **Toba** Japan
42B2 **Toba and Kakar Ranges** *Mts* Pakistan
69E4 **Tobago** *I* Caribbean Sea
27F6 **Tobelo** Indonesia
64C1 **Tobermory** Canada
8B3 **Tobermory** Scotland
27G6 **Tobi** *I* Pacific Ocean
59C2 **Tobin,Mt** USA
29C3 **Tobi-shima** *I* Japan
27D7 **Toboah** Indonesia
24H4 **Tobol** *R* Russian Federation
27F7 **Toboli** Indonesia
24H4 **Tobol'sk** Russian Federation
Tobruk = Tubruq
20J2 **Tobseda** Russian Federation
73J4 **Tocantins** *R* Brazil
73J6 **Tocantins** *State* Brazil
67B2 **Toccoa** USA
74B2 **Tocopilla** Chile
74C2 **Tocorpuri** Bolivia/Chile
72E1 **Tocuyo** *R* Venezuela
42D3 **Toda** India
28B3 **Todong** S Korea
73L6 **Todos os Santos, Baia de** *B* Brazil
56B4 **Todos Santos** Mexico
59C4 **Todos Santos,B de** Mexico
33H2 **Tofua** *I* Tonga
32B1 **Togian, Kepulauan** *I* Indonesia
48C4 **Togo** *Republic* W Africa
31C1 **Togtoh** China
62A1 **Tohatchi** USA
29E2 **Tokachi** *R* Japan
29C3 **Tokamachi** Japan
50D2 **Tokar** Sudan
26F4 **Tokara Retto** *Arch* Japan
40C1 **Tokat** Turkey
28B3 **Tok-do** *I* S Korea
33H1 **Tokelau Is** Pacific Ocean
39F1 **Tokmak** Kirgizia
35C1 **Tokomaru Bay** New Zealand
26F4 **Tokuno** *I* Ryukyu Is, Japan
29C4 **Tokushima** Japan
28B4 **Tokuyama** Japan
29D3 **Tōkyō** Japan
35C1 **Tolaga Bay** New Zealand
51E6 **Tôlañaro** Madagascar
73H8 **Toledo** Brazil
15B2 **Toledo** Spain
64C2 **Toledo** USA
63D2 **Toledo Bend Res** USA
51E6 **Toliara** Madagascar
72C2 **Tolina** *Mt* Colombia
19F2 **Toločhin** Belarus
15B1 **Tolosa** Spain
28A4 **Tolsan-do** *I* S Korea
74B5 **Toltén** Chile
70C3 **Toluca** Mexico
20H5 **Tol'yatti** Russian Federation
64A2 **Tomah** USA
64B1 **Tomahawk** USA
29E2 **Tomakomai** Japan
15A2 **Tomar** Portugal
19E2 **Tomaszów Mazowiecka** Poland
63E2 **Tombigbee** *R* USA
51B4 **Tomboco** Angola
75D3 **Tombos** Brazil
48B3 **Tombouctou** Mali
59E4 **Tombstone** USA
51B5 **Tombua** Angola
47D1 **Tomburke** South Africa
74B5 **Tomé** Chile
15B2 **Tomelloso** Spain
28A4 **Tomie** Japan
8D3 **Tomintoul** Scotland
32B3 **Tomkinson Range** *Mts* Australia
25O4 **Tommot** Russian Federation
17E2 **Tomorrit** *Mt* Albania
24K4 **Tomsk** Russian Federation
68C3 **Toms River** USA
70C3 **Tonalá** Mexico
58C1 **Tonasket** USA
7E4 **Tonbridge** England
33H3 **Tonga** *Is, Kingdom* Pacific Ocean
47E2 **Tongaat** South Africa
33H3 **Tongatapu** *I* Tonga
33H3 **Tongatapu Group** *Is* Tonga
33H3 **Tonga Trench** Pacific Ocean
28A2 **Tongchang** N Korea
31D3 **Tongcheng** China
31B2 **Tongchuan** China
31A2 **Tongde** China
13C2 **Tongeren** Belgium
30E2 **Tonggu Jiao** *I* China
31A5 **Tonghai** China
28B2 **Tonghua** China
28B3 **Tongjosŏn-Man** *S* N Korea
30D1 **Tongkin,G of** China/Vietnam
31E1 **Tongliao** China
31D3 **Tongling** China
28A3 **Tongnae** S Korea
34B2 **Tongo** Australia
31B4 **Tongren** Guizhou, China
31A2 **Tongren** Qinghai, China
43G3 **Tongsa** Bhutan
30B1 **Tongta** Burma
26C3 **Tongtian He** *R* China
8C2 **Tongue** Scotland
60B1 **Tongue** *R* USA
31D2 **Tong Xian** China
31B2 **Tongxin** China
28A2 **Tongyuanpu** China
31B4 **Tongzi** China
25L5 **Tonhil** Mongolia
56C4 **Tónichi** Mexico
50C3 **Tonj** Sudan
42D3 **Tonk** India
63C1 **Tonkawa** USA
30C3 **Tonle Sap** *L* Cambodia
13C4 **Tonnerre** France
29D3 **Tono** Japan
59C3 **Tonopah** USA
58D2 **Tooele** USA
34D1 **Toogoolawah** Australia
34B1 **Toompine** Australia
34D1 **Toowoomba** Australia
66C1 **Topaz L** USA
61D3 **Topeka** USA
59D4 **Topock** USA
56C4 **Topolobampo** Mexico
20E2 **Topozero, Ozero** *L* Russian Federation
58B1 **Toppenish** USA
68E1 **Topsfield** USA
50D3 **Tor** Ethiopia
17F3 **Torbalı** Turkey
41G2 **Torbat-e-Heydarīyeh** Iran
15A1 **Tordesillas** Spain
18C2 **Torgau** Germany
13B2 **Torhout** Belgium
26H3 **Tori** *I* Japan
Torino = Turin
50D3 **Torit** Sudan
75B2 **Torixoreu** Brazil
15A1 **Tormes** *R* Spain
12J5 **Torne** *R* Sweden
12H5 **Torneträsk** *L* Sweden
55M4 **Torngat** *Mts* Canada
12J5 **Tornio** Finland
74C3 **Toro, Cerro del** *Mt* Argentina/Chile
65D2 **Toronto** Canada
20E4 **Toropets** Russian Federation
50D3 **Tororo** Uganda
Toros, Dağlari = Taurus Mts
7C4 **Torquay** England
66C4 **Torrance** USA
15A2 **Torrão** Portugal
15C1 **Torreblanca** Spain
16C2 **Torre del Greco** Italy
15B1 **Torrelavega** Spain
15B2 **Torremolinos** Spain
32C4 **Torrens, L** Australia
56C4 **Torreón** Mexico
33F2 **Torres Is** Vanuatu
32D2 **Torres Str** Australia
15A2 **Torres Vedras** Portugal
7B4 **Torridge** *R* England
8C3 **Torridon, Loch** *Inlet* Scotland
68D2 **Torrington** Connecticut, USA
60C2 **Torrington** Wyoming, USA
12D3 **Tórshavn** Faeroes
15C1 **Tortosa** Spain
15C1 **Tortosa, Cabo de** *C* Spain
72C3 **Tortugas, Golfo de** Colombia
41G2 **Torūd** Iran
19D2 **Toruń** Poland
10B2 **Tory I** Irish Republic
9B2 **Tory Sol** Irish Republic
20E4 **Torzhok** Russian Federation
29B4 **Tosa** Japan
28C4 **Tosashimizu** Japan
29C4 **Tosa-Wan** *B* Japan
29C4 **To-shima** *I* Japan
12L7 **Tosno** Russian Federation
28B4 **Tosu** Japan
40B1 **Tosya** Turkey
15B2 **Totana** Spain
20G4 **Tot'ma** Russian Federation
7C4 **Totnes** England
73G2 **Totness** Surinam
34C2 **Tottenham** Australia
29C3 **Tottori** Japan
48B4 **Touba** Ivory Coast
48A3 **Touba** Senegal
48B1 **Toubkal** *Mt* Morocco
13B4 **Toucy** France
48B3 **Tougan** Burkina
48C1 **Touggourt** Algeria
48A3 **Tougué** Guinea
13C3 **Toul** France
14D3 **Toulon** France
14C3 **Toulouse** France
48B4 **Toumodi** Ivory Coast
30B2 **Toungoo** Burma
13B2 **Tourcoing** France
48A2 **Tourine** Mauritius
13B2 **Tournai** Belgium
14C2 **Tours** France
47C3 **Touws River** South Africa
29E2 **Towada** Japan
29E2 **Towada-ko** *L* Japan
68B2 **Towanda** USA
66D2 **Towne P** USA
60C1 **Towner** USA
58D1 **Townsend** USA
32D2 **Townsville** Australia
68B3 **Towson** USA
7C4 **Towy** *R* Wales
62B2 **Toyah** USA
29D2 **Toya-ko** *L* Japan
29D3 **Toyama** Japan
29C3 **Toyama-wan** *B* Japan
29C4 **Toyohashi** Japan
29C4 **Toyonaka** Japan
29B3 **Toyooka** Japan
29D3 **Toyota** Japan
48C1 **Tozeur** Tunisia
13D3 **Traben-Trarbach** Germany
Trâblous = Tripoli
40C1 **Trabzon** Turkey
61D2 **Tracy** Minnesota, USA
66B2 **Tracy** USA
15A2 **Trafalgar, Cabo** *C* Spain
54G5 **Trail** Canada
10B3 **Tralee** Irish Republic
9C3 **Tramore** Irish Republic
12G7 **Tranås** Sweden
30B4 **Trang** Thailand
27G7 **Trangan** *I* Indonesia
34C2 **Trangie** Australia
76E3 **Transantarctic Mts** Antarctica
47D3 **Transkei** *Self-governing homeland* South Africa
Transylvanian Alps *Mts* **= Munţii Carpaţii Meridionali**
16C3 **Trapani** Italy
34C3 **Traralgon** Australia
48A3 **Trarza** *Region* Mauritius
30C3 **Trat** Thailand
34B2 **Traveller's L** Australia
18C2 **Travemünde** Germany
64B2 **Traverse City** USA
35B2 **Travers,Mt** New Zealand
62C2 **Travis,L** USA
18D3 **Třebíč** Czech Republic
17D2 **Trebinje** Bosnia-Herzegovina
18C3 **Trebon** Czech Republic
74F4 **Treinta y Tres** Uruguay
74C6 **Trelew** Argentina
12G7 **Trelleborg** Sweden
7B3 **Tremadog B** Wales
65E1 **Tremblant,Mt** Canada
16D2 **Tremiti, Is** Italy
68B2 **Tremont** USA
58D2 **Tremonton** USA
19D3 **Trenčín** Slovakia
74D5 **Trenque Lauquén** Argentina
7D3 **Trent** *R* England
16C1 **Trento** Italy
65D2 **Trenton** Canada
61E2 **Trenton** Missouri, USA
68C2 **Trenton** New Jersey, USA
55N5 **Trepassey** Canada
74D5 **Tres Arroyos** Argentina
75C3 **Três Corações** Brazil
15B2 **Tres Forcas, Cabo** *C* Morocco
75B2 **Três Irmãos, Reprêsa** *Res* Brazil
74F2 **Três Lagoas** Brazil
66B2 **Tres Pinos** USA
74C7 **Tres Puntas, Cabo** Argentina
75D3 **Três Rios** Brazil
16C1 **Treviso** Italy
7B4 **Trevose Hd** *Pt* England
13E2 **Treysa** Germany
62B1 **Tribune** USA
44B3 **Trichūr** India
34C2 **Trida** Australia
13D3 **Trier** Germany
16C1 **Trieste** Italy

45B1 **Trikomo** Cyprus
9C3 **Trim** Irish Republic
44C4 **Trincomalee** Sri Lanka
52G6 **Trindade** *I* Atlantic Ocean
72F6 **Trinidad** Bolivia
74E4 **Trinidad** Uruguay
62B1 **Trinidad** USA
69E4 **Trinidad** *I* Caribbean Sea
69E4 **Trinidad & Tobago** *Is Republic* Caribbean Sea
63C2 **Trinity** USA
56D3 **Trinity** *R* USA
55N5 **Trinity B** Canada
67A2 **Trion** USA
45C1 **Tripoli** Lebanon
49D1 **Tripoli** Libya
17E3 **Trípolis** Greece
43G4 **Tripura** *State* India
52H6 **Tristan da Cunha** *Is* Atlantic Ocean
19D3 **Trnava** Slovakia
32E1 **Trobriand Is** Papua New Guinea
65F1 **Trois Pistoles** Canada
65E1 **Trois-Riviéres** Canada
20L5 **Troitsk** Russian Federation
20K3 **Troitsko Pechorsk** Russian Federation
12G7 **Trollhättan** Sweden
12F6 **Trollheimen** *Mt* Norway
46K9 **Tromelin** *I* Indian Ocean
47D3 **Trompsburg** South Africa
12H5 **Tromsø** Norway
66D3 **Trona** USA
12G6 **Trondheim** Norway
12G6 **Trondheimfjord** *Inlet* Norway
45B1 **Troödos Range** *Mts* Cyprus
8C4 **Troon** Scotland
52J3 **Tropic of Cancer**
52K6 **Tropic of Capricorn**
48B2 **Troudenni** Mali
55J4 **Trout L** Ontario, Canada
58E2 **Trout Peak** *Mt* USA
68B2 **Trout Run** USA
7C4 **Trowbridge** England
67A2 **Troy** Alabama, USA
58C1 **Troy** Montana, USA
68D1 **Troy** New York, USA
64C2 **Troy** Ohio, USA
68B2 **Troy** Pennsylvania, USA
17E2 **Troyan** Bulgaria
13C3 **Troyes** France
59C3 **Troy Peak** *Mt* USA
41F5 **Trucial Coast** *Region* UAE
59B3 **Truckee** *R* USA
70D3 **Trujillo** Honduras
72C5 **Trujillo** Peru
15A2 **Trujillo** Spain
72D2 **Trujillo** Venezuela
59D3 **Trumbull,Mt** USA
34C2 **Trundle** Australia
55M5 **Truro** Canada
7B4 **Truro** England
62A2 **Truth or Consequences** USA
26C2 **Tsagaan Nuur** *L* Mongolia
26C1 **Tsagan-Tologoy** Russian Federation
51E5 **Tsaratanana** Madagascar
51C6 **Tsau** Botswana
50D4 **Tsavo** Kenya
50D4 **Tsavo Nat Pk** Kenya
60C1 **Tschida,L** USA
24J4 **Tselinograd** Kazakhstan
47B2 **Tses** Namibia
26D2 **Tsetserleg** Mongolia
48C4 **Tsévié** Togo
47C2 **Tshabong** Botswana
47C1 **Tshane** Botswana
21F6 **Tshchikskoye Vdkhr** *Res* Russian Federation
50B4 **Tshela** Zaïre
51C4 **Tshibala** Zaïre
50C4 **Tshikapa** Zaïre
50C4 **Tshuapa** *R* Zaïre
21G6 **Tsimlyanskoye Vodokhranilishche** *Res* Russian Federation
Tsinan = Jinan
Tsingtao = Qingdao
51E6 **Tsiombe** Madagascar
51E5 **Tsiroanomandidy** Madagascar
19F2 **Tsna** *R* Belarus
31B1 **Tsogt Ovoo** Mongolia
47D3 **Tsomo** South Africa
26D2 **Tsomog** Mongolia
29C4 **Tsu** Japan
29C3 **Tsubata** Japan
29E3 **Tsuchiura** Japan
29E2 **Tsugarū-kaikyō** *Str* Japan
51B5 **Tsumeb** Namibia
51B6 **Tsumis** Namibia
29D3 **Tsuruga** Japan
29C3 **Tsurugi** Japan
29D3 **Tsuruoka** Japan
29C3 **Tsushima** Japan
28B4 **Tsushima** *Is* Japan
Tsushima-Kaikyō = Korea Str
29C3 **Tsuyama** Japan
15A1 **Tua** *R* Portugal
37M5 **Tuamotu, Îles** Pacific Ocean
21F7 **Tuapse** Russian Federation
35A3 **Tuatapere** New Zealand
59D3 **Tuba City** USA
37M6 **Tubai, Îles** Pacific Ocean
74G3 **Tubarão** Brazil
45C2 **Tubas** Israel
18B3 **Tübingen** Germany
49E1 **Tubruq** Libya
68C3 **Tuckerton** USA
59D4 **Tucson** USA
74C3 **Tucumán** *State* Argentina
62B1 **Tucumcari** USA
72F2 **Tucupita** Venezuela
15B1 **Tudela** Spain
40C3 **Tudmur** Syria
47E2 **Tugela** *R* South Africa
34D2 **Tuggerah L** Australia
27F5 **Tuguegarao** Philippines
25P4 **Tugur** Russian Federation
31D2 **Tuhai He** *R* China
27F7 **Tukangbesi, Kepulauan** *Is* Indonesia
54E3 **Tuktoyaktuk** Canada
19E1 **Tukums** Latvia
25O4 **Tukuringra, Khrebet** *Mts* Russian Federation
51D4 **Tukuyu** Tanzania
42B1 **Tukzar** Afghanistan
20F5 **Tula** Russian Federation
66C2 **Tulare** USA
66C2 **Tulare Lake Bed** USA
62A2 **Tularosa** USA
72C3 **Tulcán** Ecuador
21D6 **Tulcea** Romania
19F3 **Tul'chin** Ukraine
66C2 **Tule** *R* USA
51C6 **Tuli** Zimbabwe
47D1 **Tuli** *R* Zimbabwe
62B2 **Tulia** USA
45C2 **Tulkarm** Israel
67A1 **Tullahoma** USA
9C3 **Tullarnore** Irish Republic
14C2 **Tulle** France
63D2 **Tullos** USA
9C3 **Tullow** Irish Republic
68B1 **Tully** USA
63C1 **Tulsa** USA
72C3 **Tuluá** Colombia
40C3 **Tulūl ash Shāmīyah** *Desert Region* Iran/ Syria
25M4 **Tulun** Russian Federation
72C3 **Tumaco** Colombia
25R3 **Tumany** Russian Federation
34C3 **Tumbarumba** Australia
72B4 **Tumbes** Ecuador
28B2 **Tumen** China
28B2 **Tumen R** China/N Korea
44B3 **Tumkūr** India
30C4 **Tumpat** Malaysia
42D4 **Tumsar** India
48B3 **Tumu** Ghana
73H3 **Tumucumaque, Serra** *Mts* Brazil
34C3 **Tumut** Australia
34C3 **Tumut** *R* Australia
69L1 **Tunapuna** Trinidad
7E4 **Tunbridge Wells, Royal** England
40C2 **Tunceli** Turkey
51D4 **Tunduma** Zambia
51D5 **Tunduru** Tanzania
17F2 **Tundzha** *R* Bulgaria
44B2 **Tungabhadra** *R* India
26E4 **Tungkang** Taiwan
12B2 **Tungnafellsjökull** *Mts* Iceland
25M3 **Tunguska** *R* Russian Federation
44C2 **Tuni** India
16C3 **Tunis** Tunisia
16C3 **Tunis, G de** Tunisia
48C1 **Tunisia** *Republic* N Africa
72D2 **Tunja** Colombia
68C2 **Tunkhannock** USA
Tunxi = Huangshan
66C2 **Tuolumne Meadows** USA
75B3 **Tupã** Brazil
75C2 **Tupaciguara** Brazil
63E2 **Tupelo** USA
19G1 **Tupik** Russian Federation
72E8 **Tupiza** Bolivia
66C3 **Tupman** USA
65E2 **Tupper Lake** USA
74C4 **Tupungato** *Mt* Argentina
43L3 **Tura** India
25L3 **Tura** Russian Federation
20L4 **Tura** *R* Russian Federation
41G2 **Turān** Iran
25L4 **Turan** Russian Federation
40C3 **Turayf** Saudi Arabia
38E3 **Turbat** Pakistan
72C2 **Turbo** Colombia
17E1 **Turda** Romania
24K5 **Turfan Depression** China
24H5 **Turgay** Kazakhstan
25L5 **Turgen Uul** *Mt* Mongolia
40A2 **Turgutlu** Turkey
40C1 **Turhal** Turkey
12K7 **Türi** Estonia
15B2 **Turia** *R* Spain
16B1 **Turin** Italy
20L4 **Turinsk** Russian Federation
26G2 **Turiy Rog** Russian Federation
50D3 **Turkana, L** Ethiopia/Kenya
38E1 **Turkestan** *Region* C Asia
40C2 **Turkey** *Republic* W Asia
38D1 **Turkmenistan** *Republic* Asia
41F2 **Turkmenskiy Zaliv** *B* Turkmenistan
69C2 **Turks Is** Caribbean Sea
12J6 **Turku** Finland
50D3 **Turkwel** *R* Kenya
66B2 **Turlock** USA
66B2 **Turlock L** USA
35C2 **Turnagain,C** New Zealand
70D3 **Turneffe I** Belize
68D1 **Turners Falls** USA
13C2 **Turnhout** Belgium
17E2 **Turnu Măgurele** Romania
17E2 **Turnu-Severin** Romania
25K5 **Turpan** China
69B2 **Turquino** *Mt* Cuba
8D3 **Turriff** Scotland
38E1 **Turtkul'** Uzbekistan
61D3 **Turtle Creek Res** USA
25K3 **Turukhansk** Russian Federation
26D1 **Turuntayevo** Russian Federation
75B2 **Turvo** *R* Goias, Brazil
75C3 **Turvo** *R* São Paulo, Brazil
19E2 **Tur'ya** *R* Ukraine
63E2 **Tuscaloosa** USA
68B2 **Tuscarora Mt** USA
64B3 **Tuscola** Illinois, USA
62C2 **Tuscola** Texas, USA
63E2 **Tuscumbia** USA
41G3 **Tusharīk** Iran
68A2 **Tussey Mt** USA
Tutera = Tudela
44B4 **Tuticorin** India
17F2 **Tutrakan** Bulgaria
18B3 **Tuttlingen** Germany
33H2 **Tutuila** *I* American Samoa
26D2 **Tuul Gol** *R* Mongolia
25L4 **Tuva Republic** Russian Federation
33G1 **Tuvalu** *Is* Pacific Ocean
45C4 **Tuwayīlel Hāj** *Mt* Jordan
70B2 **Tuxpan** Mexico
70C2 **Tuxpan** Mexico
70C3 **Tuxtla Gutiérrez** Mexico
15A1 **Túy** Spain
30D3 **Tuy Hoa** Vietnam
40B2 **Tuz Gölü** *Salt L* Turkey
41D3 **Tuz Khurmātū** Iraq
17D2 **Tuzla** Bosnia-Herzegovina
20F4 **Tver'** Russian Federation
8D4 **Tweed** *R* England/ Scotland
34D1 **Tweed Heads** Australia
8D4 **Tweedsmuir Hills** Scotland
59C4 **Twentynine Palms** USA
55N5 **Twillingate** Canada
58D1 **Twin Bridges** USA
62B2 **Twin Buttes Res** USA
58D2 **Twin Falls** USA
35B2 **Twins,The** *Mt* New Zealand
66B3 **Twitchell Res** USA
64A1 **Two Harbors** USA
58D1 **Two Medicine** *R* USA
64B2 **Two Rivers** USA
25O4 **Tygda** Russian Federation
63C2 **Tyler** USA
26H1 **Tymovskoye** Russian Federation
26F1 **Tynda** Russian Federation
6D2 **Tyne** *R* England
6D2 **Tyne and Wear** *Metropolitan County* England
6D2 **Tynemouth** England
12G6 **Tynset** Norway
Tyr = Tyre
45C2 **Tyre** Lebanon
62A2 **Tyrone** New Mexico, USA
68A2 **Tyrone** Pennsylvania, USA
9C2 **Tyrone** *County* Northern Ireland
34B3 **Tyrrell,L** Australia
16C2 **Tyrrhenian S** Italy
21J7 **Tyuleni, Ova** *Is* Kazakhstan
24H4 **Tyumen'** Russian Federation
25O3 **Tyung** *R* Russian Federation
7B3 **Tywyn** Wales
47E1 **Tzaneen** South Africa
17E3 **Tzoumérka** *Mt* Greece

U

75D3 **Ubá** Brazil
75D2 **Ubaí** Brazil
75E1 **Ubaitaba** Brazil
50B3 **Ubangi** *R* Central African Republic/Congo/Zaïre
40D3 **Ubayyid, Wadi al** *Watercourse* Iraq
28B4 **Ube** Japan
15B2 **Ubeda** Spain
55N2 **Ubekendt Ejland** *I* Greenland
75C2 **Uberaba** Brazil
75A2 **Uberaba, Lagoa** Brazil
75C2 **Uberlândia** Brazil
30D2 **Ubon Ratchathani** Thailand
19F2 **Ubort** *R* Belarus
50C4 **Ubundu** Zaïre
72D5 **Ucayali** *R* Peru
42C3 **Uch** Pakistan
25P4 **Uchar** *R* Russian Federation
29E2 **Uchiura-wan** *B* Japan
13E1 **Uchte** Germany
58A1 **Ucluelet** Canada
25L4 **Uda** *R* Russian Federation
42C4 **Udaipur** India
43F3 **Udaipur Garhi** Nepal
12G7 **Uddevalla** Sweden
12H5 **Uddjaur** *L* Sweden
44B2 **Udgir** India
42D2 **Udhampur** India
16C1 **Udine** Italy
20J4 **Udmurt Republic** Russian Federation
30C2 **Udon Thani** Thailand
25P4 **Udskaya Guba** *B* Russian Federation
44A3 **Udupi** India
25N2 **Udzha** Russian Federation
29C3 **Ueda** Japan
50C3 **Uele** *R* Zaïre
25U3 **Uelen** Russian Federation
18C2 **Uelzen** Germany
50C3 **Uere** *R* Zaïre
20K5 **Ufa** Russian Federation
20K4 **Ufa** *R* Russian Federation
51B6 **Ugab** *R* Namibia
50D4 **Ugaila** *R* Tanzania
50D3 **Uganda** *Republic* Africa
45C3 **'Ugeiqa, Wadi** Jordan
26H2 **Uglegorsk** Russian Federation
20F4 **Uglich** Russian Federation
28C2 **Uglovoye** Russian Federation
20F5 **Ugra** *R* Russian Federation
8B3 **Uig** Scotland
51B4 **Uige** Angola
28A3 **Üijŏngbu** S Korea
21J6 **Uil** Kazakhstan
58D2 **Uinta Mts** USA
28A3 **Üiryŏng** S Korea
28A3 **Uisŏng** S Korea
47D3 **Uitenhage** South Africa
19E3 **Újfehértó** Hungary
29C4 **Uji** Japan
50C4 **Ujiji** Tanzania
74C2 **Ujina** Chile
42D4 **Ujjain** India
32A1 **Ujung Pandang** Indonesia
50D4 **Ukerewe I** Tanzania
43G3 **Ukhrul** India
20J3 **Ukhta** Russian Federation
59B3 **Ukiah** California, USA
58C1 **Ukiah** Oregon, USA
56A3 **Ukiah** USA
19E1 **Ukmerge** Lithuania
21D6 **Ukraine** *Republic* Europe
28A4 **Uku-jima** *I* Japan
26D2 **Ulaanbaatar** Mongolia
26C2 **Ulaangom** Mongolia
31C1 **Ulaan Uul** Mongolia
Ulan Bator = Ulaanbaatar
39G1 **Ulangar Hu** *L* China
26F2 **Ulanhot** China
26D1 **Ulan Ude** Russian Federation
26C3 **Ulan Ul Hu** *L* China
25Q3 **Ul'beya** *R* Russian Federation
28B3 **Ulchin** S Korea
17D2 **Ulcinj** Montenegro, Yugoslavia
26E2 **Uldz** Mongolia
26C2 **Uliastay** Mongolia
27G5 **Ulithi** *I* Pacific Ocean
19F1 **Ulla** Belarus
34D3 **Ulladulla** Australia
8C3 **Ullapool** Scotland
12H5 **Ullsfjorden** *Inlet* Norway
6C2 **Ullswater** *L* England
28C3 **Ullung-do** *I* Japan
18C3 **Ulm** Germany
34A1 **Uloowaranie,L** Australia
28B3 **Ulsan** S Korea
9C2 **Ulster** *Region* Northern Ireland
24K5 **Ulungur He** *R* China
24K5 **Ulungur Hu** *L* China
8B3 **Ulva** *I* Scotland
6C2 **Ulverston** England
34C4 **Ulverstone** Australia
25O4 **Ulya** *R* Russian Federation
19G3 **Ulyanovka** Ukraine
20H5 **Ul'yanovsk** Russian Federation
62B1 **Ulysses** USA
21E6 **Uman'** Ukraine
55N2 **Umanak** Greenland
43E4 **Umaria** India
42B3 **Umarkot** Pakistan
58C1 **Umatilla** USA
20E2 **Umba** Russian Federation
50D4 **Umba** *R* Kenya/Tanzania
32D1 **Umboi I** Papua New Guinea
12H6 **Ume** *R* Sweden
12J6 **Umea** Sweden
45C2 **Um ed Daraj, Jebel** *Mt* Jordan
45C4 **Um el Hashīm, Jebel** *Mt* Jordan
47E2 **Umfolozi** *R* South Africa
54C3 **Umiat** USA
45C4 **Um Ishrīn, Jebel** *Mt* Jordan
47E3 **Umkomaas** *R* South Africa
41G4 **Umm al Qaiwain** UAE
50C2 **Umm Bell** Sudan
50C2 **Umm Keddada** Sudan
40C4 **Umm Lajj** Saudi Arabia
50D2 **Umm Ruwaba** Sudan
41F5 **Umm Sa'id** Qatar
51C5 **Umniaiti** *R* Zimbabwe
58B2 **Umpqua** *R* USA
42D4 **Umred** India
Umtali = Mutare
47D3 **Umtata** South Africa
75B3 **Umuarama** Brazil
47D3 **Umzimkulu** South Africa
47E3 **Umzimkulu** *R* South Africa
47D3 **Umzimvubu** *R* South Africa
47D1 **Umzingwane** *R* Zimbabwe
75E2 **Una** Brazil
16D1 **Una** *R* Bosnia-Herzegovina/Croatia
68C1 **Unadilla** USA
68C1 **Unadilla** *R* USA
75C2 **Unaí** Brazil
54B3 **Unalakleet** USA
41D4 **Unayzah** Saudi Arabia
68D2 **Uncasville** USA
60B3 **Uncompahgre Plat** USA
47D2 **Underberg** South Africa
60C1 **Underwood** USA
20E5 **Unecha** Russian Federation
45C3 **Uneisa** Jordan
55M4 **Ungava B** Canada
28C2 **Unggi** N Korea
74F3 **União de Vitória** Brazil
63D1 **Union** Missouri, USA
67B2 **Union** S Carolina, USA
65D2 **Union City** Pennsylvania, USA
63E1 **Union City** Tennessee, USA
47C3 **Uniondale** South Africa
67A2 **Union Springs** USA
65D3 **Uniontown** USA
41F5 **United Arab Emirates** Arabian Pen
4E3 **United Kingdom of Gt Britain & N Ireland** NW Europe
53H4 **United States of America**
55K1 **United States Range** *Mts* Canada
58C2 **Unity** USA
62A2 **University Park** USA
13D2 **Unna** Germany
43E3 **Unnāo** India
28A2 **Unsan** N Korea
8E1 **Unst** *I* Scotland
40C1 **Ünye** Turkey
20G4 **Unzha** *R* Russian Federation
72F2 **Upata** Venezuela
51C4 **Upemba Nat Pk** Zaïre
55N2 **Upernavik** Greenland
47C2 **Upington** South Africa
66D3 **Upland** USA
33H2 **Upolu** *I* Western Samoa
35C2 **Upper Hutt** New Zealand
58B2 **Upper Klamath L** USA
58B2 **Upper L** USA
9C2 **Upper Lough Erne** *L* Northern Ireland

69L1 **Upper Manzanilla** Trinidad
61E1 **Upper Red L** USA
68B3 **Upperville** USA
12H7 **Uppsala** Sweden
61E1 **Upsala** Canada
60C2 **Upton** USA
40D4 **'Uqlat as Suqūr** Saudi Arabia
72C2 **Uraba, Golfo de** Colombia
31B1 **Urad Qianqi** China
41E4 **Urairah** Saudi Arabia
29D2 **Urakawa** Japan
21J5 **Ural** *R* Kazakhstan
34D2 **Uralla** Australia
20M4 **Ural Mts** Russian Federation
21J5 **Ural'sk** Kazakhstan
24G4 **Ural'skiy Khrebet** *Mts* Russian Federation
75D1 **Urandi** Brazil
54H4 **Uranium City** Canada
27G8 **Urapunga** Australia
60B3 **Uravan** USA
29C3 **Urawa** Japan
20L3 **Uray** Russian Federation
64B2 **Urbana** Illinois, USA
64C2 **Urbana** Ohio, USA
16C2 **Urbino** Italy
15B1 **Urbion, Sierra de** *Mt* Spain
6C2 **Ure** *R* England
20H4 **Uren'** Russian Federation
38E1 **Urgench** Uzbekistan
24J3 **Urengoy** Russian Federation
42B2 **Urgun** Afghanistan
17F3 **Urla** Turkey
17E2 **Uroševac** Serbia, Yugoslavia
75C1 **Uruaçu** Brazil
70B3 **Uruapan** Mexico
75C2 **Urucuia** *R* Brazil
74E3 **Uruguaiana** Brazil
74E4 **Uruguay** *R* Argentina/ Uruguay
74E4 **Uruguay** *Republic* S America
41E2 **Urumīyeh** Iran
39G1 **Ürümqi** China
26J2 **Urup** *I* Kuril Is, Russian Federation
24J1 **Urup, Ostrov** *I* Russian Federation
42B2 **Uruzgan** Afghanistan
29D2 **Uryū-ko** *L* Japan
21G5 **Uryupinsk** Russian Federation
20J4 **Urzhum** Russian Federation
17F2 **Urziceni** Romania
39G1 **Usa** China
28B4 **Usa** Japan
20L2 **Usa** *R* Russian Federation
40A2 **Uşak** Turkey
47B1 **Usakos** Namibia
24J1 **Ushakova, Ostrov** *I* Russian Federation
50D4 **Ushashi** Tanzania
24J5 **Ush Tobe** Kazakhstan
74C8 **Ushuaia** Argentina
25O4 **Ushumun** Russian Federation
7C4 **Usk** *R* Wales
40A1 **Üsküdar** Turkey
20H3 **Usogorsk** Russian Federation
25M4 **Usolye Sibirskoye** Russian Federation
26G2 **Ussuri** *R* China/Russian Federation
28C2 **Ussuriysk** Russian Federation
25T3 **Ust'-Belaya** Russian Federation
25R4 **Ust'Bol'sheretsk** Russian Federation
16C3 **Ustica** *I* Sicily, Italy
18C2 **Ústi-nad-Laben** Czech Republic
24J4 **Ust'Ishim** Russian Federation
18D2 **Ustka** Poland
25S4 **Ust'Kamchatsk** Russian Federation
24K5 **Ust'-Kamenogorsk** Kazakhstan
20L2 **Ust' Kara** Russian Federation
25L4 **Ust Karabula** Russian Federation
20K5 **Ust' Katav** Russian Federation
25M4 **Ust'-Kut** Russian Federation
21F6 **Ust Labinsk** Russian Federation
25P3 **Ust'Maya** Russian Federation
20K3 **Ust' Nem** Russian Federation
25Q3 **Ust'Nera** Russian Federation
25O4 **Ust'Nyukzha** Russian Federation
25M4 **Ust'Ordynskiy** Russian Federation
20J2 **Ust' Tsil'ma** Russian Federation
25P4 **Ust-'Umal'tu** Russian Federation
20G3 **Ust'ya** *R* Russian Federation
20M2 **Ust' Yuribey** Russian Federation
21J7 **Ustyurt Plateau** *Plat* Kazakhstan
28B4 **Usuki** Japan
70C3 **Usumacinta** *R* Guatemala/Mexico
47E2 **Usutu** *R* Swaziland
28A4 **Usuyŏng** S Korea
19G1 **Usvyaty** Russian Federation
56B3 **Utah** *State* USA
59D2 **Utah L** USA
19F1 **Utena** Lithuania
42B3 **Uthal** Pakistan
68C1 **Utica** USA
15B2 **Utiel** Spain
18B2 **Utrecht** Netherlands
47E2 **Utrecht** South Africa
15A2 **Utrera** Spain
12K5 **Utsjoki** Finland
29D3 **Utsonomiya** Japan
30C2 **Uttaradit** Thailand
43E3 **Uttar Pradesh** *State* India
7D3 **Uttoxeter** England
12J6 **Uusikaupunki** Finland
62C3 **Uvalde** USA
24H4 **Uvat** Russian Federation
33F3 **Uvéa** *I* New Caledonia
50D4 **Uvinza** Tanzania
50C4 **Uvira** Zaïre
55N2 **Uvkusigssat** Greenland
26C1 **Uvs Nuur** *L* Mongolia
28C4 **Uwajima** Japan
50C1 **Uweinat, Jebel** *Mt* Sudan
31B2 **Uxin Qi** China
25Q3 **Uyandina** *R* Russian Federation
25L4 **Uyar** Russian Federation
72E8 **Uyuni** Bolivia
45B4 **Uyûn Mûsa** *Well* Egypt
38E1 **Uzbekistan** *Republic* Asia
14C2 **Uzerche** France
19F2 **Uzh** *R* Ukraine
17D2 **Užice** Serbia, Yugoslavia
19E3 **Uzhgorod** Ukraine
20F5 **Uzlovaya** Russian Federation
40A1 **Uzunköprü** Turkey

V

47C2 **Vaal** *R* South Africa
47D2 **Vaal Dam** *Res* South Africa
47D1 **Vaalwater** South Africa
12J6 **Vaasa** Finland
19D3 **Vác** Hungary
74F3 **Vacaria** Brazil
75B3 **Vacaria** *R* Mato Grosso do, Brazil
75D2 **Vacaria** *R* Minas Gerais, Brazil
59B3 **Vacaville** USA
42C4 **Vadodara** India
12K4 **Vadsø** Norway
16B1 **Vaduz** Liechtenstein
20G3 **Vaga** *R* Russian Federation
19D3 **Váh** *R* Slovakia
45C3 **Vahel** Israel
44B3 **Vaigai** *R* India
8E1 **Vaila, I** Scotland
33G1 **Vaitupu** *I* Tuvalu
74C6 **Valcheta** Argentina
20E4 **Valday** Russian Federation
20E4 **Valdayskaya Vozvyshennost'** *Upland* Russian Federation
72E2 **Val de la Pascua** Venezuela
15B2 **Valdepeñas** Spain
54D3 **Valdez** USA
74B5 **Valdivia** Chile
13B3 **Val d'Oise** *Department* France
65D1 **Val-d'Or** Canada
67B2 **Valdosta** USA
58C2 **Vale** USA
75E1 **Valença** Bahia, Brazil
75D3 **Valença** Rio de Janeiro, Brazil
14C3 **Valence** France
15B2 **Valencia** Spain
72E1 **Valencia** Venezuela
Valencia *Region* = **Comunidad Valenciana**
15A2 **Valencia de Alcantara** Spain
15C2 **Valencia, Golfo de** *G* Spain
13B2 **Valenciennes** France
60C2 **Valentine** Nebraska, USA
62B2 **Valentine** Texas, USA
6D2 **Vale of Pickering** England
6D2 **Vale of York** England
72D2 **Valera** Venezuela
12K7 **Valga** Russian Federation
7E3 **Valiant** *Oilfield* N Sea
17D2 **Valjevo** Serbia, Yugoslavia
12J6 **Valkeakoski** Finland
70D2 **Valladolid** Mexico
15B1 **Valladolid** Spain
69D5 **Valle de la Pascua** Venezuela
72D1 **Valledupar** Colombia
72F7 **Valle Grande** Bolivia
66A1 **Vallejo** USA
74B3 **Vallenar** Chile
75D1 **Valle Pequeno** Brazil
61D1 **Valley City** USA
58B2 **Valley Falls** USA
65E1 **Valleyfield** Canada
15C1 **Valls** Spain
19F1 **Valmiera** Latvia
14B2 **Valognes** France
75B3 **Valparaíso** Brazil
74B4 **Valparaíso** Chile
67A2 **Valparaiso** USA
47D2 **Vals** *R* South Africa
42C4 **Valsād** India
21F5 **Valuyki** Russian Federation
15A2 **Valverde del Camino** Spain
12J6 **Vammala** Finland
41D2 **Van** Turkey
25M3 **Vanavara** Russian Federation
63D1 **Van Buren** Arkansas, USA
65F1 **Van Buren** Maine, USA
13C3 **Vancouleurs** France
54F5 **Vancouver** Canada
58B1 **Vancouver** USA
54F5 **Vancouver I** Canada
64B3 **Vandalia** Illinois, USA
64C3 **Vandalia** Ohio, USA
54F4 **Vanderhoof** Canada
27G8 **Van Diemen,C** Australia
32C2 **Van Diemen G** Australia
12G7 **Vänern** *L* Sweden
12G7 **Vänersborg** Sweden
68B1 **Van Etten** USA
51E6 **Vangaindrano** Madagascar
40D2 **Van Gölü** *Salt L* Turkey
29C2 **Vangou** Russian Federation
30C2 **Vang Vieng** Laos
62B2 **Van Horn** USA
65D1 **Vanier** Canada
33F2 **Vanikoro** *I* Solomon Islands
26G2 **Vanino** Russian Federation
25U3 **Vankarem** Russian Federation
12H6 **Vännäs** Sweden
14B2 **Vannes** France
47B3 **Vanrhynsdorp** South Africa
55K3 **Vansittart I** Canada
33F2 **Vanua Lava** *I* Vanuatu
33G2 **Vanua Levu** *I* Fiji
37K5 **Vanuatu** *Is, Republic* Pacific Ocean
64C2 **Van Wert** USA
47C3 **Vanwyksvlei** South Africa
14D3 **Var** *R* France
41F2 **Varāmīn** Iran
43E3 **Vārānasi** India
20K2 **Varandey** Russian Federation
12K4 **Varangerfjord** *Inlet* Norway
12L4 **Varangerhalvøya** *Pen* Norway
16D1 **Varazdin** Croatia
12G7 **Varberg** Sweden
12F7 **Varde** Denmark
12L4 **Vardø** Norway
13E1 **Varel** Germany
19E2 **Varéna** Lithuania
16B1 **Varese** Italy
75C3 **Varginha** Brazil
12K6 **Varkaus** Finland
17F2 **Varna** Bulgaria
12G7 **Värnamo** Sweden
20K2 **Varnek** Russian Federation
67B2 **Varnville** USA
75D2 **Várzea da Palma** Brazil
20H3 **Vashka** *R* Russian Federation
21E5 **Vasil'kov** Ukraine
64C2 **Vassar** USA
12H7 **Västerås** Sweden
12H7 **Västervik** Sweden
16C2 **Vasto** Italy
16C2 **Vaticano, Citta del** Italy
12B2 **Vatnajökull** *Mts* Iceland
17F1 **Vatra Dornei** Romania
12G7 **Vättern** *L* Sweden
62A2 **Vaughn** USA
72D3 **Vaupés** *R* Colombia
33H2 **Vava'u Group** *Is* Tonga
44C4 **Vavuniya** Sri Lanka
12G7 **Växjö** Sweden
20K1 **Vaygach, Ostrov** *I* Russian Federation
13D1 **Vecht** *R* Germany/ Netherlands
13E1 **Vechta** Germany
13D1 **Veendam** Netherlands
62B1 **Vega** USA
12G5 **Vega** *I* Norway
15A2 **Vejer de la Frontera** Spain
12F7 **Vejle** Denmark
47B3 **Velddrif** South Africa
16D2 **Velebit** *Mts* Croatia
16D1 **Velenje** Slovenia
75D2 **Velhas** *R* Brazil
25T3 **Velikaya** *R* Russian Federation
19F1 **Velikaya** *R* Russian Federation
12K7 **Velikaya** *R* Russian Federation
20E4 **Velikiye Luki** Russian Federation
20H3 **Velikiy Ustyug** Russian Federation
17F2 **Veliko Tŭrnovo** Bulgaria
48A3 **Vélingara** Senegal
19G1 **Velizh** Russian Federation
33E1 **Vella Lavella** *I* Solomon Islands
44B3 **Vellore** India
13E2 **Velmerstat** *Mt* Germany
20G3 **Vel'sk** Russian Federation
13C1 **Veluwe** *Region* Netherlands
60C1 **Velva** USA
44B4 **Vembanad L** India
74D4 **Venado Tuerto** Argentina
75C3 **Vençeslau Braz** Brazil
13C3 **Vendeuvre-sur-Barse** France
14C2 **Vendôme** France
Venezia = **Venice**
16C1 **Venezia, G di** Italy
72E2 **Venezuela** *Republic* S America
69C4 **Venezuela,G de** Venezuela
44A2 **Vengurla** India
16C1 **Venice** Italy
44B3 **Venkatagiri** India
18B2 **Venlo** Netherlands
19E1 **Venta** *R* Latvia
47D2 **Ventersburg** South Africa
7D4 **Ventnor** England
19E1 **Ventspils** Latvia
72E3 **Ventuarí** *R* Venezuela
66C3 **Ventura** USA
20E3 **Vepsovskaya Vozvyshennost'** *Upland* Russian Federation
74D3 **Vera** Argentina
15B2 **Vera** Spain
70C3 **Veracruz** Mexico
75A4 **Verá, L** Paraguay
42C4 **Verāval** India
16B1 **Vercelli** Italy
75A1 **Vérde** *R* Brazil
75B2 **Verde** *R* Goias, Brazil
75B2 **Verde** *R* Mato Grosso do Sul, Brazil
59D4 **Verde** *R* USA
Verde,C = **Cap Vert**
75D2 **Verde Grande** *R* Brazil
13E1 **Verden** Germany
14D3 **Verdon** *R* France
13C3 **Verdun** France
47D2 **Vereeniging** South Africa
20J4 **Vereshchagino** Russian Federation
48A3 **Verga,C** Guinea
15A1 **Verin** Spain
25N4 **Verkh Angara** *R* Russian Federation
20K5 **Verkhneural'sk** Russian Federation
25O3 **Verkhnevilyuysk** Russian Federation
20H3 **Verkhnyaya Toyma** Russian Federation
25P3 **Verkhoyansk** Russian Federation
25O3 **Verkhoyanskiy Khrebet** *Mts* Russian Federation
25K3 **Verkneimbatskoye** Russian Federation
20H3 **Verkola** Russian Federation
75B2 **Vermelho** *R* Brazil
13B4 **Vermenton** France
54G4 **Vermilion** Canada
61E1 **Vermilion L** USA
61D2 **Vermillion** USA
57F2 **Vermont** *State* USA
58E2 **Vernal** USA
66B2 **Vernalis** USA
47C3 **Verneuk Pan** *Salt L* South Africa
54G4 **Vernon** Canada
62C2 **Vernon** USA
67B3 **Vero Beach** USA
17E2 **Véroia** Greece
16C1 **Verona** Italy
13B3 **Versailles** France
48A3 **Vert, Cap** *C* Senegal
47E2 **Verulam** South Africa
13C2 **Verviers** Belgium
13B3 **Vervins** France
19G3 **Veselinovo** Ukraine
13C3 **Vesle** *R* France
14D2 **Vesoul** France
12G5 **Vesterålen** *Is* Norway
12G5 **Vestfjorden** *Inlet* Norway
12A2 **Vestmannaeyjar** Iceland
16C2 **Vesuvio** *Vol* Italy
19D3 **Veszprém** Hungary
12H7 **Vetlanda** Sweden
20G4 **Vetluga** *R* Russian Federation
13B2 **Veurne** Belgium
16B1 **Vevey** Switzerland
13C3 **Vézelise** France
Viangchan = **Vientiane**
15A1 **Viana do Castelo** Portugal
16C2 **Viareggio** Italy
12F7 **Viborg** Denmark
16D3 **Vibo Valentia** Italy
Vic = **Vich**
76G2 **Vice-commodoro Marambio** *Base* Antarctica
16C1 **Vicenza** Italy
15C1 **Vich** Spain
72E3 **Vichada** *R* Colombia/ Venezuela
20G4 **Vichuga** Russian Federation
14C2 **Vichy** France
63D2 **Vicksburg** USA
75D3 **Vicosa** Brazil
32C4 **Victor Harbor** Australia
63C3 **Victoria** USA
32C2 **Victoria** *R* Australia
34B3 **Victoria** *State* Australia
69B2 **Victoria de las Tunas** Cuba
51C5 **Victoria Falls** Zambia/ Zimbabwe
54G2 **Victoria I** Canada
34B2 **Victoria,L** Australia
50D4 **Victoria,L** C Africa
76F7 **Victoria Land** *Region* Antarctica
43G4 **Victoria,Mt** Burma
27H7 **Victoria,Mt** Papua New Guinea
50D3 **Victoria Nile** *R* Uganda
35B2 **Victoria Range** *Mts* New Zealand
32C2 **Victoria River Downs** Australia
54H3 **Victoria Str** Canada
65E1 **Victoriaville** Canada
47C3 **Victoria West** South Africa
59C4 **Victorville** USA
67B2 **Vidalia** USA
17F2 **Videle** Romania
17E2 **Vidin** Bulgaria
42D4 **Vidisha** India
19F1 **Vidzy** Belarus
74D6 **Viedma** Argentina
74B7 **Viedma, Lago** Argentina
69A4 **Viejo** Costa Rica
Vielha = **Viella**
15C1 **Viella** Spain
18D3 **Vienna** Austria
64B3 **Vienna** Illinois, USA
64C3 **Vienna** W Virginia, USA
14C2 **Vienne** France
14C2 **Vienne** *R* France
30C2 **Vientiane** Laos
14C2 **Vierzon** France
16D2 **Vieste** Italy
27D5 **Vietnam** *Republic* SE Asia
30D1 **Vietri** Vietnam
69P2 **Vieux Fort** St Lucia
27F5 **Vigan** Philippines
14B3 **Vignemale** *Mt* France/ Spain
15A1 **Vigo** Spain
44C2 **Vijayawāda** India
17D2 **Vijosë** *R* Albania
17E2 **Vikhren** *Mt* Bulgaria
12G6 **Vikna** *I* Norway
51D5 **Vila da Maganja** Mozambique
51D5 **Vila Machado** Mozambique
51D6 **Vilanculos** Mozambique
Vilanova i la Geltrú = **Villanueva-y-Geltrú**
15A1 **Vila Real** Portugal
51D5 **Vila Vasco da Gama** Mozambique
75D3 **Vila Velha** Brazil

19F2 Vileyka Belarus
12H6 Vilhelmina Sweden
73G6 Vilhena Brazil
19F2 Viliya Belarus
20D4 Viljandi Estonia
47D2 Viljoenskroon South Africa
25L2 Vilkitskogo, Proliv *Str* Russian Federation
19F3 Vilkovo Ukraine
62A2 Villa Ahumada Mexico
15A1 Villaba Spain
16C1 Villach Austria
74C4 Villa Dolores Argentina
74E5 Villa Gesell Argentina
75A4 Villa Hayes Paraguay
70C3 Villahermosa Mexico
74D4 Villa Huidobro Argentina
74D4 Villa María Argentina
72F8 Villa Montes Bolivia
15A1 Villa Nova de Gaia Portugal
15A2 Villanueva de la Serena Spain
15C1 Villanueva-y-Geltrú Spain
15B2 Villarreal Spain
74E3 Villarrica Paraguay
15B2 Villarrobledo Spain
62B3 Villa Unión Coahuila, Mexico
72D3 Villavicencio Colombia
14C2 Villefranche France
55L5 Ville-Marie Canada
15B2 Villena Spain
13B3 Villeneuve-St-Georges France
14C3 Villeneuve-sur-Lot France
13B3 Villeneuve-sur-Yonne France
63D2 Ville Platte USA
13B3 Villers-Cotterêts France
14C2 Villeurbanne France
47D2 Villiers South Africa
13E3 Villingen-Schwenningen Germany
44B3 Villupuram India
19F2 Vilnius Lithuania
25N3 Vilyuy *R* Russian Federation
25O3 Vilyuysk Russian Federation
15C1 Vinaroz Spain
64B3 Vincennes USA
12H5 Vindel *R* Sweden
42D4 Vindhya Range *Mts* India
68C3 Vineland USA
68E2 Vineyard Haven USA
30D2 Vinh Vietnam
30D3 Vinh Cam Ranh *B* Vietnam
30D4 Vinh Loi Vietnam
30D3 Vinh Long Vietnam
63C1 Vinita USA
17D1 Vinkovci Croatia
19F3 Vinnitsa Ukraine
76F3 Vinson Massif *Upland* Antarctica
61E2 Vinton USA
74B4 Viõna del Mar Chile
51B5 Virei Angola
75D2 Virgem da Lapa Brazil
59D3 Virgin *R* USA
47D2 Virginia South Africa
61E1 Virginia USA
57F3 Virginia *State* USA
65D3 Virginia Beach USA
59C3 Virginia City USA
69E3 Virgin Is Caribbean Sea
64A2 Viroqua USA
16D1 Virovitica Croatia
13C3 Virton Belgium
44B4 Virudunagar India
16D2 Vis *I* Croatia
66C2 Visalia USA
12H7 Visby Sweden
54H2 Viscount Melville Sd Canada
17D2 Višegrad Bosnia-Herzegovina
15A1 Viseu Portugal
44C2 Vishākhapatnam India
20K3 Vishera *R* Russian Federation
16B2 Viso, Monte *Mt* Italy
59C4 Vista USA
Vistula *R* = Wisła
44A2 Vite India
19G1 Vitebsk Belarus
16C2 Viterbo Italy
15A1 Vitigudino Spain
25N4 Vitim *R* Russian Federation
73K8 Vitória Brazil
15B1 Vitoria Spain
73K6 Vitória da Conquista Brazil
14B2 Vitré France
13C3 Vitry-le-François France
12J5 Vittangi Sweden
13C3 Vittel France
16C3 Vittoria Sicily, Italy
26J2 Vityaz Depth Pacific Ocean
Viviero = Vivero
15A1 Vivero Spain
25L3 Vivi *R* Russian Federation
15B1 Vizcaya, Golfo de Spain
25M4 Vizhne-Angarsk Russian Federation
44C2 Vizianagaram India
20J3 Vizinga Russian Federation
17E1 Vlădeasa *Mt* Romania
21G7 Vladikavkaz Russian Federation
20G4 Vladimir Russian Federation
19E2 Vladimir Volynskiy Ukraine
28C2 Vladivostok Russian Federation
18A2 Vlieland *I* Netherlands
13B2 Vlissingen Netherlands
47B2 Vloosdrift South Africa
17D2 Vlorë Albania
18C3 Vltara *R* Czech Republic
18C3 Vöcklabruck Austria
30D3 Voeune Sai Cambodia
13E2 Vogelsberg *Region* Germany
Vohemar = Vohimarina
Vohibinany = Ampasimanolotra
51F5 Vohimarina Madagascar
50D4 Voi Kenya
48B4 Voinjama Liberia
14D2 Voiron France
17D1 Vojvodina *Region* Serbia, Yugoslavia
60B1 Volborg USA
69A5 Volcán Barú *Mt* Panama
Volcano Is = Kazan Retto
20K4 Volchansk Russian Federation
21H6 Volga *R* Russian Federation
21G6 Volgodonsk Russian Federation
21G6 Volgograd Russian Federation
21H5 Volgogradskoye Vodokhranilishche *Res* Russian Federation
20E4 Volkhov Russian Federation
20E4 Volkhov *R* Russian Federation
19E2 Volkovysk Belarus
47D2 Volksrust South Africa
25L2 Volochanka Russian Federation
20G4 Vologda Russian Federation
17E3 Vólos Greece
21H5 Vol'sk Russian Federation
66B2 Volta USA
48B3 Volta Blanche *R* Burkina/Ghana
48B4 Volta, L Ghana
48B3 Volta Noire *R* W Africa
75D3 Volta Redonda Brazil
48B3 Volta Rouge *R* Burkina/Ghana
21G6 Volzhskiy Russian Federation
20F3 Vonguda Russian Federation
55R3 Vopnafjörður Iceland
18C1 Vordingborg Denmark
21C8 Voriái *I* Greece
20L2 Vorkuta Russian Federation
12G6 Vorma *R* Norway
21F5 Voronezh Russian Federation
12M5 Voron'ya *R* Russian Federation
21F6 Voroshilovgrad Ukraine
12K7 Võru Estonia
13D3 Vosges *Department* France
14D2 Vosges *Mts* France
12F6 Voss Norway
25L4 Vostochnyy Sayan *Mts* Russian Federation
76F9 Vostok *Base* Antarctica
20J4 Votkinsk Russian Federation
13C3 Vouziers France
61E1 Voyageurs Nat Pk USA
20K3 Voy Vozh Russian Federation
21E6 Voznesensk Ukraine
17E2 Vranje Serbia, Yugoslavia
17E2 Vratsa Bulgaria
17D1 Vrbas Serbia, Yugoslavia
16D2 Vrbas *R* Bosnia-Herzegovina
16C1 Vrbovsko Croatia
47D2 Vrede South Africa
47B3 Vredendal South Africa
73G2 Vreed en Hoop Guyana
44B3 Vriddhāchalam India
17E1 Vršac Serbia, Yugoslavia
16D2 Vrtoče Bosnia-Herzegovina
47C2 Vryburg South Africa
47E2 Vryheid South Africa
17D1 Vukovar Croatia
20K3 Vuktyl' Russian Federation
7F3 Vulcan *Oilfield* N Sea
16C3 Vulcano *I* Italy
30D3 Vung Tau Vietnam
12J5 Vuollerim Sweden
20E3 Vyartsilya Russian Federation
20J4 Vyatka *R* Russian Federation
26G2 Vyazemskiy Russian Federation
20E4 Vyaz'ma Russian Federation
20G4 Vyazniki Russian Federation
20D3 Vyborg Russian Federation
20F3 Vygozero, Ozero *L* Russian Federation
20J3 Vym *R* Russian Federation
7C3 Vyrnwy *R* Wales
20E4 Vyshniy-Volochek Russian Federation
18D3 Vyškov Czech Republic
20F3 Vytegra Russian Federation

W

48B3 Wa Ghana
13C2 Waal *R* Netherlands
54G4 Wabasca *R* Canada
64B2 Wabash USA
64B3 Wabash *R* USA
64C1 Wabatongushi L Canada
54J4 Wabowden Canada
55M4 Wabush Canada
67B3 Waccasassa B USA
68E1 Wachusett Res USA
63C2 Waco USA
42B3 Wad Pakistan
49D2 Waddān Libya
13C1 Waddenzee *S* Netherlands
54F4 Waddington,Mt Canada
7B4 Wadebridge England
61D1 Wadena USA
45C3 Wadi es Sir Jordan
50D1 Wadi Halfa Sudan
45C3 Wādi Mūsā Jordan
50D2 Wad Medani Sudan
28A3 Waegwan S Korea
28A2 Wafang China
41E4 Wafra Kuwait
13C2 Wageningen Netherlands
55K3 Wager B Canada
55J3 Wager Bay Canada
34C3 Wagga Wagga Australia
32A4 Wagin Australia
61D2 Wagner USA
66E5 Wahiawa Hawaiian Islands
61D2 Wahoo USA
61D1 Wahpeton USA
44A2 Wai India
66E5 Waialua Hawaiian Islands
35B2 Waiau New Zealand
35B2 Waiau *R* New Zealand
27G6 Waigeo *I* Indonesia
35C1 Waihi New Zealand
35C1 Waikaremoana,L New Zealand
35C1 Waikato *R* New Zealand
34A2 Waikerie Australia
35B3 Waikouaiti New Zealand
66E5 Wailuku Hawaiian Islands
35B2 Waimakariri *R* New Zealand
35B2 Waimate New Zealand
66E5 Waimea Hawaiian Islands
32B1 Waingapu Indonesia
54G4 Wainwright Canada
54B2 Wainwright USA
35C1 Waioura New Zealand
35B2 Waipara New Zealand
35C2 Waipukurau New Zealand
35C2 Wairarapa,L New Zealand
35B2 Wairau *R* New Zealand
35C1 Wairoa New Zealand
35C1 Wairoa *R* New Zealand
35B2 Waitaki *R* New Zealand
35B1 Waitara New Zealand
35C1 Waitomo New Zealand
35B1 Waiuku New Zealand
29C3 Wajima Japan
50E3 Wajir Kenya
29C3 Wakasa-wan *B* Japan
35A3 Wakatipu,L New Zealand
29D4 Wakayama Japan
60D3 Wa Keeney USA
7D3 Wakefield England
69H1 Wakefield Jamaica
64B1 Wakefield Michigan, USA
68E2 Wakefield Rhode Island, USA
30B2 Wakema Burma
29E1 Wakkanai Japan
34B3 Wakool *R* Australia
18D2 Wałbrzych Poland
34D2 Walcha Australia
18D2 Wałcz Poland
13D2 Waldbröl Germany
68C2 Walden USA
13E4 Waldshut Germany
54B3 Wales USA
7C3 Wales *Principality* U K
55K3 Wales I Canada
34C2 Walgett Australia
76F4 Walgreen Coast *Region* Antarctica
50C4 Walikale Zaïre
61E1 Walker USA
66C1 Walker L USA
66C3 Walker Pass USA
64C2 Walkerton Canada
60C2 Wall USA
58C1 Wallace USA
32C4 Wallaroo Australia
34C3 Walla Walla Australia
58C1 Walla Walla USA
68D2 Wallingford USA
37K5 Wallis and Futuna *Is* Pacific Ocean
33H2 Wallis, Îles Pacific Ocean
58C1 Wallowa USA
58C1 Wallowa Mts USA
34C1 Wallumbilla Australia
6C2 Walney *I* England
63D1 Walnut Ridge USA
68D1 Walpole USA
7D3 Walsall England
62B1 Walsenburg USA
67B2 Walterboro USA
67A2 Walter F George Res USA
62C2 Walters USA
68E1 Waltham USA
68C1 Walton USA
7E4 Walton-on-the Naze England
47A1 Walvis Bay Namibia
52J6 Walvis Ridge Atlantic Ocean
48C4 Wamba Nigeria
50B4 Wamba *R* Zaïre
61D3 Wamego USA
58E2 Wamsutter USA
42B2 Wana Pakistan
34B1 Wanaaring Australia
35A2 Wanaka New Zealand
35A2 Wanaka,L New Zealand
64C1 Wanapitei L Canada
28A4 Wando S Korea
34C1 Wandoan Australia
34B3 Wanganella Australia
35B1 Wanganui New Zealand
35C1 Wanganui *R* New Zealand
34C3 Wangaratta Australia
13D1 Wangerooge *I* Germany
28B2 Wangqing China
28A3 Wanjialing China
Wankie = Hwange
50E3 Wanleweyne Somalia
30E2 Wanning China
44B2 Wanparti India
6D2 Wansbeck, R England
7D4 Wantage England
31B3 Wanxian China
31B3 Wanyuan China
63D1 Wappapello,L USA
68D2 Wappingers Falls USA
61E2 Wapsipinicon *R* USA
44B2 Warangal India
34C4 Waratah Australia
34C3 Waratah B Australia
13E2 Warburg Germany
34C3 Warburton Australia
34C1 Ward *R* Australia
47D2 Warden South Africa
42D4 Wardha India
35A3 Ward,Mt New Zealand
54F4 Ware Canada
68D1 Ware USA
7C4 Wareham England
68E2 Wareham USA
13D2 Warendorf Germany
34D1 Warialda Australia
30D2 Warin Chamrap Thailand
47B2 Warmbad Namibia
51C6 Warmbad South Africa
7C4 Warminster England
68C2 Warminster USA
59C3 Warm Springs USA
18C2 Warnemünde Germany
58B2 Warner Mts USA
67B2 Warner Robins USA
34B3 Warracknabeal Australia
32D3 Warrego *R* Australia
63D2 Warren Arkansas, USA
34C2 Warren Australia
61D1 Warren Minnesota, USA
64C2 Warren Ohio, USA
65D2 Warren Pennsylvania, USA
68E2 Warren Rhode Island, USA
9C2 Warrenpoint Northern Ireland
61E3 Warrensburg USA
47C2 Warrenton South Africa
65D3 Warrenton USA
48C4 Warri Nigeria
7C3 Warrington England
63E2 Warrington USA
34B3 Warrnambool Australia
61D1 Warroad USA
19E2 Warsaw Poland
68A1 Warsaw USA
50E3 Warshiikh Somalia
Warszawa = Warsaw
19D2 Warta *R* Poland
34D1 Warwick Australia
7D3 Warwick England
68C2 Warwick New York, USA
68E2 Warwick Rhode Island, USA
7D3 Warwick *County* England
59D3 Wasatch Range *Mts* USA
47E2 Wasbank South Africa
66C3 Wasco USA
61E2 Waseca USA
64A1 Washburn USA
54H2 Washburn L Canada
58D2 Washburn,Mt USA
42D4 Wāshīm India
57F3 Washington District of Columbia, USA
67B2 Washington Georgia, USA
64B3 Washington Indiana, USA
61E2 Washington Iowa, USA
61E3 Washington Missouri, USA
67C1 Washington N Carolina, USA
68C2 Washington New Jersey, USA
64C2 Washington Pennsylvania, USA
59D3 Washington Utah, USA
56A2 Washington *State* USA
64C3 Washington Court House USA
55M1 Washington Land *Region* Canada
65E2 Washington,Mt USA
62C1 Washita *R* USA
7E3 Wash,The *B* England
42A3 Washuk Pakistan
51L4 Waskaganish Canada
69A4 Waspán Nicaragua
66C1 Wassuk Range *Mts* USA
13C3 Wassy France
27F7 Watampone Indonesia
47D3 Waterberge *Mts* South Africa
68D2 Waterbury USA
10B3 Waterford Irish Republic
9C3 Waterford *County* Irish Republic
9C3 Waterford Harbour Irish Republic
13C2 Waterloo Belgium
61E2 Waterloo USA
64B1 Watersmeet USA
58D1 Waterton-Glacier International Peace Park USA
65D2 Watertown New York, USA
61D2 Watertown S Dakota, USA
64B2 Watertown Wisconsin, USA
47E2 Waterval-Boven South Africa
65F2 Waterville Maine, USA
68C1 Waterville New York, USA
68D1 Watervliet USA
54G4 Waterways Canada
7D4 Watford England
60C1 Watford City USA
68B1 Watkins Glen USA
62C1 Watonga USA
56C1 Watrous Canada
62B1 Watrous USA
50C3 Watsa Zaïre
54F3 Watson Lake Canada
66B2 Watsonville USA
27H7 Wau Papua New Guinea
50C3 Wau Sudan
34D2 Wauchope Australia
67B3 Wauchula USA
64B2 Waukegan USA
64B2 Waukesha USA
64B2 Waupaca USA
64B2 Waupun USA
63C2 Waurika USA
64B2 Wausau USA
64B2 Wauwatosa USA
32C2 Wave Hill Australia
7E3 Waveney *R* England
60E2 Waverly Iowa, USA
68B1 Waverly New York, USA
64C3 Waverly Ohio, USA
13C2 Wavre Belgium
64C1 Wawa Canada
49D2 Wāw Al Kabīr Libya
49D2 Wāw an Nāmūs *Well* Libya

66C2 **Wawona** USA
63C2 **Waxahachie** USA
67B2 **Waycross** USA
61D2 **Wayne** USA
67B2 **Waynesboro** Georgia, USA
63E2 **Waynesboro** Mississippi, USA
68B3 **Waynesboro** Pennsylvania, USA
65D3 **Waynesboro** Virginia, USA
63D1 **Waynesville** Missouri, USA
67B1 **Waynesville** N Carolina, USA
42B2 **Wazi Khwa** Afghanistan
8E1 **W Burra** *I* Scotland
7E4 **Weald,The** *Upland* England
6C2 **Wear** *R* England
62C1 **Weatherford** Oklahoma, USA
63C2 **Weatherford** Texas, USA
58B2 **Weaverville** USA
64C1 **Webbwood** Canada
68B1 **Webster** New York, USA
61D1 **Webster** S Dakota, USA
68E1 **Webster** USA
61E2 **Webster City** Massachusetts, USA
64A3 **Webster Groves** USA
74D8 **Weddell** *I* Falkland Islands
76G2 **Weddell Sea** Antarctica
58B2 **Weed** USA
68A2 **Weedville** USA
47E2 **Weenen** South Africa
34C2 **Wee Waa** Australia
31D1 **Weichang** China
18C3 **Weiden** Germany
31D2 **Weifang** China
31E2 **Weihai** China
31C3 **Wei He** *R* Henan, China
31C2 **Wei He** *R* Shaanxi, China
34C1 **Weilmoringle** Australia
13E3 **Weinheim** Germany
31A4 **Weining** China
32D2 **Weipa** Australia
64C2 **Weirton** USA
58C2 **Weiser** USA
31D3 **Weishan Hu** *L* China
18C2 **Weissenfels** Germany
67A2 **Weiss L** USA
64C3 **Welch** USA
50E2 **Weldiya** Ethiopia
66C3 **Weldon** USA
47D2 **Welkom** South Africa
65D2 **Welland** Canada
7D3 **Welland** *R* England
32C2 **Wellesley Is** Australia
68E2 **Wellfleet** USA
7D3 **Wellingborough** England
34C2 **Wellington** Australia
60C2 **Wellington** Colorado, USA
7C4 **Wellington** England
63C1 **Wellington** Kansas, USA
66C1 **Wellington** Nevada, USA
35B2 **Wellington** New Zealand
47B3 **Wellington** South Africa
62B2 **Wellington** Texas, USA
55J2 **Wellington Chan** Canada
74B7 **Wellington, Isla** Chile
7C4 **Wells** England
58D2 **Wells** Nevada, USA
68C1 **Wells** New York, USA
68B2 **Wellsboro** USA
35B1 **Wellsford** New Zealand
32B3 **Wells,L** Australia
7E3 **Wells-next-the-Sea** England
68B1 **Wellsville** USA
18C3 **Wels** Austria
7C3 **Welshpool** Wales
7D4 **Welwyn Garden City** England
55L4 **Wemindji** Canada
58B1 **Wenatchee** USA
58C1 **Wenatchee** *R* USA
48B4 **Wenchi** Ghana
31E2 **Wendeng** China
58D2 **Wendover** USA
31E4 **Wenling** China
31A5 **Wenshan** China
6D2 **Wensleydale** England
7E3 **Wensum** *R* England
34B2 **Wentworth** Australia
31A3 **Wen Xian** China
31E4 **Wenzhou** China
31C4 **Wenzhu** China
47D2 **Wepener** South Africa
47C2 **Werda** Botswana
50E3 **Werder** Ethiopia
18C2 **Werra** *R* Germany
34D2 **Werris Creek** Australia
13D2 **Wesel** Germany
18B2 **Weser** *R* Germany
60C3 **Weskan** USA
63C3 **Weslaco** USA
55N5 **Wesleyville** Canada
32C2 **Wessel Is** Australia
60D2 **Wessington Springs** USA
64B2 **West Allis** USA
36F5 **West Australian Basin** Indian Ocean
36F6 **West Australian Ridge** Indian Ocean
63E3 **West B** USA
43F4 **West Bengal** *State* India
68C1 **West Branch Delaware** *R* USA
68A2 **West Branch Susquehanna** *R* USA
7D3 **West Bromwich** England
65E2 **Westbrook** USA
64A2 **Westby** USA
68C3 **West Chester** USA
67C3 **West End** Bahamas
66D3 **Westend** USA
13D2 **Westerburg** Germany
18B2 **Westerland** Germany
68E2 **Westerly** USA
32B3 **Western Australia** *State* Australia
51B7 **Western Cape** *Province* South Africa
44A2 **Western Ghats** *Mts* India
8B3 **Western Isles** *Region* Scotland
48A2 **Western Sahara** *Region* Morocco
33H2 **Western Samoa** *Is* Pacific Ocean
13B2 **Westerschelde** *Estuary* Netherlands
13D1 **Westerstede** Germany
13D2 **Westerwald** *Region* Germany
14D1 **Westfalen** *Region* Germany
74D8 **West Falkland** *Is* Falkland Islands
68D1 **Westfield** Massachusetts, USA
65D2 **Westfield** New York, USA
68B2 **Westfield** Pennsylvania, USA
64B3 **West Frankfort** USA
34C1 **Westgate** Australia
7C4 **West Glamorgan** *County* Wales
65F1 **West Grand L** USA
52E3 **West Indies** *Is* Caribbean Sea
64C3 **West Liberty** USA
64C2 **West Lorne** Canada
9C3 **Westmeath** *County* Irish Republic
63D1 **West Memphis** USA
7D3 **West Midlands** *County* England
7D4 **Westminster** England
68B3 **Westminster** Maryland, USA
67B2 **Westminster** S Carolina, USA
47D1 **West Nicholson** Zimbabwe
27E6 **Weston** Malaysia
64C3 **Weston** USA
7C4 **Weston-super-Mare** England
67B3 **West Palm Beach** USA
63D1 **West Plains** USA
66B1 **West Point** California, USA
63E2 **West Point** Mississippi, USA
61D2 **West Point** Nebraska, USA
68D2 **West Point** New York, USA
35B2 **Westport** New Zealand
10C2 **Westray** *I* Scotland
6E3 **West Sole** *Oilfield* N Sea
57E3 **West Virginia** *State* USA
66C1 **West Walker** *R* USA
34C2 **West Wyalong** Australia
58D2 **West Yellowstone** USA
7D3 **West Yorkshire** *County* England
27F7 **Wetar** *I* Indonesia
54G4 **Wetaskiwin** Canada
50D4 **Wete** Tanzania
13E2 **Wetter** *R* Germany
13E2 **Wetzlar** Germany
Wevok = Lisburne, Cape
32D1 **Wewak** Papua New Guinea
63C1 **Wewoka** USA
9C3 **Wexford** Irish Republic
9C3 **Wexford** *County* Irish Republic
7D4 **Weybridge** England
54H5 **Weyburn** Canada
7C4 **Weymouth** England
68E1 **Weymouth** USA
35C1 **Whakatane** New Zealand
35C1 **Whakatane** *R* New Zealand
8E1 **Whalsay** *I* Scotland
35B1 **Whangarei** New Zealand
6D3 **Wharfe** *R* England
63C3 **Wharton** USA
60B2 **Wheatland** USA
68B3 **Wheaton** Maryland, USA
61D1 **Wheaton** Minnesota, USA
59D3 **Wheeler Peak** *Mt* Nevada, USA
62A1 **Wheeler Peak** *Mt* New Mexico, USA
66C3 **Wheeler Ridge** USA
64C2 **Wheeling** USA
65D2 **Whitby** Canada
6D2 **Whitby** England
7C3 **Whitchurch** England
63D1 **White** *R* Arkansas, USA
60B2 **White** *R* Colorado, USA
64B3 **White** *R* Indiana, USA
60C2 **White** *R* S Dakota, USA
55N4 **White B** Canada
60C1 **White Butte** *Mt* USA
34B2 **White Cliffs** Australia
10C2 **White Coomb** *Mt* Scotland
58D1 **Whitefish** USA
64B1 **Whitefish Pt** USA
55M4 **Whitegull L** Canada
65E2 **Whitehall** New York, USA
68C2 **Whitehall** Pennsylvania, USA
64A2 **Whitehall** Wisconsin, USA
6C2 **Whitehaven** England
54E3 **Whitehorse** Canada
35C1 **White I** New Zealand
63D3 **White L** USA
34C4 **Whitemark** Australia
59C3 **White Mountain Peak** *Mt* USA
66C2 **White Mts** California, USA
65E2 **White Mts** New Hampshire, USA
50D2 **White Nile** *R* Sudan
68D2 **White Plains** USA
55K5 **White River** Canada
60C2 **White River** USA
65E2 **White River Junction** USA
White Russia = Belarus
58B1 **White Salmon** USA
20F2 **White Sea** Russian Federation
58D1 **White Sulphur Springs** USA
67C2 **Whiteville** USA
48B4 **White Volta** W Africa
64B2 **Whitewater** USA
8C4 **Whithorn** Scotland
67B2 **Whitmire** USA
66C2 **Whitney,Mt** USA
66C4 **Whittier** California, USA
7D3 **Whittlesey** England
54H3 **Wholdaia** Canada
32C4 **Whyalla** Australia
64C2 **Wiarton** Canada
8B3 **Wiay, I** Scotland
60C1 **Wibaux** USA
63C1 **Wichita** USA
62C2 **Wichita** *R* USA
62C2 **Wichita Falls** USA
62C2 **Wichita Mts** USA
8D2 **Wick** Scotland
59D4 **Wickenburg** USA
9C3 **Wicklow** Irish Republic
9C3 **Wicklow** *County* Irish Republic
9C3 **Wicklow Hd** *Pt* Irish Republic
9C3 **Wicklow Mts** Irish Republic
34C1 **Widgeegoara** *R* Australia
7C3 **Widnes** England
13D2 **Wied** *R* Germany
19D2 **Wielun** Poland
Wien = Vienna
18D3 **Wiener Neustadt** Austria
19E2 **Wieprz** *R* Poland
13E2 **Wiesbaden** Germany
13D4 **Wiese** *R* Germany
7C3 **Wigan** England
63E2 **Wiggins** USA
7D4 **Wight, I of** *County* England
6C2 **Wigton** England
8C4 **Wigtown** Scotland
8C4 **Wigtown B** Scotland
58C1 **Wilbur** USA
34B2 **Wilcannia** Australia
59C3 **Wildcat Peak** *Mt* USA
13E1 **Wildeshausen** Germany
16C1 **Wildspitze** *Mt* Austria
67B3 **Wildwood** Florida, USA
68C3 **Wildwood** New Jersey, USA
62B1 **Wiley** USA
47D2 **Wilge** *R* South Africa
32D1 **Wilhelm,Mt** Papua New Guinea
18B2 **Wilhelmshaven** Germany
68C2 **Wilkes-Barre** USA
76F8 **Wilkes Land** *Region* Antarctica
58B2 **Willamette** *R* USA
34B2 **Willandra** *R* Australia
58B1 **Willapa B** USA
59E4 **Willcox** USA
69D4 **Willemstad** Curaçao
34B3 **William,Mt** Australia
59D3 **Williams** Arizona, USA
59B3 **Williams** California, USA
65D3 **Williamsburg** USA
54F4 **Williams Lake** Canada
64C3 **Williamson** USA
68B2 **Williamsport** USA
67C1 **Williamston** USA
68D1 **Williamstown** Massachusetts, USA
64C3 **Williamstown** W Virginia, USA
68D2 **Willimantic** USA
68C2 **Willingboro** USA
32E2 **Willis Group** *Is* Australia
67B3 **Williston** Florida, USA
60C1 **Williston** N Dakota, USA
47C3 **Williston** South Africa
61D1 **Willmar** USA
34A3 **Willoughby,C** Australia
60B1 **Willow Bunch** Canada
47C3 **Willowmore** South Africa
58B2 **Willow Ranch** USA
59B3 **Willows** USA
63D1 **Willow Springs** USA
34A2 **Wilmington** Australia
68C3 **Wilmington** Delaware, USA
67C2 **Wilmington** N Carolina, USA
68D1 **Wilmington** Vermont, USA
60D3 **Wilson** Kansas, USA
67C1 **Wilson** N Carolina, USA
68A1 **Wilson** New York, USA
57F3 **Wilson** USA
34B1 **Wilson** *R* Australia
55K3 **Wilson,C** Canada
60D3 **Wilson L** USA
66C3 **Wilson,Mt** California, USA
62A1 **Wilson,Mt** Colorado, USA
58B1 **Wilson,Mt** Oregon, USA
34C3 **Wilson's Promontory** *Pen* Australia
13E1 **Wilstedt** Germany
7D4 **Wiltshire** *County* England
13C3 **Wiltz** Luxembourg
32B3 **Wiluna** Australia
64B2 **Winamac** USA
47D2 **Winburg** South Africa
7C4 **Wincanton** England
68D1 **Winchendon** USA
65D1 **Winchester** Canada
7D4 **Winchester** England
64C3 **Winchester** Kentucky, USA
68D1 **Winchester** New Hampshire, USA
65D3 **Winchester** Virginia, USA
58E2 **Wind** *R* USA
60C2 **Wind Cave Nat Pk** USA
6C2 **Windermere** England
6C2 **Windermere** *L* England
47B1 **Windhoek** Namibia
61D2 **Windom** USA
32D3 **Windorah** Australia
58E2 **Wind River Range** *Mts* USA
34D2 **Windsor** Australia
68D2 **Windsor** Connecticut, USA
7D4 **Windsor** England
67C1 **Windsor** N Carolina, USA
55M5 **Windsor** Nova Scotia, Canada
64C2 **Windsor** Ontario, Canada
65E1 **Windsor** Quebec, Canada
67B2 **Windsor Forest** USA
68D2 **Windsor Locks** USA
69E4 **Windward Is** Caribbean Sea
69C3 **Windward Pass** Caribbean Sea
63E2 **Winfield** Alabama, USA
63C1 **Winfield** Kansas, USA
34D2 **Wingham** Australia
55K4 **Winisk** *R* Canada
55K4 **Winisk L** Canada
30B2 **Winkana** Burma
58B1 **Winlock** USA
48B4 **Winneba** Ghana
61E2 **Winnebago** USA
64B2 **Winnebago,L** USA
58C2 **Winnemucca** USA
60D2 **Winner** USA
63D2 **Winnfield** USA
61E1 **Winnibigoshish L** USA
54J4 **Winnipeg** Canada
54J4 **Winnipeg,L** Canada
54J4 **Winnipegosis** Canada
65E2 **Winnipesaukee,L** USA
61E2 **Winona** Minnesota, USA
63E2 **Winona** Mississippi, USA
55J5 **Winona** USA
65E2 **Winooski** USA
13D1 **Winschoten** Netherlands
59D4 **Winslow** USA
68D2 **Winsted** USA
67B1 **Winston-Salem** USA
13E2 **Winterberg** Germany
67B3 **Winter Garden** USA
67B3 **Winter Park** USA
66B1 **Winters** USA
13D2 **Winterswijk** Netherlands
16B1 **Winterthur** Switzerland
61E2 **Winthrop** USA
32D3 **Winton** Australia
35A3 **Winton** New Zealand
7E3 **Wisbech** England
64A2 **Wisconsin** *R* USA
57E2 **Wisconsin** *State* USA
64B2 **Wisconsin Dells** USA
55K5 **Wisconsin Rapids** USA
54C3 **Wiseman** USA
19D2 **Wisła** *R* Poland
18C2 **Wismar** Germany
13D3 **Wissembourg** France
73G2 **Witagron** Surinam
47D2 **Witbank** South Africa
56D3 **Witchita Falls** USA
7E3 **Witham** England
7D3 **Witham** *R* England
6E3 **Withernsea** England
7D4 **Witney** England
13D2 **Witten** Germany
18C2 **Wittenberg** Germany
16B1 **Wittenberg** France/Italy
18C2 **Wittenberge** Germany
32A3 **Wittenoom** Australia
13D2 **Wittlich** Germany
47B1 **Witvlei** Namibia
19D2 **Władysławowo** Poland
19D2 **Włocławek** Poland
19E2 **Włodawa** Poland
34C3 **Wodonga** Australia
27G7 **Wokam** *I* Indonesia
7D4 **Woking** England
68B1 **Wolcott** USA
27H6 **Woleai** *I* Pacific Ocean
64B1 **Wolf** *R* USA
13E3 **Wolfach** Germany
58B2 **Wolf Creek** USA
62A1 **Wolf Creek P** USA
60B1 **Wolf Point** USA
18C3 **Wolfsberg** Austria
18C2 **Wolfsburg** Germany
74C9 **Wollaston, Islas** Chile
54H4 **Wollaston L** Canada
54H4 **Wollaston Lake** Canada
54G3 **Wollaston Pen** Canada
34D2 **Wollongong** Australia
47D2 **Wolmaransstad** South Africa
18D2 **Wołow** Poland
34B3 **Wolseley** Australia
7C3 **Wolverhampton** England
7D3 **Wolverton** England
68B2 **Womelsdorf** USA
34D1 **Wondai** Australia
28B3 **Wŏnju** S Korea
28B3 **Wŏnsan** N Korea
34C3 **Wonthaggi** Australia
68C3 **Woodbine** USA
7E3 **Woodbridge** England
65D3 **Woodbridge** USA
54G4 **Wood Buffalo Nat. Pk** Canada
34D1 **Woodburn** Australia
58B1 **Woodburn** USA
68C3 **Woodbury** USA
54D3 **Woodchopper** USA
66C1 **Woodfords** USA
66C2 **Woodlake** USA
59B3 **Woodland** California, USA
66B1 **Woodland** USA
58B1 **Woodland** Washington, USA
33E1 **Woodlark** *I* Papua New Guinea
32C3 **Woodroffe,Mt** Australia
61E1 **Woods,L of the** Canada/USA
64B2 **Woodstock** Illinois, USA
65F1 **Woodstock** New Brunswick, Canada
64C2 **Woodstock** Ontario, Canada
68A3 **Woodstock** Virginia, USA
68C3 **Woodstown** USA
35C2 **Woodville** New Zealand
63D2 **Woodville** USA
62C1 **Woodward** USA
6D2 **Wooler** England
32C4 **Woomera** Australia
65E2 **Woonsocket** USA
64C2 **Wooster** USA
7D4 **Wootton Bassett** England
7C3 **Worcester** England
47B3 **Worcester** South Africa
68E1 **Worcester** USA
6C2 **Workington** England
7D3 **Worksop** England
58E2 **Worland** USA
13E3 **Worms** Germany
7B4 **Worms Head** *Pt* Wales
7D4 **Worthing** England
61D2 **Worthington** USA
64C2 **Worthington** USA
60C2 **Wounded Knee** USA
27F7 **Wowoni** Indonesia
25T2 **Wrangel I** Russian Federation
54E4 **Wrangell** USA
54D3 **Wrangell Mts** USA

10B2 **Wrath,C** Scotland
60C2 **Wray** USA
7C3 **Wrexham** Wales
59D4 **Wrightson, Mt** USA
67B2 **Wrightsville** USA
66D3 **Wrightwood** USA
54F3 **Wrigley** Canada
18D2 **Wrocław** Poland
19D2 **Września** Poland
26F2 **Wuchang** China
30E1 **Wuchuan** China
31E2 **Wuda** China
31C2 **Wuding He** *R* China
31A3 **Wudu** China
31C4 **Wugang** China
31B2 **Wuhai** China
31C3 **Wuhan** China
31D3 **Wuhu** China
31D5 **Wuhua** China
42D2 **Wūjang** China
31B1 **Wujia He** *R* China
31B4 **Wu Jiang** *R* China
48C4 **Wukari** Nigeria
31B4 **Wuling Shan** *Mts* China
31A4 **Wumeng Shan** *Upland* China
13E1 **Wümme** *R* Germany
13E1 **Wunstorf** Germany
43H4 **Wuntho** Burma
13D2 **Wuppertal** Germany
31B2 **Wuqi** China
31D2 **Wuqing** China
18B3 **Würzburg** Germany
18C2 **Wurzen** Germany
31C2 **Wutai Shan** *Mt* China
27H7 **Wuvulu** *I* Pacific Ocean
31A2 **Wuwei** China
31E3 **Wuxi** China
31E3 **Wuxing** China
31C2 **Wuyang** China
31D4 **Wuyi Shan** *Mts* China
31B1 **Wuyuan** China
30D2 **Wuzhi Shan** *Mts* China
31B2 **Wuzhong** China
31C5 **Wuzhou** China
64C2 **Wyandotte** USA
34C1 **Wyandra** Australia
7C4 **Wye** *R* England
7C4 **Wylye** *R* England
7E3 **Wymondham** England
32B2 **Wyndham** Australia
63D1 **Wynne** USA
54G2 **Wynniatt B** Canada
34C4 **Wynyard** Australia
64B2 **Wyoming** USA
56C2 **Wyoming** *State* USA
58D2 **Wyoming Peak** *Mt* USA
58D2 **Wyoming Range** *Mts* USA
34D2 **Wyong** Australia
64C3 **Wytheville** USA

X

42D1 **Xaidulla** China
47E2 **Xai Xai** Mozambique
51B5 **Xangongo** Angola
13D2 **Xanten** Germany
17E2 **Xánthi** Greece
31D1 **Xar Moron He** *R* China
47C1 **Xau,L** Botswana
64C3 **Xenia** USA
Xiaguan = Dali
31A2 **Xiahe** China
31D5 **Xiamen** China
31B3 **Xi'an** China
31B4 **Xianfeng** China
31C3 **Xiangfan** China
31C4 **Xiang Jiang** *R* China
31C4 **Xiangtan** China
31C4 **Xianning** China
31B3 **Xianyang** China
26F2 **Xiao Hinggan Ling** *Region* China
31C4 **Xiao Shui** *R* China
31D4 **Xiapu** China
31A4 **Xichang** China
30C2 **Xieng Khouang** Laos
31B4 **Xifeng** China
28A2 **Xifeng** China
43F3 **Xigazê** China
31A1 **Xi He** *R* China
28A2 **Xi He** *R* China
31B2 **Xiji** China
31C5 **Xi Jiang** *R* China
31E1 **Xiliao He** *R* China
31B5 **Xilin** China
28A2 **Xinbin** China
28A2 **Xinchengzi** China
31D4 **Xinfeng** China
31C1 **Xinghe** China
31D5 **Xingning** China
31B4 **Xingren** China
31C2 **Xingtai** China
73H4 **Xingu** *R* Brazil
26C2 **Xingxingxia** China
31A4 **Xingyi** China
31A2 **Xining** China
31E2 **Xinjin** Liaoning, China
31A3 **Xinjin** Sichuan, China
28A2 **Xinlitun** China
28A2 **Xinmin** China
31D2 **Xinwen** China
31C2 **Xin Xian** China
31C2 **Xinxiang** China
31C3 **Xinyang** China
31C5 **Xinyi** Guangdong, China
31D3 **Xinyi** Jiangsu, China
28B2 **Xinzhan** China
28A2 **Xiongyuecheng** China
31D1 **Xi Ujimqin Qi** China
28A2 **Xiuyan** China
31D3 **Xuancheng** China
31B3 **Xuanhan** China
31D1 **Xuanhua** China
31A4 **Xuanwei** China
31C3 **Xuchang** China
50E3 **Xuddur** Somalia
28A2 **Xujiatun** China
31A2 **Xunhua** China
31C5 **Xun Jiang** *R* China
26F2 **Xunke** China
31D5 **Xunwu** China
31C4 **Xupu** China
43N1 **Xurgru** China
30E1 **Xuwen** China
31B4 **Xuyong** China
31D3 **Xuzhou** China

Y

31A4 **Ya'an** China
34B3 **Yaapeet** Australia
50B3 **Yabassi** Cameroon
26D1 **Yablonovyy Khrebet** *Mts* Russian Federation
45D2 **Yabrūd** Syria
58B2 **Yachats** USA
72F8 **Yacuiba** Bolivia
44B2 **Yādgīr** India
49D1 **Yafran** Libya
29D2 **Yagishiri-tō** *I* Japan
19G2 **Yagotin** Ukraine
50C3 **Yahuma** Zaïre
29C3 **Yaita** Japan
29C4 **Yaizu** Japan
31A4 **Yajiang** China
54D3 **Yakataga** USA
58B1 **Yakima** USA
58B1 **Yakima** *R* USA
48B3 **Yako** Burkina
50C3 **Yakoma** Zaïre
29E2 **Yakumo** Japan
25O3 **Yakut Republic** Russian Federation
54E4 **Yakutat** USA
54E4 **Yakutat B** USA
25O3 **Yakutsk** Russian Federation
30C4 **Yala** Thailand
58B1 **Yale** Canada
50C3 **Yalinga** Central African Republic
34C3 **Yallourn** Australia
26C3 **Yalong** *R* China
31A4 **Yalong Jiang** *R* China
17F2 **Yalova** Turkey
21E7 **Yalta** Ukraine
28B2 **Yalu Jiang** *R* China/ N Korea
29D3 **Yamada** Japan
29E3 **Yamagata** Japan
28C4 **Yamaguchi** Japan
24J2 **Yamal, Poluostrov** *Pen* Russian Federation
26E1 **Yamarovka** Russian Federation
34D1 **Yamba** New S Wales, Australia
34B2 **Yamba** S Australia, Australia
50C3 **Yambio** Sudan
17F2 **Yambol** Bulgaria
27G7 **Yamdena** *I* Indonesia
30B1 **Yamethin** Burma
Yam Kinneret = Tiberias,L
34B1 **Yamma Yamma,L** Australia
48B4 **Yamoussoukro** Ivory Coast
60B2 **Yampa** *R* USA
25R4 **Yamsk** Russian Federation
42D3 **Yamuna** *R* India
43G3 **Yamzho Yumco** *L* China
25P3 **Yana** *R* Russian Federation
34B3 **Yanac** Australia
28B4 **Yanagawa** Japan
44C2 **Yanam** India
31B2 **Yan'an** China
40C5 **Yanbu'al Baḩr** Saudi Arabia
34B2 **Yancannia** Australia
31E3 **Yancheng** China
31B2 **Yanchi** China
34B1 **Yandama** *R* Australia
50C3 **Yangambi** Zaïre
28A3 **Yanggu** S Korea
31C1 **Yang He** *R* China
31C5 **Yangjiang** China
Yangon = Rangoon
31C2 **Yangquan** China
28A3 **Yangsan** S Korea
31C5 **Yangshan** China
31C3 **Yangtze Gorges** China
31E3 **Yangtze,Mouths of the** China
28A3 **Yangyang** S Korea
31D3 **Yangzhou** China
31B4 **Yanhe** China
28B2 **Yanji** China
34C3 **Yanko** Australia
61D2 **Yankton** USA
26B2 **Yanqqi** China
39G1 **Yanqqi** China
31D1 **Yan Shan** *Hills*
25P2 **Yanskiy Zaliv** *B* Russian Federation
34B1 **Yantabulla** Australia
31E2 **Yantai** China
28B2 **Yantongshan** China
31D2 **Yanzhou** China
50B3 **Yaoundé** Cameroon
27G6 **Yap** *I* Pacific Ocean
27G7 **Yapen** *I* Indonesia
70B2 **Yaqui** *R* Mexico
20H4 **Yaransk** Russian Federation
7E3 **Yare** *R* England
20H3 **Yarenga** Russian Federation
20H3 **Yarensk** Russian Federation
72D3 **Yari** *R* Colombia
29D3 **Yariga-take** *Mt* Japan
39F2 **Yarkant He** *R* China
43G3 **Yarlung Zangbo Jiang** *R* China
55M5 **Yarmouth** Canada
45C2 **Yarmūk** *R* Jordan/Syria
20F4 **Yaroslavl'** Russian Federation
45C2 **Yarqon** *R* Israel
34C3 **Yarram** Australia
34D1 **Yarraman** Australia
34C3 **Yarrawonga** Australia
20N2 **Yar Sale** Russian Federation
20E4 **Yartsevo** Russian Federation
25L3 **Yartsevo** Russian Federation
72C2 **Yarumal** Colombia
48C3 **Yashi** Nigeria
48C4 **Yashikera** Nigeria
21G6 **Yashkul'** Russian Federation
42C1 **Yasin** Pakistan
19E3 **Yasinya** Ukraine
34C2 **Yass** Australia
34C2 **Yass** *R* Australia
28B3 **Yasugi** Japan
63C1 **Yates Center** USA
54J3 **Yathkyed L** Canada
50C3 **Yatolema** Zaïre
45C3 **Yatta** Israel
72D4 **Yavari** Peru
42D4 **Yavatmāl** India
28C4 **Yawatahama** Japan
30D2 **Ya Xian** China
41F3 **Yazd** Iran
41F3 **Yazd-e Khvāst** Iran
63D2 **Yazoo** *R* USA
63D2 **Yazoo City** USA
30B2 **Ye** Burma
19F3 **Yedintsy** Moldavia
20F5 **Yefremov** Russian Federation
21G6 **Yegorlyk** *R* Russian Federation
50D3 **Yei** Sudan
20L4 **Yekaterinburg** Russian Federation
21F5 **Yelets** Russian Federation
25Q4 **Yelizavety, Mys** *C* Russian Federation
10C1 **Yell** *I* Scotland
44C2 **Yellandu** India
56B1 **Yellowhead P** Canada
54G3 **Yellowknife** Canada
34C2 **Yellow Mt** Australia
Yellow R = Huang He
26F3 **Yellow Sea** China Korea
56C2 **Yellowstone** *R* USA
58D2 **Yellowstone L** USA
58D2 **Yellowstone Nat Pk** USA
8E1 **Yell Sd** Scotland
19G2 **Yel'nya** Russian Federation
19F2 **Yel'sk** Belarus
55K1 **Yelverton B** Canada
48C3 **Yelwa** Nigeria
38C4 **Yemen** *Republic* Arabian Pen
30C1 **Yen Bai** Vietnam
48B4 **Yendi** Ghana
30B1 **Yengan** Burma
24K3 **Yenisey** *R* Russian Federation
25L4 **Yeniseysk** Russian Federation
25L3 **Yeniseyskiy Kryazh** *Ridge* Russian Federation
24J2 **Yeniseyskiy Zaliv** *B* Russian Federation
7C4 **Yeo** *R* England
34C2 **Yeoval** Australia
7C4 **Yeovil** England
25M3 **Yerbogachen** Russian Federation
21G7 **Yerevan** Armenia
59C3 **Yerington** USA
20J2 **Yermitsa** Russian Federation
59C4 **Yermo** USA
25O4 **Yerofey-Pavlovich** Russian Federation
45C3 **Yeroham** Israel
25S3 **Yeropol** Russian Federation
21H5 **Yershov** Russian Federation
Yerushalayim = Jerusalem
40C1 **Yeşil** *R* Turkey
25M3 **Yessey** Russian Federation
45C2 **Yesud Hama'ala** Israel
34D1 **Yetman** Australia
48B2 **Yetti** Mauritius
43H4 **Yeu** Burma
14B2 **Yeu, Ile d'** *I* France
21H7 **Yevlakh** Azerbaijan
21E6 **Yevpatoriya** Ukraine
31E2 **Ye Xian** China
21F6 **Yeysk** Russian Federation
45B3 **Yi'allaq, Gebel** *Mt* Egypt
45C1 **Yialousa** Cyprus
17E2 **Yiannitsá** Greece
31A4 **Yibin** China
31C3 **Yichang** China
26F2 **Yichun** China
31B2 **Yijun** China
17F2 **Yıldız Dağları** *Upland* Turkey
40C2 **Yıldızeli** Turkey
31A5 **Yiliang** China
31B2 **Yinchuan** China
31D3 **Ying He** *R* China
28A2 **Yingkou** China
31D3 **Yingshan** Hubei, China
31B3 **Yingshan** Sichuan, China
31D4 **Yingtan** China
39G1 **Yining** China
31B1 **Yin Shan** *Upland* China
50D3 **Yirga' Alem** Ethiopia
50D3 **Yirol** Sudan
25N5 **Yirshi** China
31B5 **Yishan** China
31D2 **Yishui** China
17E3 **Yíthion** Greece
28B2 **Yitong** China
28A2 **Yi Xian** China
31C4 **Yiyang** China
20D2 **Yli-Kitka** *L* Finland
12J5 **Ylitornio** Sweden
12J6 **Ylivieska** Finland
63C3 **Yoakum** USA
27E7 **Yogyakarta** Indonesia
50B3 **Yokadouma** Cameroon
29C4 **Yokkaichi** Japan
29D3 **Yokobori** Japan
29C3 **Yokohama** Japan
29C3 **Yokosuka** Japan
29D3 **Yokote** Japan
48D4 **Yola** Nigeria
29C3 **Yonago** Japan
28A3 **Yŏnan** N Korea
29E3 **Yonezawa** Japan
28A4 **Yongam** S Korea
31D4 **Yong'an** China
31A2 **Yongchang** China
28B3 **Yŏngch'ŏn** S Korea
31B4 **Yongchuan** China
31A2 **Yongdeng** China
31D5 **Yongding** China
31D2 **Yongding He** *R* China
28B3 **Yŏngdŏk** S Korea
28A3 **Yŏnggwang** S Korea
28B3 **Yŏnghŭng** N Korea
28A3 **Yŏnghŭng-man** *I* N Korea
28A3 **Yŏngil-man** *B* S Korea
28B2 **Yongji** China
28B3 **Yongju** S Korea
31B2 **Yongning** China
28A3 **Yŏngsanp'o** S Korea
28A3 **Yŏngyang** S Korea
68D2 **Yonkers** USA
13B4 **Yonne** *Department* France
14C2 **Yonne** *R* France
6D3 **York** England
61D2 **York** Nebraska, USA
68B3 **York** Pennsylvania, USA
32D2 **York,C** Australia
55J4 **York Factory** Canada
55M2 **York, Kap** *C* Greenland
27F8 **York Sd** Australia
6C4 **Yorkshire Dales Nat Pk** England
10C3 **Yorkshire Moors** England
7D2 **Yorkshire Wolds** *Upland* England
56C1 **Yorkton** Canada
65D3 **Yorktown** USA
68E1 **York Village** USA
66B2 **Yosemite L** USA
66C1 **Yosemite Nat Pk** USA
29B3 **Yoshii** *R* Japan
29B4 **Yoshino** *R* Japan
20H4 **Yoshkar Ola** Russian Federation
28B4 **Yŏsu** S Korea
45C4 **Yotvata** Israel
10B3 **Youghal** Irish Republic
31B5 **You Jiang** *R* China
34C2 **Young** Australia
35A2 **Young Range** *Mts* New Zealand
68A1 **Youngstown** New York, USA
64C2 **Youngstown** Ohio, USA
66A1 **Yountville** USA
31B4 **Youyang** China
40B2 **Yozgat** Turkey
75A3 **Ypané** *R* Paraguay
58B2 **Yreka** USA
12G7 **Ystad** Sweden
7C3 **Ystwyth** *R* Wales
8D3 **Ythan** *R* Scotland
31C4 **Yuan Jiang** *R* Hunan, China
31A5 **Yuan Jiang** *R* Yunnan, China
31A4 **Yuanmu** China
31C2 **Yuanping** China
59B3 **Yuba City** USA
29E2 **Yūbari** Japan
48A2 **Yubi,C** Morocco
70D3 **Yucatan** *Pen* Mexico
70D2 **Yucatan Chan** Cuba/ Mexico
59D4 **Yucca** USA
31C2 **Yuci** China
25P4 **Yudoma** *R* Russian Federation
31D4 **Yudu** China
31A4 **Yuexi** China
31C4 **Yueyang** China
20L2 **Yugorskiy Poluostrov** *Pen* Russian Federation
17D2 **Yugoslavia** *Federal Republic* Europe
31B5 **Yu Jiang** *R* China
54D3 **Yukon** *R* Canada/USA
54E3 **Yukon Territory** Canada
30E1 **Yulin** Guangdong, China
31C5 **Yulin** Guangxi, China
31B2 **Yulin** Shaanxi, China
59D4 **Yuma** USA
26C3 **Yumen** China
31C5 **Yunkai Dashan** *Hills* China
34A2 **Yunta** Australia
31C3 **Yunxi** China
31C3 **Yun Xian** China
31B3 **Yunyang** China
72C5 **Yurimaguas** Peru
31E5 **Yu Shan** *Mt* Taiwan
20E3 **Yushkozero** Russian Federation
39H2 **Yushu** Tibet, China
31D2 **Yutian** China
75A4 **Yuty** Paraguay
31A5 **Yuxi** China
29D3 **Yuzawa** Japan
19F3 **Yuzhnyy Bug** *R* Ukraine
26H2 **Yuzhno-Sakhalinsk** Russian Federation
20K5 **Yuzh Ural** *Mts* Russian Federation

Z

13C1 **Zaandam** Netherlands
18A2 **Zaanstad** Netherlands
21G8 **Zab al Asfal** *R* Iraq
41D2 **Zāb al Babīr** *R* Iraq
41D2 **Zāb aş Şaghīr** *R* Iraq
26E2 **Zabaykal'sk** Russian Federation
18D3 **Zabreh** Czech Republic
19D2 **Zabrze** Poland
70B2 **Zacatecas** Mexico
16D2 **Zadar** Croatia
30B4 **Zadetkyi** *I* Burma
15A2 **Zafra** Spain
49F1 **Zagazig** Egypt
16C3 **Zaghouan, Dj** *Mt* Tunisia
48B1 **Zagora** Morocco
16D1 **Zagreb** Croatia
Zagros Mts = Kūhhā-ye Zāgros
38E3 **Zāhedān** Iran
45C2 **Zahle** Lebanon
15C2 **Zahrez Chergui** *Marshland* Algeria
20J4 **Zainsk** Russian Federation
50B4 **Zaïre** *R* Congo/Zaïre
50C4 **Zaïre** *Republic* Africa
17E2 **Zaječar** Serbia, Yugoslavia
26D1 **Zakamensk** Russian Federation
21H7 **Zakataly** Azerbaijan
40D2 **Zakho** Iraq
17E3 **Zákinthos** *I* Greece
19D3 **Zakopane** Poland
18D3 **Zalaegerszeg** Hungary
17E1 **Zalău** Romania
18C2 **Zalew Szczeciński** *Lg* Poland
40D5 **Zalim** Saudi Arabia
50C2 **Zalingei** Sudan

25P4 **Zaliv Akademii** *B* Russian Federation
25M2 **Zaliv Faddeya** *B* Russian Federation
21J7 **Zaliv Kara-Bogaz-Gol** *B* Turkmenistan
25R3 **Zaliv Shelikhova** *B* Russian Federation
49D2 **Zaltan** Libya
51C5 **Zambezi** Zambia
51C5 **Zambezi** *R* Africa
51C5 **Zambia** *Republic* Africa
27F6 **Zamboanga** Philippines
19E2 **Zambrów** Poland
72C4 **Zamora** Ecuador
70B2 **Zamora** Mexico
15A1 **Zamora** Spain
66B1 **Zamora** USA
19E2 **Zamość** Poland
31A3 **Zamtang** China
50B4 **Zanaga** Congo
15B2 **Záncara** *R* Spain
42D2 **Zanda** China
64C3 **Zanesville** USA
42D2 **Zangla** India
41E2 **Zanjān** Iran
     Zante = Zákinthos
50D4 **Zanzibar** Tanzania
50D4 **Zanzibar** *I* Tanzania
48C2 **Zaouatallaz** Algeria
31D3 **Zaozhuang** China
41D2 **Zap** *R* Turkey
19G1 **Zapadnaya Dvina** Russian Federation
20L3 **Zapadno-Sibirskaya Nizmennost'** Lowland, Russian Federation
25L4 **Zapadnyy Sayan** *Mts* Russian Federation
74C5 **Zapala** Argentina
62C3 **Zapata** USA
20E2 **Zapolyarnyy** Russian Federation
21F6 **Zaporozh'ye** Ukraine
40C2 **Zara** Turkey
15B1 **Zaragoza** Spain
41F2 **Zarand** Iran
41G3 **Zarand** Iran
38E2 **Zaranj** Afghanistan
72E2 **Zarara** Venezuela
19F1 **Zarasai** Lithuania
41E3 **Zard Kuh** *Mt* Iran
42B2 **Zarghun Shahr** Afghanistan
42B2 **Zargun** *Mt* Pakistan
48C3 **Zaria** Nigeria
40C3 **Zarqa** Jordan
45C2 **Zarqa** *R* Jordan
72C4 **Zaruma** Ecuador
18D2 **Zary** Poland
48D1 **Zarzis** Tunisia
42D2 **Zāskār** *R* India
42D2 **Zāskār Mts** India
47D3 **Zastron** South Africa
45D2 **Zatara** *R* Jordan
     Zatoka Gdańska = Gdańsk,G of
26F1 **Zavitinsk** Russian Federation
19D2 **Zawiercie** Poland
45D1 **Zāwīyah, Jabal az** *Upland* Syria
25M4 **Zayarsk** Russian Federation
45D2 **Zaydī, Wadi az** Syria
24K5 **Zaysan** Kazakhstan
24K5 **Zaysan, Ozero** Kazakhstan
43H3 **Zayü** China
26C4 **Zayü** China
19D2 **Zduńska Wola** Poland
13B2 **Zeebrugge** Belgium
45C3 **Zeelim** Israel
47D2 **Zeerust** South Africa
45C2 **Zefat** Israel
48C3 **Zegueren** *Watercourse* Mali
50E2 **Zeila** Somalia
18C2 **Zeitz** Germany
31A2 **Zêkog** China
20E2 **Zelenoborskiy** Russian Federation
20H4 **Zelenodol'sk** Russian Federation
12K6 **Zelenogorsk** Russian Federation
50C3 **Zemio** Central African Republic
24F1 **Zemlya Aleksandry** *I* Russian Federation
24F2 **Zemlya Frantsa Iosifa** *Is* Russian Federation
24F1 **Zemlya Georga** *I* Russian Federation
24H1 **Zemlya Vil'cheka** *I* Russian Federation
17D2 **Zenica** Bosnia-Herzegovina
45C3 **Zenifim** *R* Israel
31B4 **Zenning** China
21G7 **Zestafoni** Georgia
13E1 **Zeven** Germany
45B1 **Zevgari, C** Cyprus

25O4 **Zeya** Russian Federation
25O4 **Zeya Res** Russian Federation
15A1 **Zêzere** *R* Portugal
45C1 **Zghorta** Lebanon
19D2 **Zgierz** Poland
31D1 **Zhangjiakou** China
31D4 **Zhangping** China
31D2 **Zhangwei He** *R* China
31E1 **Zhangwu** China
31A2 **Zhangye** China
31D5 **Zhangzhou** China
31C5 **Zhanjiang** China
31A4 **Zhanyi** China
31C5 **Zhaoqing** China
31A4 **Zhaotong** China
31D2 **Zhaoyang Hu** *L* China
21K6 **Zharkamys** Kazakhstan
19G1 **Zharkovskiy** Russian Federation
19G3 **Zhashkov** Ukraine
25O3 **Zhatay** Russian Federation
31D4 **Zhejiang** *Province* China
20J3 **Zheleznodorozhnyy** Russian Federation
31C3 **Zhengzhou** China
31D3 **Zhenjiang** China
31A4 **Zhenxiong** China
31B4 **Zhenyuan** China
21G5 **Zherdevka** Russian Federation
31C3 **Zhicheng** China
26D1 **Zhigalovo** Russian Federation
25O3 **Zhigansk** Russian Federation
31B4 **Zhijin** China
19F2 **Zhitkovichi** Belarus
19F2 **Zhitomir** Ukraine
19F2 **Zhlobin** Belarus
19F3 **Zhmerinka** Ukraine
42B2 **Zhob** Pakistan
19F2 **Zhodino** Belarus
43E3 **Zhongba** China
31B2 **Zhongning** China
31C5 **Zhongshan** China
76F10 **Zhongshan** *Base* Antarctica
31B2 **Zhongwei** China
26C4 **Zhougdian** China
31E3 **Zhoushan Qundao** *Arch* China
19G3 **Zhovten'** Ukraine
31E2 **Zhuanghe** China
31A3 **Zhugqu** China
31C3 **Zhushan** China
31C4 **Zhuzhou** China
31D2 **Zibo** China
32C3 **Ziel,Mt** Australia
18D2 **Zielona Góra** Poland
45A3 **Zifta** Egypt
30A1 **Zigaing** Burma
31A4 **Zigong** China
48A3 **Ziguinchor** Senegal
45C2 **Zikhron Ya'aqov** Israel
19D3 **Žilina** Slovakia
19F1 **Zilupe** Latvia
25M4 **Zima** Russian Federation
47D1 **Zimbabwe** *Republic* Africa
45C3 **Zin** *R* Israel
48C3 **Zinder** Niger
59D3 **Zion Nat Pk** USA
31C4 **Zi Shui** *R* China
18C2 **Zittau** Germany
31D2 **Ziya He** *R* China
31A3 **Ziyang** China
20K4 **Zlatoust** Russian Federation
19D3 **Zlin** Czech Republic
24K4 **Zmeinogorsk** Russian Federation
19D2 **Znin** Poland
18D3 **Znojmo** Czech Republic
47D1 **Zoekmekaar** South Africa
31A3 **Zoigê** China
19E3 **Zolochev** Ukraine
19G3 **Zolotonosha** Ukraine
51D5 **Zomba** Malawi
50B3 **Zongo** Zaïre
40B1 **Zonguldak** Turkey
48B4 **Zorzor** Liberia
48A2 **Zouerate** Mauritius
13D1 **Zoutkamp** Netherlands
17E1 **Zrenjanin** Serbia, Yugoslavia
16B1 **Zug** Switzerland
21G7 **Zugdidi** Georgia
13C1 **Zuidelijk Flevoland** *Polder* Netherlands
15A2 **Zújar** *R* Spain
51D5 **Zumbo** Mozambique
61E2 **Zumbrota** USA
48C4 **Zungeru** Nigeria
62A1 **Zuni** USA
62A1 **Zuni Mts** USA
31B4 **Zunyi** China
30D1 **Zuo** *R* China
31B5 **Zuo Jiang** *R* China
14D2 **Zürich** Switzerland
13D1 **Zutphen** Netherlands
49D1 **Zuwārah** Libya

49D2 **Zuwaylah** Libya
20J4 **Zuyevka** Russian Federation
19G3 **Zvenigorodka** Ukraine
51C6 **Zvishavane** Zimbabwe
19D3 **Zvolen** Slovakia
17D2 **Zvornik** Bosnia-Herzegovina
26G1 **Zvoron, Ozero** *L* Russian Federation
13D3 **Zweibrücken** Germany
18C2 **Zwickau** Germany
18B2 **Zwolle** Netherlands
19E2 **Zyrardów** Poland
25R3 **Zyryanka** Russian Federation
24K5 **Zyryanovsk** Kazakhstan
19D3 **Żywiec** Poland
45B1 **Zyyi** Cyprus